Handbook of Research on Biomimicry in Information Retrieval and Knowledge Management

Reda Mohamed Hamou
Dr. Tahar Moulay University of Saida, Algeria

A volume in the Advances in Web Technologies
and Engineering (AWTE) Book Series

Published in the United States of America by
IGI Global
Engineering Science Reference (an imprint of IGI Global)
701 E. Chocolate Avenue
Hershey PA, USA 17033
Tel: 717-533-8845
Fax: 717-533-8661
E-mail: cust@igi-global.com
Web site: http://www.igi-global.com

Library of Congress Cataloging-in-Publication Data

Names: Hamou, Reda Mohamed, 1967- editor.
Title: Handbook of research on biomimicry in information retrieval and
  knowledge management / Reda Mohamed Hamou, editor.
Description: Hershey, PA : Engineering Science Reference, [2018] | Includes
  bibliographical references.
Identifiers: LCCN 2017013839| ISBN 9781522530046 (hardcover) | ISBN
  9781522530053 (ebook)
Subjects: LCSH: Data mining--Handbooks, manuals, etc. | Information
  technology--Handbooks, manuals, etc. | Big data--Handbooks, manuals, etc.
  | Knowledge management--Handbooks, manuals, etc. |
  Bioinformatics--Handbooks, manuals, etc. | Machine learning--Handbooks,
  manuals, etc. | Information storage and retrieval systems--Handbooks,
  manuals, etc.
Classification: LCC QA76.9.D343 H397 2018 | DDC 006.3/12--dc23 LC record available at https://lccn.loc.
gov/2017013839

This book is published in the IGI Global book series Advances in Web Technologies and Engineering (AWTE) (ISSN: 2328-2762; eISSN: 2328-2754)

British Cataloguing in Publication Data
A Cataloguing in Publication record for this book is available from the British Library.

All work contributed to this book is new, previously-unpublished material. The views expressed in this book are those of the authors, but not necessarily of the publisher.

For electronic access to this publication, please contact: eresources@igi-global.com.

Advances in Web Technologies and Engineering (AWTE) Book Series

Ghazi I. Alkhatib
The Hashemite University, Jordan
David C. Rine
George Mason University, USA

ISSN:2328-2762
EISSN:2328-2754

MISSION

The **Advances in Web Technologies and Engineering (AWTE) Book Series** aims to provide a platform for research in the area of Information Technology (IT) concepts, tools, methodologies, and ethnography, in the contexts of global communication systems and Web engineered applications. Organizations are continuously overwhelmed by a variety of new information technologies, many are Web based. These new technologies are capitalizing on the widespread use of network and communication technologies for seamless integration of various issues in information and knowledge sharing within and among organizations. This emphasis on integrated approaches is unique to this book series and dictates cross platform and multidisciplinary strategy to research and practice.

The **Advances in Web Technologies and Engineering (AWTE) Book Series** seeks to create a stage where comprehensive publications are distributed for the objective of bettering and expanding the field of web systems, knowledge capture, and communication technologies. The series will provide researchers and practitioners with solutions for improving how technology is utilized for the purpose of a growing awareness of the importance of web applications and engineering.

COVERAGE

- Metrics-based performance measurement of IT-based and web-based organizations
- Web user interfaces design, development, and usability engineering studies
- Data and knowledge capture and quality issues
- Integrated Heterogeneous and Homogeneous Workflows and Databases within and Across Organizations and with Suppliers and Customers
- Strategies for linking business needs and IT
- Web systems performance engineering studies
- Case studies validating Web-based IT solutions
- Knowledge structure, classification, and search algorithms or engines
- Integrated user profile, provisioning, and context-based processing
- Web systems engineering design

IGI Global is currently accepting manuscripts for publication within this series. To submit a proposal for a volume in this series, please contact our Acquisition Editors at Acquisitions@igi-global.com or visit: http://www.igi-global.com/publish/.

Titles in this Series

For a list of additional titles in this series, please visit: www.igi-global.com/book-series

701 East Chocolate Avenue, Hershey, PA 17033, USA
Tel: 717-533-8845 x100 ● Fax: 717-533-8661
E-Mail: cust@igi-global.com ● www.igi-global.com

Editorial Advisory Board

List of Contributors

Table of Contents

Detailed Table of Contents

Chapter 1

Shonak Bansal, PEC University of Technology, India
Kuldeep Sharma, PEC University of Technology, India

Multi-objective nature-inspired-based approaches are powerful optimizing algorithms to solve the multiple objectives in NP-complete engineering design problems. This chapter proposes a nature-inspired-based modified multi-objective big bang-big crunch (M-MOBB-BC) optimization algorithm to find the Optimal Golomb rulers (OGRs) in a reasonable timeframe. The OGRs have their important application as channel-allocation algorithm that allow suppression of the four-wave mixing crosstalk in optical wavelength division multiplexing systems. The presented simulation results conclude that the proposed hybrid algorithm is superior to the existing conventional classical algorithms, namely extended quadratic congruence and search algorithm and nature-inspired-based algorithms, namely genetic algorithms, biogeography-based optimization, and simple BB-BC optimization algorithm to find near-OGRs in terms of ruler length, total occupied optical channel bandwidth, bandwidth expansion factor, computation time, computational complexity, and non-parametric statistical tests.

Chapter 2

Ahmed Chaouki Lokbani, Dr. Tahar Moulay University of Saida, Algeria
Mohamed Amine Boudia, Dr. Tahar Moulay University of Saida, Algeria

In this paper, the authors propose a meta-heuristic for intrusion detection system by scenario, inspired by the protection system of social bees to their hive. This approach is based on a specialized multi-agent system where the authors give limited responsibility to each guard bee agent: to secure only one port.

This specialization aims to better exploit the training set and the hardware and software performance. The authors start this paper with a short introduction where they show the importance of IT security. Then they give a little insight into the state of the art, before starting the essential part of a scientific paper: "Our Approach," where they explain the natural model. Finally, they simplify their model in a modelling table to share their vision and philosophy to switch from natural model to artificial model.

Chapter 3

Mohamed Amine Boudia, Dr. Tahar Moulay University of Saida, Algeria
Mohamed Elhadi Rahmani, Dr. Tahar Moulay University of Saida, Algeria
Amine Rahmani, Dr. Tahar Moulay University of Saida, Algeria

This chapter is a comparative study between two bio-inspired approaches based on swarm intelligence for detection and filtering of SPAM: social bees vs. inspiration from the human renal. The authors took inspiration from biological model and use two meta-heuristics because the effects allow the authors to detect the characteristics of unwanted data. Messages are indexed and represented by the n-gram words and characters independent of languages (because a message can be received in any language). The results are promising and provide an important way to use this model for solving other problems in data mining. The authors start this paper with a short introduction where they show the importance of IT security. Then they give a little insight into the state of the art, before starting the essential part of a scientific paper, where they explain and experiment with two original meta-heuristics, and explain the natural model. Then they detail the artificial model.

Chapter 4

Mekour Norreddine, Dr. Tahar Moulay University of Saida, Algeria

One of the problems that gene expression data resolved is feature selection. There is an important process for choosing which features are important for prediction; there are two general approaches for feature selection: filter approach and wrapper approach. In this chapter, the authors combine the filter approach with method ranked information gain and wrapper approach with a searching method of the genetic algorithm. The authors evaluate their approach on two data sets of gene expression data: Leukemia, and the Central Nervous System. The classifier Decision tree (C4.5) is used for improving the classification performance.

Chapter 5

Ishak H. A. Meddah, Oran University of Science and Technology – Mohamed Boudiaf,
    Algeria
Khaled Belkadi, Oran University of Science and Technology – Mohamed Boudiaf, Algeria

Process mining provides an important bridge between data mining and business process analysis. This technique allows for the extraction of information from event logs. In general, there are two steps in process mining: correlation definition or discovery and then process inference or composition. Firstly, the authors mine small patterns from log traces of two applications; those patterns are the representation of the execution traces of a business process. In this step, the authors use existing techniques. The patterns are represented by finite state automaton or their regular expression. The final model is the combination of only two types of small patterns that are represented by the regular expressions (ab)* and (ab*c)*. Secondly, the authors compute these patterns in parallel and then combine those small patterns using the composition rules. They have two parties. The first is the mine, where the authors discover patterns from execution traces, and the second is the combination of these small patterns. The pattern mining and the composition is illustrated by the automaton existing techniques.

Inverted index is used in most Information Retrieval Systems (IRS) to achieve the fast query response time. In inverted index, compression schemes are used to improve the efficiency of IRS. In this chapter, the authors study and analyze various compression techniques that are used for indexing. They also present a new compression technique that is based on FastPFOR called New FastPFOR. The storage structure and the integers' representation of the proposed method can improve its performances both in compression and decompression. The study on existing works shows that the recent research works provide good results either in compression or in decoding, but not in both. Hence, their decompression performance is not fair. To achieve better performance in decompression, the authors propose New FastPFOR in this chapter. To evaluate the performance of the proposed method, they experiment with TREC collections. The results show that the proposed method could achieve better decompression performance than the existing techniques.

Chapter 7

Day after day the cases of plagiarism increase and become a crucial problem in the modern world caused by the quantity of textual information available in the web. As data mining becomes the foundation for many different domains, one of its chores is a text categorization that can be used in order to resolve the impediment of automatic plagiarism detection. This chapter is devoted to a new approach for combating plagiarism named MML (Multi-agents Machine Learning system) composed of three modules: data preparation and digitalization, using n-gram character or bag of words as methods for the text representation, TF*IDF as weighting to calculate the importance of each term in the corpus in order to transform each document to a vector, and learning and vote phase using three supervised learning algorithms (decision tree c4.5, naïve Bayes, and support vector machine).

A container terminal is a complicated system made up of several components in interdependence. Several materials handle possible to move containers at the port to better meet the needs of ships awaiting loading or unloading. In order to effectively manage this area, it is necessary to know the location of each container. Containers search times can be considerable and lead to delays that cause financial penalties for terminal management operators. In this chapter, the authors propose an approach to solve the problem of placement of containers through the description of a model that optimizes available storage space to handle the distance travelled between the containers and the storage locations in a seaport. In other words, a model that minimizes the total number of unnecessary movement while respecting the constraints of space and time. This work develops a software tool enabling identification of the best location of a container using the methodological resolution Branch and Bound.

In recent years, social networks analysis has attracted the attention of many researchers. Community detection is one of the highly studied problems in this field. It is considered an NP-hard problem, and several algorithms have been proposed to solve this problem. In this chapter, the authors present a new algorithm for community detection in social networks based on the Black Hole optimization algorithm. The authors use the modularity density evaluation measure as a function to maximize. They also propose the enhancement of the algorithm by using two new strategies: initialization and evolution. The proposed algorithm has been tested on famous synthetic and real-world networks; experimental results compared with three known algorithms show the effectiveness of using this algorithm for community detection in social networks.

Diabetes is a major health problem and a disease that can be very dangerous in developing and developed countries, and its incidence is increasing dramatically. In this chapter, the authors propose a system of automatic detection of diabetes based on a bioinspired model called a swarm of fish (fish swarm or AFSA). AFSA (artificial fish swarm algorithm) represents one of the best methods of optimization among swarm intelligence algorithms. This algorithm is inspired by the collective, the movement of fish and their different social behaviors in order to achieve their objectives. There are several parameters to be adjusted in the AFSA model. The visual step is very significant, given that the fish artificial essentially moves according to this parameter. Large parameter values increase the capacity of the global search algorithm, while small values tend to improve local search capability. This algorithm has many advantages, including high speed convergence, flexibility, and high accuracy. In this chapter, the authors evaluate their model of AFSA for the purpose of automatic detection of diabetes.

Chapter 11

Shonak Bansal, PEC University of Technology, India

Nature-inspired-based approaches are powerful optimizing algorithms to solve the NP-complete problems having multiple objectives. In this chapter, two nature-inspired-based multi-objective optimization algorithms (MOAs) and their hybrid forms are proposed to find the optimal Golomb rulers (OGRs) in a reasonable time. The OGRs can be used as a channel-allocation algorithm that allows suppression of the four-wave mixing crosstalk in optical wavelength division multiplexing systems. The presented results conclude that the proposed MOAs outperforms the existing conventional classical and nature-inspired-based algorithms to find near-OGRs in terms of ruler length, total occupied optical bandwidth, bandwidth expansion factor, computation time, and computational complexity. In order to find the superiority of proposed MOAs, the performances of the proposed algorithms are also analyzed by using statistical tests.

Chapter 12

Ayan Chatterjee, Sarboday Public Academy, India
Mahendra Rong, Bangabasi Evening College, India

The communication through wireless medium is very popular to the developed society. More specifically, the use of the internet as well as the use of social networking sites is increasing. Therefore, information security is an important factor during wireless communication. Three major components of it are confidentiality, integrity, and availability of information among authorized users. Integrity level is maintained through various digital authentication schemes. Fuzzy logic is an important soft computing tool that increases the digital watermarking system in various ways. In this chapter, different popular and high secured watermarking schemes using fuzzy logic are analyzed with their mathematical and experimental efficiency. A comparative analysis is developed here with corresponding different parameters.

Chapter 13

Mohamed Elhadi Rahmani, Dr. Tahar Moulay University of Saida, Algeria

Ecological systems are known by their relationships with the environment. They affect and are affected by various external factors such as climate and the basic materials that form the soil. Good distinctions of relationships is the first important point in the modeling of ecosystems. The diversity of these systems caused a large amount of data that became hard to analyze, which made researchers classify it as NP-Hard problems. This chapter presents a study of application of bio-inspired algorithms for ecosystem data analysis. The chapter contains application of four different approaches that were inspired by authors of the paper from four different phenomena, and they were applied for analysis of four different ecosystem data collected from real life cases. Results showed a very high accuracy and proved the efficiency of bio-inspired algorithms for supervised classification of real ecosystem data.

Chapter 14

Hanane Menad, Dr. Tahar Moulay University Saida, Algeria
Abdelmalek Amine, Dr. Tahar Moulay University of Saida, Algeria

Medical data mining has great potential for exploring the hidden patterns in the data sets of the medical domain. These patterns can be utilized for clinical diagnosis. Bio-inspired algorithms is a new field of research. Its main advantage is knitting together subfields related to the topics of connectionism, social behavior, and emergence. Briefly put, it is the use of computers to model living phenomena and simultaneously the study of life to improve the usage of computers. In this chapter, the authors present an application of four bio-inspired algorithms and meta heuristics for classification of seven different real medical data sets. Two of these algorithms are based on similarity calculation between training and test data while the other two are based on random generation of population to construct classification rules. The results showed a very good efficiency of bio-inspired algorithms for supervised classification of medical data.

Chapter 15

Mohamed Amine Boudia, Dr. Tahar Moulay University of Saida, Algeria

This chapter is a comparative study between two bio-inspired approach based on the swarm intelligence for automatic text summaries: Social Spiders and Social Bees. The authors use two techniques of extraction, one after the other: scoring of phrases and similarity that aims to eliminate redundant phrases without losing the theme of the text. While the optimization uses the bio-inspired approach to perform the results of the previous step, the objective function of the optimization is to maximize the sum of similarity between phrases of the candidate summary in order to keep the theme of the text and minimize the sum of scores in order to increase the summarization rate. This optimization will also give a candidate's summary where the order of the phrases changes compared to the original text. For the third and final step concerning choosing a best summary from all candidate summaries generated by optimization layer, the authors opted for the technique of voting with a simple majority.

Chapter 16

Fatima Kabli, Dr. Tahar Moulay University of Saida, Algeria

The mass of data available on the Internet is rapidly increasing; the complexity of this data is discussed at the level of the multiplicity of information sources, formats, modals, and versions. Facing the complexity of biological data, such as the DNA sequences, protein sequences, and protein structures, the biologist cannot simply use the traditional techniques to analyze this type of data. The knowledge extraction process with data mining methods for the analysis and processing of biological complex data is considered a real scientific challenge in the search for systematically potential relationships without prior knowledge of the nature of these relationships. In this chapter, the authors discuss the Knowledge Discovery in Databases process (KDD) from the Biological Data. They specifically present a state of the art of the best known and most effective methods of data mining for analysis of the biological data and problems of bioinformatics related to data mining.

Chapter 17

Dharmendra Trikamlal Patel, Charotar University of Science and Technology, India

Voluminous data are being generated by various means. The Internet of Things (IoT) has emerged recently to group all manmade artificial things around us. Due to intelligent devices, the annual growth of data generation has increased rapidly, and it is expected that by 2020, it will reach more than 40 trillion GB. Data generated through devices are in unstructured form. Traditional techniques of descriptive and predictive analysis are not enough for that. Big Data Analytics have emerged to perform descriptive and predictive analysis on such voluminous data. This chapter first deals with the introduction to Big Data Analytics. Big Data Analytics is very essential in Bioinformatics field as the size of human genome sometimes reaches 200 GB. The chapter next deals with different types of big data in Bioinformatics. The chapter describes several problems and challenges based on big data in Bioinformatics. Finally, the chapter deals with techniques of Big Data Analytics in the Bioinformatics field.

Chapter 18

Zakaria Bendaoud, University of Saida, Algeria
Yachba Khadidja, University of Oran, Algeria
Bouamrane Karim, University of Oran, Algeria

The number of individuals using public transportation is increasing. Transport companies want to ensure, at best, the satisfaction of the travellers. Nevertheless, a significant number of these companies sometimes pushes the travellers to confusion to compose their itineraries and obtain the required information. The authors suggest in this chapter integrating several traveller information systems into the same global system. This chapter aims to provide information to the traveller without concern for their location and optimize processing by limiting the number of involved nodes. They opted for a multi-agent system associated with the Voronoï decomposition of the global network.

Chapter 19

Kijpokin Kasemsap, Suan Sunandha Rajabhat University, Thailand

This chapter indicates the overview of Brain-Machine Interfaces (BMIs); the aspects of BMIs; BMIs, human-machine interfaces, and electrooculography interfaces; BMIs, Amyotrophic Lateral Sclerosis (ALS), and stroke motor recovery; speech BMIs; BMIs and neuroplasticity; and BMIs and transcranial doppler (TCD). BMIs are the computerized approaches to gaining the brain signals, investigating them, and translating them into computerized functions in order to organize the required practices. BMIs can allow people to manipulate computerized networks and various electrical devices. With the support of modern technologies, BMIs are functional and able to operate in operational settings. The chapter argues that applying BMIs has the potential to increase organizational performance and reach strategic goals in the digital age.

Chapter 20

MapReduce is a solution for the treatment of large data. With it we can analyze and process data. It does this by distributing the computation in a large set of machines. Process mining provides an important bridge between data mining and business process analysis. This technique allows for the extraction of information from event logs. Firstly, the chapter mines small patterns from log traces. Those patterns are the representation of the traces execution from a business process. The authors use existing techniques; the patterns are represented by finite state automaton; the final model is the combination of only two types of patterns that are represented by the regular expressions. Secondly, the authors compute these patterns in parallel, and then combine those patterns using MapReduce. They have two parties. The first is the Map Step. The authors mine patterns from execution traces. The second is the combination of these small patterns as reduce step. The results are promising; they show that the approach is scalable, general, and precise. It minimizes the execution time by the use of MapReduce.

Foreword

In a world where information is the code of life, biomimicry represents an interesting line of research that can be a solution for designing systems to solve any problem application in the real life of human.

In the last decade, the modern digital world is photographed as an "ocean" fueled by Google searches, social networks, blogs and commercial websites. This ocean has led to a renewed interest and enthusiasm for information retrieval (IR) technology. the need for IR is that we have too much data, applications and services, but we do not have useful information, which can cause a lot of confusion and perplexity for user. One of the strengths of this technology is its ability to find the required needle in a haystack of digital data.

The biomimicry is the innovation that seeks sustainable solutions to human challenges by emulating models and proven strategies of nature. For example, imitating termites to create sustainable buildings, imitating humpback whales to create efficient wind energy and imitating dolphins to send submarine signals, or imitating ants to search for the shortest path in a graph, etc.

Computer science and nature share a long history together by possessing many properties in common since they can be used together to solve several application problems especially when conventional methods are too costly or difficult to implement. These two directions have been convergent based on the idea that biological processes are intrinsically algorithms designed by nature to solve computational problems. Nowadays, the information has become the blood circulating in the digital body and the biomimicry is the system of reoxygination which ensures the access to the relevant information.

This book offers a journey on the theory and applications of the innovations issued from nature to learn how to separate the wheat (relevant information) from the chaff (irrelevant information). These applications grouped in term of Biomimicry is the process of inspiring intelligent systems from biological phenomena in order to benefit from its power in solving hard problems. The bio-inspired techniques are used in many computer science fields since they have proven a good efficiency in finding optimal solutions; they are inspired from the connectionism, social or evolutionary behavior in different sources. It touches a variety of issues and concerns such as, plagiarism detection, bioinformatics, traveling, intrusion detection, clustering, control systems, image processing, parallel and distributed computing, game theory, biometrics, automatic summarization, etc.

Benyahia Kadda
Taher Moulay University of Saida, Algeria

Benyahia Kadda *received an engineering degree in Computer Science from the Computer Science Department of Djillali Liabes University of Sidi-Belabbes, Algeria and PhD from the same university. His research interests include data mining, computational intelligence, and Semantic Web. Dr. Benyahia is currently a lecturer and Assistant at the Computer Science Department, Taher Moulay University of Saida, Algeria.*

Preface

Nature is an immense laboratory of efficient strategies and processes adapted to disturbances.

Biomimicry is an innovation approach, based on the principles and Strategies developed by living organisms and ecosystems.

It aims to produce goods and services in a sustainable way and to make human societies compatible with the biosphere. It also consists of identifying, understanding and imitating what it does best to design products, processes, or Innovative systems.

The main steps of the biomimicry approach are to identify an interesting natural property related to a scientific, technological or ecological problem.

There are three levels of inspiration for living things: shapes and surfaces; processes and materials; and ecosystems that inspire our organizations.

Nature has always inspired man in the study of forms and surfaces. But it is also an invaluable source of inspiration for research and innovation on processes and materials, while at the same time being a promising framework for our organizations.

Under the term biomimicry, all engineering inspired by living organisms is grouped together. Hence also, the qualification of bio-inspiration. It is thus not a matter of copying, but rather of taking inspiration from the solutions invented by nature, selected over billions of years of evolution, in order to respond to a problem that confronts our human society. All this with much lower environmental and energy costs than those offered by other types of engineering.

Biomimicry, an immense potential since the terrestrial environment is full of ecosystems that can be inspiring. The marine environment, whose biodiversity is poorer but whose species are much more specialized, could contain the most interesting ideas.

The biomimetic approach is by nature interdisciplinary. The starting point is given by fundamental research that observes, analyzes and models the living. The most interesting biological models are then captured by the engineering sciences, which translate them into technical concepts. Finally, the contractors took over and moved on to industrial development.

Possible drift thanks to the biomimicry that researchers and engineers hope to succeed in improving a host of materials and technologies. But the method could also lead to much less noble achievements. Thus, the wings of fighter planes are more and more often inspired by flying animals. Drones, which can be used for combat missions, derive their name from the bumblebee. And do not forget that the most powerful poisons are in nature.

Several bio-inspired approaches as well as several biomimetic techniques are discussed in this book. The editor wishes to thank the authors of the book for the quality of the chapters proposed.

This handbook is intended for a wide audience, in particular academic researchers, engineers wishing to implement or test new bio-inspired techniques or a large number of doctoral students working in the field of biomimetism as well as researchers in laboratories specializing in the field of biomimetics (World of life), and in the search for information and knowledge management.

The book consists of 20 chapters.

Multi-objective nature-inspired-based approaches are the powerful optimizing algorithms to solve the multiple objectives in NP-complete engineering design problems. In the first chapter of Shonak Bansal, the author proposes a nature-inspired-based modified multi-objective Big bang–Big crunch (M-MOBB-BC) optimization algorithm to find the Optimal Golomb rulers (OGRs) at a reasonable time. The OGRs have their important application as channel-allocation algorithm that allows suppression of the four-wave mixing crosstalk in optical wavelength division multiplexing systems. The presented simulation results conclude that the proposed hybrid algorithm is superior to the existing conventional classical algorithms, namely, Extended quadratic congruence and Search algorithm and nature–inspired based algorithms, namely, Genetic algorithms, Biogeography based optimization, and simple BB-BC optimization algorithm to find near–OGRs in terms of ruler length, total occupied optical channel bandwidth, bandwidth expansion factor, computation time, computational complexity, and non-parametric statistical tests.

In the second chapter of Dr. ahmed Chaouki Lokbani, the authors will propose a meta-heuristic for intrusion detection system by scenario, inspired from the protection system of social bees to their hive. This approach is based on a specialized multi agent system where we will give a limited responsibility to each guard bee agent: to secure only one port, this specialization aims to better exploit the training set and the hardware and software performance. we will start this paper by a short introduction where we will see the importance of IT security especially today, then the authors will give a little insight into the state of the art, before starting the essential part of a scientific paper: "their approach" where they will explain the natural model, and then they simplified their model in a modelling table to share their vision and philosophy to switch from natural model to artificial model. The authors will discuss the results and make comparison.

The third chapter of Dr. Mohamed Amine Boudia is a comparative study between two bio-inspired approach based on the swarm intelligence for detection and filtering of SPAM: Social bees Vs inspiration from the Human Renal. The authors took inspiration from biological model, we use two meta-heuristics because it presents effects allow the authors to detect the characteristics of unwanted data. Messages are indexed and represented by the n-gram words and characters independent of languages (because a message can be received in any language). The results are promising and provide an important way for the use of this model for solving other problems in data mining. The authors will start this paper by a short introduction where they will see the importance of IT security especially today, then they will give a little insight into the state of the art, before starting the essential part of a scientific paper, where they explain and experiment a two original meta-heuristic, and explain the natural model and then they will detail the artificial model

The fourth chapter of Mekour Norreddine who proposed a solution that represents the selection of features for one of the most modern problems solved by gene expression data. There is an important process to choose which characteristics are important for prediction. Two general approaches exist for the selection of functionalities: the filter approach and the wrapper approach. In this chapter, the author combines the filter approach with method-classified information gain and the wrapper approach with a genetic algorithm search method. The evaluation of the approach is developed on two sets of gene expression data: Leukemia and the central nervous system; The classifier decision tree (C4.5) is used to improve classification performance.

The fifth chapter of Ishak H. A. Meddah who proposed in the framework of information retrieval one of the techniques in the extraction of the processes that provides an important bridge between the exploration of data and the analysis of the business processes. Its techniques make it possible to extract information from the event logs. Generally, there are two steps in process extraction, correlation definition or discovery, then inference or composition of the process. First, the work developed in this chapter is to exploit small models from a log traces of two applications; these models are the representation of the execution traces of a business process. In this step, the authors use existing techniques; The patterns are represented by the automaton of the finite states or their regular expression; The final model is the combination of only two types of small patterns represented by the regular expressions (ab) * and (ab * c) *. In the second step, the authors compute these models in parallel, then combine these small patterns using the composition rules. For these rules there are two parts, the first is the mine, we discover patterns from the traces of execution and the second is the combination of these small models. The patterns mining and composition are illustrated by the existing techniques of the automaton.

The sixth chapter of V Glory which also proposed in the framework of the research of information a new technique of compression, based on FastPFOR called New FastPFOR. The reverse index was used in most information retrieval systems (IRS) to obtain fast response time. In reverse index, compression schemes are used to improve the efficiency of the IRS. The storage structure and the full representation of the proposed method can improve its compression and decompression performance. The study of existing work shows that recent research provides good results either in compression or in decoding, but not in both. Therefore, their decompression performance is not fair. To evaluate the performance of the proposed method, the authors carried out experiments with TREC collections. The results show that the proposed method could achieve better decompression performance than existing techniques.

The seventh chapter of Dr. Hadj Ahmed Bouarara who proposed a new approach to combat plagiarism called MML "Multi-agent machine learning system" composed of three modules: data preparation and digitization, using the n-gram character or bag Of words as textual representation methods, TF * IDF as a weighting to calculate the importance of each term in the corpus in order to transform each document into a vector; Learning and voting phase using three supervised learning algorithms (c4.5 decision tree, naive bayes and support vector machine). This approach was elaborated since day after day the cases of plagiarism increase and become a crucial problem in the modern world caused by the quantity of textual information available in the web. The data mining becomes the foundation for many of different domains one of its chores is the text categorization that can be used in order to resolve the impediment of automatic plagiarism detection.

The eighth chapter of Khedidja Yachba et al. proposed an approach to solving the problem of placing containers by describing a model that optimizes the available storage space to manage the distance traveled between containers and storage locations in a sea port. In other words, a model that minimizes the total number of unnecessary movements while respecting the constraints of space and time. The interest of this work is in the development of a software tool allowing to identify the best location of a container using the methodological solution Branch and Bound. The approach was elaborated because of the following problem: A container terminal is a complicated system made up of several components in interdependence. Several materials handling possible to move containers at the port to better meet the needs of ships awaiting loading or unloading. In order to effectively manage this area, it is necessary to know the location of each container. Containers search times can be considerable and lead to delays that cause financial penalties for terminal management operators.

In last years, social networks analysis has attracted the attention of many researchers, community detection is one of the highly studied problems in this field, it is considered as an NP-hard problem several algorithms have been proposed to solve this problem. In this ninth chapter of Mohamed Guendouz et al., the authors present a new algorithm for community detection in social networks based on the Black Hole optimization algorithm. The authors use the modularity density evaluation measure as a function to maximize, they propose also to enhance the algorithm by using two new strategies: initialization and evolution. The proposed algorithm has been tested on famous synthetic and real world networks; experimental results compared with other three known algorithms show the effectiveness of using this algorithm for community detection in social networks.

Diabetes is a major health problem and a disease that can be very dangerous in developing and developed countries and its incidence increases dramatically. In this the tenth chapter of Dr. Reda Mohamed Hamou et al., the authors propose a system of automatic detection of diabetes based on A bioinspired model called a swarm of fish (FISH SWARM or AFSA). AFSA (artificial fish swarm algorithm) which represents one of the best methods of optimization among swarm intelligence algorithms. This algorithm is inspired by the collective, the movement of fish and their different social behaviors in order to achieve their objectives. There are several parameters to be adjusted in the AFSA model. The visual step is very significant, given that the fish Artificial essentially moves according to this parameter. Large parameter values increase the capacity of the global search algorithm, while small values tend to improve local search capability. This algorithm has many advantages, including high speed convergence, flexibility and high accuracy. In this chapter, the authors will evaluate her model of AFSA for the purpose of automatic detection of diabetes.

Nowadays, nature-inspired-based approaches are powerful optimizing algorithms to solve the NP-complete problems having multiple objectives. In this eleventh chapter of Shonak Bansal, two nature-inspired-based multi-objective optimization algorithms (MOAs) and their hybrid forms are being proposed to find the optimal Golomb rulers (OGRs) at a reasonable time. The OGRs can be used as a channel-allocation algorithm that allows suppression of the four-wave mixing crosstalk in optical wavelength division multiplexing systems. The presented results conclude that the proposed MOAs outperforms the existing conventional classical and nature–inspired based algorithms to find near-OGRs in terms of ruler length, total occupied optical bandwidth, bandwidth expansion factor, computation time, and computational complexity. In order to find the superiority of proposed MOAs, the performances of the proposed algorithms are being also analyzed by using statistical tests.

Today, in the digitalized world, the communication through wireless medium is very much popular to the developed society. More specifically, use of internet as well as use of social networking sites increases the use of wireless communication from a decade approximately. So, information security is an important factor during wireless communication. Three major components of it are confidentiality, integrity and availability of information among authorized users. Integrity level is maintained through various digital authentication schemes. Fuzzy logic is an important soft computing tool which increases the digital watermarking system in various ways. In this twelfth chapter of Ayan Chatterjee, different popular and high secured watermarking schemes using fuzzy logic are analyzed with their mathematical and experimental efficiency. A comparative analysis is developed here with corresponding different parameters.

Ecological systems are known by their relationships with the environment, they affect and affected by various external factors such as climate, and the basic materials that form the soil. It is for his good distinction of relationships is the first important point in the modeling of ecosystems. The diversity of these systems caused a large amount of data that became hard for analysis, which made researches to classify it as NP-Hard problems. In this thirteenth chapter of Mohamed Elhadi Rahmani, the authors presented a study of application of bio inspired algorithms for ecosystem data analysis. The study contains application of four different approaches that were inspired by authors of the paper from four different phenomena, and they were applied for analysis of four different ecosystem data collected from real life cases. Results showed a very high accuracy and proved the efficiency of bio inspired algorithms for supervised classification of real ecosystem data.

Chapter 14

Medical data mining has high potential for exploring the hidden patterns in the data sets of the medical domain. These patterns can be utilized for clinical diagnosis for widely distributed in raw medical data which is heterogeneous in nature and voluminous. Bio inspired algorithms is new field of research, its main advantage is knitting together subfields related to the topics of connectionism, social behavior and emergence. Briefly put, it is the use of computers to model the living phenomena, and simultaneously the study of life to improve the usage of computers. In this fourteenth chapter of Hanane Menad, the author presents an application of four bio-inspired algorithms and meta heuristics for classification of seven different real medical data set, two of these algorithms are based on similarity calculation between training and test data while the other two are based on random generation of population to construct classification rules. The results showed a very good efficiency of bio inspired algorithms for supervised classification of medical data.

The fifteenth chapter of Mohamed Amine Boudia represents a comparative study between two bio-inspired approaches based on the swarm intelligence for automatic text summaries: Social Spiders and Social Bees. We use two techniques of extraction, one after the other: scoring of phrases, and similarity that aims to eliminate redundant phrases without losing the theme of the text. While the optimization use the bio-inspired approach to perform the results of the previous step. Its objective function of the optimization is to maximize the sum of similarity between phrases of the candidate summary in order to keep the theme of the text, minimize the sum of scores in order to increase the summarization rate; this optimization also will give a candidate's summary where the order of the phrases changes compared to the original text. The third and final step concerned in choosing a best summary from all candidates summaries generated by optimization layer, we opted for the technique of voting with a simple majority.

The mass of data available on Internet is rapidly increased; the complexity of these data is discussed at the level of the multiplicity of information sources, formats, modals and versions, Facing the huge amount complexity of biological data, such as the DNA sequences, protein sequences, and protein structures, the biologist cannot simply use the traditional techniques to analyze this types of data. The knowledge extraction process with data mining methods for the analysis and processing of biological complex data is considered as a real scientific challenge in the search for systematically potential relationships without prior knowledge of the nature of these relationships. In this sixteenth chapter of Fatima Kabli, the author discuss about the Knowledge Discovery in Databases process (KDD) from the Biological Data, specifically the author present a state of the art of the best known and most effective methods of data mining for analysis the biological data and Problems of bioinformatics related to data mining.

In modern information age voluminous data are being generated by various means. Internet of Things (IoT) concept has emerged recently to group all manmade artificial things around us Due to such kind of intelligent devices the annual growth of data generation increase in rapid manner and it is expected that by 2020 it will reach near about more than 40 trillion GB. Data generated through devices are in unstructured form and it is in voluminous amount, tradition techniques of descriptive and predictive analysis are not enough for that. Big Data Analytics have emerged to perform descriptive and predictive analysis on such voluminous data. This seventeenth chapter of Dharmendra Trikamlal Patel first deals with the introduction to Big Data Analytics. Big Data Analytics is very essential in Bioinformatics field as the size of human genome sometimes reaches near about 200 GB. This chapter next deals with different types of big data in Bioinformatics. This chapter will describe the several problems and challenges based on big data in Bioinformatics. Finally, this chapter deals with techniques of Big Data Analytics in Bioinformatics field.

The number of individuals using public transportation is increasing more and more. Transport companies want to ensure, at best, the satisfaction of the travellers. Nevertheless, the significant number of these companies sometimes pushes the travellers to confusion to compose their itineraries and obtain the required information. The authors suggest In this eighteenth chapter of Dr. Zakaria Bendaoud integrating several traveller information systems into a same global system. This chapter aims to provide information to the traveller with-out concern for their location and optimize processing by limiting the number of involved nodes. In this optics, the authors opted for a multi-agents system associated with the Voronoï decomposition of the global network.

This nineteenth chapter of Kijpokin Kasemsap indicates the overview of Brain-Machine Interfaces (BMIs); the aspects of BMIs; BMIs, human-machine interfaces, and electrooculography interfaces; BMIs, Amyotrophic Lateral Sclerosis (ALS), and stroke motor recovery; speech BMIs; BMIs and neuroplasticity; and BMIs and transcranial doppler (TCD). BMIs are the computerized approaches to gaining the brain signals, investigate them, and translate them into the computerized functions in order to organize the required practices. BMIs can allow people to manipulate computerized networks and various electrical devices. With the support of modern technologies, BMIs are functional and able to operate in operational settings. This chapter argues that applying BMIs has the potential to increase organizational performance and reach strategic goals in the digital age.

MapReduce is a solution for the treatment of large data, with-it we can analyze and process data, it does this by distributing the computational in a large set of machines. Process mining provides an important bridge between data mining and business process analysis, his techniques allow for extracting information from event logs. Firstly, the work consists to mine small patterns from a log traces, those patterns are the representation of the traces execution from a business process. In this twentieth and last chapter of Ishak H. A. Meddah, the authors use existing techniques; the patterns are represented by finite state automaton; the final model is the combination of only two types of patterns whom are represented by the regular expressions. Secondly, the authors compute these patterns in parallel, and then combine those patterns using MapReduce, we have two parties the first is the Map Step, the authors mine patterns from execution traces and the second is the combination of these small patterns as reduce step. The results are promising; they show that the approach is scalable, general and precise. It minimizes the execution time by the use of MapReduce.

Acknowledgment

This project was completed with the participation of several people, including members of the Editorial Advisory Board, as well as reviewing them for help and collaboration for their comments and suggestions. I would like to highlight the help of all the actors involved in the process, review and publication of the manual, without which the project could not be satisfactorily finished.

A great thank you and a deep gratitude are due to all the commentators and in particular the GeCoDe laboratory board members who spent their time providing their comments and suggestions and headed Pr Amine Abdelmalek.

Special thanks to the publishing team at IGI Global, whose contributions throughout the process, from the initial idea to the final publication, were invaluable. In particular, Courtney Tychinski, Managing Editor – Development & Acquisitions.

In closing, I would like to thank all the authors for their ideas and excellent contributions to this manual.

Reda Mohamed Hamou
Dr. Tahar Moulay University of Saida, Algeria
September 2017

Chapter 1
Nature–Inspired–Based Modified Multi–Objective BB–BC Algorithm to Find Near–OGRs for Optical WDM Systems and Its Performance Comparison

Shonak Bansal
PEC University of Technology, India

Kuldeep Sharma
PEC University of Technology, India

ABSTRACT

Multi-objective nature-inspired-based approaches are powerful optimizing algorithms to solve the multiple objectives in NP-complete engineering design problems. This chapter proposes a nature-inspired-based modified multi-objective big bang-big crunch (M-MOBB-BC) optimization algorithm to find the Optimal Golomb rulers (OGRs) in a reasonable timeframe. The OGRs have their important application as channel-allocation algorithm that allow suppression of the four-wave mixing crosstalk in optical wavelength division multiplexing systems. The presented simulation results conclude that the proposed hybrid algorithm is superior to the existing conventional classical algorithms, namely extended quadratic congruence and search algorithm and nature-inspired-based algorithms, namely genetic algorithms, biogeography-based optimization, and simple BB-BC optimization algorithm to find near-OGRs in terms of ruler length, total occupied optical channel bandwidth, bandwidth expansion factor, computation time, computational complexity, and non-parametric statistical tests.

DOI: 10.4018/978-1-5225-3004-6.ch001

1. INTRODUCTION

Finding optimal solutions for engineering and industrial design problems having multiple objectives (multi–objective) are computationally very time consuming and tough due to their high degree of complexities, dimensionality, nonlinearities, and inhomogeneity. In order to solve the multi–objective problems in a reasonable time, several nature–inspired based multi–objective optimization algorithms (MOAs) are being proposed (Abbass and Sarker, 2002; Deb, 1999; Deb, 2001; Yang, 2011; Yang et al., 2014). Nature–inspired based MOAs can have several distinct solutions instead of single optimal solution which often conflict with each other and makes it difficult to use any single design option without compromise. The compromise solution is optimal in the wider sense since there is no other better solution present in the search space while taking into consideration all other objectives. Pareto optimal is the best compromise solutions from several different solutions that cannot be dominated as no objective can be better without making some other objective worse. The set of all Pareto optimal solution is designated as Pareto front (Koziel and Yang, 2011; Yang, 2011; Yang et al., 2014). Pareto–optimality is estimated in MOAs to provide flexibility for the design engineer. The aim of MOAs is to search for either the Pareto optimal solutions or the solutions near to Pareto front.

This chapter proposes the application of a nature–inspired based modified multi–objective Big bang–Big crunch (M–MOBB–BC) algorithm to solve an NP–complete optimal Golomb ruler (OGR) sequence problem (Babcock, 1953; Bloom and Golomb, 1977; Colannino, 2003; Distributed.net, 2017; Meyer and Papakonstantinou, 2009; Memarsadegh, 2013; Robinson, 1979; Shearer, 1990; Shearer, 1998) in optical wavelength division multiplexing (WDM) systems. The OGRs can be used as unequally spaced channel–allocation algorithm in optical WDM systems to suppress one of the nonlinear optical effects.

Among the numerous different fiber nonlinear optical effects proposed by researchers Aggarwal (2001), Babcock (1953), Chraplyvy (1990), Forghieri et al. (1994), Kwong and Yang (1997), Saaid (2010), and Thing et al. (2004), the crosstalk due to four–wave mixing (FWM) signal is the major dominant noise effect in optical WDM systems. The performance of the system can be improved if FWM crosstalk signal generation at the channel frequencies is avoided. The efficiency of FWM signal depends on the fiber dispersion and channel–allocation. If the frequency separation of any two channels in an optical WDM system is different from that of any other pair of channels, no FWM crosstalk signals will be generated at any of the channel frequencies (Aggarwal; 2001; Babcock, 1953; Chraplyvy, 1990; Forghieri et al., 1994; Kwong and Yang, 1997; Saaid, 2010; Thing et al., 2004).

To suppress the FWM crosstalk in optical WDM systems, numerous unequally spaced channel–allocation algorithms have been formulated by the many researchers (Atkinson et al., 1986; Forghieri et al., 1995; Hwang and Tonguz, 1998; Kwong and Yang, 1997; Randhawa et al. 2009; Sardesai, 1999; Tonguz and Hwang, 1998) that have the drawback of increased bandwidth requirement when compared with equally spaced channel–allocation. This chapter proposes an unequally spaced bandwidth efficient channel–allocation algorithm by taking into consideration the concept of near–OGRs (Babcock, 1953; Bloom and Golomb, 1977; Shearer, 1990; Thing et al., 2003) to suppress FWM crosstalk in optical WDM systems.

In order to tackle Golomb ruler problem, numerous algorithms have been presented by Galinier et al. (2001), Leitao (2004), Rankin (1993), Robinson (1979), and Shearer (1990). The successful realization of nature–inspired based optimization algorithms such as Tabu search (TS) (Cotta et al., 2006), Memetic approach (MA) (Cotta et al., 2006), Genetic algorithms (GAs) (Ayari et al., 2010; Bansal, 2014; Robinson, 2000; Soliday et al., 1995) and its hybridizations with TS (HGA) (Ayari et al., 2010), hybrid evolutionary (HE) algorithms (Dotú and Hentenryck, 2005), Biogeography based optimization (BBO) (Bansal et al., 2011, Bansal, 2014), simple Big bang–Big crunch (BB–BC) (Bansal et al., 2013; Vyas et al., 2016), simple Firefly algorithm (FA) (Bansal et al., 2014) and its improved form (Bansal et al., 2016), multi–objective Bat algorithm (BA) and its hybridization with differential evolution (DE) mutation strategy (Bansal et al., 2017a; Bansal et al., 2017b; Ritu et al., 2016), Cuckoo search algorithm (CSA) and its hybridization (Bansal et al., 2014; Bansal et al., 2017b; Kumari et al., 2016), and multi–objective Flower pollination algorithm (MOFPA) and its hybridization (Bansal et al., 2017b; Jain et al., 2015) in finding OGR sequences provides a good starting point for algorithms for finding near–OGRs. Therefore, nature–inspired based algorithms seem to be very effective solutions to such NP–complete problems. The proposed hybrid MOA solves the bi–objective (two objectives) in OGR as optical WDM channel–allocation problem. The performances of the proposed algorithms are compared with the existing classical and nature–inspired based optimization algorithms to find near–OGRs for optical WDM systems.

The organization of the chapter is as follows: Section 2 presents the concept of optimal Golomb rulers. Section 3 describes a brief account of nature–inspired based multi–objective BB–BC optimization algorithm and its modified hybrid forms. Section 4 presents the formulation of the OGR problem as a channel–allocation. Section 5 provides simulation results comparing with existing classical and nature–inspired based optimization algorithms for finding unequally spaced channel–allocation in optical WDM systems. Conclusions and future work are outlined in Section 6.

2. OPTIMAL GOLOMB RULERS

The concept of *Golomb rulers* was firstly introduced by W. C. Babcock (1953) which was further described by Bloom and Golomb (1977). An *n*–marks Golomb ruler *G* is an ordered sequence of *n* distinct positive integer numbers

$$G = \left\{ x_1, x_2, ..., x_{n-1}, x_n \right\}, x_1 < x_2 < ... < x_{n-1} < x_n \tag{1}$$

such that all the positive differences

$$\left| x_i - x_j \right|, x_i, x_j \in G, \forall i > j \; or \; i \neq j \tag{2}$$

are distinct.

The positive integer numbers are referred to as *order* or *marks*. The number of marks on a ruler is referred to as the *ruler size*. The difference between the largest and smallest number is referred to as the *ruler length RL* (Bloom and Golomb, 1977; Cotta et al., 2007; Distributed.net, 2017; Drakakis, 2009; Drakakis and Rickard, 2010), i.e.

$$RL = \max(G) - \min(G) = x_n - x_1 \tag{3}$$

where

$$\max(G) = \max\left\{x_1, x_2, ..., x_{n-1}, x_n\right\} = x_n \tag{4}$$

and

$$\min(G) = \min\left\{x_1, x_2, ..., x_{n-1}, x_n\right\} = x_1 \tag{5}$$

Generally the first mark of Golomb ruler sequence G i.e. x_1 can be assumed on position 0. That is, if

$$x_1 = 0 \tag{6}$$

then the n–marks Golomb ruler sequence G becomes

$$G = \left\{0, x_2, ..., x_{n-1}, x_n\right\} \tag{7}$$

The ruler length RL of such n–marks Golomb ruler sequence G is given by

$$RL = x_n \tag{8}$$

Figure 1 shows an example of a 4–marks Golomb ruler sequence $G = \{0, 1, 4, 6\}$ having ruler length 6. The distance associated with each pair of marks is also illustrated in Figure 1.

A perfect Golomb ruler measures all the positive integer distances from 1 to length of the ruler RL (Soliday et al., 1995). That is, an n–marks Golomb ruler sequence G is called perfect if for every integer, say d, $1 \leq d \leq \left(x_n - x_1\right)$, there is at least one solution to

$$d = x_i - x_j, x_i, x_j \in G, \forall i > j.$$

Figure 1 also shows a 4–marks perfect Golomb ruler which measures all the integer distances from 1 to 6. The only available perfect Golomb rulers are up to 4–marks that is there exist no perfect Golomb rulers for $n > 4$ (Colannino, 2003). The ruler length RL of a n–mark perfect Golomb ruler is given by (Leitao, 2004; Soliday, 1995)

Figure 1. A 4–marks OGR and its associated distances

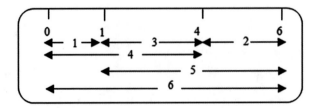

$$RL = \frac{n(n-1)}{2} = \sum_{i=1}^{n-1} i \qquad\qquad (9)$$

An n–marks Golomb ruler sequenced $G = \left\{0, x_2, ..., x_{n-1}, x_n\right\}$ is said to be as optimal if it is of minimal possible length (Weisstein, 2017a; Weisstein, 2017b). There can be several different OGRs for a specific mark values. The unique 4–marks OGR, which measures all the distances from 0 to 6 is illustrated in Figure 1. In a case where optimal Golomb ruler sequence not exists, but its length is near to optimal it will be considered as a near–optimal Golomb ruler. For example, the sequence G = {0,1,3,7,12,20} is a 6–marks near–OGR since its differences are {1 = 1 – 0; 2 = 3 – 1; 3 = 3 – 0; 4 = 7 – 3; 5 = 12 – 7; 6 = 7 – 1; 7 = 7 – 0; 8 = 20 – 12; 9= 12 – 3; 11 = 12 – 1; 12 = 12 – 0; 13 = 20 – 7; 17 = 20 – 3; 19 = 20 – 1}, all of which are distinct. As clear from the differences that the integer numbers 10, 14, 15, 16, 18 are absent so it is not a perfect Golomb ruler. An n–marks Golomb ruler G is an optimal Golomb ruler if and only if, (Bansal, 2014)

1. There is no other n–marks Golomb ruler with the minimal ruler length, and
2. The ruler is represented in canonical form as the smaller of the equivalent rulers $\left\{0, x_2, ..., x_{n-1}, x_n\right\}$ and $\left\{0, ..., x_n - x_2, x_n\right\}$. The smaller means that the difference distance between the first two marks in the ruler set is less than the corresponding distance in the equivalent ruler.

According to the literatures (Colannino, 2003; Dimitromanolakis, 2002; Dollas et al., 1998), all of rulers' up to 8–marks introduced by Babcock (1953) are optimal; the 9 and 10–marks are near–optimal Golomb ruler. Till date the OGR sequences for up to 27–marks are well known and there are some predictions for OGRs up to 158–marks (Shearer, 2001a; Shearer, 2001b). Distributed.net (2017) is now actively searching the OGRs for $n > 27$.

Several algebraic and exact methods are formulated by various researchers (Dewdney, 1985; Dewdney, 1986; Dimitromanolakis, 2002; Drakakis, 2009; Kwong and Yang, 1997; Randhawa et al. 2009) that are impractical in terms of computational resources and it took several months or even years of calculation to prove the optimality with high computational power. Different nature–inspired based optimization algorithms and their hybridization, (Ayari, 2010; Bansal, et al. 2011; Bansal et al., 2013; Bansal et al., 2014; Bansal, 2014; Bansal et al., 2016; Bansal et al., 2017a; Bansal et al., 2017b; Cotta et al., 2006; Dotú and Hentenryck, 2005; Jain et al., 2015; Kumari et al., 2016; Ritu et al., 2016; Robinson, 2000; Soliday et al., 1995; Vyas et al., 2016) have been proposed to find either optimal or near–OGRs at a reasonable time. Therefore, the nature–inspired based optimization algorithms appear to be efficient solutions for such NP–complete OGR problem.

The OGRs found their variety of applications in radio communication, sensor placement in X–ray crystallography, computer communication network, circuit layout, pulse phase modulation, geographical mapping, self–orthogonal codes, very large scale integration (VLSI) architecture, coding theory, linear arrays, fitness landscape analysis, radio astronomy, antenna design for radar missions, sonar applications and NASA missions in astrophysics, planetary and earth sciences (Babcock, 1953; Bloom and Golomb, 1977; Blum et al., 1974; Cotta and Fernández, 2005; Dimitromanolakis, 2002; Dollas et al., 1998; Fang and Sandrin, 1977; Lam and Sarwate, 1988; Lavoie et al., 1991; Leitao, 2004; Memarsadegh, 2013; Robinson and Bernstein, 1967; Soliday et al., 1995).

With the application of OGR sequences in the optical WDM systems, it is possible that the smallest distinct number can be used as the WDM channel–allocation sequence. Since the difference between any two numbers is different, the new FWM crosstalk signals generated would not fall into the one already allocated for the carrier channels.

3. MULTI–OBJECTIVE NATURE–INSPIRED BASED BIG BANG–BIG CRUNCH OPTIMIZATION ALGORITHM AND ITS MODIFIED HYBRID FORMS

The exact or classical computing algorithms in finding optimal solutions to a multi–objective design problem are unreasonable in terms of computational resources and are not considered best for global optimization. Nature–inspired based MOAs are very powerful in dealing with such kind of optimization (Koziel and Yang, 2011; Yang, 2011; Yang, 2013; Yang et al., 2014). The guiding principle is to improve algorithms computationally that lead to an acceptable solution at low cost by seeking for an approximate solution to a precisely or imprecisely formulated problem (Cotta and Hemert, 2008; Rajasekaran and Pai, 2004; Yang, 2010; Koziel and Yang, 2011; Yang, 2013).

This section presents the brief overview of multi–objective nature–inspired optimization algorithm based on the two theories of big bang and big crunch called BB–BC.

In nature–inspired based MOAs, an engineering design problem with M objective functions, having h and g as nonlinear equality and inequality constraints, respectively, can be written as (Yang, 2011; Yang et al., 2014)

$$\text{Minimize} \rightarrow f_1(x), f_2(x), \ldots, f_M(x), \tag{10}$$

$$h_i(x) = 0, \ (i = 1, 2, \ldots, I), \tag{11}$$

$$g_j(x) \leq 0, \ (j = 1, 2, \ldots, J), \tag{12}$$

There are different general approaches to deal with multi–objective optimization. One is to combine the individual objective functions into a single composite function f. A single objective function can be determined with approaches such as weighted sum, utility theory, etc. For simplicity, a weighted sum approach is used to composite all objective functions into a single objective function (Yang, 2011; Yang et al., 2014)

$$f = \sum_{m=1}^{M} w_m f_m \tag{13}$$

with

$$\sum_{i=1}^{M} w_i = 1, w_i > 0, \tag{14}$$

where w_i are randomly generated positive weight values from a uniform distribution. A set of random numbers u_i are generated from a uniform distribution $U[0,1]$. Then, the weight values w_i are normalized by

$$w_i = \frac{u_i}{\sum\limits_{i=1}^{M} u_i} \qquad (15)$$

These normalized weight values w_i ($i = 1,2,...,M$) serves as preferences for optimizing the multi–objective functions. As the weights are generated randomly from a uniform distribution, it is possible to vary the weight values with sufficient diversity so that the Pareto front can be estimated correctly.

Although the nature–inspired based MOAs in their simplified form works well in the exploitation (the acceptable search around a local optimal), still there are some problems in the global exploration (diversification) of the search space. Exploration is the process of finding the diverse solutions so as to explore the search space on a global scale, whereas exploitation is to focus the search in a local region knowing that a current good solution is found in that region. In order to find the best solution, a search algorithm needs to find a good balance between exploration and exploitation. If all the solutions in the initial phase of the MOA are collected in a small part of search space, the algorithm may not search the optimal result and with a high probability, it may be trapped in that sub–domain. One can consider a large number for solutions to avoid this problem, but it will increase in the function calculations as well as the computation time and costs. So for the nature–inspired based MOAs, there is a need by which exploration and exploitation can be improved and the algorithms can work more efficiently. By considering these two features, fitness (cost) based DE mutation strategy and random walk i.e. Lévy–flight distribution is introduced in the proposed nature–inspired based MOAs. In the proposed modified MOAs the mutation rate probability is estimated based on the fitness value. The mutation rate probability MR_i^t of each solution x_i at iteration index t is (Bansal et al., 2017a)

$$MR_i^t = \frac{f_i^t}{Max(f^t)} \qquad (16)$$

where f_i^t is the fitness value of solution x_i at the iteration index t, and $Max(f^t)$ is the maximum fitness value of the population at iteration t. For the proposed multi–objective algorithms, the mutation equation used in this chapter is given by (Price et al., 2005; Storn et al., 1997)

$$x_i^t = x_i^{t-1} + p_m\left(x_{best}^{t-1} - x_i^{t-1}\right) + p_m\left(x_{r_1}^{t-1} - x_{r_2}^{t-1}\right) \qquad (17)$$

where x_i^t is the population at iteration t, $x_{best}^{t-1} = x_*^{t-1}$ is the current global best solution at iteration one less than running iteration index t, p_m is mutation operator, r_1 and r_2 are randomly generated integer numbers between 1 to size of the given problem. The numbers r_1 and r_2 are different from running index. The mutation strategy enhances the probabilities for a good solution, but a high mutation rate results in too much exploration and is disadvantageous to the improvement of candidate solutions. As p_m decreases from 1.0 to 0.01, optimization ability increases greatly, but as p_m continues to decrease to 0.001, optimization ability decreases rapidly. A small value of p_m is not able to sufficiently increase solution diversity (Bansal, 2014).

The Lévy flight distribution used in the proposed nature–inspired MOAs in this chapter is given by (Yang, 2012)

$$L(\lambda) \sim \frac{\lambda \Gamma(\lambda) \sin(\pi \lambda / 2)}{\pi} \frac{1}{s^{1+\lambda}}, (s >> s_0 > 0) \tag{18}$$

Here, $\Gamma(\lambda)$ is the standard gamma distribution valid for large steps i.e. for $s > 0$. Throughout the chapter, $\lambda = 1.5$ is used. In theory, it is required that $|s_0| \gg 0$, but in practice s_0 can be as small as 0.1 (Yang, 2012).

With these two features in the simplified forms of proposed nature–inspired MOA, the basic concept of the search space is modified, i.e. the proposed MOAs can explore new search space by the mutation and random walk strategies. A fundamental benefit of using mutation and Lévy flight strategies with nature–inspired MOA in this chapter is their ability to improve its solutions over time, which does not seem in the other algorithms (Ayari, 2010; Bansal et al., 2011; Bansal et al., 2013; Bansal, 2014; Bansal et al., 2014; Cotta et al., 2006; Dotú and Hentenryck, 2005; Robinson, 2000; Soliday, 1995) to find near–OGR sequences.

Erol and Eksin (2006), inspired by the theories of the evolution of the universe; namely, the Big bang and Big crunch theory, formulated an optimization algorithm called Big bang–Big crunch (BB–BC) algorithm. BB–BC algorithm has two phases: Big bang phase where candidate solutions are randomly distributed over the search space and Big crunch phase where a contraction procedure calculates a center of mass or the best fit individual for the population (Erol and Eksin, 2006; Tabakov, 2011). In BB–BC, the center of mass mathematically is computed by (Erol and Eksin, 2006)

$$x_c = \frac{\sum_{i=1}^{Popsize} \frac{1}{f_i} x_i}{\sum_{i=1}^{Popsize} \frac{1}{f_i}} \tag{19}$$

where x_c = position of the center of mass, x_i = position of candidate i, f_i = fitness (cost) value of candidate i, and *Popsize* = population size. Instead of the center of mass, the best fit individual can also be chosen as the starting point in the Big bang phase. The new candidates (x_{new}) around the center of mass are calculated by adding or subtracting a normal random number whose value decreases as the iterations elapse. This can be formalized by (Erol and I. Eksin, 2006)

$$x_{new} = x_c + r \times c_1 \times \frac{\left(x_{max} - x_{min}\right)}{1 + t / c_2} \tag{20}$$

where r is a random number with a standard normal distribution, c_1 is a parameter for limiting the size of the search space, parameter c_2 denotes after how many iterations the search space will be restricted to half, x_{max} and x_{min} are the upper and lower limits of elite pool, and t is the iteration index.

If fitness based mutation strategy is introduced in the simple BB–BC algorithm, a new *Big bang–Big crunch algorithm with mutation* (BB–BCM) can be formulated.

By applying Lévy–flight distributions in the simple BB–BC algorithm, another new *Lévy–flight Big bang–Big crunch algorithm* (LBB–BC) can be formulated. For LBB–BC, equation (20) is randomized via Lévy flights as given by

$$x_{new} = x_c + r \times c_1 \times \frac{\left(x_{max} - x_{min}\right)}{1 + t / c_2} \oplus L(\lambda) \qquad (21)$$

The product $\oplus$ means entry wise multiplications and $L(\lambda)$ is the Lévy flight based step size given mathematically by the equation (18).

If fitness based mutation strategy is applied to LBB–BC algorithm, *Lévy flight Big bang–Big crunch with Mutation* (LBB–BCM) algorithm can be formulated.

With the same approximated rules and equations, this chapter extends the basic BB–BC algorithm and its modified forms to solve multi–objective problems and named as multi–objective BB–BC (MOBB–BC) algorithm and modified multi–objective BB–BC algorithm (M–MOBB–BC). The only difference is that MOBB–BC and M–MOBB–BC deals with multiple objectives, rather than a single objective.

Based upon the above discussion, the corresponding general pseudo–code for M–MOBB–BC algorithm can be summarized in Figure 2. If the lines 17 to 22 in Figure 2 are removed and Lévy flight distributions in line 16 are not used, then Figure 2 represents the general pseudo–code for MOBB–BC algorithm. If from line 16 Lévy flight distributions is not used, then Figure 2 corresponds to the general pseudo–code for multi–objective BB–BCM (MOBB–BCM) algorithm. If no modifications in Figure 2 are performed, then it represents the general pseudo–code for multi–objective LBB–BCM (MOLBB–BCM) algorithm.

4. PROBLEM FORMULATION: FINDING NEAR–OGRS

In order to find a bandwidth efficient approach to optical WDM system, two research problems are examined: *generation* and *optimization*. The first problem is to find or generate Golomb ruler sequences for channel–allocation in optical WDM systems. The second problem is to optimize Golomb rulers through nature–inspired based MOA by optimizing both the *ruler length* and *total occupied optical channel bandwidth*. Thus the use of Golomb ruler sequences as the channel–allocation algorithm has bi–objectives which are to be optimized.

If each individual element in an obtained sequence (i.e. positive integer location) is a Golomb ruler, the sum of all elements of an individual sequence form the total occupied optical channel bandwidth. Thus, if the spacing between any pair of channels in a Golomb ruler sequence is denoted as CS, an individual element is as IE and the total number of channels/marks is n, then the ruler length RL and the unequally spaced total optical channel bandwidth TBW_{un} are given by the equations (22) and (23) respectively as

Figure 2. General pseudo–code for M–MOBB–BC algorithm

1. **Modified MOBB–BC (M–MOBB–BC) algorithm**
2. **Begin**
3.   /* **Big bang phase** */
4.   Define Pareto front points N and objective functions $f_1(x),...,f_M(x)$, $x = (x_1, ..., x_d)^T$;
                                                                /* d is dimension of the problem */
5.   Generate a random set of NP candidates (population);
6.   Generate M weights $_{w_m \geq 0}$ so that equation (14) is satisfies;
7.   Form a single objective by using equation (13);
8.   Based on fitness value, find the global best solution x_* among the population of NP candidates;
9.   /* **End of Big bang phase** */
10. **For** $i = 1 : N$
11.   Generate M weights randomly which satisfies equation (14);
12.   **While** not TC /* TC is the termination criterion */
13.   /* **Big crunch phase** */
14.   Compute the center of mass;
15.   /* **End of Big crunch phase** */
16.   Calculate new candidates around the center of mass by adding or subtracting a normal random number whose value decreases as the iterations elapse via Lévy flight;   /* **Big bang phase** */
17.   /* **Mutation** */
18.   Compute mutation rate probability MR_i via equation (16);
19.   **If** ($MR_i < rand$)
20.   Perform mutation via equation (17);
21.   **End if**
22.   /* **End of mutation** */
23.   Re–evaluate fitness values of all the generated candidates;
24.   Rank the candidates and find the global best Pareto front solution x_* solutions;
25.   **End while**
26.   Record x_* as a non–dominated solution;
27.   **End for** i
28.   Postprocess results and visualization;
29. **End**

4.1 Ruler Length (*RL*)

$$f_1 = RL = \sum_{i=1}^{n-1}(CS)_i = IE(n) - IE(1) \tag{22}$$

subject to $(CS)_i \neq (CS)_j$ and $(IE)_i \neq (IE)_j$

Total occupied optical channel bandwidth (TBW_{un})

$$f_2 = TBW_{un} = \sum_{i=1}^{n}(IE)_i \tag{23}$$

subject to $(IE)_i \neq (IE)_j$

where $i, j = 1, 2, ..., n$ with $i \neq j$ are distinct in both equations (22) and (23).

These two objective functions f_1 and f_2 are combined into a single objective function f by using equations (10) to (15) so that the Pareto front i.e. best compromise solution can be estimated correctly.

The lower bound on the unequally spaced total optical channel bandwidth can be achieved from (Forghieri et al., 1995)

$$TBW_{un} \geq \left[1 + \left(\left(n/2 - 1 \right) \Big/ S \right) \right] TBW_{eq} \tag{24}$$

where S is minimum channel separation and TBW_{eq} is total occupied channel bandwidth of an optical WDM system where channel are equally spaced and is given mathematically by (Forghieri et al., 1995; Randhawa et al., 2009)

$$TBW_{eq} = (n - 1)\Delta f_c \tag{25}$$

where $\Delta f_c = CS$ is the channel–to–channel separation. Thus equation (24) can also be re-written as

$$TBW_{un} \geq (1 + ((n/2 - 1)/S))(n - 1)\Delta f_c \tag{26}$$

With the optimization of TBW_{un}, the bandwidth expansion factor (*BEF*) (Forghieri et al., 1995; Randhawa et al., 2009) as given by equation (27) is also get optimized.

$$BEF = \frac{TBW_{un}}{TBW_{eq}} \tag{27}$$

The general pseudo–code to find near–OGRs with proposed multi–objective nature–inspired based optimization algorithms and their modified forms is shown in Figure 3. The core of the proposed algorithms is lines 10 to 21 which find OGR sequences for a number of iterations or until either an optimal or near–optimal solution is found.

5. SIMULATION RESULTS

In this section the performance evaluation of proposed nature–inspired based hybrid MOA to find near–OGRs for optical WDM systems is presented. The performance of proposed algorithm has been compared with best known OGRs (Bloom and Golomb, 1977; Dollas et al, 1998; Leitao, 2004; Meyer and Papakonstantinou, 2009; Shearer, 1990; Shearer, 2001a; Shearer, 2001b; Weisstein, 2017b), classical computing algorithms, i.e. Extended quadratic congruence (EQC) and Search algorithm (SA) (Kwong and Yang, 1997; Randhawa et al., 2009) and existing nature–inspired based algorithms, i.e. GAs (Bansal, 2014), BBO (Bansal et al., 2011; Bansal, 2014) and simple BB–BC (Bansal et al., 2013), of finding near–OGRs as channel–allocation algorithm in optical WDM systems.

Figure 3. General pseudo–code to find near–OGRs by using modified multi–objective BB–BC algorithm

1. **Modified multi–objective nature–inspired based BB–BC optimization algorithm to find near–OGRs**
2. **Begin**
3. /* Parameter initialization */
4. Define operating parameters for nature–inspired based multi–objective BB–BC algorithm;
5. Initialize the number of channels, Pareto front points, lower and upper bound on the ruler length;
6. Generate a integer set of populations of size *NP* randomly and each integer population corresponding to Golomb ruler to the specified marks/channels;
    /* Number of integers in population is being equal to the number of channels */
7. Compute the fitness values by using equations (13) to (15), (22), and (23);
    /* fitness value represents the cost value i.e. ruler length and total optical channel bandwidth */
8. Based on fitness value, among *NP* solutions select the globally best solution $x*$;
9. /* End of parameter initialization */
10. **While not** *TC*   /* *TC* is a termination criterion */
11. *A:*   Call multi–objective BB–BC optimization algorithm to determine new set of optimal candidates;
12. Recheck Golombness of updated candidates;
13. **If** Golombness is satisfied
14.   Retain that candidate and then go to *B*;
15. **Else**
16.   Retain the previous generated candidate and then go to *A*;
17.   /* Previous generated candidate is being equal to the candidate generated into the parameter initialization step*/
18. **End if**
19 *B:*   Recompute the fitness values of the modified candidates;
20. Rank the candidates from best to worst based on fitness values and find the global best solution;
21. **End while**
22. Display the near–OGR sequences;
23. **End**

The proposed hybrid MOA have been written and tested in Matlab language running under Windows 7, 64–bit operating system. The proposed hybrid algorithm has been implemented on Intel(R) core™ 2 Duo CPU T6600 @ 2.20 GHz processor Laptop having a hard drive of 320 GB and RAM of 3 GB.

5.1 Parameters Selection for the Proposed M–MOBB–BC Algorithm

Selecting a best suitable parameter value of nature–inspired based MOA is problem specific as there are no concrete rules. The proposed M–MOBB–BC algorithm generates 100 Pareto fronts points *N*.

For M–MOBB–BC algorithm the value of parameter $c_2 = 5$ is assumed a priori as this parameter denotes after how many iterations the search space will be restricted to half. All the other parameter values for M–MOBB–BC were varied from 0.0 to 1.0. After looking wisely at the obtained near–optimal solutions, it was concluded that $c_1 = 0.1$, $p_m = 0.05$ are the best choices for M–MOBB–BC to obtain optimal solutions.

The choice of the best population size (*Popsize*) and maximum iteration (*Maxiter*) for nature–inspired based optimization algorithms are problem specific (Bansal et al., 2017a). The increased *Popsize* helps to explore the search space and increases the diversity of possible solutions. But as the *Popsize* increase, the computation time required to get desirable solutions increase slightly as the diversity of possible solutions increase. After certain limit, it is not useful to increase the *Popsize*, as it does not help in solving the problem quickly.

Golomb rulers realized from 10 to 16–marks by TS algorithm (Cotta et al., 2006), maximum *Popsize* was 190. The hybrid approach proposed by Ayari et al. (2010) to find Golomb rulers from 11 to 23–marks, the *Popsize* were set between 20 and 2000. The algorithms GAs and BBO realized by Bansal, 2014, to find near–OGRs sequences the maximum *Popsize* was 30. For the hybrid evolutionary (HE) algorithms (Dotú and Hentenryck, 2005), the maximum *Popsize* was set to 50 to find near–OGRs. To realize OGRs by the BB–BC algorithm (Bansal et al., 2013), the maximum *Popsize* was set to 10, whereas for the bat algorithm and its hybrid form (Bansal et al. 2017a), the maximum *Popsize* was 20 and 200, respectively.

In this chapter *Popsize* has little significant effect on the performance of proposed M–MOBB–BC. After carefully looking at the results, the *Popsize* of 10 was found to be appropriate for proposed M–MOBB–BC in finding near–OGRs for optical WDM systems.

Increasing the number of iterations tends to decrease the total occupied optical channel bandwidth (TBW_{un}). This indicates that the rulers reach their optimal or near–optimal values after certain iterations and no further improvement is needed.

It is noted that the iterations have little effect for low value channels. But for higher order channels, the iterations have a great effect on the total occupied optical iterations have a great effect on the total occupied optical channel bandwidth, i.e. total occupied optical channel bandwidth gets optimized after a certain number of iterations.

To find Golomb rulers by TS algorithm proposed by Cotta et al. (2006) and Ayari et al. (2010), the *Maxiter* were set to 10000 and 30000, respectively. The hybrid approach proposed by Ayari et al. (2010), finds Golomb ruler sequences within the *Maxiter* of 100000. Bansal (2014) reported that to find near–OGRs, GAs and BBO algorithms stabilized in and around *Maxiter* of 5000, whereas the hybrid evolutionary algorithms proposed by Dotú and Hentenryck (2005) get stabilized at and around *Maxiter* of 10000. By carefully looking at the results, it was noted that to find either optimal or near–optimal Golomb rulers, the proposed algorithm M–MOBB–BC stabilized at or around 1000 iterations. In general, to find *n*–channels near–OGR, the *Maxiter* parameter in this chapter was set to 100 times number of channel (*n*) during simulations, i.e.

$$Maxiter = 100 \times n \tag{27}$$

With the same parameters setting as reported above, the large numbers of sets of trials for various marks/channels were conducted. The proposed M–MOBB–BC was executed 20 times until near–optimal solution was found. Although the proposed M–MOBB–BC find same near–OGRs, but the difference is in the computational time, computational complexity and their statistical analysis which are discussed in the following subsections.

5.2 Performance Comparison of Proposed M–MOBB–BC Algorithm With Existing Algorithms in Terms of Ruler Length and Total Occupied Optical Channel Bandwidth

Table 1 reports the ruler length and total occupied optical channel bandwidth by different sequences obtained from the proposed nature–inspired based M–MOBB–BC after 20 executions and its performance comparison with best known OGRs, EQC, SA, GAs, BBO, and simple BB–BC. Kwong and Yang (1997) stated that the algorithms EQC and SA have their applications limited to prime powers only, so the ruler length and total occupied optical channel bandwidth for EQC and SA are shown by a dash line in Table 1. Comparing the ruler length and total occupied optical channel bandwidth obtained from

Table 1. Performance comparison of proposed M–MOBB–BC optimization algorithm to optical WDM channel–allocation

n	Best Known OGRs (Bloom and Golomb, 1977; Dollas et al, 1998; Leitao, 2004; Meyer and Papakonstantinou, 2009; Shearer, 1990; Shearer, 2001a; Shearer, 2001b; Weisstein, 2017b)		Algorithms															
			Conventional Algorithms				Existing Nature–Inspired Algorithms						Proposed Hybrid Algorithm M–MOBB–BC					
			EQC (Kwong and Yang, 1997; Randhawa et al., 2009)		SA (Kwong and Yang, 1997; Randhawa et al., 2009)		GAs (Bansal, 2014)		BBO (Bansal, 2014)		BB–BC (Bansal, 2013; Bansal et al. 2017a)		MOBB–BCM		MOLBB–BC		MOLBB–BCM	
	RL	TBW_{un} (Hz)	RL	TBW_{un} (Hz)	RL	TBW_{un} (Hz)	RL	TBW_{un} (Hz)	RL	TBW_{un} (Hz)	RL	TBW_{un} (Hz)	RL	TBW_{un} (Hz)	RL	TBW_{un} (Hz)	RL	TBW_{un} (Hz)
3	3	4	6	10	6	4	3	4	3	4	3	4	3	4	3	4	3	4
4	6	11	15	28	15	28	6 7	11	6 7	11	6 7	11	6 7	11	6 7	11	6 7	11
5	11	25 28	—	—	—	—	12 13	23 25 29	12 13	23 24	11 12	23 25	11 12	23 25	11 12 13	23 24 25	11 12	23 25 28
6	17	44 47 50 52	45	140	20	60	17 18 21	42 44 45	17 18 20 21	42 43 44 45 49	17 18	42 44	17 18	42 44 46	17 18	42 44	17 18	42 44 46
7	25	77 81 87 90 95	—	—	—	—	27 28 29 30 31 32	73 78 79 80 83 86 95	27 29 30 31 32 33	73 82 83 84 91 95	25 26 28 30	73 74 77 81	25 27 28 30	73 74 77 79	25 30	73 77 81	25 28 30	73 74 77
8	34	117	91	378	49	189	35 41 42 45 46	121 126 128 129 131 133	34 39 40 42	121 125 127 131	39 41 42	113 118 119	39 41	113 118	39 41	113 118	34 39	113 117
9	44	206	—	—	—	—	52 56 59 61 63 65	192 193 196 203 225	49 56 61 62 64	187 200 201 206 215	44 45 46 61	179 248 253 262	44 57	183 215 226	46 47 58	177 204 217 228	44 55	176 208
10	55	249	—	—	—	—	75 76	283 287 301	74	274	77	258	55 58 74	274 299 311	55 77	258 321 341	55	259 309
11	72	386 391	—	—	—	—	94 96	395 456	86 103 104 114 118	378 435 440 491	72 105	377 490 456	72 105	377 435	72 103	378 439	72 96	369 397 434
12	85	503	231	1441	132	682	123 128 137	532 581 660	116 124 138	556 590 605	85 91	550 580 613	85 90	549 565	85 90	565 567	85 91 93	520 551 550
13	106	660	—	—	—	—	203 241	1015 1048	156 171 187	768 786 970	110 113	768 753	106 110	736 755 848	109 111	700 751 763	106 111	725 744
14	127	924	325	2340	286	1820	206 228 230	1172 1177 1285	169 206 221	991 1001 1166	221	1166	229	996	221	1166	206 226	993 1285
15	151	1047	—	—	—	—	275 298	1634 1653	260 267	1322 1554	267	1322	267	1322	267	1322	260	1554
16	177	1298	—	—	—	—	316	1985	283	1804	316	1985	316	1985	316	1985	283	1804

continued on following page

Table 1. Continued

	Best Known OGRs (Bloom and Golomb, 1977; Dollas et al, 1998; Leitao, 2004; Meyer and Papakonstantinou, 2009; Shearer, 1990; Shearer, 2001a; Shearer, 2001b; Weisstein, 2017b)		Algorithms														
			Conventional Algorithms				Existing Nature–Inspired Algorithms						Proposed Hybrid Algorithm					
													M–MOBB–BC					
n			EQC (Kwong and Yang, 1997; Randhawa et al., 2009)		SA (Kwong and Yang, 1997; Randhawa et al., 2009)		GAs (Bansal, 2014)		BBO (Bansal, 2014)		BB–BC (Bansal, 2013; Bansal et al. 2017a)		MOBB–BCM		MOLBB–BC		MOLBB–BCM	
	RL	*TBW$_{un}$ (Hz)*	*RL*	*TBW$_{un}$ (Hz)*	*RL*	*TBW$_{un}$ (Hz)*	*RL*	*TBW$_{un}$ (Hz)*	*RL*	*TBW$_{un}$ (Hz)*	*RL*	*TBW$_{un}$ (Hz)*	*RL*	*TBW$_{un}$ (Hz)*	*RL*	*TBW$_{un}$ (Hz)*	*RL*	*TBW$_{un}$ (Hz)*
17	199	1661	—	—	—	—	355	2205	354 369	2201 2208	369	2201	369	2201	369	2201	355	2205
18	216	1894	561	5203	493	5100	427 463	2599 3079	362 445	2566 2912	427	3079	445	2566	436	2872	436	2872
19	246	2225	—	—	—	—	567 597	3432 5067	467 475 584	3337 3408 4101	584	4101	567	3432	584	4101	467	3337
20	283	2794	703	7163	703	6460	615 673 680 691	4660 4826 4905 4941	578 593 649	4306 4517 4859	691	4941	673	4826	673	4826	649	4517

the proposed M–MOBB–BC with best known OGRs and existing algorithms, it is noted that there is a significant improvement in the results that is, the results gets better.

From Table 1, it is also noted that the simulation results are particularly impressive. First, observe that for all the proposed M–MOBB–BC, the ruler length obtained up to 13–marks are same as that of best known OGRs and the total occupied optical channel bandwidth for marks 5 to 9 and 11 is smaller than the best known OGRs, while all the other rulers obtained are either optimal or near–optimal. Second, observe that the algorithms MOBB–BCM and MOLBB–BC does not find best known OGRs for *n* > 7, but finds near–OGRs for 8 ≤ *n* ≤ 20. The algorithm MOLBB–BCM can find best optimal rulers up to 8–marks, but finds near–optimal rulers for *n* > 8 efficiently and effectively at a reasonable time.

From the simulation results illustrated in Table 1, it is further noted that the proposed nature–inspired based M–MOBB–BC to find near–OGR sequences for optical WDM systems, outperforms the algorithms presented in their simplified forms. Thus, it is concluded that the algorithm MOLBB–BCM outperforms the other existing algorithms in terms of both the ruler length and total occupied optical channel bandwidth.

5.3 Performance Comparison of Proposed M–MOBB–BC Algorithm in Terms of Bandwidth Expension Factor

The bandwidth expansion factor (*BEF*), gives the factor of expanded bandwidth with the use of unequally spaced channel–allocation for a given number of channels *n* to that of equally spaced channel–allocation for the same number of channels. Table 2 reports the calculated *BEF* (using equation (27)) for different number of channels by the proposed M–MOBB–BC. From Table 2, it can be seen that the *BEF*, as expected, increases with the number of channels for all the proposed algorithms. The *BEF* for algorithm MOLBB–BCM is less than the other existing and proposed algorithms. The obtained *BEF* indicates that the algorithm MOLBB–BCM needs lesser bandwidth requirements than the other algorithms.

Table 2. Comparison of proposed M–MOBB–BC optimization algorithm in terms of BEF for various channels

n	TBW_{eq} (Hz) (Randhawa et al., 2009)	BEF								
		Known OGRs (Bloom and Golomb, 1977; Dollas et al, 1998; Leitao, 2004; Meyer and Papakonstantinou, 2009; Shearer, 1990; Shearer, 2001a; Shearer, 2001b; Weisstein, 2017b)	EQC (Randhawa et al., 2009)	SA (Randhawa et al., 2009)	GAs (Bansal, 2014)	BBO (Bansal, 2014)	BB–BC (Bansal, 2013; Bansal et al. 2017a)	MOBB–BCM	MOLBB–BC	MOLBB–BCM
4	12	0.9166	2.3333	2.3333	0.9166	0.9166	0.9166	0.9166	0.9166	0.9166
6	35	1.2571	4.0	1.7142	1.2857	1.2857	1.2571	1.2571	1.2571	1.2571
8	70	1.6714	5.4	2.7	1.8	1.7286	1.6857	1.6857	1.6857	1.6714
12	176	2.8579	8.1875	3.875	3.0227	3.1591	3.125	3.2102	3.1193	2.9545
14	247	3.7408	9.4736	7.3684	4.7449	4.7206	4.7206	4.0526	4.0324	4.7206
18	425	4.4564	12.2423	12.0	6.7576	6.1153	7.2447	6.0376	6.7576	6.0376
20	532	5.2518	13.4642	12.1428	9.2875	8.7594	9.0714	9.0714	8.094	8.4906

5.4 Performance Comparison of Proposed M–MOBB–BC Algorithm in Terms of Computational Time

The search for Golomb ruler sequences and proving their optimality is tremendously complex and challenging problem. The OGRs generation by classical computing and exhaustive parallel search algorithms for higher order marks is computationally very time consuming, which took several hours, months and even years of calculations on several thousand computers (Distributed.net, 2017; Dollas et al., 1998; Leitao, 2004; Shearer, 1998; Shearer, 2001a; Shearer, 2001b). For example, OGRs with 20 to 27–marks were found by distributed.net (2017) which took several years of calculations on many computers.

Table 3 enlists the average *CPU time* in seconds taken by proposed MOAs to find near–OGRs for up to 20– marks and their comparison with the *CPU time* taken by existing algorithms (Ayari et al., 2010; Bansal et al., 2013; Bansal, 2014; Distributed.net, 2017; Dollas et al., 1998; Leitao, 2004; Shearer, 1990; Soliday et al., 1995). Soliday et al. (1995) reported that to find Golomb ruler sequences from heuristic based exhaustive search algorithm, the computation times varied from 0.035 seconds for 5–marks to 6 weeks for 13–marks ruler, whereas non–heuristic exhaustive search algorithms took approximately 12.57 minutes, 2.28 years, 2.07e+04 years, 3.92e+09 years, 1.61e+15 years, and 9.36e+20 years of, calculations for 10, 12, 14, 16, 18 and 20–marks, respectively. Ayari et al. (2010) identified that to find OGRs by TS algorithm the computational *CPU time* in seconds was around 0.1, 720, 960, 1913, and 2516, for 5, 10, 11, 12, and 13–marks, respectively. The OGRs realized by hybrid GAs proposed by Ayari et al. (2010) the *CPU time* in hours was 5, 8, and 11 for 11, 12, and 13–marks, respectively. The exhaustive computer search algorithms (Shearer, 1990) find OGRs for 14 and 16–marks in an around one and hundred hours, respectively, whereas 17, 18 and 19–marks OGR realized by Rankin (1993) and Dollas et al. (1998), took around 1440, 8600 and 36200 CPU hours (around seven months) of calculations, respectively, on a Sun SPARC Classic workstation. The near–OGRs realized by algorithms GAs and BBO (Bansal, 2014) up to 20–marks the maximum *CPU time* was approximately 31 hours, i.e. nearly 1.3 days, while for algorithm BB–BC (Bansal et al., 2013; Bansal et at., 2017a) the maximum execution time was around 28 hours, i.e. almost 1.1 days.

From Table 3, it is clear that with the applications of mutation and Lévy flight strategies the proposed M–MOBB–BC, the computation *CPU time* for 20–marks ruler is approximately 27 hours. This signifies the improvement realized by the use of proposed M–MOBB–BC to find near–OGRs for optical WDM systems. From Table 3, it is also noted that algorithm MOLBB–BCM outperforms the other algorithms followed by MOLBB–BC, MOBB–BCM, BB–BC, BBO, and GAs in terms of computational *CPU time*.

5.5 Performance Comparison of Proposed M–MOBB–BC Algorithm in Terms of Maximum Computation Complexity

In order to search for the near–OGRs, the proposed hybrid MOA algorithm has an initialization stage and a subsequent stage of iterations. The computational complexity of proposed hybrid algorithm depends upon *Popsize*, *Maxiter*, and Pareto front points (*N*) as (Bansal et al., 2017a)

$$Computation\ Complexity = Popsize \times Maxiter \times N \tag{28}$$

Table 3. Comparison of average CPU time taken by proposed M–MOBB–BC optimization algorithm for various channels

n	Existing Nature–Inspired Algorithms			Proposed Hybrid Algorithm		
	GAs (Bansal, 2014)	BBO (Bansal, 2014)	BB–BC (Bansal et al. 2017a)	MOBB–BCM	MOLBB–BC	MOLBB–BCM
	CPU Time (Sec.)	*CPU Time (Sec.)*	*CPU Time (Sec.)*	*CPU Time (Sec.)*	*CPU Time (Sec.)*	*CPU Time (Sec.)*
3	0.000	0.000	0.000	0.000	0.000	0.000
4	0.001	0.000	0.000	0.000	0.000	0.000
5	0.021	0.020	0.009	0.011	0.001	0.001
6	0.780	0.7432	0.659	0.4398	0.0589	0.0584
7	1.120	1.180	1.170	0.8520	0.0936	0.0935
8	1.241	1.239	1.210	1.0227	0.1986	0.1984
9	1.711	1.699	1.698	1.4890	1.3190	1.3170
10	5.499e+01	5.491e+01	5.450e+01	5.211e+01	3.321e+01	3.319e+01
11	7.200e+02	7.110e+02	6.990e+02	6.710e+02	4.982e+02	4.982e+02
12	8.602e+02	8.600e+02	7.981e+02	7.890e+02	5.865e+02	5.864e+02
13	1.070e+03	1.030e+03	1.020e+03	1.010e+03	8.989e+02	8.980e+02
14	1.028e+03	1.027e+03	1.021e+03	1.019e+03	1.019e+03	1.018e+03
15	1.440e+03	1.480e+03	1.291e+03	1.270e+03	1.187e+03	1.185e+03
16	1.680e+03	1.677e+03	1.450e+03	1.439e+03	1.367e+03	1.366e+03
17	5.048e+04	5.040e+04	4.075e+04	4.041e+03	3.759e+03	3.760e+03
18	6.840e+04	6.839e+04	5.897e+04	5.875e+04	4.087e+04	4.085e+04
19	8.280e+04	8.280e+04	7.158e+04	7.132e+04	6.988e+04	6.986e+04
20	1.12428e+05	1.1196e+05	1.0012e+05	9.876e+04	9.859e+04	9.810e+04

The maximum computation complexity for the TS algorithm (Ayari et al., 2010) to find Golomb ruler sequences was found to be 57e+05, whereas for hybrid GAs proposed by Ayari et al. (2010) was 2e+08. The maximum computation complexity for algorithms GAs and BBO (Bansal, 2014) was 15e+04, whereas for the bat algorithm and its hybrid form (Bansal et al., 2017a) was 4e+06 and 4e+07, respectively.

For example, to find 16–mark near–OGR sequences the computation complexity for MOBB–BCM, MOLBB–BC, and MOLBB–BCM, is 66e+04, 65e+04, and 62e+04, respectively. Thus, it is clear that the algorithm MOLBB–BCM outperforms the other proposed MOBB–BCM and MOLBB–BC algorithms in terms of computation complexity. It is also further concluded that by introducing the concept of mutation and Lévy flight strategies in the simplified form of nature–inspired based MOA the computation complexity is reduced.

Theoretically, the maximum computation complexity for all proposed hybrid MOA to generate near–OGRs upto 20–marks is $10 \times 2000 \times 100 = 2e+06$. As described in above subsection, to generate near–OGRs up to 20–marks, M–MOBB–BC stabilized in *Maxiter* of 1000. Thus, practically, the maximum computation complexity of M–MOBB–BC to generate 20–marks OGR is $10 \times 1000 \times 100 = 1e+06$.

5.6 Performance Comparison of Proposed M–MOBB–BC Algorithm in Terms of Non–Parametric Statistical Analysis

To evaluate whether the near–OGRs found by the proposed hybrid MOA is significant or not, the non–parametric Friedman's statistical analysis (Derrac et al., 2011) of each modified algorithm is performed. For performing the statistical analysis, each proposed hybrid MOA was executed 20 times using the same parameter values as reported in the above subsections. The optimal values of *RL*, TBW_{un} (Hz), *BEF*, and computational *CPU time* (Sec.) after each trial were estimated for the non–parametric statistical analysis.

Two hypotheses: the null hypothesis H_0 and the alternative hypothesis H_1 are defined in non–parametric statistical analysis. The null hypothesis indicates that there is no change or no difference, whereas the alternative hypothesis signifies the presence of a change or difference among the proposed M–MOBB–BC algorithm. In order to reject the null hypothesis, a 95% significance level of confidence is used to analyze at which level the null hypothesis can be rejected. In non–parametric statistical analysis, a *p*–value is estimated to determine whether a statistical hypothesis analysis for the proposed M–MOBB–BC algorithm is significant or not, and it also gives information about how significant the results are. Table 4 enlists the mean ranking calculated from Friedman's statistical test in terms of *RL*, TBW_{un} (Hz), *BEF*, and *CPU time* (Sec.). At a 95% significance level of confidence with 5 as degrees of freedom the critical value in χ^2 distribution is 1.145. As clear from Table 4, the calculated Friedman's statistic value for *RL*, TBW_{un} (Hz), *BEF*, and *CPU time* (Sec.) are larger than the critical values in χ^2 distribution. It suggests that there is a significant difference between the performances of proposed M–MOBB–BC algorithm, i.e. the null hypothesis H_0 is rejected. The algorithm MOLBB–BCM is with the lowest rank and potentially outperforms the other existing and proposed algorithms. The estimated *p*–value in Friedman's statistic is <0.00001 for *RL*, TBW_{un} (Hz), *BEF*, and *CPU time* (Sec.).

Using MOLBB–BCM as a control algorithm, the Holm's post–hoc statistical test (Holm, 1979) is performed to determine the statistical better performance of the algorithm MOLBB–BCM to find OGRs for optical WDM systems. The unadjusted and adjusted *p*–values estimated through the Holm's post–hoc statistical procedure is mentioned in Table 5. It is clear from Table 5 that the algorithm MOLBB–BCM outperforms the other existing and proposed algorithms for OGRs problem in terms of both efficiency and success rate at 95% significance level of confidence. This is no surprise as the objective of for-

Table 4. Mean rankings of the proposed M–MOBB–BC optimization algorithm obtained by Friedman's non–parametric test for OGRs problem

Algorithm	Friedman's Non–Parametric Statistical Test			
	Mean Rank			
	RL	TBW$_{un}$ (Hz)	BEF	CPU Time (Sec.)
MOLBB-BCM	5.1667	5.1944	4.7857	5.0278
MOLBB-BC	5.4167	6.25	5.5	5.7222
MOBB-BCM	6.2778	6.2778	6.2857	6.8333
BB-BC	6.6944	6.6944	7.4286	7.6944
BBO	6.8333	7.5556	7.4286	8.7222
GAs	7.5278	8.0833	8.3571	9.5556
Friedman's statistic value	6.7777	13.6972	5.9551	120.2153
p–value	<0.00001	<0.00001	0.00001	<0.00001

Table 5 Unadjusted and adjusted p–values found for RL, TBW$_{un}$, BEF, and CPU time through Holm's post–hoc procedure with MOLBB–BCM as control algorithm

Algorithm	RL		TBW$_{un}$ (Hz)		BEF		CPU Time (Sec.)	
	Unadjusted *p*–Value	Adjusted *p*–Value	Unadjusted *p*–Value	Adjusted *p*–Value	Unadjusted *p*–Value	Adjusted *p*–Value	Unadjusted *p*–Value	Adjusted *p*–Value
MOLBB-BC	0.8188	0.0269	8.9043e-11	1.6696e-11	0.4005	0.0468	8.7790e-27	8.4958e-28
MOBB-BCM	0.3303	0.0747	3.0e-06	2.85e-07	1.0	0.0993	1.5098e-20	1.3065e-21
BB-BC	1.0	0.3746	1.4e-05	1.0e-06	1.0	0.0993	3.3418e-11	2.9837e-12
BBO	1.0	0.7641	0.0119	0.001	1.0	0.1463	2.0e-06	2.8439e-07
GAs	1.0	0.7641	0.1124	0.01	1.0	0.3304	0.0193	0.003618

mulating the MOBB–BC algorithm and its modified forms to find OGRs was to use the advantages of mutation and Lévy–flight strategies. The performance comparison of proposed algorithm suggests that the algorithm MOLBB–BCM is theoretically more dominant and thus should be further examined in several complex applications of industrial and engineering multi–objective optimization problems.

6. CONCLUSION

A bandwidth efficient unequally spaced channel–allocation algorithm by considering the concept of near–OGRs for optical WDM system to suppress FWM crosstalk was presented. The search for Golomb ruler sequences and proving their optimality through either classical computing or exact algorithms is computationally NP–complete problem. This is because as the number of marks increases, the search for Golomb rulers becomes computationally complex and tough optimization problem. The application of OGR sequences in optical WDM systems as channel–allocation can be considered as multi–objective optimization problem. The purpose to use nature–inspired based hybrid MOA was not essential to find the best solutions, but to produce the best compromise near–optimal solutions under the certain constraints. In this chapter, the application of nature–inspired based MOBB–BC algorithm and its modified forms (i.e. MOBB–BCM, MOLBB–BC, and MOLBB–BCM) to find the near–OGR sequences for optical WDM systems. The proposed MOBB–BC algorithm was modified by introducing fitness value based differential evolution mutation and Lévy flight strategies in its standard forms, which is the main contribution of this research. The proposed hybrid algorithm outperform the other existing algorithms to find near–OGRs in terms of ruler length, total occupied optical channel bandwidth, bandwidth expansion factor, computation time, and statistical analysis. It has also been observed that modified forms, finds near–OGRs very efficiently and effectively than their simplified forms.

The simulated results suggest that for large order marks, the algorithm MOLBB–BCM potentially outperforms the others followed by MOLBB–BC, MOBB–BCM, BB–BC, BBO, and GAs in terms of ruler length, total occupied optical channel bandwidth, bandwidth expansion factor, computation time, and statistical analysis to find near–OGRs. The obtained promising results motivate us to extend the proposed hybrid MOBB–BC study by applying them to real–optical WDM systems and in the future, the proposed modifications will be considered.

REFERENCES

Abbass, H. A., & Sarker, R. (2002). The Pareto Differential Evolution Algorithm. *International Journal of Artificial Intelligence Tools, 11*(4), 531–552. doi:10.1142/S0218213002001039

Aggarwal, G. P. (2001). *Nonlinear Fiber Optics* (2nd ed.). San Diego, CA: Academic Press.

Atkinson, M. D., Santoro, N., & Urrutia, J. (1986). Integer Sets with Distinct Sums and Differences and Carrier Frequency Assignments for Nonlinear Repeaters. *IEEE Transactions on Communications, 34*(6), 614–617. doi:10.1109/TCOM.1986.1096587

Ayari, N., Luong, T. V., & Jemai, A. (2010). A Hybrid Genetic Algorithm for Golomb Ruler Problem. *Proceedings of ACS/IEEE International Conference on Computer Systems and Applications (AICCSA–2010)*, 1–4. doi:10.1109/AICCSA.2010.5586955

Babcock, W. (1953). Intermodulation Interference in Radio Systems. *The Bell System Technical Journal, 32*(1), 63–73. doi:10.1002/j.1538-7305.1953.tb01422.x

Bansal, S. (2014). Optimal Golomb Ruler Sequence Generation for FWM Crosstalk Elimination: Soft Computing Versus Conventional Approaches. *Applied Soft Computing, 22*, 443–457. doi:10.1016/j.asoc.2014.04.015

Bansal, S., Chauhan, R., & Kumar, P. (2014). A Cuckoo Search based WDM Channel Allocation Algorithm. *International Journal of Computers and Applications, 96*(20), 6–12. doi:10.5120/16908-6988

Bansal, S., Gupta, N., & Singh, A. K. (2017b). Nature-Inspired Metaheuristic Algorithms to Find Near–OGR Sequences for WDM Channel Allocation and their Performance Comparison. *Open Mathematics, 15*(1), 520–547. doi:10.1515/math-2017-0045

Bansal, S., Jain, P., Singh, A. K., & Gupta, N. (2016). Improved Multi–Objective Firefly Algorithms to Find OGR Sequences for WDM Channel–Allocation. *International Journal of Mathematical, Computational, Physical, Electrical and Computer Engineering*, 10(7), 315–322.

Bansal, S., Kumar, S., & Bhalla, P. (2013). A Novel Approach to WDM Channel Allocation: Big Bang–Big Crunch Optimization. *Proceeding of Zonal Seminar on Emerging Trends in Embedded System Technologies (ETECH–2013)*, 80–81.

Bansal, S., Kumar, S., Sharma, H., & Bhalla, P. (2011). Golomb Ruler Sequences Optimization: A BBO Approach. *International Journal of Computer Science and Information Security*, 9(5), 63–71.

Bansal, S., Singh, A. K., & Gupta, N. (2017a). Optimal Golomb Ruler Sequences Generation: A Novel Parallel Hybrid Multi–Objective Bat Algorithm. *Journal of The Institution of Engineers (India): Series B, 98*(1), 43–64, doi:10.1007/s40031-016-0249-1

Bansal, S., & Singh, K. (2014). A Novel Soft–Computing Algorithm for Channel Allocation in WDM Systems. *International Journal of Computers and Applications*, 85(9), 19–26. doi:10.5120/14869-3244

Bloom, G. S., & Golomb, S. W. (1977). Applications of Numbered Undirected Graphs. *Proceedings of the IEEE*, 65(4), 562–570. doi:10.1109/PROC.1977.10517

Blum, E. J., Biraud, F., & Ribes, J. C. (1974). On Optimal Synthetic Linear Arrays with Applications to Radio Astronomy. *IEEE Transactions on Antennas and Propagation*, 22(1), 108–109. doi:10.1109/TAP.1974.1140732

Chraplyvy, A. R. (1990). Limitations on Lightwave Communications Imposed by Optical–Fiber Non-linearities. *Journal of Lightwave Technology*, 8(10), 1548–1557. doi:10.1109/50.59195

Colannino, J. (2003). *Circular and Modular Golomb Rulers*. Available at http://cgm.cs.mcgill.ca/~athens/cs507/Projects/2003/JustinColannino/

Cotta, C., Dotú, I., Fernández, A. J., & Hentenryck, P. V. (2006). *A Memetic Approach to Golomb Rulers*. In Lecture Notes in Computer Science: Vol. 4193. *Parallel Problem Solving from Nature–PPSN IX* (pp. 252–261). Springer–Verlag Berlin Heidelberg. doi:10.1007/11844297_26

Cotta, C., Dotu, I., Fernandez, A. J., & Hentenryck, P. V. (2007). Local Search–Based Hybrid Algorithms for Finding Golomb Rulers. Kluwer Academic Publishers.

Cotta, C., & Fernández, A. J. (2005). *Analyzing Fitness Landscapes for the Optimal Golomb Ruler Problem*. In J. Gottlieb & G. Raidl (Eds.), *In* Lecture Notes in Computer Science: *Evolutionary Computation in Combinatorial Optimization* (Vol. 3448, pp. 68–79). Springer–Verlag Berlin. doi:10.1007/978-3-540-31996-2_7

Cotta, C., & Hemert, J. V. (2008). Recent Advances in Evolutionary Computation for Combinatorial Optimization. *Studies in Computational Intelligence, Springer, 153*. doi:10.1007/978-3-540-70807-0

Deb, K. (1999). Evolutionary Algorithms for Multi–Criterion Optimization in Engineering design. In *Evolutionary Algorithms in Engineering and Computer Science* (pp. 135–161). New York: Wiley.

Deb, K. (2001). *Multi-Objective Optimization Using Evolutionary Algorithms*. New York: Wiley.

Derrac, J., García, S., Molina, D., & Herrera, F. (2011). A Practical Tutorial on the Use of Nonparametric Statistical Tests as A Methodology for Comparing Evolutionary and Swarm Intelligence Algorithms. *Swarm and Evolutionary Computation, 1*(1), 3–18. doi:10.1016/j.swevo.2011.02.002

Dewdney, A. (1985). Computer Recreations. *Scientific American, 253*(2), 16–26. doi:10.1038/scientificamerican0885-16

Dewdney, A. (1986). Computer recreations. *Scientific American, 255*(3), 14–21. doi:10.1038/scientificamerican0986-14

Dimitromanolakis, A. (2002). *Analysis of the Golomb Ruler and the Sidon Set Problems, and Determination of Large, Near–Optimal Golomb Rulers* (Master's thesis). Department of Electronic and Computer Engineering, Technical University of Crete.

Distributed.net. (2017). *Project OGR*. Retrieved January 2017 from http://www.distributed.net/ogr

Dollas, A., Rankin, W. T., & McCracken, D. (1998). A New Algorithm for Golomb Ruler Derivation and Proof of the 19 Mark Ruler. *IEEE Transactions on Information Theory, 44*(1), 379–382. doi:10.1109/18.651068

Dotú, I., & Hentenryck, P. V. (2005). A Simple Hybrid Evolutionary Algorithm for Finding Golomb Rulers. *Proceedings of 2005 IEEE Congress on Evolutionary Computation, 3*, 2018–2023. doi:10.1109/CEC.2005.1554943

Drakakis, K. (2009). A Review of The Available Construction Methods for Golomb Rulers. *Advances in Mathematics of Communications, 3*(3), 235–250. doi:10.3934/amc.2009.3.235

Drakakis, K., & Rickard, S. (2010). On the Construction of Nearly Optimal Golomb Rulers by Unwrapping Costas Arrays. *Contemporary Engineering Sciences, 3*(7), 295–309.

Erol, O. K., & Eksin, I. (2006). A New Optimization Method: Big Bang–Big Crunch. *Advances in Engineering Software, 37*(2), 106–111. doi:10.1016/j.advengsoft.2005.04.005

Fang, R. J. F., & Sandrin, W. A. (1977). Carrier Frequency Assignment for Non–Linear Repeaters. *C.O.M.S.A.T. Technical Review, 7*, 227–245.

Forghieri, F., Tkach, R. W., & Chraplyvy, A. R. (1995). WDM Systems with Unequally Spaced Channels. *Journal of Lightwave Technology, 13*(5), 889–897. doi:10.1109/50.387806

Forghieri, F., Tkach, R. W., Chraplyvy, A. R., & Marcuse, D. (1994). Reduction of Four–Wave Mixing Crosstalk in WDM Systems Using Unequally Spaced Channels. *IEEE Photonics Technology Letters, 6*(6), 754–756. doi:10.1109/68.300184

Galinier, P., Jaumard, B., Morales, R., & Pesant, G. (2001). A constraint–Based Approach to the Golomb Ruler Problem. *Proceedings of 3rd International Workshop on Integration of AI and OR Techniques (CP–AI–OR 2001)*.

Holm, S. (1979). A Simple Sequentially Rejective Multiple Test Procedure. *Scandinavian Journal of Statistics, 6*(2), 65–70.

Hwang, B., & Tonguz, O. K. (1998). A Generalized Suboptimum Unequally Spaced Channel Allocation Technique—Part I: In IM/DDWDMsystems. *IEEE Transactions on Communications, 46*(8), 1027–1037. doi:10.1109/26.705403

Jain, P., Bansal, S., Singh, A. K., & Gupta, N. (2015). Golomb Ruler Sequences Optimization for FWM Crosstalk Reduction: Multi–population Hybrid Flower Pollination Algorithm. *Proceeding of Progress in Electromagnetics Research Symposium (PIERS)*, 2463–2467.

Koziel, S., & Yang, X.-S. (2011). *Computational Optimization, Methods and Algorithms*. Springer. doi:10.1007/978-3-642-20859-1

Kumari, N., Singh, T., & Bansal, S. (2016). Optimal Golomb Ruler Sequences as WDM Channel–Allocation Algorithm Generation: Cuckoo Search Algorithm with Mutation. *International Journal of Computers and Applications, 142*(9), 21–27. doi:10.5120/ijca2016909910

Kwong, W. C., & Yang, G. C. (1997). An Algebraic Approach to the Unequal–Spaced Channel–Allocation Problem in WDM Lightwave Systems. *IEEE Transactions on Communications, 45*(3), 352–359. doi:10.1109/26.558698

Lam, A. W., & Sarwate, D. V. (1988). On Optimal Time–Hopping Patterns. *IEEE Transactions on Communications, 36*(3), 380–382. doi:10.1109/26.1464

Lavoie, P., Haccoun, D., & Savaria, Y. (1991). New VLSI Architectures for Fast Soft-Decision Threshold Decoders. *IEEE Transactions on Communications, 39*(2), 200–207. doi:10.1109/26.76456

Leitao, T. (2004). Evolving the Maximum Segment Length of a Golomb Ruler. *Proceedings of Genetic and Evolutionary Computation Conference*.

Memarsadegh, N. (2013). Golomb Patterns: Introduction, Applications, and Citizen Science Game. *Information Science and Technology (IS&T), Seminar Series NASA GSFC*. Available at http://istcolloq.gsfc.nasa.gov/fall2013/presentations/memarsadeghi.pdf

Meyer, C., & Papakonstantinou, P. A. (2009). On the complexity of constructing Golomb Rulers. *Discrete Applied Mathematics, 157*(4), 738–748. doi:10.1016/j.dam.2008.07.006

Price, K., Storn, R., & Lampinen, J. (2005). *Differential Evolution–A Practical Approach to Global Optimization*. Berlin, Germany: Springer.

Rajasekaran, S., & Pai, G. A. V. (2004). *Neural Networks, Fuzzy Logic, and Genetic Algorithms–Synthesis and Applications*. New Delhi: Prentice Hall of India Pvt. Ltd.

Randhawa, R., Sohal, J. S., & Kaler, R. S. (2009). Optimum Algorithm for WDM Channel Allocation for Reducing Four–Wave Mixing Effects. *Optik (Stuttgart), 120*(17), 898–904. doi:10.1016/j.ijleo.2008.03.023

Rankin, W. T. (1993). *Optimal Golomb Rulers: An Exhaustive Parallel Search Implementation* (Master's thesis). Duke University. Available at http://people.ee.duke.edu/~wrankin/golomb/golomb.html

Ritu, B. (2016). A Novel Bat Algorithm for Channel Allocation to Reduce FWM Crosstalk in WDM Systems. *International Journal of Computers and Applications, 136*(4), 33–42. doi:10.5120/ijca2016908459

Robinson, J. P. (1979). Optimum Golomb Rulers. *IEEE Transactions on Computers, 28*(12), 183–184.

Robinson, J. P. (2000). Genetic Search for Golomb Arrays. *IEEE Transactions on Information Theory*, *46*(3), 1170–1173. doi:10.1109/18.841202

Robinson, J. P., & Bernstein, A. J. (1967). A Class of Binary Recurrent Codes with Limited Error Propagation. *IEEE Transactions on Information Theory*, *IT–13*(1), 106–113. doi:10.1109/TIT.1967.1053951

Saaid, N. M. (2010). Nonlinear Optical Effects Suppression Methods in WDM Systems with EDFAs: A Review. *Proceedings of International Conference on Computer and Communication Engineering (ICCCE–2010)*, 1–4. doi:10.1109/ICCCE.2010.5556802

Sardesai, H. P. (1999). A Simple Channel Plan to Reduce Effects of Nonlinearities In Dense WDM Systems. Proceedings of Lasers and Electro–Optics (CLEO '99), 183-184. doi:10.1109/CLEO.1999.834058

Shearer, J. B. (1990). Some New Optimum Golomb Rulers. *IEEE Transactions on Information Theory*, *36*(1), 183–184. doi:10.1109/18.50388

Shearer, J. B. (1998). Some New Disjoint Golomb Rulers. *IEEE Transactions on Information Theory*, *44*(7), 3151–3153. doi:10.1109/18.737546

Shearer, J. B. (2001a). *Golomb Ruler Table*. Mathematics Department, IBM Research. Available at http://www.research.ibm.com/people/s/shearer/grtab.html

Shearer, J. B. (2001b). *Smallest Known Golomb Rulers*. Mathematics Department, IBM Research. Available at http://www.research.ibm.com/people/s/shearer/gropt.html

Soliday, S. W., Homaifar, A., & Lebby, G. L. (1995). Genetic Algorithm Approach to the Search for Golomb Rulers. *Proceedings of the Sixth International Conference on Genetic Algorithms (ICGA–95)*, 528–535.

Storn, R., & Price, K. V. (1997). Differential Evolution—A Simple and Efficient Heuristic for Global Optimization Over Continuous Spaces. *Journal of Global Optimization*, *11*(4), 341–359. doi:10.1023/A:1008202821328

Tabakov, P. Y. (2011). Big Bang–Big Crunch Optimization Method in Optimum Design of Complex Composite Laminates, *World Academy of Science, Engineering and Technology, International Journal of Mechanical, Aerospace, Industrial Mechatronic and Manufacturing Engineering*, *5*(5), 835–839.

Thing, V. L. L., Rao, M. K., & Shum, P. (2003). Fractional Optimal Golomb Ruler Based WDM Channel Allocation. *Proceedings of the 8th Opto-Electronics and Communication Conference (OECC–2003)*, 23, 631–632.

Thing, V. L. L., Shum, P., & Rao, M. K. (2004). Bandwidth–Efficient WDM Channel Allocation for Four–Wave Mixing–Effect Minimization. *IEEE Transactions on Communications*, *52*(12), 2184–2189. doi:10.1109/TCOMM.2004.838684

Tonguz, O. K., & Hwang, B. (1998). A Generalized Suboptimum Unequally Spaced Channel Allocation Technique—Part II: In coherent WDM systems. *IEEE Transactions on Communications*, *46*(9), 1186–1193. doi:10.1109/26.718560

Vyas, J., Bansal, S., & Sharma, K. (2016). Generation of Optimal Golomb Rulers for FWM Crosstalk Reduction: BB–BC and FA Approaches. In *Proceeding of 2016 International Conference on Signal Processing and Communication (ICSC–2016)*. Jaypee Institute of Information Technology. doi:10.1109/ICSPCom.2016.7980551

Weisstein, E. W. (2017a). *Perfect Ruler from MathWorld--A Wolfram Web Resource*. Available at http://mathworld.wolfram.com/PerfectRuler.html

Weisstein, E. W. (2017b). *Golomb Ruler from MathWorld--A Wolfram Web Resource*. Available at http://mathworld.wolfram.com/GolombRuler.html

Yang, X.-S. (2010). *Nature–Inspired Metaheuristic Algorithms* (2nd ed.). Luniver Press.

Yang, X.-S. (2011). Bat Algorithm for Multi–objective Optimization. *International Journal of Bio-inspired Computation*, *3*(5), 267–274. doi:10.1504/IJBIC.2011.042259

Yang, X.-S. (2012). Flower Pollination Algorithm for Global Optimization. In Lecture Notes in Computer Science: Vol. 7445. Proceeding of Unconventional Computation and Natural Computation (UCNC 2012). Springer. doi:10.1007/978-3-642-32894-7_27

Yang, X.-S. (2013). Optimization and Metaheuristic Algorithms in Engineering. In X. S. Yang, A. H. Gandomi, S. Talatahari, & A. H. Alavi (Eds.), *Metaheursitics in Water, Geotechnical and Transport Engineering* (pp. 1–23). Elsevier. doi:10.1016/B978-0-12-398296-4.00001-5

Yang, X.-S., Karamanoglu, M., & He, X. S. (2014). Flower Pollination Algorithm: A Novel Approach for Multiobjective Optimization. *Engineering Optimization*, *46*(9), 1222–1237. doi:10.1080/0305215X.2013.832237

Chapter 2

A New Meta-Heuristics for Intrusion Detection System by Scenario Inspired From the Protection System of Social Bees

Ahmed Chaouki Lokbani
Dr. Tahar Moulay University of Saida, Algeria

Mohamed Amine Boudia
Dr. Tahar Moulay University of Saida, Algeria

ABSTRACT

In this paper, the authors propose a meta-heuristic for intrusion detection system by scenario, inspired by the protection system of social bees to their hive. This approach is based on a specialized multi-agent system where the authors give limited responsibility to each guard bee agent: to secure only one port. This specialization aims to better exploit the training set and the hardware and software performance. The authors start this paper with a short introduction where they show the importance of IT security. Then they give a little insight into the state of the art, before starting the essential part of a scientific paper: "Our Approach," where they explain the natural model. Finally, they simplify their model in a modelling table to share their vision and philosophy to switch from natural model to artificial model.

INTRODUCTION AND PROBLEM

After that people realized that the "war: a massacre of people who don't know each other for the profit of people who know each other but don't massacre each other" Paul Valery. They have decided to change the field of wars form reality to virtual world. today the development of science gives birth to an electronic war. we can even predict that World War III will be purely electronic.

A proverb known and recited in the area of intelligence and espionage issues: "Who has information wins the war". The human had known lot of wars. The development of wars and strategies are based on the sensible information of the enemy and gives a favour to the camp that holds the last update of

DOI: 10.4018/978-1-5225-3004-6.ch002

information. In the history the data holder was always leaking under attack to intercept, modify or destroy information.

Nowadays everything, is computerized, personal information from birth to death: name, address, weight, height, date of birth, CV, health.... Are computerized and stored in servers and even money and fortune became as property files or tuples in a databases for mayor or numbers to the bank. It will not stop there, the arrival social networks and computerized our personal lives, opinions and feelings. We the IT professionals, aims to replicate the world in virtual mode. What makes servers and computer systems have become targets of attacks and crime.

This also leads us to predict the end of the old-style crime where robbers have to be writer and director and main actor, the end of improvisation as well, and the end of exposing the victim and criminal's life at risk. At present, The robber must have a great knowledge of computer science, he must write an algorithm instead of scenario, it must be implemented his computer programs and skipping all the security protocols. Now, robbers are able to work from a warm office listening to a Mozart symphony and drinking a cup of coffee. the challenge is big!!!!!

Electronic crime generally begins as a trend and a challenge between young and novice hackers, but it is rapidly evolving to the point where it becomes the subject of secret international tenders for large institutions and even countries. Companies and countries are under attack which can result in significant losses. The establishment of IT security has become more important than the establishment of the internal security for the place and people (scanner, metal detector, door guard,, weapon, intelligence ...). Must control the input data stream and the output data stream of the telephone cable, or fiber optic and wireless connections that the company spend a large sum to get them, for the installation and maintain them; all that with their total grateful(company), more than that, that she considers it like a pride and added value in its performance.

A good IT security is based on the robustness of the implementation of security policy, it is designed and defined by a number of characteristics: it occurs when the levels, the objectives of this polished and finally tick the tools used to ensure safety.

To ensure a protection of company data, different tools are available. They usually used together, in order to secure the various existing flaws in a system. But the first and the most important tools in the security system is the IDS (intrusion detection system); firstly because the majority of attacks are made after an intrusion or by introducing a malicious program and secondly because the IDS is the only tool that ensures permanence. It is responsible for start or stop strategies and response in case of attack.

IDS stands for Intrusion Detection System. It is an equipment that ensures on-the activity of a network or a given host to detect intrusion attempts and possibly react to this at-tempt. There are different kinds of IDS in the literature, it differs in the area of monitoring, operating mode or answer mode.

The theory cites two response mode: where the passive save attack in a log file that will be analysed by the security manager. And active response: rather aim is to stop an attack at the time of detection: by interrupting a connection where even against attack. We can classify the IDS by the response mode: passive IDS where IDS save intrusion and communicates it to the manager of IT security, and Active IDS that make an action when an intrusion is detected. While re-looking scientific and the software industry there are only passive IDS answer.

The approach of the security of information systems that prevails today is too passive. We expect to detect an attack while we trust the multiple protection tools that we have developed and which are not infallible.

If you back up toward the end of the third paragraph of this introduction, you will find a striking sentences: "We are IT professionals, we aim to replicate the world in virtual mode". We had searched in nature a strong security system. We were attracted by a quote from Albert Einstein that "if bees disappear, mankind has for four years to live," how social bees can protect themselves and their honey facing the law of the strongest?

I do not even know the crazy person who can approach a bees hive without protection, because not only can't do it but it will be pursued and attacked hundreds of meters by the bees of this hive who sacrifice themselves for the safety of their hive. This inspired us to model an intrusion detection system based on a meta-heuristic, in this case the system of protection of social bees.

In this paper, we propose a theoretical model modelling a new intrusion detection sys-tem based on bio-inspired metaheuristic namely "social bees" that we nicknamed it "IDS-bee" having an active response mode; and we propose dubbed the given computer system of this IDSbee a "hive" system.

INTRUSTION DETECTION SYSTEM LITERATURE REVIEW

Today's information systems are becoming more open to the outside world that is the Internet, which nevertheless raises a critical issue from the perspective of the attacks suf-fered by these systems. Hence the need to set up around these systems security policies.

To detect attacks, it is necessary to have a specialized software in the monitoring of data transmitted on a system, and is able to react if data seem suspicious. They are called IDS (Intrusion Detection Systems).

An intrusion detection system is a mechanism to identify anomalous or suspicious activity on the analysed target (network B) at an operation illustrated in Figure 1.

We have a Intrusion prevention systems (IPS). that prevent any detected suspi-cious activity in a system, actively acting on the attack by blocking the connection unlike IDS, which are rather passive.

In general, we classify the IDS according to the using approaches:behavioral, scenari-os or hybrid approach, but it is possible to classify the IDS according to other parameters that is to say in terms of the response that he brings to the intrusion they have detected. Some IDS are content to issue an alarm to

Figure 1. Function manner of an IDS

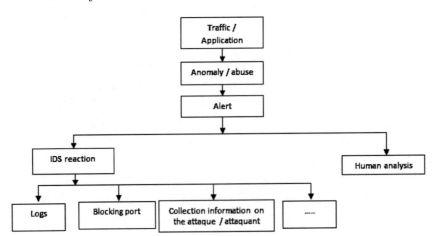

the administrator (passive response) tan tell others try to counter the ongoing attack by packet filtering from the attacker (active response).

The Scenario Approach

Using to detect a known attack by a set of characteristics to identify an intrusion: unusual packet size, unusual format of packet... we have four main technique in this approach:

- Pattern matching. The first use of Pattern Matching was done by Kumer et al in 1994 and the system was improved and called IDIOT which is based on coloured Petri networks. after many works have been developed, we cite her the work of Boyer-Moore, Counting Algorithm, Genetic Algorithms.
- Protocol analysis
- Detection of anomaly using the heuristics methods as genetic algorithms proposed in 1970 that were used by L. M for the implementation of the system GASSATA for example.
- Statistical analysis or statistical model that represent the Probabilistic analysis using the Bayesian networks in the most algorithm

The Behavioural Approach

It consists of detected suspicious activity in the behaviour of the user relative to his usual behaviour and thus trigger an alarm. It was proposed by Anderson in 1980 who proposed to describe the user profile by a set of relevant measures modelling at its best behaviour to detect by a following any deviation from normal behaviour learned while Denning taken over by in 1987, his model contains six components: subjects, objects, audit education, profiles, anomaly education and rule of activity.

It most known algorithms:

- Neural networks
- Expert systems
- Immunology
- Data Mining
- Graphs

OUR PROPOSED APPROACH

Our work aims at modelling a method bio-inspired which is the protection system of social bees to problems in computer science, in this case the intrusion detection system. Before explaining and detailing our approach we must describe at first the natural model of the functioning of the protection system of social bees and shed light on the aspects which directed us to choose this metaheuristics for our problem which is the intrusion detection system. Then we draw up a table of modelling (the natural model vs the artificial model). Finally we shall explain the artificial model which is the pulp of our approach.

Natural Model

Bees have different properties from those of other insect species. They live in colonies, building their hive in tree trunks or similar closed spaces.

A bee colony consists of:

- **A Queen:** A female bees we found one queen for each colony, its size is much larger than other bees. Its main task is to lay eggs. In addition to laying eggs, the queen also secretes important communicative substances that keep the unity of the colony and the proper functioning of different systems within it.
- **Males:** Larger than the working females, but they do not sting and organs necessary to harvest their own food. Their only function is to fertilize the queen
- **Workers Bees:** Perform all other tasks: cleaning the hive, caring for the larvae, feeding the queen and males, make honey, construct and maintain the hive, ventilate the hive, harvest and storing substances like nectar, pollen, water and resin. Ensure the safety and security of the hive.

German scientist Gustav Rosch sought the secret of this fantastic distributions of tasks, he concluded that the tasks performed by the workers in the hive depends on their age. Ac-cording to these results, the worker bees perform completely different roles during the first three weeks of life. but in an emergency, bees can also change their tasks. This is a huge advantage in a society as crowded as the hive. For example, in the case of an attack, if only the sentinel bees were involved in combat and the others continued to perform their own tasks, it would represent a serious danger to the hive. However, what happens in reality is that much of the colony except that stands guard over the other entries took part in the defense and security is an immediate priority.

Worker bees are starting earlier work:

1. After hatching from the cell, they clean their own cell and can they clean the hive, during the first phase of their life that lasts three days and cleaning hive
2. In second phase, they will be responsible for the care and feeding larvae,
3. The third stage, they will be responsible for the construction and maintenance of the hive.
4. In the fourth phase of their lives, worker bees will be the military defence of the hive, their main role will be to ensure the safety and security of the hive, honey and in the worst case ensure the safety of the queen and the leak and why they sacrificed their lives.
5. In the last period of their lives the working bee will make the task of foraging is collecting food.

In this article we sum interest by the fourth phase All bees are very similar, however, the foreign bees entering the hive are immediately identified. Scientists who have studied the question of how bees accomplish this have come to some surprising conclusions: The smell of the hive is the most important factor that allows the bees to recognize each other; with this smell, the bees are able to distinguish from each other. Those who do not have the distinctive smell of the hive therefore represent a danger. Without exception, all foreigners who do not have the smell of the hive is attacked by sentinel bees. The bees that are trying to get into another hive are immediately identified by the sentinels because of their different smell and they are deported or killed by the guards.

When a stranger arrives at the entrance of the hive, sentinel immediately show a strong reaction, using their stings. Immediately after the initial response of the guards, the other bees in the hive usually join the attack. The signal that initiates a general attack by worker bees in the hive is a chemical (pheromone) issued by the pricks sentinel during an attack against the intruder.

In addition to the emission of pheromones that initiate the attack, the characteristic posture and agitated behavior of bees also an alarm signal for the other bees in the hive. Following the release of chemical agents warning, hundreds of bees are grouped at the entrance of the hive. The attack was leading by the bee will stop as soon as the intruder is dead or near the perimeter of the hive, this scope has totalled some hundred meters.

When a bee stings, the lancets stay outside their body, in the body of the enemy more precisely. During this process, the entire lancets mechanism is torn, leaving the mortally wounded bee.

The defense of the hive is a major responsibility regarding the entire colony, the guard bees assume that, even at the cost of their own lives. Each bee in the hive behaves in the same way and when the hive is under attack, they assume the role of protecting the hive.

The guard bees have two strategies to response to any intrusion, the two strategies are based on the principle of offensive defence:

1. The first strategy is based on the pursuit and attack until the intruder leaves the perimeter of hive or died, this strategy and deadly to bees because the sting mechanism is mortal for bees.
2. The second strategy that bees use to defend what is the use of heat to destroy the enemy with a vulnerability to heat.

In case the guardian bees fail to defend the hive and the intruder win, bees that are not made part of the offensive defense are relocated maximum food and content to hive of other place. They choose even in the worst case to relocated the queen and drones providing escort during relocation. Queen of relocation, fake embroider and food designed to ensure a hive of life and continuity melt another life in a more secure location.

In this paper we will focus on odor recognition: intrusion detection by scenario. In previous work, the implementation of intrusion detection systems by scenario, whether it's a single or a multi agent, we give a big responsibility to the agent or agents: they must detect all intrusions on the network (on all ports).

The construction of the intrusion model is made by a general training set globalizing all connection (intrusion and non-intrusion) on all ports. So we will have one intrusion model only for all agents, which we are not even sure that he take into consideration every possible intrusion on all ports.

We have noted that in a bee hive, each guardian bee stands guard over the entry that she is responsible, and she does not care about the other entries, and will continue to en-sure that its entry even in worst case.

The Artificial Model

In our approach dedicated to the intrusion detection we propose to model the protection system of social bees where the artificial model involves two states:

Initial State

According to the modelling table above our intrusion detection system will be implemented:

Table 1. Transition from natural model of security of bees to artificial model of IDS by scenario

	Natural Model	Artificial Model
	Hive	Network
E	Entry of hive	port
A	Queen	Sensitive data
B	Males	Applications
D	Guardian workers	Guardian agent: security service
F	Odor recognition (recognized or unrecognized)	Training Set (intrusion, no-intrusion)
G	Limited responsibility for each Guardian workers	Spliting of Training set

Figure 2. Artificial modal of IDS by scenario based on bees protection system

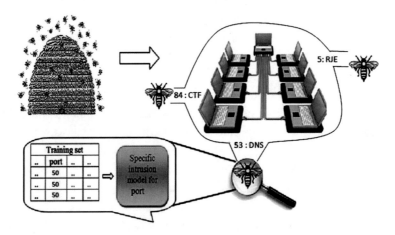

1. Sensitive Data characters that represent the queen,
2. Priority of applications.
3. Determine the minimum required services for stability of system
4. The ports to be secure; each port a Guardian agent showed the guard. The number of active agents guards equals the number of the port in addition to the numbers of guards maintain order within the hive.
5. The training set base two-class learning which represents the intrusion scenarios where the class has two possible values: 'intrusion' or 'non-intrusion', the learning base will be divided according to the number of existing ports. Each guardian agent posted on port X will be take a part of the training set where the attribute 'port' value is equal to X.

State of Activity: Build and Update of an Action Model

To use intrusion detection system IDS by scenario based on social bees, All bees will be posted, one bee at every port of the network and she is responsible on its security, and attribute to every bee the part of training set concerning the port which she is responsible to secure it to build a model of attack by using several algorithms for Data Mining; we propose to use the algorithm known by their high performance bi-class classification: Naive Bayes, SVM and ID3 or C4.5. After the application of these three classic data mining algorithms on learning bases we have three different classification models. The class assignment to a new incoming connection, or user acting in the network will be made by the method of bagging which is a simple majority vote.

EXPERIMENTATION

In the experiment we used three classical algorithm of data mining to build three models for each intrusion gardian bee, noting that decision making and the attribution of the class for the new instances will be by the bagging method (simple majority vote).

We have use the baysien classifier, k-means algorithm with k = 2 and c.45 as decision tree algorithm.

Used Corpus

Since 1999, KDD'99 has been the most wildly used data set for the evaluation of anomaly detection methods. This data set is prepared by Stolfo et al. The two weeks of test data have around 2 million connection records. KDD training dataset consists of approximately 4,900,000 single connection vectors each of which contains 41 features and is labeled as either normal or an attack, with exactly one specific attack type.

The simulated attacks fall in one of the following four categories:

- Denial of Service Attack (DoS)
- User to Root Attack (U2R)
- Remote to Local Attack (R2L)
- Probing Attack

Result

We randomly generated from the general corpus 51 training set and 51 test set, that corre-spond to 51 existing logic port in KDDCUP 99 (attribut = service); each pair (training set, test set) contains the tuple where the value of the service_attribute is the same.

Each agent generates three intrusion models using the three algorithm Naives Bayes, K-Means, and C.45, with training set. Finally, we apply these three intrusion models on the test set, the class allocation shall be by a simple majority vote.

- **In Yellow:** The performance of agent is good, the port is secure
- **In Green:** The performance of the agent is very good, the port is very well secured
- **In Red:** The performance of the agent is bad, the port is not very secure and can be a source of attack because it is vulnerable

If we assume that the performance of our system is the sum of the performance of all agents applied to each network port, we will have the overall result.

If we assume that the performance of our system is the sum of the performance of all agents applied to each network port, we will have the overall result (see Table 3).

Figure 3. Evaluation result of each agent posted on port (part 1/3)

Port n° 0 : OTHER			Port n° 5 : RJE			Port n° 7 : Echo		
1005	415	Precision = 0.662	1031	144	Precision = 0.844	1193	87	Precision = 0. 937
344	671	Recall = 0.694	248	1077	Recall = 0.845	68	1152	Recall = 0.938
	F-Measure= 0.689			F-Measure= 0.844			F-Measure= 0.938	
Port n° 9 : DISCARD			Port n° 11 : SYSTAT			Port n° 13 : DAYTIME		
1005	232	Precision = 0.759	1051	144	Precision = 0.829	1101	184	Precision = 0.824
377	88	Recall = 0.66	291	1014	Recall = 0.828	257	958	Recall = 0.822
	F-Measure= 0.768			F-Measure= 0.828			F-Measure= 0.823	
Port n° 15 : NETSTAT			Port n° 21 : FTP			Port n° 22 : SSH		
999	191	Precision = 0.766	1257	64	Precision = 0.942	1248	151	Precision = 0.869
418	403	Recall = 0.773	81	1098	Recall = 0.941	173	928	Recall = 0.867
	F-Measure= 0.764			F-Measure= 0.941			F-Measure= 0.868	
Port n° 23 : TELNET			Port n° 25 : SMTP			Port n° 35 : PRINTER		
1110	101	Precision = 0.842	1178	121	Precision = 0.919	993	285	Precision = 0.727
315	974	Recall = 0.836	79	1122	Recall = 0.920	405	804	Recall = 0.736
	F-Measure= 0.839			F-Measure= 0.920			F-Measure= 0.737	
Port n° 42 : HOSTNAMES			Port n° 53 : DNS			Port n° 56 : AUTH		
1144	151	Precision = 0.882	1055	157	Precision = 0.858	1288	44	Precision = 0.968
143	1062	Recall = 0.882	198	1090	Recall = 0.858	35	1133	Recall = 0.968
	F-Measure= 0.882			F-Measure= 0.858			F-Measure= 0.968	

*For a more accurate representation see the electronic version.

Figure 4. Evaluation result of each agent posted on port (part 2/3)

Port n° 63 : WHOIS			Port n° 69 : TFTP			Port n° 70 : GOPHER		
1197	81	Precision = 0.908	1219	50	Precision = 0.951	987	272	Precision = 0.802
153	1069	Recall = 0.908	72	1159	Recall = 0.951	223	1018	Recall = 0.802
	F-Measure= 0.908			F-Measure= 0. 951			F-Measure= 0.802	
Port n° 79 : FINGER			Port n° 80 : HTTP			Port n° 84 : CTF		
1014	163	Precision = 0.74	1235	30	Precision = 0.957	927	200	Precision = 0.828
288	835	Recall = 0.78	79	1156	Recall = 0.956	225	1148	Recall = 0.0.829
	F-Measure= 0.76			F-Measure= 0. 956			F-Measure= 0.0.828	
Port n° 87 : PRIVATE			Port n° 95 : SUPDUP			Port n° 102 : ISO_TSAP		
1214	160	Precision = 0.880	1116	271	Precision = 0.837	1061	163	Precision = 0.823
134	992	Recall = 0.882	135	978	Recall = 0.841	286	990	Recall = 0.821
	F-Measure= 0.881			F-Measure= 0. 839			F-Measure= 0.822	

*For a more accurate representation see the electronic version.

Figure 5. Evaluation result of each agent posted on port (part 3/3)

Port n° 194 : IRC			Port n° 196 : RED I			Port n° 209 : MTP		
1159	185	Precision = 0.838	1176	174	Precision = 0.861	1118	187	Precision = 0.841
218	938	Recall = 0.836	171	979	Recall = 0.861	208	987	Recall = 0.841
F-Measure= 0.837			F-Measure= 0. 861			F-Measure= 0.841		
Port n° 210 : Z39 50			Port n° 245 : LINK			Port n° 387 : URP I		
1108	154	Precision = 0.861	1155	180	Precision = 0.872	1079	146	Precision = 0.846
194	1044	Recall = 0.860	136	1029	Recall = 0.874	241	1034	Recall = 0.845
F-Measure= 0.860			F-Measure= 0. 873			F-Measure= 0.846		
Port n° 389 : LDAP			Port n° 407 : TIM I			Port n° 433 : NNSP		
1187	112	Precision = 0.868	1121	157	Precision = 0.855	1218	120	Precision = 0.892
225	976	Recall = 0.863	205	1017	Recall = 0.854	149	1013	Recall = 0.891
F-Measure= 0.866			F-Measure= 0. 855			F-Measure= 0.891		
Port n° 472 : KLOGIN			Port n° 491 : LOGIN			Port n° 495 : ECO I		
1169	71	Precision = 0.904	1142	114	Precision = 0.901	1097	338	Precision = 0.821
174	1086	Recall = 0.902	133	1111	Recall = 0.901	114	951	Recall = 0.828
F-Measure= 0.903			F-Measure= 0. 901			F-Measure= 0.825		

*For a more accurate representation see the electronic version.

Table 2. The global evaluation result of our approach

Globale: 127.500 instance		
TP=57.429	FN=10.116	Precision = 0.856
FP=8.190	TN=51.765	Recall = 0.855
F-Measure= 0.856		

Table 3. Result of classical approach

Traditionnel technic: 10.000 instance max		
TP=4.784	FN=758	Precision = 0. 832
FP=901	TN=3.557	Recall = 0.830
F-Measure= 0.831		

INTERPRETATION AND DISCUSSION

In the results we can see clearly that each bees is autonomous and independent to the another bees, it has its proper training set, and it generates its own intrusion model and take its own class allocation decision.

In case of attack we risk losing the agent is applied to the port whose attack is incoming, the other agents are not going to be vulnerable, and ensures the security of their port without the concerned about the attack. In the approach of a single agent or multiple agents who secure all networks, if an attack occurs, the agent or agents are giving different port security and focuses on the harbour in danger, creating of another vulnerability that can be used by cybercrime.

Table 4. Representativeness of approach

	The Number of Instance	**Against 10% KDDCUP'99**	**Against KDDCUP'99**
Our approach	127.500	127.500/500.000 = 25%	127.500/5.000.000 = 2,5%
Traditional approach	10.000	10.000/500.000 = 2%	10.000/500.000 = 0,2%

We finds that 40% of ports have a ordinar security, et and we point that there are only 12% of bad secured port and vulnerable.

We have experiments the same method: three algorithm with the same allocation class made by the method of bagging which is a simple majority vote. with a single agent to secure a totally of network. knowing that the greatest defect kddcup'99 is its huge size, that cannot be used in the whole, our hardware allows us to go up using 10.000 instances for the test, here below the result

Our approach is better than the traditional approach every level, it has: Recall, precesion, F-Measure, and true alarm greater than that of the traditional approach and has an entropy and the false alarm rate also less than traditional approach.

We want to put the light representativeness of our approach rapport the complete works and much more important than traditional, as shown in Table 4.

CONCLUSION AND PERSPECTIVE

In this paper, we proposed a new method bio-inspired in this case the protection system in bees, we have developed an artificial model for intrusion detection based on this natural model.

The first highlight of our approach based on the system protection of bees is the intelli-gent use of resources: training set, set and test our hardware. Another strength of our ap-proach is that the security of permanence is guaranteed even in case of attack the other network logical port will not be disturbed, you can even stop connection on port in attack and let the other operational, this will increase the profitability of our network. Another strong point of our approach is that the training set is not static, in fact the learning base is updated as and measure; to ensure greater representation of possible cases. Our approach ensures fault tolerance, indeed launching two threads, even if either intentionally or acci-dentally stops the other thread assured the service.

In the future, we plan to experiment and our artificial simulated model for intrusion detection IDS with several other algorithms of data mining to have an idea on the influence of algorithm on performance of IDS . We plan after the experiments to bring some improvement according to the results by pressing the strong point and try to rectify the maximum weaknesses.

REFERENCES

Alanou, L. M. V. (1996). *Détection d'intrusion dans un système informatique: méthodes et outils*. Academic Press.

Anderson, D., Frivold, T., Tamaru, A., & Valdes, A. (1994). *Next generation intrusion detection expert system (nides), software users manual*. Academic Press.

Beauquier, D., Bcrstcl, J., & Chrétienne, P. (1992). *Éléments d'algorithmique* (Vol. 8). Paris: Masson.

Boudia, M. A., Hamou, R. M., & Amine, A. (2015). A New Meta-Heuristic based on Human Renal Function for Detection and Filtering of SPAM. *International Journal of Information Security and Privacy*, *9*(4), 26–58. doi:10.4018/IJISP.2015100102

Cikala, F., Lataix, R., & Marmeche, S. (2005). *Les IDS/IPS*. Intrusion Detection/Prevention Systems.

Dagorn, N. (2006). Détection et prévention d'intrusion: présentation et limites. *HAL archives-ouvertes*.

Debar, H. (1993). *Application des reseaux de neurones a la detection d'intrusions sur les systemes informatiques* (Doctoral dissertation).

Debar, H., Becker, M., & Siboni, D. (1992, May). A neural network component for an intrusion detection system. In *Research in Security and Privacy, 1992. Proceedings., 1992 IEEE Computer Society Symposium on* (pp. 240-250). IEEE. doi:10.1109/RISP.1992.213257

Denning, D. E. (1987). An intrusion-detection model. *Software Engineering, IEEE Transactions on*, (2), 222-232.

Evangelista, T. (2004). *Les IDS: les systèmes de détection d'intrusions informatiques*. Dunod.

Forrest, S., Hofmeyr, S. A., Somayaji, A., & Longstaff, T. A. (1996, May). A sense of self for unix processes. In *Security and Privacy, 1996. Proceedings., 1996 IEEE Symposium on* (pp. 120-128). IEEE. doi:10.1109/SECPRI.1996.502675

Hamou, R. M., Amine, A., & Boudia, A. (2013). A New Meta-Heuristic Based on Social Bees for Detection and Filtering of Spam. *International Journal of Applied Metaheuristic Computing*, *4*(3), 15–33. doi:10.4018/ijamc.2013070102

Hamou, R. M., Amine, A., & Lokbani, A. C. (2013). Study of Sensitive Parameters of PSO Application to Clustering of Texts. *International Journal of Applied Evolutionary Computation*, *4*(2), 41–55. doi:10.4018/jaec.2013040104

Ilgun, K., Kemmerer, R. A., & Porras, P. A. (1995). State transition analysis: A rule-based intru-sion detection approach. *Software Engineering. IEEE Transactions on*, *21*(3), 181–199.

Kumar, S., & Spafford, E. H. (1994). *An application of pattern matching in intrusion detection*. Purdue University. Computer Science Technical Reports.

Lindqvist, U., & Porras, P. A. (1999). Detecting computer and network misuse through the pro-duction-based expert system toolset (P-BEST). In *Security and Privacy, 1999. Proceedings of the 1999 IEEE Symposium on* (pp. 146-161). IEEE.

MIT Lincoln Labs. (1998). *DARPA Intrusion Detection Evaluation*. Available on: http://www.ll.mit.edu/mission/communications/ist/corpora/ideval/ index.html

Percher, J. M., & Jouga, B. (2003). Détection d'intrusions dans les réseaux Ad hoc. *Projet*.

Chapter 3
Comparative Study Between a Swarm Intelligence for Detection and Filtering of SPAM:
Social Bees vs. Inspiration From the Human Renal

Mohamed Amine Boudia
Dr. Tahar Moulay University of Saida, Algeria

Mohamed Elhadi Rahmani
Dr. Tahar Moulay University of Saida, Algeria

Amine Rahmani
Dr. Tahar Moulay University of Saida, Algeria

ABSTRACT

This chapter is a comparative study between two bio-inspired approaches based on swarm intelligence for detection and filtering of SPAM: social bees vs. inspiration from the human renal. The authors took inspiration from biological model and use two meta-heuristics because the effects allow the authors to detect the characteristics of unwanted data. Messages are indexed and represented by the n-gram words and characters independent of languages (because a message can be received in any language). The results are promising and provide an important way to use this model for solving other problems in data mining. The authors start this paper with a short introduction where they show the importance of IT security. Then they give a little insight into the state of the art, before starting the essential part of a scientific paper, where they explain and experiment with two original meta-heuristics, and explain the natural model. Then they detail the artificial model.

DOI: 10.4018/978-1-5225-3004-6.ch003

INTRODUCTION AND PROBLEMATIC

The appearance of the Internet and the incredibly rapid development of telecommunication technology have made the world a global village. The Internet has become a major channel for communication. Email is one among the tools for communication that Internet users take advantage of as it is available free of charge and supplies the transfer of files.

According to the most recent report of the Radicati Group (2014), who supplies quantitative and qualitative researches with details on the e-mail, the security, the Instant messaging (IM), the social networks, the archiving of the data, the regulatory compliance, the wireless technologies, the Web's technologies and the unified communications, there was exactly:

- 4.116 trillion Of active emails accounts in the world.
- 2.504 Billion People who use e-mails regularly to over 2.8 billion in 2018.
- 196,3billion is the number of e-mails that are sent to by day in 2014in the world on average. This number will increase to 227,7 billion in 2018.
- 1,6 is the number of accounts detained by each person and which should increase to 1,8 in four years.

According to the same reports of the Radicati Group, unsolicited mail, or SPAM, can reach more than 89,1%; 262 million SPAMS a day. Although the decision "spam / no-spam" is most often easy to take for a human. Messages in circulation, prevents address manually sorting the emails acceptable and others. Spam is a global phenomenon and massive. According to the CNIL (The National Commission of The computing and Freedoms), spam is defined as follows: "The" spamming "or" spam "is to send massive and sometimes repeated, unsolicited electronic mail, to individuals with whom the sender has had no contact and he has captured the email address erratically. ".

From the above statistics, the detection and filtering of spam is a major stake to the Internet community making the detection and filtering of spam a crucial task.

It is only the late 90s that the problem of detection and spam filtering by content, drew attention to three areas of research that were not directly affected by e-mail: the Information Retrieval (IR), the Data Mining (DM) and Machine Learning (ML).

This whole issue leads us to a study as to the representation of data (message corpus) to try to identify sensitive parameters that can improve the results of classification and categorization, around detections and spam filtering. We know very well that supervised learning techniques give the best results, and it is for this reason that we tried to experiment a new meta-heuristic to solve the problem of detecting and filtering spam.

The literature gives two broad approaches for the filtering and the detection of SPAM: The approach based on the machine learning and the approach not based on the machine learning. The first approach is based on feature selection which is an important stage in the systems of classification. It aims to reduce the number of features while trying to preserve or improve the performance of the used classifier. On the other hand, the second approach (not based on the machine learning) is based on many existing techniques and algorithms: content analysis, the block-lists, black-lists and white-lists, the authentication of mailbox and the heuristics and finally meta-heuristics.

We compare between two approach bio-inspired: from the human renal system and the social bees for the detection and the filtering of the SPAM.

MATERIALS AND METHODS

To apply the Naive Bayes algorithm on textual data we must use one this document model:

- Bernoulli document model: binary vector.
- Multinomial document model: frequency vector.

$$P(C \mid D) = \frac{P(D \mid C)P(C)}{P(D)} \tag{1}$$

STATE OF THE ART

It is only in the late 90's that the problem of the detection and the filtering of SPAM drew the attention of the researchers; the works were included in three axes: information retrieval, data mining and Machine Learning. The detection and filtering of SPAM is a binary classification problem in which emails are classified as HAM or SPAM.

There are two types of approaches for the detection and the filtering of SPAM (see Figure 1): the approach that is not based on Machine Learning and the Machine Learning-Based Approach.

The Approach Non-Based on Machine Learning

This approach consists of using one of the techniques or strategies of detection and filtering of SPAM as analysis of contents, black-lists, white-lists and authentication of a mailbox or a heuristic and meta-heuristics.

Content Analysis

Content analysis is an application implemented on the mail server as a complement to the user's mail application (Mueller, and al, 2009). Its role is to give a probability to an email to be a SPAM (or HAM) according to its contents. (O'Brien, C., and al, 2003) have proposed a Bayesian weighting or a Chi2 weighting between the candidates emails and the references emails labeled beforehand; The authors used two representations: bag of words and bag of sentences for calculate the probability that an email is a SPAM or HAM. (Sebastiani, F., 2002) (Zhang, L., and Al, 2004) (Van Staden, F., and al, 2009) and (Sanz, E. P., and al, 2008) have suggested and improved many of scanner of contents textual, image, and code HTM for filtering and the detection of the spam.

Block List, Blacklist, Whitelist, and the Authentication of Mailbox

The block list contains viral email's adresses so that we should block any email that is sent from one of these addresses. It is filled and modified by the end who are not enough competent in computing will not be able to use this technique effectively and appropriately.

(Zdziarski, J. A., 2005) and (Lueg, C., and al, 2007) have proposed that it is the Internet service provider who must generate this list because they monitor the traffic and can determine accounts suspected of sending of bulk mail (by definition SPAM what are email sent in a massive way) what allows them to block these emails and consequently to reduce the load of the traffic.

Unlike to the blacklist, (Sanz, E. P., and al, 2008) et (Kågström, J., 2005) have proposed white lists which are used to mark the confidence mail accounts, and authorize to receive their emails.The major drawback of the two aforementioned techniques is that they do not deal to identity theft. In order to face the problem of identity theft, one of the most known techniques was proposed by (Faynberg, I., and al., 2010) which is consisted of the authentication of mailboxes. Each gateway server authenticates the mail by sending a request to the original mail server asking if the received email came from the specified mailbox. This technique has been improved by (Yegin, A. E., and al, 2005) using the technique of Authentication, Authorization and Accounting (AAA) where each mail server must be approved and verified to attest that it is a trusted server and gives a real answer.

Legal Computing

In the works of (De Vel, O., and al, 2001) and (Gupta, G., and al, 2004), the authors used the principles of the legal computing to verify the signature of the email's author (authenticate the physical or real sender). (Yerazunis, W. S., 2004) And (Obied, A., and al, 2009) used the principles of the legal computing to trace an email to detect proxys and diversions of routing which the spammers use to bypass the others techniques of detection and filtering of SPAM.

Meta-Heuristics

Many of meta-heuristics have been proposed. Among these remarkable works, we can quote the Modelling of immune systems for the detection and the filtering of SPAM by (Murphy K., and al, 2008), the immune system is known for its extremely complex resistance which has the capacity to identify foreign substances (Nonself or pathogenic cells) and to know the difference between harmless and harmful substances.

(Oda, T., and al, 2005) have proposed the immune system for the filtering of spam. In their work, antibodies and antigens were created by using regular expressions. In 2009, (Tan, Y., and al, 2009) have proposed a technique of concentration based on the characteristics of construction. In 2010, (Ruan, G., and Tan, Y., 2010) have proposed a new meta-heuristic based on Artificial neural network with three layers. In 2013, (Hamou, R. M., and al, 2013) we have proposed a new meta-heuristic based on social bees for the filtering of the SPAM, We took inspiration from the lifestyle of bees in a hive and how the bees maintain a maintain a clean hive. Consequently, we have proposed a method based on triple filter that is clearly improved the the quality of the current results.

The Approach Based on Machine Learning

The researchers of the Data mining have proposed and presented many works which handle the problem of filtering of SPAMS by using methods of machine learning.

In 1998, (Sahami M., and al, 1998) have proposed applying the Bayesian classifiers to build what they have called the Bayesian filter of SPAM which was the object of a comparison done by (Provost, J., and al, 1999) and the results showed the robustness of the Bayesian filters.

During the same year (Drucker, H., and al, 1999) have suggested to apply the SVM classifier for the filtering of SPAMS and compared their results with other classification algorithms results such as Ripper, Rocchio and decision tree; The performance of SVM were much better. This work was taken over by (Sculley, D., and Wachman, G. M., 2007) which have applied the Non-linear SVM algorithm afterwards (Xiao-li C., and al, 2009) have applied the SVM in 3D to increase it's performance.

In 2004, (Chhabra, S., and al, 2004) have presented an anti-spam classifier based on the MRF model (Markov random field). This approach allows to the SPAM classifier to take consideration of the neighborhood relationship between the words of the electronic message to be filtered by the dependence between the words of natural language that can be incorporated into the process of the classification, which is generally ignored by Bayesian classifiers.

(Chou, C. H., and al, 2008) have proposed to use the KNN algorithm with Euclidean distance for filtering of SPAM. All these works have been collected by (Guzella, T.S., and al, 2009) where they present a complete review on the application of machine learning algorithms for the filtering of SPAMS.

In 2010, (Lakshmi, R. D., and Radha, N., 2010) have made a comparison between the methods mentioned above: naive Bayes, SVM, decision tree (J48), LDA, MFR and KNN; their studies led to show the high robustness of Bayesian spam filters and SVM, Moreover their comparison indicates a performance reduced to decision trees (the decision trees behave badly in the case of classification problem with a reduced number of classes); And acceptable results averagely for the other methods of filtering of the SPAM by machine learning.

Whatever the learning method used, to treat ot to test the filtering of SPAM based on the machine learning, it is necessary to build a wide corpus of SPAMS and HAM; and E-mails must be pretreated to extract their feature.(Youn, S., and McLeod, D., 2007) have conducted a study on the impact of the size of the SpamBase (corpus) explored on the performance of the classification.

The results showed that the SpamBase (corpus) must be large-sized (big number of mes-sage) and the number of SPAM must be upper to that of HAM for evaluated properly the classification. Another recent work led by (Sharma, V., and al, 2013) where they estimated the behaviour of 24 SpamBase by using 24 classifiers of WEKA.

The number of features in a corpus can be very high so that the selection of the most representative features must be done before making the learning of the filter. The features selection is an active domain in recent years. It comes to selecting a subset of features from an original set according to certain evaluation criteria (Liu, Z., et al, 2005)]. The main objective is to reduce the number of features used while trying to maintain and improve the performances of the classification system

Many works were made and as (Dash, M., and al, 1997) and (Mendez, J. R., and al, 2006) works, the authors present a detailed analysis showing the influence of the change of the dimension of the representation of a message on the precision of certain classic techniques of filtering of SPAMS.

Our most recent work in this axis is tjehe one of (Hamou, R. M., and al, 2013) (35) we studied the impact of the representation of textual data on the quality of the results of clustering and filtering of SPAM.

Figure 1. Different approaches for filtering of spam

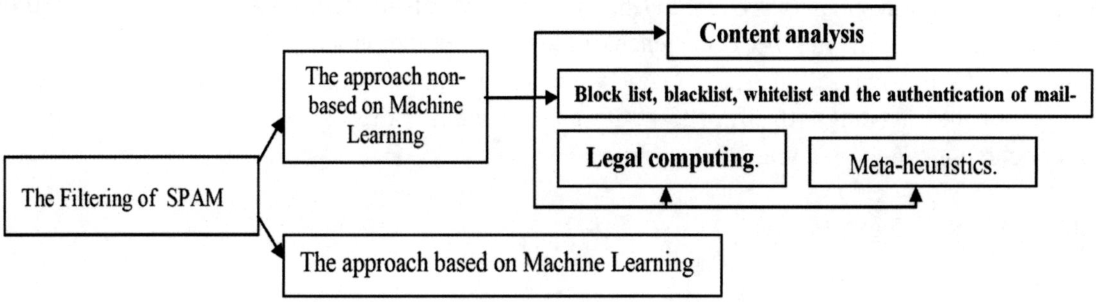

DATA REPRESENTATION

The machine learning algorithms cannot process directly the unstructured data: image, video, and of course the texts written in natural language. Thus, we are obliged to pass by an indexing step. Indexing step is simply a representation of the text as a vector where each entry corresponds to a different word and the number at that entry corresponds to how many times that word was present in the document (or some function of it); this is very delicate and very important at the same time: a poor or bad representation will lead certainly to bad results (Chhabra and al, 2006).

We will represent each text as a vector where each entry corresponds to a different word and the number at that entry corresponds to how many times that word was present in the document (or some function of it). In this way, we shall have a vector which represents the text and which is exploitable by machine learning algorithms at the same time(Chhabra and al, 2006).

Several approaches for the representation of texts exist in the literature, among whom the bag-of-words representation which is the simplest and the most used, the bag-of-sentences representation, lexical-roots representation and of course the n-gram representation which is a representation independent from the natural language (Chhabra and al, 2006) .

Stop words will not be removed, because the method of automatic summarization by extraction aims to extract the most informative phrases without modifying them: if we remove Stop words without information on their morph syntactic impact on the phrases, we risk having an inconsistent summary in a morphological part. Then cleaning is to remove emoticons, to replace spaces with "_" and remove special characters (#, \, [,] ....).

For automatic summarization by extraction, we will need two representations: Bag of words representation or Bag of sentences representation.

Both representations are introduced in the vector model.

The first representation consists to transform the text i into a vector v_i $(w_1, w_2,...., w_{|T|})$ where T is the number of all words that appear at least once in the text i, The weight w_k indicated the occurrence of the word t_k in the text i.

The second representation consists to transform the text i into a vector v_i $(w_1, w_2,...., w_{|T|})$ where T is the number of all phrases that appear at least once in the text i, The weight w_k indicated the occurrence of the word t_k in the text i.

And finally the "word-phrases" occurrence matrix will be generated after the two previous performances, the size of this matrix is equal to (the number of words in the text) X (the number of words in the text), p_{ik} weight is the number occurrence of the word i in the phrase j;

Once the "Word-Phrase" matrix is ready, we calculate the weighting of "Word-Phrase" matrix by using one of the encodings (tf-idf, or tfc) with a small modification to adapt it with the concept of a mono-document summarization.

$$TfIdf(tk, i) = Nb * \log(A / B) \tag{2}$$

Nb: The number of occurrences of the term t_k in the text i;
A: The total number of phrase in the text;
B: The number of phrase in which the t_k term appears at least once.

$$tfc\left(t_k, p_i\right) = \frac{tf - idf\left(t_k, p_i\right)}{\sqrt{\sum_{i=1}^{|p|} tf - idf\left(t_k, p_i\right)^2}} \tag{3}$$

After calculating the frequency of each word, a weight is assigned to each phrase. The generated summary is then generated by displaying the highest score of the source document phrases.

FIRST PROPOSED APPROACH: SOCIAL BEES (HAMOU AND AL, 2013)

Natural or Biological Model

According to the lifestyle of the species, there are several types of bees: the phrase "bee" is one of the common names of the European honeybee (Apis mellifera), but it can also be used for any other domesticated bee by humans. By contrast, called "wild bee" a bee undomesti¬cated. The term "social bee" means a species of bee that lives in colonies, if it is a "solitary bee" constituting rather aggregations of individual burrows. Other species are "parasitic bees" that practice the kleptoparasitism. Among all categories of bees exist, we are interested in social bees. (Faustino, Silva-Matos, Mateus, & Zucchi, 2002).

Social Bees and the Notion of Swarm

Such as ants, bees are social insects; they cannot have an isolated existence and need to live in colonies. A very highly organized colony always composed of workers, drones and one queen.

The workers are exclusively female bees, the most numerous of the colony (about 30,000 to 70,000 per hive). In the colony, where they work tirelessly, they are responsible for all tasks related to the proper functioning of the hive. But unlike ants who does one specific task throughout their lives, the bees perform all successively, in a life that, on average, lasts only a few weeks (about 45 days).

Organizational Cycles of Social Bees

During the first four days of his life, the worker cleans the alveoli and maintains the hive. From 5th to the 11th day, it is the nurse and gave larvae royal jelly of the royal cells. The 11th and 13th days, it becomes storekeeper: its role is to store pollen and nectar in the cells and to ventilate the hive, waving its wings quickly, so as to maintain a constant temperature. From the 14th to the 17th day, the wax glands of its abdo¬men is being developed, it becomes waxy, and built the shelves. From the 18th to the 21st day she is sentry and stands guard at the entrance of the hive to chase all intruders, wasps, butterflies and even drones. From the 22nd day, and until his death she will go from flower to flower to collect nectar, pollen and propolis: becomes forager and brings food to the hive.

Drones are the only male in the colony. The number of hundreds, they are bigger, rounder, more hairy than the workers. They are tolerated within the hive as "fertilizers" potential and live in spring and summer.

Not being able to feed themselves, they are fed by the workers. Having no stinger, they cannot protect the colony. However, they participate in certain tasks in the hive, but especially for essential mission to fertilize the queen. Only a few succeed, in a unique and deadly nuptial flight.

Because once accomplished their mission of spawners, they die, gutted by the Queen. Once they are out of the hive, the workers do not let enter, because they are considered useless mouths to feed, and those who remained inside were ruthlessly expelled and left to fend for themselves. Unable to meet their needs, they are condemned to death. In a bee colony, there can be only one queen. She was born in a royal cell, a cell larger than the other, oblong, specially built by the workers to house the larvae royal. To ensure the survival of the species, the hive still has several queen cells each containing a larva fed with royal jelly and likely to become queen (Chinh, Sommeijer, Boot, & Michener, 2005).

Just born, the first queen's mission is to kill all the larvae of other royal cells, because it is undivided sway over the colony. If a second queen is born at the same time, the two queens fought a battle no thank and victorious is the queen who took command of the hive. Three to six days after his birth, the young queen flies to a nuptial flight only where it will join five or six times a dozen drones. Once fertilized, she returns to the hive, begins his life of laying eggs. She did not come out again for four or five years lasts his life, and will have only one mission lay tirelessly to 2000 eggs per day! (About 1 egg per minute). Constantly surrounded, protected, fed by the workers, it is the object of all their care.

First, because of all the bees, it is the only one with the reproductive function, the workers being ster-ile. She lays eggs at will, male or female according to their fertilization: fertilized eggs produce workers; those unfertilized give birth to drones. Secondly, because this is what determines the life of the hive. It secretes a chemical called pheromone specific to each hive, essential to social cohesion. Bees, touching and licking this secretion, including draw all the necessary information to the organization of work.

Communication is an individual emission of a stimulus that causes a reaction in another individual, the reaction being beneficial to party who issues the stimulus, or for anyone who receives it (Wilson, 1971). Communication can take place between individuals of different species. In the bee, the term re-fers to social communication signal exchange between individuals of the same colony. We traditionally distinguish two modes of communication, one based on chemical signals (pheromones), the other on vibration signals (dances, noise).

Among the extras bees in a colony or a swarm (queens, false spoil, workers ...), we are particularly interested in workers (workers) and more specifically to the tasks they perform (Cleaner, manifold and supervisor), that the we formalize the artificial model, especially to solve our problem that is detection and spam filtering.

Artificial Model

In our artificial model dedicated to detecting and filtering spam, we are interested in social bees workers and more precisely the roles they perform in their life ie cleaning, monitoring and collection.

To try to solve the problem of detection and spam filtering we need to have a test database and a training base. For artificial model, the test database is equated with fields of flowers where each flower is a document or message (spam or ham) to analyze.

The role of manifold is simply to collect a text document or message of the test database (corpus) as the criterion collection "Criter_collect" and therefore it did not need to look for the flower field or need has to indicate to his colleagues.

Criter_Collect: The Manifold Uses a Distance and a Threshold

For each flower (document or message), a distance with all documents based learning (spam and ham) is calculated and an average distance is calculated respecting a certain threshold (the average distance is calculated only for the document collected and all spam based learning). the same process is performed for all the hams based learning. If the average distances of spam is smaller than the average distance of ham then manifold considers that the document collected is spam and do not collect it otherwise she collects it.

The role of the supervisor is identical to that of the manifold but only with the documents collected by the manifold in other words the new test database is the base of documents collected. It should be noted that monitoring is established by a distance, and a threshold different than that established by the manifold. The role of the Cleaner is identical to that of the supervisor. The difference lies on the basis of those documents which are filtered by the supervisor with a distance, and a threshold different from the previous step. Worker bees act as filters leaving went inside the hive that the documents purporting non spam (ham) and those who do not spend at least the last filter and stay outside the hive are supposed documents to be spam. (Figure 2).

SECOND PROPOSED APPROACH: INSPIRATION FROM HUMAN KIDNEY (BOUDIA AND AL, 2015)

This work aims at modelling a method bio-inspired which is the renal System to problems in computer science, in this case the detection and the filtering of the SPAM. Before explaining and detailing our approach we must describe at first the natural model of the functioning of the renal system and shed light on the aspects which directed us to choose this meta heuristics for our problem which is the detection and the filtering of the SPAM. Then we draw up a table of modelling (the natural model vs the artificial model). Finally we shall explain the artificial model which is the pulp of our approach.

Natural Model

Physiology of the Renal System

The urinary system consists of:

Figure 2. Artificial model of social bees to detect and filtering of spam (our first approach)

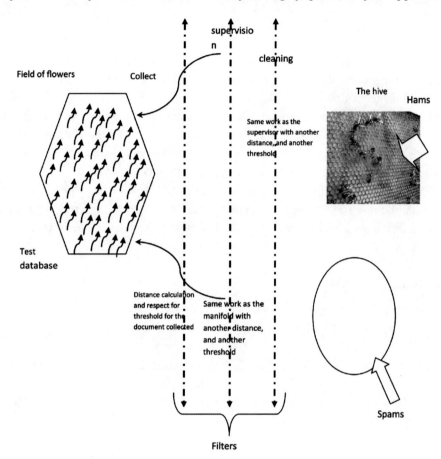

- Two kidneys,
- Ureters,
- Urinary bladder,
- Urethra.

In our current research, we will focus on the kidneys as it is the functional unit of the renal system. Furthermore, the kidneys are bean-shaped organs that lie in the retroperitoneal, exactly, in the superior lumbar region. The main role of the kidney is to ensure the elimination of toxins and exogenous substances from the blood. Thus, it plays a great role in the regularization of the blood pressure.

Functioning of the Renal System

The Nephrons are supplied by two capillary systems:

- The Glomerulus where a glomerular filtration occurs to produce the primitive urine.
- The peritubular capillary network where the processes of reabsorption and of secretion are produced. Once these two processes finished, one will have the definitive urine.

The functioning of renal System is divided into two steps:

Step 1: The Glomerular Filtration

The blood comes from the afferent arteriole and enters the glomerular room (glomerulus + Bowman capsule) to undergo the glomerular filtration. Noting that the renal blood flow is equal to 20% of cardiac output, i.e., 1.1 to 1.2 liters of blood per minute.

Glomerular filtration is a nonselective, passive mechanical process. It does not consume energy; the blood pressure in the glomerular represents the dynamic element of the filtration. It is not selective because any molecule which has a smaller size than the Bowman's capsule hole will be filtered. The glomerular filtration stops when the blood pressure falls below 60 mm Hg.

Once the first step was completed, the primitive urine will follow the path of renal tubule where its composition will be modified during the second step. Consequently, filtered blood primitively will join the efferent arteriole and the efferent arteriole will bypass the renal tubule forming the peritubular capillary network.

Step 2: Renal Tubular Transfer

The composition of the primitive urine which is produced by glomerular filtration will be modified in the renal tubule by two processes which they will happen in parallel:

- **Reabsorption:** It consists of the transfer of certain constituents of the primitive urine to the peritubular capillary, i.e., to the blood (e.g. water, mineral salts, glucose ...)
- **Secretion:** The toxic or exogenous substances that are escaped from the glomerular filtration will be added to the tubular urine.

At the connecting tubule (CNT), the volume and acidity of the urine will be controlled by two operations respectively; the ADH stimulus so that to make the second reabsorption of water and acidified urine or the ADH inhibition which dilutes the urine and adjustment of the balance of fluid in the blood.

At the end of the process, we shall firstly have definitive urine which is going to be driven by ureters towards the bladder then outside the body. Secondly, the cleansed Blood which is going to join the general blood circulation (the tip of the peritubular capillary network joined the interlobular vein). Noticeably, the blood pressure will be stabilized in the normal upstream.

The Artificial Model of Renal System for Filtering of Spam

Our approach is devoted to the detection and filtering of the SPAM. Therefore, we suggest the modeling of the renal system so that the artificial model will have three states (see Figure 3):

Initial State

To solve the problem of filtering and detection of SPAM, we need a training set and a test set. In parallel, the training set represents the consumption of oxygen by the kidney which is between 10 to 15% of the blood supply.

On the other hand, the test set is all the messages (SPAM and HAM) that must be treated. In equivalent with the natural model, the test set is represented by the coming blood from the afferent arteriole.

Initially, the kidneys must be active enough and well-fed to do their role appropriately. In the artificial model, we begin to fill the training set by 15% of the number of messages.

We propose to launch several threads of the application on the server; each thread will represent a kidney. The goal of this parallelism is to accelerate the process of filtering and to give a fault tolerance so that even if a thread stops accidentally or intentionally, the other thread ensures the minimum services during the time of maintenance in addition to the re-launching of the thread which was broken down.

Moreover, each kidney contains a predefined large number of nephrons which is sufficient in our artificial model to not consume too much from the virtual memory and CPU. Nephrons are identical, i.e., the same parameters are generalized for the whole of nephrons. Obviously, the parameters of the nephrons are identical. If an email is considered SPAM by the first nephrons then it will be also considered SPAM by other nephrons and vice versa. We propose that Each message (email) passes by only nephron randomly in each iteration. In our artificial model, 15% of the number of artificial nephrons (filtering agent) of each kidney are used to update the training set by messages after the application of the filtering process and optimization. It is the same for the juxtamedullary nephrons which feeds kidney.

State of Activity

The arrival of blood (message) by the afferent arteriole increases the blood pressure within the glomerulus and activates the process of filtration of blood (filtering of SPAM). Thus, this process is divided into two steps.

Step 1: Artificial Glomerular Filtration

Before beginning this step, we have to allocate a score to each message so that the HAM messages will have a high score and they will not be filtered by the artificial Bowman's capsule (the sieve) and the SPAM message will have a weak score.

Therefore, they will be filtered by artificial Bowman's capsule (the sieve) (see Figure 2).

There are several techniques and methods of scoring. However, we have chosen the Bayesian classifier as a technique for our research with less modification.

We propose to use a notion of Naive Bayes classifier for scoring and the score of each message will be equal to its probability to be HAM. In this way, each message having a big probability to be a HAM will not be filtered by the artificial Bowman's capsule and will join the efferent arteriole (classified as primitive-HAM) Whereas those who will have a weak probability to be a HAM will be filtered and will join the renal tubule (classified as primitive-SPAM).

The only change that will occur on the Bayesian classifier is in the step of class assignments. We will not assign the class according to the biggest probability and we will not even use both of two probability (SPAM and HAM).

We will define a hole diameter of the artificial Bowman's capsule (the sieve).It is the artificial filtering glomerular threshold; each message having a score bigger or equal to this threshold will not be filtered by the artificial Bowman's capsule and will join the efferent arteriole (classified as primitive-HAM) whilst those who will have a score smaller to the threshold will be filtered and will join the renal tubule (classified as primitive-SPAM); Let us remind that the score represents the probability that the message is a HAM by using the Bayesian classifier.

In the natural model, the glomerular filtration is very important with producing up to 180 liters of primitive urine per day. This must be taken up in the artificial model by choosing a big artificial filtering glomerular threshold so as to have a very harsh filtering of SPAM.

At the end of this first step, we will have:

- A set of primitive SPAM that represents the primitive urine and which they will join the renal tubule.
- A set of primitive HAM that represents the filtered blood primitively and which they will join the efferent arteriole.

It is worth noting that there are two different types of nephron. The messages which are in the juxtamedullary nephrons will be used in the next steps to update the training set.

Step 2: Artificial Renal Tubular Transfer (Optimization)

The renal tubular transfer is made by two processes: Reabsorption and Secretion in the Proximal tubule, loop of Henle and distal convoluted tubule. Let us remember that these two processes will be performed in a automatic way (without intervention of brain).

At the level of the connecting tubule (CNT) two operations will be done; Stimulus ADH to get back the water from urine and Inhibition ADH to reject the water in urine. These two operations (Stimulus ADH and Inhibition ADH) are controlled by a hormone ordered by brain, therefore they are semi automatic operations. In our work and in parallel to the natural model, we propose to use a clustering algorithm which its initial state will be the result of the first step so that the renal tubular transfer takes in input the results of glomerular filtration.

At the same time, the K-means algorithm must represent the reabsorption process and secretion process. Thus, we propose to use the K-Means algorithm with k = 2. Initially the centroids will be calculated by the classification resulting from the first step (glomerular filtration) as follows: The centroid of the HAM class will be calculated by the set of primitive-HAM (result of step 1: glomerular filtration) likewise the centroid of the SPAM class will be calculated by the set of primitive-SPAM (result of step 1: glomerular filtration).

The philosophy of the K-Means algorithm in every iteration is the changing of documents to join the class that they are close to its centroid(class), in our case K = 2 (SPAM and HAM). In each iteration, we have some messages classified as HAM which change class: from HAM class to the SPAM class (this is the secretion process) and other messages classified as SPAM that change class: from SPAM class to the HAM class (this is the reabsorption process). At the end of both processes of renal tubular transfer (reabsorption + secretion) in the natural model, two operations are followed: the Stimulus ADH and / or the inhibition ADH. In the artificial model, we have employed the Stimulus ADH through the use of white-list technique (which will be generated by the user or the service provider); then, we have used the Inhibition ADH by the technique of blacklist (which will be also generated by the user or the service provider).

Updating of the Training Set

In the artificial model, 15% of nephrons are juxtamedullary nephrons and the messages which are treated by those nephrons will be used to update the training set. It is worth noting that messages are distributed randomly and that SPAM messages (of test set) are in the renal tubule. On the other hand, HAM messages (of test set) are in the peritubular capillary network which surrounds the renal tubule.

The training set must not grow up to avoid Over fitting. So, we must make a crushing of the most repeated message in it to create diversity in this training set so that a maximum number of cases will be included in the training set.

Choosing an Outbound HAM and an Outbound SPAM From Training Set

We calculate the similarity between the HAM messages in the training set and also for SPAM message. Then we calculate the centroid of each class (SPAM and HAM of training set).

Furthermore, we choose the most similar two HAM (SPAM respectively) (the biggest similarity for each class). It is supposed that HAM1 and HAM2 (SPAM1 and SPAM2 respectively) are most similar among all HAM messages in the training set (SPAM respectively). The HAM message to crush (outbound) is the closest to the centroid of HAM class of the training set (SPAM respectively) because it is more similar to the other HAM in the training set (respectively SPAM). Consequently, we shall call it the HAM-outbound (SPAM-outbound respectively).

The HAM-outbound message from the training set will be crushed and replaced with a copy of the HAM which is in the peritubular capillary network (test set) respectively The SPAM-outbound message from the training set will be crushed and replaced with a copy of the SPAM which is in the renal tubule (test set).

Figure 3. Artificial Bowman's capsule

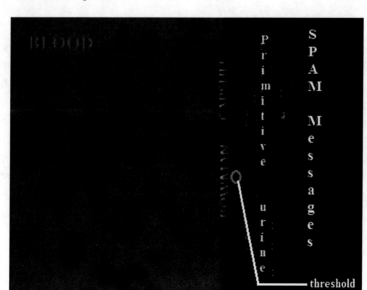

Figure 4. Artificial model vs. natural model

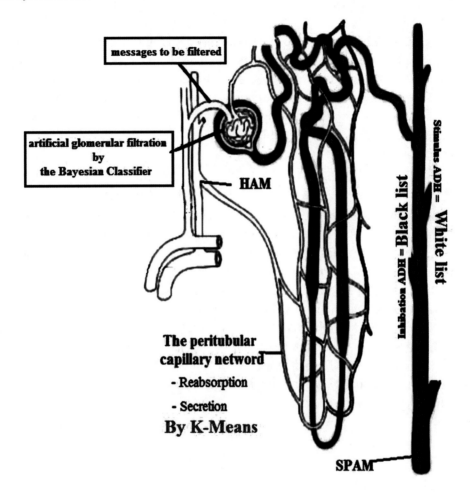

The Final State

After a finite and sufficient number of iterations; All messages that are classified as spam are considered as the final urine. Therefore, they will be removed outside the body (system) to not return to the blood stream. On the other hand, all the messages that are classified as HAM represent the purified blood as they will join the interlobular vein.

The training set will be updated and the recommendations of the user or service provider will be taken into consideration (Blacklist and White-list) as a part of the training set (by the updating).

It is of great importance to note that the training set is quite reduced (15% of SpamBase) so that these recommendations (Blacklist and White-list) are the starting point for more advanced investigations and will have a weight in decision-making by the Bayesian classifier (in probability calculation).

At the end of our proposed process, the results are as follow:

- The SPAM class contains the set of messages classified as SPAM representing the final urine.
- The HAM class contains the set of messages classified as HAM representing the purified blood.

- A training set is updated to the next use (fed kidneys).

EXPERIMENTATION

In our experiments, we used a corpus of data, already categorized, that we will explain in details in the next section as we will talk about for it learning base after representation of textual documents corpus of spam by various techniques.

The Data Used

The SMS Spam Corpus v.0.2 (hereafter the corpus) is a set of SMS tagged messages that have been collected for SMS Spam research. It contains two collections of SMS messages in English of 1799 and other 1319 messages that are tagged according to being legitimate (HAM) or SPAM. This corpus has been collected from free or free for research sources at the Web.

The SMS Spam Corpus v.0.1 (hereafter the corpus) is a set of SMS tagged messages that have been collected for SMS Spam research. It contains two collections of SMS messages in English of 1084 and 1319 messages, tagged according being legitimate (ham) or spam.

This corpus has been collected from free or free for research sources at the Web:

- A list of 202 legitimate messages, probably collected by Jon Stevenson, according to the HTML code of the Webpage. Only the text of the messages is available. We will call this corpus the Jon Stevenson Corpus (JSC). It is available at: http://www.demo.inty.net/Units/SMS/corpus.htm
- A subset of the NUS SMS Corpus (NSC), which is a corpus of about 10,000 legitimate messages collected for research at the Department of Computer Science at the National University of Singapore.

Evaluation Metrics

Confusion Matrix

Confusion matrix is a tool often used when it is desired to study the relationship between two variables that take discrete values (or categories).

From this matrix in Table 1 we will calculate all of this metric of evaluations: Recall, Precision, F-Measure, Kappa Statistic, Entropy and Accuracy. We present some evaluation metrics that we used in our experiments to validate our results.

$$F - measure = \frac{2 * Precision * Recall}{Precision + Recall} \qquad (4)$$

$$Entropy = -Precision \ln\left(Precision\right) \qquad (5)$$

Table 1. Confusion matrix

	Classified as HAM	**Classified as SPAM**
Real HAM	TP	FN
Real SPAM	FP	TN

where:

TP: True Positive: HAM classified by our filter as HAM or HAM correctly classified.

FP: **False Positive:** SPAM classified by our filter as HAM or SPAM not correctly classified.

VN: True Negatives: SPAM classified by our filter as SPAM or SPAM correctly classified.

FN: False Negative: HAM classified by our filter as SPAM or HAM not correctly classified.

$$Accuracy = \frac{\left(TP + TN\right)}{\left(TP + FP + TN + FN\right)} \tag{6}$$

RESULTS

We start by give the result of the first approach: The threshold S is a rate that allows decision making whether or not a document is similar to a document based learning to S meadows. For the choice of threshold we have made a lot of experimentation to find the best threshold for distance (similarity) given. It should be noted that the results reported in this article represent the best results selected from all experiments performed. The results are summarized in Table 2, Table 3, Table 4, and Table 5, show the classification results from experimentation with our algorithm (first approach: bees social). All modes of data representation have been presented.

Three types of bees have been anti spam filter, in this case the manifold the supervisor and cleaner. For each type of bee, we presented the results of classification and evaluation measures.

The classification results are grouped by mode of representation of unstructured data. We note that after each filter (manifold, Supervisor, Cleaner) there is improved performance, and the last step called final step we have the best results.

Five distances of similarity have been used by various workers in this case the cosine, Manahalobis, Euclidean, Manhattan and Minkowski. Each filter model based on social bees, different distances are used.

We proceeded to view the best results. Each type of bee performs its task with a distance and a given threshold such as:

- 3-gram character without cleaning with TFC weighting
- **Manifold:** Manhattan (threshold = 0.22)
- **Supervisor:** Minkowski of order 3 (threshold = 0.17)
- **Cleaner:** Mahalanobis (threshold = 0.5)

In the following series of results (Table 6, 7 and 8), we have fixed some parameters that their impacts on quality of the results found to be not very important or almost nil. We have made several preliminary pre-test to measure the impact of each parameter on quality of result of detection and filtering of spam. Our judgment is based on a series of preliminary tests. We have found that changing the parameter

Table 2. Results of 1-gram word without data cleaning (first approach: social bees)

Representation	Confusion Matrix		Recall	Precesion	F-Measure	Accuracy	Entropy
Manifold	703	299	0,81	0,73	0,77	0,75	0,16
	26	296					
Supervisor	716	0	0,66	0,98	0,79	0,97	0,029
	19	9					
Cleaner	716	0	0,50	/	/	0,97	/
	20	0					
Final	716	286	0,83	0,74	0,78	0,77	0,22
	19	303					

Table 3. Results of 2-gram characters without data cleaning (first approach: social bees)

Representation	Confusion Matrix		Recall	Precesion	F-Measure	Accuracy	Entropy
Manifold	1002	0	0,63	0,90	0,74	0,82	0,09
	238	84					
Supervisor	1001	1	0,59	0,90	0,71	0,83	0,09
	206	43					
Cleaner	1002	0	0,54	0,92	0,68	0,83	0,08
	204	16					
Final	1001	1	0,68	0,91	0,78	0,84	0,085
	206	116					

Table 4. Results of 3-gram characters without data cleaning (first approach: social bees)

Representation	Confusion Matrix		Recall	Precesion	F-Measure	Accuracy	Entropy
Manifold	1002	0	0,66	0,91	0,77	0,84	0,086
	217	105					
Supervisor	1002	0	0,53	0,91	0,67	0,83	0,086
	206	11					
Cleaner	839	163	0,82	0,73	0,77	0,83	0,23
	42	171					
Final	839	163	0,85	0,79	0,82	0,85	0,19
	42	280					

Table 5. Results of 4-gram characters without data cleaning (first approach: social bees)

Representation	Confusion Matrix		Recall	Precesion	F-Measure	Accuracy	Entropy
Manifold	1002	0	0,74	0,93	0,82	0,87	0,067
	167	155					
Supervisor	1002	0	0,52	0,91	0,66	0,83	0,086
	213	9					
Cleaner	1002	0	0,50	0,91	0,65	0,83	0,086
	211	2					
Final	1002	0	0,74	0,93	0,82	0,87	0,87
	167	155					

Table 6a. Results of 3-gram characters and weighing TFC

Step 1 Artificial Glomerular Filtration			Confusion Matrix		Recall	Precesion	F-Measure	Kappa Statistic	Accuracy	Entropy
Bernoulli	artificial filtering glomerular threshold	40	1068	27	0.5650	0.7218	0.6339	0.1520	0.6542	0.2352
			595	109						
		50	972	123	0.7165	0.7548	0.7352	0.4559	0.7537	0.2122
			320	384						
		60	793	302	0.7541	0.7427	0.7484	0.4896	0.7476	0.2208
			152	552						
		70	676	419	0.7838	0.7828	0.7833	0.5172	0.7476	0.1916
			35	669						
		80	526	569	0.7252	0.7535	0.7391	0.3955	0.6720	0.2132
			21	683						
Multinomial	artificial filtering glomerular threshold	40	1072	23	0.6052	0.7704	0.6779	0.2423	0.6864	0.2009
			541	163						
		50	993	102	0.7467	0.7876	0.7666	0.5183	0.7815	0.1880
			291	413						
		60	689	406	0.8011	0.8005	0.8008	0.5484	0.7637	0.1781
			19	685						
		70	810	285	0.7952	0.7814	0.7882	0.5647	0.7832	0.1927
			105	599						
		80	529	566	0.7301	0.7596	0.7446	0.4040	0.6764	0.2088
			16	688						

Table 6b. Results of 3-gram characters and weighing TFC

Step 2 (Final) Artificial Renal Tubular Transfer(Optimization)			Confusion Matrix		Recall	Precesion	F-Measure	Kappa Statistic	Accuracy	Entropy	ERTS
Bernoulli	artificial filtering glomerular threshold	40	1081	14	0.9006	0.8359	0.8671	0.7092	0.8688	0.0941	1,28%
			222	482							
		50	1046	49	0.9129	0.8973	0.9051	0.8078	0.9099	0.0831	1,26%
			113	591							
		60	998	107	0.8319	0.8137	0.8227	0.6474	0.8382	0.1530	1,16%
			194	510							
		70	1018	77	0.9408	0.9520	0.9464	0.8907	0.9471	0.0573	1,18%
			18	686							
		80	866	229	0.8619	0.8798	0.8707	0.7217	0.8604	0.1280	1,12%
			22	682							
Multinomial	artificial filtering glomerular threshold	40	1073	22	0.8764	0.8003	0.8366	0.6404	0.8393	0.1156	2,39%
			267	437							
		50	1062	33	0.9284	0.9096	0.9189	0.8347	0.9227	0.0689	2,15%
			106	598							
		60	1041	54	0.9560	0.9639	0.9599	0.9191	0.9610	0.0429	2,03%
			16	688							
		70	997	98	0.9360	0.9517	0.9437	0.8825	0.9427	0.0618	1,97%
			5	699							
		80	933	162	0.8275	0.8368	0.8321	0.6633	0.8371	0.1567	1,77%
			75	629							

ERTS*: exchange rate training set

"Number of nephron." does not affect in any way the classification quality, that affect the execution time: increasing "number of nephron" reduces the execution time and vice versa.

In our experiments, the number of nephron equal to 1500. In the next section, we will present a table where we will put the light on the influence of the "number of nephron" on the execution time (see Table 9).

We also opted to set other parameters according to the natural model to build an artificial model similar as possible to the natural model. These parameters are as follow:

- In the proportion of initial set training, we have set at 15%, like a consumption of oxygen by kidney in natural model.
- Concerning Blood flow which represents the proportion of email to be treated each iteration, we have set it at 20% by reference to the natural model, i.e., at each iteration, we deal only with 20% of the incoming message.
- Moreover, the proportion of juxtamedullary nephrons represents the number of update attempt on the training set at the end of each iteration. We have set it at 15% of messages processed by iteration and through reference to the natural model.

Table 7a. Results of 4-gram characters and weighing TFC

Step 1 Artificial Glomerular Filtration			Confusion Matrix		Recall	Precesion	F-Measure	Kappa Statistic	Accuracy	Entropy
Bernoulli	artificial filtering glomerular threshold	40	1074	21	0.7892	0.6267	0.6987	0.2896	0.7037	0.1867
			512	192						
		50	981	112	0.7682	0.7271	0.7471	0.4780	0.7632	0.2025
			312	392						
		60	743	352	0.7867	0.7945	0.7806	0.5488	0.7693	0.1910
			63	641						
		70	812	283	0.7665	0.7791	0.7727	0.5373	0.7709	0.2038
			129	575						
		80	572	523	0.7370	0.7249	0.7307	0.4018	0.6809	0.2251
			51	653						
Multinomial	artificial filtering glomerular threshold	40	1069	26	0.7818	0.6294	0.6974	0.2947	0.7048	0.1924
			505	199						
		50	1001	94	0.8014	0.7603	0.7803	0.5403	0.7937	0.1774
			277	427						
		60	851	244	0.8074	0.8218	0.8145	0.6200	0.8121	0.1727
			94	610						
		70	732	363	0.7661	0.7767	0.7713	0.5164	0.7531	0.2041
			81	623						
		80	587	508	0.7783	0.7595	0.7688	0.4610	0.7109	0.1950
			12	692						

- Last but not least, we launch our application in two threads.

We have chosen a stagnation of results as stopping criteria for k-means which represents the second step: artificial renal tubular transfer (optimization) and we have used a Euclidian similarity in k-means Algorithm.

From the superposition graphs between the two Bayesian model: Bernoulli and Multinomial, we can see clearly that the multinomial model gives better results compared with the model Bernoulli, because the Multinomial model takes into consideration the frequency of the term to generate the model Bayesian; whereas the Bernoulli model generate the model Bayesian simply by the presence or absence of the term. Consequently, we will interpret and discuss only the results of the model Multinomial in the rest of this section.

The data representation affects the quality of results: with the 4 gram character and TFC weighting, we have got the best result. Whereas with the 3 gram character and TFC weighting, we have got the medium result. Finally, we can see that with the 1 gram word and TFC weighting, we have got the worst results that are unstable and difficult to interpret. The combination, 4gram character and TFC weighting, and by choosing the multinomial Bayesian model with "glomerular filtering the artificial threshold"=60%, is the best combination that returns the best result: a very low entropy (equal to 3%), the F-Measure which

Table 7b. Results of 4-gram characters and weighing TFC

Step 2 (Final) Artificial Renal Tubular Transfer(Optimization)			Confusion Matrix		Recall	Precesion	F-Measure	Kappa Statistic	Accuracy	Entropy	ERTS
Bernoulli	artificial filtering glomerular threshold	40	1077	18	0.8898	0.8206	0.8538	0.6796	0.8560	0.1038	2,43%
			241	463							
		50	1059	49	0.9135	0.8976	0.9055	0.8197	0.9171	0.0826	2,31%
			113	591							
		60	997	108	0.9311	0.8133	0.8221	0.6463	0.8376	0.1536	2,10%
			194	510							
		70	1023	72	0.9438	0.9543	0.9490	0.8964	0.9499	0.0545	2,29%
			18	686							
		80	894	201	0.8741	0.8725	0.8832	0.7510	0.8760	0.1175	2,04%
			22	682							
Multinomial	artificial filtering glomerular threshold	40	1084	11	0.8981	0.8252	0.8601	0.6903	0.8610	0.0965	4,06%
			239	465							
		50	1063	32	0.9473	0.9391	0.9432	0.8858	0.9460	0.0512	3,87%
			65	639							
		60	1057	39	0.9678	0.9734	0.9706	0.9408	0.9716	0.0316	3,69%
			13	691							
		70	1048	47	0.9505	0.9529	0.9517	0.9034	0.9538	0.0482	3,61%
			36	668							
		80	977	118	0.8992	0.9106	0.9048	0.8072	0.9066	0.0955	3,57%
			50	654							

ERTS*: exchange rate training set

is almost perfect (equal to 97%) and high Kappa-Statistic (equal to 94%), this is due to the strength of each element of this combination. The 4 gram character representation is a powerful data representation and it often gives the best results.

TFC weighting is a correction of Tf-Idf over the length of texts through standardization cosine, not to favor longer documents. Remember that Tf-Idf gives more importance to words that appear often inside the same text because as long as the term is frequent in a text, it will be more related to the topic of this text, and also gives less weight to words that belong to several documents because when the term is common in a body and in most documents, it will be less used to the difference between the documents. Secondly, we should remember what we have seen before: the Multinomial Bayesian model take into account the frequency of the term in generation of the model Bayesian which gives this model a strength and credibility.

The "glomerular filtering the artificial threshold" = 60%, which is greater than the traditional threshold of the Naive Bayes (50%) has decided that Naive Bayes model is more severe. In fact, even though the probability of a message being a HAM is 55% (so its probability of being SPAM is 45%), this message will be considered SPAM because its probability of being a HAM does not exceed the confidence level of 60%. Consequently, this threshold provides additional security and confidence.

Table 8a. Results of 1-gram word and weighing TFC

Step 1 Artificial Glomerular Filtration			Confusion Matrix		Recall	Precesion	F-Measure	Kappa Statistic	Accuracy	Entropy
Bernoulli	artificial filtering glomerular threshold	40	1002	93	0.5666	0.5264	0.5457	0.0677	0.6108	0.3218
			607	97						
		50	**771**	**324**	**0.7091**	**0.7185**	**0.7137**	**0.4224**	**0.7153**	**0.2437**
			188	**516**						
		60	928	167	0.6901	0.6602	0.6748	0.3379	0.7009	0.2559
			371	333						
		70	622	473	0.6688	0.6739	0.6713	0.3219	0.6509	0.2690
			155	549						
		80	465	630	0.7071	0.6775	0.6920	0.3094	0.6225	0.2450
			49	655						
Multinomial	artificial filtering glomerular threshold	40	1034	61	0.6607	0.5637	0.6084	0.1466	0.6464	0.2737
			575	129						
		50	952	143	0.7262	0.6918	0.7086	0.4039	0.7304	0.2322
			342	362						
		60	**657**	**438**	**0.7582**	**0.7595**	**0.7588**	**0.4733**	**0.7248**	**0.2098**
			57	**647**						
		70	768	327	0.7447	0.7569	0.7508	0.4896	0.7448	0.2194
			132	572						
		80	498	597	0.6929	0.6755	0.6841	0.3099	0.6275	0.2541
			73	631						

In the results that are presented in tables (those result after step 2), we can plainly see that the Training set changes from 1% to 4%, this change allows the system to update the training set gradually as system running. It is worth remembering that this change is between iterations, the advantage of this operation is to rectify mistakes and take into consideration the results of each filter.

COMPARISON STUDY

In the following tables, we will compare the results of this approach: "human Renal Function for detection and Filtering of SPAM" with previous results: ABC (Artificial bee colony) algorithm for Detection and Filtering of spam (Hamou and al, 2013) and a Social Bees approach for Detection and Filtering of Spam (Hamou and al, 2013). Based on some evaluation criteria, we present Table 9 for comparison between the two algorithms studied.

Based on some evaluation criteria, Table 10 is presented for comparison between the two algorithms studied. In terms of results and based on several evaluation measure, we find that our model based on Human Renal Function for detection and spam filtering algorithm gives the best results even in the worst case.

Table 8b. Results of 1-gram word and weighing TFC

Step 2 (Final) Artificial Renal Tubular Transfer (Optimization)			Confusion Matrix		Recall	Precesion	F-Measure	Kappa Statistic	Accuracy	Entropy	ERTS
Bernoulli	artificial filtering glomerular threshold	40	1033	62	0.8278	0.7699	0.7978	0.5721	0.8067	0.1563	2,33%
			284	420							
		50	998	97	0.8396	0.8193	0.8293	0.6544	0.8393	0.1467	2,04%
			192	512							
		60	898	197	0.7265	0.7161	0.7213	0.4408	0.7387	0.2320	1,88%
			273	431							
		70	**957**	**138**	**0.8536**	**0.8581**	**0.8558**	**0.7114**	**0.8615**	**0.1350**	**1,89%**
			111	**593**							
		80	793	302	0.7739	0.7875	0.7806	0.5476	0.7737	0.1983	1,85%
			105	599							
Multinomial	artificial filtering glomerular threshold	40	1039	56	0.8367	0.7776	0.8061	0.5883	0.8148	0.1491	2,43%
			277	427							
		50	**966**	**129**	**0.8749**	**0.8825**	**0.8789**	**0.7566**	**0.8827**	**0.1168**	**2,31%**
			82	**622**							
		60	1001	94	0.8472	0.8285	0.8377	0.6718	0.8471	0.1404	2,10%
			181	523							
		70	915	180	0.8144	0.8205	0.8174	0.6340	0.8237	0.1671	2,29%
			137	567							
		80	854	241	0.7536	0.7599	0.7567	0.5124	0.7643	0.2131	2,04%
			183	521							

ERTS*: exchange rate training set

Table 9. Number of nephrons vs execution time

Configuration		Number of Nephrons		
		500	1000	1500
Bernoulli	3 Gram characters - TFC	13713 ms	8819 ms	7435 ms
	4 Gram characters – TFC	18513 ms	10520 ms	8294 ms
	1 Gram word - TFC	10937 ms	7270 ms	4592 ms
Multinomial	3 Gram characters - TFC	18812 ms	11374 ms	8824 ms
	4 Gram characters – TFC	20182 ms	13276 ms	9488 ms
	1 Gram word - TFC	18174 ms	9731 ms	6213 ms

Table 10. Result of evaluation of the three approaches (ABC, Bees and Renal Approach)

	The Worst Case			The Best Case		
	ABC Algorithm	**Social Bees Approach**	**Humain Renal Approach**	**ABC Algorithm**	**Social Bees Approach**	**Humain Renal Approach**
Recall	0.4853	0.8277	0.7536	0.5464	0.7406	0.9678
Precision	0.4959	0.7442	0.7599	0.5130	0.9285	0.9734
F-Measure	0.4905	0.7838	0.7567	0.5292	0.8240	0.9706
Kappa-Statistic	0.1281	0.5116	0.5124	0.1827	0.5841	0.9408
Entropy	0.4935	0.2198	0.2131	0.219	0.0688	0.0316
Accuracy	0.1914	0.7696	0.7643	0.4991	0.8738	0.9716

In the best case, the best results of our approach are obtained by 4 grams characters, TFC and with "glomerular filtering the artificial threshold "equal to 60% it has the greatest F-measure (97%) and accuracy (97%) and the lowest entropy (3.1%), as shown in Table 7, by cons the best results obtained by the ABC algorithm are the work of 3 grams characters with the Manhattan distance for f-measure of 52.43% and an accuracy of 49.9% and an entropy of 21.9% which represents a loss information fairly consistent for this type of problem. Moreover, the best results of the model based on artificial social bees for detection and spam filtering algorithm are obtained by 4 grams characters for the F-measure (82%) and accuracy (87%) and the entropy (6.7%). We can see that even in the worst case, our approach gives the best result, even more, the worst result returned by our approach can compete with the best result of the two other approaches.

In terms of results and based on several evaluation measure we find that our model based on artificial social bees for detection and spam filtering algorithm gives the best results. The best results obtained our approach are obtained by 4 grams characters since they have the greatest F-measure (82%) and accuracy (87%) and the lowest entropy (6.7%), as shown in Table 8, by cons the best results obtained by the ABC algorithm are the work of 3 grams characters with the Manhattan distance for fmeasure of 52.43% and an accuracy of 49.9% and an entropy of 21.9% which represents a loss information fairly consistent for this type of problem. We clearly see the difference between the two approaches.

CONCLUSION AND PERSPECTIVE

In this paper, we have proposed a comparison between two bio-inspired method which is the renal system and social bees. In the second part, we explain our platform for the experimentation.. In the second part we are interested in experimenting with our model in textual data because emails are unstructured documents. For this reason, our interest is focused on the modes of representation of textual data in this case the n-grams character and words because these modes operate regardless of language, lexical roots are automatically captured and they are tolerant to the misspellings. The advantages of n-grams have led us to use as a spam text is a document written in any language and can contain text full of mistakes and written by anyone.

In the future, we plan to compare our artificial model for the filtering of the SPAM based on human renal function with other algorithms as well as other techniques of SPAM's filtering and to optimize its performance. Last but not least, we plan to, hopefully, create an appropriate model of functioning parallel to our approach.

To conclude, the results of human Renal Function for detection and Filtering of SPAM" approach found to be more effective and workable than the previous approaches. Taking into consideration the fact that the white and black lists have not been used in the current research, it will be interesting to employ them in the next research as the starting point for better results and more advanced investigations in the field of detection and Filtering of SPAM.

REFERENCES

Boudia, M. A., Hamou, R. M., & Amine, A. (2015). A New Meta-Heuristic based on Human Renal Function for Detection and Filtering of SPAM. *International Journal of Information Security and Privacy, 9*(4), 26–58. doi:10.4018/IJISP.2015100102

Boudia, M. A., Hamou, R. M., & Amine, A. (2017). A New Meta-Heuristics for Intrusion Detection System Inspired from the Protection System of Social Bees. . *International Journal of Information Security and Privacy, 11*(1), 18–34. doi:10.4018/IJISP.2017010102

Chhabra, S., Yerazunis, W. S., & Siefkes, C. (2004, November). Spam filtering using a markov random field model with variable weighting schemas. In *Data Mining, 2004. ICDM'04. Fourth IEEE International Conference on* (pp. 347-350). IEEE. doi:10.1109/ICDM.2004.10031

Chou, C. H., Sinha, A. P., & Zhao, H. (2008). A text mining approach to Internet abuse detection. *Information Systems and e-Business Management, 6*(4), 419–439. doi:10.1007/s10257-007-0070-0

da Cruz, J. M. M. (2009). Méthodologie d'évaluation des filtres anti-spam. *Journées Réseaux, Nante du, 1*.

De Vel, O., Anderson, A., Corney, M., & Mohay, G. (2001). Mining e-mail content for author identification forensics. *SIGMOD Record, 30*(4), 55–64. doi:10.1145/604264.604272

Drucker, H., Wu, S., & Vapnik, V. N. (1999). Support vector machines for spam categorization. *Neural Networks. IEEE Transactions on, 10*(5), 1048–1054. PMID:18252607

Faynberg, I., Lu, H. L., Perlman, R., & Zeltsan, Z. (2010). *U.S. Patent No. 7,752,440*. Washington, DC: U.S. Patent and Trademark Office.

Gupta, G., Mazumdar, C., & Rao, M. S. (2004). Digital Forensic Analysis of E-mails: A trusted E-mail Pro-tocol. *International Journal of Digital Evidence, 2*(4).

Guzella, T. S., & Caminhas, W. M. (2009). A review of machine learning approaches to spam filtering. *Expert Systems with Applications, 36*(7), 10206–10222. doi:10.1016/j.eswa.2009.02.037

Hamou, R. M., Amine, A., & Boudia, A. (2013). A New Meta-Heuristic Based on Social Bees for Detection and Filtering of Spam. *International Journal of Applied Metaheuristic Computing, 4*(3), 15–33. doi:10.4018/ijamc.2013070102

Hamou, R. M., Amine, A., & Lokbani, A. C. (2013). Study of Sensitive Parameters of PSO Application to Clustering of Texts. *International Journal of Applied Evolutionary Computation*, *4*(2), 41–55. doi:10.4018/jaec.2013040104

Kågström, J. (2005). *Improving naive Bayesian spam filtering* (Doctoral dissertation). Mid Sweden University.

Lakshmi, R. D., & Radha, N. (2010, September). Spam classification using supervised learning techniques. In *Proceedings of the 1st Amrita ACM-W Celebration on Women in Computing in India* (p. 66). ACM.

Lokbani, A. C., Lehireche, A., & Hamou, R. M. (2013). Experimentation of Data Mining Technique for System's Security: A Comparative Study. In *Advances in Swarm Intelligence* (pp. 248–257). Springer Berlin Heidelberg. doi:10.1007/978-3-642-38715-9_30

Lueg, C., & Martin, S. (2007, July). Users dealing with spam and spam filters: some observations and rec-ommendations. In *Proceedings of the 8th ACM SIGCHI New Zealand chapter's International Conference on Computer-Human Interaction: Design Centered HCI* (pp. 67-72). ACM.

Lueg, Mueller, & Scott. (2009). *Fight Spam on the Internet!* Retrieved from spam.abuse.net

Murphy, K., Travers, P., & Walport, M. (2008). *Janeway's immunology*. Garland Science.

O'Brien, C., & Vogel, C. (2003, September). Spam filters: Bayes vs. chi-squared; letters vs. words. In *Proceedings of the 1st international symposium on Information and communication technologies* (pp. 291-296). Trinity College Dublin.

Obied, A., & Alhajj, R. (2009). Collection and Analysis of Web-based Exploits and Malware. *Journal of Applied Intelligence*, *30*(2), 112–120. doi:10.1007/s10489-007-0102-y

Oda, T., & White, T. (2005). Immunity from spam: An analysis of an artificial immune system for junk email detection. In *Artificial Immune Systems* (pp. 276–289). Springer Berlin Heidelberg. doi:10.1007/11536444_21

Provost, J. (1999). *Naive-Bayes vs. Rule-Learning in Classification of Email*. University of Texas at Austin.

Ruan, G., & Tan, Y. (2010). A three-layer back-propagation neural network for spam detection using artifi-cial immune concentration. *Soft Computing*, *14*(2), 139–150. doi:10.1007/s00500-009-0440-2

Sahami, M., Dumais, S., Heckerman, D., & Horvitz, E. (1998, July). A Bayesian approach to filtering junk e-mail. In *Learning for Text Categorization: Papers from the 1998 workshop* (*Vol. 62*, pp. 98-105). Academic Press.

Sanz, E. P., Gómez Hidalgo, J. M., & Cortizo Pérez, J. C. (2008). Email spam filtering. *Advances in Computers*, *74*, 45–114. doi:10.1016/S0065-2458(08)00603-7

Sculley, D., & Wachman, G. M. (2007, July). Relaxed online SVMs for spam filtering. In *Proceedings of the 30th annual international ACM SIGIR conference on Research and development in information retrieval* (pp. 415-422). ACM.

Sebastiani, F. (2002). Machine learning in automated text categorization. *ACM computing surveys (CSUR)*, *34*(1), 1-47.

Shannon, C. E. (1948). *A Mathematical Theory of Communication'-BSTJ*. Juillet et Octobre.

Tan, Y., Deng, C., & Ruan, G. (2009, June). Concentration based feature construction approach for spam detection. In *Neural Networks, 2009. IJCNN 2009. International Joint Conference on* (pp. 3088-3093). IEEE. doi:10.1109/IJCNN.2009.5178651

Van Staden, F., & Venter, H. S. (2009). The State of the Art of Spam and Anti-Spam Strategies and a Possi-ble Solution using Digital Forensics. ISSA, 437-454.

Xiao-li, C., Pei-yu, L., Zhen-fang, Z., & Qiu, Y. (2009, August). A method of spam filtering based on weighted support vector machines. In *IT in Medicine & Education, 2009. ITIME'09. IEEE International Symposium on* (Vol. 1, pp. 947-950). IEEE.

Yegin, A. E., & Watanabe, F. (2005). Authentication, Authorization, and Accounting. *Next Generation Mobile Systems 3G and Beyond*, 315-343.

Yerazunis, W. S. (2004, January). The spam-filtering accuracy plateau at 99.9% accuracy and how to get past it. *Proceedings of the 2004 MIT Spam Conference*.

Zdziarski, J. A. (2005). *Ending spam: Bayesian content filtering and the art of statistical language classifica-tion*. No Starch Press.

Zhang, L., Zhu, J., & Yao, T. (2004). An evaluation of statistical spam filtering techniques. *ACM Trans-actions on Asian Language Information Processing*, *3*(4), 243–269. doi:10.1145/1039621.1039625

Chapter 4
Methods for Gene Selection and Classification of Microarray Dataset

Mekour Norreddine
Dr. Tahar Moulay University of Saida, Algeria

ABSTRACT

One of the problems that gene expression data resolved is feature selection. There is an important process for choosing which features are important for prediction; there are two general approaches for feature selection: filter approach and wrapper approach. In this chapter, the authors combine the filter approach with method ranked information gain and wrapper approach with a searching method of the genetic algorithm. The authors evaluate their approach on two data sets of gene expression data: Leukemia, and the Central Nervous System. The classifier Decision tree (C4.5) is used for improving the classification performance.

INTRODUCTION

DNA microarray technology is a revolutionary method enabling the measurement of expression levels of thousands of genes in a single experiment under diverse experimental conditions. Since its invention, this technology has proved to be a valuable tool for many biological and medical applications (Beatrice et al., 1999). Microarray data analysis can be carried out according to at least two different and complementary perspectives. In one hand, data clustering (non supervised classification) aims to identify groups of genes, or groups of experimental conditions that exhibit similar expression patterns. In such a context bi-clustering is particularly interesting since it allows the simultaneous identification of groups of genes that show similar expression patterns across specific groups of experimental conditions (samples) (Beatrice et al., 1999).

Nowadays, people can obtain the expression datasets of thousands of genes simultaneously using microarray technology. One of the important fields in using these gene expression datasets is to classify and predict the diagnostic category of a sample. Actually, precise diagnosis and classification is crucial

DOI: 10.4018/978-1-5225-3004-6.ch004

for successful treatment of illness (Zhen et al., 2009a). Knowledge Data Discovery (KDD) consists of several phases like Data selection, Data mining.

Data mining is one of the important phases of knowledge data discovery, There is a technique which is used to find new, hidden and useful patterns of knowledge from large databases. There are several data mining methods such as Prediction, Clustering and Classification (D.Lavanya et al., 2011).The problem of classification of data is identified as one of the major problems in extracting knowledge from data.

BIOLOGICAL BACKGROUND

Cells are the basic operating units of each living system. All the directions required to direct their actions are contained inside the chemical DNA or shortly deoxyribonucleic acid. A deoxyribonucleic acid molecule may be a double-stranded compound composed of 4 basic molecular units specifically nucleotides. The nitrogen bases include adenine (A), guanine (G), cytosine (C) and thymine (T).

The ordering provides a example for the synthesis of a range of ribonucleic acid molecules. the method of transcribing a gene's deoxyribonucleic acid sequence into ribonucleic acid is termed organic phenomenon. A gene's expression level indicates the approximate variety of copies that gene's ribonucleic acid created in a very cell and it's correlative with the quantity of the corresponding proteins created. This mechanism controls that genes are expressed in a very cell and acts as a "volume control" that will increase or decreases the extent of expression of explicit genes as necessary (Nagamma et al., 2013b).

MICROARAY DATA FORMAT

A gene expression data set from a microarray experiment can be represented by a real-valued.

Expression matrix = { $G(i,j)$ | $1 \leq i \leq n, 1 \leq j \leq m$ }

where the columns G= { $\overleftarrow{g_1}$, $\overleftarrow{g_2}$,....., $\overleftarrow{g_m}$ } form the expression patterns of genes, the rows S= { $\overleftarrow{s_1}$, $\overleftarrow{s_2}$,...., $\overleftarrow{s_n}$ } . An example of a gene expression microarray dataset for Leukemia is shown (in Table 1). the table organizes data into m columns (genes) and n rows (samples) where m mostly varies from thousand to hundred thousand according to the accuracy of microarray image processing technique, while n is always less than 200 samples according to the previously collected datasets (Zeeshan et al., 2014a). Category column presents the actual class of the sample. For the shown example AML stands for acute myeloid leukemia disease and ALL represents acute lymphoblastic.

PROBLEM DEFINITION

The selection of attributes has become a very active research topic a few years in the fields of artificial learning (Jain et al.,1997; Dash et al.,1997; Kohavi et al.,1997; Blum et al.,1997; Duch et al.,2006) Data mining, image processing (Singh et al., 2002; Fukunaga et al.,1990) and data analysis in bioinformatics.

Table 1. Microarray data decision table

Samples	Attributes (Genes)	Category
	Gene1 Gene2 ... Gene m	
1	G(1,1) G(1,2) ... G(1,m)	ALL
2	G(2,1 G(2,2) ... G(2,m)	ALL
...	... ...	ALL
...	... ...	AML
n	G(n,1) G(n,2) ... G(n,m)	AML

In all these domains, applications need to process data described by a very large number of attributes. Thus, one may have to deal with web pages described by several hundred descriptors, images described by several thousands of pixels or data in bioinformatics giving the expression levels of several thousand genes (Guyon et al.,2003; Dai et al., 2006).

INFORMAL PRESENTATION OF THE PROBLEM

We first present a formalization of the relevance of the attributes that allows distinguishing the different contributions of an attribute to the definition of a function of Classification. Similarly, we present a definition of redundancy that allows us to propose a mechanism for eliminating redundant attributes.

RELVANCE OF ATTRIBUTES

In (Liu et al.,2005), the authors define relevance in the case of Boolean attributes and functions and assuming that the data is non-noisy. A broader definition proposed by (Kohavi et al.,1997) defines relevant attributes such as those whose values systematically vary with class values. In other words, an attribute fi Is relevant if knowing its value changes the probabilities on the values of the class C. But this definition can be clarified to distinguish strongly Relevant attributes and attributes with the following definitions. Is F A complete set of attributes, Fi An attribute, and $Si = F - \{Fi\}$ we suppose that we work with a probability space where the probability is denoted P. $P(C \mid S)$ is the probability of class C knowing the attributes of the set S.

Definition 1

An attribute f is highly relevant iff:

$$P(C \mid F_i, S_i) \neq P(C \mid S_i) \tag{1}$$

Definition 2

An attribute f is weakly relevant iff:

$$P\left(C \mid F_i, S_i\right) = P\left(C \mid S_i\right) \text{ and } \exists S_i' \subset S_i \text{ such as } P\left(C \mid F_i, S_i'\right) \neq P\left(C \mid S_i'\right) \tag{2}$$

Definition 3

An attribute f is irrelevant iff:

$$P\left(C \mid F_i, S_i\right) = P\left(C \mid S_i\right) \text{ and } \forall S_i' \subseteq P\left(C \mid F_i, S_i'\right) = P\left(C \mid S_i'\right) \tag{3}$$

According to these definitions, highly relevant attributes are therefore should appear in any selected optimal subset because their absence should lead to a target function recognition fault. The low relevance suggests that the attribute is not always important, but it can become necessary for an optimal subset under certain conditions. The irrelevance of an attribute is simply defined in relation (23.1) and (2.3.2) and in that an attribute is not at all necessary in an optimal subset of attributes. If we return to Example, we can say that the attribute $F1$ Is highly relevant, Than $F2$ and $F3$ are of little relevance, and then $F4$ and $F5$ are irrelevant.

An optimal subset of attributes should include only highly relevant attributes, no irrelevant attributes, and a subset of weakly relevant attributes. To know how to choose which weakly relevant attributes one should select, it is necessary to highlight the notion of redundancy.

REDUNDANCY OF ATTRIBUTES

The notion of attribute redundancy is intuitively understood and is generally expressed in terms of the correlation between attributes. We can say that two attributes are redundant (between them) if their values are completely correlated (for example, the attributes $F2$ and $F3$ of example 1).This definition is not broadly generalized for a subset of attributes. One finds in (Koller et al.,1996) a formal definition of the redundancy which makes it possible to conceive an approach to identify and eliminate the redundant attributes. A formal definition of redundancy that allows an approach to identify and eliminate redundant attributes. This formalization is based on the notion of Markov blanket of an attribute which makes it possible to identify the irrelevant and redundant attributes (Koller et al.,1996; Yu et al.,2004).

Definition 4

Let F be the total set of attributes and C the class. Let F_i an attribute and M_i a subset of attributes that does not contain F_i, that is: $M_i \subseteq F$ and $M_i \notin F_i$.

M_i is a Markov cover for F_i ffi:

$$P\left(F - M_{i} - \left\{F_{i}\right\}, C \mid F_{i}, M_{i}\right) = P\left(F - M_{i} - \left\{F_{i}\right\}, C \mid M_{i}\right) \tag{4}$$

The Markov definition defines that M_{i} Not only the information that F_{i} brings on C But also the information it brings about all the others Attributes.In (koller et al.,1996) it is shown that an optimal subset of attributes can be obtained by a downward elimination procedure known as Markov blanket Filtering and defined as follows: Let G The current set of attributes ($G = F$ at the beginning).At each step of the procedure, if there is a Markov cover for the attribute F_{i} in the set G current F_{i} Is removed from G.

METHODS

Information Gain

Information gain (IG) is a ranking method of feature selection based on decision trees, This measure used in filter approach of feature selection for measures the amount of information in bits and discard irrelevant or redundant features from a given feature vector (Cheng et al.,2009;Ahmed et al.,2013). Entropy is a foundation of the IG attribute ranking methods, this measure is given by:

Figure 1. The two approaches to selecting attributes

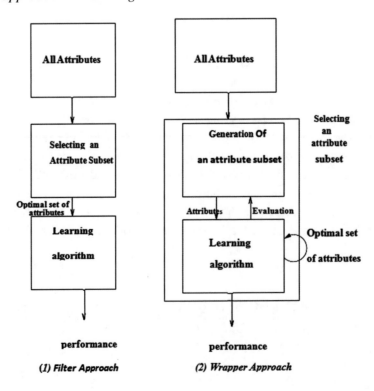

$$H(S) = -\sum p(s) \log_2(p(s)) \tag{5}$$

where $p(s)$ is the marginal probability density function for the random variable S. If the observed values of S in the training data set M are partitioned according to the values of a second feature X, and the entropy of S with respect to the partitions induced by X is less than the entropy of S prior to partitioning, then there is a relationship between features S and X. The entropy of S after observing X is:

$$H(S \mid X) = -\sum p(x) - \sum p(s \mid x) \log_2(p(s \mid x)) \tag{6}$$

where p($s \mid x$) is the conditional probability of s given x. Given the entropy as a criterion of impurity in a training set M, we can define a measure reflecting additional information about S provided by X that represents the amount by which the entropy of S decreases. This measure is known as IG. It is given by

$$IG = p(S) - p(S \mid X) = p(X) - p(X \mid S) \tag{7}$$

IG is a symmetrical measure (refer to equation (7)). The information gained about S after observing X is equal to the information gained about X after observing S. A weakness of the IG criterion is that it is biased in favor of features with more values even when they are not more informative.

Genetic Algorithms

Genetic algorithms (GA) are search algorithms inspired by the mechanisms of the natural evolution of living beings and genetics in biological systems. They can be applied in many problem optimizations and machine learning problem.The microarray data classification requires the selection of a subset of relevant genes in order to achieve good classification performance. The selection of genes can be modeled as a combinatorial optimization problem. GA works with a set of candidate solutions called a population and obtain the optimal solution after a series of iterative computations. As in the case of biological evolution, it has a mechanism of selecting fitter chromosomes at each generation. To simulate the process of evolution, the selected chromosomes undergo genetic operations, such as crossover and mutation.For a given problem optimization, an individual represents a point in the search space, a potential solution. It is associated with the value of the test to optimize its adaptation.On generates after iteratively populations of individuals on which are applied selection process of crossing and selection mutation.The aims to promote the best elements of the population for the criterion considered (most suitable), the crossover and mutation ensure the exploration and exploitation of the search space. These are the main components of a genetic algorithm (see Figure 2).

Figure 2. General Process of GA

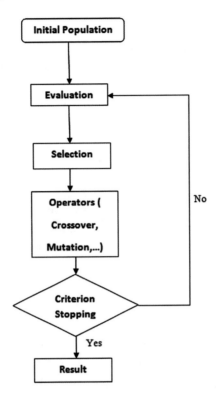

DECISION TREE (C4.5)

Decision trees are one of the best-known methods in classification. The principle decision trees are to achieve the classification of a sample through a series of tests on the attributes that describe it. Concretely, in the graphical representation of a tree.

1. An internal node corresponds to a test of the value of an attribute.
2. A branch from a node corresponds to one or more values of this test.
3. A leaf is a node which does not leave any branch corresponds to a class.

A decision rule (of the form if ... then ...) is created for each path by as the root of the tree and traversing the tests (by conjunctions) to the sheet that is beyond the class label. Decision trees are particularly popular because they allow easy understanding, but at a relatively complex classification task, the user is no longer able to effectively explore the results in text form.

The main construction algorithms of a decision tree are C4.5 (J. Ross Quinlan,1993) and *CART* (Breiman et al.,1984). In these algorithms, at each step of creating a node, a criterion of separation between classes is used to decide which attribute is most relevant for classification. In this study, the feature subset was measured by the one-out cross-validation of the Decision tree. Genetic algorithms (*GA*) are search algorithms inspired by the mechanisms of the natural evolution of living beings and genetics in biological systems.

Figure 3. Process of our system

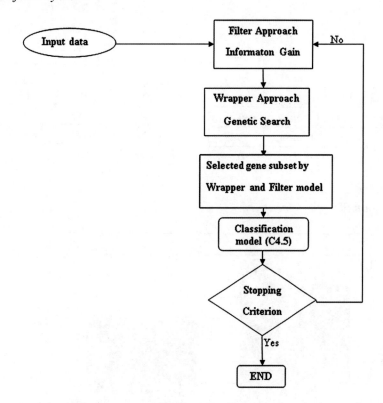

EXPRIMENTAL STUDIES

In this study, we present new approach to select feature gene in microarrays data and used the classifier decision tree ($C4.5$) for evaluate the performance of our method.

We used Waikato Environment for Knowledge Analysis ($WEKA$) version 3.6.12 to measure the performance of each feature selection algorithm. $WEKA$ is a well-known machine learning tool based on JAVA (Ahmed et al.,2013).

These feature subsets measured and analyzed with 10-fold Cross-Validation (CV). The classification models are evaluated using the accuracy and AUC (Area under Receiver Operating Characteristic Curve) performance metric.

In this works, we compared our Hybrid approach ($IG+GA$) with ranking techniques Information Gain (IG), Gain Ratio (GR) and Symmetrical Uncertainty(SU) by the classification accuracy and AUC values.

Table 2. Classification accuracy using C4.5 classifier for Leukemia dataset

Bestofgene	IG	GR	SU	Our Methods
70	83.33	86.11	83.33	84.72
50	83.33	84.72	83.33	94.44
20	81.94	86.11	91.84	93.06
10	83.33	86.11	81.94	90.28
Average	82.98	85.76	85.11	90.63

Table 3. Classification accuracy using C4.5 classifier for CNS dataset

Bestofgene	IG	GR	SU	Our Methods
70	63.33	65	65	63.33
50	65	66.67	68.33	68.33
20	75	68.33	71.67	73.33
10	68.33	78.33	75	76.67
Average	67.92	69.58	70	70.42

Figure 4. Comparison of testing accuracy

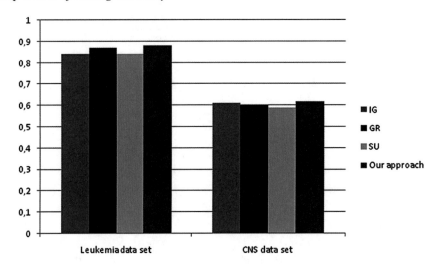

Table 4. AUC values using C4.5 classifier for Leukemia dataset

Bestofgene	IG	GR	SU	Our Methods
70	0.85	0.88	0.85	0.85
50	0.85	0.86	0.85	0.94
20	0.83	0.85	0.83	0.90
10	0.81	0.88	0.82	0.82
Average	0.84	0.87	0.84	0.88

Table 5. AUC values using C4.5 classifier for CNS dataset

Bestofgene	IG	GR	SU	Our Methods
70	0.57	0.58	0.58	0.63
50	0.59	0.58	0.60	0.56
20	0.65	0.58	0.51	0.61
10	0.66	0.65	0.65	0.65
Average	0.61	0.60	0.59	0.62

Figure 5. Comparison of testing AUC values

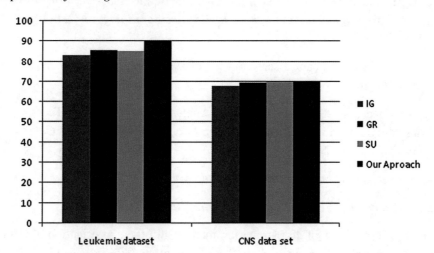

CONCLUSION AND FUTURE WORKS

In this paper, we propose a method hybrid for gene selection between Information Gain (IG) for filter methods and Genetic Algorithm (GA) for Wrappers methods. The results confirm that the C4.5 classifier gives best results of Accuracy and AUC values for proposed hybrid technique than other methods ranked. Finally, our approach has better performance than filter and wrapper methods. We can also Applied other methods of meta-heuristics based on bio-inspired techniques such as immune systems, and other evolution algorithms, the experiments carried out have led to positive results and many perspectives are yet to be explored in this rapidly expanding field.

REFERENCES

Abou-Taleb, Mohamedet, Mohamed, & Abedelhalim. (2013c). Hybridizing Filters and Wrapper Approaches for Improving the Classification Accuracy of Microarray Dataset. *International Journal of Soft Computing and Engineering, 3*(3), 155-159.

Ahmed & Zeeshan. (2014a). Applying weka towards machine learning with genetic algorithm and back propagation neural networks. *International Journal of Soft Computing and Engineering, 3*(3), 155-159.

Ben-Dor, A., Bruhn, L., Friedman, N., Nachman, I., Schummer, M., & Yakhini, Z. (2000a). Classification with Gene Expression Profiles. *Proceedings of the 4th Annual Intemational Conference on Computational Molecular Biology, 7*(3/4), 559-84.

Blum, A., & Langley, P. (1997c). Selection of relevant features and examples in machine learning. *Artificial Intelligence, 97*(1-2), 245–271. doi:10.1016/S0004-3702(97)00063-5

Breiman, Friedman, Olshen, & Stone. (1984). *Classification and Regression Trees.* Wadsworth.

Brown & Grundy. (2000). Knowledge-based analysis of microarray gene expression data by using support vector machines. *International Journal of Web Engineering and Technology, 97*(1), 262-267.

Dai, J. J., Lieu, L., & Rocke, D. (2006a). TDimension reduction for classification with gene expression microarray data. *Statistical Applications in Genetics and Molecular Biology, 5*(1), 1–19. doi:10.2202/1544-6115.1147 PMID:16646870

Dash, M., & Liu, H. (1997b). Feature selection for classification. *Intelligent Data Analysis, 1*(1-4), 131–156. doi:10.1016/S1088-467X(97)00008-5

David, Saeb, & Al Rubeaan. (2013a). Comparative Analysis of Data Mining Tools and Classification Techniques using WEKA in Medical Bioinformatics. *International Journal of Computer Engineering and Intelligent Systems, 4*(13), 28-38.

Duch, W. (2006). *Feature extraction, foundations and applications.* Springer.

Duda & Hart. (1973). *Pattern Classification and scene analysis.* Wiley.

Dudoit, S. (2002b). Comparison of discrimination methods for the classification of tumors using gene expression data. *Journal of the American Statistical Association, 97*(457), 77-87.

Duvaland & Hao. (1999). *Advances in metaheuristics for gene selection and classification of Microarray data.* Addison-Wesley.

Fukunaga, K. (1990). *Statistical pattern recognition* (2nd ed.). Morgan Kaufmann.

Golub, T. R. (1999a). Molecular classification of cancer: Class discovery and class prediction by gene expression monitoring. *Science, 286*(5439), 531–539. doi:10.1126/science.286.5439.531 PMID:10521349

Guyon, I., & Elisseeff, A. (2003). An introduction to variable and feature selection. *Journal of Machine Learning Research, 3*, 1157–1182.

Guyon, I., Weston, J., Barnhill, S., & Vapnik, V. (2002a). Gene selection for cancer classification using support vector machine. *SMachine Learning., 46*(13), 389–422. doi:10.1023/A:1012487302797

Hassan & Abou-Taleb. (2013). A hybrid feature selection approach of ensemble multiple Filter methods and wrapper method for Improving the Classification Accuracy of Microarray Data Set. *International Journal of Computer Science and Information Technology and Security, 3*(2).

Hernandez, J. (2007). *A Genetic Embedded Approach for Gene Selection and Classification of Microarray Data.* EvoBIO.

Jain, A., & Zongker, D. (1997a). Feature selection: Evaluation, application, and small sample performance. *IEEE Transactions on Pattern Analysis and Machine Intelligence, 19*(2), 153–157. doi:10.1109/34.574797

Jantawan & Tsai. (2014). A Comparison of Filter and Wrapper Approaches with Data Mining Techniques for Categorical Variables Selection. *International Journal of Innovative Research in Computer and Communication Engineering, 2*(6).

Kohavi, R., & John, G. H. (1997). Wrappers for feature subset selection. *Artificial Intelligence, 97*(1-2), 273–334. doi:10.1016/S0004-3702(97)00043-X

Koller, D., & Sahami, M. (1996). Toward optimal feature selection. *13th International conference on machines learning*, 1-15.

Lavanya & Usha Rani. (2011). Analysis of feature selection with classification: Breast Cancer Datasets. *Indian Journal of Computer Science and Engineering, 2.*

Liu, H., & Yu, L. (2005). Toward Integrating Feature Selection Algorithms for Classification and Clustering. *IEEE Trans. on Knowledgeand Data Engineering., 17*(4), 491–502. doi:10.1109/TKDE.2005.66

Mei, Shen, & Ye. (2009a). Hybridized KNN and SVM for gene expression data classification. *Life Science Journal, 6*(1), 61-65.

Patil, N., Toshniwa, D., & Garg, K. (2013b). *Genome data classification based on fuzzy matching.* Addison-Wesley.

Quinlan. (1993). C4.5: programs for machine learning. Morgan Kaufmann Publishers Inc.

Singh, S., Singh, M., & Markou, M. (2002). Feature selection for face recognition based on data partitioning. *ICPR, 1*, 680–683.

Wang, X. L., Jing, Z., & Yang, H. Z. (2011a). Service selection constraint model and optimization algorithm for web service composition. *Journal of Information Technology, 10*(5), 1024–1030. doi:10.3923/itj.2011.1024.1030

Xiong, M., Jin, L., & Li, W. (2000b). Computational methods for gene expression-based tumor classification. *BioTechniques, 29*(6), 264–268, 1270. PMID:11126130

Yang, Chuang, & Yang. (2009). A Hybrid Filter/Wrapper Method for Feature Selection of Microarray Data. *International Journal of Medical and Biological Engineering, 30*(1), 23-28.

Yang, J., & Honovar, V. (1998). feature subset selection using a genetic algorithm. *IEEE Intelligent Systems, 13*(2), 44–49. doi:10.1109/5254.671091

Yu, L., & Liu, H. (2004a). Efficient feature selection via analysis of relevance and redundancy. *Journal of Machine Learning Research, 5*, 1205–1224.

Chapter 5
Mining Patterns Using Business Process Management

Ishak H. A. Meddah
Oran University of Science and Technology – Mohamed Boudiaf, Algeria

Khaled Belkadi
Oran University of Science and Technology – Mohamed Boudiaf, Algeria

ABSTRACT

Process mining provides an important bridge between data mining and business process analysis. This technique allows for the extraction of information from event logs. In general, there are two steps in process mining: correlation definition or discovery and then process inference or composition. Firstly, the authors mine small patterns from log traces of two applications; those patterns are the representation of the execution traces of a business process. In this step, the authors use existing techniques. The patterns are represented by finite state automaton or their regular expression. The final model is the combination of only two types of small patterns that are represented by the regular expressions (ab)* and (ab*c)*. Secondly, the authors compute these patterns in parallel and then combine those small patterns using the composition rules. They have two parties. The first is the mine, where the authors discover patterns from execution traces, and the second is the combination of these small patterns. The pattern mining and the composition is illustrated by the automaton existing techniques.

INTRODUCTION

Many techniques have been proposed that mine patterns from execution traces. However; existing techniques mine only simple patterns, or a single complex pattern that is limited to a particular set of manually selected events.

Authors (Ammons, G and al., 2002) has recognized that patterns can be specified as regular languages, That allows the compact representation of patterns as regular expressions or finite state automata, and it allows the characterization of the pattern mining as a language learning problem.

DOI: 10.4018/978-1-5225-3004-6.ch005

Process mining approaches are fundamentally similar; each takes as input a static program or a dynamic traces or profile and produces one or more compact regular languages that specify the pattern representation or the workflow. However; the individual solutions differ in key ways.

In this paper, we present a new general approach to patterns mining that addresses several of the limitations of current techniques. Our insight is twofold. First, we recognize that instances of smaller patterns can be composed in parallel into larger patterns. Second, we observed also that the composition of small pattern can be in parallel.

We then leverage this insight to divide our work into two parties; The first one, we use a technique how we can mine two types of small patterns and we compose them by using standard algorithms for finite state automaton manipulation, and some special rules using by M.Gabel and Z.Su [(Gabel, M., & Su, Z, 2008), (Ammons, G and al., 2002)], the mining is also performed by symbolic mining algorithm [(Gabel, M & Su, Z, 2008, May), (Gao, X, 2013), (Guyet, T., & Quiniou, R, 2011)].

Our approach is an amelioration of existing work in pattern mining, it has been implemented in the java programming language with more log files of two application; the SKYPE and VIBER applications. The size of those applications log files is 10 GB, 15 GB, 18 GB, and 20 GB which are generated by log file generator.

The executions traces in our applications are the user's actions like call, the answer, and the messages...

RELATED WORK

Many techniques are suggested in the domain of process mining, we quote:

M.Gabel and al (Gabel, M., & Su, Z, 2008) present a new general technique for mining temporal specification, they realized their work in two steps; firstly they discovered the simple patterns using existing techniques, then combine these patterns using the composition and some rules like Branching and Sequencing rules.

Temporal specification expresses formal correctness requirement of an application's ordering of specific actions and events during execution, they discovered patterns from traces of execution or program source code; The simples patterns are represented using regular expression (ab)* or (ab*c)* and their representation using finite state automaton, after they combine simple patterns to construct a temporal specification using a finite state automaton.

G.Greco and al (Greco, G and al., 2006) discovered several clusters by using a clustering technique, and then they calculate the pattern from each cluster, they combine these patterns to construct a final model, they discovered a workflow scheme from, and then they mine a workflow using a Mine Workflow Algorithm, after they define many clusters from a log traces by using clustering technique and Process Discover Algorithm and some rules cluster.

Then they use a Find Features Algorithm to find a patterns of each cluster, finally they combine these patterns to construct a completely hierarchical workflow model.

In their clustering algorithm, clusters reflect only structural similarities among traces; they say that in future works extending their techniques to take care of the environment so that clusters may reflect not only structural similarities among traces, but also information about, e.g., users and data values.

H.R.Motahari-Nezhed and al (2008) use a service conversation log; first they split a log into several partitions, 2nd they discovered a model from each partition, and 3rd, they annotate the discover protocol model with various metadata to construct a protocol model from real-word service conversation logs.

The protocol is the specification of all possible conversations that a service can have with its partners and the conversation consists of a sequence of messages exchanged between two or more services.

During the split they discovered a simple precise protocol models by analyzing messages sequences in the log, they eliminate conversations considered noisy or not presented in the log; they augmently discovered protocol with various metadata including state and transition supports to get a final protocol model of the log a most generalized model based splitting.

"Mining frequent patterns and finding associations among them require handling large and distributed databases. As FP-tree considered being the best compact data structure to hold the data patterns in memory there has been efforts to make it parallel and distributed to handle large databases" (Itkar, & Kulkarni, 2013) . However, it incurs lot of communication over head during the mining. Parallel and distributed frequent pattern mining algorithm using Hadoop Map Reduce framework is proposed, which shows best performance results for large databases. Proposed algorithm partitions the database in such a way that, it works independently at each local node and locally generates the frequent patterns by sharing the global frequent pattern header table. These local frequent patterns are merged at final stage (Itkar, & Kulkarni, 2013) .

This reduces the complete communication overhead during structure construction as well as during pattern mining. The item set count is also taken into consideration reducing processor idle time. Hadoop Map Reduce framework is used effectively in all the steps of the algorithm. Their experiments are carried out on a PC cluster with 5 computing nodes which shows execution time efficiency as compared to other algorithms. Their experimental result shows that proposed algorithm efficiently handles the scalability for very large data bases (Itkar, & Kulkarni, 2013) .

Ranjan, J., & Bhatnagar, V (Ranjan, & Bhatnagar, 2010) present the advantages of the application of data mining techniques in the management of client relationship in the financial sectors like banking, forecasting stock market, currency exchange rate and bank bankruptcies, say they; there are a big concurrence in the society financial sectors, and they find a difficult to sustain the ever-changing behavior of the customer.

"Data mining techniques is helping the firms to achieve profitable and efficient CRM by providing them with advance techniques to analyze the already existing data in the databases of the firms using the complex modeling algorithms" (Ranjan, & Bhatnagar, 2010); their work demonstrated that data mining is able to automate the process of searching to mountain of customer's related data to find patterns that are good predictors of the behaviors of the clients.

Authors propose an idea of how data mining provide the increased customer, and minimize the risk involved in the financial sectors to obtain the advantages and conclude by providing the limitations of opportunities in the field.

Ranjan, J., & Bhatnagar, V (Ranjan, & Bhatnagar, 2011) propose to provide the analysis of the concepts of business intelligence (BI), knowledge management (KM) and analytical CRM (aCRM) and to establish a framework for integrating all the three to each other. They seek to establish a KM and aCRM based framework using data mining (DM) techniques, which helps in the enterprise decision-making. "The objective is to share how KM and aCRM can be integrated into this seamless analytics framework to sustain excellence in decision making using effective data mining techniques and to explore how working on such aCRM system can be effective for enabling organizations delivering complete solutions" (Ranjan, & Bhatnagar, 2011)

"Social tagging is one of the important characteristics of WEB2.0. The challenge of Web 2.0 is a huge amount of data generated over a short period. Tags are widely used to interpret and classify the web 2.0 resources. Tag clustering is the process of grouping the similar tags into clusters" (Azar, & Hassanien, 2015). Hannah Inbarani H and Al say that tag clustering is very useful for searching and organizing the web2.0 resources and also important for the success of Social Bookmarking systems. In their work, they proposed a hybrid Tolerance Rough Set Based Particle Swarm optimization (TRS-PSO) clustering algorithm for clustering tags in social systems. Then they compared their method to the benchmark algorithm K-Means clustering and Particle Swarm optimization (PSO) based Clustering technique. The experimental analysis of this work illustrates the effectiveness of the proposed approach. (Azar, & Hassanien, 2015)

They proposed a TRS-PSO clustering algorithm for social systems and their techniques are implemented and tested against a various social tagging dataset. The performance of their techniques is compared based on 'goodness of clustering' evaluation measures.

The work (Azar, & Hassanien, 2015) consists of Data Extraction: Fetching data from social systems and the Data set are converted into matrix representation. "Delicious" (del.icio.us) is a famous social bookmarking web service for storing, sharing, and determining web bookmarks.

- **Data Formatting:** Data formatting consists of mapping the tags and bookmarks based on tag weights represented in matrix format.
- **Bookmark Selection:** BMS is the progression of selecting more useful tagged bookmarks from a set of bookmarks associated with tags.
- **Tag Clustering:** To cluster relevant tags based on tag weights associated with selected bookmarks.

"Data clustering is a key field of research in the pattern recognition arena. Although clustering is an unsupervised learning technique, numerous efforts have been made in both hard and soft clustering. In hard clustering, K-means is the most popular method and is being used in diversified application areas" (Kanungo, D. P, 2016). D.P. Kanungo and Al (Kanungo, D. P, 2016) have proposed an approach with a recently developed population based metaheuristic called Elitist based teaching learning based optimization (ETLBO) for data clustering. This ETLBO has been hybridized with K-means algorithm (ETLBO-K-means) to get the optimal cluster centers and effective fitness values. They say that performance of their method has been compared with other techniques by considering standard benchmark real life datasets as well as some synthetic datasets. The simulation and comparison results demonstrate the effectiveness and efficiency of their method. (Kanungo, D. P, 2016)

"Frequent sub graph mining (FSM) is an important task for exploratory data analysis on graph data. Over the years, many algorithms have been proposed to solve this task" (Bhuiyan, & Al Hasan, 2015). Their algorithms assume that the data structure of the mining task is small enough to fit in the main memory of a computer. However, as the real-world graph data grows, both in size and quantity, such an assumption does not hold any longer. Some graph database-centric methods have been proposed in recent years for solving FSM; however, a distributed solution using MapReduce paradigm has not been explored extensively. Since MapReduce is becoming the de-facto paradigm for computation on massive data, an efficient FSM algorithm on this paradigm is of huge demand. In this work, they propose a frequent sub graph mining algorithm called FSM-H which uses an iterative MapReduce based framework. FSM-H is complete as it returns all the frequent sub graphs for a given user-defined support, and it is efficient as it applies all the optimizations that the latest FSM algorithms adopt. Their experiments with real life and large synthetic datasets validate the effectiveness of FSM-H for mining frequent sub graphs from large graph datasets. (Bhuiyan, & Al Hasan, 2015)

Bhuiyan, M. A., & Al Hasan, M propose, a distributed frequent sub graph mining method over MapReduce. This distributed method generates a complete set of frequent sub graphs for a given minimum support threshold. To ensure completeness, it constructs and retains all patterns that have a non-zero support in the map phase of the mining, and then in the reduce phase, it decides whether a pattern is frequent by aggregating its support from different computing nodes (Bhuiyan, & Al Hasan, 2015).

PROCESS MINING

Recently, process mining has become a vivid research area [(Van der Aalst, W, and al., 2004), (V der Aalst, W., Weijters, T., & Maruster, L, 2004)]. The basic idea of process mining is to diagnose business processes by mining event logs for knowledge. Process mining techniques and tools provide the means for discovering process, control, data, organizational, and social structures from event logs. [(Van der Aalst, W, 2004), (Van der Aalst, W, and al., 2004), (V der Aalst, W., Weijters, T., & Maruster, L, 2004), (Van der Aalst, W. M, 2015)]

It provides an important bridge between data mining and business process analysis [(Weske, M, 2012), (Gao, X, 2013), (De Weerdt, J and al, 2013)], and even allow for extracting information from event logs.

The idea is that process mining is:

- **Process Discovery:** What processes are executed in our company, supported by enterprise information systems (ERP, BPM, total ad-hoc, e-mail).
- **Conformance Checking:** Business processes are executed according to the rules defined, or human variants exist.
- **Performance Analysis:** Where are the bottlenecks?
- **Process Prediction:** When will the process end?
- **Process Improvement:** How to redesign a process?

For example, the audit trails of a workflow management system or the transaction logs of an enterprise resource planning system can be used to discover models describing processes, organizations, and products. Moreover, it is possible to use process mining to monitor deviations (e.g., comparing the observed events with predefined models or business rules in the context of SOX)." [(Gao, X, 2013), (De Weerdt, J and al, 2013)]

In addition, Process mining is interesting (Gao, X, 2013):

In enterprise architecture, when analysts and people who work in your company lost time going fishing for processes that exist, in order to establish process and system architecture. Process Mining plays an indispensable role in the discovery of true enterprise architecture.

- **Process Conformity:** How many times people discovered that the processes are not performed according to the rules (our human nature love finding new ways to execute). This does not mean that the process should be executed according to the rules, because sometimes the rules were not correctly set up.
- **Process Optimization:** People that has the experience to perform process analysis by looking at process flows usually indicate easily where are the bottleneck, duplication, repetition, but nowadays (!) in the world of knowledge management where flows do not dictate the manner of execu-

tion is necessary to sit side by side with the people who perform work to understand what are the obstacles (in a large company this is a daunting task). But it is also true that normally escapes analysis teams some of the problem sources, or because there are based opinions, or simply … bad reasoning. [(V.D.Aalst, W, 2004), (Deng, & Lv, 2015)]

Business Intelligence helps to understand how we do things, but does have predictive capabilities needed to understand how work could be performed.

BUSINESS PROCESS

Business process is a set of activities occurring within a company that lead to a specific end [20]. Most often, it focuses on meeting the needs of the customer and delivering a good or service that will fulfill that need. This process is actually often a collection of interrelated processes that function in a logical sequence to achieve the ultimate goal. [(Versteeg, G., & Bouwman, H, 2006), (V.D.Aalst, W, 2004), (Van Der Aalst, W, 2013), (Tsourakakis, C. E. 2010)].

The log files correspond to the actions or traces of the business process. The following example, which is very simple, represents a sequence of characters:

1x Case1 A B C D E G

1x Case2 A C B D G

1x Case3 A E D

Simple Log File

A= Send e-mail, B= check credit, C= calculate capacity, D= check system, E= accept, F= reject, G=send e-mail.

There are many techniques to discover micro patterns from event log or process traces [(Shang, W and al, 2009), (Stewart, R.J and al., 2011)], the next section describes how we mine small patterns from business process.

In our work we use the user applications as business process, the SKYPE and VIBER; the traces are the actions of users, like call, answer, message.

We give a character for each trace, like A=Call, B=answer,….

For the SKTPE we have 11 traces, and for VIBER we have 8 actions.

IMPLEMENTATION AND RESULTS

Implementation and Experimental Setup

We implemented our approach in the java programing language. The first phase, which consists of mining micro patterns, is performed by an existing symbolic specification-mining algorithm [(Gabel, M & Su, Z, 2008, May), (Gao, X, 2013), (Braun, P and al., 2014), (White, B and al., 2010)]. This algorithm leverages Binary Decision Diagrams [(Bryant, R. E, 1986), (Itkar, & Kulkarni, 2013)] to maintain a compact state throughout its execution, despite simultaneously tracking up to billions of potential micro patterns. This algorithm is currently the most scalable pattern-based approach, and it is the only algorithm capable of scalably mining micro patterns with alphabets of size three.

Our small patterns were represented by using regular expression or their finite state automaton, to compose these small patterns; our patterns are the regular expressions (ab)* and (ab*c)* we use the standard algorithm for finite state automaton, using the following rules:

- **Definition (Projection):** The projection π of a string s over an alphabet $\sum$, $\pi_{\sum}$ (s), is defined as s with all letters not in $\sum$ deleted.
- The projection of a language L over $\sum$ is defined as $\pi_{\sum}$ $(L) = \{\pi_{\sum}$ (s) | s $\in L\}$.
- **Definition (Specification Pattern):** A specification pattern is a finite state automaton A= $(Q, \sum, \delta, q_0, F)$, where Q is a finite set of states, $\sum$ is a set of input symbols, $\delta: Q$ x $\sum \rightarrow Q$ is the transition function, q_0 is the single starting state, and F is a set of final states. A pattern is satisfied over a trace T with alphabet $\sum' \supseteq \sum$ if $\pi_{\sum}$ $(T) \in L$ (A).
- **Definition (Expansion) [Gabel and Su, [(Gabel, M & Su, Z, 2008, May)] §2.6]:** Assume a regular language defined by finite state automaton A= $(Q, \sum, \delta, q_0, F)$. The expansion of $(L$ (A)) over an arbitrary alphabet $\sum'$, written $E_{\sum'}$ $(L$ (A)), is the maximal language over $\sum \cup \sum'$ whose projection over $\sum$ is L (A).
- An automaton accepting $E_{\sum'}$ $(L$ (A)) can be constructed by first duplicating A and then adding a looping transition δ (q, a) = q to each state q for each letter a $\in \sum' \backslash \sum$.
- Expansion can be thought of maximal inverse of projection. For example, an expression corresponding to $E_{\{a, b, c\}}$ ((a b)*) is c*(a c*b c*)*.
- Note that projecting this new language over {a, b} yields the original language, (a b)*. The composition of two patterns is defined as follows:
- **Definition (Composition):** The composition of two patterns A_1 and A_2 is the intersection of the expansion of each pattern over their combined alphabets, $E_{\sum_1}$ $(A_1) \cap E_{\sum_2}$ (A_2)
- Intuitively, the composition of two patterns defines a language of traces in which both patterns hold.

We could use this general definition to arbitrary compose patterns by using standard algorithms for finite state automaton manipulation. However, in general, performing these pairwise compositions directly is undesirable. Given a reasonably large set of patterns, the finite state expansion, intersection, and minimization operations become more expensive as the automata grow.

There is some difficulty of treatment with the use of those rules, however, we use some other rules used by Gabel and Su (Gabel, M., & Su, Z, 2008) in their framework Javert.

They recognize special cases of composition in which the result of composition is compact and intuitive. Then they formulate these cases as inference rules, which lead to straightforward implementation in which composition is a constant time operation. [(Dean, J., & Ghemawat, S., 2008), (Itkar, & Kulkarni, 2013), (Aridhi, S and al., 2014)]

They suggest two rules: the branching rule and the sequencing rule:

Branching Rule describes the composition of two patterns with identical "endpoint", i.e., the first and the last letters of a single iteration of the pattern. Defining $\sum'$ as $\{a, b\} \cup \sum_{L1} \cup \sum_{L2}$, the correctness of the branching rule follows [Gabel and Su(Gabel, M., & Su, Z, 2008) §3. (Gabel, M & Su, Z, 2008, May)]:

$$E_{\sum'}(aL_1*b)* \cap E_{\sum'}(aL_2*b)* = (a(L_1|L_2)*b)*$$

This rule performs the composition, of two patterns that describe legal operations at the same logical state. For example, from the patterns: [Call answer* Close]*, and [Call not answer* Close]*

We can infer a third pattern [Call (answer | not answer)* Close]*

Sequencing Rule describes the sequencing of two patterns with compatible endpoints.as with the previous rule, L_1 and L_2 must have disjoint alphabets, which must in turn be disjoint from $\{a, b, c\}$. Redefining $\sum'$ as $\{a, b, c\} \cup \sum_{L1} \cup \sum_{L2}$, the correctness of the sequencing rule follows from the following fact [Gabel and Su(Gabel, M., & Su, Z, 2008) §3.6]:

$$E_{\sum'}(a\,L_1\,b)* \cap E_{\sum'}(b\,L_2\,c)* \cap E_{\sum'}(a\,c)* = (a\,L_1\,b\,L_2\,c)*$$

Continuing the earlier example, from the patterns:

[Call (answer | not answer)* Close]*, [Connect Call]*, and [Connect close]*

We can infer a fourth pattern

[Connect Call (answer | not answer)* Close]*

Both of these rules are general; they apply to both micro patterns and any intermediate assembly thereof. [(Tsourakakis, C. E. 2010), (Seki, Jinno, & Uehara, 2013), (Koundinya, A. K. and al., 2012), (Fournier-Viger, P, 2014),]

For the second party, we computed and composed the small patterns.

As an input we have log file of two applications, in this log file we have all applications traces, from those traces we mine small patterns, after we compose them in order to get the final pattern that represents the whole model of the process, this model generates a lot of cases, Unfortunately there are two cases can't be generated by our approach.

The next section presents our result in all steps.

RESULTS

The Table 1 presents the result of our approach; we used a log file of size 10 GB of two Applications Skype and Viber. The number of traces is the actions effected by users, and total trace events are the number of all actions contained in the log file, we know that we have two steps; the pattern mining and the composition of patterns whom are executed in limited times.

The Table 2 presents the result of our approach; we used a log file of size 15 GB of two Applications Skype and Viber. The number of traces is the actions effected by users, and total trace events are the number of all actions contained in the log file, we know that we have two steps; the pattern mining and the composition of patterns whom are executed in limited times.

The Table 3 presents the result of our approach; we used a log file of size 18 GB of two Applications Skype and Viber. The number of traces is the actions effected, and total trace events are the number of all actions contained in the log file, we know that we have two steps; the pattern mining and the composition of patterns whom are executed in limited times.

The Table 4 presents the result of our approach; we used a log file of size 20 GB of two Applications Skype and Viber. The number of traces is the actions effected, and total trace events are the number of all actions contained in the log file, we know that we have two steps; the pattern mining and the composition of patterns whom are executed in limited times.

Table 1. Trace data and analysis time of log file of size 10 GB

Execution Time				
Application	**Num. of Traces Total**	**Trace Events**	**Pattern Mining**	**Composition**
Skype	11	825,458,970	5432,8s	462,0s
Viber	8	332,697,321	3951,0s	589,4s

Table 2. Trace data and analysis time of log file of size 15 GB

Execution Time				
Application	**Num. of Traces Total**	**Trace Events**	**Pattern Mining**	**Composition**
Skype	11	825,458,970	6821,0s	629,8s
Viber	8	332,697,321	5002,3s	770,2s

Table 3. Trace data and analysis times of log file of size 18 GB

Execution Time				
Application	**Num. of Traces Total**	**Trace Events**	**Pattern Mining**	**Composition**
Skype	11	935,478,970	7432,8s	962,0s
Viber	8	424,707,321	5951,0s	809,4s

Table 4. Trace data and analysis times of log file of size 20 GB

	Execution Time			
Application	Num. of Traces Total	Trace Events	Pattern Mining	Composition
Skype	11	935,478,970	7980,1s	1099,7s
Viber	8	424,707,321	6214,3s	900,1s

CONCLUSION AND FUTURE WORK

A scalable patterns mining solution should be efficient, scalable. In this paper, we propose to use a general framework to mining micro patterns from process traces. To validate our approach, we presented our experience of mining small patterns and compose them. Our experiments demonstrate that our solution minimizes the execution time, and we conclude that the compute have an inverse relationship with the execution time, with the grow of the machines, the time execution decreases. In addition to the existence of a proportional relationship between the grow of computers and the efficiency of treatment.

There are a number of directions for future work, including and evaluating our method in a big number of computers in cloud, also for big log file size of different applications.

We would like to thank the anonymous reviewers for their insightful comments and helpful suggestions.

REFERENCES

Ammons, G., Bodík, R., & Larus, J. R. (2002). Mining specifications. *ACM SIGPLAN Notices*, *37*(1), 4–16. doi:10.1145/565816.503275

Aridhi, S., D'Orazio, L., Maddouri, M., & Mephu, E. (2014, June). A novel MapReduce-based approach for distributed frequent subgraph mining. In *Reconnaissance de Formes et Intelligence Artificielle*. RFIA.

Azar, A. T., & Hassanien, A. E. (2015). Hybrid TRS-PSO clustering approach for Web2. 0 social tagging system. *International Journal of Rough Sets and Data Analysis*, *2*(1), 22–37. doi:10.4018/ijrsda.2015010102

Bhuiyan, M. A., & Al Hasan, M. (2015). An iterative MapReduce based frequent subgraph mining algorithm. *Knowledge and Data Engineering*. *IEEE Transactions on*, *27*(3), 608–620.

Braun, P., Cameron, J. J., Cuzzocrea, A., Jiang, F., & Leung, C. K. (2014). Effectively and efficiently mining frequent patterns from dense graph streams on disk. *Procedia Computer Science*, *35*, 338–347. doi:10.1016/j.procs.2014.08.114

Bryant, R. E. (1986). Graph-based algorithms for Boolean function manipulation. *Computers. IEEE Transactions on*, *100*(8), 677–691.

De Weerdt, J., Schupp, A., Vanderloock, A., & Baesens, B. (2013). Process Mining for the multi-faceted analysis of business processes—A case study in a financial services organization. *Computers in Industry*, *64*(1), 57–67. doi:10.1016/j.compind.2012.09.010

Dean, J., & Ghemawat, S. (2008). MapReduce: Simplified data processing on large clusters. *Communications of the ACM, 51*(1), 107–113. doi:10.1145/1327452.1327492

Deng, Z. H., & Lv, S. L. (2015). PrePost+: An efficient N-lists-based algorithm for mining frequent itemsets via Children–Parent Equivalence pruning. *Expert Systems with Applications, 42*(13), 5424–5432. doi:10.1016/j.eswa.2015.03.004

Fournier-Viger, P., Gomariz, A., Šebek, M., & Hlosta, M. (2014). VGEN: fast vertical mining of sequential generator patterns. In Data Warehousing and Knowledge Discovery (pp. 476-488). Springer International Publishing. doi:10.1007/978-3-319-10160-6_42

Gabel, M., & Su, Z. (2008, November). Javert: fully automatic mining of general temporal properties from dynamic traces. In *Proceedings of the 16th ACM SIGSOFT International Symposium on Foundations of software engineering* (pp. 339-349). ACM. doi:10.1145/1453101.1453150

Gabel, M., & Su, Z. (2008, May). Symbolic mining of temporal specifications. In *Proceedings of the 30th international conference on Software engineering* (pp. 51-60). ACM.

Gao, X. (2013). Towards the next generation intelligent BPM–in the era of big data. In *Business Process Management* (pp. 4–9). Springer Berlin Heidelberg. doi:10.1007/978-3-642-40176-3_2

Greco, G., Guzzo, A., Pontieri, L., & Sacca, D. (2006). Discovering expressive process models by clustering log traces. *Knowledge and Data Engineering. IEEE Transactions on, 18*(8), 1010–1027.

Guyet, T., & Quiniou, R. (2011, July). Extracting temporal patterns from interval-based sequences. In *IJCAI Proceedings-International Joint Conference on Artificial Intelligence* (Vol. 22, No. 1, p. 1306). Academic Press.

Itkar, S. A., & Kulkarni, U. V. (2013). Distributed Algorithm for Frequent Pattern Mining using Hadoop-Map Reduce Framework. *Proc. of Int. Conf. on Advances in Computer Science, AETACS.*

Kanungo, D. P., Nayak, J., Naik, B., & Behera, H. S. (2016). Hybrid Clustering using Elitist Teaching Learning-Based Optimization: An Improved Hybrid Approach of TLBO. *International Journal of Rough Sets and Data Analysis, 3*(1), 1–19. doi:10.4018/IJRSDA.2016010101

Koundinya, A. K., Sharma, K. A. K., Kumar, K., & Shanbag, K. U. (2012). *Map/Reduce Deisgn and Implementation of Apriori Alogirthm for handling voluminous data-sets.* arXiv preprint arXiv:1212.4692

Motahari-Nezhad, H. R., Saint-Paul, R., Benatallah, B., & Casati, F. (2008). Deriving protocol models from imperfect service conversation logs. *Knowledge and Data Engineering. IEEE Transactions on, 20*(12), 1683–1698.

Ranjan, J., & Bhatnagar, V. (2010). Application of data mining techniques in the financial sector for profitable customer relationship management. *International Journal of Information and Communication Technology, 2*(4), 342–354. doi:10.1504/IJICT.2010.034976

Ranjan, J., & Bhatnagar, V. (2011). Role of knowledge management and analytical CRM in business: Data mining based framework. *The Learning Organization, 18*(2), 131–148. doi:10.1108/09696471111103731

Seki, K., Jinno, R., & Uehara, K. (2013). Parallel distributed trajectory pattern mining using hierarchical grid with MapReduce. *International Journal of Grid and High Performance Computing, 5*(4), 79–96. doi:10.4018/ijghpc.2013100106

Shang, W., Jiang, Z. M., Adams, B., & Hassan, A. E. (2009). *Mapreduce as a general framework to support research in mining software repositories.* MSR.

Stewart, R. J., Trinder, P. W., & Loidl, H. W. (2011). Comparing high level mapreduce query languages. In *Advanced Parallel Processing Technologies* (pp. 58–72). Springer Berlin Heidelberg. doi:10.1007/978-3-642-24151-2_5

Tsourakakis, C. E. (2010). *Data Mining with MAPREDUCE: Graph and Tensor Algorithms with Applications* (Doctoral dissertation). Carnegie Mellon University.

van der Aalst, W. (2004). Discovering coordination patterns using process mining. *Workshop on Petri Nets and Coordination*, 49-64.

Van Der Aalst, W. (2013). Service mining: Using process mining to discover, check, and improve service behavior. *Services Computing. IEEE Transactions on, 6*(4), 525–535.

Van der Aalst, W., Weijters, T., & Maruster, L. (2004). Workflow mining: Discovering process models from event logs. *Knowledge and Data Engineering. IEEE Transactions on, 16*(9), 1128–1142.

van der Aalst, W. M. (2015). Extracting event data from databases to unleash process mining. In *BPM-Driving innovation in a digital world* (pp. 105–128). Springer International Publishing. doi:10.1007/978-3-319-14430-6_8

Van der Aalst, W. M., & Weijters, A. J. M. M. (2004). Process mining: A research agenda. *Computers in Industry, 53*(3), 231–244. doi:10.1016/j.compind.2003.10.001

Versteeg, G., & Bouwman, H. (2006). Business architecture: A new paradigm to relate business strategy to ICT. *Information Systems Frontiers, 8*(2), 91–102. doi:10.1007/s10796-006-7973-z

Weske, M. (2012). *Business process management: concepts, languages, architectures.* Springer Science & Business Media. doi:10.1007/978-3-642-28616-2

White, B., Yeh, T., Lin, J., & Davis, L. (2010, July). Web-scale computer vision using mapreduce for multimedia data mining. In *Proceedings of the Tenth International Workshop on Multimedia Data Mining* (p. 9). ACM. doi:10.1145/1814245.1814254

Chapter 6
New FastPFOR for Inverted File Compression

V. Glory
Periyar University, India

S. Domnic
National Institute of Technology Tiruchirappalli, India

ABSTRACT

Inverted index is used in most Information Retrieval Systems (IRS) to achieve the fast query response time. In inverted index, compression schemes are used to improve the efficiency of IRS. In this chapter, the authors study and analyze various compression techniques that are used for indexing. They also present a new compression technique that is based on FastPFOR called New FastPFOR. The storage structure and the integers' representation of the proposed method can improve its performances both in compression and decompression. The study on existing works shows that the recent research works provide good results either in compression or in decoding, but not in both. Hence, their decompression performance is not fair. To achieve better performance in decompression, the authors propose New FastPFOR in this chapter. To evaluate the performance of the proposed method, they experiment with TREC collections. The results show that the proposed method could achieve better decompression performance than the existing techniques.

INTRODUCTION

Information Retrieval System (IRS) is receiving substantial attention due to the exponential increase of the quantity of information available in recent years. Digital Library, Search engines, E-commerce and Electronic news are the some of the applications of the information retrieval system (Kobayashi & Takeda, 2000; Williams & Zobel, 2002). The main objective of IRS is to provide the maximum efficiency (speed) and effectiveness (relevance) with proper balance between them. Particularly, IR effectiveness deals with retrieving the most relevant information to a user's need, while IR efficiency deals with providing fast and ordered access to huge amounts of information. Indexing is one of the efficient ways to improve the fast retrieval in IRS. Compared to the Signature file (Faloutsos,1985), Bitmaps (Chan &

DOI: 10.4018/978-1-5225-3004-6.ch006

Ioannidis, 1998) and Pat Tree (Morrison, 1968), the inverted index is the most suitable indexing structure to locate the data quickly, offers quick response time and supports the various searching techniques (Zobel & Moffat, 2006).

An inverted index contains two parts: lexicon file (dictionary) which stores a distinct list of terms found in the collection and document frequency (total number of documents in which term appears). For each term, an inverted list (posting list) is maintained and it contains a sequence of document identifiers (id), term frequency (tf) (number times the particular term appears) and positions. In each inverted list, the increasing order of document identifiers is replaced by D-Gap (difference between the document identifiers except the first one to enable efficient compression). The compression of inverted index is essential because it is potentially taking the less storage space and gives faster query performance to improve the efficiency of IRS. Compression techniques are classified into two categories such as integer compression and integer list compression techniques. Each integer is processed individually in integer compression whereas the group of integers are processed in integer list compression. Unary code (UC) (Salomon, 2004), Golomb code (GC) (Golomb, 1966), Rice code (RC) (Rice, 1979), Elias Gamma code (EC) (Elias, 1975), Elias Delta code (DC) (Elias, 1975), Variable Byte code (VBC) (Salomon, 2007), Fast Extended Golomb code (FEGC) (Domnic & Glory, 2012) and Re-ordered Fast Extended Golomb code (RFEGC) (Glory & Domnic, 2013) are the some of the integer compression techniques. VBC is faster than GC, RC, EC and DC. Compared to VBC, RFEGC gives better compression and decompression when the occurrence of middle and large range of integers are more in the data (Glory & Domnic, 2013). Some of the integer list compression techniques are Interpolative Code (Moffat & Stuiver, 2000), Simple Family (Anh & Moffat, 2005), Frame-Of-Reference (FOR) (Goldstein, Ramakrishnan & Shaft, 1998; Ng, & Ravishankar, 1997) and Patched coding techniques (PFORDelta, NewPFD, OptPFD and FastPFOR) (Zukowski et al., 2006; Yan, Ding & Suel, 2009; Lemire & Boytsov, 2015). Interpolative code is slower than GC (Anh & Moffat, 2005; Yan et al., 2009). Simple Family coding is generally slower and it is slightly better in compression. FOR and Patched coding techniques are the faster decoding coder in the recent years (Zukowski et al., 2006; Yan et al., 2009; Lemire & Boytsov, 2015). Depending on the range of integers, sometimes FOR gives the poor compression. FastPFOR is one of the recent patched coding techniques, which gives the better compression rate and fast decoding performance compared to other patched techniques. But the decompression performance (disk access time + decoding time) of FastPFOR is not fair.

In this paper, we propose a new patched coding technique called New FastPFOR to achieve the better compression and decompression performances. New FastPFOR is based on FastPFOR technique, but it uses new cost formula to determine optimal b value. In the proposed scheme, the positional values of the exceptions, the number of exceptions and maximum bit width are together represented by unary code, which leads the better result than FastPFOR. In our work, we have used TREC dataset to evaluate the performance of proposed method and other existing methods.

The rest of the paper is organized as the review of some of the compression techniques, the proposed method, the experimental results and conclusions are derived.

COMPRESSION TECHNIQUES

Some of the compression techniques which have been used for inverted list compression are discussed in this section

Integer Encoders

Unary Code

An integer n is represented in Unary code (Salomon, 2004) as n-1 one bits followed by single zero bit or n-1 zero bits followed by single one bit. In this code, the small range integers get shorter code length than large range of integers.

Golomb Rice Code

Golomb (GC) (Golomb, 1966) / Rice code (RC) (Rice, 1979) is a parameterized code. It encodes an integer into two parts which are the quotient part and the remainder part. Depending on the divisor, the GC and the RC can be categorized. Here, the integer n is divided by the divisor d. Then, the quotient q is coded by unary code and the remainder r is coded by binary code in $\log_2 d$ bits. Depending on the distribution of the integers, the parameter d is chosen in Golomb code (Golomb, 1966) Making more efficient in implementation with use of bitwise operators, the parameter is chosen as the power of two, called as Rice code (Rice, 1979).

Elias Gamma Code

Elias Gamma code (EC) (Elias, 1975) represents an integer n as the unary representation for the length of the binary representation (B(n)) of the integer n i.e unary (|B(n)|) and the binary representation of the integer n without its most significant bit i.e ~B(n). EC does not suite when the large range of integers occur in the data to be compressed. Elias delta code (DC) (Elias, 1975) was proposed to overcome the drawback of EC. The integer n is represented by DC as two parts: in the first part, the length of the binary representation of the integer (|B(n)|) using the Elias gamma code and the second part is ~B(n). Both the codes are slower than variable byte code (Lemire & Boytsov, 2015), hence, these coders have not considered in our experiment.

Fast Extended Golomb Code and Re-Ordered Fast Extended Golomb Code (RFEGC)

Fast Extended Golomb Code (FEGC) (Domnic & Glory, 2012) is the extension of Extended Golomb Code (EGC) (Somasundaram & Domnic, 2007). In FEGC, the integer n is divided repeatedly M times by the divisor d until the quotient (q) becomes zero and the divisor is restricted to powers of two. In each division the remainders r_i (i=1 to M) are saved. M is coded by unary code and remainders are coded by binary code.

In RFEGC (Glory & Domnic, 2013), the ideas of RC and FEGC are used to encode the non-negative integer n. The given integer n is divided by a divisor d (2^k), a power of 2, recursively L times until the condition either $q_1 + 1 \leq (L-1)k + L$ or $q_L = 0$ is satisfied, where $q_1 = n / 2^k$. Then, each remainder is coded as two parts which are the flag bit and the data bits. The flag bit is used to identify whether the next remainder is still in the part of current integer or not and the data bits are binary representation of the remainder.

Variable Byte Code

The integer n is represented as the sequence of bytes in Variable Byte code (VBC) (Salomon, 2007). In each byte, the highest bit is used to indicate whether the next byte is still part of the current integer or not and the lower-order seven bits are used to store the data part. VBC requires a single branching condition for each byte which is more cost-effective in term of CPU cycles, so VBC is better in decoding speed compared to other bitwise coders.

Integer List Encoders

Simple Family

The Simple family coders: Simple-9 and Simple-16 use only the single 32-bit to code the groups of integers. In simple-9, nine possible ways are used to encode a list of positive integers, but it wastes some of the bits of the 32 bit when encoding some combinations of integers. Simple-16 technique was proposed by Anh and Moffat (Anh & Moffat, 2005) to overcome the drawback of Simple- 9 technique. It uses sixteen possible ways to encode the list of integers. In Simple- 9 & 16, each 32 bit is partitioned into 28-bits used for *data bits* and 4-bits used for describing the organization of the data bits. These codes may sometimes lead to slightly better compression, but generally slow (Lemire & Boytsov, 2015).

Frame of Reference

Frame of Reference (FOR) (Goldstein et al., 1998 ; Ng & Ravishankar, 1997) uses fixed size blocks of integers for compression. For each block, a bit width (b) is calculated with the use of finding the maximum M and the minimum m value in the block to represent all the integers of the block. The formula used to calculate the bit width (b) is $\left\lceil \log_2 \left(M + 1 - m \right) \right\rceil$ and then all the values are encoded by b bits each in that block.

PFOR

PFOR (Zukowski et al., 2006) approach is a Patched Frame-Of-Reference and sometimes it is called as PForDelta when used in conjunction with delta coding. It uses a small bit width (b) which is reasonably selected from a block such that most of the values in the block are represented by b bits and the values larger than 2^b are treated as exceptions, which are stored in a separate location. PFOR could achieve better compression than FOR, in which the presence of single large value increases the bit width (b) and it affects the compression performance of FOR.

In PFOR, the given set of integers are divided into different pages, each contains 2^{16} integers. For every page, the small bit width b is calculated, but the data is encoded in blocks of 128 integers with two storage arrays. In the first storage array, the normal values (smaller than 2^b) and the offsets to the locations of the exceptions ($\geq 2^b$) are stored in b bits each. This array is maintained for every block of 128 integers in a page. The second array is used to store the exceptions (c) in 32 bits each. This array is maintained for every page. These two storage arrays are preceded by a 32-bit word containing two pointers. The first pointer is pointing to the location of the first exception in the block of 128 integers and the second pointer points to the location of the first exception value in the storage array of the exceptions. Each exception value and the offset value are stored in 32 bits and b bits respectively. The disadvantage of PFOR is that compulsive exceptions may occur in the first array when the bit width b is too small to represent an offset value. The storage structure used in PFD is given in Table 1.

NewPFD and OptPFD

NewPFD and OptPFD schemes are proposed by Yan et.al for getting better compression than PFOR with an improvement in handling the exceptions. NewPFD divides the data into blocks of fixed length 128 integers and for each block, the small bit width b is calculated. Like PFOR, NewPFD uses two storage arrays, but these two arrays are maintained for every block of 128 integers. The first one is for storing the normal values ($<2^b$) and lower b bits of the exceptions ($\geq 2^b$); the second one is for storing the locations of the exceptions and the (32-b) higher bits of the exceptions and it is compressed by simple family techniques. These two arrays are preceded by a 32 bit word used to store the b, the number of exceptions, and the number of 32 bit words used to store the compressed exceptions values. NewPFD does not allow more than 10% of integers as exceptions during the selections of bit width (b).

The another technique, OptPFD, is similar to NewPFD except that OptPFD uses optimal cost formula to compute small bit width b in order to optimize the compression ratio and the decompression speed. The storage structure used by OptPFD and NewPFD for implementation is given in Table 2.

FastPFOR

FastPFOR technique is similar in design to OptPFD and NewPFD to offer better decoding speed and compression rate; which is proposed by D.Lemire et al., 2015. In this technique, the small bit width b is calculated for every block of 128 integers and the (max$b$ - b) higher bits of the exceptions are stored in one of 32 arrays for every page of 2^{16} integers, where max b is the number of bits required to represent the largest integer of the block. In order to locate the storage array (1 to 32) of the exceptions, the difference of the maximal bit width (max$b$) and b is used. Since the decoding of integers is done in bulk, FastPFOR achieves better decoding speed.

Table 1. PFOR storage structure

Header Section	Normal Data Section (Storage Array-1)	Exception Data Section (Storage Array-2)
32 – bits	BlockSize * b – bits	c * 32 – bits

Table 2. NewPFD/ OptPFD storage structure

Header Section	Normal Data Section (Storage Array-1)	Exception Data Section (Storage Array-2)
32 bits	128×b bits	Simple Family Techniques- {Exception Value, Location}

The selection of *b* and the method used to store and compress the exceptions will determine the performance of FastPFOR. The compression and decompression performances of FastPFOR depend on the number of exceptions identified from each block of 128 integers. FastPFOR uses the cost optimization formula: $8 + (b \times 128) + C \times (8 + \max b - b)$ in which the values of *b* and *C* (number of exceptions are varied to determine *b* for identifying the exceptions), So that it could achieve better search performance (disk access cost + decoding cost) than NewPFD and OptPFD.

FastPFOR compression technique has the following header section for each block of a page and it contains the sequence of bytes to store the following information:

- The bit width (*b*) – One byte
- Maximal bit width (max*b*) – One byte
- The Number of Exceptions (C) – One byte
- Location of the exceptions – C bytes.

The storage structure used by FastPFOR is given in Table 3.

PROPOSED WORK: NEW FASTPFOR

In FastPFOR, the storage requirements for the exceptions and the positional values of the exceptions depend on the number of exceptions. Hence, when the number of exceptions is more, the storage costs as well as the disk access costs will be increased, so that disk access speed will be reduced. FastPFOR could achieve fast decoding speed, but it may fail to achieve fast disk access due to the storage requirements for the exceptions and the positional values of the exceptions, because the increase of the storage cost will slow the disk access speed. So that decompression speed (decoding speed + disk access speed) of FastPFOR may not be better. In order to improve the performance of FastPFOR, a new scheme, called New FastPFOR, is proposed and presented in this section. The proposed scheme uses variable bit-length code to identify the locations of the exceptions and to store the exceptions in the storage arrays where as FastPFOR uses fixed bit-length code to store the exceptions in the storage arrays and to keep the locations of the exceptions. Hence, the proposed scheme can achieve storage space reduction than FastPFOR, which leads to fast disk access. The steps used in the proposed scheme to encode and decode the given set of integers are given below.

Table 3. Fast PFOR storage structure (used per page)

Header Section									Normal Data Section (Storage Array)			Exception Data Section (32 Storage Arrays)		
Block 1				...	Block n				Block1	...	Block n			
b8 bits	Maxb 8 bits	C8 bits	(C×8) bits		b 8 bits	Maxb 8 bits	C 8 bits	(C×8) bits	Block Size * *b* bits		Block Size * *b* bits	(Maxb – b) bits	(Maxb – b) bits	

Algorithm for Encoding

The following steps are used to encode the given set of integers.

1. The given set of integers is divided into the pages of 2^{16} integers each.
2. Each page is divided into the blocks of 128 integers each.
3. Optimal b value is computed in each block using the optimal cost formula until get the minimum bit width b is calculated for each block of the page using the equation given in Equation (1).

$$Optimal\ cost = b \times Blocksize + \left(2 \times \sum_{i=1}^{NE}\left(\left|B(e_i)\right| - b\right)\right) + Blocksize \tag{1}$$

where NE is the number of exceptions and e_i is the ith exception value.

4. The normal values which are smaller than 2^b and lower b bits of the exception values ($e_i > 2^b$) are stored using b bits each in a separate storage array (Normal data section).
5. The $\left(d = \left|B(e_i)\right| - b\right)$ higher order bits of the exception values are stored in one of 32 storage arrays (Exception data section). There are 32 arrays maintained for every page of 2^{16} integers. The d value determines the storage array of a exception value i.e the exception value with d.

Algorithm for Decoding

The following steps are used to decode the compressed data.

1. For each page, all the exception arrays (1 to 32) are read from the exception data section.
2. Then, for each block in a page, read b from header section and read the flag bit which is used to identify the existence of the exceptions in that block . If the flag bit is 1, then exceptions are there, so read the bits (C_i) and decode using unary code. If the decoded value (d) is greater than one, it is used to locate the position of the exception and read the $d\text{-}1$ higher bits of the exception from the $(d\text{-}1)^{th}$ storage array of exception data section.
3. Decode each normal value of the block using b bits; each exception value using higher d bits and lower b bits. Then, put the exception value in its right location by making use of flag bit i.e when flag bit =1, the corresponding C_i location is the location of that exception value.

Repeat 1 to 3 until all the pages are decoded.

Illustration

The selection of minimal bit width *b* is best illustrated with an example.
Let a set of integers be:

< 3, 1, 2, 40, 2, 3, 1, 1, 3, 3, 3, 50, 2, 2, 60, 2>

The selection of bit width *b* will be done by applying 3rd step of the encoding algorithm as follows:
The optimal cost formula is given in Equation (1). For the given set of integers, the value of Block size in Equation (1) is taken as 16, because, the number of integers in the example data is 16. Initially, b value of the formula is assigned to 6 (the number of bits required to represent the largest value (60) of the set).
For the given example, initially *b* = 6; For *b*=6, the number of exceptions = 0, So the last two terms of the Equation (1) can be avoided according to the encoding steps.
Initially the best_cost = 16×*b* = 16 × 6 = 96; Then *b* is decremented by one in each iteration until *b*=0.

1. *b* is decremented by one, now *b* = 5, the no. of exceptions is 3 for b=5

this_cost = 16×5 + (2×(1+1+1)) + 16= 80+ 6+16 = 102;

Check If (this_cost < best_cost) = > (102 < 96) => false

2. Now *b* = 4, no. of exceptions = 3;

this_cost = 16×4 + (2×(2+2+2) + 16 = 64 + 12 + 16 = 92;

So, 92 < 96 is true then best_cost is 92 and assign *b* = 4 &

No.of exceptions = 3;

3. Now *b* = 3, number of exceptions = 3;

this_cost = 16×3 + (2×(3+3+3)) + 16 = 48 + 18 + 16 = 82;

So, 82 < 92 is true then best_cost is 82 and assign *b* = 3 &

No.of exceptions = 3;

4. Now *b* = 2, the number of exceptions = 3;

this_cost = 16×2 + (2×(4+4+4)) + 16 = 32 + 24 + 16 = 72;

So, 72 < 82 is true then the best_cost is 72 and $b = 2$ &

No.of exceptions = 3;

5.   Now $b = 1$, the number of exceptions = 13;

this_cost=16×1+(2×(1+1+5+1+1+1+1+1+5+1+1+5+1))+16 = 16 + 50 + 16= 82;

So, 82 < 72 is false then the best_cost is 72, b is decremented by one so $b = 0$ then stop the iterations. Finally $b = 2$ is selected according to the cost formula.

The number of exceptions and the locations of the exceptions are found after the selection of (b). The proposed scheme needs 32 (2 * 16) bits for the storage in normal data section, 37 (8 + 1 + 28) bits in header section and 12 bits for exceptions according to the storage structure given Table 4. So New FastPFOR totally uses 81 bits to compress the data.

But FastPFOR requires 92 bits including 48 (8+8+8+3*8) bits for header section, 32 bits for normal data section and 12 bits for exceptions, to compress the same data for the determined b according to the cost formula. Compared to FastPFOR, New FastPFOR needs less number of bits.

EXPERIMENTAL RESULTS

We have used TREC data collections such as: Clueweb 09, Gov2 and Yandex to test the performance of proposed technique and existing compression techniques which are implemented in Java. The Gov2 contains 25 millions of HTML, Text and PDF documents and the Clueweb 09 collection is a collection of about 50 million crawled HTML documents. For all the document collections, the storage requirements (compression) and the query processing time (decompression performance) for each integer encoding method are measured using compression rate and search time respectively. We have used some of the open source codes which are available in (Lemire & Boystov, 2013) and done the experiments using Intel Xeon processor machine equipped with 16 GB of RAM and 64-bit version of windows 7 OS. In our experiments, we have used the document identifiers of the inverted lists which were constructed from the TREC collections (Boystov, 2012; Silvestri & Venturini, 2010) and applied the compression techniques to compress d-gap values of the document identifiers.

Table 4. New Fast PFOR storage structure (used per page)

Header Section								Normal Data Section (Storage Array)			Exception Data Section (32 Storage Arrays)			
Block 1					Block n									
B	Flag Bit	Exception Locations		.	B	Flag Bit	Exception Locations		Block 1	...	Block n	1	2	..	3
8 bits	1/0bit	C_1	.	C_{128}	8 bits	1/0 bit	C_1	C_{128}	128*b bits		128*b bits	.	...	..	...

To calculate compression rate (bits per integer) in our experiment, we use the formula given in Equation (2).

$$Compression(orBit)Rate = \frac{Compressed\ Size\ of\ Inverted\ List\ (docids)}{Total\ number\ of\ Document\ Identifiers\ in\ the\ List} \qquad (2)$$

Table 5 shows the compression performance of New FastPFOR and other encoding methods. New FastPFOR achieves 14.13%, 9.12% and 5.32% reduction in storage space for Gov2, Clueweb and Yandex collections compared to FastPFOR technique. Our method also gives better results in compression compared to other existing methods. The search performance (or query processing time) of the integer encoding algorithms is also measured using the equation given in Equation (3).

$$Search\ Time\ (ST) = Disk\ Access\ time\ (AT) + Decoding\ Time\ (DT) \qquad (3)$$

To measure the search performance, a set of random queries is generated from each document collection. For each query, approx. 100000 docid's are retrieved and decoded. Then, the time taken to retrieve the compressed data from the disk and to decode the compressed data is calculated. The search performance of the various algorithms is given in Table 6. Table 6 shows that New FastPFOR achieved better results than other methods, because it has the lower bit rate. Lower bit rate has the benefits of getting the lesser time for accessing the data from the disk. Based on the minimum bit rate and minimum query processing time, a good compression technique can be characterized. So compared to other techniques, New FastPFOR can be the better compression technique for IR applications.

Table 5. Bit rate (bits per docid) for TREC data collections

Compression Techniques	Gov2	Clueweb09	Yandex
New FastPFOR	**4.002**	**6.244**	**5.169**
FastPFOR	4.661	6.871	5.460
New PFD	4.682	7.055	5.860
Opt PFD	4.509	6.708	5.384
RFEGC	4.957	6.444	5.799
FEGC	4.957	6.444	5.799
Rice	14.07	13.66	13.748
VBC	8.631	9.23	9.23

Table 6. Search performance time (in milliseconds) for TREC data collections

Compression Techniques	Gov2	Clueweb09	Yandex
New Fast PFOR			
Disk Access Time (AT)	8330	4321	4228
Decoding Time (DT)	125	94	62
Search Time (ST)	8455	4415	4290
Fast PFOR			
Disk Access Time (AT)	12527	7425	5647
Decoding Time (DT)	63	31	47
Search Time (ST)	12590	7456	5694
New PFD			
Disk Access Time(AT)	14305	8159	7504
Decoding Time (DT)	63	31	47
Search Time (ST)	14368	8190	7551
Opt PFD			
Disk Access Time(AT)	12730	7612	5944
Decoding Time (DT)	62	62	47
Search Time (ST)	12792	7674	5991
RFEGC			
Disk Access Time(AT)	12074	8253	8767
Decoding Time (DT)	125	93	78
Search Time (ST)	12199	8346	8845
FEGC			
Disk Access Time(AT)	12074	8253	8767
Decoding Time (DT)	202	140	156
Search Time (ST)	12276	8393	8923
Rice			
Disk Access Time(AT)	38501	29921	30560
Decoding Time (DT)	140	125	125
Search Time (ST)	38641	30046	30685
VBC			
Disk Access Time(AT)	23681	21653	22511
Decoding Time (DT)	78	78	78
Search Time (ST)	23759	21731	22589

CONCLUSION

In this paper, we have proposed a new method called New FastPFOR which reduces the storage space of the integers to be encoded; which in turn achieves fast disk access. Hence, it could achieve better compression and fast decompression (disk access + decoding time). To reduce the storage space lower than FastPFOR, New FastPFOR uses variable bit-length code to identify the positions of the exception values and store the exception values where as FastPFOR uses fixed bit-length code. We have used TREC data collections in our experiments to evaluate the performance of the compression techniques. The results show that the proposed method performs better both in compression and searching (decompression) for the different random queries than the existing methods. So, the proposed technique can be used in IR applications.

REFERENCES

Anh, V. N., & Moffat, A. (2005). Inverted index compression using word-aligned binary codes. *Information Retrieval, 8*(1), 151–166. doi:10.1023/B:INRT.0000048490.99518.5c

Boystov, L. (2012). *Clueweb09 posting list data set*. Retrieved from http://boytsov.info/datasets/clueweb09gap/

Chan, C. Y., & Ioannidis, Y. E. (1998, June). Bitmap index design and evaluation. *SIGMOD Record, 27*(2), 355–366. doi:10.1145/276305.276336

Domnic, S., & Glory, V. (2012). Inverted file compression using EGC and FEGC. *Procedia Technology, 6*, 493–500. doi:10.1016/j.protcy.2012.10.059

Elias, P. (1975). Universal codeword sets and representations of the integers. *IEEE Transactions on Information Theory, 21*(2), 194–203. doi:10.1109/TIT.1975.1055349

Faloutsos, C. (1985). Access methods for text. *ACM Computing Surveys, 17*(1), 49–74. doi:10.1145/4078.4080

Glory, V., & Domnic, S. (2013). Re-Ordered FEGC and Block Based FEGC for Inverted File Compression. *International Journal of Information Retrieval Research, 3*(1), 71–88. doi:10.4018/ijirr.2013010105

Goldstein, J., Ramakrishnan, R., & Shaft, U. (1998). Compressing relations and indexes. In *Data Engineering, 1998. Proceedings., 14th International Conference on* (pp. 370-379). IEEE. doi:10.1109/ICDE.1998.655800

Golomb, S. W. (1966). Run Length Coding. *IEEE Transactions on Knowledge and Data Engineering, 12*(3), 399–401.

Kobayashi, M., & Takeda, K. (2000). Information retrieval on the web. *ACM Computing Surveys, 32*(2), 144–173. doi:10.1145/358923.358934

Lemire, D., & Boystov, L. (2013). *FastPFOR Java code, 2013*. Retrieved from https://github.com/lemire/JavaFastPFOR

Lemire, D., & Boytsov, L. (2015). Decoding billions of integers per second through vectorization. *Software, Practice & Experience*, *45*(1), 1–29. doi:10.1002/spe.2203

Moffat, A., & Stuiver, L. (2000). Binary interpolative coding for effective index compression. *Information Retrieval*, *3*(1), 25–47. doi:10.1023/A:1013002601898

Morrison, D. R. (1968). PATRICIA—practical algorithm to retrieve information coded in alphanumeric. *Journal of the Association for Computing Machinery*, *15*(4), 514–534. doi:10.1145/321479.321481

Ng, W. K., & Ravishankar, C. V. (1997). Block-oriented compression techniques for large statistical databases. *IEEE Transactions on Knowledge and Data Engineering*, *9*(2), 314–328. doi:10.1109/69.591455

Rice, R. F. (1979). *Some practical universal noiseless coding techniques*. Academic Press.

Salomon, D. (2004). *Data compression: the complete reference*. Springer Science & Business Media.

Salomon, D. (2007). *Variable-length codes for data compression*. Springer Science & Business Media. doi:10.1007/978-1-84628-959-0

Silvestri, F., & Venturini, R. (2010). VSEncoding: efficient coding and fast decoding of integer lists via dynamic programming. In *Proceedings of the 19th ACM international conference on Information and knowledge management* (pp. 1219-1228). ACM. doi:10.1145/1871437.1871592

Somasundaram, K., & Domnic, S. (2007). Extended golomb code for integer representation. *IEEE Transactions on Multimedia*, *9*(2), 239–246. doi:10.1109/TMM.2006.886260

Williams, H. E., & Zobel, J. (2002). Indexing and retrieval for genomic databases. *IEEE Transactions on Knowledge and Data Engineering*, *14*(1), 63–78. doi:10.1109/69.979973

Yan, H., Ding, S., & Suel, T. (2009). Inverted index compression and query processing with optimized document ordering. In *Proceedings of the 18th international conference on World wide web* (pp. 401-410). ACM. doi:10.1145/1526709.1526764

Zobel, J., & Moffat, A. (2006). Inverted files for text search engines. *ACM Computing Surveys*, *38*(2), 6, es. doi:10.1145/1132956.1132959

Zukowski, M., Heman, S., Nes, N., & Boncz, P. (2006). Super-scalar RAM-CPU cache compression. In *22nd International Conference on Data Engineering (ICDE'06)* (pp. 59-59). IEEE. doi:10.1109/ICDE.2006.150

Chapter 7
Multi–Agents Machine Learning (MML) System for Plagiarism Detection

Hadj Ahmed Bouarara
Dr. Tahar Moulay University of Saida, Algeria

ABSTRACT

Day after day the cases of plagiarism increase and become a crucial problem in the modern world caused by the quantity of textual information available in the web. As data mining becomes the foundation for many different domains, one of its chores is a text categorization that can be used in order to resolve the impediment of automatic plagiarism detection. This chapter is devoted to a new approach for combating plagiarism named MML (Multi-agents Machine Learning system) composed of three modules: data preparation and digitalization, using n-gram character or bag of words as methods for the text representation, TF*IDF as weighting to calculate the importance of each term in the corpus in order to transform each document to a vector, and learning and vote phase using three supervised learning algorithms (decision tree c4.5, naïve Bayes, and support vector machine).

INTRODUCTION AND BACKGROUND

The information revolution jostled by the large-scale development of Internet / Intranet of networks access has detonated the amount of textual data available online or offline and the popularization of computer science in the world of business, government and individuals, has created large volumes of electronic documents written in natural language. It is very difficult to estimate the quantities of textual data created each month in government, corporations, institutions, or the amount of scientific publications in various search fields. This resolution gave the birth to a big problem called plagiarism which has received much attention from both the academic and commercial communities, in recent years. Instead of producing original work, some students or researcher prefer to directly take ideas things or content found in books, encyclopedias, newspaper articles or previous work submitted by others or on one of the many cheat sites available recently on the Internet, sites with existing equipment perfectly organized by

DOI: 10.4018/978-1-5225-3004-6.ch007

subject and level for easy access, either intentionally or un-intentionally without putting it in quotation marks and / or without citing source.

Many examples of text reuse surround us today, including the creation of literary and historical texts, summarization, translation or revision of existing texts. Many factors influence plagiarism including translating an original text into a different language, restyling an original to fit different authorial or consumer needs (e.g. rewriting a scientific text to be readable by the layman), reducing or expanding the size of the original text and the competency and production requirements of the writer. Recent advances in technology are making plagiarism much easier. For example, the Google web search engine claims to index over 3 billion web pages1 providing a large variety of source texts on a diverse range of topics in many different languages. Word processors have also become more sophisticated, enabling users to easily cut and paste, merge and format pre-existing texts from a variety of sources.

Depending on the behavior of plagiarist, we can distinguish several types of plagiarism as a plagiarism verbatim when the plagiarist copied the words or sentence from a book, magazine or web page as like it without putting it in quotation marks and / or without citing source or buy a work online, the paraphrase when the words or the syntax of sentence copied are changing and finally the cases of plagiarism the most difficult to detect are plagiarism with translation and plagiarism of ideas when summarizing the original idea of the author expressed in his own words partially or completely (Stein, 2007).

The Plagiarism problem can be regarded as a categorization problem for this we have studied the different learning algorithms for the supervised classification of texts (two classes plagiarism or no-plagiarism), which produce a prediction model. These techniques based on a single agent are face to limitations when we sought to develop more complex models for the classification of a gigantic textual database. These limitations can be easily felt by a considerable performance degradation of the best classifiers in response time that increases proportionally with the size of the volumes treated and even the quality of results. In our work we had the idea of decentralizing the classification process using multiple agents that will communicate with each other to share knowledge to improve the performance and efficiency of our classification system. We have developed a model based on an architecture composed of several parts; each part will deal with the problem of categorization of a textual database in a specific way, but can communicate and share their knowledge.

Aims of our work:

- Construction of a multi-agents supervised classification system for the detection of the plagiarism cases.
- Find the best representation of the data set 09 Pan used in our experiment
- Find the number of ideal agent for each learning algorithm used
- Vary the algorithm used by each agent in order to find the best combination.
- Compare the obtained results with the results of the classical technique
- Make decisions that can be used by another researcher in the fields of plagiarism detection, classification and multi-agents systems.
- The Construction of a visualization method to help experts in the field of analyzing the results obtained.

Our work is organized as follows in section 2 we describe some existed plagiarism detection systems. Section three we will give you a detailed view of our contribution and the different steps used in the realization of a distributed architecture using different agent of machine learning algorithm. Section 4 we detailed the different experiment realized and the validation tool developed. Section 5 gives a comparative study. Section 6 detailed the visualization method proposed. Finally we conclude with a general conclusion and some future works.

STATE OF THE ART

Text plagiarism is perhaps one of the oldest forms of plagiarism, which, to this day, remains difficult to be identified in practice. Therefore, a lot of research has been conducted to detect plagiarism automatically. However, much of this research lacks proper evaluation, rendering it irreproducible at times and mostly incomparable across papers. This section is devoted to the different works of automatic plagiarism detection existed in literature:

The technique of clustering has been used by SI and Al in (Si & Leong, 1997) for reducing the comparison time for plagiarism detection. This technique is based on specific words (keywords) to find similar clusters between documents. Hoad et al in (Hoad, 2003) propose a method based on the representation of texts fingerprint block and a comparison between the suspect document and source document gonna be done to detect common blocks this proposal will give good results but it does not work well when the plagiarized part will change or word order will change in the suspect text. Kang et al in (Kang & Gelbukh, 2006) have used the thesaurus wordnet which is a lexical database to exploit the Degree relationship between words in order to calculate the semantic similarity between suspicious and original documents.

A set of methods have been developed in 2009 by Grozea in (Grozea & Gehl, 2009), and by Kasparzak & al in (Kasprzak & Brandejs, 2009) which consists of comparing the suspect document with the original document based on the n-gram character representation (16-gram and 8- gram respectively) and the degree of similarity between the chains grams depends on the number of identical character between them. In (Basile, 2009) the author present a novel system using information retrieval with the help of the Nutch this system is made up of three phases: preparation of the Nutch (search engine) index using corpus and formulating queries from the suspect paper, finally the retrieved of the source plagiarism document, with an account of similarity for each query of the suspicious document.

A very interesting system was developed by Nawab et al in (Nawab & Stevenson, 2011) for plagiarism detection. This system consists of three main modules: preprocessing and indexing candidate selection (using an information retrieval based approach) and detailed analysis (using runing Rabbi Karp string tiling greedy algorithm). Bouarara et al in (Bouarara & Hamou, 2015) have used a boosting algorithm for classifying documents as plagiarism or not plagiarism and the results obtained have been optimized by genetic algorithms.

A major problem for plagiarism detection systems is the paraphrase, in (Barrón-Cedeño & Vila, 2013) an original idea has been proposed to address and detect similar sentences. Another marking system was proposed in (Sanchez-Perez & Sidorov, 2014) which is based on a recursive algorithm to extend the maximum sentence length to matching passages and a tip to resolve the overlapping boxes plagiarism. .Finally, in (Shet & Acharya, 2012) the Proposed approach is based on ontology mapping

MULTI-AGENT MACHINE LEARNING (MML) SYSTEM

For instance, let's consider an international conference where the reviewers must detect if the received papers are plagiarized or not, so in classical ways each reviewer will treat some papers but this can't ensure a fully detection of plagiarism, the presence of an automatic detection of plagiarism has become mandatory

The automatic plagiarism detection can be seen as a problem of supervised classification bi-classes (plagiarism and no-plagiarism), but caused by the number of documents available online and offline the classical methods that treat this problem by a single algorithm has not sacrificed the best answers. Our solution is inhaled by the principle that the purpose of a group (set of agents) can deliver more serious and precision detection than a single agent facing to any problem, we employ a set of algorithms (agents) to resolve the problem of automatic plagiarism detection where each member of the group solve the problem with its own way, they will communicate between them to solve the final problem and every agent must analyse all suspicious texts and the final decision that for each text must be after a vote(plagiarism or not plagiarism)where the vote that has the majority will be selected (the final solution is oriented by the vote) as showing in the Figure 1 and the number of selected agents will fully odd to avoid perfect equality in voting.

The realization of our idea is composed of four modules: i) pre-processing and indexation ii) learning and vote: using multi-agent machine learning (MML) system with the variation of the machine learning algorithm used by each agent (that can decision tree C4.5, Support vector machine (SVM) or naïve bayes) iii) classification step that depending on the vote of each agent. iiii) visualization step.

Figure 1. Architecture of multiagents machine learning system

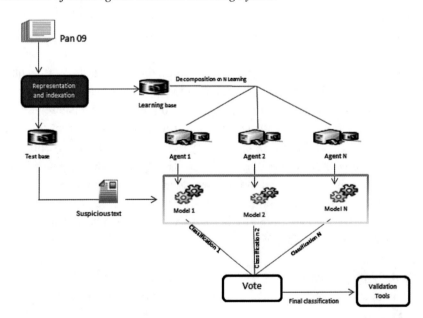

Pre-Processing

We are face to a supervised classification problem so the main dataset will be decomposed into two parts: learning part that will be used for the construction of models by the agents and the test part that representation the evaluation basis (new text to be classified by our system in order to evaluate the performance of the final classification). Each text must be transformed into a vector in order to be interpretable by machine. The vectoring of text is achieved following the next steps:

- **Data Preparation:** The substance of the text must be converted to lowercase and eliminate all non-alphabetic characters (numbers and limited graphic symbols).
- **Elimination of Stop Words:** In any textual documents, there's a set of words that are repeated a lot and others that are uncommon, this kind of words are not discriminant and does not incorporate data,for this reason, it is necessary to eliminate them (stop words) specialized for each language (Bouarara, 2014).
- **Texts Representation:** This is a simplification of texts ensures the enactment of any text into a set of terms (indexing unit chosen) can be words using a bag of words method, concepts using Wordnet, and linguistic processing or sentences (using a bag of sentences) finally the n-gram characters. We adopt for our work the next two methods:
- **Bag of Words:** First a word is a set of characters linked and separated by punctuations or white separator this method allows to render the text into a list of words for e.g. the sentence "I am a PhD student" Becomes a list of words {I, am, PhD, student}.
- **N-Gram Character:** This method is directly linked to a parameter N where a window of N cells will be built, that it moves in all the text from beginning to end with a single step and each n-gram captured will be saved in a list (Bouarara[2], 2015).
- **Coding and Indexation:** It is the conversion of each text to a digital vector where each one of its components represents the importance (the weight) of the term in the corpus that will be figured utilizing the composite weighting tf*idfthat is the most used in the literature

$$\boldsymbol{TF} \times \boldsymbol{IDF}\left(\boldsymbol{D}, \boldsymbol{T}_i\right) = TF\left(T_i, D\right) \times IDF\left(T_i\right) \tag{1}$$

where: term frequency TF (T_i, Di) =number of occurrences of term ti in document Di.

$$\boldsymbol{IDF}\left(\boldsymbol{T}, \boldsymbol{Di}\right) = \log \frac{|N|}{DF\left(T\right)} \tag{2}$$

DF (T) represents the number of documents that comprise the term T, and N is the number of documents used. The final outcome of previous phases is a matrix (documents*terms) showing in Figure 2.

*Figure 2. Matrix (documents*terms)*

$$
\begin{array}{ccccc}
 & T_1 & T_2 & \cdots & T_t \\
D_1 & w_{11} & w_{21} & \cdots & w_{t1} \\
D_2 & w_{12} & w_{22} & \cdots & w_{t2} \\
\vdots & \vdots & \vdots & & \vdots \\
\vdots & \vdots & \vdots & & \vdots \\
D_n & w_{1n} & w_{2n} & \cdots & w_{tn}
\end{array}
$$

Learning Bases Construction

Our system was based on multiple agents, so each one of them must have a learning base, for this reason our main learning base will be decomposed into a set of sub-learning-bases where every agent must have its own training base completely different to others. For e.g. our main learning base is equal to600 documents and we chose to use three agents, then the mini-learning-corpusforanyagentis600/3=200 documents.

Learning Phase

Every agent is a machine learning algorithm which uses its owner learning base for the construction of prediction model. In our work we have tested three algorithms that produce three different prediction models (naïve bayes algorithm produce a probabilistic model, decision tree algorithm produce a model as a set of decision rules, and the support vector machine (SVM) algorithm produce a linear function model). The yield of this part is a succession of model (created by each agent). We have used the weka API in the development of each machine learning algorithm because it offers us a set of algorithm ready to be used directly. We give you a global description of each algorithm used:

Naïve Bayes

Bayes theorem provides assigns to each text a probability of belonging to a possible class (no-plagiarism or plagiarism). It supposed that the effect of the value of a predictor (Xn) for a given class (Ci) is independent of the values of other predictors (McCallum & Nigam, 1998).

$$P\left(Ci\,/\,Tn\right) = P(x_1, C_i)^* \; P(x_2, C_i)^* \ldots \ldots \ldots *P(C_i)$$

- **P (C_i | T_n):** The probability that the text Tn is classified in the class (Ci) (posterior probability).
- **P (C_i):** The prior probability of the class Ci.
- **P (x | C_i):** The probability that the component X generates the class Ci.

Decision Tree (c4.5)

The first classification algorithms for decision trees are old but the most significant work is C4.5 that represent an improvement of ID3 and consists to construct a consistent tree with the most of data dividing recursively and efficiently as possible examples of the training set until the subset example containing (almost) is obtained as such belong to the same class, we chose this method because it represents a set of rules and it is easily interpretable, can handle attributes with null values or missing opportunity to work with continuous value, ranges and reduce the size using pruning and solve the problem of over-fitting (Sayad, 2010).

Support Vector Machine Algorithm (SVM)

The SVM is a classifier based on two key ideas and reformulates the classification problem as a problem of quadratic optimization. The first key idea is the concept of maximum margin. The margin is the distance between the separation boundary and the nearest samples. These are called support vector. In SVM, the separation boundary is chosen as that which maximizes the margin. This is justified by the theory Vapnik-Chervonenkis (or statistical learning theory). The problem is to find the optimal separating border, from a training set. This is done by formulating the problem as a problem of quadratic optimization.

In order to deal with cases where the data are not linearly separable, the second key idea of SVM is to transform the space of input data representation in a space of larger (possibly infinite dimensional), in which it is likely that there is a linear division. This is achieved through a kernel function, which must meet the conditions of Mercer's theorem, which has the advantage of not requiring the explicit knowledge of the transformation to apply the changing of the space (Hearst & Dumais, 1998).

Vote and Evaluation

Each model will be evaluated by all test documents and the communication between the models is based on a vote where all models must classify each test document, the final decision (concerning if a text is plagiarism or not) is the majority class among all classes obtained after the vote for e.g. we have 7 agents each of them construct a model, when a new document comes to be examined will be classified by all agents and we count the number of occurrences of each class, if more than 3 models classified the document as plagiarism, then the final class is plagiarism else the final class is no-plagiarism.

EXPERIMENTATION

Before presenting the obtained results, we detail our data source that represents the benchmark pan 09

Corpus PAN 09

PAN Corpus 09 (PAN-PC-09) is a corpus for the detection of plagiarism used in international competition plagiarism detection pan 09. This corpus contains a set of brute document plagiarized in which plagiarism has been inserted manually and non-plagiarized text documents (source document).

The corpus is constructed 22,874 documents that are in the public domain, so this corpus is available to other researchers as a benchmark. 50% of the documents are small (pages 1-10), 35% of medium-sized (10-100 pages), and 15% large (100-1000 pages). 90% of documents are unilingual English. 50% of documents are identified as suspicious documents, and 50% are designated as source documents. The length of a case of plagiarism is equally distributed between 50 and 5000 words. In our case we chose only 1500 documents 800 papers as plagiarism and 900 no-plagiarism papers (Weimar, 2009). In our case we use 60% of our data set for learning phase and 40% for evaluation phase.

Validation Tools

All methods of quantifying the difference between an expected result and a result obtained for this a panoply of Metrics were introduced comprised between 0 and 1 for our system we use the f-measure (F) and entropy (E) based on a traditional operators Recall (R) and precision (P)

$$F-measure = \frac{2*Recall*precision}{\left(Recall+precision\right)} \tag{6}$$

Entropy= -precision* (log (precision)) (7)

RESULT

After experimentation, we grouped our results in the accompanying tables and shapes offering a series of comparison, putting in competition our results obtained after the change many of the different parameters

1.   The first comparison shows confrontation the best f-measure and entropy given by the method multi-agents Machine learning using the decision tree C4.5 algorithm with the variation of the number of agents and the method of representation of text.

Discussion in Term of f-Measure

By analysing the previous Table 1 and the Figure 3, we observe that the majority of the method (1,3 and 5 agents) their best outcomes are obtained using the 3-gram character except for the method using (7 agents) that will perform using 4-gram text representation (yellow boxes).The badly f-measure using 3, 5,and 7 agents was obtained using 2-gram character (red boxes). The best detector is obtained with the 3-gram representation validated by the f-measure=0.906 (blue circle in the Figure 3) and consequently a better precision and recall.

Table 1. F-measure of machine learning agents oriented supervised with several text representations

	Bag of Words		2-Gram		3-Gram		4-Gram		5-Gram	
	Entropy	F-Measure	Entropy	F-Measure	Entropy	F-Measure	Entropy	F-Measure	Entropy	F-Measure
3 agents	0,195	0,78	0,213	0,79	0,151	0,849	0,125	0,819	0,201	0,827
5 agents	0,123	0,756	0,18	0,816	0,121	0, 906	0,14	0,805	0,07	0,786
7 agents	0,15	0,764	0,16	0,70	0,093	0,83	0,11	0,847	0,05	0,744
1 agent	0,187	0,701	0.151	0,761	0.13	0,832	0.169	0,799	0.182	0,795

Figure 3. Curve of F-measure between variation of text representation and agent number using decision tree C4.5 algorithm

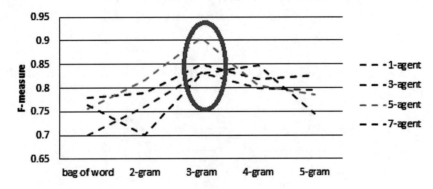

Figure 4. Curve of entropy between variation of text representation and agent number using decision tree C4.5 algorithm

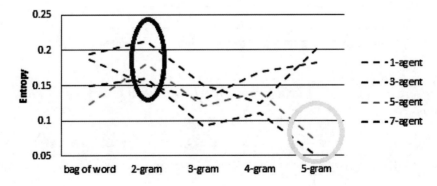

In Term of Entropy

We clearly detected by the first glance in Figure 5 (yellow circle) that the best entropy is given by the 5-gram character representation and the number of agents = 7 (yellow box in table). On the other hand the worst entropy is given by the 2-gram representation (red circle in figure 4) and the number of agents = 3 (red box in table).

Influence of Text Representation

The 5-gram representation allows to the multi-agent decision tree system with the number equal to 5 or 7 agents to get the best performance in terms of loss of information, which allows that this representation technique allows obtaining a better precision in term of classification and N = 5 allows to generate only the discriminant terms that ensure more cohesion between the rules produced by each agent.

Influence of the Number of Agents

The number of agents equal to 5 achieves the best result which explains that the vote done by 5 agents is more effective than the vote done by 3 or 7 agents which explains the distribution of the learning base in five parts can produce more effective classification model than other distribution.

The different results obtained using MML system with the naïve Bayes algorithm with the variation of text representation are grouped in the next Table 2 and Figures (6 and 7).

Figure 5. Curve of F-measure between variation of text representation and agent number using naïve Ayes algorithm

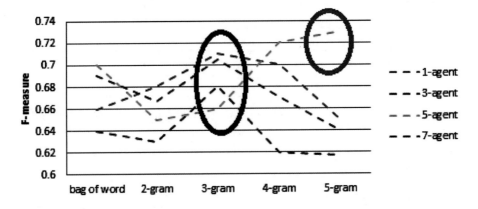

Table 2. F-measure of multi-agent machine learning with variation of text representations using naïve bayes algorithm

	Bag of Words		2-Gram		3-Gram		4-Gram		5-Gram	
	Entropy	F-Measure	Entropy	F-Measure	Entropy	F-Measure	Entropy	F-Measure	Entropy	F-Measure
3 agents	0.271	0.64	0.312	0.63	0.251	0.68	0.332	0.62	0.29	0.617
5 agents	0.238	0.70	0.3058	0.65	0.269	0.66	0.263	0.72	0.207	0.73
7 agents	0.2345	0.69	0.2817	0.667	0.26	0.705	0.281	0.67	0.262	0.64
1 agent	0.209	0.66	0.2733	0.68	0.24	0.71	0.25	0.70	0.276	0.65

Figure 6. Curve of entropy between variation of text representation and agent number using naïve ayes algorithm

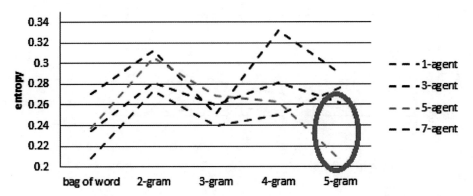

After observed the previous Table 2 and Figure 5, we see that in term of f-measure the best performance with F = 0.73 is obtained with 5-gram representation and number of agents = 5 (blue circle in the Figure 5). By-cons, regarding the number of agents equal to 1, 3 or 7 then the best performance is obtained with N = 3 (black circle in Figure 5).

In term of entropy as present the Figure 6 (green circle), N = 5 provides less loss of information. Finally we go out with a strong decision is that the distribution with a large number of agents is not necessary because the results with 5 agents began to relapse slightly.

The different results obtained using MML system using the Support vector machine algorithm with the variation of representation of text and the number of agent, are grouped in the next Table 3 and Figures (7 and 8).

The Figures (7 and 8), and the Table 3 show that the best performance of multi-agents support vector machine system is given with 3-gram representation technique and number of agents=5 validated by the f-measure =0.88 and entropy=0.112.

Table 3. F-measure of Multiagent Machine Learning with variation of text representations using support vector machine algorithm

	Bag of Words		2-Gram		3-Gram		4-Gram		5-Gram	
	Entropy	F-Measure	Entropy	F-Measure	Entropy	F-Measure	Entropy	F-Measure	Entropy	F-Measure
3 agents	0.214	0..711	0.142	0.73	0.189	0.76	0.203	0.759	0.21	0.751
5 agents	0.163	0.801	0.1325	0.83	0.112	0.88	0.14	0.81	0.19	0.79
7 agents	0.175	0.741	0.17	0.77	0.15	0.79	0.164	0.809	0.234	0.73
1 agent	0.16	0.76	0.139	0.82	0.13	0.83	0.131	0.84	0.1907	0.807

Figure 7. Curve of F-measure between variation of text representation and agent number using support vector machine algorithm

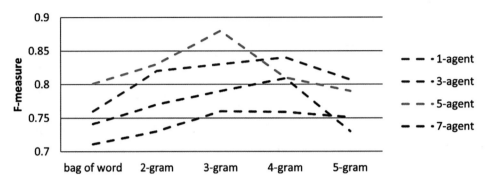

Figure 8. Curve of entropy between variation of text representation and agent number using Support vectors machine algorithm

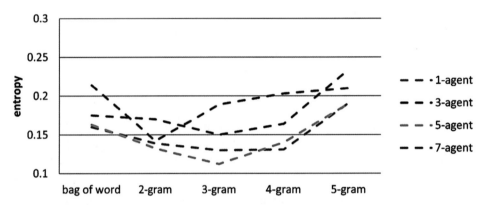

DECISIONS AND DISCUSSION

After the testes realized and the analysis carries out on the different results obtained we go out with a series of decisions:

1. The representation N-gram give best results compared to the representation bag of word because the first representation offers several advantages such as:
    a. Multilingual or it can be applied to any language.
    b. It is not necessary to use a language processing.
        Unfortunately, the representation bag of word suffers from different drawbacks such as:
    c. Difficulty to delimited text written in the Chinese language.
    d. The necessity of linguistic processing (semantic and conceptual syntax is required) view the ambiguity of natural speech
    e. Problem of composed word, words of the same family and abbreviations
2. The variation of parameter N in N-gram representation was an interesting experience. We notice that using algorithms Naive Bayes and decision tree, N = 5 is the optimal values and using the

SVM algorithm N = 3 is the optimal value. A value of N is called optimal when it helps generate the most discriminating terms in order to give a best representation of the data set 09 pan.

3. The optimal number of agents is equal to 5 for the three types of algorithms (naive Bayes, support vector machines and decision tree) because the distribution of learning base in 5 parts allows to each classifier to produce the most efficient model for the prediction.

4. The multi-agents decision tree c4.5 gives best performance compared to the multi-agents naïve Bayes and multi-agents support vector machine because it is based on a pruning phase which eliminate the redundancy of term and the over-fitting.

Comparative Study

The best result obtained by our system MML will be compared to the public presentation of other systems applied to the data set pan 09 that are:

1. Similarity between sentences proposed in (Kasprzak & Brandejs, 2009).
2. Method in three steps (selection, matching and squares) proposed in (Grozea & Gehl, 2009)
3. The Enclopot system proposed in (Basile, 2009)

This comparison is shown in Table 4 in order to move over our results some credibility.

View the table 6 and Figure 8 shows that our approach is vastly superior compared to the classical methods based on a simple method of matching between documents validated by the f-measure that

Table 4. Comparison between the best result of our approach with the result of other systems

	f-Measure
Multiagents decision tree C4.5 system	0, 906
Simple similarity measure	0.6192
Similarity between sentence	0.6976
Selection, matches and squares	0.6491

Figure 9. The F-measure of our system face to several other plagiarism detection systems

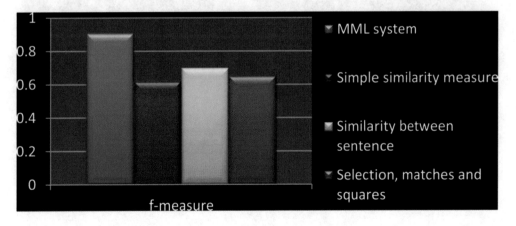

has been preferred because it is grounded on the recall and precision unlike the entropy based simply on the precision.

VISUALIZATION OF RESULTS

One of the advantages of our organisation is the visualisation of the plagiarized documents as a cobweb and whenever a new text identifies as plagiarism a thread will be weaving between this document and the nearest document among the documents already detected as plagiarism the wire of the same colour links the nearest papers with a threshold of 0.4 using the Euclidian distance as shown in the pattern which represents a general survey with a rear zoom

This component of our system is characterised by a set of attributes:

- Forward a rear Zoom for the purpose of better visualize the result
- Rotation option to examine the effects of different posts
- Offers data about each document detected as plagiarism
- It permits the extraction of knowledge and information partially known

Text files are represented by a white dot and when we approach the mouse on this white point it gives us the information about the document author's name and placement as shown in Figure 11 that exhibit a detail of the outcome using the property of prior zooms

Figure 10. Global view of plagiarism documents as a cobweb

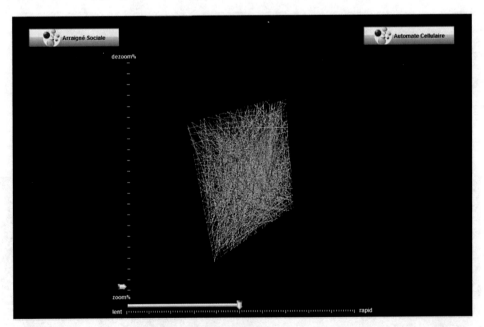

*For a more accurate representation see the electronic version.

Figure 11. Detailed visualization of paper plagiarism as a white picket

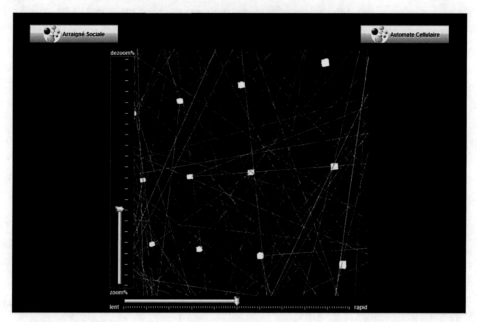

For a more accurate representation see the electronic version.

CONCLUSION AND FUTURE WORK

The plagiarism detection problem has been proved in the last years as a major area looking for businesses and particle. This dynamism is partly due to significant demand from users for this technology. It is becoming increasingly important in many situations where the amount of textual documents makes any manual processing impossible.

We presented a multi-agents plagiarism detection system which derives its profit from the use of N-grams as method of text representation, three supervised learning algorithms different (support vector machine (SVM), naive Bayes, decision tree C4 .5) but especially the contribution of our proposed idea is the distribution process of the classification based on the paradigm of agents and vote. We analyzed the results of this approach on the pan dataset 09. The Experimentation has shown that the system multi-agents C4.5 decision tree gives better results validate the measure of evaluation (entropy and f-measure). Finally a comparison was carried out with the plagiarism detection techniques that were developed in the 2009 on the Pan competition. The second part of our system is a visualization tool was developed to help experts of the areas to find more effective solution.

This application offers an original coupling of methods derived from the Natural Language Processing (NLP), methods of machine learning (ML) and Distributed Artificial Intelligence (DAI). With this combined use, it is possible to have a large learning base and very representative of the problem that we are looking to learn. Our system can be used as a service in Google search engine, by a professor in order to detect the cases of plagiarism in the works of their students, by conference or journal in order to check the originality of the paper or university in order to check the percentage of plagiarism in the thesis of PHD students.

Future works can instead utilize the same algorithm we can apply different algorithms in which each agent uses a different representation of text so that can increase the number of agents using other bio-inspired meta-heuristic method as PSO, social spider, cellular automaton, treating the problem of plagiarism with a translation using Google translation. We can treat the case of idea plagiarism using the automatic summarisation because two text have the same idea if the theirs summary are similar. Concerning the paraphraser problem we use the representation bag of sentences.

REFERENCES

Barrón-Cedeño, A., Vila, M., Martí, M. A., & Rosso, P. (2013). Plagiarism meets paraphrasing: Insights for the next generation in automatic plagiarism detection. *Computational Linguistics, 39*(4), 917–947. doi:10.1162/COLI_a_00153

Basile, C. (2009). A plagiarism detection procedure in three steps: Selection, matches and squares. In *Proceeding of the SEPLN '09 pan 09 3rd workshop and 1st international compétition on plagiarism* (pp. 19-23). IEEE.

Bouarara, H. A., Hamou, R. M., & Amine, A. (2014). Text Clustering using Distances Combination by Social Bees: Towards 3D Visualisation Aspect. *International Journal of Information Retrieval Research, 4*(3), 34–53. doi:10.4018/IJIRR.2014070103

Bouarara, H. A., Hamou, R. M., & Amine, A. (2015). New Swarm Intelligence Technique of Artificial Social Cockroaches for Suspicious Person Detection Using N-Gram Pixel with Visual Result Mining. *International Journal of Strategic Decision Sciences, 6*(3), 65–91. doi:10.4018/IJSDS.2015070105

Bouarara, H. A., Hamou, R. M., & Amine, A. (2015). A Novel Bio-Inspired Approach for Multilingual Spam Filtering. *International Journal of Intelligent Information Technologies, 11*(3), 45–87. doi:10.4018/IJIIT.2015070104

Bouarara, H. A., Hamou, R. M., Rahmani, A., & Amine, A. (2015). Boosting Algorithm and Meta-Heuristic Based on Genetic Algorithms for Textual Plagiarism Detection. *International Journal of Cognitive Informatics and Natural Intelligence, 9*(4), 65–87. doi:10.4018/IJCINI.2015100105

Bouarara, H. A., Hamou, R. M., Rahmani, A., & Amine, A. (2015). Boosting Algorithm and Meta-Heuristic Based on Genetic Algorithms for Textual Plagiarism Detection. *International Journal of Cognitive Informatics and Natural Intelligence, 9*(4), 65–87. doi:10.4018/IJCINI.2015100105

Grozea, C., Gehl, C., & Popescu, M. (2009, September). ENCOPLOT: Pairwise sequence matching in linear time applied to plagiarism detection. *3rd PAN Workshop. Uncovering Plagiarism, Authorship and Social Software Misuse,* 10.

Hearst, M. A., Dumais, S. T., Osman, E., Platt, J., & Scholkopf, B. (1998). Support vector machines. *Intelligent Systems and their Applications, IEEE, 13*(4), 18-28.

Hoad, T. C., & Zobel, J. (2003). Methods for identifying versioned and plagiarized documents. *Journal of the American Society for Information Science and Technology*, *54*(3), 203–215. doi:10.1002/asi.10170

Kang, N., Gelbukh, A., & Han, S. (2006, September). PPChecker: Plagiarism pattern checker in document copy detection. In Text, Speech and Dialogue (pp. 661-667). Springer Berlin Heidelberg.

Kasprzak, J., Brandejs, M., & Kripac, M. (2009, September). Finding plagiarism by evaluating document similarities. In *Proc. SEPLN* (*Vol. 9*, pp. 24-28). Academic Press.

McCallum, A., & Nigam, K. (1998, July). A comparison of event models for naive bayes text classification. In AAAI-98 workshop on learning for text categorization (Vol. 752, pp. 41-48). Academic Press.

Nawab, R. M. A., Stevenson, M., & Clough, P. (2011). External Plagiarism Detection using Information Retrieval and Sequence Alignment-Notebook for PAN at CLEF 2011. *Proceedings of the 5th International Workshop on Uncovering Plagiarism, Authorship, and Social Software Misuse.*

Sayad, D. S. (2010). *decision_tree*. Retrieved November 20, 2013, from saedsayad: http://www.saedsayad.com/

Shet, K. C., & Acharya, U. D. (2012). Semantic plagiarism detection system using ontology mapping. *Advances in Computers*, *3*(3).

Si, A., Leong, H. V., & Lau, R. W. (1997, April). Check: a document plagiarism detection system. In *Proceedings of the 1997 ACM symposium on Applied computing* (pp. 70-77). ACM. doi:10.1145/331697.335176

Stein, B. (2007). Principles of Hash-Based Text Retrieval. *30th Annual International ACM SIGIR Conference*, 527–534.

Weimar, B.-U. (2009, September 10). *webis groupe weimer*. Retrieved november 9, 2013, from webis: http://www.webis.de/research/events/pan-09

Chapter 8
A Technique for Resolution of the Assignment Problem Containers in a Container Terminal

Khedidja Yachba
University Center of Relizane, Algeria

Zakaria Bendaoud
University of Saida, Algeria

Karim Bouamrane
University of Oran, Algeria

ABSTRACT

A container terminal is a complicated system made up of several components in interdependence. Several materials handle possible to move containers at the port to better meet the needs of ships awaiting loading or unloading. In order to effectively manage this area, it is necessary to know the location of each container. Containers search times can be considerable and lead to delays that cause financial penalties for terminal management operators. In this chapter, the authors propose an approach to solve the problem of placement of containers through the description of a model that optimizes available storage space to handle the distance travelled between the containers and the storage locations in a seaport. In other words, a model that minimizes the total number of unnecessary movement while respecting the constraints of space and time. This work develops a software tool enabling identification of the best location of a container using the methodological resolution Branch and Bound.

DOI: 10.4018/978-1-5225-3004-6.ch008

INTRODUCTION

To Upon arrival at a port, the ships docked remain inactive for the duration of loading and unloading. Handling port terminal operators receive a schedule indicating the dates of loading and unloading of containers and their locations in the storage areas. The challenge for the port authority is to determine the storage plan containers so as to minimize the total processing time (loading or unloading) of the latter. The processing time depends on various parameters such as:

1. The distance between the ship and the storage area.
2. The arrival and exit date of containers.
3. The time required to perform container movements (movement required of a container in a buffer space before the processing of another container).

This work's objective is to minimize the container investment cost and to increase the efficiency of transport companies by minimizing the time occupied by a container or ship in port. This amounts to revise the placement of containers in the storage area (taking into consideration the distance between the container and the storage area, and within each type of a container) by minimizing the number of unnecessary movements.

In this sense the authors are studying how to organize the container storage area, so that the authors find the optimum location for each container.

Consequently, the authors in this chapter are interested in the development of an optimization model that allows the identification of the best location for a container at a seaport.

This chapter is structured as follows: Section 2: presents a state of art concerning the various works in the field of containerization while positioning the contribution. Section 3: shows the model proposed, section 4: demonstrates the results obtained in the implementation of this approach. Section 5: illustrates the conclusion and some perspectives.

RELATED WORK AND CONTRIBUTION

In The container storage problem the authors are concerned is a decision problem representing the container storage business, predominant component of the whole process of managing a port.

The resolution of the container storage problem in a container terminal is a logistical problem that has captivated scientists for decades. Two main lines of storage resolutions are usually studied: optimization of storage time and optimize storage space. These two questions are often treated separately. Therefore, the authors offer some of the work in this area on the optimization of the storage space.

In the work of Kim et al. (1997) planning of container loading sequences to be exported in a seaport was made by using an optimal routing algorithm. Korbaa et al. (2004) using a dynamic programming algorithm based on a stochastic arrival barges law to solve the real-time allocation problem of containers unloaded to storage areas while minimizing the number of unwanted movements .

In the work of Murthy et al. (2005) a decision support system for minimizing the time allocation of ships to berths was proposed. Dubreuil (2008) used an intelligent transport system for treating containers transition problem in port. Kefi (2008) used the greedy heuristics in a multi-agent architecture to optimize the storage containers.

Chebli (2011) proposed in his work a heuristic approach to solve the planning problem of container loading operations.

Ndèye (2014) provided a branch-and-cut algorithm for solving the container storage problem and taking into account additional constraints to prevent alterations to the docks and in the order in which the containers are unloaded by ships.

Dkhil (2015) proposed a single-objective optimization for handling time container and multi-objective optimization of the overall operating cost; the authors of this approach studied the problem of integrated scheduling considering the three equipment of an automated container terminal, namely: self-guided vehicles, dockside cranes and rack cranes.

They Study also the problem of allocating storage locations to containers, in import, in integration with the scheduling problem of jumpers.

The contribution is to propose a model for the container placement optimization in port. The challenge is to determine the storage plan containers in order to minimize the total processing time (loading or unloading) of the latter.

The processing time depends on various parameters such as the distance between ships and the storage area.

The implementation of this optimization model is characterized by the development of a container of the storage process in the storage area.

POSITIONING OUR CONTRIBUTION

This work forms part of the research work in the field of decision support system, optimization and simulation (Yachba et al., 2015; Yachba et al., 2016; Yachba, 2017; Belayachi et al., 2017). The authors address the problem with the placement of full containers in the storage area, where we propose a model that simulates the container allocation operation in a seaport. The model allows to the users to make analyzes of the marine transportation system and helps them later to make predictions on the container storage management in a seaport.

JUSTIFICATION OF THE CHOICE OF THE BRANCH AND BOUND ALGORITHM

The choice to implement the Branch and Bound (BB) algorithm in this work was opted for the following reasons:

1. It is an exact algorithm so it allows finding exact solutions.
2. Branch and Bound offers a performance and this through its ability to exclude partial solutions as soon as possible.

THE PROPOSED MODEL

This job combines the concepts of mathematical programming and optimization using an exact algorithm (Branch and Bound). This offering an optimization model that combines on one hand, the characteristics of mathematical programming supported by accurate or optimal algorithms based on the formulation of the problem.

Container investment optimization system in a seaport that the authors developed using the algorithm Branch and Bound, the following objectives:

1. Minimizing the time spent by a ship in the port taking into account various operations taking place in a port (optimal choice of container placement).
2. Speeding up the loading / unloading of containers import / export minimizing unproductive movements and "covered" by these distances containers.
3. Finding the best location for a container minimizing the cost of loading and unloading of goods in port.
4. Improving management of container storage process.

The proposed decision model inspired from the work of (Hamdadou and Bouamrane, 2007) consists mainly of three phases: the structuring of the model, its Exploitation and Achievement of results. Figure 1 illustrates the different phases and stages of use of the proposed decision model.

1. The objective of the structuring phase of the model is to identify the problem (Data collection, location of Ships, Containers, identification of the initial state of the storage area) and basic choices on how to approach it.
2. The Exploitation phase of the model is the analytical part of the Study Process. Its two main objectives are the evaluation of Constraints, then optimization via Brunch and Bound method.
3. The Achievement of the results essentially aims at the social acceptance of the result. However, it also includes the implementation of the decision, recommendation and decision support.

To describe the different stages of optimization in this work, the authors opted for the UML language for several reasons:

1. A language used to describe models of a system (real or software) based on object-oriented concepts.
2. System of notations for modelling systems using object-oriented concepts.
3. Represents a modelling standard, a notation: it is therefore a tool and not a method; everyone can use the method most appropriate to their needs.
4. It allows representing the treatment aspect of the system as well as the given aspect.

The use of class and sequence diagrams is necessary in order to model the decision support system proposed in this chapter.

THE CLASS DIAGRAM

The authors recommend the use of class diagrams (Matignon, 2013) to present the classes and interfaces of container placement systems and the various relationships between them. The class diagram in the proposed model consists of five classes (the Stack class, the container class, the ship class, the Dock class and the Area class). Classes are connected together by links (see Figure 2).

Figure 1. The proposed model

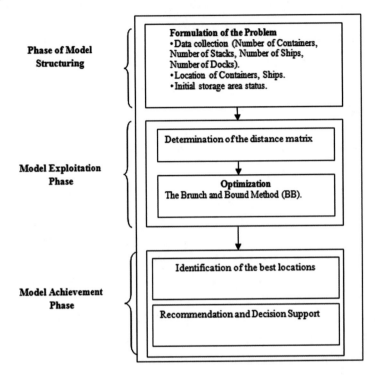

1. A ship has arrival and departure dates when mooring on a dock; it contains several containers as it can happen to load empty containers.
2. In a port, there are many docks; a dock has one or more storage areas.
3. Each storage area contains container stacks.
4. There may be one or more types of container such as container 20 ', 40'.. etc.
5. Each container is positioned in a stack of the same type.
6. A ship has a role loading or unloading of containers in an area.

THE SEQUENCE DIAGRAM

At any time T, the users configure the initial state of our system by choosing the distribution of containers on ships or on stacks or storage area (initially a container can be stored in the stack or it can be in a Ship waiting to be unloaded or it may be waiting to be stored in the stacks).

After displaying this distribution, insertion of the initial distribution is necessary before starting Branch and Bound processing.

Then the parameterization of the Branch and Bound algorithm is important, when the different distance matrices (type 1 matrix, type 2 matrix, type 3 matrix) are entered, the algorithm is launched which goes through several steps to Namely: to estimate the problem in sub-problems, to calculate the terminals and the final result of the algorithm.

Figure 2. The class diagram

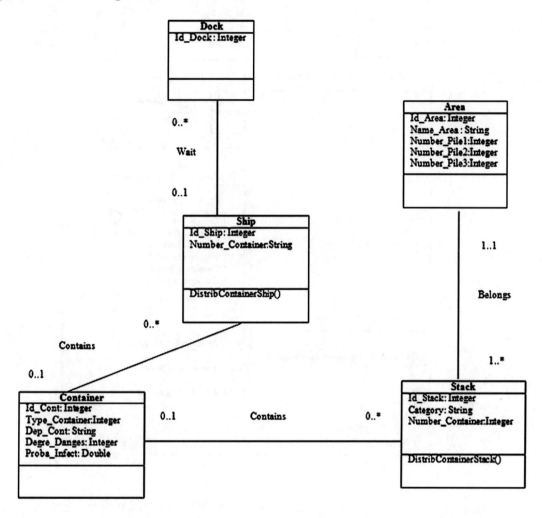

As a result the Branch and Bound algorithm provides optimal locations for the containers in the storage area (see Figure 3).

IMPLEMENTATION

The algorithm Branch and Bound is a method for global optimization in nonconvex problems (Stephen et al., 2003). Branch and Bound is a method used for scheduling and optimization; it builds an exploration shaft which lists all the solutions. Then using some properties of the problem in question, the authors must find a smart way to explore this tree.

This method uses a function to determine one or more terminals (depending on the treaty issue) to evaluate some solutions to either exclude them or keep them as potential solutions. Of course, the performance of a Branch and Bound method depends, inter alia, the quality of this function (for its ability to exclude partial solutions as soon as possible). The method of Branch and Bound algorithm also

Figure 3. The sequence diagram

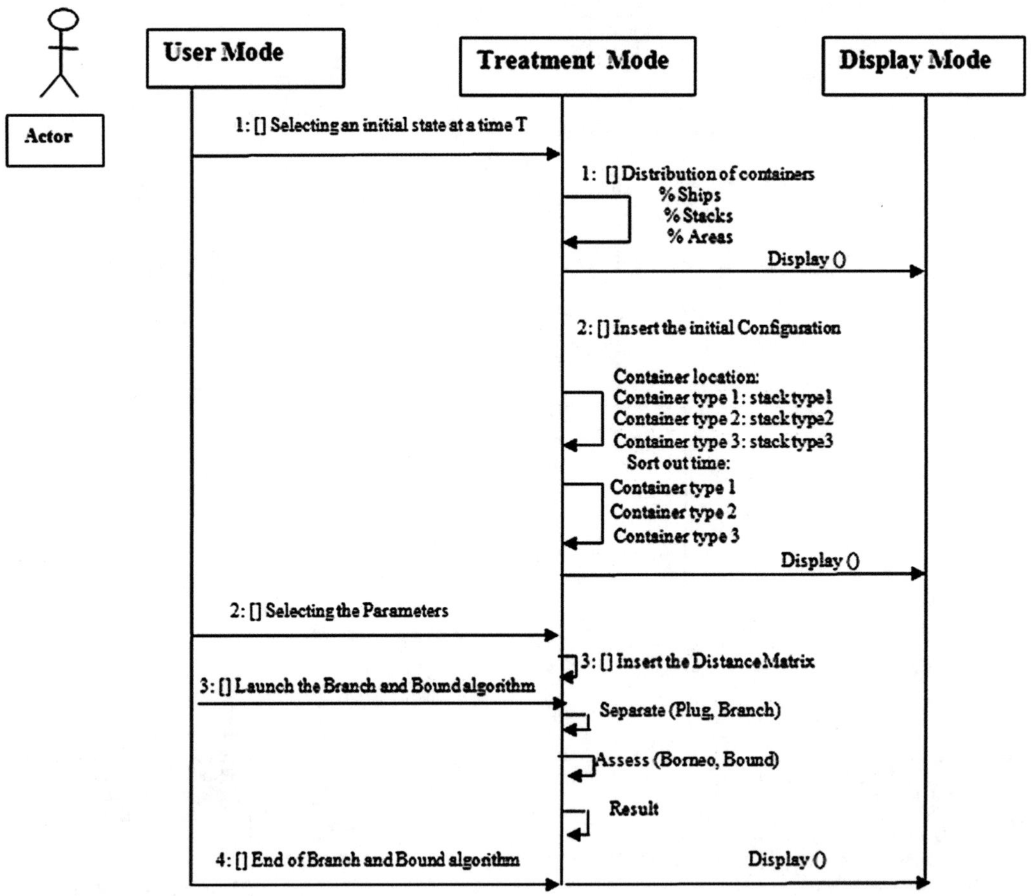

known's as separation and evaluation. The principle of this method is to build the enumeration tree node by node while making use terminals (primal and dual) to avoid the generation of all nodes of the tree.

THE FUNCTIONAL ARCHITECTURE

The application is part of the wide range of linear programming. The developed tool allows the identification of the optimal locations of the containers. The work provides the user with an accurate programming evaluation module around the Branch and Bound method (see Figure 4).

MECHANISMS

In Branch and Bound algorithm the mechanism is as follows:

1.   **Separate (Plug, Branch):** Divide the problem into sub-problems ("divide and rule").

Figure 4. The functional architecture of the proposed model

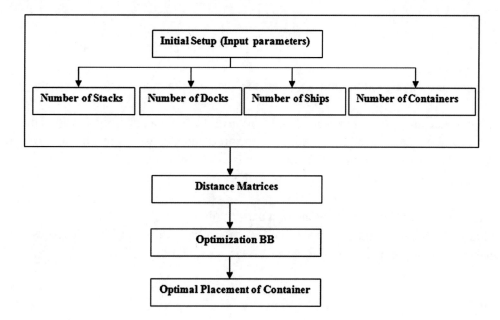

2.   **Assess (Borner, Bound):** Calculate an estimate of the optimal solution of a sub- problem.
3.   Calculate a good feasible solution (primal terminal) is an element that can be important.

(Peng et al., 1997) apply the principle of Branch and Bound allocation problem communicating periodic tasks.

DEVELOPMENT CRITERIA

To develop the Branch and Bound method in our study, the authors consider the following constraints:

1.   The category of container: each container has a category, in which the containers of the same class will be placed in a stack.
2.   The maximum height of the stack: each cell at a maximum height if the stack is full, you cannot insert a container.
3.   The distance between the container and the empty slots in accordance to the category of the stack and the type of container.

BRANCH AND BOUND ALGORITHM EXECUTION SCENARIO

In this section, the authors show the achievable results by the Branch and Bound algorithm to identify the best location for a container.

The method Branch and Bound is also called separation algorithm and evaluation. The principle of this method is as follows:

1. It consists in constructing the node tree by node while using terminals to avoid the generation of all the nodes of the tree.
2. The calculation of a good feasible solution is an element that may prove important.

For convenience, the authors represent the execution of the Branch and Bound method through a tree. The root of this tree represents all the solutions of the problem in question. In what follows, the authors summarize the Branch and Bound method on minimization problems.

To apply the Branch and Bound method, the authors must be in possession:

1. An idea for calculating a lower bound of a partial solution.
2. A strategy to subdivide the search space to create smaller and smaller search spaces.
3. A means for calculating an upper limit for at least one solution.

HYPOTHESES

In this work the authors consider the following hypotheses:

1. n containers to assign to n locations
2. Any container occupies 1 and only 1 location
3. cij: cost of allocating container i to location j
4. Non-segregation method.
5. Storage by group (Type).
6. The storage method is indirect (container placement in the stack is not initially scheduled).

1. The containers are stored in the same type.
2. The arrival dates and the unloading order of the containers are known before the unloading begins. Containers are assumed to be numbered in ascending order of arrival, and containers unloaded with the same means of transport are numbered according to their discharge.
3. Each container has its own storage cost depending on its load.

Problem: Find the assignment of containers to locations that minimize the total cost?

BRANCH AND BOUND SUMMARY EXAMPLE

The authors assume in the following example that the users have 4 stacks (P1, P2, P3, P4) and four containers (C1, C2, C3, C4) to place (containers and stacks in this example are Type1 (20')). The distance matrix is shown in Table 1.

In this example the lower bound (LB) is the optimal solution, it has a cost at least equal to: $2 + 3 + 1 + 4 = 10$ (sum of the minimum costs of each line). (See Table 2).

Table 1. The distance matrix

	P1	P2	P3	P4
C1	9	2	7	8
C2	6	4	3	7
C3	5	8	1	8
C4	7	6	9	4

Table 2. The lower bound

	P1	P2	P3	P4
C1	9	2	7	8
C2	6	4	3	7
C3	5	8	1	8
C4	7	6	9	4

The method begins by considering the starting problem with its set of solutions, called the root. Lower and upper boundary procedures are applied to the root (Table 2). If these two bounds are equal, then an optimal solution is found, and the authors stop there. Otherwise, the set of solutions is divided into two or more sub-problems, thus becoming children of the root (see Figure 5).

The method is then applied recursively to these sub problems, thus generating a tree structure. If an optimal solution is found for a sub-problem, it is feasible, but not necessarily optimal, for the initial problem. As it is feasible, it can be used to eliminate all its progeny: if the lower bound of a node exceeds the value of an already known solution then it can be asserted that the global optimal solution cannot be contained in the sub- Solution set represented by this node. The search continues until all nodes are either scanned or eliminated (see Figure 5).

The optimal solution for placing the four containers in this example (Fig.5) is as follows:

- The container C1 must be placed in the P2 stack
- The container C2 must be placed in the P1 stack
- The container C3 must be placed in the P3 stack
- The container C4 must be placed in the P4 stack

The investment cost in this case is 13 (the sum of the various investment costs).

Figure 5. The tree structure generated until the optimal solution is obtained

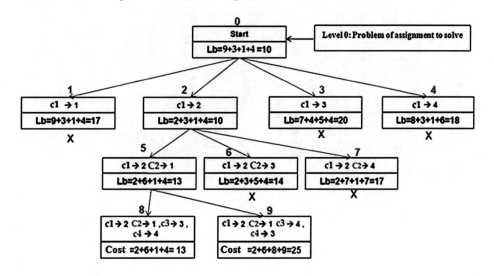

DISCUSSION OF RESULTS

This method uses a function that allows to fix a lower bound (according to the problem treated) in order to evaluate some solutions to either exclude them or to maintain them as potential solutions. Of course, the performance of the Branch and Bound method depends, among other things, on the quality of this function (its ability to exclude partial solutions as soon as possible).

The solution given by the Branch and Bound algorithm is better than that of a random solution where containers are classified according to their arrival in the storage areas without taking into account the constraints treated in this work (type, distance, etc.). The solution proposed this chapter makes it possible to identify the best available location in the storage area (stack) instead of randomly assigning the container.

COMPARATIVE ANALYSIS

The result obtained is a consequence of an initial configuration duly identified with respect to the environment of a maritime transport network in its storage part.

The optimization algorithm Branch and Bound allowed us to find optimal locations, which induced a reduced cost of container storage, the authors carried out a comparative study between the three algorithms: Branch and Bound (Yachba, 2017), genetic algorithm (Yachba et al., 2016) and the ant colony algorithm . The experimental results illustrated in Figure 6 are obtained.

In the latter, the X axis represents the number of iterations and the Y axis represents the execution time of the three algorithms in units of time (second).

The Brunch and Bound algorithm is an exact algorithm, but the comparison is interesting. The experimental results related to the execution time of the proposed algorithms show that the three algo-

Figure 6. Comparative study of the three algorithms

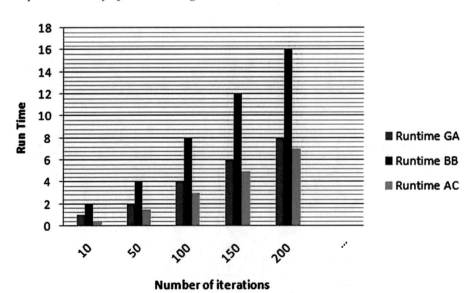

rithms increase as a function of the number of iterations. The genetic algorithm (AG) and the ant colony (AC) are faster than the Brunch and Bound (BB) algorithm, but a better solution can be expected. The proposed solution (Branch and Bound) identifies the best available location in the storage area (stack).

Of all the scenarios the authors examined, the ant colony and the genetic algorithm always find the solution faster than the Brunch and Bound algorithm. However, all three algorithms converge towards a solution.

The ant colony algorithm can be a good solution to solve a problem both with respect to the time and quality of solutions. However, its use must be conditioned by certain characteristics of the problem. For example:

1. Number of important solutions: the performances of the ants colony compared to the classical algorithms are more significant when the spaces of research are important. Indeed, for a confined space, it may be safer to explore this space exhaustively in order to obtain the optimal solution in a time that will remain completely correct.
2. When the users prefers to have a relatively quick solution rather than having the optimal solution in an indefinite time.

Branch and bound is preferred when the user wants a solution with a good quality, it makes the journey of all the space of solutions in order to find the best solution it is for this it takes much more time if compared with the genetic algorithm or the ant colony algorithm.

CONCLUSION AND PERSPECTIVES

In this chapter, the authors presented the steps for the realization of the proposal. The authors proposed an optimization model. Indeed, the result is the fruit of an initial configuration duly identified in relation to the environment of a marine transportation network in the storage part. A calculation of distances matrices representing an entry for the Branch and Bound algorithm which gives the best containers locations with the least cost.

The authors aim as appraisals of the work to implement other algorithms and complete the comparative study of the results. Hybridization with other algorithms to increase the number of factors which are taken into account and the use of simulation software to simulate the different movements in a seaport.

REFERENCES

Belayachi, N., Yachba, K., Gelareh, S., & Bouamrane, K. (2017). Storage the logistic of empty containers' return in the liner-shipping network. *Tansport and Telecommunication Journal*, *18*(3), 207–219.

Chebli, K. (2011). Optimisation des mouvements des conteneurs dans un terminal maritime, mémoire présenté en vue de l'obtention du diplôme de maîtrise des sciences appliquées (Génie Industriel). École polytechnique de Montréal, Canada.

Dkhil, H. (2015). *Optimisation des systèmes de stockage de conteneurs dans les terminaux maritimes automatisés* (Doctoral thesis). Mathématiques générales [math.GM], Université du Havre.

Dubreuil, J. (2008). La logistique des terminaux portuaires de conteneurs, Centre interuniversitaire de recherche sur les réseaux d'entreprise. Mémoire, Centre Universitaire de Recherche sur les Réseaux d'Entreprise la Logistique et Transport, Montréal, Canada.

Hamdadou, D., & Bouamrane, K. (2007). A Multicriterion SDSS for the Space Process Control: Towards a Hybrid Approach, MICAI 2007. *Advances in Artificial Intelligence*, *1611*(3349), 139–150.

Kefi, G. M. (2008). *Optimisation Heuristique Distribuée du Problème de Stockage de Conteneurs dans un Port* (Doctoral thesis). l'Ecole Centrale de Lille, France.

Kim, K., & Kim, H. (1997). A routing algorithm for a single transfer crane to load export containers onto a containership. *Computers & Industrial Engineering*, *33*(3-4), 673–676. doi:10.1016/S0360-8352(97)00219-2

Korbaa, O., & Yim. (2004). Container Assignment to stock in a fluvial port. *Proceedings of The International Conference on Systems, Man and Cybernetics*. doi:10.1109/ICSMC.2004.1401369

Matignon, L. (2013). *UML: Unified Modeling Language, Diagrammes dynamiques*. Lyon: Université Claude Bernard.

Murty, K. G., Liu, J., Wan, Y. W., & Linn, R. (2005). A decision support system for operations in a container shipping terminal. *Decision Support Systems*, *39*(3), 309–332. doi:10.1016/j.dss.2003.11.002

Ndèye, F. N. (2014). A Branch-and-Cut Algorithm to Solve the Container Storage Problem. In *Proceedings of The Ninth International Conference on Systems*. University of Le Havre.

Peng, D. T., Shin, K. G., & Abdezaher, T. F. (1997). Assignment and Scheduling communicating periodic tasks in distributed real time systems. *Software Engineering*, *23*(12), 745–758. doi:10.1109/32.637388

Stephen, B., Arpita, G., & Alessandro, M. (2003). *Branch and Bound Methods*. Notes for EE392o, Stanford University. Available from: https://web.stanford.edu/class/ee364b/lectures/bb_slides.pdf

Yachba, K. (2017). *Vers une contribution dans le transport maritime de marchandises: Optimisation de placement des conteneurs dans un port maritime* (PhD thesis). Computer Science Department, University of Oran1 Ahmed Benbella.

Yachba, K., Bouamrane, K., & Gelareh, S. (2015). Containers storage optimization in a container terminal using a multimethod multi-level approach. *Proceedings of The 45th International Conference on Computers & Industrial Engineering (CIE45)*.

Yachba, K., Gelareh, S., & Bouamrane, K. (2016). Storage management of hazardous containers using the genetic algorithm. *Transport and Telecommunication Journal*, *17*(4), 371–383. doi:10.1515/ttj-2016-0033

Chapter 9
A Discrete Black Hole Optimization Algorithm for Efficient Community Detection in Social Networks

Mohamed Guendouz
Dr. Moulay Tahar University of Saida, Algeria

ABSTRACT

In recent years, social networks analysis has attracted the attention of many researchers. Community detection is one of the highly studied problems in this field. It is considered an NP-hard problem, and several algorithms have been proposed to solve this problem. In this chapter, the authors present a new algorithm for community detection in social networks based on the Black Hole optimization algorithm. The authors use the modularity density evaluation measure as a function to maximize. They also propose the enhancement of the algorithm by using two new strategies: initialization and evolution. The proposed algorithm has been tested on famous synthetic and real-world networks; experimental results compared with three known algorithms show the effectiveness of using this algorithm for community detection in social networks.

INTRODUCTION

In last years, the use of online social networks has increased significantly due to the increasing use of Internet in general and the large availability of various kinds of connected devices such as: desktop computers, laptops and smartphones. Every day millions of people connect to social networking websites to communicate with each other and to share information, which made these websites very popular among others, Facebook and Twitter are the most famous ones. Facebook which was created in 2008 has now more than one billion active users from around the world, this huge number of users makes it the most popular social networking website in the world. Twitter known as the first microblogging website created earlier in 2006 has now more than 200 million active user. The huge amount of data and information shared between people on these websites has made social networks analysis a very important research field.

DOI: 10.4018/978-1-5225-3004-6.ch009

Social Networks are generally represented by graphs where nodes represent individuals and edges represent the relation between them, for example, in Facebook individuals are people and the relation between them is friendship. A social network is usually found to be grouped into a set of interconnected groups which means that individuals who are very similar between them have strong possibility to be in a same group, these groups are generally known as communities, one can classify communities into two types: Explicit and Implicit ones (Kadushin, 2012). In an explicit community members know that they belong to it and nonmembers know who its members are, Facebook groups are famous example of this type of communities where members can post messages and images, comment on other's posts and see activities of other people. In the contrary, an implicit community is a community where individuals interact with each other in a form of unknown connections which means that members of such communities do not know that there is a community and that they are members of it, for example people who use same hashtags in their tweets or follow the same celebrities in Twitter form implicit communities. In social networks, researchers are typically interested in finding implicit communities since explicit ones are already known and identified; this task is known as community detection or community discovery.

Community detection is defined as the process of identifying interconnected groups also known as clusters or partitions in a network, it assigns each individual in the network to his/her suitable group. Community detection algorithms are often provided with a graph $G\left(V, E\right)$ where nodes $\left(V\right)$ represent individuals and edges $\left(E\right)$ represent relations between individual, Formally, the task of community detection is to find a set of communities $\left\{C_i\right\}_{i=1}^{n}$ in G such that $U_{i=1}^{n}C_i \subseteq V$. Community detection algorithms are not specific only to detect communities inside social networks, they have many applications in different domains such us: Biology (Girvan & Newman, 2002), Social (Lozano et al., 2007) and Communications (Faloutsos et al., 1999). In fact, they can be applied to any complex problem that takes the form of a complex network; social networks are a specific type of complex networks. However, these algorithms are extensively used on social networks because of the important applications that can be done, for instance, community detection algorithms are widely used by marketing agencies to find potential clients among millions of people or to detect group of people who have the same food taste to recommend for them a special food product or may be a specific restaurant.

The problem of community detection in complex networks and especially in social networks has known in the last years an enormous interest by many researchers from different domains, several methods for community detection have been proposed and applied on many real world problems. One can classify these methods into different types (Fortunato, 2010); traditional methods can be classified into two groups: Graph Partitioning and Hierarchical Clustering. Graph Partitioning methods cluster a network into a predetermined number of communities, usually with equal size, these methods require the number and the size of communities before partitioning, the Kernighan-Lin algorithm proposed in (Suaris & Kedem, 1988) is one of the earliest methods for graph partitioning. Hierarchical Clustering methods cluster a network into groups of nodes based on their similarity which means that similar nodes are grouped into communities according to a similarity measure. Cosine similarity, Hamming distance and Jaccard (Singhal, 2001) index are frequently used measures. These methods are classified into two categories:

1. **Agglomerative Algorithms:** Initially each node represents a partition of its own, then partitions are successively merged until the desired network partition structure is obtained.

2. **Divisive Algorithms:** All nodes initially belong to one partition, and then the partition is divided into sub-partitions, which are successively divided into their own sub-partitions. This process continues until the desired network partition structure is obtained.

Hierarchical methods have the advantage of not requiring a predefined number and size of partitions. However, they do not provide a way to choose the better partition that represents the community structure of the network from those obtained by the procedure, a detailed classification of community detection algorithms can be found in (Fortunato, 2010). Other algorithms and methods will be discussed later in the next section.

Nature inspired algorithms have been extensively studied in the last years, various methods have been proposed to solve real world optimization problems in different fields, these algorithms which are inspired from nature represent nowadays an active research area and a popular research avenue for many researchers. Nature inspired algorithms can be inspired from evolutionary phenomena, collective behavior of creatures (swarm intelligence techniques), physical rules, and human-related concepts. Some of the recent and popular algorithms in each of these subclasses are as follows:

- **Evolutionary Techniques:** Genetic Algorithms (GA) (Holland, 1992), Genetic Programming (GP) (Koza, 1992), Biogeography-Based Optimization algorithm (BBO) (Simon, 2008), and Evolution Strategy (ES) (Dasgupta & Michalewicz, 2013).
- **Swarm Intelligence Techniques:** Ant Colony Optimization (ACO) (Dorigo et al., 2006), Particle Swarm Optimization (PSO) (Eberhart & Kennedy, 1995), and Artificial Bee Colony (ABC) algorithm (Basturk & Karaboga, 2006).
- **Physics-Based Techniques:** Gravitational Search Algorithm (GSA) (Rashedi et al., 2009) and Black Hole (BH) (Hatamlou, 2013).
- **Human-Related Techniques:** League Championship Algorithm (LCA) (Kashan, 2014), Mine Blast Algorithm (MBA) (Sadollah et al., 2013), and Teaching-Learning-Based Optimization (TLBO) (Rao et al., 2011).

Nature inspired algorithms are known for their efficiency in solving optimization problems, they have been applied on many problems like: Data Mining (Rana et al., 2011; Yeh, 2012), Information Retrieval (Alloui et al., 2015; Joshi & Srivastava, 2013), Engineering (Fox et al., 2007). The Black Hole Algorithm is one of the latest proposed nature-inspired metaheuristic optimization algorithms; this algorithm inspired from the natural phenomenon of black holes in the space was originally proposed by Hatamlou in (Hatamlou, 2013). Since its first apparition, the Black Hole algorithm has taken the attention of many researchers in many fields of computer sciences and engineering, it was successfully applied on many real world problems such as: Data Clustering by the original author, Job Scheduling on Parallel Machines (). Optimal power flow (Bouchekara, 2014), Engineering (Heidari & Abbaspour, 2014; Lenin et al., 2014; Ghaffarzadeh & Heydari, 2015; Bouchekara, 2013).

The effectiveness of the Black Hole algorithm in solving many optimization problems has influenced the authors to propose in this paper a discrete variant of the original algorithm for solving the problem of community detection in social networks, the essential aim of the authors is to investigate the capabilities of this algorithm in solving this problem, their main contributions in this paper are as follows:

Figure 1. Classification of nature inspired metaheuristic algorithms

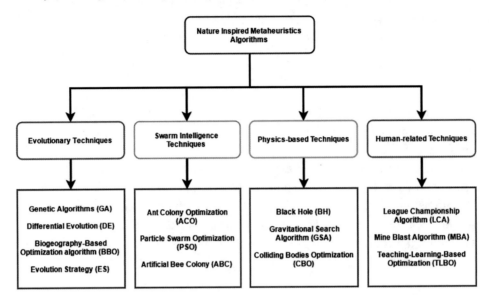

- They propose a new discrete variant of the Black Hole algorithm to solve community detection problem.
- They introduce a new population initialization strategy.
- They introduce a new evolution operator based on the label propagation strategy to enhance algorithm results and speed up its convergence.
- They test their proposed algorithm on synthetic and real world networks to show their algorithm's performance.

The rest of this paper is organized as follows: Section 2 reviews and discusses some popular methods for community detection proposed in literature. Section 3 defines the problem of community detection as an optimization problem. Section 4 gives an overview of the Black Hole algorithm. Section 5 shows the methodology of the proposed algorithm. Section 6 reports and discusses the results of performed experiments on a synthetic network benchmark as well on some real world networks. Section 7 concludes the paper.

LITERATURE REVIEW

Community detection in complex networks can be a difficult computational task because communities or groups have different sizes and their number is usually unknown, in fact it is considered as an NP-hard problem (Fortunato, 2010). Even with these difficulties several methods have been proposed to deal with this particular problem. The Girvan-Newman algorithm proposed in (Girvan & Newman, 2002; Newman & Girvan, 2004; Newman, 2004) is one of the popular methods; this algorithm is classified under Divisive algorithms methods. Divisive algorithms identify communities in graphs by detection edges that connect vertices of different communities and remove them, so that the clusters get disconnected from each other. The essential task in this type of algorithms is how to detect the intercommunity edges; in the Girvan-Newman algorithm authors propose the edge centrality to measure the importance of edges in the graph, the edge with the highest centrality value is removed. The steps of the algorithm are as follows:

1. Computation of the centrality for all edges;
2. Removal of edge with largest centrality: in case of ties with other edges, one of them is picked at random;
3. Recalculation of centralities on the running graph;
4. Iteration of the cycle from step 2.

The Girvan-Newman algorithm uses the edge betweenness measure to calculate the centrality value of edges, which is a variable expressing the number of shortest paths between all vertex pairs that run along the edge. Girvan and Newman proposed also the modularity as a stopping criterion for their proposed algorithm, the modularity (Q) is a measure that evaluates the quality of a network partition; Q is a real value in the range [−0.5, 1]. The larger the value of Q, the more accurate a network partition is and it is defined by the following equation:

$$Q = \frac{1}{2m} \sum_{ij} \left(A_{ij} - \frac{k_i k_j}{2m} \right) \delta(i, j) \tag{1}$$

where k_i and k_j are respectively degrees of nodes i and j, m is the total number of nodes in the network, $\delta(i, j) = 1$ if nodes i and j are in the same community, otherwise 0.

The modularity has been used later in many other methods as quality function to evaluate obtained results or as a fitness function to optimize for many optimization algorithms and especially bio-inspired metaheuristics algorithms. A greedy method proposed by Newman in (Newman, 2004b) was the first attempt to maximize the modularity; this method is an agglomerative hierarchical clustering method, where groups of vertices are successively joined to form larger communities such that modularity increases after the merging.

A fast greedy modularity optimization method was proposed by Clauset et al. in (Clauset et al., 2004) which is in fact a fast implementation of the original Girvan-Newman algorithm (), this algorithm has a complexity of *O(md log n)*, where *d* is the depth of the dendrogram which describes the successive partitions found during the execution of the algorithm. The greedy optimization of Clauset et al. is by far one of the few algorithms that can be used to estimate the modularity on large graphs; this algorithm is abbreviated by CNM acronym which represents the first characters of author's names.

Another famous method for community detection is the GA-Net algorithm proposed by Pizzuti (Pizzuti, 2008), this method uses Genetic Algorithms to detect communities, Pizzuti introduces a new evaluation metric called Community Score (CS) which was used as a fitness function for the proposed genetic algorithm, community score is a powerful metric to evaluate network portions. Pizzuti proposed also a modification to the variation operators to take into consideration only the actual correlations among the nodes therefore the search space for potential solutions is reasonably reduced, experiments on synthetic and real life networks show the capability of the method to successfully detect the network structure.

The great success of different evolutionary and swarm intelligence optimization algorithms on solving various real world problems has influenced many researchers to apply them to community detection problems. These methods try to optimize one or more fitness functions to detect the best network partition or a good one. One can classify these methods into two groups: single objective and multi objective optimization methods (Cai et al., 2016), while the first methods try to optimize one only fitness function, the second methods use a combination of two or more fitness functions. Many single objective bio-inspired metaheuristics optimization algorithms optimize the modularity (Q) to find the community structure with biggest Q value such as: Collaborative Evolutionary Algorithms (Gog et al., 2007), Genetic Algorithms (Tasgin et al., 2007; He et al., 2009), Particle Swarm Optimization (Xiaodong et al., 2008; Shi et al., 2009a) and Artificial Bee Colony (Naser et alshattnawi, 2014). However, the modularity has been found to have many disadvantages. First, Brandes et al. (Brandes et al., 2006) prove that the maximization of the modularity value is an NP-hard problem. Second, authors in (Guimera et al., 2004) found that large modularity value does not mean necessarily better community structure. Third, Fortunato and Barthelemy (Fortunato & Barthelemy, 2007) show the big disadvantage that modularity has a resolution limitation.

To overcome this limitation, the modularity density (denoted as D) has been proposed by Li et al. in (Li et al., 2008). The modularity density is a quantitative measure that uses the average modularity degree to evaluate a community structure, the larger the value of D, the more accurate a partition is. Authors proved also that maximizing modularity density can overcome the resolution limit of modularity. As a result, many algorithms have been proposed to find partitions in networks by maximizing the modularity density value including (Guoqiang & Xiaofang, 2010; Gong et al., 2011; Gong et al., 2012). A detailed survey on community detection using evolutionary algorithms can be found in (Cai et al., 2016).

COMMUNITY DETECTION PROBLEM

This section presents the problem of community detection and gives some definitions.

A network can be presented by a graph $G(V, E)$, where $V = \{v_1, v_2 \dots v_n\}$ represents vertices or nodes and $E \subseteq V \times V$ represents edges. The network structure can be presented by a $n \times n$ adjacency matrix A, each element A_{ij} can be either 1 or 0, $A_{ij} = 1$ if there is an edge e_{ij} between vertices v_i and v_j otherwise $A_{ij} = 0$. Assume that $S \subset G$ is a subgraph where node i belongs to it, $k_i^{in} = \sum_{i,j \in S} A_{ij}$ and $k_i^{out} = \sum_{i \in S, j \notin S} A_{ij}$ are respectively the internal and the external degree of node i, then the community of network represented by the subgraph S has usually the following property:

$$\sum_{i \in S} k_i^{in} > \sum_{i \in S} k_i^{out} \tag{2}$$

This property means that the sum of all degrees within the community is larger than the sum of all degrees toward the rest of the network.

The community detection problem can be formulated as a modularity (Q) maximization problem, the modularity (Q) was proposed by Newman in (Newman, 2006) to evaluate a community structure of a network. Q is mathematically described by the following equation:

$$Q = \frac{1}{2m} \sum_{ij} \left(A_{ij} - \frac{k_i k_j}{2m} \right) \delta(i,j) \tag{3}$$

where k_i and k_j are respectively degrees of nodes i and j, m is the total number of nodes in the network, $\delta(i,j) = 1$ if nodes i and j are in the same community, otherwise 0. Large Q value means better community structure, otherwise the structure is more ambiguous. Li (Gong et al., 2011) proposes another mathematical form for writing the modularity, it is described as follows:

$$Q = \sum_{i=1}^{N} \left[\frac{L(V_i, V_i)}{L(V,V)} - \left(\frac{L(V_i, V)}{L(V,V)} \right)^2 \right] \tag{4}$$

where N is the number of communities, $L(V_n, V_m) = \sum_{i \in V_n, j \in V_m} A_{ij}$, $L(V,V) = 2m$ and $L(V_i, V) = \sum_{j \in V_i, k \in V} Ajk$

The modularity has been used in many community detection methods as an objective function to maximize or as evaluation criterion. Until, when Fortunato and Barthelemy (Fortunato & Barthelemy, 2007) prove that the modularity has a resolution limitation, to overcome this limitation Li et al. (Gong et al., 2011) propose the modularity density (D) which is based on the average modularity degree, it is defined as follows:

$$D = \sum_{i=1}^{N} \frac{L(V_i, V_i) - L(V_i, \bar{V})}{|V_i|} \tag{5}$$

where $\dfrac{L(V_i, V_i)}{|V_i|}$ and $\dfrac{L(V_i, \bar{V})}{|V_i|}$ represent the average internal and external degrees of the i th community, D aims to maximize the internal degree and minimize the external degree of the community structure.

In this paper the authors propose a new method for detecting communities in complex networks based on the Black Holes algorithm by maximizing the value of modularity density (D).

BLACK HOLE ALGORITHM OVERVIEW

The Black Hole Algorithm (BHA) is a nature inspired metaheuristic optimization algorithm proposed originally by Hatamlou in (Hatamlou, 2013) to solve the problem of data clustering, this algorithm is inspired from the phenomenon of black holes in universe, a black hole is a region in the space with a high gravitational force that appears when a huge star collapses. The gravitational force of black holes is too high that no object can escape from it even the light, the surface around a black hole is a sphere shape known as the event horizon, every object that acroases the event horizon will be swallowed by the black hole and disappears. The event horizon radius is called the Schwarzschild radius, at this radius, the escape speed is equal to the speed of light and nothing can escape from within the event horizon because nothing can go faster than light. The Schwarzschild radius is calculated by the following equation:

$$R = \frac{2GM}{c^2}$$
(6)

where G is the gravitational constant, M is the mass of the black hole, and c is the speed of light, these are the physical characteristics of black holes that have been used to formulate the mathematical model of the algorithm.

The Black Hole algorithm shares many features with other population-based methods like PSO where the first phase consists in the generation and the distribution of a population of random candidate solutions in the search space, in the next phase the algorithm evolves this population towards the optimal solution by using some procedures. These procedures change from one algorithm to another, they are very important since they are responsible for exploring the search space to find better candidate solutions. The Black Hole algorithm uses a particular displacement operator to evolve its population of candidate solutions, at each iteration, the algorithm moves all the candidates – stars – towards the best candidate – the black hole – and each candidate solution that enters the event horizon of the black hole is replaced by a new randomly generated one, this operator is defined as follows:

$$X_i(t+1) = X_i(t+1) + rand \times \left(X_{BH} - X_i(t) \right), i = 1 \ldots N$$
(7)

where $X_i(t)$ and $X_i(t+1)$ are the locations of the ith star at iterations t and $t+1$, respectively. X_{BH} is the location of the black hole in the search space, rand is a random number in the interval [0,1]. N is the number of stars (candidate solutions). The steps of the Black Hole algorithm are summarized as follows:

- Initialize a population of stars with random locations in the search space

Loop

- For each star, evaluate the objective function
- Select the best star that has the best fitness value as the black hole
- Change the location of each star according to Eq.(3)
- If a star reaches a location with lower cost than the black hole, exchange their locations
- If a star crosses the event horizon of the black hole, replace it with a new star in a random location in the search space
- If a termination criterion (a maximum number of iterations or a sufficiently good fitness) is met, exit the loop

End loop

THE PROPOSED DISCRETE BLACK HOLE ALGORITHM

In this section the authors present their proposed discrete variant of the Black Hole algorithm, they illustrate the encoding schema used to represent solutions, then they give the objective function – the fitness function – used to evaluate each solution, after that they present their proposed initialization strategy used by the algorithm to initialize the first population of solutions, finally they present the mutation operator.

Individual Encoding

In community detection literature there are two famous encoding schemas: Locus-based and String-based schemas (Cai et al., 2016). In the two schemas individuals are represented by a vector of N positions where N is equal to the size of the network – number of nodes –, in locus-based representation schema each position in the vector corresponds to a node in the network, and each position i can takes an arbitrary j value in the range {1, 2...n} which means a link between node i and j existing in the corresponding graph, this also means that nodes i and j might be in the same community in the network. Although this encoding schema takes the advantage of network structure information but it has some drawbacks such as the difficulty of designing mutation and evolution operations.

In string-based representation schema each position in the vector is an integer value in the range {1, 2...m} where m is the number of communities in the network, each position i takes a j value, this means that node i is in the community j – node i is in the cluster labeled by j –. Formally, this encoding schema is defined as follows: assume that X_i is an individual and X_i^k is its kth position then X_i^k represents the community's label of node k in the network denoted by $L(k)$. For example, if $X_i^1 = X_i^3 = 1$ then nodes 1 and 3 are in the same community labeled by 1, we write $L(1) = L(3) = 1$.

The string-based encoding schema has many advantages such as: the number of communities is automatically determined and it is equal the number of unique labels, it can provide great convenience to the diversity promotion strategies and it is easier to code and decode. These advantages have influenced the authors in this paper to use the string-based encoding schema.

An illustrative example of the solution encoding and corresponding network is shown in Figure 3. As indicated by Figure 3(a) the network consists of six nodes numbered from 1 to 6, a possible optimal solution is given in Figure 3(b), nodes 1 to 4 are clustered into the first community labeled by 1 while nodes 5 and 6 are in the second community labeled by 2, this solution is translated in the community structure shown in Figure 3(c).

Objective Function

In this paper the authors use the modularity density (D) evaluation criterion as a fitness function to maximize for their proposed algorithm, the modularity density was proposed by Li et al. (Gong et al., 2011) in the goal of trying, the authors have already discussed this measure in details in Section 3.

Figure 2. An illustrative example of the string-based encoding schema: (a) network graph; (b) individual encoding; (c) network community structure

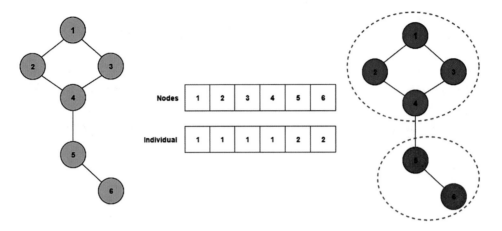

Population Initialization

In bio-inspired metaheuristics algorithms the initialization of the first population of candidate solutions plays an important role because this population will be used as a start point to search for other candidates, therefore a good initial population will generate better solutions and will speed up the convergence of the algorithm while searching in the search space. The Black Hole algorithm uses a random strategy to initialize the first population of individuals without taking into consideration any information about the specified problem, in this paper the authors propose a new initialization strategy to generate a better population of candidate solutions, the authors take the advantages of network linkage relations found in the graph and use them as rules for their proposed strategy. The proposed initialization strategy is summarized as follows:

1.   Generate a population of N stars.
2.   For each star X_i, $X_i^k = k$, each node will be in its own community.
3.   For each star, select a random node j, get node k from neighbors of j which has the highest degree. Assign all neighbors of k to the same community of k.

If the randomly chosen node j in Step 2 has no neighbors, select another one.

Evolution Phase

The evolution phase is an important step in bio-inspired metaheuristics algorithms, operations in this phase are responsible for generating the new positions of candidate solutions after each iteration, these operations have a great impact on the final optimal solution. In Black Hole algorithm this phase is achieved by the evolution operator defined in Equation 7, as we can see from this equation that the evolution is made in a random way. Another problem with this operator is the fact that it is designed for continuous search space while the proposed approach in this paper considers the community detection problem as a discrete optimization problem, therefore Equation cannot be used in the proposed algorithm, we must create a new evolution operator for discrete search space, this is done using a transfer function.

A transfer function is a specific function that receives in input a continuous value – real value – and returns a number in the range [0, 1] which represents a probability of changing positions. By using this technique we will convert the algorithm from a continuous one to a discrete one without affecting or modifying its structure. The authors choose the sigmoid function as a transfer function for their proposed algorithm, sigmoid function is defined as follows:

$$sigmoid\left(x\right) = \frac{1}{1 + \exp^{-x}} \tag{8}$$

The new proposed evolution strategy is then defined as follows:

$$X_i^k = \begin{cases} Nbest_k & if \quad random\left(0,1\right) < sigmoid\left(f_{BH} - f_i\right) \\ X_i^k & if \quad random\left(0,1\right) \geq sigmoid\left(f_{BH} - f_i\right) \end{cases} \tag{9}$$

where x_i^k is the current k^{th} position of star i, which is representing the current label of node k. $random\left(0,1\right)$ is a randomly generated number between 0 and 1. $Nbest_k$ is the most common used label by neighbors of node k. $sigmoid\left(f_{BH} - f_i\right)$ is the sigmoid value of the difference between the fitnees value of the Black Hole (f_{BH}) and the fitness value of the current star (f_i).

By using this strategy, positions of stars will be changed according to their distances from the black hole which is the current optimal solution; stars that are far from the black hole will have a great probability of changing their positions to new ones while the stars that are near the black hole will not change their positions.

An illustrative example of this new defined evolution operator for discrete Black Hole algorithm can be found in Figure 8. In this figure, $X_i\left(t\right)$ represents the current location of star X_i, the label of node 3 is 2 which means that it is in the community labeled by 2 with node 6, when updating the current star location to the new location $X_i\left(t+1\right)$, the label of node 3 is changed to 1, because, the label 1 is the mot frequently used one in its neighborhood nodes.

EXPERIMENTAL RESULTS AND DISCUSSION

This section reports and discusses obtained results from evaluating the proposed algorithm against other three famous algorithms: FTQ, CNM and GA-Net. The authors have tested each algorithm on synthetic and real world networks.

Fine-tuned modularity density (denoted as FTQ) is a fine-tuned community detection algorithm proposed by Chen et al. in (Chen et al., 2014), this algorithm iteratively improves the modularity density metric by splitting and merging the given network community structure. The CNM algorithm proposed by Clauset et al. in (Clauset et al., 2004) is a fast implementation of the Girvan-Newman approach. GA-

Figure 3. Illustrative example of the proposed evolution strategy

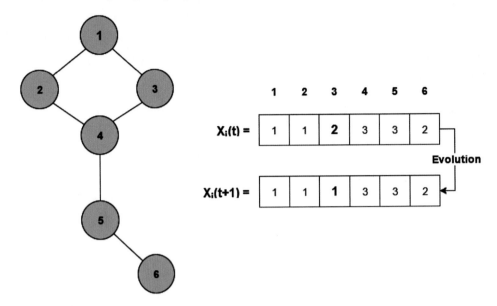

Net proposed by Pizzuti in (Pizzuti, 2008) is a genetic based optimization algorithm that optimizes the community score metric to detects communities.

Experimental Settings

The authors choose two evaluation metrics: the modularity (Q) and the Normalized Mutual Information (NMI) metrics to test their proposed algorithm against the other three ones, the modularity (Q) is a popular metric to evaluate network community structure, it has already discussed in previous sections.

The Normalized Mutual Information (Wu & Huberman, 2004) is a measure that calculates the similarity between two community detection results; the true known communities of the network and the detected ones, it is used when the network structure is known in advance. Suppose that A and B are two partitions of a network and C is the confusion matrix where C_{ij} is the number of nodes that are in both communities i and j of partitions A and B respectively. Then $NMI(A,B)$ is calculated as follows:

$$NMI(A,B) = \frac{-2\sum_{i=1}^{C_A}\sum_{j=1}^{C_B} C_{ij} \log\left(C_{ij}N / C_{i.}C_{.j}\right)}{\sum_{i=1}^{C_A}C_{i.} \log\left(C_{i.} / N\right) + \sum_{j=1}^{C_B}C_{.j} \log\left(C_{.j} / N\right)}$$

where $C_A\left(C_B\right)$ is the number of communities in partition $A(B)$, $C_{i.}\left(C_{.j}\right)$ is the sum of elements of C in row i (column j), and N is the number of nodes of the network. If $A = B$, then $NMI(A,B) = 1$; if A and B are totally different, then $NMI(A,B) = 0$.

The Black Hole algorithm does not take much parameters, just two parameters must be fiexd before executing it: the number of stars in the first population (N) and the number of itarations (I). In this paper the number of stars was fixed by 100 and the maximimum number of iterations was fixed to 1000.

Experiments on Synthetic Networks

The authors present here the obtained results from testing their proposed algorithm on a synthetic network benchmark, they used the GN Extended networks benchmark from (Lancichinetti et al., 2008) which is in fact an extension of the classical GN networks benchmark (Girvan & Newman, 2002). This benchmark consists of a computer generated network with 128 nodes grouped into four communities; each community has a size of 32 nodes with an average node degree equal to 16. GN Extended benchmark has a controlling parameter u which is a mixing parameter in the range of [0, 1] that controls the percentage of node links between the nodes of its own community and the total nodes in the network, When $\mu < 0.5$ the network has a strong community structure. In the contrarily, the community structure is ambiguous, and the detection of its structure will be difficult.

The authors have generated 10 GN Extended networks with mixing parameter u ranging from 0.05 to 0.5 and with an interval of 0.05. Figure shows obtained NMI values from different algorithms on generated benchmark networks with different mixing parameter values, we can see from this figure that FTQ, CNM, GA-Net and the proposed algorithm can successfully detect the valid network structure when the mixing parameter u is under 0.15. However, when u is greater than 0.2 the community structure of the network becomes more and more ambiguous and the community detection task becomes difficult, CNM algorithm first shows its weakness on detecting the true community structure and its detection capability decreases dramatically from u > 0.2. Then, the capability of FTQ and GA-Net algorithms on detecting network's communities decreases from u > 0.3, in contrary the proposed algorithm shows its dominance over other algorithms and its detection capacity is stable on the ten generated networks.

Figure reports the modularity (Q) values obtained from different algorithms on the same previously generated networks, as is shown in this figure, when u < 0.15 algorithms have approximately the same detection capability, this is observed from the modularity (Q) values of their detection results. But when the mixing parameter increasing, CNM, GA-Net and FTQ algorithms fail respectively and their detection capability becomes more and more weak, this figure clearly exhibit the advantage of our proposed algorithm against the other three algorithms.

Experiments on Real Worlds Networks

The authors present here results of evaluating their proposed algorithm on four popular real world networks described as follows:

1. **Zachary's Karate Club Network:** This is one of the most famous networks that has been widely used in literature. This network represents a social network of a karate club members studied by (Zachary, 1977), it consists of 34 nodes, each node represents a member of this club. However, during this study a dispute occurred between the administrator (node 34) and the instructor (node 1), which led to separate the club members into two smaller club groups, one group formed around the administrator contains 16 members, the rest 18 members formed a group around the instructor.

Figure 4. Obtained NMI values from different algorithms on the GN extended networks benchmark

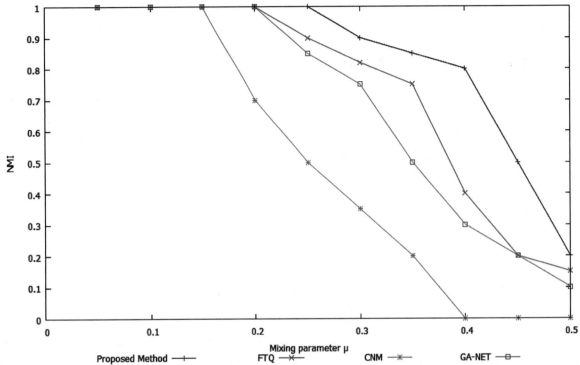

Figure 5. Obtained Q values from different algorithms on the GN extended networks benchmark

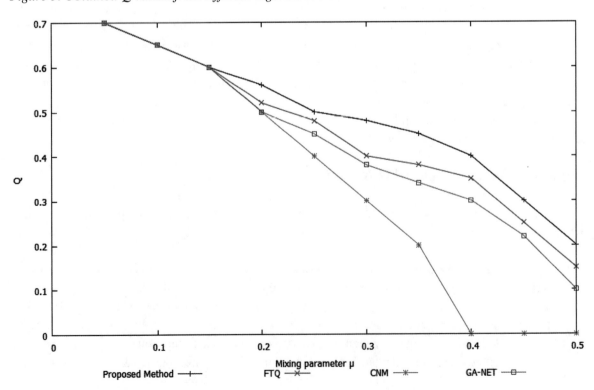

2. **Dolphins Social Network:** This network represents result from studying the behavior of 62 bottlenose dolphins among seven years in Doubtful Sound, New Zealand (Lusseau et al., 2003).
3. **Kreb's Politics Books:** Network which contains 105 US politics books collected by Krebs that have been sold by Amazon.com.
4. **American Football:** Which consists of 115 US Football team from 12 different regions of the USA playing a championship game between each other during the season of fall 2000, each link represents a game between two teams, a total 616 games have been played.

Table 1 shows statistics of used networks.

Table 2 shows obtained NMI and Q results from different algorithms on four real world networks: Zachary's Karate Club, Dolphins social network, Kreb's Politics Books and American Football network. As is reported in this table, better NMI and Q values are always obtained from the proposed algorithm on each real world network. However, the FTQ algorithm shows also a good capacity on detecting communities but the proposed algorithm outperforms it, for example: on Zachary's Karate Club the two algorithms have the same NMI value which is equal to 1 but there is a difference between the obtained Q values, FTQ has a Q value of 0.4202 and the proposed algorithm has a Q value of 0.4351 which greater than FTQ' value, this is due to the efficiency of the proposed initialization/evolution strategies. These results reported in Table 2 show plainly the effectiveness of the proposed algorithm on detecting communities on networks.

Table 1. Characteristics of used real world networks

Network	Nodes	Edges	True Communities
Zachary's Karate Club	34	78	2
Dolphins social network	62	159	2
Kreb's Politics Books	105	613	3
American Football	115	616	12

Table 2. Experiment result on real world networks from different algorithms

Network	Index	Proposed Algorithm	FTQ	CNM	GA-Net
Zachary's Karate Club	NMI	1	1	0.8	0.9
	Q	0.4351	0.4202	0.2851	0.4036
Dolphins social network	NMI	1	0.75	0.65	0.7
	Q	0.5218	0.4851	0.3613	0.4634
Kreb's Politics Books	NMI	0.8	0.62	0.50	0.55
	Q	0.5903	0.5058	0.3108	0.4508
American Football	NMI	0.92	0.54	0.43	0.48
	Q	0.6102	0.5695	0.3508	0.5369

Figure 6. The comparison of different initialization and evolution strategies on the NMI values

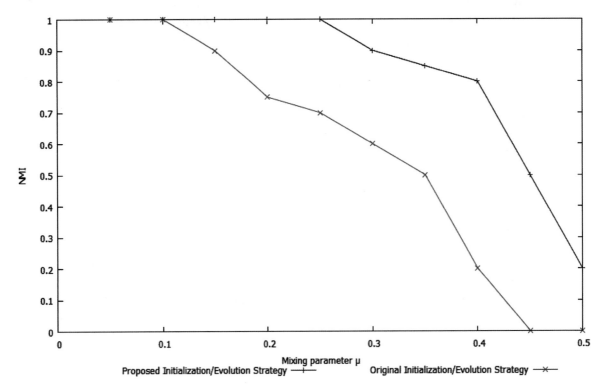

Figure 7. The comparison of different initialization and evolution strategies on the Q values

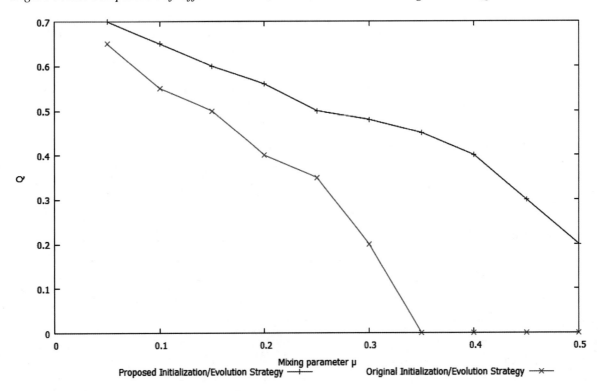

Impact of Proposed Initialization and Evolution Strategies

In order to show the performance of the proposed two strategies: the initialization and the evolution strategy on the quality of community detection results, the authors have tested two versions of their proposed algorithm, one by using the proposed initialization/evolution strategy and other using the random initialization/evolution strategies of the original Black Hole algorithm.

Figures 6 and 7 show respectively the obtained NMI and Q values from the two versions of the proposed algorithm, as is shown in Figure 6, the initialization and the evolution strategies have a great impact on final results, the proposed strategies give better results than the original ones. As seen from Figure 7, the same conclusion could be drawn from obtained Q values. These two figures show the effectiveness of the proposed initialization and evolution strategies on overall results and how can such strategies affect the performance of the Black Hole algorithm

CONCLUSION

In this paper, a discrete Black Hole algorithm was proposed to solve the problem of community detection in social networks by maximizing the modularity density measure (D), two strategies: initialization and evolution have been proposed by the authors to increase the capacity of the algorithm. The proposed algorithm has been tested on synthetic and real world networks, obtained results have been compared against three other famous algorithms, comparison shows the effectiveness of this algorithm on detecting true communities in networks.

REFERENCES

Alloui, T., Boussebough, I., & Chaoui, A. (2015). A Particle Swarm Optimization Algorithm for Web Information Retrieval: A Novel Approach. *International Journal of Intelligent Information Technologies*, *11*(3), 15–29. doi:10.4018/IJIIT.2015070102

Basturk, B., & Karaboga, D. (2006, May). An artificial bee colony (ABC) algorithm for numeric function optimization. In IEEE swarm intelligence symposium (Vol. 8, No. 1, pp. 687-697). IEEE.

Bouchekara, H. R. (2013). Optimal design of electromagnetic devices using a black-hole-based optimization technique. *IEEE Transactions on Magnetics*, *49*(12), 5709–5714. doi:10.1109/TMAG.2013.2277694

Bouchekara, H. R. E. H. (2014). Optimal power flow using black-hole-based optimization approach. *Applied Soft Computing*, *24*, 879–888. doi:10.1016/j.asoc.2014.08.056

Brandes, U., Delling, D., Gaertler, M., Görke, R., Hoefer, M., Nikoloski, Z., & Wagner, D. (2006). *Maximizing modularity is hard*. arXiv preprint physics/0608255

Cai, Q., Ma, L., Gong, M., & Tian, D. (2016). A survey on network community detection based on evolutionary computation. *International Journal of Bio-inspired Computation*, *8*(2), 84–98. doi:10.1504/IJBIC.2016.076329

Chen, M., Kuzmin, K., & Szymanski, B. K. (2014). Community detection via maximization of modularity and its variants. *IEEE Transactions on Computational Social Systems*, *1*(1), 46–65. doi:10.1109/TCSS.2014.2307458

Clauset, A., Newman, M. E., & Moore, C. (2004). Finding community structure in very large networks. *Physical Review. E*, *70*(6), 066111. doi:10.1103/PhysRevE.70.066111 PMID:15697438

Cuevas, E., Oliva, D., Zaldivar, D., Pérez-Cisneros, M., & Sossa, H. (2012). Circle detection using electro-magnetism optimization. *Information Sciences*, *182*(1), 40–55. doi:10.1016/j.ins.2010.12.024

Dasgupta, D., & Michalewicz, Z. (Eds.). (2013). *Evolutionary algorithms in engineering applications*. Springer Science & Business Media.

Dorigo, M., Birattari, M., & Stutzle, T. (2006). Ant colony optimization. *IEEE Computational Intelligence Magazine*, *1*(4), 28–39. doi:10.1109/MCI.2006.329691

Eberhart, R. C., & Kennedy, J. (1995, October). A new optimizer using particle swarm theory. In *Proceedings of the sixth international symposium on micro machine and human science* (Vol. 1, pp. 39-43). doi:10.1109/MHS.1995.494215

Faloutsos, M., Faloutsos, P., & Faloutsos, C. (1999, August). On power-law relationships of the internet topology. *Computer Communication Review*, *29*(4), 251–262. doi:10.1145/316194.316229

Fortunato, S. (2010). Community detection in graphs. *Physics Reports*, *486*(3), 75–174. doi:10.1016/j.physrep.2009.11.002

Fortunato, S., & Barthelemy, M. (2007). Resolution limit in community detection. *Proceedings of the National Academy of Sciences of the United States of America*, *104*(1), 36–41. doi:10.1073/pnas.0605965104 PMID:17190818

Fox, B., Xiang, W., & Lee, H. P. (2007). Industrial applications of the ant colony optimization algorithm. *International Journal of Advanced Manufacturing Technology*, *31*(7-8), 805–814. doi:10.1007/s00170-005-0254-z

Ghaffarzadeh, N., & Heydari, S. (2015). Optimal Coordination of Digital Overcurrent Relays using Black Hole Algorithm. *World Applied Programming*, *5*(2), 50–55.

Girvan, M., & Newman, M. E. (2002). Community structure in social and biological networks. *Proceedings of the National Academy of Sciences of the United States of America*, *99*(12), 7821–7826. doi:10.1073/pnas.122653799 PMID:12060727

Gog, A., Dumitrescu, D., & Hirsbrunner, B. (2007, September). Community detection in complex networks using collaborative evolutionary algorithms. In *European Conference on Artificial Life* (pp. 886-894). Springer Berlin Heidelberg. doi:10.1007/978-3-540-74913-4_89

Gong, M., Cai, Q., Li, Y., & Ma, J. (2012, June). An improved memetic algorithm for community detection in complex networks. In *2012 IEEE Congress on Evolutionary Computation* (pp. 1-8). IEEE.

Gong, M., Fu, B., Jiao, L., & Du, H. (2011). Memetic algorithm for community detection in networks. *Physical Review. E*, *84*(5), 056101. doi:10.1103/PhysRevE.84.056101 PMID:22181467

Guimera, R., Sales-Pardo, M., & Amaral, L. A. N. (2004). Modularity from fluctuations in random graphs and complex networks. *Physical Review. E, 70*(2), 025101. doi:10.1103/PhysRevE.70.025101 PMID:15447530

Guoqiang, C., & Xiaofang, G. (2010, December). A genetic algorithm based on modularity density for detecting community structure in complex networks. In *Computational Intelligence and Security (CIS), 2010 International Conference on* (pp. 151-154). IEEE. doi:10.1109/CIS.2010.40

Hatamlou, A. (2013). Black hole: A new heuristic optimization approach for data clustering. *Information Sciences, 222*, 175–184. doi:10.1016/j.ins.2012.08.023

He, D., Wang, Z., Yang, B., & Zhou, C. (2009, November). Genetic algorithm with ensemble learning for detecting community structure in complex networks. In *Computer Sciences and Convergence Information Technology, 2009. ICCIT'09. Fourth International Conference on* (pp. 702-707). IEEE. doi:10.1109/ICCIT.2009.189

Heidari, A. A., & Abbaspour, R. A. (2014). Improved black hole algorithm for efficient low observable UCAV path planning in constrained aerospace. *Advances in Computer Science: an International Journal, 3*(3), 87–92.

Holland, J. H. (1992). Genetic algorithms. *Scientific American, 267*(1), 66–72. doi:10.1038/scientificamerican0792-66

Holland, J. H., & Reitman, J. S. (1977). Cognitive systems based on adaptive algorithms. *ACM SIGART Bulletin*, (63), 49-49.

Joshi, M., & Srivastava, P. R. (2013). Query optimization: An intelligent hybrid approach using cuckoo and tabu search. *International Journal of Intelligent Information Technologies, 9*(1), 40–55. doi:10.4018/jiit.2013010103

Kadushin, C. (2012). *Understanding social networks: Theories, concepts, and findings*. OUP USA.

Karaboga, D., & Basturk, B. (2007). A powerful and efficient algorithm for numerical function optimization: Artificial bee colony (ABC) algorithm. *Journal of Global Optimization, 39*(3), 459–471. doi:10.1007/s10898-007-9149-x

Kashan, A. H. (2014). League Championship Algorithm (LCA): An algorithm for global optimization inspired by sport championships. *Applied Soft Computing, 16*, 171–200. doi:10.1016/j.asoc.2013.12.005

Koza, J. R. (1994). Genetic programming II: Automatic discovery of reusable subprograms. Cambridge, MA: Academic Press.

Lancichinetti, A., Fortunato, S., & Radicchi, F. (2008). Benchmark graphs for testing community detection algorithms. *Physical Review. E, 78*(4), 046110. doi:10.1103/PhysRevE.78.046110 PMID:18999496

Lenin, K., Reddy, B. R., & Kalavathi, M. S. (2014). Black Hole Algorithm for Solving Optimal Reactive Power Dispatch Problem. *International Journal of Research in Management, Science & Technology, 2*, 10-15.

Li, Z., Zhang, S., Wang, R. S., Zhang, X. S., & Chen, L. (2008). Quantitative function for community detection. *Physical Review. E, 77*(3), 036109. doi:10.1103/PhysRevE.77.036109 PMID:18517463

Lozano, S., Duch, J., & Arenas, A. (2007). Analysis of large social datasets by community detection. *The European Physical Journal. Special Topics, 143*(1), 257–259. doi:10.1140/epjst/e2007-00098-6

Lusseau, D., Schneider, K., Boisseau, O. J., Haase, P., Slooten, E., & Dawson, S. M. (2003). The bottlenose dolphin community of Doubtful Sound features a large proportion of long-lasting associations. *Behavioral Ecology and Sociobiology, 54*(4), 396–405. doi:10.1007/s00265-003-0651-y

Naser, A. M. A., & Alshattnawi, S. (2014). An Artificial Bee Colony (ABC) Algorithm for Efficient Partitioning of Social Networks. *International Journal of Intelligent Information Technologies, 10*(4), 24–39. doi:10.4018/ijiit.2014100102

Newman, M. E. (2004). Fast algorithm for detecting community structure in networks. *Physical Review. E, 69*(6), 066133. doi:10.1103/PhysRevE.69.066133 PMID:15244693

Newman, M. E. (2006). Modularity and community structure in networks. *Proceedings of the National Academy of Sciences of the United States of America, 103*(23), 8577–8582. doi:10.1073/pnas.0601602103 PMID:16723398

Newman, M. E., & Girvan, M. (2004). Finding and evaluating community structure in networks. *Physical Review. E, 69*(2), 026113. doi:10.1103/PhysRevE.69.026113 PMID:14995526

Pizzuti, C. (2008, September). Ga-net: A genetic algorithm for community detection in social networks. In *International Conference on Parallel Problem Solving from Nature* (pp. 1081-1090). Springer Berlin Heidelberg. doi:10.1007/978-3-540-87700-4_107

Rana, S., Jasola, S., & Kumar, R. (2011). A review on particle swarm optimization algorithms and their applications to data clustering. *Artificial Intelligence Review, 35*(3), 211–222. doi:10.1007/s10462-010-9191-9

Rao, R. V., Savsani, V. J., & Vakharia, D. P. (2011). Teaching–learning-based optimization: A novel method for constrained mechanical design optimization problems. *Computer Aided Design, 43*(3), 303–315. doi:10.1016/j.cad.2010.12.015

Rashedi, E., Nezamabadi-Pour, H., & Saryazdi, S. (2009). GSA: A gravitational search algorithm. *Information Sciences, 179*(13), 2232–2248. doi:10.1016/j.ins.2009.03.004

Sadollah, A., Bahreininejad, A., Eskandar, H., & Hamdi, M. (2013). Mine blast algorithm: A new population based algorithm for solving constrained engineering optimization problems. *Applied Soft Computing, 13*(5), 2592–2612. doi:10.1016/j.asoc.2012.11.026

Shi, Z., Liu, Y., & Liang, J. (2009, November). PSO-based community detection in complex networks. In *Knowledge Acquisition and Modeling, 2009. KAM'09. Second International Symposium on* (Vol. 3, pp. 114-119). IEEE.

Simon, D. (2008). Biogeography-based optimization. *IEEE Transactions on Evolutionary Computation, 12*(6), 702–713. doi:10.1109/TEVC.2008.919004

Singhal, A. (2001). Modern information retrieval: A brief overview. *IEEE Data Eng. Bull.*, *24*(4), 35–43.

Storn, R., & Price, K. (1997). Differential evolution–a simple and efficient heuristic for global optimization over continuous spaces. *Journal of Global Optimization*, *11*(4), 341–359. doi:10.1023/A:1008202821328

Suaris, P. R., & Kedem, G. (1988). An algorithm for quadrisection and its application to standard cell placement. *IEEE Transactions on Circuits and Systems*, *35*(3), 294–303. doi:10.1109/31.1742

Tasgin, M., Herdagdelen, A., & Bingol, H. (2007). *Community detection in complex networks using genetic algorithms.* arXiv preprint arXiv:0711.0491

Wu, F., & Huberman, B. A. (2004). Finding communities in linear time: A physics approach. *European Physical Journal. B, Condensed Matter and Complex Systems*, *38*(2), 331–338. doi:10.1140/epjb/e2004-00125-x

Xiaodong, D., Cunrui, W., Xiangdong, L., & Yanping, L. (2008, June). Web community detection model using particle swarm optimization. In *2008 IEEE Congress on Evolutionary Computation (IEEE World Congress on Computational Intelligence)* (pp. 1074-1079). IEEE. doi:10.1109/CEC.2008.4630930

Yeh, W. C. (2012). Novel swarm optimization for mining classification rules on thyroid gland data. *Information Sciences*, *197*, 65–76. doi:10.1016/j.ins.2012.02.009

Yin, H., Li, J., & Niu, Y. (2014). Detecting Local Communities within a Large Scale Social Network Using Mapreduce. *International Journal of Intelligent Information Technologies*, *10*(1), 57–76. doi:10.4018/ijiit.2014010104

Zachary, W. W. (1977). An information flow model for conflict and fission in small groups. *Journal of Anthropological Research*, *33*(4), 452–473. doi:10.1086/jar.33.4.3629752

Zhang, Y., & Li, X. (2014). Relative Superiority of Key Centrality Measures for Identifying Influencers on Social Media. *International Journal of Intelligent Information Technologies*, *10*(4), 1–23. doi:10.4018/ijiit.2014100101

Zhang, Y., Li, X., & Wang, T. W. (2013). Identifying influencers in online social networks: The role of tie strength. *International Journal of Intelligent Information Technologies*, *9*(1), 1–20. doi:10.4018/jiit.2013010101

Chapter 10
The Automatic Detection of Diabetes Based on Swarm of Fish

Reda Mohamed Hamou
Dr. Moulay Tahar University of Saida, Algeria

ABSTRACT

Diabetes is a major health problem and a disease that can be very dangerous in developing and developed countries, and its incidence is increasing dramatically. In this chapter, the authors propose a system of automatic detection of diabetes based on a bioinspired model called a swarm of fish (fish swarm or AFSA). AFSA (artificial fish swarm algorithm) represents one of the best methods of optimization among swarm intelligence algorithms. This algorithm is inspired by the collective, the movement of fish and their different social behaviors in order to achieve their objectives. There are several parameters to be adjusted in the AFSA model. The visual step is very significant, given that the fish artificial essentially moves according to this parameter. Large parameter values increase the capacity of the global search algorithm, while small values tend to improve local search capability. This algorithm has many advantages, including high speed convergence, flexibility, and high accuracy. In this chapter, the authors evaluate their model of AFSA for the purpose of automatic detection of diabetes.

INTRODUCTION AND PROBLEM

The diagnosis of diabetes disease via an abstract interpretation of the data is an important classification problem. Diabetes occurs when the body is unable to produce or respond properly to the insulin that is needed to regulate glucose. Diabetes is not only a factor contributing to the

Heart disease, but also increases the risk of developing kidney disease, blindness, nerve damage, and damage to blood vessels. Statistics show that more than 80% of people with diabetes die from some form of heart disease or blood vessels.

Currently, there is no cure for diabetes; However, it can be controlled by insulin injection, changing eating habits, and doing physical exercises.

DOI: 10.4018/978-1-5225-3004-6.ch010

Meta-heuristics and biomimetic methods are a class of methods that provide good quality solutions to difficult problems for which there are no more efficient conventional methods. They are generally stochastic, iterative methods that progress.

Towards an optimum by evaluating an objective function. Poisson Swarm Optimization is a branch of swarm intelligence (a population-based meta-heuristic), inspired by the behavior of real Fish.

The AFSA algorithm is well suited for discrete optimization problems such as quadratic assignment problems, bioinformatics and data mining.

Data from the dataset is abstract data for the machine. What do they tell us about this data? And what is the reliability of the information derived from them? Such is the problematic of this research work as well as to see how Meta heuristics contributes to the improvement of data mining tasks. More precisely, an NP-difficult optimization problem is solved which is the detection of diabetic disease and improve the supervised classification (an acceptable (high) accuracy rate) of the data mining, using the Bio-inspired and Meta heuristics.

A promising solution is to use an inspired Bio Method (AFSA) that assigns a category to a data set, classifies these data into two different classes, the first class contains data from the sick and the second contains data from the normal people.

Objective of Work

The aim of this work is to propose a Bioinspired technique for the resolution of a Data Mining task capable of giving good results compared to others obtained by other classical classification methods.

There are other works that use this algorithm but none of them is used for classification. That is the advantage of our work.

We used a Bioinspired method. Its principle is to learn how to organize elements in predefined categories according to their characteristics.

Knowing how to automatically assign a category to an item can be very useful and calculate validation measures by trying to improve those measures obtained by classical classification algorithms.

In this chapter we will evaluate our AFSA approach with the aim of Automatic detection of diabetes.

The AFSA Approach (Artificial Fish Swarm Algorithm)

AFSA is an optimization algorithm that simulates the behavior of swarms of fish, such as hunting for food and movement. For example, the position of most fish in a basin is typically the position at which most foodstuffs can be obtained. There are three main stages in AFSA, which are tracking, moving in swarm, and feeding. In the AFSA, these three steps are repeated in order to determine the optimal solution. Similar to other bioinspired algorithms, AFSA is used to determine the optimum or most satisfactory solution within a limited time. In the AFSA approach, the position of each fish is considered a solution, and each solution has a fitness value that is evaluated using the fitness function. The fitness function changes when different objectives are set.

Let us suppose that the state vector of the artichoke swarm is $X = (x_1, x_2,,, x_n)$ where $(x_1, x_2,,, x_n)$ is the state of the fish. The variable "Visual" is the visual distance, the artificial fish only activates in the inner radius of the circle to the length of the field of vision. The food concentration in the fish position is expressed as $y = f(x)$ where y is the value of the objective function. The distance between the fishes

Figure 1. The concept of vision of artificial fish

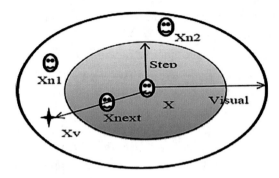

is d$_{ij}$ = |X$_i$-X$_j$|, i and j are of random fish. The variable "Step" is the maximum step of the artificial fish. α Is the degree of congestion factor.

Suppose that X$_v$ is the visual position at a given moment. X$_{next}$ is the new position. Then the movement procedure is defined as follows:

$$X_v = X_i + Visual * rand(), i \in \left[0,1\right]$$ (1)

$$X_{next} = X + \frac{X_v - X}{\left\|X_v - X\right\|} * Step * rand()$$ (2)

where rand () produces random numbers between 0 and 1. The basic behaviors of artificial fish are:

- **The Behavior of Food (Prey Behavior):** This is a basic biological behavior that tends to food. The state of artistic fish is Xi, select a state Xj in its random detection range. If Xj is greater than Xj, then move to Xj;

The state Xj is chosen randomly. Determine whether it must meet the requirement to complete the processes, repeated several times, if still the conditions of moving forward are not realized, moving a step at random.

$$X_j = x_i + Visual * rand()$$

If Y$_i$ <Y$_j$, then move a step towards this direction.

$$X_i^{t+1} = X_i^t + \frac{X_j - X_i^t}{\left\|X_j - X_i^t\right\|} * step * rand()$$

- **The Behavior of Swarm (Swarm Behavior):** Suppose the current state of artificial fish is X_i ($d_{i,j}$ <Visual) and n_f is the number of artificial fish, If $n_f < \delta$ Which indicates that the partners have more food and fewer people, if Y_c is better than Y_i, Then go to the front towards the center of the direction of the swarm, otherwise go back to the food behavior.

$$X_i^{t+1} = X_i^t + \frac{X_j - X_i^t}{\left\| X_c - X_i^t \right\|} * step * rand()$$

- **The Behavior of Follow (Follow Behavior):** Given the state of artificial fish is X_i, explore its optimal X_{max} state of visual neighbors, the number of Partners of X_{max} is n_f, If nf < δ Indicates that it is near the distance in addition to food and not too crowded, go farther to the front of the X_{max} position; Otherwise do a food search process.

$$X_i^{t+1} = X_i^t + \frac{X_j - X_i^t}{\left\| X_j - X_i^t \right\|} * step * rand()$$

The AFSA Process Proposed in this Work

fi represents the fish; And Ci represents the center of the fish. The process is as follows:

1. **Initialization:** Encode the optimization problem to be integrated with AFSA, create the fitness function and the initial fish randomly, and include the position and parameters.
2. **Evaluation:** Use the fitness function to assess the fitness of each fish.
3. **Movement of Fish:** Treat movements Follow, swarm and feed for all fish and determine the optimal solution.

To Follow

At this stage, the f_i are compared with neighboring fish on the basis of fitness function value; If the optimum shape of its neighbor is higher and the world's degree of this fish does not exceed the maximum crowded degree, then f_i moves to the position of the neighboring fish, indicating that the subset function of f_i is replaced by the subspace function of the neighboring fish. This also indicates that the tracking step is complete. If step Follow-up fails, then implement swarm stage or follow the next fish.

Swarm

In this step, the f_i are compared with the fitness value of their own C_i; If the fitness value of C_i is greater and the degree of world of f_i is not greater than the degree Maximum of world, then the f_i moves to the C_i; This indicates that the functionality of the subset of f_i is replaced by the C_i and here the step is completed. If the swarm step fails, implement the food step for the next fish.

Food

At this stage, the fish has nothing to predict that the food is in the middle of the swarm, whereas it is moving towards the middle, which means taking the characteristics of the fish from the middle of the swarm, Whose feed is finished. If the feed step fails, the algorithm repeats this step until the number repeated reaches the maximum number of tests.

The AFSA process is summarized as follows

```
Initialize the swarm of fish
while (i = 0; i <NUM of fish; i ++)
Calculate FITNESS of fish
DO follow step
IF (follow failure) THEN
DO step swarm
IF (swarm failure) THEN
DO step food
IF (follow failure) THEN
END
END
EndFor
EndWhile
Optimal solution output
```

The AFSA Parameters

- **The Distance:** The distance between f_i and f_j is obtained by the formula below. These two fish have the same number of functionalities k, and if the first characteristic of f_i is 0 and the first characteristic of f_j 0, then the distance between f_i and f_j will remain the same. But if the first characteristic of f_i is different from the first characteristic of f_j then a distance between will be plus one. The distance between two fishes is the sum of the differences of each function:

$$Distance\left(F_i, F_j\right) = \sum_{k=1}^{K} \left\| F_i\left(k\right) - F_j\left(k\right) \right\|$$

The visibility of a fish and also the maximum distance that this fish can move. In other words, it is the maximum number of features that one can choose.

- **The Neighbor:** The neighbor of f_i, is any fish that is in the vision of f_i; If the distance between f_k and f_i is greater than 0 and less than or equal to the vision, f_k is the neighbor of f_i. It is obtained by the following formula:

$$Neighbor\left(F_i\right) = \left\{F_k \mid 0 < distance\left(F_i, F_k\right) \le vision\right\}$$

The center of f_i is the center of the neighbor of f_i. It can be considered as a fish; The center function is obtained by the formula below; If the function of more than half the neighbors of f_i are equal to 0, then the center of f_i will be 0, and vice versa:

$$F_{center}\left(i\right) = \left\{0 \sum_{k=1}^{K} F_k\left(i\right) < \frac{k}{2} 1 \sum_{k=1}^{K} F_k\left(i\right) \ge \frac{k}{2}\right.$$

- **The Degree of Congestion:** The degree of congestion of the f_i is the parameter which represents the position density of f_i. It is obtained by the following formula.

$$Crowded\ Degree\left(F_i\right) = \frac{Neighbours\ of\ F_i}{Total\ number\ of\ fishes}$$

RESULTS AND DISCUSSIONS

The Dataset Used

In this study, we use the UCI dataset i.a set of input data By Black CL [Blake C. L., 1998]. This database contains 768 samples, each sample with 8 characteristics that represent eight clinical outcomes:

1. Number of times pregnant.
2. plasma glucose concentration at 2 hours in an oral glucose tolerance test.
3. Diastolic blood pressure (mm Hg).

Figure 2. The initiation step of AFSA

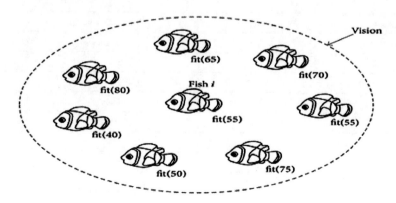

Figure 3. The follow step of AFSA

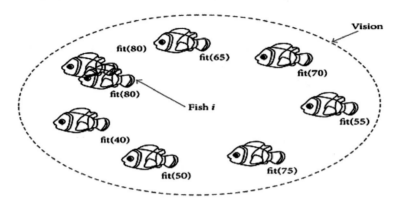

4.   Thick fold thickness of the triceps (mm).
5.   serum insulin at 2 hours (mu U / ml).
6.   Body mass index BMI (kg = m2).
7.   Diabetes pedigree function.
8.   Age.

These characteristics are detailed in the following table. All patients in this data set are women aged at least 21 years old and living near Phoenix, Arizona, United States. The binary target variable takes values '0' or '1'. While '1' means a positive test for diabetes, '0' is a negative test. There are 268 cases in class '1' and 500 cases in class '0'.

Distance Used in Model

In our model, a single distance was used entitled Euclidian distance. In a hyperspace, n-dimensional space, the Euclidian distance between $X(x_1,x_2,....,x_n)$ and $Y(y_1,y_2,....,y_n)$ is:

Table 1. Brief statistical analysis of the dataset

Characteristics	Average	Standard Deviation	Min/Max
1	3.8	3.4	0/17
2	120.9	32.0	0/199
3	69.1	19.4	0/122
4	20.5	16.0	0/99
5	79.8	115.2	0/846
6	32.0	7.9	0/67.1
7	0.5	0.3	0.078/2.42
8	33.2	11.8	21/81

Table 2. Biological model vs. artificial model

Biological Model	Artificial Model
Set of fish	Set of documents
Physical distance between fish	Euclidean distance between documents
Global visual threshold	The documents to be reached
Target search	Choice of place or class
Local visual threshold	Almost identical documents
Swarm step	Swarm step algorithm
To follow step	To follow step algorithm
Food step	Food step algorithm

$$d = \sqrt{\sum_{i=1}^{n} \left(x_i - y_i \right)^2}$$

Performance Measures of Classifiers

We consider here a simple classification problem for which we are interested in a single class C and we want to evaluate the system that tells us whether or not an instance can be associated with this class C.

This problem is a classification problem with two classes (C and not C noted: C '). If we can master this simple problem (bi-class), we can also master the validation measures of several classes or multi-class.

Contingency Matrix (Confusion Matrix)

To evaluate a classification system, we use a labeled corpus (learning corpus and even for the test) for which we know the true category of each connection or instance, and the result obtained by the classifier. For this corpus, we can construct the contingency matrix for each class, which provides four essentials information:

- **True Positive (VP):** A person who is sick and who has a positive test.
- **False Positive (FP):** A person who is not sick and who has a positive test.
- **False Negative (FN):** A person who is sick and who has a negative test.
- **True Negative (VN):** A person who is not ill and has a negative test.

Precision and Recall

Some evaluation principles are commonly used in the various fields. Performance in terms of classification is generally measured from two indicators traditionally used are recall and precision measurements. Initially they were designed for information retrieval systems, but subsequently the text classification community adopted them. Formally, for each class Ci, two probabilities are calculated which can be

Table 3. The contingency matrix

Category C$_i$		Judgment of the Expert	
		Normal	Abnormal
Judgment of the Classifier	Normal	VP$_i$	FP$_i$
	Abnormal	FN$_i$	VN$_i$

estimated from the corresponding contingency matrix, so these two measurements can be defined in the following way:

$$Recall\left(C_i\right) = \frac{Number\ of\ documents\ well\ classified\ in\ C_i}{Number\ of\ documents\ in\ class\ C_i}$$

$$R_i = \frac{VP_i}{VP_i + FN_i}$$

The recall being the proportion of documents correctly classified by the system in relation to all the documents of the Ci class.

The recall measures the ability of a classifier to detect correctly classified documents.

However, a classification system that would consider all documents as relevant would get a 100% recall. A strong or weak recall is not sufficient to evaluate the performance of a system. For this purpose, precision is defined.

$$P_i = \frac{VP_i}{VP_i + FP_i}$$

Precision is the proportion of documents correctly classified among those classified by the system in Ci.

Precision measures the ability of a classification system not to classify a document into a class, a document that is not. As it can also be interpreted by the conditional probability that a document chosen randomly in the class is well classified by the classifier. These two indicators Independently of each other, allow only one aspect of the classification system to be assessed: quality or quantity.

Success Rate and Error Rate

Accuracy rate (Accuracy rate) is a measure often used by the automated learning community. The success rate refers to the percentage of examples well classified by the classifier by cons the error rate refers to the percentage of misclassified examples. Both rates are estimated as Follows:

$$Accuracy = \frac{VP + VN}{VP + VN + FP + FN}$$

$$Error = \frac{VP + FN}{VP + VN + FP + FN}$$

Noise and Silence

The Noise (B) and the Silence (S) are respectively complementary notions of precision and recall.

Noise is the percentage of documents incorrectly associated with a class by the system; Silence is the percentage of documents to associate with a class incorrectly not classified by the system.

$$Noise = 1 - Precision = \frac{FP}{VP + FP}$$

$$Silence = 1 - Recall = \frac{FN}{VP + FN}$$

Rate of Fall and Specificity

$$Rate\,of\,fall = \frac{FP}{FP + VN}$$

$$Specificity = \frac{VN}{FP + VN}$$

Overlap and Generality

$$Overlap = \frac{VP_i}{VP_i + FP_i + FN_i}$$

$$Generality = \frac{VP}{VP + VN + FP + FN}$$

F-Measure and Entropy

When viewed together, the most famous indicators, recall and accuracy, are a common estimate of the performance of a classification system.

However, several measures have been developed to synthesize this dual information. F-measurement is the commonly used synthesis measure since the 1980s to evaluate algorithms for classifying textual data from precision and recall.

It is used indifferently for the classification (Unsupervised) or the categorization (Supervised), in the problematic of "Information Retrieval" or classification. It therefore makes it possible to combine, according to a parameter, recall and precision. The measurement is thus noted:

$$F_{measure} = \frac{2 * precision * recall}{precision + recall}$$

Entropy: it is the loss of information; it is calculated by the formula:

$$Entropy = -precision - \log\left(precision\right)$$

THE RESULTS

Several experiments have been established and are grouped in Table 4.

Table 4.

Measures	LVT-GVT																		
	5-6		10-11		21-20		31-30		41-40		51-50		61-60		71-70		81-80		91-90
Recall	0,247		0,388		0,611		0,712		0,739		0,755		0,758		0,759		0,760		0,762
Precision	0,155		0,291		0,595		0,747		0,786		0,808		0,811		0,813		0,813		0,813
F-measure	0,190		0,332		0,603		0,728		0,762		0,781		0,784		0,785		0,786		0,787
Entropy	1,860		0,234		0,518		0,295		0,239		0,212		0,209		0,206		0,206		0,206
Noise	0,844		0,708		0,404		0,255		0,213		0,191		0,188		0,186		0,186		0,186
Silence	0,752		0,611		0,388		0,287		0,260		0,244		0,241		0,240		0,239		0,237
Accuracy	0,143		0,241		0,491		0,638		0,680		0,705		0,709		0,710		0,712		0,713
Overlap	0,105		0,199		0,432		0,578		0,615		0,640		0,644		0,646		0,647		0,648
Exec.time(S)	3		1		1		1		1		1		1		1		1		1
Confusion matrix	70	380	131	319	268	181	335	115	354	96	364	86	365	85	365	85	366	84	366	84
	213	29	206	36	170	72	135	107	125	117	118	124	116	126	116	126	115	127	114	128

Note: LVT-GVT: Local Visual Threshold - Global Visual Threshold

Figure 4. Graphic illustration of the results

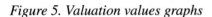

*For a more accurate representation see the electronic version.

Figure 5. Valuation values graphs

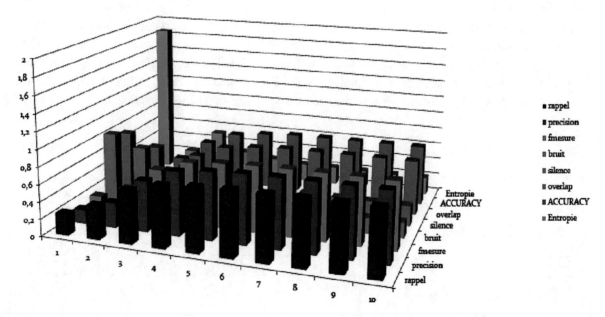

DISCUSSION

According to the three preceding figures, at each increment of the local visual threshold and the overall visual threshold, the accuracy is progressively increased from (6-5) to (71-70), and from (71- 70) it starts to stabilize with a percentage of 81.3% approximately.

For the recall, at each increment of the local visual threshold and the overall visual threshold it is seen that it increases progressively from (6-5) to (71-70), and from (71-70) it begins to Stabilize with a percentage of approximately 76.2%.

For the f-measure and success rate, the same thing is observed as for the recall and the precision with a stabilization of 78.7% and 71.3% respectively.

At each increment of the LVT-GVT, we notice a gradual decrease from (6-5) to (11-10) of the entropy then an increase to (21-20) and finally stabilization at (71-70) with Percentage of 20.6% and consequently the loss of information decreases progressively.

For noise and silence, at each increment of the LVT-GVT, we notice a gradual decrease from (6-5) to (71-10) and then stabilization with a percentage of 18.6% and 23.7 respectively.

NB: For these experiments carried out and incrementing the two thresholds we could not know the best parameters to achieve better results and more we know not the most important parameter. For this we will try other experiments and in this case we will set the local visual threshold at 80 and we will increment the global visual threshold.

The increment of the global threshold will be as follows: 81, 91, 101, 111, 121, 131.

DISCUSSION

According to this experiment we note that all validity measurements remain stable with the same percentage in all the tests with the increment of the global threshold and the fixing of the local threshold.

NB: this stage of the experiment allowed us to know that the single increment of the global threshold does not give good results and one can also conclude that a global threshold alone is not so important.

In the next and third experiment, we will vary the local visual threshold and set the global visual threshold to 120 which represents an experimental value giving satisfactory results.

Table 6. The results of the second experiment

Measures	LVT-GVT											
	80-81		80-91		80-101		80-111		80-121		80-131	
Recall	0,760		0,760		0,760		0,760		0,760		0,760	
Precision	0,813		0,813		0,813		0,813		0,813		0,813	
F-measure	0,786		0,786		0,786		0,786		0,786		0,786	
Entropy	0,206		0,206		0,206		0,206		0,206		0,206	
Noise	0,186		0,186		0,186		0,186		0,186		0,186	
Silence	0,239		0,239		0,239		0,239		0,239		0,239	
Accuracy	0,712		0,712		0,712		0,712		0,712		0,712	
Overlap	0,647		0,647		0,647		0,647		0,647		0,647	
Exec.time(S)	3		1		1		1		1		1	
Confusion matrix	366	84	366	84	366	84	366	84	366	84	366	84
	114	128	114	128	114	128	114	128	114	128	114	128

Figure 6. Graphic illustration of the results

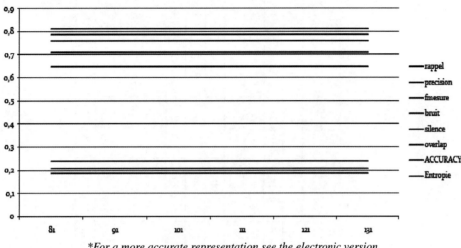

*For a more accurate representation see the electronic version.

Figure 7. Evaluation graphs

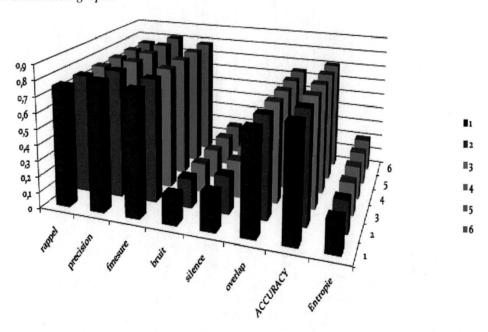

Evaluation Graphs

In this experimental phase, by incrementing the local visual threshold and fixing the overall visual threshold at 120, we notice that precision, recall, f-measure and entropy increase progressively from (120-5) to (120- 60), and from (120-70) they began to stabilize with a percentage of 81.3%, 76.2%, 78.7% and 20.6%, respectively.

Table 7. The results of the third experiment

Measures		5	10	20	30	40	50	60	65	70	75	80	100
							LVT						
Recall		0,230	0,366	0,600	0,710	0,739	0,754	0,758	0,759	0,759	0,760	0,760	0,762
Precision		0,142	0,268	0,584	0,740	0,876	0,811	0,813	0,813	0,813	0,813	0,813	0,813
F-measure		0,175	0,310	0,592	0,724	0,762	0,781	0,784	0,785	0,785	0,786	0,786	0,787
Entropy		1,750	1,310	0,537	0,301	0,239	0,209	0,209	0,206	0,206	0,206	0,206	0,206
Noise		0,857	0,730	0,415	0,260	0,213	0,188	0,188	0,186	0,186	0,180	0,180	0,180
Silence		0,769	0,630	0,399	0,289	0,260	0,245	0,240	0,240	0,240	0,230	0,230	0,230
Accuracy		0,130	0,233	0,476	0,634	0,680	0,705	0,710	0,710	0,710	0,710	0,712	0,713
Overlap		0,090	0,180	0,420	0,568	0,615	0,541	0,644	0,646	0,646	0,647	0,647	0,650
Exec. time(S)		3	1	1	1	1	1	1	1	1	1	1	1
Confusion matrix		64 386	121 329	263 187	333 117	354 96	365 85	366 84	366 84	366 84	366 84	366 84	366 84
		214 28	208 34	175 67	136 106	125 117	119 123	116 126	116 126	116 126	115 127	115 127	114 128

Figure 8. Graphic illustration of the results

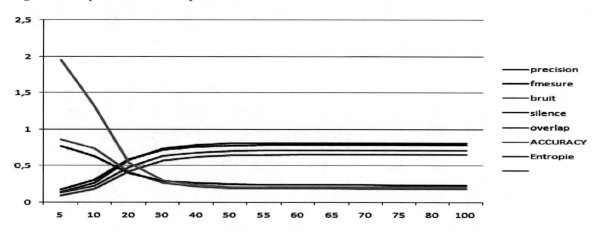

Figure 9.

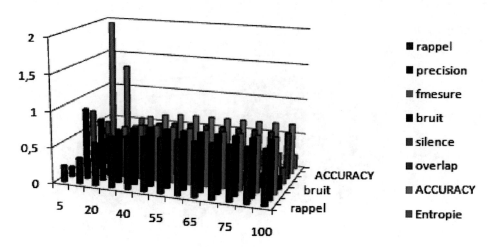

Table 8. The results of the last experiment

Measures	LVT-GVT											
	80-80		**120-80**		**120-120**		**394-394**		**597-597**		**999-999**	
Recall	0,760		0,760		0,762		0,762		0,762		0,762	
Precision	0,813		0,8133		0,8133		0,8133		0,8133		0,8133	
F-measure	0,786		0,786		0,787		0,787		0,787		0,787	
Entropy	0,206		0,2066		0,2066		0,2066		0,2066		0,2066	
Noise	0,186		0,186		0,1866		0,1866		0,1866		0,1866	
Silence	0,239		0,237		0,237		0,237		0,237		0,237	
Accuracy	0,712		0,712		0,713		0,713		0,713		0,713	
Overlap	0,647		0,647		0,648		0,648		0,648		0,648	
Exec.time(S)	3		1		1		1		1		1	
Confusion matrix	366	84	366	84	366	84	366	84	366	84	366	84
	116	126	115	127	114	128	114	128	114	128	114	128

Figure 10. Graphic illustration of the results

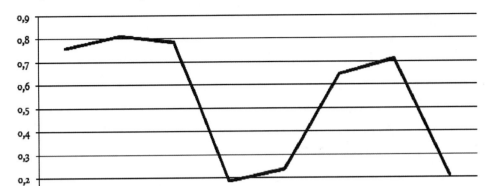

Figure 11. Evaluation graphs

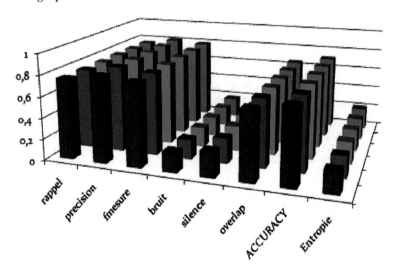

Table 8. Optimal contingency matrix

Category		Expert Judgment	
		Normal	**Sick**
Judgment of the Classifier	**Normal**	366	84
	Sick	114	128

Under the same conditions, we notice that noise and silence gradually increase from (120-5) to (120-70), and from (120-70) they begin to stabilize with a percentage of 18.6% and 36, 7% respectively.

On the other hand, the success rate increases gradually from (120-5) to (120-50), and from (71-60) it begins to stabilize with a percentage of 71.3%.

NB: In this step, we made sure that the use of the two parameters, global visual threshold and local visual threshold is necessary and it is noticed that the first step is almost identical than the third step, which means that The local visual threshold is extremely important than the global visual threshold. .

To validate our results we will do a final parallel increment test with a larger number. Test with the pairs: 80-80, 120-80, 120-20, 394-394, 597-597, 999-999.

We note that from (120-120), the measurement measures stabilize with the same percentage in all cases, which confirms the stability of the measurements and also confirms the results obtained in the first three experiments.

Therefore, and according to our tests, the optimal contingency matrix is:

COMPARISON OF OUR APPROACH WITH OTHER ALGORITHMS

Comparison in Terms of Confusion Matrix

We experimented our algorithm on a sample of 78 individuals categorized into 50 non-diabetic individuals and 28 diabetic individuals.

This sample has been experimented by several researchers with different methods that will be explored in the table below in terms of confusion matrix.

With accuracy of 71% and for a new bio-inspired technique the results obtained are very satisfactory.

At the beginning and during the development of the approach we do not expect to achieve such results given the limitations and the major problem of our algorithm which resides in its global visual threshold which represents the maximum threshold to be reached for fish.

Table 9. Comparison in terms of confusion matrix

Approach	Confusion Matrix	
AFSA (Our Approach)	42	8
	14	14
LS-SVM (Polat et al., 2008)	44	6
	11	17
PCA-LS-SVM	45	5
	9	19
PCA-MI-LS-SVM	44	6
	4	24
PCA-PSO-LS-SVM	45	5
	4	24
MI-MCS-SVM	48	2
	3	25

Table 10. Comparison in terms of accuracy

Authors	Method	Accuracy
Ster & al.	QDA	59.5
Zarndt	C4.5 rules	67
Yildirim & al.	RBF	68.23
R.M Hamou & al. (our approach)	AFSA	71
Bennet & al.	C4.5 (5xCV)	72
Zarndt	Bayes	72.2
Statlog	Kohonen	72.8
Ster & al.	ASR	74.3
Shang et al	. DB-CART	74.4
Friedman	Naïve Bayes	74.5
Zarndt	CART DT	74.7
Statlog	BP	75.2
Ster & al.	SNB	75.4
Ster & al.	NB	75.5
Grudzinski	KNN	75.5
Zarndt	MML	75.5
Statlog	RBF	75.7
Ster & al.	LVQ	75.8
Friedman	Semi-Naïve Bayes (5xCV)	76
Ster & al.	MLP + BP	76.4
Ster & al.	FDA	76.5
Ster & al.	ASI	76.6
Statlog	SMART	76.8
Bennet & al.	GTO DT (5xCV)	76.8
Yildirim & al.	BFGS quasi Newton	77.08
Yildirim & al.	LM	77.08
Statlog & al	. LDA	77.5
Yildirim & al.	GD	77.6
Bennet & al.	SVM (5xCV)	77.6
Polat & al.	GDA-LS-SVM	79.16
Yildirim & al.	GRNN	80.21
Calisir & al.	LDA-MWSVM	89.74

CONCLUSION AND PERSPECTIVES

In this study, we saw one of the most important contributions of Metaheuristics in improving the tasks of data mining. We proposed an approach to improve the task of supervised classification of data mining. In recent years the volume of data of all kinds is growing more and more. With so much data available, it is necessary to develop algorithms that can extract meaningful information from this vast volume. The search for useful nuggets of information among huge amounts of data has become known as the field of data mining. This interdisciplinary field draws these techniques and tasks from several other fields. One task in particular is supervised classification.

The study of this problem is justified by the fact that an exact search has an exponential cost in terms of computation time and memory space indeed it is part of the NP-difficult problems and which can be solved by the meta heuristics.

We propose in this paper the resolution of an NP-diffcult optimization problem which is the detection of diabetes by the metaheuristic of AFSA (swarm of fish) for the improvement of the task of the supervised classification of data mining by improving the accuracy and comprehension of the classifier.

The experiments are carried out on databases of the UCI (University of California, Irvine). The AFSA approach aims to select the best solutions from a large dataset that contains redundant, noisy or irrelevant data. The aim was to improve one of the tasks of data mining, which is supervised classification. With the experimental results, we have observed that the proposed approach is competitive with other metaheuristics.

This work presents an automatic model to diagnose diabetes disease based on the swarm of fish. The results show that the model is satisfactory. The results show that the proposed model is faster and much more reliable to other metaheuristics. We can merger several methods with that if to achieve very high performance. This method can be coupled with medical software to help physicians make more accurate decisions about diabetes disease.

REFERENCES

Abdessemed, M. R., Slimane, M., Aupetit, S., & Bilami, A. (2009, March). Une approche de groupement orienté dans un entourage de robots homogènes. *5th international conference SETIT: Sciences of Electronic, Technologies of Information and Telecommunications*.

Alaoui, A. (2012). *Application des techniques des métaheuristiques pour l'optimisation de la tâche de la classification de la fouille de données* (Doctoral dissertation). USTO, Oran, Algeria.

Azizi, R. (2014). *Empirical study of artificial fish swarm algorithm*. arXiv preprint arXiv:1405.4138

El-bayoumy, M. A., Rashad, M. Z., Elsoud, M. A., & El-dosuky, M. A. (2014). Job Scheduling in Grid Computing with Fast Artificial Fish Swarm Algorithm. *International Journal of Computers and Applications*, *96*(14).

Farzi, S. (2009). Efficient job scheduling in grid computing with modified artificial fish swarm algorithm. *International Journal of Computer Theory and Engineering, 1*(1), 13.

Giveki, D., Salimi, H., Bahmanyar, G., & Khademian, Y. (2012). *Automatic detection of diabetes diagnosis using feature weighted support vector machines based on mutual information and modified cuckoo search.* arXiv preprint arXiv:1201.2173

Hamidi, Y. N. E. (2015). *L'utilisation de l'approche boosting pour le diagnostic du diabéte* (Doctoral dissertation). Tlemcen university, Algeria.

Hu, J., Zeng, X., & Xiao, J. (2010, December). Artificial fish school algorithm for function optimization. In *Information Engineering and Computer Science (ICIECS), 2010 2nd International Conference on* (pp. 1-4). IEEE. doi:10.1109/ICIECS.2010.5678350

Huang, Z., & Chen, Y. (2015). Log-linear model based behavior selection method for artificial fish swarm algorithm. *Computational Intelligence and Neuroscience, 2015*, 10. doi:10.1155/2015/685404 PMID:25691895

Jiang, M., & Cheng, Y. (2010, July). Simulated annealing artificial fish swarm algorithm. In *Intelligent Control and Automation (WCICA), 2010 8th World Congress on* (pp. 1590-1593). IEEE.

Kameche, Z. (2011). *Sélection des Web Services à Base Des Essaimes Particulaires.* Tlemcen University.

Karabatak, M., & Ince, M. C. (2009). An expert system for detection of breast cancer based on association rules and neural network. *Expert Systems with Applications, 36*(2), 3465–3469. doi:10.1016/j.eswa.2008.02.064

Neshat, M., Sepidnam, G., Sargolzaei, M., & Toosi, A. N. (2014). Artificial fish swarm algorithm: A survey of the state-of-the-art, hybridization, combinatorial and indicative applications. *Artificial Intelligence Review*, 1–33.

Saidi, M. (2011). *Traitement de données médicales par un Système Immunitaire Artificiel Reconnaissance Automatique du Diabète.* Tlemcen University.

Wei, X. X., Zeng, H. W., & Zhou, Y. Q. (2010, October). Hybrid artificial fish school algorithm for solving ill-conditioned linear systems of equations. In *Intelligent Computing and Intelligent Systems (ICIS), 2010 IEEE International Conference on* (Vol. 1, pp. 290-294). IEEE. doi:10.1109/ICICISYS.2010.5658678

Yazdani, D., Toosi, A. N., & Meybodi, M. R. (2010, December). Fuzzy adaptive artificial fish swarm algorithm. In *Australasian Joint Conference on Artificial Intelligence* (pp. 334-343). Springer Berlin Heidelberg.

Zhu, K. K., Jiang, M., & Cheng, Y. (2010, October). Niche artificial fish swarm algorithm based on quantum theory. In *Signal Processing (ICSP), 2010 IEEE 10th International Conference on* (pp. 1425-1428). IEEE.

Zhu, K., & Jiang, M. (2010, July). Quantum artificial fish swarm algorithm. In *Intelligent Control and Automation (WCICA), 2010 8th World Congress on* (pp. 1-5). IEEE.

Chapter 11
Nature–Inspired–Based Multi–Objective Hybrid Algorithms to Find Near–OGRs for Optical WDM Systems and Their Comparison

Shonak Bansal
PEC University of Technology, India

ABSTRACT

Nature-inspired-based approaches are powerful optimizing algorithms to solve the NP-complete problems having multiple objectives. In this chapter, two nature-inspired-based multi-objective optimization algorithms (MOAs) and their hybrid forms are proposed to find the optimal Golomb rulers (OGRs) in a reasonable time. The OGRs can be used as a channel-allocation algorithm that allows suppression of the four-wave mixing crosstalk in optical wavelength division multiplexing systems. The presented results conclude that the proposed MOAs outperforms the existing conventional classical and nature-inspired-based algorithms to find near-OGRs in terms of ruler length, total occupied optical bandwidth, bandwidth expansion factor, computation time, and computational complexity. In order to find the superiority of proposed MOAs, the performances of the proposed algorithms are also analyzed by using statistical tests.

INTRODUCTION

Due to the high degree of dimensionality, complexities, and nonlinearities, finding optimal solutions to any problem with multi–objective are very time consuming and tough. To solve the multi–objective problems, numerous nature–inspired based multi–objective optimization algorithms (MOAs) are being formulated by Abbass and Sarker (2002), Deb (2001), and Yang et al., (2014). Nature–inspired based MOAs can have several conflicting solutions instead of having single optimal solution, making it

DOI: 10.4018/978-1-5225-3004-6.ch011

impossible to use any single design option without compromise. Pareto optimal solution called Pareto front (Koziel and Yang, 2011; Yang et al., 2014) is the best compromise optimal solutions from several solutions that cannot be dominated as no objective can be better without making some other objective worse. The MOAs either search the Pareto optimal solutions or solutions near to Pareto front to provide flexibility for the design engineer.

This chapter proposes the application of nature–inspired based multi–objective Big bang–Big crunch (MOBB–BC) algorithm, multi–objective Firefly algorithm (MOFA) and their modified hybrid forms, namely, modified MOBB–BC (M–MOBB–BC) algorithm, and modified MOFA (M–MOFA) to solve an NP–complete optimal Golomb ruler (OGR) problem (Babcock, 1953; Bloom and Golomb, 1977; Colannino, 2003; Distributed.net, 2017; Meyer and Papakonstantinou, 2009; Memarsadegh, 2013; Robinson, 1979; Shearer, 1990; Shearer, 1998) in optical wavelength division multiplexing (WDM) systems. The OGRs found their application as unequally spaced channel–allocation algorithm (USCA) in optical WDM systems to suppress one of the dominant nonlinear optical effects formulated in literatures (Aggarwal, 2001; Babcock, 1953; Chraplyvy, 1990; Forghieri et al., 1994; Kwong and Yang, 1997; Saaid, 2010; Singh and Bansal, 2013; Thing et al., 2004), i.e. four–wave mixing (FWM) crosstalk. The performance of the system can be improved if FWM crosstalk signals generation at the channel frequencies is avoided. If the frequency separation of any two channels in an optical WDM system is different from that of any other pair of channels, no FWM crosstalk signals will be generated (Aggarwal, 2001; Babcock, 1953; Chraplyvy, 1990; Saaid, 2010; Thing et al., 2004).

To suppress the FWM crosstalk, several USCAs have been proposed by Atkinson et al. (1986), Forghieri et al. (1995), Hwang and Tonguz (1998), Kwong and Yang (1997), Randhawa et al. (2009), Sardesai (1999), and Tonguz and Hwang (1998) with the limitation of increased bandwidth requirement as compared to equally spaced channel–allocation. This chapter proposes a bandwidth efficient USCA by taking into consideration near–OGRs (Babcock, 1953; Bloom and Golomb, 1977; Shearer, 1990; Thing et al., 2003) to suppress FWM crosstalk.

Cota et al. (2006), Galinier et al. (2001), Leitao, (2004), Rankin (1993), Robinson (1979), and Shearer (1990), presented numerous algorithms to solve OGR problem. Many authors has successfully realized the algorithms such as Tabu search (TS) (Cota et al., 2006), Memetic approach (MA) (Cota et al., 2006), Genetic algorithms (GAs) (Ayari et al., 2010; Bansal, 2014; Robinson, 2000; Soliday et al., 1995) and its hybridizations with TS (Ayari et al., 2010), hybrid evolutionary (HE) (Dotú and Hentenryck, 2005), Biogeography based optimization (BBO) (Bansal et al., 2011; Bansal, 2014), simple Big bang–Big crunch (BB–BC) (Bansal et al., 2013; Jyoti et al., 2016), simple Firefly algorithm (FA) (Bansal et al., 2014), multi–objective Bat algorithm (MOBA) (Ritu et al., 2016) and its modified forms (Bansal et al., 2017a; Bansal et al., 2017b), Cuckoo search algorithm (Bansal et al., 2014) and its hybridization (Bansal et al., 2017b; Kumari et al., 2016), and multi–objective Flower pollination algorithm and its hybridization (Bansal et al., 2017b; Jain et al., 2015) in finding near–OGRs. Therefore, nature–inspired based algorithms seem to be very effective solutions to such NP–complete problems. The proposed MOAs solve the bi–objective in OGR problem as optical WDM channel–allocation problem. The performances of the proposed algorithms are compared with the existing algorithms to find near–OGRs.

OPTIMAL GOLOMB RULERS AND ITS BACKGROUND

Firstly, Babcock (1953) introduced the concept of *Golomb rulers* and was described by Bloom and Golomb (1977). An *n*-marks Golomb ruler G is an ordered sequence of n distinct positive integer numbers

$$G = \left\{ x_1, x_2, ..., x_{n-1}, x_n \right\}, x_1 < x_2 < ... < x_{n-1} < x_n \tag{1}$$

such that all the positive differences

$$\left| x_i - x_j \right|, x_i, x_j \in G, \forall i > j \text{ or } i \neq j \tag{2}$$

are distinct.

The positive integer numbers are referred to as *marks*. The number of marks on a ruler is referred to as the *ruler size*. The difference between the largest and smallest number is referred to as the *ruler length* (RL) (Bloom and Golomb, 1977; Cotta et al., 2007; Distributed.net, 2017; Drakakis, 2009; Drakakis and Rickard, 2010), i.e.

$$RL = \max(G) - \min(G) = x_n - x_1 \tag{3}$$

where

$$\max(G) = \max \left\{ x_1, x_2, ..., x_{n-1}, x_n \right\} = x_n \tag{4}$$

and

$$\min(G) = \min \left\{ x_1, x_2, ..., x_{n-1}, x_n \right\} = x_1 \tag{5}$$

Alternatively, the sequence of n distinct positive integer numbers

$$G = \left\{ x_1, x_2, ..., x_{n-1}, x_n \right\}, x_1 < x_2 < ... < x_{n-1} < x_n$$

is an *n*-marks Golomb ruler if and only if (Colannino, 2003)

$$\forall i, j, k, l \in \left\{ 1, 2, ..., n-1, n \right\}, x_i - x_j = x_k - x_l \Leftrightarrow i = k \wedge j = l \tag{6}$$

Generally,

$$x_1 = 0 \tag{7}$$

then

$$G = \left\{0, x_2, ..., x_{n-1}, x_n\right\} \tag{8}$$

and

$$RL = x_n \tag{9}$$

Figure 1 shows an example of a 4–marks Golomb ruler sequence $G = \{0, 1, 4, 6\}$ having ruler length 6. The distance associated with each pair of marks is also illustrated in Figure 1.

A perfect Golomb ruler measures all the positive integer distances from 1 to the RL (Soliday et al., 1995). That is, an n-marks Golomb ruler is called perfect if for every integer, say d, $1 \le d \le \left(x_n - x_1\right)$, there is at least one solution to

$$d = x_i - x_j, x_i, x_j \in G, \forall i > j.$$

Figure 1 also shows a 4–marks perfect Golomb ruler which measures all the integer distances from 1 to 6. The only available perfect Golomb rulers are up to 4–marks, i.e there exist no perfect Golomb rulers for $n > 4$. The RL of an n–mark perfect Golomb ruler (Leitao, 2004; Soliday, 1995) is

$$RL = \frac{n(n-1)}{2} = \sum_{i=1}^{n-1} i \frac{1}{2} n \left(n - 1\right) \tag{10}$$

An n-marks Golomb ruler sequenced $G = \left\{0, x_2, ..., x_{n-1}, x_n\right\}$ is optimal if it is associated with shortest possible length (Bansal, 2014; Weisstein, 2017a; Weisstein, 2017b). There can be several different OGRs for a specific mark value. The unique 4–marks OGR, which measures all the distances from 0 to

Figure 1. A 4–marks OGR with its associated distances

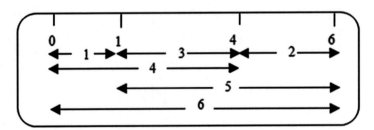

6 is illustrated in Figure 1. In a case where OGR didn't exist, but its length is near to optimal it will be considered as a near–OGR.

Till date the OGRs for up to 27–marks are well known and there are some predictions for OGRs up to 158–marks (Shearer, 2001a; Shearer, 2001b). Distributed.net (2017) is now actively searching the OGRs for $n > 27$.

Several algebraic and exact methods are proposed by Dewdney (1986), Dimitromanolakis (2002), Drakakis (2009), Kwong and Yang (1997), and Randhawa et al. (2009) that are impractical in terms of computational resources and it took several months or even years of calculation to prove the optimality with high computational power. Several nature–inspired based algorithms and their hybridization (Ayari, 2010; Bansal et al., 2011; Bansal et al., 2013; Bansal and Singh, 2014; Bansal et al., 2014; Bansal, 2014; Bansal et al., 2017a; Bansal et al., 2017b; Cotta et al., 2006; Dotú and Hentenryck, 2005; Jain et al., 2015; Kumari et al., 2016; Ritu et al., 2016; Robinson, 2000; Soliday et al., 1995, Vyas et al., 2016) have been proposed efficiently to find either optimal or near–OGRs at a reasonable time.

The OGRs found their applications in radio communication, circuit layout, self–orthogonal codes, sensor placement in X–ray crystallography, geographical mapping, pulse phase modulation, computer communication network, coding theory, very large scale integration architecture, linear arrays, fitness landscape analysis, radio astronomy, antenna design for radar missions, sonar applications and NASA missions in astrophysics, planetary and earth sciences (Babcock, 1953; Bloom and Golomb, 1977; Blum et al., 1974; Cotta and Fernández, 2005; Dimitromanolakis, 2002; Dollas et al., 1998; Fang and Sandrin, 1977; Lam and Sarwate, 1988; Lavoie et al., 1991; Leitao, 2004; Memarsadegh, 2013; Robinson and Bernstein, 1967; Soliday et al., 1995).

Using OGRs in the optical WDM systems, it is possible that the smallest distinct number can be used as the WDM channel–allocation sequence to suppress the FWM crosstalk signals.

NATURE–INSPIRED BASED MULTI–OBJECTIVE OPTIMIZATION ALGORITHMS

The classical or exact algorithms in finding optimal solutions to a multi–objective problem are unreasonable in terms of computational resources and are not considered best for global optimization. According to Koziel and Yang (2011), Yang (2013), and Yang et al. (2014), nature–inspired based MOAs are very powerful in dealing with such kind of optimization. The guiding principle is to improve algorithms computationally that lead to an acceptable solution at low cost (Cotta and Hemert, 2008; Rajasekaran and Pai, 2004; Yang, 2010a; Koziel & Yang, 2011; Yang, 2012; Yang, 2013).

Generally, in nature–inspired based MOAs, a problem with M objectives, having g and h as non-linear inequality and equality constraints, respectively, can be written as (Yang et al., 2014)

$$\text{Minimize} \rightarrow f_1(x), f_2(x), ..., f_M(x), \tag{11}$$

$$g_j(x) \leq 0, (j = 1, 2, ..., J), \tag{12}$$

$$h_i(x) = 0, (i = 1, 2, ..., I),$$ (13)

To deal with MOAs, the individual objective functions are combined into a single function f. Generally, weighted sum approach is used to combine all objective functions into a single objective function

$$f = \sum_{m=1}^{M} w_m f_m$$ (14)

with

$$\sum_{i=1}^{M} w_i = 1, w_i > 0,$$ (15)

where w_i are randomly generated positive weight values. A set of random numbers u_i are generated from a uniform distribution $U[0,1]$. The weight values w_i are normalized by

$$w_i = \frac{u_i}{\sum_{i=1}^{M} u_i}, (i = 1, 2, ..., M)$$ (16)

These weight values serve as preferences for optimizing the multi–objective functions in order to estimate the Pareto front correctly.

Although the MOAs in their simplified form works well in the exploitation, still there are some problems in the global exploration of the search space. In order to find the best solution, a search algorithm needs to find a good balance between exploitation and exploration. So for the MOAs, there is a need by which exploitation and exploration can be improved and the algorithms can work more efficiently. By considering these two features, fitness value based differential evolution mutation and Lévy–flight strategies are introduced in the proposed MOAs. The mutation rate probability MR_i^t (Bansal et al., 2017a) of each solution is

$$MR_i^t = \frac{f_i^t}{Max(f^t)}$$ (17)

where f_i^t is the fitness value of solution x_i at the iteration t, and $Max(f^t)$ is the maximum fitness value of the population at iteration t. The mutation equation (Price et al., 2005; Storn et al., 1997) used here is

$$x_i^t = x_i^{t-1} + p_m \left(x_{best}^{t-1} - x_i^{t-1} \right) + p_m \left(x_{r_1}^{t-1} - x_{r_2}^{t-1} \right)$$ (18)

where x_i^t is the population at iteration t, $x_{best}^{t-1} = x_*^{t-1}$ is the current global best solution at iteration one less than running iteration index, p_m is mutation operator, r_1 and r_2 are randomly generated integer numbers between 1 to size of the problem and are different from running iteration index. The mutation strategy enhances the probabilities for a good solution, but a high mutation rate results in too much exploration and is disadvantageous to the improvement of candidate solutions. As p_m decreases from 1.0 to 0.01, optimization ability increases greatly, but as p_m continues to decrease to 0.001, optimization ability decreases rapidly. A small value of p_m is not able to sufficiently increase solution diversity (Bansal, 2014).

The Lévy flight distribution (Yang, 2012) used here is

$$L(\lambda) \sim \frac{\lambda \Gamma(\lambda) \sin(\pi \lambda / 2)}{\pi} \frac{1}{s^{1+\lambda}}, (s >> s_0 > 0) \tag{19}$$

where $\Gamma(\lambda)$ is the standard gamma distribution valid for $s > 0$. Throughout the chapter, $\lambda = 1.5$ is used. In theory, it is required that $|s_0| >> 0$, but in practice s_0 can be as small as 0.1 (Yang, 2012).

With these two features in the simplified forms of proposed MOAs, the basic concept of the search space is modified, i.e. the proposed MOAs can explore new search space by the mutation and Lévy flight strategies. A fundamental benefit of using mutation and Lévy flight strategies with proposed MOAs is their ability to improve its solutions over time, which does not seem in the other algorithms (Ayari, 2010; Bansal et al., 2011; Bansal et al., 2013; Bansal, 2014; Bansal et al., 2014; Cotta et al., 2006; Dotú & Hentenryck, 2005; Robinson, 2000; Soliday, 1995) to find near–OGRs.

MOBB–BC Algorithm and Its Modified Forms

Erol and Eksin (2006), inspired by the theories of the evolution of the universe: Big bang and Big crunch, formulated an optimization algorithm called BB–BC algorithm. BB–BC algorithm has two phases: Big bang phase where candidate solutions are randomly distributed over the search space and Big crunch phase where a contraction procedure calculates a center of mass (Erol & Eksin, 2006)

$$x_c = \frac{\sum_{i=1}^{Popsize} \frac{1}{f_i} x_i}{\sum_{i=1}^{Popsize} \frac{1}{f_i}} \tag{20}$$

where x_c = position of the center of mass, x_i = position of candidate i, f_i = fitness value of candidate i, and $Popsize$ = population size. Instead of the center of mass, the best fit individual can also be chosen as the starting point in the big bang phase. The new candidates (x_{new}) around the center of mass are calculated by adding or subtracting a normal random number whose value decreases as the iterations elapse and is

$$x_{new} = x_c + r \times c_1 \times \frac{\left(x_{max} - x_{min}\right)}{1 + t / c_2} \tag{21}$$

where r is a random number with a standard normal distribution, c_1 is a parameter for limiting the size of the search space, c_2 denotes after how many iterations the search space will be restricted to half, x_{max} and x_{min} are the upper and lower limits of elite pool, respectively.

If fitness based mutation strategy is introduced in the simple BB–BC algorithm, *BB–BC algorithm with mutation* (BB–BCM) can be formulated.

By applying Lévy–flight distributions in the simple BB–BC algorithm, *Lévy–flight BB–BC algorithm* (LBB–BC) can be formulated. For LBB–BC, equation (21) is randomized via Lévy flights

$$x_{new} = x_c + r \times c_1 \times \frac{\left(x_{max} - x_{min}\right)}{1 + t / c_2} \oplus L(\lambda) \tag{22}$$

The product $\oplus$ meant entry wise multiplications and $L(\lambda)$ is the Lévy flight based step size.

If fitness based mutation strategy is applied to LBB–BC algorithm, *Lévy flight BB–BC algorithm with mutation* (LBB–BCM) algorithm can be formulated.

With the same approximated rules, this chapter extends the basic BB–BC algorithm and its modified forms to solve multi–objective problems and named as MOBB–BC algorithm and modified MOBB–BC algorithm (M–MOBB–BC).

The general pseudo–code for M–MOBB–BC can be summarized in Figure 2. If the lines 17 to 22 in Figure 2 are removed and Lévy flight distributions in line 16 are not used, then Figure 2 represents the general pseudo–code for MOBB–BC. If from line 16 Lévy flight distributions are not used, then Figure 2 illustrates the general pseudo–code for multi–objective BB–BCM (MOBB–BCM) algorithm. If no modifications in Figure 2 are performed, then it represents the general pseudo–code for multi–objective LBB–BCM (MOLBB–BCM) algorithm.

MOFA and Its Modified Forms

Yang (2009; 2010; 2012; 2013) inspired by the flashing pattern and characteristics of fireflies, formulated an optimization algorithm called Firefly inspired algorithm or simply FA. Yang (2013) further extended this simple FA for single optimization to solve multiple objectives and named MOFA.

In MOFA, the variation of light intensity and the formulation of attractiveness are two main issues. For maximum optimization problems, the brightness I of a firefly at a particular location X can simply be proportional to the objective function i.e. $I(X) \propto f(X)$ (Yang; 2009; Yang, 2010a; Yang, 2010b; Yang, 2010c, Yang, 2012; Yang, 2013). With a fixed light absorption coefficient γ, the light intensity $I(r)$ varies with the distance r between any two fireflies by (Yang, 2009)

$$I = I_0 e^{-\gamma r} \tag{23}$$

where I_0 = original light intensity.

Figure 2. General pseudo–code for M–MOBB–BC algorithm

```
1. Modified MOBB–BC (M–MOBB–BC) algorithm
2. Begin
3.    /* Big bang phase */
4.       Define Pareto front points N and objective functions f₁(x),...f_M(x),   x= (x₁, ..., x_d)ᵀ;
                                                    /* d is dimension of the problem */
5.       Generate a random set of NP candidates (population);
6.       Generate M weights w_m ≥ 0 so that equation (15) is satisfied;
7.       Form a single objective by using equation (14);
8.       Based on fitness value, find the global best solution x* among the population of NP candidates;
9.    /* End of Big bang phase */
10. For i = 1 : N
11.      Generate M weights randomly which satisfies equation (15);
12.      While not TC                                /* TC is the termination criterion */
13.        /* Big crunch phase */
14.           Compute the center of mass;
15.        /* End of Big crunch phase */
16.        Calculate new candidates around the center of mass by adding or subtracting a normal random
             number whose value decreases as the iterations elapse via Lévy flight;
                                                               /* Big bang phase */
17.        /* Mutation */
18.           Compute mutation rate probability MR_i via equation (17);
19.         If ( MR_i < rand)
20.             Perform mutation via equation (18);
21.         End if
22.        /* End of mutation */
23.        Re–evaluate fitness values of all the generated candidates;
24.        Rank the candidates and find the global best Pareto front solution x* solutions;
25.      End while
26.      Record x* as a non–dominated solution;
27. End for i
28. Postprocess results and visualization;
29. End
```

As attractiveness of a firefly is proportional to the light intensity seen by the neighboring fireflies, therefore the attractiveness β of a firefly with the distance r is

$$\beta\left(r\right) = \beta_0 e^{-\gamma r^2} \tag{24}$$

where β_0 = attractiveness at $r = 0$.

The Cartesian distance between any two fireflies i and j at locations X_i and X_j, respectively, is (Yang, 2009)

$$r_{ij} = \left\|X_i - X_j\right\| = \sqrt{\sum_{k=1}^{d}\left(x_{i,k} - x_{j,k}\right)^2} \tag{25}$$

where $x_{i,k}$ is the kth component of the spatial coordinate X_i of ith firefly and d is the number of dimensions in the search space. The movement of a firefly i is attracted to another more brighter firefly j is estimated by (Yang, 2009)

$$X_i = X_i + \beta_0 e^{-\gamma r_{ij}^2} \left(X_j - X_i \right) + \alpha \left(rand - 0.5 \right) \tag{26}$$

where the second term is due to the attraction and the third term is randomization with a control parameter α, which makes the more efficient exploration of the search space. For most cases in the implementation, $\beta_0 = 1$ and $\alpha \in [0,1]$.

If the mutation strategy is combined with MOFA algorithm, *MOFA with mutation* (MOFAM) can be formulated.

All the parameters and equations for MOFAM are same as for MOFA. Only the difference between algorithms MOFAM and MOFA is that mutation is added to MOFA.

By combining the characteristics of Lévy flights with the MOFA, another new algorithm named, *multi–objective Lévy flight FA* (MOLFA) can be formulated. For MOLFA, the third term in the equation (26) is randomized via Lévy flights. The modified firefly's movement equation for MOLFA is

$$X_i = X_i + \beta_0 e^{-\gamma r_{ij}^2} \left(X_j - X_i \right) + \alpha.sign\left(rand - 0.5 \right) \oplus L(\lambda) \tag{27}$$

The term $sign(rand - 0.5)$, where $rand \in [0,1]$ essentially provides a random direction, while the random step length is drawn from a Lévy distribution having an infinite variance with an infinite mean. In MOLFA the steps of firefly motion are essentially a random walk process.

If both MOFAM and MOLFA are combined into a single algorithm, *MOLFA with mutation* (MOLFAM) can be formulated.

The general pseudo–code for modified MOFA (M–MOFA) is shown in Figure 3. If lines 20 to 25 in Figure 3 are removed and in line 18 Lévy flight distributions are not used, then illustrates the general pseudo–code for MOFA. If Lévy flight distributions in line 18 are not used in Figure 3, then it represents the general pseudo–code for MOFAM and if no modifications in Figure 3 are performed then it represents the general pseudo–code for MOLFAM.

FINDING NEAR–OGRs

In order to find a bandwidth efficient approach to optical WDM system, two problems: generation of Golomb ruler sequences and optimization of the generated sequences through MOAs by optimizing both the *ruler length* and *total occupied optical bandwidth* are examined. Thus the use of Golomb rulers as the channel–allocation algorithm has bi–objectives which are to be optimized.

If each individual element in an obtained sequence is a Golomb ruler, the sum of all elements of an individual sequence form the total occupied optical bandwidth. Thus, if the spacing between any pair of channels in a Golomb ruler sequence is denoted as CS, an individual element is as IE and the total number of channels/marks is n, then the RL and the unequally spaced total optical channel bandwidth TBW_{un} are

$$f_1 = RL = \sum_{i=1}^{n-1} \left(CS \right)_i = IE\left(n \right) - IE\left(1 \right) \tag{28}$$

Figure 3. General pseudo–code for M–MOFA

1. Modified MOFA (M–MOFA) algorithm
2. Begin
3. /* parameter initialization */
4. Define Pareto front points N and objective functions $f_1(x),...,f_M(x)$, $x = (x_1,...,x_d)^T$;
                   /* d is dimension of the problem */
5. Generate initial population of NP fireflies x_i ($i = 1, 2,...NP$);
6. Define light absorption coefficient γ;
8. Generate M weights $w_m \geq 0$ so that equation (15) is satisfies;
9. Form a single objective i.e. light intensity I_i by using equation (14);
10. Based on fitness value, find the global best solution $x*$ among the population of NP fireflies;
11. /* End of parameter initialization */
12. For $i = 1 : N$
13. Generate M weights randomly which satisfies equation (15);
14. **While not** TC /* TC is a termination criterion */
15.   For $j = 1 : NP$ /*all NP fireflies*/
16.   For $k = 1 : j$
17.   If ($I_k > I_j$)
18.   Move firefly j towards k in d-dimension via Lévy flights;
19.   **End if**
20.   /* Mutation */
21.   Compute mutation rate probability MR_i via equation (17);
22.   If ($MR_i < rand$)
23.   Perform mutation via equation (18);
24.   **End if**
25.   /* End of mutation */
26.   Vary attractiveness with distance r via exp$[-\gamma r]$;
27.   Re–evaluate fitness values of all the generated solutions to update light intensity;
28.   Rank the solutions and find the current best Pareto front solution;
29.   **End for** k
30.   **End for** j
31.   Find the global best Pareto front solution $x*$ among NP solutions;
32. **End while**
33. Record $x*$ as a non–dominated solution;
34. **End for** i
35. Postprocess results and visualization;
36. End

subject to $(CS)_i \neq (CS)_j$ and $(IE)_i \neq (IE)_j$

$$f_2 = TBW_{un} = \sum_{i=1}^{n}\left(IE\right)_i \tag{29}$$

subject to

$$(IE)_i \neq (IE)_j$$

where $i, j = 1, 2,..., n$ with $i \neq j$ are distinct in both equations (28) and (29).

The objectives f_1 and f_2 are combined into a single objective f to estimate the Pareto front.

The lower bound on TBW_{un} can be achieved from (Forghieri et al., 1995)

$$TBW_{un} \geq \left[1 + ((n/2 - 1)/S)\right] TBW_{eq} \tag{30}$$

where S is minimum channel separation and TBW_{eq} is equally spaced total occupied channel bandwidth of an optical WDM system (Forghieri et al., 1995; Randhawa et al., 2009) and is

$$TBW_{eq} = (n - 1)\Delta f_c \tag{31}$$

where $\Delta f_c = CS$ is the channel–to–channel separation. Thus equation (30) becomes

$$TBW_{un} \geq (1 + ((n/2 - 1)/S))(n - 1)\Delta f_c \tag{32}$$

With the optimization of TBW_{un}, the bandwidth expansion factor (BEF) as given by equation (33) is also get optimized.

$$BEF = \frac{TBW_{un}}{TBW_{eq}} \tag{33}$$

The pseudo–code to find near–OGRs with proposed MOAs is shown in Figure 4.

SIMULATION RESULTS

This section presents the performance evaluation of proposed MOAs to find near–OGRs. The performance of proposed MOAs has been compared with best known OGRs (Bloom & Golomb, 1977; Colannino, 2003; Dollas et al, 1998; Leitao, 2004; Meyer & Papakonstantinou, 2009; Shearer, 1990; Shearer, 2001a; Shearer, 2001b; Weisstein, 2017b), existing classical computing, i.e. Extended quadratic congruence (EQC) and Search algorithm (SA) (Kwong & Yang, 1997; Randhawa et al., 2009) and nature–inspired based algorithms, i.e. GAs (Bansal, 2014), BBO (Bansal et al., 2011; Bansal, 2014), and simple BB–BC (Bansal et al., 2013), of finding near–OGRs as USCA in optical WDM systems.

Parameters Selection for the Proposed Algorithms

Selecting a best suitable parameter values of nature–inspired based MOAs are problem specific as there are no concrete rules. To find near–OGRs as optical WDM channel–allocation algorithm, Tables 1 and 2 shows the selected optimal parameter values for proposed MOAs.

For M–MOBB–BC the value of parameter $c_2 = 5$ is assumed a priori as this parameter denotes after how many iterations the search space will be restricted to half. All the other parameter values for M–MOBB–BC, MOFA and M–MOFA were varied from 0.0 to 1.0. After looking wisely at the obtained

Figure 4. General pseudo–code to find near–OGRs by using nature–inspired based MOAs

```
1.  Multi–objective nature–inspired based optimization algorithms to find near–OGRs
2.  Begin
3.      /* Parameter initialization */
4.          Define operating parameters for nature–inspired based multi–objective optimization algorithms;
5.          Initialize the number of channels, Pareto front points, lower and upper bound on the ruler length;
6.          Generate a integer set of populations of size NP randomly and each integer population corresponding to
            Golomb ruler to the specified marks/channels;
                                    /* Number of integers in population is being equal to the number of channels */
7.          Compute the fitness values by using equations (14) to (16), (28), and (29);
                                    /* fitness value represents the cost value i.e. ruler length and total optical channel bandwidth */
8.          Based on fitness value, among NP solutions select the globally best solution x∗;
9.      /* End of parameter initialization */
10.     While not TC                                                    /* TC is a termination criterion */
11. A:      Call any multi–objective nature–inspired based optimization algorithm to determine new set of
            optimal candidates;
12.         Recheck Golombness of updated candidates;
13.         If Golombness is satisfied
14.             Retain that candidate and then go to B;
15.         Else
16.             Retain the previous generated candidate and then go to A;
                            /* Previous generated candidate is being equal to the candidate generated into
                            the parameter initialization step*/
17.         End if
18. B:      Recompute the fitness values of the modified candidates;
19.         Rank the candidates from best to worst based on fitness values and find the global best solution;
20.     End while
21.     Display the near–OGR sequences;
22. End
```

Table 1. Simulation parameters for M–MOBB–BC

Parameter	Value
c_1	0.1
c_2	5
p_m	0.05
Pareto front points (N)	100

Table 2. Simulation parameters for MOFA and M–MOFA

Parameter	Value
α	0.5
β	0.2
γ	1.0
p_m	0.01
Pareto front points (N)	100

solutions, it was concluded that $c_1 = 0.1$, $p_m = 0.05$ are the best choices for M–MOBB–BC (Table 1), and $\alpha = 0.5$, $\beta = 0.2$, $\gamma = 1.0$, $p_m = 0.01$ are the best choices for MOFA and M–MOFA (Table 2) to obtain optimal solutions.

With these parameters setting, each proposed MOA was executed 20 times until near–optimal solution was found. A set of 10 trials for various marks/channels for M–MOBB–BC is reported in Table 3, whereas for MOFA and M–MOFA are reported in Table 4. Although the proposed MOAs find same near–OGRs, but the difference is in a required maximum number of iterations $(Maxiter)$, BEF, CPU time, *computational complexity* and their statistical analysis which is discussed in the following subsections.

Table 3. Performance of proposed M–MOBB–BC algorithms to find near–OGRs for various channels in a set of 10 trials

Trials	n=6			n=8			n=15		
	RL	*TBW_un* (Hz)	*CPU Time* (Sec.)	*RL*	*TBW_un* (Hz)	*CPU Time* (Sec.)	*RL*	*TBW_un* (Hz)	*CPU Time* (Sec.)
MOBB–BCM									
1	17	44	0.0592	39	113	0.1984	267	1322	1.174e+03
2	18	42	0.0589	41	118	0.1988	267	1322	1.194e+03
3	17	44	0.0577	39	113	0.1989	267	1322	1.191e+03
4	18	42	0.0590	39	113	0.1984	267	1322	1.187e+03
5	17	44	0.0588	39	113	0.1989	267	1322	1.188e+03
6	17	44	0.0587	41	118	0.1986	267	1322	1.187e+03
7	17	44	0.0589	41	118	0.1988	267	1322	1.178e+03
8	18	42	0.0612	39	113	0.1982	267	1322	1.189e+03
9	17	44	0.0586	39	113	0.1985	267	1322	1.191e+03
10	17	44	0.0588	39	113	0.1983	267	1322	1.186e+03
	Optimal *RL* = 17 Optimal *TBW_un* = 42 Hz Minimum *CPU time* = 0.0577 Sec. Average *CPU time* = 0.05898 Sec			Optimal *RL* = 39 Optimal *TBW_un* = 113 Hz Minimum *CPU time* = 0.1982 Sec. Average *CPU time* = 0.19858 Sec.			Optimal *RL* = 267 Optimal *TBW_un* = 1322 Hz Minimum *CPU time* = 1.174e+03 Sec. Average *CPU time* = 1.187e+03 Sec.		
MOLBB–BC									
1	17	44	0.0581	39	113	0.1987	267	1322	1.165e+03
2	17	44	0.0575	39	113	0.1981	267	1322	1.187e+03
3	17	44	0.0594	39	113	0.213	267	1322	1.185e+03
4	18	42	0.0610	39	113	0.1985	267	1322	1.169e+03
5	17	44	0.0582	39	113	0.1984	267	1322	1.187e+03
6	17	44	0.0574	39	113	0.1845	267	1322	1.184e+03
7	17	44	0.0575	41	118	0.1984	267	1322	1.178e+03
8	17	44	0.0581	39	113	0.1982	267	1322	1.190e+03
9	18	42	0.0574	39	113	0.1983	267	1322	1.188e+03
10	17	44	0.0576	39	113	0.1984	267	1322	1.189e+03
	Optimal *RL* = 17 Optimal *TBW_un* = 42 Hz Minimum *CPU time* = 0.0574 Sec. Average *CPU time* = 0.0582 Sec.			Optimal *RL* = 39 Optimal *TBW_un* = 113 Hz Minimum *CPU time* = 0.1845 Sec. Average *CPU time* = 0.1984 Sec.			Optimal *RL* = 267 Optimal *TBW_un* = 1322 Hz Minimum *CPU time* = 1.165e+03 Average *CPU time* = 1.182e+03 Sec.		
MOLBB–BCM									
1	17	44	0.0551	34	117	0.1965	260	1554	1.172e+03
2	17	44	0.0548	39	113	0.1979	260	1554	1.171e+03
3	17	44	0.055	34	117	0.1964	260	1554	1.164e+03
4	17	44	0.0547	34	117	0.1961	260	1554	1.163e+03
5	18	42	0.0552	34	117	0.1847	260	1554	1.153e+03

continued on following page

Table 3. Continued

Trials	n=6			n=8			n=15		
	RL	TBW_un (Hz)	CPU Time (Sec.)	RL	TBW_un (Hz)	CPU Time (Sec.)	RL	TBW_un (Hz)	CPU Time (Sec.)
6	18	42	0.0549	34	117	0.1967	260	1554	1.166e+03
7	17	44	0.0548	34	117	0.1964	260	1554	1.165e+03
8	17	44	0.0547	34	117	0.2110	260	1554	1.161e+03
9	17	44	0.0549	34	117	0.1885	260	1554	1.162e+03
10	17	44	0.0548	34	117	0.1965	260	1554	1.163e+03
	Optimal RL = 17 Optimal TBW_{un} = 42 Hz Minimum CPU time = 0.0547 Sec. Average CPU time = 0.05489 Sec.			Optimal RL = 34 Optimal TBW_{un} = 113 Hz Minimum CPU time = 0.1847 Sec. Average CPU time = 0.1960 Sec.			Optimal RL = 260 Optimal TBW_{un} = 1554 Hz Minimum CPU time = 1.153e+03 Sec. Average CPU time = 1.164e+03 Sec.		

Table 4. Performance of proposed MOFA and M–MOFA algorithms for various channels in a set of 10 trials

Trials	n=6			n=8			n=15		
	RL	TBW_un (Hz)	CPU Time (Sec.)	RL	TBW_un (Hz)	CPU Time (Sec.)	RL	TBW_un (Hz)	CPU Time (Sec.)
MOFA									
1	18	42	0.5122	34	117	1.0810	260	1554	1.282e+03
2	17	44	0.4378	34	117	1.0200	260	1554	1.267e+03
3	17	44	0.4388	34	117	1.0131	260	1554	1.270e+03
4	17	44	0.4378	34	117	1.0177	260	1554	1.245e+03
5	18	42	0.4379	39	113	1.0179	260	1554	1.280e+03
6	17	44	0.4371	39	113	1.0158	260	1554	1.271e+03
7	18	42	0.3852	34	117	1.0189	260	1554	1.269e+03
8	18	42	0.4369	34	117	1.0144	260	1554	1.268e+03
9	18	42	0.4379	34	117	1.0157	260	1554	1.272e+03
10	17	44	0.4365	39	113	1.0134	260	1554	1.266e+03
	Optimal RL = 17 Optimal TBW_{un} = 42 Hz Minimum CPU time = 0.3852 Sec. Average CPU time = 0.43981 Sec.			Optimal RL = 34 Optimal TBW_{un} = 113 Hz Minimum CPU time = 1.0131 Sec. Average CPU time = 1.02279 Sec.			Optimal RL = 260 Optimal TBW_{un} = 1554 Hz Minimum CPU time = 1.245e+03 Sec. Average CPU time = 1.269e+03 Sec.		
MOFAM									
1	17	44	0.0542	34	117	0.1447	151	1047	1.159e+03
2	17	44	0.0534	34	117	0.1445	151	1047	1.167e+03
3	17	44	0.0489	34	117	0.1442	151	1047	1.166e+03
4	17	44	0.0533	39	113	0.1441	151	1047	1.167e+03
5	18	42	0.0556	39	113	0.1451	151	1047	1.163e+03
6	17	44	0.0567	34	117	0.1442	151	1047	1.164e+03

continued on following page

Table 4. Continued

Trials	n=6			n=8			n=15		
	RL	*TBW$_{un}$* (Hz)	*CPU Time* (Sec.)	*RL*	*TBW$_{un}$* (Hz)	*CPU Time* (Sec.)	*RL*	*TBW$_{un}$* (Hz)	*CPU Time* (Sec.)
7	17	44	0.0562	34	117	0.1435	151	1047	1.166e+03
8	17	44	0.0539	34	117	0.1441	151	1047	1.164e+03
9	17	44	0.0529	34	117	0.1432	151	1047	1.165e+03
10	17	44	0.0530	34	117	0.1446	151	1047	1.175e+03
	Optimal *RL* = 17 Optimal *TBW$_{un}$* = 42 Hz Minimum *CPU time* = 0.0489 Sec. Average *CPU time* = 0.05381 Sec.			Optimal *RL* = 34 Optimal *TBW$_{un}$* = 113 Hz Minimum *CPU time* = 0.1432 Sec. Average *CPU time* = 0.14422 Sec.			Optimal *RL* = 151 Optimal *TBW$_{un}$* = 1047 Hz Minimum *CPU time* = 1.159e+03 Sec. Average *CPU time* = 1.166e+03 Sec.		
MOLFA									
1	17	44	0.0519	39	113	0.1446	151	1047	1.168e+03
2	17	44	0.0538	34	117	0.1442	151	1047	1.166e+03
3	18	42	0.0481	34	117	0.1437	151	1047	1.157e+03
4	17	44	0.0549	34	117	0.1436	151	1047	1.176e+03
5	17	44	0.0577	34	117	0.1443	151	1047	1.160e+03
6	18	42	0.0565	34	117	0.1439	151	1047	1.161e+03
7	17	44	0.0542	39	113	0.1434	151	1047	1.157e+03
8	17	44	0.0519	39	113	0.1435	151	1047	1.169e+03
9	17	44	0.0557	34	117	0.1439	151	1047	1.168e+03
10	18	42	0.0519	34	117	0.1451	151	1047	1.167e+03
	Optimal *RL* = 17 Optimal *TBW$_{un}$* = 42 Hz Minimum *CPU time* = 0.0481 Sec. Average *CPU time* = 0.05366 Sec.			Optimal *RL* = 34 Optimal *TBW$_{un}$* = 113 Hz Minimum *CPU time* = 0.1434 Sec. Average *CPU time* = 0.14402 Sec.			Optimal *RL* = 151 Optimal *TBW$_{un}$* = 1047 Hz Minimum *CPU time* = 1.157e+03 Sec. Average CPU Time = 1.165e+03 Sec.		
MOLFAM									
1	18	42	0.0511	34	117	0.1387	151	1047	1.088e+03
2	18	42	0.0520	34	117	0.1411	151	1047	1.070e+03
3	18	42	0.0512	34	117	0.1386	151	1047	1.091e+03
4	18	42	0.0529	34	117	0.1388	151	1047	1.095e+03
5	17	44	0.0439	34	117	0.1389	151	1047	1.090e+03
6	17	44	0.0488	34	117	0.1386	151	1047	1.089e+03
7	17	44	0.0519	39	113	0.1385	151	1047	1.092e+03
8	17	44	0.0512	34	117	0.1391	151	1047	1.096e+03
9	17	44	0.0567	34	117	0.1392	151	1047	1.087e+03
10	17	44	0.0518	34	117	0.1385	151	1047	1.091e+03
	Optimal *RL* = 17 Optimal *TBW$_{un}$* = 42 Hz Minimum *CPU time* =0.0439 Sec. Average *CPU time* = 0.05115 Sec.			Optimal *RL* = 34 Optimal *TBW$_{un}$* = 113 Hz Minimum *CPU time* = 0.1385 Sec. Average *CPU time* = 0.1390 Sec.			Optimal *RL* = 151 Optimal *TBW$_{un}$* = 1047 Hz Minimum *CPU time* = 1.070e+03 ec. Average *CPU time* = 1.089e+03 Sec.		

Influence of Popsize

This subsection examines the influence of selecting the different *Popsize* on the performance of proposed MOAs for different values of channels. The increased *Popsize* helps to explore the search space and increases the diversity of possible solutions. After certain limit, it is not useful to increase the *Popsize*, as it does not help in solving the problem quickly. The choice of the best *Popsize* for nature–inspired based algorithms is problem specific (Bansal et al., 2017a). With the same parameter settings as reported in Tables 1 and 2, Table 5 reports the influence of selecting different *Popsize* on the performance of proposed MOAs for various channels.

Golomb rulers realized from 10 to 16–marks by TS proposed by Cotta et al. (2006), *Popsize* of 190 was fixed. The hybrid approach proposed by Ayari et al. (2010) to find Golomb rulers from 11 to 23–marks, the *Popsize* were set between 20 and 2000. The OGRs realized by GAs and BBO (Bansal, 2014), the *Popsize* was set to 30. For the hybrid algorithms (Dotú and Hentenryck, 2005), the *Popsize* was set to 50 to find near–OGRs. To realize OGRs by the BB–BC (Bansal et al., 2013), the *Popsize* was set to 10, whereas for the MOBA and its hybrid form proposed by Bansal et al. (2017a), the *Popsize* was 20 and 200, respectively.

From Table 5, it is clear that *Popsize* has little significant effect on the performance of proposed MOAs. By carefully looking at the results, the *Popsize* of 10 was found to be appropriate for proposed MOAs.

Influence of Iterations

Increasing the numbers of iteration, the possibility of finding the optimal solutions will increase. This will helps in promoting the exploitation of the search space. The choice of the best *Maxiter* for proposed MOAs is always critical for particular problem.

Increasing the number of iterations tends to decrease the total occupied optical bandwidth. This indicates that the rulers reach their optimal or near–optimal values after certain iterations. The influence of increasing iterations for various channels on the performance of MOBB–BC is illustrated in Table 6, whereas for MOFA and M–MOFA is illustrated in Table 7. It is noted that the iterations have little effect for low value channels, whereas for higher order channels, the iterations have a great effect on the total occupied optical bandwidth.

To find Golomb rulers by TS proposed by authors (Cotta et al., 2006; Ayari et al., 2010), the *Maxiter* were set to 10000 and 30000, respectively. The hybrid approach proposed by Ayari et al. (2010), finds Golomb ruler sequences within the *Maxiter* of 100000. Bansal (2014), reported that to find near–OGRs, GAs and BBO stabilized with *Maxiter* of 5000, whereas the hybrid algorithms (Dotú and Hentenryck, 2005) get stabilized in and around *Maxiter* of 10000. By carefully looking at the results, it is concluded that to find either optimal or near–OGRs, the M–MOBB–BC and MOFA stabilized at or around 1000 iterations, whereas M–MOFA stabilized at or around 900 iterations. In general, to find the n-channels near–OGR, the *Maxiter* in this chapter was set to 100 times number of channel (n), i.e.

$$Maxiter = 100 \times n \qquad (34)$$

Table 5. Influence of Popsize on the performance of M–MOBB–BC, MOBB–BC, MOFA and M-MOFA for various channels

MOBB–BCM

Popsize	n=7 RL	n=7 TBW$_{un}$ (Hz)	n=9 RL	n=9 TBW$_{un}$ (Hz)	n=14 RL	n=14 TBW$_{un}$ (Hz)
10	30	73	44	215	229	996
20	30	73	44	215	229	996
50	30	73	44	215	229	996
80	28	74	44	226	229	996
100	25	81	57	183	229	996

MOFAM

Popsize	n=7 RL	n=7 TBW$_{un}$ (Hz)	n=9 RL	n=9 TBW$_{un}$ (Hz)	n=14 RL	n=14 TBW$_{un}$ (Hz)
10	25	77	44	206	206	991
20	25	77	44	206	206	991
50	25	77	44	206	206	991
80	27	73	44	206	206	991
100	28	74	44	206	206	991

MOFA

Popsize	n=7 RL	n=7 TBW$_{un}$ (Hz)	n=9 RL	n=9 TBW$_{un}$ (Hz)	n=14 RL	n=14 TBW$_{un}$ (Hz)
10	27	73	44	208	206	991
20	27	73	44	208	206	991
50	27	73	44	208	206	991
80	26	77	44	208	206	991
100	25	80	49	206	169	1001

M-MOBB-BC — **MOLBB–BC**

Popsize	n=7 RL	n=7 TBW$_{un}$ (Hz)	n=9 RL	n=9 TBW$_{un}$ (Hz)	n=14 RL	n=14 TBW$_{un}$ (Hz)
10	25	77	46	204	221	1166
20	25	77	46	204	221	1166
50	25	77	46	204	221	1166
80	25	77	57	186	221	1166
100	30	73	58	177	221	1166

M-MOMFA — **MOLFA**

Popsize	n=7 RL	n=7 TBW$_{un}$ (Hz)	n=9 RL	n=9 TBW$_{un}$ (Hz)	n=14 RL	n=14 TBW$_{un}$ (Hz)
10	27	73	49	206	169	1001
20	26	77	44	206	169	1001
50	26	77	44	206	169	1001
80	25	80	44	206	169	1001
100	25	80	44	206	169	1001

MOLBB–BCM

Popsize	n=7 RL	n=7 TBW$_{un}$ (Hz)	n=9 RL	n=9 TBW$_{un}$ (Hz)	n=14 RL	n=14 TBW$_{un}$ (Hz)
10	25	77	44	208	206	1285
20	25	77	44	208	206	1285
50	25	77	44	208	206	1285
80	28	74	55	176	226	993
100	30	73	44	208	206	1285

MOLFAM

Popsize	n=7 RL	n=7 TBW$_{un}$ (Hz)	n=9 RL	n=9 TBW$_{un}$ (Hz)	n=14 RL	n=14 TBW$_{un}$ (Hz)
10	25	77	44	206	127	927
20	25	77	44	206	127	927
50	25	77	44	206	127	927
80	25	77	49	206	127	927
100	28	74	44	206	127	927

Table 6. Influence of increasing iterations on the performance of M–MOBB–BC algorithm in terms on TBW$_{un}$ in Hz for various channels

Iterations	n=7	n=8	n=9	n=10	n=11	n=12	n=13	n=14	n=16	n=18
MOBB–BCM										
5	115	212	655	479	689	971	1230	2467	4113	7185
50	74	117	199	346	613	766	1087	2295	3460	6825
100	73	113	186	333	459	581	1048	2176	2745	6660
150	73	113	183	285	388	562	970	1920	2497	6312
250	73	113	183	274	377	549	904	1746	2338	6214
350	73	113	183	274	377	549	736	1477	2143	5817
500	73	113	183	274	377	549	736	1308	2040	5516
600	73	113	183	274	377	549	736	996	2026	4814
700	73	113	183	274	377	549	736	996	1985	3264
800	73	113	183	274	377	549	736	996	1985	2669
900	73	113	183	274	377	549	736	996	1985	2566
1000	73	113	183	274	377	549	736	996	1985	2566
1200	73	113	183	274	377	549	736	996	1985	2566
1800	73	113	183	274	377	549	736	996	1985	2566
2000	73	113	183	274	377	549	736	996	1985	2566
MOLBB–BC										
5	96	174	373	619	671	864	1190	2274	4261	7088
50	74	113	190	583	519	682	970	2138	3623	6767
100	73	113	177	336	490	679	881	1937	3032	6591
150	73	113	177	304	437	567	823	1723	2745	6244
250	73	113	177	258	378	565	768	1583	2592	5819
350	73	113	177	258	378	565	700	1332	2215	5620
500	73	113	177	258	378	565	700	1219	2100	4817
600	73	113	177	258	378	565	700	1166	2061	4019
700	73	113	177	258	378	565	700	1166	1985	3712
800	73	113	177	258	378	565	700	1166	1985	3397
900	73	113	177	258	378	565	700	1166	1985	2872
1000	73	113	177	258	378	565	700	1166	1985	2872
1200	73	113	177	258	378	565	700	1166	1985	2872
1800	73	113	177	258	378	565	700	1166	1985	2872
2000	73	113	177	258	378	565	700	1166	1985	2872
MOLBB–BCM										
5	74	139	199	405	606	758	1134	2333	3525	6887
50	73	113	183	360	461	605	1049	2242	3525	6660
100	73	113	176	295	387	581	876	1861	2901	6187

continued on following page

Table 6. Continued

Iterations	n=7	n=8	n=9	n=10	n=11	n=12	n=13	n=14	n=16	n=18
150	73	113	176	274	378	550	828	1680	2721	5820
250	73	113	176	259	369	520	786	1494	2484	5718
350	73	113	176	259	369	520	725	1290	2233	4779
500	73	113	176	259	369	520	725	1177	2149	4458
600	73	113	176	259	369	520	725	993	1985	4104
700	73	113	176	259	369	520	725	993	1804	3822
800	73	113	176	259	369	520	725	993	1804	3264
900	73	113	176	259	369	520	725	993	1804	2872
1000	73	113	176	259	369	520	725	993	1804	2872
1200	73	113	176	259	369	520	725	993	1804	2872
1800	73	113	176	259	369	520	725	993	1804	2872
2000	73	113	176	259	369	520	725	993	1804	2872

Table 7. Influence of increasing iterations on the performance of MOFA and M–MOFA in terms on TBW_{un} (Hz) for various channels

Iterations	n=7	n=8	n=9	n=10	n=11	n=12	n=13	n=14	n=16	n=18
MOFA										
5	95	149	342	408	682	831	1297	2242	3703	6244
50	73	113	268	336	523	736	1092	2125	2943	6028
100	73	113	206	287	402	711	987	1883	2497	5812
150	73	113	206	249	399	605	935	1680	2338	5626
250	73	113	206	249	391	562	786	1477	2338	5312
350	73	113	206	249	391	562	725	1434	2233	4714
500	73	113	206	249	391	562	725	1288	2215	4112
600	73	113	206	249	391	562	725	1001	2215	3512
700	73	113	206	249	391	562	725	1001	1804	3221
800	73	113	206	249	391	562	725	1001	1804	3100
900	73	113	206	249	391	562	725	1001	1804	2599
1000	73	113	206	249	391	562	725	1001	1804	2599
1200	73	113	206	249	391	562	725	1001	1804	2599
1800	73	113	206	249	391	562	725	1001	1804	2599
2000	73	113	206	249	391	562	725	1001	1804	2599
MOFAM										
5	93	124	254	336	664	746	1115	1937	2215	6187
50	73	113	206	297	559	628	1047	1937	2215	5799
100	73	113	206	249	450	558	951	1876	2143	5726
150	73	113	206	249	386	551	823	1477	2143	5594
250	73	113	206	249	386	551	786	1285	2026	5098
350	73	113	206	249	386	551	675	1166	1985	4112

continued on following page

Table 7. Continued

Iterations	n=7	n=8	n=9	n=10	n=11	n=12	n=13	n=14	n=16	n=18
500	73	113	206	249	386	551	675	991	1834	3789
600	73	113	206	249	386	551	675	991	1804	3367
700	73	113	206	249	386	551	675	991	1804	3123
800	73	113	206	249	386	551	675	991	1804	2912
900	73	113	206	249	386	551	675	991	1804	2912
1000	73	113	206	249	386	551	675	991	1804	2912
1200	73	113	206	249	386	551	675	991	1804	2912
1800	73	113	206	249	386	551	675	991	1804	2912
2000	73	113	206	249	386	551	675	991	1804	2912
MOLFA										
5	81	121	247	298	671	711	1121	2141	2497	6072
50	73	113	206	280	502	679	1065	1920	2452	5920
100	73	113	206	249	458	581	1048	1883	2143	5704
150	73	113	206	249	378	551	987	1494	2040	5484
250	73	113	206	249	378	551	951	1159	2040	4953
350	73	113	206	249	378	551	673	1114	2100	3927
500	73	113	206	249	378	551	673	1001	1958	3680
600	73	113	206	249	378	551	673	1001	1804	3113
700	73	113	206	249	378	551	673	1001	1804	2806
800	73	113	206	249	378	551	673	1001	1804	2566
900	73	113	206	249	378	551	673	1001	1804	2566
1000	73	113	206	249	378	551	673	1001	1804	2566
1200	73	113	206	249	378	551	673	1001	1804	2566
1800	73	113	206	249	378	551	673	1001	1804	2566
2000	73	113	206	249	378	551	673	1001	1804	2566
MOLFAM										
5	73	113	206	268	646	611	1230	1723	2149	5775
50	73	113	185	258	489	546	1025	1424	2149	5718
100	73	113	185	249	391	515	915	1219	2061	5509
150	73	113	185	249	378	503	786	1177	1985	5065
250	73	113	185	249	378	503	660	1001	1960	4740
350	73	113	185	249	378	503	660	991	1834	3822
500	73	113	185	249	378	503	660	924	1804	3508
600	73	113	185	249	378	503	660	924	1298	3100
700	73	113	185	249	378	503	660	924	1298	2678
800	73	113	185	249	378	503	660	924	1298	2566
900	73	113	185	249	378	503	660	924	1298	2566
1000	73	113	185	249	378	503	660	924	1298	2566
1200	73	113	185	249	378	503	660	924	1298	2566
1800	73	113	185	249	378	503	660	924	1298	2566
2000	73	113	185	249	378	503	660	924	1298	2566

Performance Comparison in Terms of RL and TBW$_{un}$

Table 8 reports the RL and TBW_{un} by different sequences obtained from the proposed MOAs and their performance comparison with best known OGRs, EQC, SA, GAs, BBO, and simple BB–BC. Kwong and Yang (1997) reported that EQC and SA have their applications limited to prime powers only, so RL and TBW_{un} for EQC and SA are shown by a dash line in Table 8. Comparing RL and TBW_{un} obtained from the proposed MOAs with best known OGRs and existing algorithms, it is noted that there is a significant improvement in the results. Figures 5 and 6 illustrate the graphical representation of Table 8 in terms of RL and TBW_{un} for various channels, respectively.

Table 8. Performance comparison in terms of RL and TBW$_{un}$ for various channels

n	RL	TBW_{un} (Hz)	RL	TBW_{un} (Hz)	RL	TBW_{un} (Hz)	RL	TBW_{un} (Hz)	RL	TBW_{un} (Hz)	RL	TBW_{un} (Hz)
						Algorithms						
	Best Known OGRs		**Conventional Algorithms**				**Existing Nature–Inspired Algorithms**					
			EQC		**SA**		**GAs**		**BBO**		**BB–BC**	
3	3	4	6	10	6	4	3	4	3	4	3	4
4	6	11	15	28	15	28	6 7	11	6 7	11	6 7	11
5	11	25 28	—	—	—	—	12 13	23 25 29	12 13	23 24	11 12	23 25
6	17	44 47 50 52	45	140	20	60	17 18 21	42 44 45	17 18 20 21	42 43 44 45 49	17 18	42 44
7	25	77 81 87 90 95	—	—	—	—	27 28 29 30 31 32	73 78 79 80 83 86 95	27 29 30 31 32 33	73 82 83 84 91 95	25 26 28 30	73 74 77 81
8	34	117	91	378	49	189	35 41 42 45 46	121 126 128 129 131 133	34 39 40 42	121 125 127 131	39 41 42	113 118 119
9	44	206	—	—	—	—	52 56 59 61 63 65	192 193 196 203 225	49 56 61 62 64	187 200 201 206 215	44 45 46 61	179 248 253 262
10	55	249	—	—	—	—	75 76	283 287 301	74	274	77	258
11	72	386 391	—	—	—	—	94 96	395 456	86 103 104 114 118	378 435 440 491	72 105	377 490 456

continued on following page

Table 8. Continued

n	RL	TBW_{un} (Hz)	RL	TBW_{un} (Hz)	RL	TBW_{un} (Hz)	RL	TBW_{un} (Hz)	RL	TBW_{un} (Hz)	RL	TBW_{un} (Hz)
12	85	503	231	1441	132	682	123 128 137	532 581 660	116 124 138	556 590 605	85 91	550 580 613
13	106	660	—	—	—	—	203 241	1015 1048	156 171 187	768 786 970	110 113	768 753
14	127	924	325	2340	286	1820	206 228 230	1172 1177 1285	169 206 221	991 1001 1166	221	1166
15	151	1047	—	—	—	—	275 298	1634 1653	260 267	1322 1554	267	1322
16	177	1298	—	—	—	—	316	1985	283	1804	316	1985
17	199	1661	—	—	—	—	355	2205	354 369	2201 2208	369	2201
18	216	1894	561	5203	493	5100	427 463	2599 3079	362 445	2566 2912	427	3079
19	246	2225	—	—	—	—	567 597	3432 5067	467 475 584	3337 3408 4101	584	4101
20	283	2794	703	7163	703	6460	615 673 680 691	4660 4826 4905 4941	578 593 649	4306 4517 4859	691	4941

Algorithms						
Proposed MOAs						
M–MOBB–BC				**M–MOFA**		
MOBB–BCM		**MOLBB–BC**		**MOLBB–BCM**		**MOFAM**

n	MOBB–BCM 3	4	MOLBB–BC 3	4	MOLBB–BCM 3	4	MOFAM 3	4	MOLFA 3	4	MOLFAM 3	4
3	3	4	3	4	3	4	3	4	3	4	3	4
4	6 7	11	6 7	11	6 7	11	6	11	6	11	6	11
5	11 12	23 25	11 12 13	23 24 25	11 12	23 25 28	11 12 13	23 24	11 12	23 24	11 12 13	23 24
6	17 18	42 44 46	17 18	42 44	17 18	42 44 46	17 18	42 44	17 18	42 44	17 18	42 44
7	25 27 28 30	73 74 77 79	25 30	73 77 81	25 28 30	73 74 77	25 27 28	73 74 77	25 26 27	73 77 80 81	25 26 27 28	73 74 77
8	39 41	113 118	39 41	113 118	34 39	113 117	34 39	113 117	34 39	113 117	34 39	113 117
9	44 57	183 215 226	46 47 58	177 204 217 228	44 55	176 208	44 49	206	44 49	206	44 47 49	185 206
10	55 58 74	274 299 311	55 77	258 321 341	55	259 309	55	249	55	249	55	249
11	72 105	377 435	72 103	378 439	72 96	369 397 434	72	386	72 103	378 391	72 103	378 386 391
12	85 90	549 565	85 90	565 567	85 91 93	520 551 550	85	503	85	503	85	503

continued on following page

Table 8. Continued

n	RL	TBW_{un} (Hz)	RL	TBW_{un} (Hz)	RL	TBW_{un} (Hz)	RL	TBW_{un} (Hz)	RL	TBW_{un} (Hz)	RL	TBW_{un} (Hz)
13	106 110	736 755 848	109 111	700 751 763	106 111	725 744	106 111	675 725	106 111	673 720	106	660
14	229	996	221	1166	206 226	993 1285	206	991	169	1001	127	924
15	267	1322	267	1322	260	1554	151	1047	151	1047	151	1047
16	316	1985	316	1985	283	1804	283	1804	283	1804	177	1298
17	369	2201	369	2201	355	2205	354	2208	354	2208	369	2201
18	445	2566	436	2872	436	2872	362	2912	445	2566	445	2566
19	567	3432	584	4101	467	3337	467	3337	475	3408	467	3337
20	673	4826	673	4826	649	4517	615	4660	615	4660	578	4306
	MOFA											
3	3	4										
4	6 7	11										
5	11 12 13	23 24 25										
6	17 18	42 44										
7	25 26 27	73 77 80 81										
8	34 39	113 117										
9	44 49	206 208										
10	55	249										
11	72	391										
12	85	515										
13	106	725 744										
14	169 206	991 1001										
15	260	1554										
16	283	1804										
17	355	2205										
18	463	2599										
19	567	3432										
20	649	4517										

The simulation results are particularly impressive. First, observe that for all the proposed MOAs, the RL obtained up to 13–marks are same as that of best known OGRs and the TBW_{un} for marks 5 to 9 and 11 is smaller than the best known OGRs, while all the other rulers obtained are either optimal or near–optimal. Second, observe that MOBB–BCM and MOLBB–BC does not find best known OGRs

Figure 5. Comparison of the RL obtained for various channels by proposed MOAs with best known OGRs, EQC, SA, GAs, BBO, and simple BB–BC

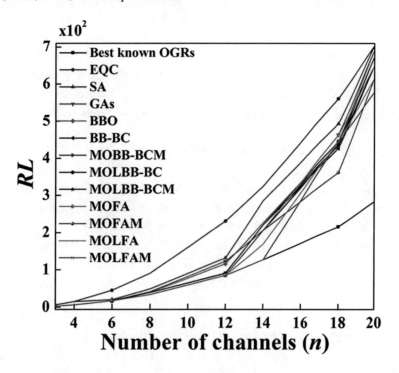

Figure 6. Comparison of the TBW$_{un}$ obtained for various channels by proposed MOAs with best known OGRs, EQC, SA, GAs, BBO, and simple BB–BC

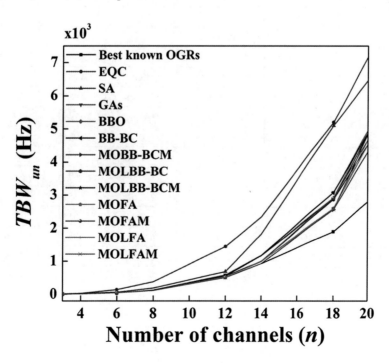

for $n > 7$, but finds near–OGRs for $8 \leq n \leq 20$. MOLBB–BCM can find best optimal rulers up to 8–marks, but finds near–optimal rulers for $n > 8$, whereas MOFA can find best rulers for up to 11–marks. MOFAM and MOLFA can find OGRs for up to 12–marks and near–OGRs for $n > 12$. By combining the features of MOFAM and MOLFA into a single composite algorithm MOLFAM, OGRs up to 16–marks and near–OGRs for $17 \leq n \leq 20$ can be find efficiently and effectively.

From the simulation results illustrated in Table 8, it is further noted that modified forms of the proposed MOAs, outperforms the algorithms presented in their simplified forms. Thus, it is concluded that MOLFAM outperforms the other existing and proposed MOAs in terms of both RL and TBW_{un}.

Performance Comparison in Terms of BEF

The *BEF* gives the factor of expanded bandwidth with the use of USCA for a given number of channels to that of equally spaced channel–allocation for the same number of channels. Table 9 reports the calculated *BEF* for different number of channels by the proposed MOAs.

From Table 9, it can be seen that the *BEF*, as expected, increases with the number of channels. The *BEF* for MOLFAM is less than the other algorithms. The obtained *BEF* indicates that MOLFAM needs lesser bandwidth requirements than the other algorithms.

Table 9. Performance comparison in terms of BEF for various channels

n	TBW_{eq} (Hz) (Randhawa et al., 2009)	Known OGRs	EQC (Randhawa et al., 2009)	SA (Randhawa et al., 2009)	GAs (Bansal, 2014)	BBO (Bansal, 2014)	BB–BC (Bansal et al. 2017a)
4	12	0.9166	2.3333	2.3333	0.9166	0.9166	0.9166
6	35	1.2571	4.0	1.7142	1.2857	1.2857	1.2571
8	70	1.6714	5.4	2.7	1.8	1.7286	1.6857
12	176	2.8579	8.1875	3.875	3.0227	3.1591	3.125
14	247	3.7408	9.4736	7.3684	4.7449	4.7206	4.7206
18	425	4.4564	12.2423	12.0	6.7576	6.1153	7.2447
20	532	5.2518	13.4642	12.1428	9.2875	8.7594	9.0714
n	MOBB–BCM	MOLBB–BC	MOLBB–BCM	MOFA	MOFAM	MOLFA	MOLFAM
4	0.9166	0.9166	0.9166	0.9166	0.9166	0.9166	0.9166
6	1.2571	1.2571	1.2571	1.2571	1.2571	1.2	1.2
8	1.6857	1.6857	1.6714	1.6714	1.6714	1.6143	1.6143
12	3.2102	3.1193	2.9545	2.9261	2.8579	2.8579	2.8579
14	4.0526	4.0324	4.7206	4.0202	4.0121	4.7206	3.7409
18	6.0376	6.7576	6.0376	6.1153	6.8517	6.0376	6.0376
20	9.0714	8.094	8.4906	8.7594	8.4906	8.7594	8.0939

Performance Comparison in Terms of CPU Time

The OGRs generation by classical computing and exhaustive parallel search for higher order marks is computationally very time consuming, which took several hours, months and even years of calculations on several thousand computers (Distributed.net, 2017; Dollas et al., 1998; Leitao, 2004; Shearer, 1998; Shearer, 2001a; Shearer, 2001b).

Table 10 enlists the average *CPU time* in seconds taken by proposed MOAs to find near–OGRs for up to 20–marks and their comparison with the *CPU time* taken by existing algorithms (Ayari et al., 2010; Bansal et al., 2013; Bansal, 2014; Distributed.net, 2017; Dollas et al., 1998; Leitao, 2004; Shearer, 1990; Soliday et al., 1995). Figure 7 illustrates the graphical representation of the Table 10. It was reported by Soliday et al. (1995) that to find Golomb ruler sequences from heuristic based exhaustive search algorithm, the computation times varied from 0.035 seconds for 5–marks to 6 weeks for 13–marks ruler, whereas non–heuristic exhaustive search algorithms took approximately 12.57 minutes, 2.28 years, 2.07e+04 years, 3.92e+09 years, 1.61e+15 years, and 9.36e+20 years of calculations for 10, 12, 14, 16, 18 and 20–marks, respectively. It was identified by Ayari et al. (2010) that to find OGRs by TS algorithm the computational *CPU time* in seconds was around 0.1, 720, 960, 1913, and 2516, for 5, 10, 11, 12, and 13–marks, respectively. The OGRs realized by hybrid GAs proposed by Ayari et al. (2010) the *CPU time* in hours was 5, 8, and 11 for 11, 12, and 13–marks, respectively. The exhaustive computer search algorithms (Shearer, 1990) find OGRs for 14 and 16–marks in an around one and hundred hours, respectively, whereas 17, 18 and 19–marks OGR realized by authors (Rankin, 1993; Dollas et al., 1998), took around 1440, 8600 and 36200 CPU hours of calculations, respectively, on a Sun SPARC Classic workstation. The near–OGRs realized by algorithms GAs and BBO (Bansal, 2014) up to 20–marks the maximum *CPU time* was approximately 31 hours, while for algorithm simple BB–BC (Bansal et al., 2013; Bansal et at., 2017a) the maximum execution time was around 28 hours.

From Table 10, it is clear that for proposed MOAs, the average *CPU time* varied from 0.0 second for 3–marks ruler to around 27 hours for 20–marks ruler. With the applications of mutation and Lévy flight strategies with the proposed MOAs, the *CPU time* for 20–marks ruler is reduced to approximately 20 hours. This signifies the improvement realized by the use of proposed MOAs to find near–OGRs. It is also noted that MOLFAM outperforms the other algorithms followed by MOLFA, MOFAM, MOFA, MOLBB–BCM, MOLBB–BC, MOBB–BCM, BB–BC, BBO, and GAs in terms of *CPU time*.

Performance Comparison in Terms of Maximum Computation Complexity

To search for the near–OGRs, the proposed MOAs have an initialization stage and a subsequent stage of iterations. The maximum *computational complexity* of proposed MOAs depends upon *Popsize*, *Maxiter*, and N (Bansal et at., 2017a)

$$Computation\ Complexity = Popsize \times Maxiter \times N \tag{35}$$

Alternatively, maximum *computational complexity* can be re–written as

$$Computation\ Complexity = Popsize \times 100 \times n \times N \tag{36}$$

Table 10. Performance comparison of average CPU time (sec.) for various channels

n	Existing Nature–Inspired Algorithms			Proposed MOAs	
	GAs	BBO	BB–BC	MOBB–BCM	MOLBB–BC
3	0.000	0.000	0.000	0.000	0.000
4	0.001	0.000	0.000	0.000	0.000
5	0.021	0.020	0.009	0.011	0.001
6	0.780	0.7432	0.659	0.4398	0.0589
7	1.120	1.180	1.170	0.8520	0.0936
8	1.241	1.239	1.210	1.0227	0.1986
9	1.711	1.699	1.698	1.4890	1.3190
10	5.499e+01	5.491e+01	5.450e+01	5.211e+01	3.321e+01
11	7.200e+02	7.110e+02	6.990e+02	6.710e+02	4.982e+02
12	8.602e+02	8.600e+02	7.981e+02	7.890e+02	5.865e+02
13	1.070e+03	1.030e+03	1.020e+03	1.010e+03	8.989e+02
14	1.028e+03	1.027e+03	1.021e+03	1.019e+03	1.019e+03
15	1.440e+03	1.480e+03	1.291e+03	1.270e+03	1.187e+03
16	1.680e+03	1.677e+03	1.450e+03	1.439e+03	1.367e+03
17	5.048e+04	5.040e+04	4.075e+04	4.041e+03	3.759e+03
18	6.840e+04	6.839e+04	5.897e+04	5.875e+04	4.087e+04
19	8.280e+04	8.280e+04	7.158e+04	7.132e+04	6.988e+04
20	1.12428e+05	1.1196e+05	1.0012e+05	9.876e+04	9.859e+04
n	Proposed MOAs				
	MOLBB–BCM	MOFA	MOFAM	MOLFA	MOLFAM
3	0.000	0.000	0.000	0.000	0.000
4	0.000	0.000	0.000	0.000	0.000
5	0.001	0.001	0.001	0.001	0.001
6	0.0584	0.0549	0.0538	0.0536	0.0512
7	0.0935	0.0919	0.0899	0.0895	0.0870
8	0.1984	0.1961	0.1442	0.1440	0.1390
9	1.3170	1.1990	1.1890	1.1880	1.1770
10	3.319e+01	3.160e+01	3.151e+01	3.149e+01	3.120e+01
11	4.982e+02	4.782e+02	4.767e+02	4.765e+02	4.656e+02
12	5.864e+02	5.658e+02	5.652e+02	5.645e+02	5.648e+02
13	8.980e+02	8.563e+02	8.550e+02	8.751e+02	8.436e+02
14	1.018e+03	1.016e+03	1.014e+03	1.012e+03	0.981e+03
15	1.185e+03	1.166e+03	1.165e+03	1.163e+03	1.090e+03
16	1.366e+03	1.342e+03	1.289e+03	1.287e+03	1.158e+03
17	3.760e+03	3.542e+03	3.460e+03	3.455e+03	3.320e+03
18	4.085e+04	3.998e+04	4.077e+04	4.076e+04	3.880e+04
19	6.986e+04	6.691e+04	6.682e+04	6.442e+04	6.390e+04
20	9.810e+04	9.356e+04	7.335e+04	7.232e+04	7.110e+04

Figure 7. Comparison of CPU time obtained for various channels by proposed MOAs with GAs, BBO, and simple BB–BC

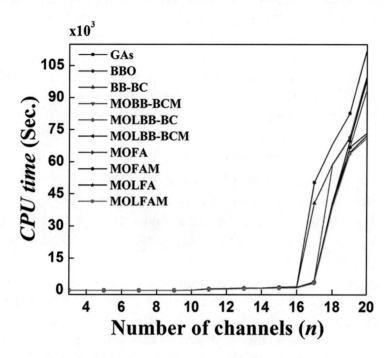

The maximum *computation complexity* of the TS algorithm (Ayari et al., 2010) to find Golomb ruler sequences was found to be 57e+05, whereas for hybrid GAs (Ayari et al., 2010) was 2e+08. The maximum *computation complexity* for algorithms GAs and BBO (Bansal, 2014) was 15e+04.

For example, to find 16–mark near–OGRs the *computation complexity* for MOBB–BCM, MOLBB–BC, MOLBB–BCM, MOFA, MOFAM, MOLFA, and MOLFAM is 66e+04, 65e+04, 62e+04, 615e+03, 55e+04, 53e+04, and 51e+04, respectively. It is also further concluded that by introducing the concept of mutation and Lévy flight strategies in the simplified form of MOAs the *computation complexity* is reduced.

Theoretically, the maximum *computation complexity* for all proposed MOAs upto 20–marks is 10×100×20×100=2e+06. As described in above subsection, to generate near–OGRs up to 20–marks, M–MOBB–BC and MOFA stabilized in *Maxiter* of 1000, whereas M–MOFA stabilized within *Maxiter* of 900. Thus, practically, the maximum computation complexity of M–MOBB–BC and MOFA to generate 20–marks OGR is 10×1000×100=1e+06, whereas for M–MOFA is 10×900×100=9e+05. Thus M–MOFA generates OGRs upto 20–marks for WDM systems efficiently than that of other proposed MOAs.

Performance Comparison in Terms of Statistical Analysis

To analyze the performance of the proposed MOAs, the non–parametric statistical analysis of each algorithm is performed. For performing the statistical analysis, each algorithm was executed 20 times using the same parameter values as reported in the above subsections. The optimal values of RL, TBW_{un} (Hz), *BEF*, and *CPU time* (Sec.) after each trial were estimated for the non–parametric statistical analysis.

From the above discussions, it is clear that MOLFAM potentially outperforms the other algorithms. To evaluate whether the near–OGRs found by MOLFAM are significant or not, non–parametric Friedman's statistical test (Derrac et al., 2011) is performed. The non–parametric statistical analysis defines the two hypotheses: the null hypothesis H_0 and the alternative hypothesis H_1. In order to reject the null hypothesis, a 95% significance level of confidence is used to analyze at which level the null hypothesis can be rejected. Here, a *p*-value is estimated to determine whether a statistical hypothesis analysis for the proposed MOAs is significant or not, and it also gives information about how significant the results are. Table 11 enlists the mean ranking calculated from Friedman's statistical test in terms of RL, TBW_{un} (Hz), *BEF*, and *CPU time* (Sec.). At a 95% significance level of confidence with 9 as degrees of freedom the critical value in χ^2 distribution is 3.325. As clear from Table 11, the calculated Friedman's statistic value for RL, TBW_{un} (Hz), *BEF*, and *CPU time* (Sec.) are larger than the critical values in χ^2 distribution. It suggests that there is a significant change among the performances of proposed MOAs, i.e. the null hypothesis H_0 is rejected. The algorithm MOLFAM is with the lowest rank and potentially outperforms the other algorithms. The estimated *p*–value in Friedman's statistic is <0.00001 for RL, TBW_{un} (Hz), *BEF*, and *CPU time* (Sec.).

Using MOLFAM as a control algorithm, the Holm's post–hoc statistical test (Holm, 1979) is performed to determine the statistical better performance of the algorithm MOLFAM to find OGRs. The unadjusted and adjusted *p*-values estimated through the Holm's post–hoc statistical procedure is mentioned in Table 12. It is clear that MOLFAM outperforms the other algorithms for OGRs problem in terms of both efficiency and success rate at 95% significance level of confidence. This is no surprise as the objective of formulating the MOAs and their modified forms to find OGRs was to use the advantages of mutation and Lévy–flight strategies. The performance comparison of proposed MOAs suggests that MOLFAM is more dominant and thus should be further examined in several complex applications of multi–objective optimization problems.

Table 11. Mean rankings obtained by Friedman's non–parametric test

Algorithms	Friedman's Non–Parametric Statistical Test			
	Mean Rank			
	RL	*TBW_{un}* (Hz)	*BEF*	*CPU Time* (Sec.)
MOLFAM	3.9722	2.1944	2.1429	1.6667
MOLFA	4.1389	3.6667	3.7857	2.5556
MOFAM	4.3056	4.0833	4.5	3.2778
MOFA	4.6667	5.0	4.7857	3.9444
MOLBB-BCM	5.1667	5.1944	4.7857	5.0278
MOLBB-BC	5.4167	6.25	5.5	5.7222
MOBB-BCM	6.2778	6.2778	6.2857	6.8333
BB-BC	6.6944	6.6944	7.4286	7.6944
BBO	6.8333	7.5556	7.4286	8.7222
GAs	7.5278	8.0833	8.3571	9.5556
Friedman's statistic value	6.7777	13.6972	5.9551	120.2153
p–value	<0.00001	<0.00001	0.00001	<0.00001

Table 12. Unadjusted and adjusted p–values found for RL, TBW$_{un}$, BEF, and CPU time through Holm's post–hoc procedure with MOLFAM as control algorithm

Algorithms	Unadjusted *p*–Value	Adjusted *p*–Value	Unadjusted *p*–Value	Adjusted *p*–Value
	RL		*TBW$_{un}$* (Hz)	
MOLFA	3.3113e-08	1.6933e-08	1.0717e-19	1.0717e-19
MOFAM	2.2e-06	4.0e-06	4.7911e-17	2.45e-17
MOFA	7.3e-05	1.1e-05	7.8513e-13	2.7388e-13
MOLBB-BCM	0.0018	0.0002	6.7988e-11	1.4924e-11
MOLBB-BC	0.8188	0.0269	8.9043e-11	1.6696e-11
MOBB-BCM	0.3303	0.0747	3.0e-06	2.85e-07
BB-BC	1.0	0.3746	1.4e-05	1.0e-06
BBO	1.0	0.7641	0.0119	0.001
GAs	1.0	0.7641	0.1124	0.01
	BEF		*CPU Time* (Sec.)	
MOLFA	0.0005	0.0005	1.5432e-57	1.5432e-57
MOFAM	0.0057	0.0019	1.4372e-51	7.3491e-52
MOFA	0.0057	0.0019	1.1757e-43	2.2044e-44
MOLBB-BCM	0.0862	0.0189	1.5849e-36	21418e-37
MOLBB-BC	0.4005	0.0468	8.7790e-27	8.4958e-28
MOBB-BCM	1.0	0.0993	1.5098e-20	1.3065e-21
BB-BC	1.0	0.0993	3.3418e-11	2.9837e-12
BBO	1.0	0.1463	2.0e-06	2.8439e-07
GAs	1.0	0.3304	0.0193	0.003618

CONCLUSION

A bandwidth efficient USCA by considering the concept of near–OGRs for an optical WDM system to suppress FWM crosstalk was presented. The search for OGRs through either classical computing or exact algorithms is computationally tough problem. This is because as the number of marks increases, the search for OGRs becomes computationally complex optimization problem. In this chapter, the application of two nature–inspired based MOAs, (MOBB–BC and MOFA) and their modified forms (M–MOBB–BC and M–MOFA) to find the near–OGRs for optical WDM systems was proposed. The proposed MOAs were modified by introducing mutation and Lévy flight strategies in their standard forms. The proposed algorithms outperformed the other existing algorithms in terms of ruler length, total occupied optical bandwidth, *BEF*, computation time, and statistical analysis. It had also been observed that modified forms, finds near–OGRs very efficiently and effectively than their simplified forms.

The simulated results suggest that for large order marks, the algorithm MOLFAM potentially out-performed the others algorithms. The obtained promising results motivate us to extend the proposed hybrid MOAs study by applying them to real–optical WDM systems and in the future, the proposed modifications will be considered.

REFERENCES

Abbass, H. A., & Sarker, R. (2002). The Pareto Differential Evolution Algorithm. *International Journal of Artificial Intelligence Tools*, *11*(4), 531–552. doi:10.1142/S0218213002001039

Aggarwal, G. P. (2001). *Nonlinear Fiber Optics* (2nd ed.). San Diego, CA: Academic Press.

Atkinson, M. D., Santoro, N., & Urrutia, J. (1986). Integer Sets with Distinct Sums and Differences and Carrier Frequency Assignments for Nonlinear Repeaters. *IEEE Transactions on Communications*, *34*(6), 614–617. doi:10.1109/TCOM.1986.1096587

Ayari, N., Luong, T. V., & Jemai, A. (2010). A Hybrid Genetic Algorithm for Golomb Ruler Problem. *Proceedings of ACS/IEEE International Conference on Computer Systems and Applications (AICC-SA–2010)*, 1–4. doi:10.1109/AICCSA.2010.5586955

Babcock, W. (1953). Intermodulation Interference in Radio Systems. *The Bell System Technical Journal*, *32*(1), 63–73. doi:10.1002/j.1538-7305.1953.tb01422.x

Bansal, S. (2014). Optimal Golomb Ruler Sequence Generation for FWM Crosstalk Elimination: Soft Computing Versus Conventional Approaches. *Applied Soft Computing*, *22*, 443–457. doi:10.1016/j.asoc.2014.04.015

Bansal, S., Chauhan, R., & Kumar, P. (2014). A Cuckoo Search based WDM Channel Allocation Algorithm. *International Journal of Computers and Applications*, *96*(20), 6–12. doi:10.5120/16908-6988

Bansal, S., Gupta, N., & Singh, A. K. (2017b). Nature–Inspired Metaheuristic Algorithms to Find Near–OGR Sequences for WDM Channel Allocation and their Performance Comparison. *Open Mathematics*, *15*(1), 520–547. doi:10.1515/math-2017-0045

Bansal, S., Kumar, S., & Bhalla, P. (2013). A Novel Approach to WDM Channel Allocation: Big Bang–Big Crunch Optimization. *Proceeding of Zonal Seminar on Emerging Trends in Embedded System Technologies (ETECH–2013)*, 80–81.

Bansal, S., Kumar, S., Sharma, H., & Bhalla, P. (2011). Golomb Ruler Sequences Optimization: A BBO Approach. *International Journal of Computer Science and Information Security*, *9*(5), 63–71.

Bansal, S., Singh, A. K., & Gupta, N. (2017a). Optimal Golomb Ruler Sequences Generation: A Novel Parallel Hybrid Multi–Objective Bat Algorithm. *Journal of The Institution of Engineers (India): Series B, 98*(1), 43–64, doi: 10.1007/s40031-016-0249-1

Bansal, S., & Singh, K. (2014). A Novel Soft–Computing Algorithm for Channel Allocation in WDM Systems. *International Journal of Computers and Applications*, *85*(9), 19–26. doi:10.5120/14869-3244

Bloom, G. S., & Golomb, S. W. (1977). Applications of Numbered Undirected Graphs. *Proceedings of the IEEE*, *65*(4), 562–570. doi:10.1109/PROC.1977.10517

Blum, E. J., Biraud, F., & Ribes, J. C. (1974). On Optimal Synthetic Linear Arrays with Applications to Radio Astronomy. *IEEE Transactions on Antennas and Propagation*, *22*(1), 108–109. doi:10.1109/TAP.1974.1140732

Chraplyvy, A. R. (1990). Limitations on Lightwave Communications Imposed by Optical–Fiber Nonlinearities. *Journal of Lightwave Technology*, *8*(10), 1548–1557. doi:10.1109/50.59195

Colannino, J. (2003). *Circular and Modular Golomb Rulers*. Available at http://cgm.cs.mcgill.ca/~athens/cs507/Projects/2003/JustinColannino/

Cotta, C., Dotú, I., Fernández, A. J., & Hentenryck, P. V. (2006). *A Memetic Approach to Golomb Rulers. In* Lecture Notes in Computer Science: Vol. 4193. *Parallel Problem Solving from Nature–PPSN IX* (pp. 252–261). Springer–Verlag Berlin Heidelberg. doi:10.1007/11844297_26

Cotta, C., Dotu, I., Fernandez, A. J., & Hentenryck, P. V. (2007). Local Search–Based Hybrid Algorithms for Finding Golomb Rulers. Kluwer Academic Publishers.

Cotta, C., & Fernández, A. J. (2005). *Analyzing Fitness Landscapes for the Optimal Golomb Ruler Problem.* In J. Gottlieb & G. Raidl (Eds.), Lecture Notes in Computer Science: Vol. 3448. *Evolutionary Computation in Combinatorial Optimization* (pp. 68–79). Springer–Verlag Berlin. doi:10.1007/978-3-540-31996-2_7

Cotta, C., & Hemert, J. V. (2008). Recent Advances in Evolutionary Computation for Combinatorial Optimization. *Studies in Computational Intelligence, Springer, 153*. doi:10.1007/978-3-540-70807-0

Deb, K. (2001). *Multi–Objective Optimization Using Evolutionary Algorithms*. New York: Wiley.

Derrac, J., García, S., Molina, D., & Herrera, F. (2011). A Practical Tutorial on the Use of Nonparametric Statistical Tests as A Methodology for Comparing Evolutionary and Swarm Intelligence Algorithms. *Swarm and Evolutionary Computation*, *1*(1), 3–18. doi:10.1016/j.swevo.2011.02.002

Dewdney, A. (1986). Computer recreations. *Scientific American*, *255*(3), 14–21. doi:10.1038/scientificamerican0986-14

Dimitromanolakis, A. (2002). *Analysis of the Golomb Ruler and the Sidon Set Problems, and Determination of Large, Near–Optimal Golomb Rulers* (Master's Thesis). Department of Electronic and Computer Engineering, Technical University of Crete.

Distributed.net. (2017). *Project OGR*. Retrieved January 2017 from http://www.distributed.net/ogr

Dollas, A., Rankin, W. T., & McCracken, D. (1998). A New Algorithm for Golomb Ruler Derivation and Proof of the 19 Mark Ruler. *IEEE Transactions on Information Theory*, *44*(1), 379–382. doi:10.1109/18.651068

Dotú, I., & Hentenryck, P. V. (2005). A Simple Hybrid Evolutionary Algorithm for Finding Golomb Rulers. *Proceedings of 2005 IEEE Congress on Evolutionary Computation*, *3*, 2018–2023. doi:10.1109/CEC.2005.1554943

Drakakis, K. (2009). A Review of The Available Construction Methods for Golomb Rulers. *Advances in Mathematics of Communications*, *3*(3), 235–250. doi:10.3934/amc.2009.3.235

Drakakis, K., & Rickard, S. (2010). On the Construction of Nearly Optimal Golomb Rulers by Unwrapping Costas Arrays. *Contemporary Engineering Sciences*, *3*(7), 295–309.

Erol, O. K., & Eksin, I. (2006). A New Optimization Method: Big Bang–Big Crunch. *Advances in Engineering Software*, *37*(2), 106–111. doi:10.1016/j.advengsoft.2005.04.005

Fang, R. J. F., & Sandrin, W. A. (1977). Carrier Frequency Assignment for Non–Linear Repeaters. *C.O.M.S.A.T. Technical Review*, 7, 227–245.

Forghieri, F., Tkach, R. W., & Chraplyvy, A. R. (1995). WDM Systems with Unequally Spaced Channels. *Journal of Lightwave Technology*, *13*(5), 889–897. doi:10.1109/50.387806

Forghieri, F., Tkach, R. W., Chraplyvy, A. R., & Marcuse, D. (1994). Reduction of Four–Wave Mixing Crosstalk in WDM Systems Using Unequally Spaced Channels. *IEEE Photonics Technology Letters*, *6*(6), 754–756. doi:10.1109/68.300184

Galinier, P., Jaumard, B., Morales, R., & Pesant, G. (2001). A constraint–Based Approach to the Golomb Ruler Problem. *Proceedings of 3rd International Workshop on Integration of AI and OR Techniques (CP–AI–OR 2001)*.

Holm, S. (1979). A Simple Sequentially Rejective Multiple Test Procedure. *Scandinavian Journal of Statistics*, *6*(2), 65–70.

Hwang, B., & Tonguz, O. K. (1998). A Generalized Suboptimum Unequally Spaced Channel Allocation Technique—Part I: In IM/DDWDMsystems. *IEEE Transactions on Communications*, *46*(8), 1027–1037. doi:10.1109/26.705403

Jain, P., Bansal, S., Singh, A. K., & Gupta, N. (2015). Golomb Ruler Sequences Optimization for FWM Crosstalk Reduction: Multi–population Hybrid Flower Pollination Algorithm. *Proceeding of Progress in Electromagnetics Research Symposium (PIERS)*, 2463–2467.

Koziel, S., & Yang, X.-S. (2011). *Computational Optimization, Methods and Algorithms*. Springer. doi:10.1007/978-3-642-20859-1

Kumari, N., Singh, T., & Bansal, S. (2016). Optimal Golomb Ruler Sequences as WDM Channel–Allocation Algorithm Generation: Cuckoo Search Algorithm with Mutation. *International Journal of Computers and Applications*, *142*(9), 21–27. doi:10.5120/ijca2016909910

Kwong, W. C., & Yang, G. C. (1997). An Algebraic Approach to the Unequal–Spaced Channel–Allocation Problem in WDM Lightwave Systems. *IEEE Transactions on Communications*, *45*(3), 352–359. doi:10.1109/26.558698

Lam, A. W., & Sarwate, D. V. (1988). On Optimal Time–Hopping Patterns. *IEEE Transactions on Communications*, *36*(3), 380–382. doi:10.1109/26.1464

Lavoie, P., Haccoun, D., & Savaria, Y. (1991). New VLSI Architectures for Fast Soft-Decision Threshold Decoders. *IEEE Transactions on Communications*, *39*(2), 200–207. doi:10.1109/26.76456

Leitao, T. (2004). Evolving the Maximum Segment Length of a Golomb Ruler. *Proceedings of Genetic and Evolutionary Computation Conference*.

Memarsadegh, N. (2013). Golomb Patterns: Introduction, Applications, and Citizen Science Game. *Information Science and Technology (IS&T), Seminar Series NASA GSFC*. Available at http://istcolloq. gsfc.nasa.gov/fall2013/presentations/memarsadeghi.pdf

Meyer, C., & Papakonstantinou, P. A. (2009). On the complexity of constructing Golomb Rulers. *Discrete Applied Mathematics, 157*(4), 738–748. doi:10.1016/j.dam.2008.07.006

Price, K., Storn, R., & Lampinen, J. (2005). *Differential Evolution–A Practical Approach to Global Optimization*. Berlin, Germany: Springer.

Rajasekaran, S., & Pai, G. A. V. (2004). *Neural Networks, Fuzzy Logic, and Genetic Algorithms–Synthesis and Applications*. New Delhi: Prentice Hall of India Pvt. Ltd.

Randhawa, R., Sohal, J. S., & Kaler, R. S. (2009). Optimum Algorithm for WDM Channel Allocation for Reducing Four–Wave Mixing Effects. *Optik (Stuttgart), 120*(17), 898–904. doi:10.1016/j.ijleo.2008.03.023

Rankin, W. T. (1993). *Optimal Golomb Rulers: An Exhaustive Parallel Search Implementation* (M.S. Thesis). Duke University. Available at http://people.ee.duke.edu/~wrankin/golomb/golomb.html

Ritu, B. (2016). A Novel Bat Algorithm for Channel Allocation to Reduce FWM Crosstalk in WDM Systems. *International Journal of Computers and Applications, 136*(4), 33–42. doi:10.5120/ijca2016908459

Robinson, J. P. (1979). Optimum Golomb Rulers. *IEEE Transactions on Computers, 28*(12), 183–184.

Robinson, J. P. (2000). Genetic Search for Golomb Arrays. *IEEE Transactions on Information Theory, 46*(3), 1170–1173. doi:10.1109/18.841202

Robinson, J. P., & Bernstein, A. J. (1967). A Class of Binary Recurrent Codes with Limited Error Propagation. *IEEE Transactions on Information Theory, IT–13*(1), 106–113. doi:10.1109/TIT.1967.1053951

Saaid, N. M. (2010). Nonlinear Optical Effects Suppression Methods in WDM Systems with EDFAs: A Review. *Proceedings of International Conference on Computer and Communication Engineering (ICCCE–2010)*, 1–4. doi:10.1109/ICCCE.2010.5556802

Sardesai, H. P. (1999). A Simple Channel Plan to Reduce Effects of Nonlinearities in Dense WDM Systems. Proceedings of Lasers and Electro–Optics (CLEO '99), 183-184. doi:10.1109/CLEO.1999.834058

Shearer, J. B. (1990). Some New Optimum Golomb Rulers. *IEEE Transactions on Information Theory, 36*(1), 183–184. doi:10.1109/18.50388

Shearer, J. B. (1998). Some New Disjoint Golomb Rulers. *IEEE Transactions on Information Theory, 44*(7), 3151–3153. doi:10.1109/18.737546

Shearer, J. B. (2001a). *Golomb Ruler Table*. Mathematics Department, IBM Research. Available at http://www.research.ibm.com/people/s/shearer/grtab.html

Shearer, J. B. (2001b). *Smallest Known Golomb Rulers*. Mathematics Department, IBM Research. Available at http://www.research.ibm.com/people/s/shearer/gropt.html

Singh, K., & Bansal, S. (2013). Suppression of FWM Crosstalk on WDM Systems Using Unequally Spaced Channel Algorithms–A Survey. *International Journal of Advanced Research in Computer Science and Software Engineering, 3*(12), 25–31.

Soliday, S. W., Homaifar, A., & Lebby, G. L. (1995). Genetic Algorithm Approach to the Search for Golomb Rulers. *Proceedings of the Sixth International Conference on Genetic Algorithms (ICGA–95)*, 528–535.

Storn, R., & Price, K. V. (1997). Differential Evolution—A Simple and Efficient Heuristic for Global Optimization Over Continuous Spaces. *Journal of Global Optimization*, *11*(4), 341–359. doi:10.1023/A:1008202821328

Thing, V. L. L., Rao, M. K., & Shum, P. (2003). Fractional Optimal Golomb Ruler Based WDM Channel Allocation. *Proceedings of the 8th Opto-Electronics and Communication Conference (OECC–2003)*, 23, 631–632.

Thing, V. L. L., Shum, P., & Rao, M. K. (2004). Bandwidth–Efficient WDM Channel Allocation for Four–Wave Mixing–Effect Minimization. *IEEE Transactions on Communications*, *52*(12), 2184–2189. doi:10.1109/TCOMM.2004.838684

Tonguz, O. K., & Hwang, B. (1998). A Generalized Suboptimum Unequally Spaced Channel Allocation Technique—Part II: In coherent WDM systems. *IEEE Transactions on Communications*, *46*(9), 1186–1193. doi:10.1109/26.718560

Vyas, J., Bansal, S., & Sharma, K. (2016). Generation of Optimal Golomb Rulers for FWM Crosstalk Reduction: BB–BC and FA Approaches. In *Proceeding of 2016 International Conference on Signal Processing and Communication (ICSC–2016)*. Jaypee Institute of Information Technology. doi:10.1109/ICSPCom.2016.7980551

Weisstein, E. W. (2017a). *Perfect Ruler from MathWorld--A Wolfram Web Resource*. Available at http://mathworld.wolfram.com/PerfectRuler.html

Weisstein, E. W. (2017b). *Golomb Ruler from MathWorld--A Wolfram Web Resource*. Available at http://mathworld.wolfram.com/GolombRuler.html

Yang, X.-S. (2009). Firefly Algorithms for Multimodal Optimization. In Lecture Notes in Computer Science: Vol. 5792. *Stochastic Algorithms: Foundations and Applications (SAGA–2009)* (pp. 169–178). Berlin: Springer–Verlag. doi:10.1007/978-3-642-04944-6_14

Yang, X.-S. (2010a). *Nature–Inspired Metaheuristic Algorithms* (2nd ed.). Luniver Press.

Yang, X.-S. (2010b). Firefly Algorithm, Stochastic Test Functions and Design Optimisation. *International Journal of Bio-inspired Computation*, *2*(2), 78–84. doi:10.1504/IJBIC.2010.032124

Yang, X.-S. (2010c). Firefly Algorithm, Levy Flights and Global Optimization. In Research and Development in Intelligent Systems XXVI. Springer London.

Yang, X.–S. (2012). Nature–Inspired Mateheuristic Algorithms: Success and New Challenges. *Journal of Computer Engineering and Information Technology,* *1*(1), 1–3. doi:104172/2324-9307.1000e101

Yang, X.-S. (2012). Flower Pollination Algorithm for Global Optimization. In Proceeding of Unconventional Computation and Natural Computation (UCNC 2012). Springer. doi:10.1007/978-3-642-32894-7_27

Yang, X.-S. (2013). Multiobjective Firefly Algorithm for Continuous Optimization. *Engineering with Computers*, *29*(2), 175–184. doi:10.1007/s00366-012-0254-1

Yang, X.-S. (2013). Optimization and Metaheuristic Algorithms in Engineering. In X. S. Yang, A. H. Gandomi, S. Talatahari, & A. H. Alavi (Eds.), *Metaheursitics in Water, Geotechnical and Transport Engineering* (pp. 1–23). Elsevier. doi:10.1016/B978-0-12-398296-4.00001-5

Yang, X.-S., Karamanoglu, M., & He, X. S. (2014). Flower Pollination Algorithm: A Novel Approach for Multiobjective Optimization. *Engineering Optimization*, *46*(9), 1222–1237. doi:10.1080/030521 5X.2013.832237

Chapter 12
A Survey on Different Digital Authentication Systems Using Fuzzy Logic

Ayan Chatterjee
Sarboday Public Academy, India

Mahendra Rong
Bangabasi Evening College, India

ABSTRACT

The communication through wireless medium is very popular to the developed society. More specifically, the use of the internet as well as the use of social networking sites is increasing. Therefore, information security is an important factor during wireless communication. Three major components of it are confidentiality, integrity, and availability of information among authorized users. Integrity level is maintained through various digital authentication schemes. Fuzzy logic is an important soft computing tool that increases the digital watermarking system in various ways. In this chapter, different popular and high secured watermarking schemes using fuzzy logic are analyzed with their mathematical and experimental efficiency. A comparative analysis is developed here with corresponding different parameters.

INTRODUCTION

Information security is a big issue in present decade during wireless communication. Actually, it is communication of privacy among authorized users. The major wings of information security are confidentiality, integrity and availability of data. According to the architecture of wireless communication, it can be realized that the internet channel, through which important and secured information are exchanged among authorized users, is not well secured from unauthorized access. So, to protect the important data from unauthorized users, i.e. to maintain the basic ingredients of information security, various approaches are developed gradually. Cryptography is the most basic approach of information security. In this particular methodology, secret message is altered to another text using a particular algorithm, i.e. encryption algo-

DOI: 10.4018/978-1-5225-3004-6.ch012

rithm with corresponding secret keys. This changed text is sent to receiver end. Then actual message is extracted from the changed text by using the decryption technique of corresponding encryption algorithm and predefined secret keys. In this approach, secret key maintains the security from unauthorized users. But the disadvantage of the scheme is the survival of communication is realized by unauthorized users. To take away this problem, next approach steganography is developed. In this methodology, secret message is embedded in a cover file, such as- image, video/audio etc. This embedded cover file is sent through wireless medium to the receiver end. Receiver extracts this secret message from the embedded file. But unauthenticated users can't realize the existence of communication. In both of cryptography and steganography, only confidentiality and availability of information are maintained among authenticated users. But integrity level is not considered in these two popular and important particular methodologies. In other words, if any unauthorized user changes the information during communication, that can't be realized at the receiver end using the approaches cryptography and steganography only. So, to increase integrity level, digital authentication, more specifically digital watermarking approach is developed. The important side of this approach is if the information is distorted by some middle hacker(s) that can be realized at the receiver end. So, here the concentration is only on digital watermarking.

Fuzzy logic is an important soft computing tool and it has major application area in optimization. But, the fuzzy rule bases are used also in the issue of digital watermarking and acts efficiently to increase integrity level. In this chapter, some popular as well as secured digital watermarking schemes using fuzzy logic are described in comparative manner. Also, efficiency of fuzzy in this particular field is analyzed. In the next section, some related survey works are described. Then the proposed discussion is developed in comparative way. Some experimental results are also shown here to observe the efficiency of the schemes. At last, a conclusion is drawn followed by future trends of proposed work.

BACKGROUND

In 2014, a survey on various digital image authentication schemes was held by Reshma Vartak & Smita Deshmukh (July 2014). In this survey, the requirements of image authentication are analyzed. More specifically, some specific types of authentication, like strict authentication, content based authentication etc. are described according to classification of various wireless security approaches. The important as well as good side of this survey is the proper categorization of the authentication schemes. But the drawback of this contribution is that no experimental analysis is developed here. An excellent survey was developed by Adil Haouzia et al (August 2007). This is very much important survey from various aspects, such as- categorization, explanation of each scheme with proper mathematical analysis, experimentation on the basis of various parameters. But the efficiency of the schemes was not developed through different numerical value based experiment. Also, here all the techniques with various dependencies are considered, but importance of soft computing is not defined here. To develop the importance of soft computing, a survey on various digital watermarking techniques was developed by Sharbani Bhattacharya in 2014 (November 2014). In that particular survey, digital watermarking techniques are categorized into seven different parts. The classified factors are type of documents, robustness, application areas of watermarking, visibility, different approaches of watermarking, original image availability to extract watermarks and the task after watermark extraction. After that, each category is divided into different sub-categories. The basic objective of this paper is efficiency analysis of security and digital forensics of the watermarking approaches. Actually, in this paper, an overall categorization of digital watermarking in security and forensics is drawn, but effectiveness of each category as well as sub category is not analyzed in comparative manner. Another survey on digital image watermarking techniques was built up by Amita Goel and Anurag Mishra (January 2015). This is one of the finest surveys of watermarking approaches using soft computing tools. The speciality of the paper is that a comparative analysis among GA, fuzzy logic and neural network based approaches of image watermarking. But, this comparison is only experimental based. More specifically, the efficiency of the tools in image watermarking is analyzed through some experimental results only. But no mathematical analysis is drawn here. In the proposed paper, a comparative analysis of some popular fuzzy logic based watermarking approaches is drawn by showing both of mathematical importance as well as experimental efficiency with some examples. In the next section, a short out of some efficient watermarking schemes using fuzzy logic are discussed.

WATERMARKING SCHEMES

In this section, some efficient watermarking schemes are discussed elaborately. Here, mathematical importance of fuzzy is shown corresponding to each watermarking scheme.

Fuzzy Logic and Multi- Resolution Based Watermarking With 3D Model

This is an important approach of digital authentication due to its security efficiency. This technique is developed by Sharvari C. Tamane and Ratnadeep R. Deshmukh (IJCSIT 2012). Here, a 3D model is developed to make a watermark. In this particular case, Haar wavelet transform is applied initially to transform the actual domain. At the time of applying the Haar wavelet transformation, four different coefficient matrices are generated and these are CA, CH, CV and CD. Again, this wavelet transformation is applied to CV and CH coefficient matrices and 8 matrices are generated. Then the process is continued until obtaining 16 coefficient matrices. After that, the watermark image is converted into binary representation. Then the watermark is scrambled with a special transform Arnold. Next, a 3D model is developed as input with the parameters area, curvature and bumpiness. This input is passed through fuzzy inference system. This inference system is used to decide about the importance of three parameters with seven membership functions, like lowest, low, lower, medium, higher etc. Combining these three facts with seven membership functions, fifteen fuzzy rules are generated. The previous obtained coefficient matrices are changed according to the rules of this FIS. Here, importance of using fuzzy logic in this particular case is according to the rules of FIS, the distortion of original image can be decided. Actually, these rules make less distortion and as a result PSNR and MSE obviously give good result. Also, in the case of security analysis, i.e. at the time of unauthorized access, the rules are very much critical to extract due to a large number of combinations. So, this scheme maintains a good security with confidentiality, integrity and availability of information to authenticated users due to fuzzification.

Digital Image Watermarking Technique With DWT and SVD Based Fuzzy Logic

This is a typical as well as popular image watermarking scheme. The approach is developed by T. Sridevi and S. Sameena Fatima (IJCA 2013). Actually, this watermarking scheme is built in the transformed domain of digital image. In other words, the watermark is not set in the actual pixel domain of digital image. At first, the image domain is transformed to another domain by using 1-D DWT (Discrete Wavelet Transform). The working formula of 1-D DWT is,

$$\varphi_{j,k} = a_0 \varphi \left(a_0^j t - k \right) \tag{1}$$

Here, $j, k \in Z$ and generally, the value of a_0 is taken as 2. The utility of using DWT in the case of image domain transformation is minimum distortion of actual image. In other words, PSNR and MSE give better results for using DWT than other transformations, like DCT, DFT etc. In the transformed domain, SVD is applied to a particular sub band HL of cover image. The term SVM (Singular Value Decomposition) is the product of three matrices- U, D, and V^T. Here U and V are two orthonormal matrices. D is the diagonal matrix by comprising the singular values of a rectangular matrix A. This particular decomposition is applied to HL sub band of discrete wavelet transformed domain corresponding to a diagonal image. The fuzzy logic is used to find the adjustment of pixels, i.e. for embedding watermark to get the fidelity. In other words, after using DWT and SVD, an inference system is developed using fuzzy knowledge base. Actually, the interconnection relation between inference engine and knowledge base is maintained by fuzzifier and defuzzifier. Here, fuzzifier is used to identify input four sub images- LL, HL, LH and HH. Each input is developed using the composition of the membership functions and these are taken on three colors of gray scale- black, gray and white. So, the insertion of sub image is converted to sub-image of manipulation to develop watermark feature. Here, fuzzy rule base increases efficiency of watermarking security. If any of deterministic rule base is applied to the domain every time after using DWT and SVD, then that can be hacked by unauthorized access using PRNG (Pseudo Random No. Generator) or any statistical attack. But, the membership functional values are very much secured. So, if any changes occur during unauthorized access, then that can be realized at the receiver end by checking previously defined membership functions and fuzzy rule base. So, the scheme becomes protective from unauthenticated users due to fuzzification of knowledge base.

Genetic Algorithm and Fuzzy Logic Based Image Watermarking

This is a good approach of authentication using soft computing tools- genetic algorithm and fuzzy logic. This technique is developed by Arun Kumar R. and Venkat Narayan Rao T. (IJCTT 2016). This technique is also DWT-SVD based, mentioned as previous scheme. In this scheme, DWT is used to transform the domain of actual intensity pixel values. SVD also maintains the same purpose as the previous. But, use of combined GA and fuzzy make it more effective than the previous one. Here, the full transformed domain of image is divided into four parts- LL, HL, HH and LH. From these four sub parts, the initial population is developed with randomly selection of intensity transformed values. Then fuzzy is applied to embed the watermark with strength 3. Here, fuzzy is used for the reference image purpose. Actually, here the input is original image and any band among four is chosen. After that, fuzzy rules are developed to grow the strength the watermark. In other words, fuzzification and defuzzification concatenating with inference engine increases the capacity of watermark from unauthorized users. The procedure of GA, i.e. combined process of selection of chromosomes, crossover and mutation is used to maintain the deep level, at which the watermark is inserted. So, analyzing the whole procedure, it is observed that the scheme becomes very much efficient due to increment of strength and that is possible for using fuzzy. So, here use of fuzzy rules makes the system very much secured from unauthorized access.

Compositions of Fuzzy Matrix and Rough Set Based Digital Image Watermarking

Fuzzy and rough set based particular digital watermarking approach is developed by Sharbani Bhattacharya (IJACSA 2014). This particular approach is effective for satisfying all the conditions of information security- confidentiality, integrity and availability. In this scheme, fuzzy is used for both of encryption of watermark as well as to embed the watermark for authentication purpose. So, here we concentrate on efficiency of fuzzy logic for both of encryption and embedding of watermark. Actually, initially it is observed that the watermark image is encrypted using fuzzy matrix. Public key and private key fuzzy matrices of encryption and decryption part are chosen randomly from data base. At the time of embedding the watermark, encrypted file is broken into three parts. These files are embedded as watermark in digital image by proper fuzzy rule. For encryption purpose, two fuzzy matrices are chosen and to embed the watermark three fuzzy matrices are selected using various compositions, like max-max, max-min, min-max etc. Actually, different type compositions of fuzzy matrices increase the authentication security as well as composition of initial two fuzzy matrices increase the confidentiality and availability through encryption process. At the time of unauthorized access, development of fuzzy matrix is more critical than a specific matrix using PRNG, as the membership functions are fractional values. It takes a wide range at the time of using PRNG. For this reason, the scheme acts as efficient approach of information security during wireless communication.

Fuzzy Clustering Based Digital Image Authentication

This is a popular and secured watermarking technique and developed by Rohit Singh and Pancholi Bhavana K. (IJSR 2016). Clustering is one of the most basic parts of data mining and it is implemented of making groups automatically from a huge set of data depending on some particular facts. Here, the clustering concept is used to insert watermarking image to a particular cover image. The procedure of the scheme is shown in Figure 1.

At first, intensity pixel values (f_i) of an NxN size cover image is taken. Mean of the pixel values is evaluated using fuzzy membership functions. Depending on the value of mean, two clusters are formed. The intensity values, which are less than the mean value, are taken in cluster 1 and which are greater than the mean value, are taken in cluster 2. Again, the means of each cluster is evaluated separately and sub-clusters are made. This process is continued until obtaining the level to which watermarking image is embedded. Here, fuzzy is used in clustering purpose, especially for pixel values which accurately matches with mean value. The advantage of fuzzy in clustering purpose is that a particular data may occur in two or more groups according to similarity. As a result, the scheme becomes efficient from various attacks. In other words, watermark embedded pixels can't be found through unauthorized access

Figure 1. Schematic diagram of fuzzy clustering based authentication

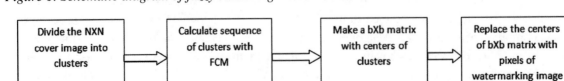

due to multi-occurrence of data in the clusters and multi-presence is formed only for use of fuzzy logic. That's why the approach is effective to the authorized users from the view of digital authentication.

EXPERIMENTS AND RESULTS

In this part, competence of each digital watermarking scheme is evaluated with various strictures. Peak Signal to Noise Ratio (PSNR), Mean Squared Error (MSE), Normalized Cross Correlation (NCC) etc. are important constraints to examine the efficiency of each scheme. Also, freeness of the schemes from different attacks, such as- low pass filtering, median filtering, Jpeg compression, histogram equalization, rotational, Gaussian Noise etc. are investigated here. The mathematical representations of PSNR and NCC are,

$$PSNR = 20\log_{10}\left(\frac{2^b - 1}{\sqrt{MSE}}\right)$$

(2)

$$NCC = \frac{1}{m}\sum \frac{\left(I(x,y) - \overline{I}\right)\left(I'(x,y) - \overline{I}'\right)}{\sigma_1 \sigma_1'}$$

(3)

The symbols hold their usual meanings. Actually, PSNR is anti proportional to square root of MSE. So, low MSE and high PSNR implies good efficiency of the scheme. Efficiency of each scheme is analyzed with the corresponding parameters separately by taking some examples in each case. The selected cover images for testing are in Figure 2.

Fuzzy Logic and Multi- Resolution Based Watermarking With 3D Model

In this scheme, three different models are used. So, the utility as well as effectiveness of three models are analyzed separately with some examples. Suppose, the testing watermark image is,

According to the experimental results of three models separately, it is observed that the correlation between original and extracted watermark is nearly equal to 1. So, watermark can be extracted easily without any attack. Also, good PSNR shows that the distortion between actual image and watermarked image is very much less.

Digital Image Watermarking Technique With DWT and SVD Based Fuzzy Logic

This scheme is DWT and SVD based. Applying the fuzzy logic, the approach is tested with specified watermark (Figure 3) on the mentioned cover images (Figure 2). Observed NCC and PSNR are shown in Table 4. The system is tested with various noises.

According to the observed experimental results, it is realized that the NCC gives good result, i.e. the difference between embedded and extracted watermark is minimum. But PSNR result shows that the distortion between original and watermarked image is high.

Figure 2. Selected cover images for testing watermarking schemes

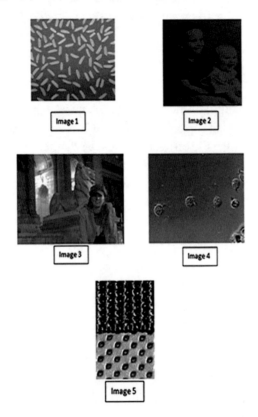

Figure 3. Watermark image

Table 1. Experimental outcomes from Model I (testing through different attacks)

Images	Correlation (Actual and Obtained Watermark)	PSNR (Original and Watermarked Image)
Image 1	0.986417	91.470216
Image 2	0.921346	92.443221
Image 3	0.931689	82.469803
Image 4	0.992547	87.443122
Image 5	0.928367	93.831562

Table 2. Experimental outcomes from Model II (testing through different attacks)

Images	Correlation (Actual and Obtained Watermark)	PSNR (Original and Watermarked Image)
Image 1	0.976423	74.829132
Image 2	0.983123	74.784531
Image 3	0.994432	74.783253
Image 4	0.934671	74.457123
Image 5	0.964273	74.627193

Table 3. Experimental outcomes from Model III (testing through different attacks)

Images	Correlation (Actual and Obtained Watermark)	PSNR (Original and Watermarked Image)
Image 1	0.937543	90.203392
Image 2	0.937452	90.213532
Image 3	0.924572	90.202432
Image 4	0.934471	90.201334
Image 5	0.924372	90.205312

Table 4. Experimental outcomes from DWT and SVD based fuzzy logic approach (testing through different attacks)

Images	NCC (Actual and Obtained Watermark)	PSNR (Original and Watermarked Image)
Image 1	0.989	40.298726
Image 2	0.987	40.137256
Image 3	0.992	39.732145
Image 4	0.997	40.232175
Image 5	0.995	39.876135

Genetic Algorithm and Fuzzy Logic Based Image Watermarking

The testing PSNR and NCC results of the specific authentication approach are shown in Table 5. In that table, a comparative result is drawn also among the techniques SVD-DWT based fuzzy logic approach and SVD-DWT based combined fuzzy & genetic approach.

According to the composition, it is observed that the approach becomes developed in comparison with previous SVD-DWT based fuzzy approach in both of NCC and PSNR values.

Compositions of Fuzzy Matrix and Rough Set Based Digital Image Watermarking

This is a secured approach from unauthorized users. Security is analyzed through the parameters PSNR. NCC values of embedded watermark and extracted watermark is near about 1. The NCC and PSNR values tested with predefined five images (Figure 2) and specified watermark (Figure 3) is shown in Table 6.

Table 5. Comparative experimental results between SVD-DWT based fuzzy and SZD-DWT based fuzzy and GA

Images	SVT-DWT Fuzzy Logic		SVT-DWT Fuzzy Logic and GA	
	NCC (Actual and Obtained Watermark)	PSNR (Original and Watermark Images)	NCC (Actual and Obtained Watermark)	PSNR (Original and Watermark Images)
Image 1	0.873	32.134568	0.998	46.234532
Image 2	0.892	31.246932	0.964	45.257159
Image 3	0.864	30.294321	0.998	44.427561
Image 4	0.853	30.174592	0.967	44.765263
Image 5	0.887	32.154271	0.987	46.325169

Figure 4. Experimental results of NCC between SVD-DWT based fuzzy and SZD-DWT based fuzzy and GA

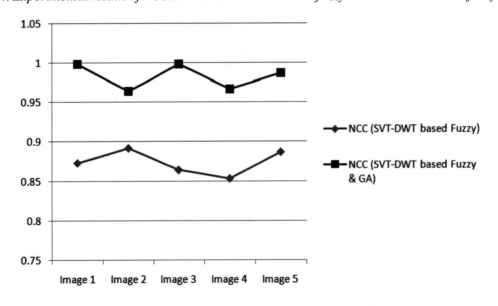

Figure 5. Experimental results of PSNR between SVD-DWT based fuzzy and SZD-DWT based fuzzy and GA

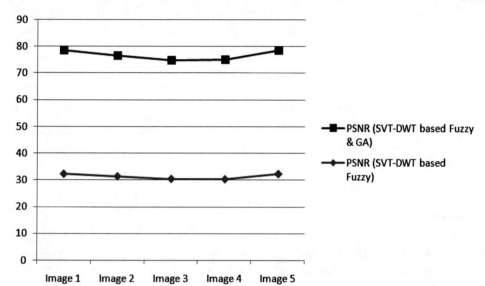

Table 6. Experimental outcomes from fuzzy matrix and rough set based watermarking (testing through different attacks)

Images	NCC (Actual and Obtained Watermark)	PSNR (Original and Watermarked Image)
Image 1	0.942	39.423179
Image 2	0.931	38.437214
Image 3	0.887	36.427534
Image 4	0.896	37.935751
Image 5	0.898	37.946576

PSNR results show that there is a large difference between actual cover image and watermarked image. But good NCC shows its efficiency from freeness of various authentication breaking schemes.

Fuzzy Clustering Based Digital Image Authentication

This is a good fuzzy watermarking approach based on clustering. The specified watermark (Figure 3) is embedded in the images (Figure 3) separately one by one and obtained NCC and PSNR are shown in Table 7.

According to tested result, it is observed that this is the best approach due to security among all other discussed approaches.

Table 7. Experimental results of fuzzy clustering based digital authentication (testing through different attacks)

Images	NCC (Actual and Obtained Watermark)	PSNR (Original and Watermarked Image)
Image 1	1.000	31.752139
Image 2	1.000	30.762438
Image 3	1.000	29.647831
Image 4	1.000	29.694574
Image 5	0.999	30.263431

CONCLUSION

Analyzing the mathematical efficiency and experimentation of fuzzy based watermarking schemes, it is observed that the authentication schemes are very much strong for using fuzzy logic. Actually, according to the results of NCC of the schemes, it is seen that the values are all near about 1. It proves that embedded watermark at the sender side and extracted watermark at the receiver end are almost similar and the minimum distortion can't be visualized. Another important parameter PSNR shows also very good result. It implies that the chance of distortion of watermarked embedded images is low during wireless communication. Among the five popular and secured discussed schemes, fuzzy clustering based watermark approach is efficient most. Other four schemes are more or less equally effective according to the experimental results. Actually, this comparative survey of fuzzy based schemes focuses on effectiveness of fuzzy rule based image authentication development sequence as well as importance of fuzzy logic in a different field other than optimization.

FUTURE TRENDS

In this particular survey, the importance of fuzzy logic is discussed in digital watermarking schemes. To do that, only five popular schemes are discussed with their efficiencies. But practically, it is observed that many other schemes are chosen here to analyze the importance of fuzzy. Category wise analysis of all the digital authentication schemes using fuzzy logic is considered as future work corresponding to this particular survey. Another thing is that some other soft computing tools, such as- genetic algorithm, artificial neural network, ant colony optimization, particle swarm optimization etc. are also used in digital authentication purpose. So, to show properly efficiency of fuzzy logic, there should be a comparison with the schemes based on other soft computing tools. This particular comparative survey is also considered as future work.

REFERENCES

Arun Kumar, R. (2016, November). Digital Image Watermarking using Fuzzy Logic and Genetic Algorithm. *International Journal of Computer Trends and Technology, 41*(02), 101–105.

Bhattacharya, S. (2014, November). Survey on Digital Watermarking- A Digital Forensics & Security Application. *International Journal of Advanced Research in Computer Science and Software Engineering, 4*(11), 1–6.

Bhattacharya, S. (2014). Watermarking Digital Image Using Fuzzy Matrix Compositions and Rough Set. *International Journal of Advanced Computer Science and Applications, 5*(06), 135–140. doi:10.14569/IJACSA.2014.050621

Chatterjee, A. (2015). A Comparative Analysis of Three Important Data Hiding Schemes in Steganography. *International Journal of Innovative Trends In Engineering, 11*(2), 61–65.

Chatterjee, A. (2015). A Survey on Different Digital Media Based Steganography Techniques Using Genetic Algorithms. *International Journal of Innovative Research in Computer and Communication Engineering, 3*(12), 12990–12998.

de Ru, W. G. (1997). Enhanced Password Authentication through Fuzzy Logic. *IEEE Intelligent Systems*, 38–45.

Dutt, D., Hedge, V., & Borse, P. T. (2015). AAKRITI[ed]: An Image and Data Encryption-Decryption Tool. *International Journal of Computer Science and Information Technology Research, 02*(02), 264–268.

Goel, A., & Mishra, A. (2015, January). Survey on Watermarking Schemes using Adaptive Soft Computing Techniques. *International Journal of Computers and Applications, 110*(04), 4–8. doi:10.5120/19302-0751

Haouzia, A., & Noumeir, R. (2007). Methods for image authentication: A survey. *Multimed Tools Appl.*, 1-46.

Harding, , & Leitner, , & Schmidhuber. (2013). Cartesian Genetic Programming for Image Processing. *Genetic and Evolutionary Computation: Genetic Programming Theory and Practice, 10*, 1–17.

Kim, J. H. (2009, July). Interleaved Hop-by-Hop Authentication using fuzzy logic to defend against of False Report Injection by Replaying an attack. *International Journal of Computer Science and Network Security, 9*(7), 91–96.

Lande, P. U. (2010). Robust image adaptive watermarking using fuzzy logic an FPGA approach. *International Journal of Signal Processing, Image Processing and Pattern Recognition, 3*(4), 43–54.

Patel, M. (2015, August). A Robust DCT Based Digital Image Watermarking Using Fusion of Computational Intelligence Techniques. *Oriental Journal of Computer Science and Technology, 8*(2), 146–153.

Singh, R., & PancholiBhavan, K. (2016). A Nobel Technique for Digital Image Watermarking Authentication Using Fuzzy Mean Clustering. *International Journal of Science and Research, 5*(4), 207–209.

Sridevi, T., & Sameena Fathima, S. (2013). Digital Image Watermarking using Fuzzy Logic approach based on DWT and SVD. *International Journal of Computers and Applications*, *74*(13), 16–20. doi:10.5120/12945-0014

Tamane, S. C., & Deshmukh, R. R. (2012). Blind 3d model watermarking based on multi-resolution representation and fuzzy logic. *International Journal of Computer Science & Information Technology*, *4*(01), 117–126. doi:10.5121/ijcsit.2012.4110

Vartak, R., & Deshmukh, S. (2014, July). Survey of Digital Image Authentication Techniques. *International Journal of Research in Advent Technology*, *2*(7), 176–179.

KEY TERMS AND DEFINITIONS

Digital Authentication: Digital authentication is the way of realizing reality of documents/information digitally.

Digital Watermarking: Digital watermarking is the way of authentication with an embedded image or audio or video.

Fuzzy Logic: Fuzzy logic is a special kind of soft computing tool and it is applicable in the field of artificial intelligence effectively.

Peak Signal to Noise Ratio (PSNR): A mathematical expression is applied to realize the alteration between the actual cover medium and watermarked cover medium.

Soft Computing: Soft Computing is the way of solution of NP hard problems through artificial intelligence.

Chapter 13
Bio-Inspired Algorithms for Ecosystem Data Analysis

Mohamed Elhadi Rahmani
Dr. Tahar Moulay University of Saida, Algeria

ABSTRACT

Ecological systems are known by their relationships with the environment. They affect and are affected by various external factors such as climate and the basic materials that form the soil. Good distinctions of relationships is the first important point in the modeling of ecosystems. The diversity of these systems caused a large amount of data that became hard to analyze, which made researchers classify it as NP-Hard problems. This chapter presents a study of application of bio-inspired algorithms for ecosystem data analysis. The chapter contains application of four different approaches that were inspired by authors of the paper from four different phenomena, and they were applied for analysis of four different ecosystem data collected from real life cases. Results showed a very high accuracy and proved the efficiency of bio-inspired algorithms for supervised classification of real ecosystem data.

INTRODUCTION

A system is together of the interactions between several components. These interactions are guided according to rules from which the nature of the components play a role in the determination of the system and also the interaction of the system itself with its environment. If we speak of a set of organs interacting within an organism to perform a biological function, this system is called an ecological system. And if we speak of a set of axioms guided by vocabularies to form rules of deductions, we speak of a logical system.

Ecosystems or ecological systems are defined by interactions between living organisms in conjunction with non-living components of their environment (Odum, 1971). These components are linked by nutrient cycles and energy flows (Smith, 2012). Ecosystems differ in their networks of interactions; small ecosystems can be found at the cellular level (a leaf of a tree), an organ of a living being (tree trunk), or a living being (a tree). And we can also find large ecosystems containing relationships between a group of individuals or a society. What is important is that to properly define the term ecosystem or ecological system is a set of interactions between ecological units formed by plant and animal organ-

DOI: 10.4018/978-1-5225-3004-6.ch013

isms and an environment defined by physical and chemical characteristics, this environment is called biotope. A key feature in ecosystems is that it is very difficult to find a closed ecological system. To say a closed system, its elements have no relation with the outside world, they have relations only among themselves. Ecological systems are known by their relationships with the environment, they affect and affected by various external factors such as climate, and the basic materials that form the soil. Unlike closed systems, open systems require a good distinction between the entities of the system that bind its entities with the environment, the relationships that bind the entities called relations within, they are Characteristics of the system. It is for his good distinction of relationships is the first important point in the modeling of ecosystems.

One of the great promising fields in the discovery of knowledge today is the detection of disturbances of the ecosystem, it includes many fields such as remote sensing, earth science, biology and oceans. Ecologists analyse the data to identify the relationships between a response and a set of predictors, using statistical models that do not accurately describe the main sources of variation in the response variable.

Knowledge discovery techniques are often more powerful, flexible and effective for exploratory analysis than statistical techniques, (Wesley, 2007) suggest useful ways in which data extraction and statistical analysis can Be integrated into an in-depth data analysis to facilitate the rapid creation of specific models by defining the distinctions between data mining analysis and parametric statistical analysis, and the strengths of data mining tools to generate Assumptions from the data. An example of done works in this field presented in (Jane, 2009) which shows one of the distribution species models as a model that relates to species distribution data with information on the environment and / or particular characteristics of Biological domains and scientific disciplines.

In technology and speed era, software plays a major role in all domains. A large part of the massive growth of energy consumption in the past few decades is due to the manufacture, the use of computing and communication technologies, and the technological advances they make possible. Software allows simulating earth system processes, assessing the implications, and exploring possible responses. All these are able by processing vast amounts of geo-scientific data, which help communities of experts to share data, explore scenarios and validate assumptions.

Nature contains a lot of sub-disciplines, a very big number of complex mechanisms that help life keep going on. Understanding these mechanisms is a principal source to inspire different algorithms and solution for problems in technology era. Over the last few decades, it has stimulated many successful algorithms and computational tools for dealing with complex and optimization problems. The 21st century became NP-hard problems era; this kind of problems took a large space in research areas. Researchers work and invent a lot of solutions for these problems. Biologically Inspired Computation is one of those areas. It is computation inspired by biological metaphor, also referred to as Bio-mimicry, and Bio-mimetics in other engineering disciplines. The intent of this field is to devise mathematical and engineering tools to generate solutions to computation problems. The field involves using procedures for finding solutions abstracted from the natural world for addressing computationally phrased problems. Bio inspired algorithms and metaheuristics in general are powerful solutions for hard problems in many technological fields. These solutions have been derived from the biological behavior systems, particle swarm optimization was developed based on the swarm behavior of birds and fish

Since ecological systems' studies are considered as NP-hard problems. The objective of this chapter is explaining the importance of using meta heuristics for study of different ecosystems. We will begin by giving an idea about ecosystems and different issues, then explaining use of meta heuristics and their advantages in order to prove their efficiency in ecosystems study.

This paper presents a synthesis of four works that have been done by authors in four different publication where we used to inspire four algorithms for ecosystem data analysis. The organization of this chapter is as following: next section presents some known problems in ecosystem and ecosystem data types, then we will present four examples of application of bio inspired algorithms for solving of ecological data by explaining the approaches, then giving the obtained results by each approach, these works were done by authors of this chapter. Finally, we give major conclusions.

Related Works to Ecological Data Analysis

This section provides some related works to four ecological data analysis examples that we have treated them in this chapter.

Climate Data and Computer Software

In technology and speed era, software plays a major role in all domains. According to (Easterbrook, 2010), a large part of the massive growth of energy consumption in the past few decades is due to the manufacture, the use of computing and communication technologies, and the technological advances they make possible. Software allows simulating earth system processes, assessing the implications, and exploring possible responses. All these are able by processing vast amounts of geo-scientific data, which help communities of experts to share data, explore scenarios and validate assumptions.

The need to find a quick solution for climate changes gave birth to a new research area in computer science, and propose a question, can computer software account for climate change? that is what Easterbrook et al. tries to illustrate in their paper (Easterbrook, 2009), in which they describe an ethnographic study of the culture and practices of climate scientists at the Met Office Hadley Centre. Their study confirms many of the general observations of earlier studies. Notable differences include the sophistication and variety of the approaches used for software Verification and Validation, and the absence of any obvious confirmation bias.

Back in 2010 Easterbrook tried to map out the space, in which software researchers and practitioners' contributions are likely to be needed, and suggest a possible research agenda. (Easterbrook, 2010), concluded that software and computational thinking are critical components of the solution for climate changes. They identified three key areas where effort might be focused: software to support the science of understanding climate change; software to support the global collective decision making; and software to reduce the carbon footprint of modern technology.

Another work was done for Software Testing and Verification in Climate Model Development in (Clune, 2011), where authors discussed what analogous tools could bring to scientific software for climate modelling, they have suggested a methodology to minimize difficulties of complex numerical algorithms by touching challenges and issues of testing them.

Gent et al. presented in (Gent, 2011) the fourth version of the Community Climate System Model (CCSM4), where they described developments to all CCSM components, and documents fully coupled preindustrial control runs compared to the previous version of the Community Climate System Model (CCSM3). Using the standard atmosphere and land resolution of $1°$ results in the sea surface temperature, biases in the major upwelling regions being comparable to the $1.4°$ -resolution CCSM3.

Lucas et al. proposed a system that allows failure analysis of parameter-induced simulation crashes in climate models in their paper (Lucas, 2013). They have experienced a series of simulation crashes within the Parallel Ocean Program (POP2) component of CCSM4.

Assessing climate model software quality: a defect density analysis of three models is a work done in (Eberhart, 1995) where authors have performed a detailed analysis of defect reports based on data collected from many big tracking systems and repositories in order to prove that climate models have low defect densities.

Seismic Hazards Detection

According to (Gale, 2001), advanced seismic and seismoacoustic monitoring systems allow a better understanding of rock mass processes, so in (Gibowicz, 2001) who ??? defined seismic hazards prediction methods, but these methods required a non-standard measuring apparatus, for this reason they are not used in seismic mining. Who? (Kornowski, 2003) proposed a linear method to predict seismoacoustic energy in a given time horizon. Works on seismic prediction continued in (Lasocki, 2005) that gave clustering methods to predict the energy of future seismic tremors emitted in a given time horizon based on probabilistic analysis, in which fuzzy numbers and Markov chains were applied. However, the accuracy of all those methods is so far from prefect. Neural Networks also appeared in many studies for prediction of seismic tremors, beginning with the work in (Rudajev, 1999) in which an application to mining tremor prediction has been tested and methodological conditions have been obtained by treatment of induced seismic activity prediction that was treated as a problem of time series extrapolation of maximum cumulative amplitudes and numbers of seismic events recorded per day, the treatment was done using multilayer perceptron, (Kabiesz, 2006) is another work that presented an approach using neural network for determining an influence of the type and shape of the input data on the efficiency of such a prediction. The considerations are based on a selected example of the seismic activity recorded during long wall mining operations conducted in one of the Polish mines. Also in Leśniak (2009), who gave a study that demonstrated the potential of the clustering technique in evaluation of the increment of the seismic hazard over a limited area.

All mentioned works reported their methods in form of bi-class problem for prediction of "Hazardous" and "Non-Hazardous" seismic, and they are the basic works in seismology for prediction of earthquake occurrences (Bodri, 2001; Sikder, 2009) in which two of the most known methods in data mining were applied, decision trees and rules induction.

SONAR DATA CLASSIFICATION

Classification of Sonar data began in 1988 by Gorman and .al in (Gorman, 1988) where authors presented a neural network learning procedure that has been applied to the classification of sonar returns from two undersea targets, a metal cylinder and a similarly shaped rock. Networks with an intermediate layer of hidden processing units achieved classification accuracy as high as 100% on a training set of 104 returns. These networks correctly classified up to 90.4% of 104 test returns not contained in the training set. (Tan, 2004) proposed a multivariate decision tree inference scheme using the minimum message length (MML) principle (Wallace, 1999). The scheme uses MML coding as an objective (goodness-of-fit) function on model selection and searches with a simple evolution strategy. And test it on UCI machine learning repository data sets containing Sonar dataset and compare with the decision tree programs C4.5 and C5. In 2013, Ravi and al. published a paper (Jade, 2013) in which they presented additional experimental data, a comparison of network classification performance to that of traditional pattern recognition techniques, and support vector classification technique.

Plants Identification and Machine Learning

Recently, plant classification became one of major researches, James S Cope and al. (James, 2010) presented Plant Texture Classification Using Gabor Co-Occurrences, Joint distributions for the responses from applying different scales of the Gabor filter are calculated. The difference between leaf textures is calculated by the Jeffrey divergence measure of corresponding distributions. Also, Kadir and al. in (Abdul Kadir, 2011) incorporate shape and vein, color, and texture features to classify leaves using probabilistic neural network and proves that it gives better result with average accuracy of 93.75%. Plant leaf images corresponding to three plant types, are analyzed using two different shape modelling techniques in Chaki and al. (Jyotismita Chaki, 2011) proposes an automated system for recognizing plant species based on leaf images. One of the last works released by Bhardwaj (Anant Bhardwaj, 2013) that present a simple computational method in computer vision to recognize plant leaves and to classify it using K nearest neighbor. Anang Hudaya also works on plant classification in his paper (Hudaya, 2013) presenting a scalable approach for classifying plant leaves using the 2-dimensional shape feature, using Distributed Hierarchical Graph Neuron (DHGN) for pattern recognition and k-nearest neighbor (k-NN) for pattern classification.

Ecological Data Classification Using Bio Inspired Algorithms

This section shows four cases were authors used bio inspired algorithms for classification of ecological data. First, we will discuss the data used in the studies, next we will give ideas about bio inspired algorithms invented by authors of this chapter. Then we will present the obtained results by these algorithms applied on the four data sets.

CASES STUDIED

Prediction of Successful Climate Model Simulations

The used dataset contains records of simulation crashes encountered during climate model uncertainty quantification (UQ) ensembles. Based on a software developed by Lawrence Livermore National Laboratory, ensemble members were constructed using three separate Latin hypercubes in order to sample the uncertainties of 18 model parameters within the Parallel Ocean Program (POP2) that is a component of the Community Climate System Model (CCSM4). Each hypercube was conducted in a different study, and it contains 180 simulations, where 46 simulations out of 540 were failed for numerical reasons during the combination of the 18 parameters. Table 1 shows the success rate in each of the three hypercubes (Lucas, 2013):

Table 1. Success rate in each study

Study	Simulations	Success	Failure	Success Rate
Study 1	180	160	20	88.89%
Study 2	180	168	12	93.3%
Study 3	180	166	14	92.2%
Total	540	494	46	91.5%

Seismic Data Classification

In the data set each row contains a summary statement about seismic activity in the rock mass within one shift (8 hours). If decision attribute has the value 1, then in the next shift any seismic bump with energy higher than 104J was registered. That task of hazards prediction bases on the relationship between the energy of recorded tremors and seismoacoustic activity with the possibility of rock burst occurrence. Hence, such hazard prognosis is not connected with accurate rock burst prediction. Moreover, with the information about the possibility of hazardous situation occurrence, an appropriate supervision service can reduce a risk of rock burst (e.g. by distressing shooting) or withdraw workers from the threatened area. Good prediction of increased seismic activity is therefore a matter of great practical importance. The presented data set is characterized by unbalanced distribution of positive and negative examples. In the data set, there are only 170 positive examples representing class 1. Table 2 shows the attributes of the data set.

SONAR Data Set

Sound Navigation and Ranging (Sonar) is underwater sound detection used in boats or submarines to navigate, communicate with or detect objects under the surface of water based on sound propagation. Sonar data contains 111 patterns obtained by bouncing sonar signals off a metal cylinder at various angles and under various conditions, and 97 patterns obtained from rocks under similar conditions. The transmitted sonar signal is a frequency-modulated chirp, rising in frequency. The data set contains signals obtained from a variety of different aspect angles, spanning 90 degrees for the cylinder and 180 degrees for the rock. Each pattern is a set of 60 numbers in the range 0.0 to 1.0. Each number represents the energy within a particular frequency band, integrated over a certain period of time. The integration aperture for higher frequencies occurs later in time, since these frequencies are transmitted later during the chirp. The label associated with each record contains the letter "R" if the object is a rock and "M" if it is a mine (metal cylinder). The numbers in the labels are in increasing order of aspect angle, but they do not encode the angle directly.

Plants Recognition From Images of Their Leaves

The 'Leaves' dataset contains one-hundred species of leaves (Mallah, 2013), each species represented by three 64 element vector for each of three distinct features extracted from images: a fine-scale margin feature histogram, a Centroid Contour Distance Curve shape signature, and an interior texture feature histogram. This dataset contains 1600 samples, whereas there are sixteen distinct specimens for each

Table 2. Attribute of seismic data set

Attribute	Description
seismic	result of shift seismic hazard assessment in the mine working obtained by the seismic method (a - lack of hazard, b - low hazard, c - high hazard, d - danger state)
seismoacoustic	result of shift seismic hazard assessment in the mine working obtained by the seismoacoustic method
shift	information about type of a shift (W - coal-getting, N -preparation shift)
genergy	seismic energy recorded within previous shift by the most active geophone (GMax) out of geophones monitoring the long wall
gpuls	a number of pulses recorded within previous shift by GMax
gdenergy	a deviation of energy recorded within previous shift by GMax from average energy recorded during eight previous shifts
gdpuls	a deviation of a number of pulses recorded within previous shift by GMax from average number of pulses recorded during eight previous shifts
ghazard	result of shift seismic hazard assessment in the mine working obtained by the seismoacoustic method based on registration coming from GMax only
nbumps	the number of seismic bumps recorded within previous shift
nbumps2	the number of seismic bumps (in energy range [102,103)) registered within previous shift
nbumps3	the number of seismic bumps (in energy range [103,104)) registered within previous shift
nbumps4	the number of seismic bumps (in energy range [104,105)) registered within previous shift
nbumps5	the number of seismic bumps (in energy range [105,106)) registered within the last shift
nbumps6	the number of seismic bumps (in energy range [106,107)) registered within previous shift
nbumps7	the number of seismic bumps (in energy range [107,108)) registered within previous shift
nbumps89	the number of seismic bumps (in energy range [108,1010)) registered within previous shift
energy	total energy of seismic bumps registered within previous shift
maxenergy	the maximum energy of the seismic bumps registered within previous shift
class	the decision attribute - "1" means that high energy seismic bump occurred in the next shift ("hazardous state"), "0" means that no high energy seismic bumps occurred in the next shift ("non-hazardous state")

species, captured as a color image on a white background using scanner. Figure 1 shows the first 27 species from the dataset.

The data set inherently consists of having a wide set of classes with a low number of samples. Additionally, many sub species resemble the appearance of other major species, as well as many sub species with a major species can resemble a radically different appearance (Mallah, 2013).

ALGORITHMS USED FOR STUDIES

In this section, we discuss four approaches developed by authors in four different studies, these approaches were inspired from different natural phenomena, beginning by social bees' algorithm, to termites' hill building, then an algorithm based on the echolocation mechanism of bats, finally another algorithm inspired from the black hole of space. First, we will give the source of inspiration from nature before detailing the artificial models

Figure 1. A silhouette image of one plant specimen each from the challenging one-hundred species leaves data set

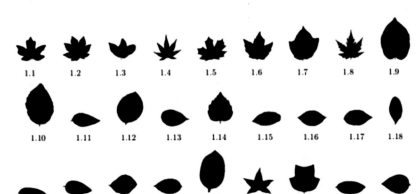

Source of Inspiration

Natural Social Bees

Honey bees are social insects. "Social bees" is a phrase used to express that they live together in large, well-organized family groups. A honey bee colony typically consists of three kinds of adult bees: workers, drones, and a queen. Several thousand worker bees cooperate in nest building, food collection, and brood rearing. Each member has a definite task to perform, related to its adult age. But surviving and reproducing take the combined efforts of the entire colony. Individual bees (workers, drones, and queens) cannot survive without the support of the colony. In this work, we were more interested on worker bees.

Worker bees, with its remarkable creatures, have a considerable amount of jobs and duties to perform in their short lives that vary as they age, in other words, they perform a brilliant team work. Initially, a worker's responsibilities include various tasks within the hive. At this stage of development, worker bees are referred to as house bees. As they get older, their duties involve work outside of the hive as field bees. We were more interested to implement our approach on three jobs as follow:

1. **Worker Bee Housekeeping (Days 1 to 3):** One of her first tasks is cleaning out the cell from which she just emerged. This and other empty cells are cleaned and polished and left immaculate to receive new eggs and to store nectar and pollen.
2. **Worker Bee Undertakers (Days 3 to 16):** During the first couple weeks of her life, the worker bee removes any bees that have died and disposes of the corpses as far from the hive as possible. Similarly, diseased or dead brood are quickly removed before becoming a health threat to the colony.
3. **Collecting Nectar for the Hive (Days 12 to 18):** Young worker bees also take nectar from foraging field bees that are returning to the hive. The house bees deposit this nectar into cells earmarked for this purpose. The workers similarly take pollen from returning field bees and pack the pollen into cells. Both the ripened honey and the pollen are food for the colony.

Termites' Hill Building in Nature

Cooperation of a large population of individuals to solve global tasks is given to us in many examples in biological life; the hill building behavior of termites is one of these examples. Individuals act independently and move only on the basis of the observed local pheromone gradient in order to gather pebbles spread over an area into one place to build a hill. Pheromone is a chemical excreted by the insect which evaporates and disperses over time. Each termite has to follow four rules:

1. A termite moves randomly, but is biased towards the locally observed pheromone gradient. If no pheromone exists, a termite moves uniformly randomly in any direction.
2. Each termite may carry only one pebble at a time.
3. If a termite is not carrying a pebble and it encounters one, the termite will pick it up.
4. If a termite is carrying a pebble and it encounters one, the termite will put the pebble down in order to build the hill. The pebble will be infused with a certain amount of pheromone so another termite coming from another hill cannot take it.

In order to understand better the hill building behavior, we have to explain five major elements of this principle:

1. A positive feedback is the general guidelines for a particular behavior. Because a termite's attraction towards the pheromone gradient biases it to adding to large piles, positive feedback is given as follow: The larger the pile is, the more pheromone it is likely to have, and thus a termite is more biased to move towards it and potentially add to the pile. The greater the bias to the hill is, the more termites are also likely to arrive faster, further increasing the pheromone content of the hill.
2. Negative feedback, in the form of pheromone decay, helps large piles grow by preventing small piles from continuing to attract termites. Diffused pheromone over the environment is a liquid, it evaporates. This evaporation consequently weakens the pheromone, which decreases the resulting gradient. When the bias to the hill is greater, more termites will arrive faster, while the lower gradient is, fewer termites will move in its direction. This may seem detrimental to the task of collecting all pebbles into one pile, it is in fact essential. As the task begins, several small piles will emerge very quickly. Those piles that are able to attract more termites will grow faster. As pheromone decays on lesser piles, termites will be less likely to visit them again, thus preventing them from growing.
3. Termites move randomly. Where piles start and how they end is entirely determined by chance. Small fluctuations in the behavior of termites may have a large influence in future events. This mechanism allows for new solutions to arise, or to direct current solutions as they evolve to fit the environment.
4. It is essential that many individuals work together at this task. If not enough termites exist, then the pheromone would decay before any more pebbles could be added to a pile. Termites would continue their random walk, without forming any significant piles.
5. Stigmergy refers to indirect communications between individuals, generally through their environment. Termites are directed to the largest hill by the pheromone gradient. There is no need for termites to directly communicate with each other or even to know of each other's existence. For this reason, termites are allowed to act independently of other individuals, which greatly simplifies the necessary rules.

Bat Echolocation in Nature

Bats are a special fascinating kind of mammals with their wings and their lifestyle, as we know bats are active only at night and in the dark places. It is estimated that there are about 996 species of bats, more than half of them rely on sounds for navigation while they fly. The use of this trick is to detect obstacles and forage for food. This mechanism is called Echolocation or SONAR (SOund Navigation And Ranging). It gives a bat the ability to generate signals that bounce off surrounding objects and using a processing of the returning echoes with extraordinary acuity, the bat can determine the direction, the distance and the features of these objects. Figure 2 shows an example of a bat hunting an insect.

The echolocation mechanisms are different and correlated with the hunting strategies of each species; the most of bats use short, frequency-modulated signals to sweep through about an octave. In this strategy, a pulse only lasts a few thousandths of a second (up to about 8 to 10 ms) in the frequency range of 25kHz to 150 kHz, the typical range of frequencies for most bat species are in the region between 25kHz and 100kHz, though some species can emit higher frequencies up to 150 kHz. During hunting, the rate of pulse emission can be sped up to about 200 pulses per second when homing on their prey. Studies show the integration time of the bat ear is typically about 300 to 400 µs, which give to the bats a fantastic ability to process the signal. Taking in mind that the speed of sound in air is typically v = 340 m/s, the wavelength λ of the ultrasonic sound bursts with a constant frequency f is given by λ= v/f.

Such echolocation behavior of bats can be formulated mathematically in such a way that it can be associated with many problems solving objective, for that and based on the original work in (Yang, 2010), we are interested in some features of the echolocation of bats to formulate a mathematical implementation for seismic assessment.

Figure 2. Bats echolocation

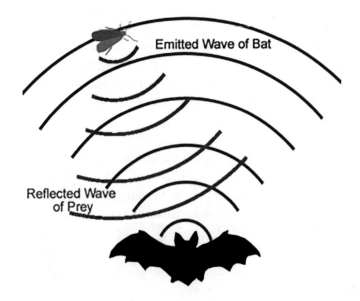

Black Holes

Eighteen-century was the birth of black holes' concept, John Michelle and Pierre Laplace were the pioneers to identify it, they formulated a new theory of a stars disappear from eyes visibility by integrate Newton's law. But the phenomenon of mass collapsing was named "Black Hole" by John Wheeler the American physicist for the first time in 1967.

A black hole in space is what forms when a star of massive size collapses. The gravitational power of the black hole is too high that even the light cannot escape from it. The gravity is so strong because matter has been squeezed into a tiny space. Anything that crosses the boundary of the black hole will be swallowed by it and vanish and nothing can get away from its enormous power. The sphere-shaped boundary of a black hole in space is known as the event horizon. The radius of the event horizon is termed as the Schwarzschild radius. At this radius, the escape speed is equal to the speed of light, and once light passes through, even it cannot escape. Nothing can escape from within the event horizon because nothing can go faster than light. The Schwarzschild radius is calculated by the following equation:

$$R = \frac{2GM}{C^2} \tag{1}$$

where G is the gravitational constant, M is the mass of the black hole, and c is the speed of light.

If anything moves close to the event horizon or crosses the Schwarzschild radius it will be absorbed into the black hole and permanently disappear. The existence of black holes can be discerned by its effect over the objects surrounding it.

Artificial Models

Those four phenomena in nature are considered as an excellent source of inspiration since they contain some parameters and a sort of filtering process which is the main idea used for inspiration of the following algorithms for the supervised classification of ecological data:

Social Bees Algorithm (SBA)

This section details the implementation of previous detailed task proposed by (Bouarara, 2015) for text clustering task, then adapted by (Rahmani, 2016) for a supervised classification of plants, where here, worker bees present vectors of the training set (50% of dataset) that perform three tasks in sort of distance calculation between these vectors and other vectors from test set, used distances described in Table 3.

In each test experiment, we calculated three different distances between vectors in training set (worker bees) and test set, where each one present a task of bee, then we calculated average distance, vectors in test set got a new class from training set depending on minimum average.

In order to avoid that some distances affect decision more than other distances, we used to normalize it before we extract minimum distance, since we know that cosine distance always be between 0 and 1, while Euclidean, Manhattan, or Chebyshev increase when number of attributes increase.

As we mentioned above, for each example from test set, we calculated the distances between it and all examples in training set, so we got the maximum distance (MaxD(x,y)) obtained and the minimum one

Table 3. Used Distances in experiment

Distance	Formula (x and y Are Two Vectors)
Manhattan (Man)	$D(x,y) = \sum \lvert x_i - y_i \rvert$
Euclidean (Euc)	$D(x,y) = \sum \sqrt{\left(xi - yi \right)^2}$
Chebyshev (Cheb)	$D(x, y) = Max\ (\lvert x_i - y_i \rvert)$
Cosine (Cos)	$D(x, y) = \dfrac{\sum xi * yi}{\sqrt{\sum xi^2} * \sqrt{\sum yi^2}}$

(MinD(x,y)) for each Manhattan, Euclidean and Chebyshev distance, then we normalized the obtained distances as following:

$$D(x,y)= x = \frac{D\left(x,y\right) - Min_D\left(x,y\right)}{Max_D\left(x,y\right) - Min_D\left(x,y\right)} \tag{2}$$

Algorithm 1 shows a detailed artificial bees algorithm

Choosing three distances to calculate their average was done during the implementation, since we based on social life of bees in the hive, we have chosen three distances that present tasks in sort of filtering where bees choose between objects, which one stays and which one dropped, in the artificial model, a hive is a class, and training set is the set of bees that work in the hive, while test set examples are the objects to keep in the hive (which means belong to the class) or dropped from the hive (which means do not belong to this class), or otherwise saying, the decision if an object belongs to a class and not the other class was taken by classifying these examples according to the minimum average of distances got.

Algorithm 1. ABC algorithm

```
Inputs: X: training set
        Y: test set
For each y in Y do
        For each x in X do
                D1 = distance_1(x, y)
                D2 = distance_2(x, y)
                D3 = distance_3(x, y)
                D_average (x, y) = D1 + D2 + D3
                                   ---------------
                                         3
        end
min (y) = minimum (D_average (x, y))
Classify y according to the min(y)
end
```

Another reason why we had chosen a combination of distances, is because by doing that we were trying to benefit from advantages of the three distances because mathematically, these distances complement each other.

Termites' Hill Building Algorithm (ATHB)

ATHB (Rahmani, 2017) is an artificial system inspired from Termite's hill building behavior; it is based on two main processes; once presents the calculation of pheromone gradient using a set of artificial termites that gather pebbles, and the second presents the hill building based on a local pheromone gradient and a distance. Figure 1 shows the architecture of ATHB:

Hill in ATHB is a class. In this step, we choose a subset from our dataset to present artificial termites that are considered as training set, whereas the rest of examples present pebbles to collect that are the test set.

Termite's Random Walk For one iteration, this step presents the random selection of an example (Pebble) of the test set.

Find a Pebble When an example from training set (Xtermite) choose one example from test set (Xpebble), a distance calculation between these two examples D (Xtermite, Xpebble) decides if this termite finds pebble or not. If not so it keeps moving randomly.

Carrying a Pebble This step presents a test of the distance calculated previously D (Xtermite, Xpebble) with a threshold that was fixed from the beginning. If it is lower than the threshold, it means the termite is not carrying a pebble, so it will pick up this pebble; else, it doesn't find a pebble, so it keeps moving randomly. If the termite is carrying a pebble, it will pass to the next task. The range of the threshold was chosen by experience according to the changes based on evaluation metrics, in which we found different results, so we took the best ones. The threshold is the controlling parameter that affects the results

Put Pebble and increment Pheromone Gradient Pheromone presents a number of instances of each class (Xtermite) that verifies the condition (D(Xtermite, Xpebble) < threshold). This step presents the fact that pheromone (initially equals zero) is incremented, after we finished with all examples, we got two pheromones (one presents failure analysis, and one presents success). Because ATHB is based on minimization problem, final pheromone gradient equals the ratio of one over pheromone as follows:

$$\text{Pheromone\_Gradient} = \frac{1}{pheromone} \tag{3}$$

We have chosen number one because in order to give the distance and the pheromone gradient the same priority in calculation, which helps us to avoid that the pheromone gradient will not affect the results more than the distance. The pheromone gradient belongs to [0,1].

In nature, each termite puts a pebble based on pheromone gradient. In ATHB, building the hill is the final decision for classification of a pebble. In this process, we calculated another distance with the centroid of each class (Hill), then we multiplied this distance by pheromone gradient. Finally, we chose the minimum result as the hill that the pebble belongs to.

Algorithm 2. Calculate pheromone gradient

```
Input
        A set of artificial termites
        A set of pebbles
        Threshold
        Distance
For each pebble Pn do
        For each class Cx do //initialize each pheromone of each class in
training set by zero
                pheromone (Pn, Cx) =0;
        End
//Calculate the pheromone
For each artificial termite Atm do
        // Calculate the distance between pebble and termite
        Calculate distance D (Pn, Atm);
        If (D (Pn, Atm) < Threshold then
                pheromone (Pn, Cx) ++;
        Else
                Atm keeps moving randomly
        End;
//Calculate pheromone gradient
```

$$\text{pheromone\_Gradient } (Pn, Cx) = \frac{1}{pheromone\left(Pn,Cx\right)}$$

```
End.
```

Bat Echolocation Algorithm (BEA)

As mentioned above, we were interested in the three rules of bat algorithm given in (Yang, 2010) to create a new model for classification of seismic data.

The proposed approach by (Rahmani, 2017b) is constructed in 6 steps in which 5 of them represents one iteration. Before beginning the treatment, we have to initialize two parameters, initial loudness A0 that decrease in each iteration, and learning parameter that is used to adjust the frequency of emitted pulses. In our approach, we considered that one bat is represented by one vector from test set, which will look for Neighbors to enjoy their class, in other words, this is a distance based approach similar to K-Nearest Neighbors algorithm with additional parameters.

To classify a bat, we first calculated the mean of each vector elements in training set as frequency of a bat (fbat) to catch that prey (vector of the training set). After that, the bat calculates the frequency of emitted pulses (fep), which initially presents the average of the bat elements. Using the two frequencies, we calculated the frequency f based on Doppler Effect of sounds, f is calculated as follow:

$$f = |fbat - fep| \tag{4}$$

Algorithm 3. Hill building

```
Input
        A set of pebbles
        A set of artificial termites
        Distance
For each class Cx do //Calculate centroid of each class
        Nbr (At) = number of termites that belongs to the class Cx;
```

$$\text{Centroid (Cx)} = \frac{\left(\sum Atm\right)}{Nbr\left(At\right)}$$

```
End
For each pebble Pn do //classify each pebble
        For each class Cx do
                //Calculate distance between pebble Pn and centroid (Cx)
                D (Pn, Cx) = distance between Pn and centroid (Cx)
                Dicision_Cx = D (Pn, Cx) * Pheromone_Gradient (Pn, Cx)
        End
Final_decision (Pn) = Min (Dicision_Cx)
End
```

After getting the frequency, we calculated a velocity as distance between the bat and the prey, in the implementation we tested the Euclidean distance as follow:

$$D(X, Y) = \sum \sqrt{\left(y_i - x_i\right)^2} \tag{5}$$

The final step before prediction of seismic hazards, we calculated a similarity between bats and preys using the velocity and the frequency. The similarity is simply the wavelength λ that each bat in real life uses it during hunting to echolocate preys, from that we conclude the formula of classification as follow:

$$\lambda = v/f \tag{6}$$

Prediction of seismic hazards presents the step of classification, in which, from all wavelengths resulted, we selected only A0 wavelengths, where A0 is an integer defined in the beginning, in other words, we selected the A0 most similar vectors from training set to classify the test vector and to use them in the next iteration. A0 presents the initial loudness. Finally, we took the maximum class appears in all selected vectors, and we associated the bat (test vector) to that class. The whole process mentioned represents one iteration. The stop criterion we tested is the loudness. According to (Yang, 2010), the loudness varies from a large (positive) A0 to a minimum constant value Amin, so we chose the loudness to stop the algorithm. By passing from iteration to iteratiom, the algorithm chooses the incorrectly classified vectors from test set and adjusts their frequencies by multiply it by the learning parameter, and decreases the loudness. The training set of an iteration i+1 will be the chosen vectors from the iteration i. We chose the initial loudness based on simple heuristic, because we deal here with a Bi-class problem, we gave the initial loudness an impair number, and it decreases by two in each iteration, that is to assure that we have always a majority neighbors that present a class than those who present the other class.

In the end of each iteration, we evaluated the classification of seismic hazards and we saved the parameters. In the end of the algorithm, we took the best parameters as a model for seismic prediction, the model is defined by: vectors of the training set, their frequencies and loudness. The algorithm 4 gives a brief description of the bat echolocation algorithm for seismic hazards prediction.

Black Hole Algorithm (BHA)

Based on Schwarzschild proposition, we present in this work a new heuristic approach for Sonar data classification; in other words, (Rahmani, in press) created a formula for classification of sonar data similar to Schwarzschild formula. To do that, we had to define the three factors used in the formula, which are the mass M, the gravity G and the light speed C. In this section, we highlighted the proposed black hole approach.

1. **Calculate the Mass of Each Class (M):** M presents the mass of a black hole, so in our case; mass of each class (Black Hole) in training set presents the number of examples that belong to each class:

$$M \text{ (class)} = \text{Number of examples that present class} \tag{7}$$

Algorithm 4. Bat echolocation algorithm for seismic hazards prediction

```
Input:    Training_Set, Test_Set
              Distance_V
              A, learning_parameter, x: constant
Frequencies_Trainig = Calculate_Frequecies(Training_Set)
Frequencies_Test - Calculate_Frequecies (Test_Set)
While (A > 0):
For each vector Dx in Test_Set do
          For each vector Dy in Training_Set do
                      F = |Frequencies_Trainig(Dy) - Frequencies_Test(Dx)|
                      G = Calculate Distance_V (Dx, Dy)
                      Velocity_V = G/F
          end for
          Min_v = Minimum_Velocities
          Classify Dx according to Min_v
end for
          A = A - x
          Save_parameters_as_model
end while
END
```

2. **Calculate the Gravity Between Objects and Black Holes (G):** Gravity (G) is the most important factor in black hole phenomenon, if objects are closer; gravity becomes stronger, so we had to present this idea as distance calculation between vectors in training set and vectors is test set, in which we used three different distances trying to figure out which one gives better results. Formulas of used distances are presented in Table 4.

3. **Initialize Light Speed (C):** C (as Schwarzschild said) is light speed, so it's constant for all objects (299 792 458 m / s). And it is also constant in our case, in which it presents number of examples in the training set.

4. **Calculate the Radius (R):** Radius (R) is the final result calculated between vectors of training set, and vectors of test set. It's the value used for classification in way that each class in training set presents a black hole, and each example in test set presents a star or moving objects:

$$R = \frac{2GM}{C^2}$$

(8)

Each vector in test set is associated to the group that contains vector from training set where radius (R) is the minimum one. And finally, basing on the final clusters, we gave to vectors of test set classes according to the group associated.

Evaluate the Classification

To evaluate our approach, we calculate some common metrics using vectors of test set (pebbles). Before detailing these metrics, we have to introduce some measures used to calculate it as follow:

1. **True Positive (TP):** Presents the average of the success simulation vectors that are correctly predicted as success simulations.

2. **True Negative (TN):** Presents the average of the failed simulation vectors that are correctly predicted as failed simulations.

3. **False Positive (FP):** Presents the average of the vectors that are predicted as success simulations but they are not.

Table 4. Used distances in experiments

Distance	Formula (x and y Are Two Vectors)
Euclidean	$D(x, y) = \sum \sqrt{\left(xi - yi\right)^2}$
Chebyshev	$D(x, y) = Max(|x_i - y_i|)$
Cosine	$D(x, y) = x = \dfrac{\sum xi * yi}{\sqrt{\sum xi^2} * \sqrt{\sum yi^2}}$

Algorithm 5. Black hole for active sonar data classification

```
Input:      Representation_of_Rocks_and_Mines_Underwater
                Distance_G
                C: constant
M_R = Calculate_Mass_Rocks(training_set)
M_M= Calculate_Mass_Mines(training_set)
For each vector Dx in test_set do
          For each vector Dy in training_set do
                  G = Calculate Distance_G (Dx, Dy)
                          if Class(Dy) = "Rock" do Radius(Dx) = (2 * G * M_R) /
C²
                          else if Class(Dy) = "Mines" do Radius(Dx) = (2 * G *
M_M) / C²
          end for
          Min_r = Minimum_Radius
          Classify Dx according to Min_r
end for
END
```

4. **False Negative (FN):** Presents the average of the vectors that are predicted as failed simulations, but they are success simulations.

Using these four measures, we calculated the most famous measures that are used to evaluate classification algorithms:

1. For classification, the accuracy estimates is the overall number of vectors correctly classified, divided by the total number of vectors in the initial data. (Han, 2011)

$$\text{Accuracy} = \frac{TP + TN}{TP + TN + FP + FN} \tag{9}$$

2. Precision and recall are the measures used in the information retrieval domain to measure how well an information retrieval system retrieves the relevant vectors requested by a user (in our case is success simulations). The measures are defined as follows (Sammut, 2011)

$$\text{Precision} = \frac{TP}{TP + FP} \tag{10}$$

$$\text{Recall} = \frac{TP}{TP + FN} \tag{11}$$

3. Instead of two measures, they are often combined to provide a single measure of retrieval performance called the F-measure as follows (Sammut, 2011)

$$\text{Fmeasure} = \frac{2*precision*recall}{precision + recall} \tag{12}$$

4. Entropy is a measure often used in data mining algorithms that measures the disorder of a set of data.

$$\text{Entropy} = \text{-precision} * \log2(\text{precision}) \tag{13}$$

RESULTS AND DISCUSSION

This section presents the obtained results of application of the four algorithms for supervised classification of the four datasets mentioned above. But first we will give a small analysis of the datasets in terms of number of attributes used to calculates distance between training and test sets since all the proposed approaches are based on distance calculation, number of examples in each dataset, also the distribution of examples on classes. Table 5 shows the datasets analysis.

Obtained Results

In the following we will present the obtained results of application of the four algorithms mentioned previously on the four datasets, Table 6 presents the obtained results.

In terms of Accuracy: The accuracy shows how well the system can classify the data. The accuracy here was calculated for evaluation of prediction of all classes of each dataset, as seen in Table 6, social bees' algorithm can correctly predict more than 85% of sonar signal vectors while it predicted more than 87% of the plants images, contrary to either climate simulations or seismic hazards, SBA predicted only about 63% and 67% of those vectors. ATHB showed better results especially for plants recognition

Table 5. Datasets analysis

Dataset	Number of Attributes	Number of Examples	Number of Classes	Class to Predict	Distribution of Examples on Classes	
Climate Model Simulations	18	540	2 classes (success and failure)	Success	Success	494
					Failure	46
Seismic Hazards	18	2584	2 classes (hazardous and non-hazardous)	Hazardous	Hazardous	170
					Non-Hazardous	2414
SONAR data	60	208	2 classes (Rock and Mines)	All Classes	Rock	97
					Mines	111
Plant Species	64	1600	100 classes (each class is a specie)	All Classes	16 examples in each class	

Table 6. Obtained results

Algorithm	Dataset	Accuracy	Precision	Recall	Fmeasure	Entropy
Social Bees Algorithm (SBA)	Climate Simulations	63.26	0.84	0.81	0.82	0.06
	Seismic Hazards	67.61	0.87	0.89	0.88	0.05
	SONAR	85.69	0.86	0.85	0.85	0.05
	Plant Species	87.62	0.88	0.89	0.88	0.04
Artificial Termites' Hill Building (ATHB)	Climate Simulations	68.89	0.89	0.99	0.95	0.04
	Seismic Hazards	71.36	0.91	0.92	0.92	0.03
	SONAR	89.37	0.90	0.91	0.90	0.04
	Plant Species	90.67	0.91	0.91	0.91	0.03
Bat Echolocation Algorithm (BEA)	Climate Simulations	68.15	0.88	0.88	0.88	0.04
	Seismic Hazards	73.41	0.89	0.94	0.91	0.04
	SONAR	87.34	0.88	0.89	0.88	0.04
	Plant Species	89.10	0.84	0.90	0.88	0.06
Black Hole Algorithm (BHA)	Climate Simulations	62	0.82	0.83	0.82	0.073
	Seismic Hazards	72.84	0.92	0.91	0.91	0.03
	SONAR	82.69	0.89	0.77	0.83	0.04
	Plant Species	86.04	0.86	0.79	0.83	0.05

and sonar data where the obtained accuracy was about 90%. Accuracy obtained by Bat Echolocation Algorithm decreased a little bit, classification of climate simulations model gave about 68%, seismic hazards gave about 73%, while classification of SONAR data and plants species exceeded 87%. Black Hole algorithm is very simple algorithm and it shows good results where plants recognition gave about 86%, and SONAR data classification resulted an accuracy of about 83%. the low accuracy given when we classified climate simulations and seismic hazards data due to the problem of unbalanced data since these two datasets are not balanced. Figure 3 shows a comparison of the obtained accuracy by each algorithm applied on all datasets.

In terms of Precision: precision presents a measure to evaluate how well the final classification by system is responding to a user request. In other words, let's say that a user requested all vectors that are classified as 'A', the precision here shows how much vectors that were correctly classified as 'A' among all vectors classified as 'A' in the final results. In our case, for climate simulation models, we requested only the successful simulations, as seen in figure 4, for all algorithms, about 82% to 89% of the predicted vectors as successful simulations were correctly classified. For seismic data, we requested the hazardous ones, so the obtained precision shown was between 87% to 92%, which is very good results. SONAR data, we asked for two requests, one to about rock vectors, and the second about mines vectors, then

Figure 3. Obtained accuracy

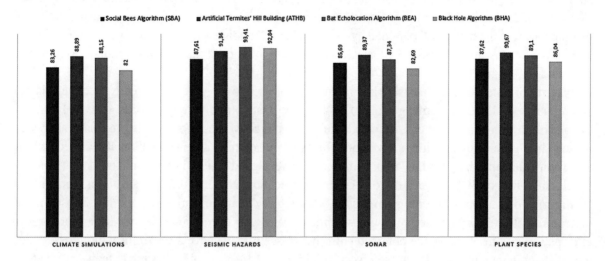

Figure 4. Obtained precision

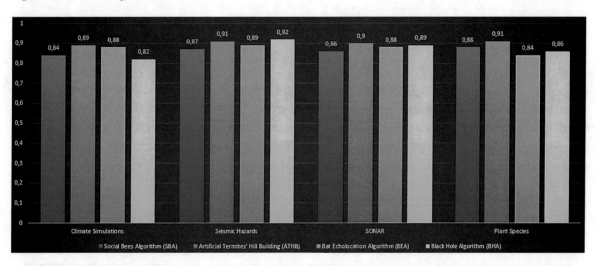

we calculated the average precision, the obtained precision was between 86% to 90%. Finally for plants recognition we do the same thing as SONAR data, we requested here 100 requests, each for a class, then we calculated the average precision that was between 84% and 91%.

In terms of Recall: if precision used to evaluate the system response in the new predicted classes, recall is used for evaluation of the system response from the original classification given by experts, since the supervised classification is based on experts' pre-classification. Back to the previous example for prediction of examples as class 'A', recall means how much examples that were originally classified as 'A' and predicted by the system as examples belong to class 'A'. Figure 5 shows the obtained recall by all algorithms applied on the four datasets, our requests here are the requests shown on Table 5 in class to predict column. As seen, all algorithms showed good results in terms of recall, where the lowest recall was given by Black Hole Algorithm for prediction of Rocks and Mines under water based on SONAR signals, while it recognized an average of about 79% of plants, then results given by Black Hole algorithm improved for prediction of successful climate model simulations, and prediction of seismic hazards. the best recall obtained by Termites' Hill Building Algorithm where it predicted more than 90% of each dataset correctly, especially for classification of climate model simulations, where it predicted 99% correctly.

In terms of Fmeasure: the fmeasure is a measure that is used to evaluate the correctly predicted classes among the new classes and among original classes at the same time. In other words, it is the harmonic average of the precision and recall. Like both measures, if it converges to one, more the results are better. As seen in Figure 6, all algorithms gave good fmeasures when they were applied on all datasets. taking for example termites hill building algorithm that gave very good results in terms of fmeasure (from 0.9 for classification of SONAR data up to 0.95 for classification of successful climate simulations).

In terms of Entropy: the entropy measure is used to evaluate information loss in the system during classification based on the precision, when it converges to one, we can say we have more loss in information. Figure 7 shows the obtained entropy, we see that we have a low information loss, which means that bio inspired algorithms were very good for classification of ecosystem data. we see that the maximum loss was when we applied black hole algorithm on climate simulations, where we loss 7% of information (entropy = 0.07).

CONCLUSION

Coined by A. G. Tansley in 1935, the term 'ecosystem' refers to an integrated system composed of a biotic community, its abiotic environment, and their dynamic interactions. A diversity of ecosystems exists through the world, from tropical mangroves to temperate alpine lakes, each with a unique set of components and dynamics, the amount of these systems made analysis of their data a very important field of study, which contains a lot of what called NP-hard problems.

Figure 5. Obtained recall

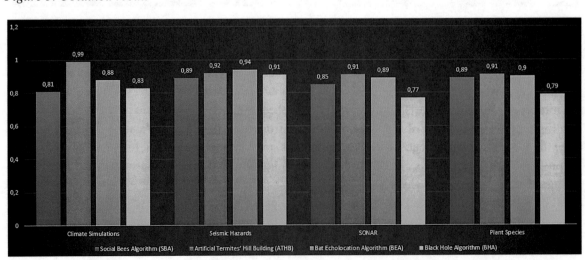

Figure 6. Obtained Fmeasure

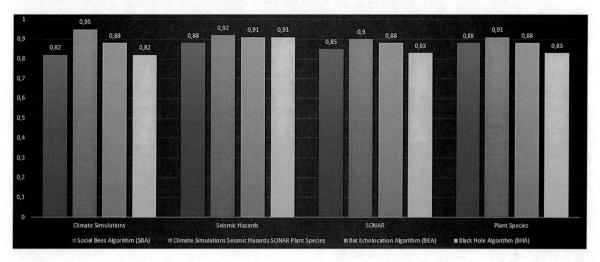

Figure 7. Obtained entropy

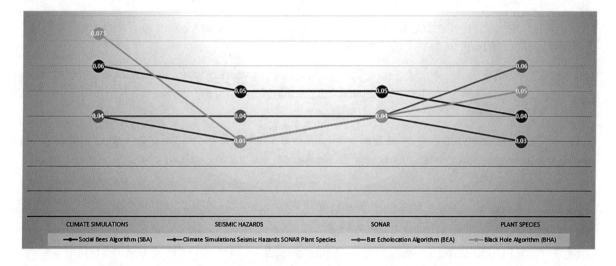

This work presented a study of application of bio inspired algorithms for ecosystem data analysis. The study contains application of four different approaches that were inspired by authors of the paper from four different phenomena, and they were applied for analysis of four different ecosystem data collected from real life cases. Results showed a very high accuracy and proved the efficiency of bio inspired algorithms for supervised classification of real ecosystem data, in terms of accuracy, the application gave very good results, whereas in terms of precision and recall, the given approaches proved that they can predict correctly different ecosystem data based on previously recorded data more than 70%. The main disadvantage of such kind of algorithms is that they cannot handle with unbalanced data like seismic and climate simulations, and that what was given during the evaluation of prediction of all classes of these two data sets.

For future work, we plan to use these approaches for other ecological problems like plant leaves classification based on their DNA sequences, land cover clustering, and different fields such as information retrieval. We also plan to combine the approaches with other approaches to optimize the results. As seen during the experiments, our approaches do not deal with unbalanced data, where number of examples of a class outnumber the other class which affect the final decision during classification, so optimizing the approaches to deal with unbalanced data like climate simulations is planned as main future work. Finally, this study belongs to a series of studies in order to develop an intelligent system for ecosystem scientists that will help them in future studies.

REFERENCES

Amin, A. H. M., & Khan, A. I. (2013). One-shot Classification of 2-D Leaf Shapes Using Distributed Hierarchical Graph Neuron (DHGN) Scheme with k-NN Classifier. *Procedia Computer Science*, *24*, 84–96. doi:10.1016/j.procs.2013.10.030

Bhardwaj, A., Kaur, M., & Kumar, A. (2013). Recognition of plants by Leaf Image using Moment Invariant and Texture Analysis. *International Journal of Innovation and Applied Studies*, *3*(1), 237–248.

Bodri, B. (2001). A neural-network model for earthquake occurrence. *Journal of Geodynamics*, *32*(3), 289–310. doi:10.1016/S0264-3707(01)00039-4

Bouarara, H. A., Hamou, R. M., & Amine, A. (2014). Text Clustering using Distances Combination by Social Bees: Towards 3D Visualisation Aspect. *International Journal of Information Retrieval Research*, *4*(3), 34–53. doi:10.4018/IJIRR.2014070103

Chaki, J., & Parekh, R. (2011). Plant leaf recognition using shape based features and neural network classifiers. *International Journal of Advanced Computer Science and Applications*, *2*(10). doi:10.14569/IJACSA.2011.021007

Clune, T., & Rood, R. (2011). Software testing and verification in climate model development. *IEEE Software*, *28*(6), 49–55. doi:10.1109/MS.2011.117

Cope, J. S., Remagnino, P., Barman, S., & Wilkin, P. (2010). Plant texture classification using gabor co-occurrences. In *Advances in Visual Computing* (pp. 669–677). Springer Berlin Heidelberg. doi:10.1007/978-3-642-17274-8_65

Easterbrook, S. M. (2010, November). Climate change: a grand software challenge. In *Proceedings of the FSE/SDP workshop on Future of software engineering research* (pp. 99-104). ACM. doi:10.1145/1882362.1882383

Easterbrook, S. M., & Johns, T. C. (2009). Engineering the software for understanding climate change. *Computing in Science & Engineering*, *11*(6), 64–74. doi:10.1109/MCSE.2009.193

Eberhart, R. C., & Kennedy, J. (1995, October). A new optimizer using particle swarm theory. In *Proceedings of the sixth international symposium on micro machine and human science* (Vol. 1, pp. 39-43). doi:10.1109/MHS.1995.494215

Elith, J., & Leathwick, J. R. (2009). Species distribution models: Ecological explanation and prediction across space and time. *Annual Review of Ecology Evolution and Systematics, 40*(1), 677–697. doi:10.1146/annurev.ecolsys.110308.120159

Gale, W. J., Heasley, K. A., Iannacchione, A. T., Swanson, P. L., Hatherly, P., & King, A. (2001, January). Rock damage characterisation from microseismic monitoring. In *DC Rocks 2001, The 38th US Symposium on Rock Mechanics (USRMS)*. American Rock Mechanics Association.

Gent, P. R., Danabasoglu, G., Donner, L. J., Holland, M. M., Hunke, E. C., Jayne, S. R., & Worley, P. H. et al. (2011). The community climate system model version 4. *Journal of Climate, 24*(19), 4973–4991. doi:10.1175/2011JCLI4083.1

Gibowicz, S. J., & Lasocki, S. (2001). Seismicity induced by mining: Ten years later. *Advances in Geophysics, 44*, 39–181. doi:10.1016/S0065-2687(00)80007-2

Gorman, R. P., & Sejnowski, T. J. (1988). Analysis of hidden units in a layered network trained to classify sonar targets. *Neural Networks, 1*(1), 75–89. doi:10.1016/0893-6080(88)90023-8

Han, J., Pei, J., & Kamber, M. (2011). *Data mining: concepts and techniques*. Elsevier.

Hochachka, W. M., Caruana, R., Fink, D., Munson, A. R. T., Riedewald, M., Sorokina, D., & Kelling, S. (2007). Data-mining discovery of pattern and process in ecological systems. *The Journal of Wildlife Management, 71*(7), 2427–2437. doi:10.2193/2006-503

Jade, R. K., Verma, L. K., & Verma, K. (2013). *Classification using Neural Network & Support Vector Machine for Sonar dataset*. Academic Press.

Kabiesz, J. (2006). Effect of the form of data on the quality of mine tremors hazard forecasting using neural networks. *Geotechnical and Geological Engineering, 24*(5), 1131–1147. doi:10.1007/s10706-005-1136-8

Kadir, A., Nugroho, L. E., Susanto, A., & Santosa, P. I. (2011). *A comparative experiment of several shape methods in recognizing plants*. arXiv preprint arXiv:1110.1509

Kornowski, J. (2003). Linear prediction of aggregated seismic and seismoacoustic energy emitted from a mining longwall. *ACTA Montana, 129*, 5–14.

Lasocki, S. (2005, March). Probabilistic analysis of seismic hazard posed by mining induced events. In *Proc. Sixth Int. Symp. on Rockburst and Seismicity in Mines "Controlling Seismic Risk"* (pp. 9-11). Academic Press.

Leśniak, A., & Isakow, Z. (2009). Space–time clustering of seismic events and hazard assessment in the Zabrze-Bielszowice coal mine, Poland. *International Journal of Rock Mechanics and Mining Sciences, 46*(5), 918–928. doi:10.1016/j.ijrmms.2008.12.003

Lucas, D. D., Klein, R., Tannahill, J., Ivanova, D., Brandon, S., Domyancic, D., & Zhang, Y. (2013). Failure analysis of parameter-induced simulation crashes in climate models. *Geoscientific Model Development, 6*(4), 1157–1171. doi:10.5194/gmd-6-1157-2013

Lucas, D. D., Klein, R., Tannahill, J., Ivanova, D., Brandon, S., Domyancic, D., & Zhang, Y. (2013). Failure analysis of parameter-induced simulation crashes in climate models. *Geoscientific Model Development, 6*(4), 1157–1171. doi:10.5194/gmd-6-1157-2013

Mallah, C., Cope, J., & Orwell, J. (2013). Plant leaf classification using probabilistic integration of shape, texture and margin features. Signal Processing. *Pattern Recognition and Applications, 5*, 1.

Odum, E. P., Odum, H. T., & Andrews, J. (1971). *Fundamentals of ecology* (Vol. 3). Philadelphia: Saunders.

Rahmani, M. E., Amine, A., & Hamou, R. M. (2017). New Approach based on Termite's Hill Building for Prediction of Successful Simulations in Climate Models. *International Journal of Swarm Intelligence Research, 8*(3), 30–60. doi:10.4018/IJSIR.2017070103

Rahmani, M. E., Amine, A., & Hamou, R. M. (2017). A Novel Bio Inspired Algorithm Based on Echolocation Mechanism of Bats for Seismic States Prediction. *International Journal of Swarm Intelligence Research, 8*(3), 1–18. doi:10.4018/IJSIR.2017070101

Rahmani, M. E., Amine, A., & Hamou, R. M. (in press). Sonar Data Classification Using a New Algorithm Inspired from Black Holes Phenomenon. *International Journal of Information Retrieval Research.*

Rahmani, M. E., Bouarara, H. A., Amine, A., Hamou, R. M., & Menad, H. (2016). New Supervised Approach for Plant Leaves Classification using Artificial Social Bees. *International Journal of Organizational and Collective Intelligence, 6*(1), 15–28. doi:10.4018/IJOCI.2016010102

Rudajev, V., & Čiž, R. (1999). Estimation of mining tremor occurrence by using neural networks. *Pure and Applied Geophysics, 154*(1), 57-72.

Sammut, C., & Webb, G. I. (Eds.). (2011). *Encyclopedia of machine learning.* Springer Science & Business Media.

Sikder, I. U., & Munakata, T. (2009). Application of rough set and decision tree for characterization of premonitory factors of low seismic activity. *Expert Systems with Applications, 36*(1), 102–110. doi:10.1016/j.eswa.2007.09.032

Smith, R. L., & Smith, T. M. (2012). *Elements of ecology.* Benjamin Cummings.

Tan, P. J., & Dowe, D. L. (2004, December). MML inference of oblique decision trees. In *Australasian Joint Conference on Artificial Intelligence* (pp. 1082-1088). Springer Berlin Heidelberg.

Wallace, C. S., & Dowe, D. L. (1999). Minimum message length and Kolmogorov complexity. *The Computer Journal, 42*(4), 270–283. doi:10.1093/comjnl/42.4.270

Chapter 14
Bio-Inspired Algorithms for Medical Data Analysis

Hanane Menad
Dr. Tahar Moulay University Saida, Algeria

Abdelmalek Amine
Dr. Tahar Moulay University of Saida, Algeria

ABSTRACT

Medical data mining has great potential for exploring the hidden patterns in the data sets of the medical domain. These patterns can be utilized for clinical diagnosis. Bio-inspired algorithms is a new field of research. Its main advantage is knitting together subfields related to the topics of connectionism, social behavior, and emergence. Briefly put, it is the use of computers to model living phenomena and simultaneously the study of life to improve the usage of computers. In this chapter, the authors present an application of four bio-inspired algorithms and meta heuristics for classification of seven different real medical data sets. Two of these algorithms are based on similarity calculation between training and test data while the other two are based on random generation of population to construct classification rules. The results showed a very good efficiency of bio-inspired algorithms for supervised classification of medical data.

INTRODUCTION

Modern medicine generates almost daily, huge amounts of heterogeneous data. For example, medical data may contain SPECT images, signals like ECG, clinical information like temperature, cholesterol levels, etc., as well as the physician's interpretation. Those who deal with such data understand that there is a widening gap between data collection and data comprehension. Computerized techniques are needed to help humans address this problem. This volume is devoted to the relatively young and growing field of medical data mining and knowledge discovery. As more and more medical procedures employ imaging as a preferred diagnostic tool, there is a need to develop methods for efficient mining in databases of images. Other significant features are security and confidentiality concerns. Moreover, the physician's

DOI: 10.4018/978-1-5225-3004-6.ch014

interpretation of images, signals, or other technical data, is written in unstructured English which is very difficult to mine.

Health care organizations are struggling to find new ways to cut healthcare utilization and costs while improving quality and outcomes. Predictive models that have been developed to predict global utilization for a healthcare organization cannot be used to predict the behavior of individuals. On the other hand, massive amounts of healthcare data are available in databases that can be used for exploring patterns and therefore knowledge discovery. Diversity and complexity of the healthcare data requires attention to the use of statistical methods. By nature, healthcare data are multivariate, making the analysis difficult as well as interesting.

Vast quantities of data are generated through the health care process. While technological advancements in the form of computer-based patient record software and personal computer hardware are making the collection of and access to health care data more manageable, few tools exist to evaluate and analyze this clinical data after it has been captured and stored. Evaluation of stored clinical data may lead to the discovery of trends and patterns hidden within the data that could significantly enhance our understanding of disease progression and management. Techniques are needed to search large quantities of clinical data for these patterns and relationships. Past efforts in this area have been limited primarily to epidemiological studies on administrative and claims databases. These data sources lack the richness of information that is available in databases comprised of actual clinical data.

In this study, we propose application of bio inspired algorithms in one of the major real life issues, medical data analysis. We have applied four bio-inspired algorithms on seven different medical datasets, the organization of the chapter was given as following: next section we give some related works to our study, then we presented the cases studied, where we give idea about the seven datasets used in experiments then we explain the four algorithms applied for classification of those datasets, and we defined measures used for evaluation, after that we discuss the obtained results. Finally, we give major conclusions.

Related Works to Medical Datasets

Predicting the outcome of a disease is one of the most interesting and challenging tasks where to develop data mining applications. In this section, we will present some related Work who used medical datasets:

Cancer Classification

Breast cancer is one of the leading cancers for women when compared to all other cancers. (Chaurasia, 2014) is a study that is made to investigate the performance of different classification techniques. This study analyses the breast Cancer data available from the Wisconsin dataset from UCI machine learning with the aim of developing accurate prediction models for breast cancer using data mining techniques.

The Disease Prediction plays an important role in data mining. Several techniques of data mining are used to predict different types of diseases. This research paper analyzes how data mining techniques are used for predicting different types of diseases it reviewed also the

research papers which mainly concentrated on predicting heart disease, Diabetes and Breast cancer . (Vijiyarani, 2013)

Lung Cancer is a disease of uncontrolled cell growth in tissues of the lung. Detection of Lung Cancer in its early stage is the key of its cure. In this paper we will use some techniques are essential to the task of medical image mining, Lung Field Segmentation, Data Processing, Feature Extraction, Classification using neural network and SVMs. The methods used in this paper work states to classify digital X-ray chest films into two categories: normal and abnormal. Different learning experiments were performed on two different data sets, created by means of feature selection and SVMs trained with different parameters; the results are compared and reported. (Kaur, 2013)

Diabetic Disease

Diabetes is a chronic, severe and progressive disease. It is characterized by a malfunction of the system of regulation of glucose in blood. Several systems of the classification system or automatic recognition of diabetes that exist in commercial biomedical systems are based on conventional techniques in the field of data mining or artificial intelligence and generally this system produce not explicit results without interpretation, on its new approach is developed an inference system based on fuzzy rules and optimized by an evolutionary learning by using the algorithm of the ant bee colony. (Nedjar, 2012)

Data mining is the process of selecting, exploring, and modeling large amounts of data to discover unknown patterns or relationships useful to the data analyst. This article describes applications of data mining for the analysis of blood glucose and diabetes mellitus data. The diabetes management context is particularly well suited to a data mining approach. This article describes and illustrates work that has been carried out in two areas in which data mining has a significant potential utility to researchers and clinical practitioners: analysis of blood glucose home monitoring data of diabetes mellitus patients and blood glucose monitoring data from hospitalized intensive care unit patients. (Bellazzi, 2009)

Heart Disease Prediction

Mrs. G. Subbalakshmi et. al. (Ansari, 2011) The main objective of this research is to develop a Decision Support in Heart Disease Prediction System using Naïve Bayes algorithm. The system extracts hidden useful information from the heart disease database. This model may possibly answer difficult queries, each one with its own potency with respect to ease of model analysis, access to complete information and accurateness.

Jyoti Soni et.al (Soni, 2011) proposed for predicting the heart diseases using the association rule data mining technique. In their work, unfortunately they have produced a large number of rules when association rules are applied to medical dataset. Most of the rules are medically irrelevant to the data.

Mai Shouman, Tim Turner, and Rob Stocker et. al. (Shouman, 2012) In this paper the author details work that applied KNN on a Cleveland Heart Disease dataset to investigate its efficiency in the prediction of heart disease. The author also investigated if the accuracy could be enhanced by integrating voting with KNN. The results show that applying KNN achieved an accuracy of 97.4% . The results also show that applying voting could not enhance the KNN accuracy in the diagnosis of heart disease. Ashish Kumar Sen, Shamsher Bahadur Patel, Dr. D. P. Shukla et. al. (Sen, 2013)

In this work, the authors have designed a system which could identify the chances of a coronary heart disease. they have divided all parameters into two levels according to criticality of the parameter and assigned each level a separate weight. Finally, both the levels are taken into consideration to arrive a final decision. The author has implemented neuro-fuzzy integrated approach at two levels. So, error rate is very low and work efficiency is high. The author concluded that this same approach could be used to perform the analysis on some other diseases also.

S.Vijiyarani et al. (Vijiyarani, 2013) the author analyze how data mining techniques are used for predicting different types of diseases it reviewed also the research papers which mainly concentrated on predicting heart disease, Diabetes and Breast cancer.

Works Using Yeast Data Set

This data is used to Predicting the Cellular Localization Sites of Proteins. In this paper they introduce a probabilistic model that generalizes classical linear discriminant analysis and gives an interpretation for the components as informative or relevant components of data. The components maximize the predictability of class distribution which is asymptotically equivalent to (i) maximizing mutual information with the classes, and (ii) finding principal components in the so-called learning or Fisher metrics. The Fisher metric measures only distances that are relevant to the classes, that is, distances that cause changes in the class distribution. (Kaski, 2003)

Processing applications with a large number of dimensions has been a challenge to the KDD community. Feature selection, an effective dimensionality reduction technique, is an essential pre-processing method to remove noisy features. In the literature there are only a few methods proposed for feature selection for clustering. And, almost all of those methods are `wrapper' techniques that require a clustering algorithm to evaluate the candidate feature subsets. In this paper they propose a `filter' method that is independent of any clustering algorithm. The proposed method is based on the observation that data with clusters has very different point-to-point distance histogram than that of data without clusters. Using this we propose an entropy measure that is low if data has distinct clusters and high otherwise. Extensive performance evaluation over synthetic, benchmark, and real datasets shows its effectiveness (Dash, 2002)

Driven by successes in several application areas, maximum entropy modeling has recently gained considerable popularity. in this work, they generalize the standard maximum entropy formulation of classification problems to better handle the case where complex data distributions arise from a mixture of simpler underlying (latent) distributions. they develop a theoretical framework for characterizing data as a mixture of maximum entropy models. They formulate a maximum-likelihood interpretation of the mixture model learning, and derive a generalized EM algorithm to solve the corresponding optimization problem. (Popescul, 2003).

Works Using Thoracic Surgery Data Set

The data is dedicated to classification problem related to the post-operative life expectancy in the lung cancer patients: class 1 - death within one year after surgery, class 2 - survival. In this paper, authors presented boosted SVM dedicated to solve imbalanced data problems. Proposed solution combines the benefits of using ensemble classifiers for uneven data together with cost-sensitive support vectors machines. Further, they presented oracle-based approach for extracting decision rules from the boosted SVM. In the next step, we examine the quality of the proposed method by comparing the performance with other algorithms which deal with imbalanced data. Finally, boosted SVM is used for medical application of predicting post-operative life expectancy in the lung cancer patients. (Zięba, 2014).

Works Using Statlog (Heart) Data Set

Current inductive machine learning algorithms typically use greedy search with limited lookahead. This prevents them to detect significant conditional dependencies between the attributes that describe training objects. Instead of myopic impurity functions and lookahead, In this paper they propose to use RELIEFF, an extension of RELIEF, for heuristic guidance of inductive learning algorithms. they have reimplemented Assistant, a system for top down induction of decision trees, using RELIEFF as an estimator of attributes at each selection step. The algorithm is tested on several artificial and several real-world problems and the results are compared with some other well-known machine learning algorithms. Excellent results on artificial data sets and two real world problems show the advantage of the presented approach to inductive learning. (Kononenko, 1997)

In this paper, they study the issue of error diversity in ensembles of neural networks. In ensembles of regression estimators, the measurement of diversity can be formalized as the Bias-Variance Covariance decomposition. In ensembles of classifiers, there is no neat theory in the literature to date. Our objective is to understand how to precisely define, measure, and create diverse errors for both cases. As a focal point we study one algorithm, Negative Correlation (NC) Learning which claimed, and showed empirical evidence, to enforce useful error diversity, creating neural network ensembles with very competitive performance on both classification and regression problems. (Brown, 2004)

Works Using Echocardiogram Data Set

Data for classifying if patients will survive for at least one year after a heart attack.

So far, boosting has been used to improve the quality of moderately accurate learning algorithms, by weighting and combining many of their weak hypotheses into a final classifier with theoretically high accuracy. It is the aim of the present paper to relax the class constraint, and extend our contribution to multiclass problems. Beyond data reduction, experimental results are also provided on twenty-three datasets, showing the benefits that our boosting-derived weighting rule brings to weighted nearest neighbor classifiers. (Sebban, 2002)

The growing access to large amounts of structured observations allows for more opportunistic uses of this data. An example of this, is the prediction of an event's class membership based on a database of observations. When these predictions are supported by a high-level representation, we refer to these as knowledge based on-line classification tasks. Two common types of algorithms from machine learning research that may be applied to on-line classification tasks make use of either lazy instance-based (k-NN, IB1) or eager model-based (C4.5,CN2) approaches. Neither approach, however, appears to provide a complete solution for these tasks. This thesis proposes a lazy model-based algorithm, named DBPredictor, that is suited to knowledge based on-line classification tasks. (Melli. 1989)

This paper analyzes experimentally discretization algorithms for handling continuous attributes in evolutionary learning. We consider a learning system that induces a set of rules in a fragment of first-order logic (Evolutionary Inductive Logic Programming), and introduce a method where a given discretization algorithm is used to generate initial inequalities, which describe subranges of attributes' values. Mutation operators exploiting information on the class label of the examples (supervised discretization) are used during the learning process for refining inequalities. The evolutionary learning system is used as a platform for testing experimentally four algorithms: two variants of the proposed method, a popular supervised discretization algorithm applied prior to induction, and a discretization method which does not use information on the class labels of the examples (unsupervised discretization). (Divina, 2005).

CASES STUDIED

Datasets

This section presents the used datasets in our studies, we have used seven different medical data downloaded from UCI Archive datasets

Diabetic Retinopathy Debrecen

This dataset contains features extracted from the Messidor image set to predict whether an image contains signs of diabetic retinopathy or not. All features represent either a detected lesion, a descriptive feature of a anatomical part or an image-level descriptor. The underlying method image analysis and feature extraction as well as classification technique is described in (Antal, 2014). Attributes of the data are:

1. The binary result of quality assessment. 0 = bad quality 1 = sufficient quality.
2. The binary result of pre-screening, where 1 indicates severe retinal abnormality and 0 its lack.
3. (2-7) The results of MA detection. Each feature value stand for the number of MAs found at the confidence levels alpha = 0.5, . . ., 1, respectively.
4. (8-15) contain the same information as 2-7) for exudates. However, as exudates are represented by a set of points rather than the number of pixels constructing the lesions, these features are normalized by dividing the number of lesions with the diameter of the ROI to compensate different image sizes.
5. (16) The euclidean distance of the center of the macula and the center of the optic disc to provide important information regarding the patient's condition. This feature is also normalized with the diameter of the ROI.
6. (17) The diameter of the optic disc.
7. (18) The binary result of the AM/FM-based classification.
8. (19) Class label. 1 = contains signs of DR (Accumulative label for the Messidor classes 1, 2, 3), 0 = no signs of DR.

Echocardiogram

These data were collected from real data of patients and used by (Salzberg, 1988). All the patients suffered heart attacks at some point in the past. Some are still alive and some are not. The survival and still-alive variables, when taken together, indicate whether a patient survived for at least one year following the heart attack.

The problem addressed by past researchers was to predict from the other variables whether or not the patient will survive at least one year. The most difficult part of this problem is correctly predicting that the patient will NOT survive.

survival -- the number of months' patient survived (has survived, if patient is still alive). Because all the patients had their heart attacks at different times, it is possible that some patients have survived less than one year but they are still alive. Check the second variable to confirm this. Such patients cannot be used for the prediction task mentioned above. The attributes are:

1. **Still-Alive:** A binary variable. 0=dead at end of survival period, 1 means still alive
2. **Age-at-Heart-Attack:** Age in years when heart attack occurred
3. **Pericardial-Effusion:** Binary. Pericardial effusion is fluid around the heart. 0=no fluid, 1=fluid
4. **Fractional-Shortening:** A measure of contracility around the heart lower numbers are increasingly abnormal
5. **Epss:** E-point septal separation, another measure of contractility. Larger numbers are increasingly abnormal.
6. **Lvdd:** Left ventricular end-diastolic dimension. This is a measure of the size of the heart at end-diastole. Large hearts tend to be sick hearts.
7. **Wall-Motion-Score:** A measure of how the segments of the left ventricle are moving
8. **Wall-Motion-Index:** Equals wall-motion-score divided by number of segments seen. Usually 12-segments are seen in an echocardiogram. Use this variable INSTEAD of the wall motion score.
9. **Mult:** A derivate var which can be ignored
10. **Name:** The name of the patient (I have replaced them with "name")
11. **Group:** Meaningless, ignore it
12. **Alive-at-1:** Boolean-valued. Derived from the first two attributes. 0 means patient was either dead after 1 year or had been followed for less than 1 year. 1 means patient was alive at 1 year.

Yeast Data Set

This data presents a set of information about Yeast protein given by (Horton, 1996), where creators of the data used the following attributes to describe it:

1. **Sequence Name:** Accession number for the SWISS-PROT database
2. **mcg:** McGeoch's method for signal sequence recognition.
3. **gvh:** von Heijne's method for signal sequence recognition.
4. **alm:** Score of the ALOM membrane spanning region prediction program.
5. **mit:** Score of discriminant analysis of the amino acid content of the N-terminal region (residues long) of mitochondrial and non-mitochondrial proteins.
6. **erl:** Presence of "HDEL" substring (thought to act as a signal for retention in the endoplasmic reticulum lumen). Binary attribute.
7. **Pox:** Peroxisomal targeting signal in the C-terminus.
8. **Vac:** Score of discriminant analysis of the amino acid content of vacuolar and extracellular proteins.
9. **Nuc:** Score of discriminant analysis of nuclear localization signals of nuclear and non-nuclear proteins.

Thoracic Surgery

The data was collected retrospectively at Wroclaw Thoracic Surgery Centre for patients who underwent major lung resections for primary lung cancer in the years 2007 and 2011. The Centre is associated with the Department of Thoracic Surgery of the Medical University of Wroclaw and Lower-Silesian Centre for Pulmonary Diseases, Poland, while the research database constitutes a part of the National Lung Cancer Registry, administered by the Institute of Tuberculosis and Pulmonary Diseases in Warsaw, Poland. Each vector of the data was presented by the following attributes (Zięba, 2014):

1. **DGN:** Diagnosis - specific combination of ICD-10 codes for primary and secondary as well multiple tumours if any (DGN3, DGN2, DGN4, DGN6, DGN5, DGN8, DGN1)
2. **PRE4:** Forced vital capacity - FVC (numeric)
3. **PRE5:** Volume that has been exhaled at the end of the first second of forced expiration - FEV1 (numeric)
4. **PRE6:** Performance status - Zubrod scale (PRZ2,PRZ1,PRZ0)
5. **PRE7:** Pain before surgery (T,F)
6. **PRE8:** Haemoptysis before surgery (T,F)
7. **PRE9:** Dyspnoea before surgery (T,F)
8. **PRE10:** Cough before surgery (T,F)
9. **PRE11:** Weakness before surgery (T,F)
10. **PRE14:** T in clinical TNM - size of the original tumour, from OC11 (smallest) to OC14 (largest) (OC11,OC14,OC12,OC13)
11. **PRE17:** Type 2 DM - diabetes mellitus (T,F)
12. **PRE19:** MI up to 6 months (T,F)
13. **PRE25:** PAD - peripheral arterial diseases (T,F)
14. **PRE30:** Smoking (T,F)
15. **PRE32:** Asthma (T,F)
16. **AGE:** Age at surgery (numeric)
17. **Risk1Y:** 1 year survival period - (T)rue value if died (T,F)

Statlog (Heart)

This data presents information about patients from a real hospital, attributes of the data are:

1. Age
2. Sex
3. Chest pain type (4 values)
4. Resting blood pressure
5. Serum cholestoral in mg/dl
6. Fasting blood sugar > 120 mg/dl
7. Resting electrocardiographic results (values 0,1,2)
8. Maximum heart rate achieved

9.   Exercise induced angina

10. Oldpeak = st depression induced by exercise relative to rest

11. The slope of the peak exercise st segment

12. Number of major vessels (0-3) colored by flourosopy

13. Thal: 3 = normal; 6 = fixed defect; 7 = reversable defect

Cardiotocogram

The dataset was presented in (Ayres, 2000), in which 2126 fetal cardiotocograms (CTGs) were automatically processed and the respective diagnostic features measured. The CTGs were also classified by three expert obstetricians and a consensus classification label assigned to each of them. Classification was both with respect to a morphologic pattern (A, B, C. ...) and to a fetal state (N, S, P). Therefore, the dataset can be used either for 10-class or 3-class experiments. In our case, we used the dataset to predict 3 classes that present the fetal state (N=normal; S=suspect; P=pathologic), but we used it in different experiments, first by integrating the class code (1 to 10) for classes A to SUSP as an attribute in representation of examples, and in another experiment, we deleted the attribute to see the impact of this attribute in cardiograms prediction. The following attributes are the standard attributes of the Cardiotocogram data recorded using Electronic Fetal Monitor (EFM):

1.   **LB:** FHR baseline (beats per minute)

2.   **AC:** Number of accelerations per second

3.   **FM:** Number of fetal movements per second

4.   **UC:** Number of uterine contractions per second

5.   **DL:** Number of light decelerations per second

6.   **DS:** Number of severe decelerations per second

7.   **DP:** Number of prolonged decelerations per second

8.   **ASTV:** Percentage of time with abnormal short term variability

9.   **MSTV:** Mean value of short term variability

10. **ALTV:** Percentage of time with abnormal long term variability

11. **MLTV:** Mean value of long term variability

12. **Width:** Width of FHR histogram

13. **Min:** Minimum of FHR histogram

14. **Max:** Maximum of FHR histogram

15. **Nmax:** Number of histogram peaks

16. **Nzeros:** Number of histogram zeros

17. **Mode:** Histogram mode

18. **Mean:** Histogram mean

19. **Median:** Histogram median

20. **Variance:** Histogram variance

21. **Tendency:** Histogram tendency

22. **CLASS:** FHR pattern class code (1 to 10)

23. **NSP:** Fetal state class code (N=normal; S=suspect; P=pathologic)

Breast Cancer

(Street, 1993) is the first paper where they use these images, where authors used Snake-generated nuclei boundaries to get ten features from images:

1. Radius of individual nucleus measured by averaging the length of the radial line segments defined by centroid of the snake and the individual snake points.
2. The total distance between the snake points constitutes the nuclear perimeter.
3. Nuclear area is measured simply by counting the number of pixels on the interior of the snake and adding one-half of the pixels in the perimeter.
4. Perimeter and area are combined to give a measure of the compactness of the cell nuclei: $perimeter^2/area$.
5. The smoothness of a nuclear contour is quantified by measuring the difference between the length of radial line and the mean length of the lines surrounding it.
6. In a further attempt to capture shape information, they measured the number and severity of concavities or indentations in a cell nucleus.
7. This feature is similar to Concavity but measures only the number, rather than the magnitude, of contour concavities.
8. They measured the length difference between lines perpendicular to the major axis to the cell boundary in both directions.
9. The fractal dimension of a cell was approximated using the "Coastline approximation" described by (Mandelbrot, 1977).
10. The texture of the cell nucleus was measured by finding the variance of the grey scale intensities in the component pixels.

Combining these ten features gave as results the "Wisconsin Diagnostic Breast Cancer" represented by 30 element vector containing 30 values. These last present ten real-valued features are computed for each cell nucleus: radius, texture, perimeter, area, smoothness, compactness, concavity, concave points, symmetry, and fractal dimension. The mean, standard error, and "worst" or largest (mean of the three largest values) of these features were computed for each image, resulting in 30 features. For instance, field 3 is Mean Radius, field 13 is Radius SE, and field 23 is Worst Radius. This dataset contains 569 samples, of which there Are two class distributions: 357 benign, 212 malignant.

Algorithms Used in Studies

Bat Echolocation Algorithm (BEA)

Bats are a special fascinating kind of mammals with their wings and their lifestyle, as we know bats are active only at night and in the dark places. It is estimated that there are about 996 species of bats, more than half of them rely on sounds for navigation while they fly. The use of this trick is to detect obstacles and forage for food. This mechanism is called Echolocation or SONAR (SOund Navigation And Ranging). It gives a bat the ability to generate signals that bounce off surrounding objects and using a processing of the returning echoes with extraordinary acuity, the bat can determine the direction, the distance and the features of these objects. Figure 1 shows an example of a bat hunting an insect.

Figure 1. Bats echolocation

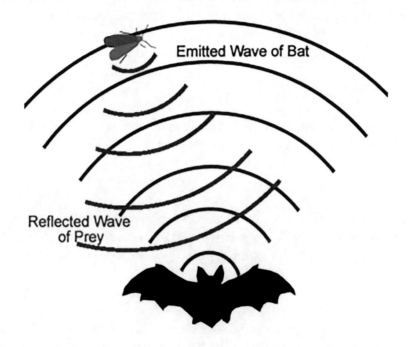

The echolocation mechanisms are different and correlated with the hunting strategies of each species; the most of bats use short, frequency-modulated signals to sweep through about an octave. In this strategy, a pulse only lasts a few thousandths of a second (up to about 8 to 10 ms) in the frequency range of 25kHz to 150 kHz, the typical range of frequencies for most bat species are in the region between 25kHz and 100kHz, though some species can emit higher frequencies up to 150 kHz. During hunting, the rate of pulse emission can be sped up to about 200 pulses per second when homing on their prey. Studies show the integration time of the bat ear is typically about 300 to 400 μs, which give to the bats a fantastic ability to process the signal. Taking in mind that the speed of sound in air is typically $v = 340$ m/s, the wavelength λ of the ultrasonic sound bursts with a constant frequency f is given by $\lambda = v/f$.

Such echolocation behavior of bats can be formulated mathematically in such a way that it can be associated with many problems solving objective, for that and based on the original work in (Yang, 2010), we are interested in some features of the echolocation of bats to formulate a mathematical implementation for seismic assessment.

We were interested in the three rules of bat algorithm given in (Yang, 2010) to create a new model for classification of seismic data.

The proposed approach by (Rahmani, 2016) is constructed in 6 steps in which 5 of them represents one iteration. Before beginning the treatment, we have to initialize two parameters, initial loudness A0 that decrease in each iteration, and learning parameter that is used to adjust the frequency of emitted pulses. In our approach, we considered that one bat is represented by one vector from test set, which will look for Neighbors to enjoy their class, in other words, this is a distance based approach similar to K-Nearest Neighbors algorithm with additional parameters.

To classify a bat, we first calculated the mean of each vector elements in training set as frequency of a bat (fbat) to catch that prey (vector of the training set). After that, the bat calculates the frequency of emitted pulses (fep), which initially presents the average of the bat elements. Using the two frequencies, we calculated the frequency f based on Doppler Effect of sounds, f is calculated as follow:

$$f = |fbat - fep| \tag{1}$$

After getting the frequency, we calculated a velocity as distance between the bat and the prey, in the implementation we tested the Euclidean distance as follow:

$$D(X, Y) = \sum \sqrt{((y\_i - x\_i)^2)} \tag{2}$$

The final step before prediction of seismic hazards, we calculated a similarity between bats and preys using the velocity and the frequency. The similarity is simply the wavelength λ that each bat in real life uses it during hunting to echolocate preys, from that we conclude the formula of classification as follow:

$$\lambda = v/f \tag{3}$$

Prediction of seismic hazards presents the step of classification, in which, from all wavelengths resulted, we selected only A0 wavelengths, where A0 is an integer defined in the beginning, in other words, we selected the A0 most similar vectors from training set to classify the test vector and to use them in the next iteration. A0 presents the initial loudness. Finally, we took the maximum class appears in all selected vectors, and we associated the bat (test vector) to that class. The whole process mentioned represents one iteration. The stop criterion we tested is the loudness. According to (Yang, 2010), the loudness varies from a large (positive) A0 to a minimum constant value Amin, so we chose the loudness to stop the algorithm. By passing from iteration to iteration, the algorithm chooses the incorrectly classified vectors from test set and adjusts their frequencies by multiply it by the learning parameter, and decreases the loudness. The training set of an iteration i+1 will be the chosen vectors from the iteration i. We chose the initial loudness based on simple heuristic, because we deal here with a Bi-class problem, we gave the initial loudness an impair number, and it decreases by two in each iteration, that is to assure that we have always a majority neighbors that present a class than those who present the other class.

In the end of each iteration, we evaluated the classification of seismic hazards and we saved the parameters. In the end of the algorithm, we took the best parameters as a model for seismic prediction, the model is defined by: vectors of the training set, their frequencies and loudness. Algorithm 1 gives a brief description of the bat echolocation algorithm for seismic hazards prediction.

Social Bees Algorithm (SBA)

Honey bees are social insects. "Social bees" is a phrase used to express that they live together in large, well-organized family groups. A honey bee colony typically consists of three kinds of adult bees: workers, drones, and a queen. Several thousand worker bees cooperate in nest building, food collection, and brood rearing. Each member has a definite task to perform, related to its adult age. But surviving and reproducing take the combined efforts of the entire colony. Individual bees (workers, drones, and queens) cannot survive without the support of the colony. In this work, we were more interested on worker bees.

Algorithm 1. Bat echolocation algorithm for seismic hazards prediction

```
Input:    Training_Set, Test_Set
              Distance_V
              A, learning_parameter, x: constant
Frequencies_Trainig = Calculate_Frequecies(Training_Set)
Frequencies_Test = Calculate_Frequecies (Test_Set)
While (A > 0):
For each vector Dx in Test_Set do
          For each vector Dy in Training_Set do
                        F = |Frequencies_Trainig(Dy) - Frequencies_Test(Dx)|
                        G = Calculate Distance_V (Dx, Dy)
                        Velocity_V = G/F
          end for
          Min_v = Minimum_Velocities
          Classify Dx according to Min_v
end for
          A = A - x
          Save_parameters_as_model
end while
END
```

Worker bees, with its remarkable creatures, have a considerable amount of jobs and duties to perform in their short lives that vary as they age, in other words, they perform a brilliant team work. Initially, a worker's responsibilities include various tasks within the hive. At this stage of development, worker bees are referred to as house bees. As they get older, their duties involve work outside of the hive as field bees. We were more interested to implement our approach on three jobs as follow:

1. **Worker Bee Housekeeping (Days 1 to 3):** One of her first tasks is cleaning out the cell from which she just emerged. This and other empty cells are cleaned and polished and left immaculate to receive new eggs and to store nectar and pollen.
2. **Worker Bee Undertakers (Days 3 to 16):** During the first couple weeks of her life, the worker bee removes any bees that have died and disposes of the corpses as far from the hive as possible. Similarly, diseased or dead brood are quickly removed before becoming a health threat to the colony.
3. **Collecting Nectar for the Hive (Days 12 to 18):** Young worker bees also take nectar from foraging field bees that are returning to the hive. The house bees deposit this nectar into cells earmarked for this purpose. The workers similarly take pollen from returning field bees and pack the pollen into cells. Both the ripened honey and the pollen are food for the colony.

This section details the implementation of previous detailed task proposed by (Bouarara, 2015) for text clustering task, then adapted by (Rahmani, 2016b) for a supervised classification of plants, where here, worker bees present vectors of the training set (50% of dataset) that perform three tasks in sort of distance calculation between these vectors and other vectors from test set, used distances described in Table 1.

263

Table 1. Used distances in experiment

Distance	Formula (x and y Are Two Vectors)
Manhattan (Man)	$D(x,y) = \sum \lvert xi\text{-}yi \rvert$
Euclidean (Euc)	$D(x,y) = \sum \sqrt{\left(xi - yi \right)^2}$
Chebyshev (Cheb)	$D(x, y) = Max\ (\lvert xi\text{-}yi \rvert)$

In our test experiment, we calculated three different distances between vectors in training set (worker bees) and test set, where each one present a task of bee, then we calculated average distance, vectors in test set got a new class from training set depending on minimum average.

Algorithm 2 shows a detailed artificial bees algorithm

Choosing three distances to calculate their average was done during the implementation, since we based on social life of bees in the hive, we have chosen three distances that present tasks in sort of filtering where bees choose between objects, which one stays and which one dropped, in the artificial model, a hive is a class, and training set is the set of bees that work in the hive, while test set examples are the objects to keep in the hive (which means belong to the class) or dropped from the hive (which means do not belong to this class), or otherwise saying, the decision if an object belongs to a class and not the other class was taken by classifying these examples according to the minimum average of distances got. Another reason why we had chosen a combination of distances, is because by doing that we were trying to benefit from advantages of the three distances because mathematically, these distances complement each other.

Evolutionary Algorithm (EA)

EAs belong to the family of nature-inspired optimization algorithms. In general, an EA can be schematized as a population-based search which is characterized by an initial creation of a set of candidate solutions

Algorithm 2. ABC algorithm

```
Inputs: X: training set
        Y: test set
For each y in Y do
        For each x in X do
                D1 = distance_1(x, y)
                D2 = distance_2(x, y)
                D3 = distance_3(x, y)
                D_average (x, y) =  (D1 + D2 + D3) / 3
        end
min (y) = minimum (D_average (x, y))
Classify y according to the min(y)
end
```

and a generation cycle, as depicted in Figure 2. A population of candidate solutions is presumed to evolve over the generation cycles utilizing some forms of natural processes such as selection and reproduction in order to refine the solutions iteratively First, a set of randomly configured candidate solutions are created. The cycle itself then starts with the evaluation of the objective values of these solutions. Based on the results, a relative fitness is assigned to each candidate solution in the population. This fitness value is the criterion on which selection algorithms operate to pick the most promising individuals for further investigation while discarding the less successful ones. The candidate solutions that managed to enter the so-called mating pool are then reproduced, i.e., combined via crossover and/or slightly changed by mutation operations. When this is done, the cycle starts again in the next generation.

Wang (2011) proposed an evolutionary algorithm for supervised classification, where they combined their proposed EA with a set of supervised classifier for test the approach. In our studies, we implemented the proposed approach with rules classification, authors used a genetic algorithm to work on a population of classifiers encoded as bit strings, each of which being a list of rules (i.e., individual classifiers which together form the classifier system). This simple rule design is chosen so that we can test the ability of the evolutionary approach to build good solutions (classifiers) of arbitrary structures. At the same time, the design allows us to encode the rules in an EA. For classification, a rule contains a classification part encoding a class $k \in K$ and a condition for each feature in the input data. Unlike conventional LCSs, the conditions of our rule-based EA are no simple ternary patterns (like 0, 1, and * for don't care) to be matched against data samples but encode a more complex relation.

Local Search Algorithm (LSA)

The local search algorithm used in our studies is the one given by (Ishibuchi, 2004), where authors first candidate fuzzy if-then rules are generated from numerical data and prescreened using two rule evaluation measures (i.e., confidence and support) in data mining. Then a small number of fuzzy if-then rules are selected from the prescreened candidate rules using multi-objective evolutionary algorithms. In rule selection, authors use three objectives: maximization of the classification accuracy, minimization of the number of selected rules, and minimization of the total rule length. Thus, the task of multi-objective evolutionary algorithms is to find a number of non-dominated rule sets with respect to these three objectives.

Figure 2. Evolutionary algorithm

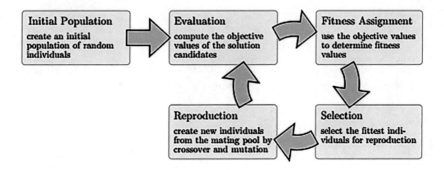

Measures Used to Evaluate the Classification

To evaluate our approach, we calculate some common metrics using vectors of test set (pebbles). Before detailing these metrics, we have to introduce some measures used to calculate it as follow:

1. **True Positive (TP):** Presents the average of the success simulation vectors that are correctly predicted as success simulations.
2. **True Negative (TN):** Presents the average of the failed simulation vectors that are correctly predicted as failed simulations.
3. **False Positive (FP):** Presents the average of the vectors that are predicted as success simulations but they are not.
4. **False Negative (FN):** Presents the average of the vectors that are predicted as failed simulations, but they are success simulations.

Using these four measures, we calculated the most famous measures that are used to evaluate classification algorithms:

1. For classification, the accuracy estimates is the overall number of vectors correctly classified, divided by the total number of vectors in the initial data. (Han, 2011)

$$\text{Accuracy} = \frac{TP + TN}{TP + TN + FP + FN} \qquad (4)$$

2. Precision and recall are the measures used in the information retrieval domain to measure how well an information retrieval system retrieves the relevant vectors requested by a user (in our case is success simulations). The measures are defined as follows (Sammut, 2011)

$$\text{Precision} = \frac{TP}{TP + FP} \qquad (5)$$

$$\text{Recall} = \frac{TP}{TP + FN} \qquad (6)$$

3. Instead of two measures, they are often combined to provide a single measure of retrieval performance called the F-measure as follows (Sammut, 2011)

$$\text{Fmeasure} = \frac{2*precision*recall}{precision + recall} \qquad (7)$$

4. Entropy is a measure often used in data mining algorithms that measures the disorder of a set of data.

Entropy = -precision * log2(precision)   (8)

Obtained Results

In this section, we discuss the obtained results by each algorithm applied for classification of the seven datasets presented in the previous section. The section is divided into four sub sections, each discusses the obtained results by an algorithm:

Bat Echolocation Algorithm

Table 2 shows the obtained results using bat echolocation algorithm:

Accuracy presents the percentage of correctly classified examples in the dataset. As seen in Table 2, bat echolocation algorithm gave a good accuracy, from 81.6% for classification of Thoracic surgery vectors up to 91.8% for classification of Breast cancer image vectors. This is due to the principle of bat echolocation algorithm, it calculates a similarity based on a distance and vectors frequency.

Precision is a measure used to evaluate the average of correctly classified vectors among all newly classified vectors, if it converges to one we can say that our system responds very well. In our cases, precision varied from 0.82 for classification of Thoracic surgery up to 0.92 for classification of Breast cancer, this means that 82% of the classified Thoracic surgery vectors were correctly classified while for Diabetic Retinopathy Debrecen, Echocardiogram, Statlog data, or Cardiotocogram data, the amount of correctly classified vectors was more than 85%, and for breast cancer vectors, 92% of vectors classified by bat echolocation algorithm were correctly classified.

As precision, recall presents the amount of correctly classified vectors, but this time, it calculates the correctly classified vectors from the original classification given by experts. Table 2 shows the recall obtained using bat echolocation algorithm, Yeast data got the bad recall (about 80%), while bat echolocation algorithm could predict more than 85% of the other dataset.

Fmeasure is the harmonic average of precision and recall, it is used to evaluate in the same time the newly predicted classes and the amount of correctly classified vectors from the original data set. As seen in Table 2, the fmeasure values were varied between 0.82 up to 0.91, which means that bat echolocation algorithm proved its efficiency for medical data classification.

Figure 3 shows the comparison of precision, recall and fmeasure obtained by classification of the seven data sets using bat echolocation algorithm.

Table 2. Obtained results by bat echolocation algorithm

Data Set	Accuracy %	Precision	Recall	Fmeasure
Diabetic Retinopathy Debrecen	87.6	0.86	0.89	0.87
Echocardiogram	89.6	0.89	0.92	0.90
Yeast	83.4	0.84	0.80	0.82
Thoracic Surgery	81.6	0.82	0.86	0.84
Statlog (Heart)	83.7	0.85	0.83	0.84
Cardiotocogram	89.4	0.89	0.93	0.91
Breast Cancer	91.8	0.92	0.90	0.91

Figure 3. Obtained results by bat echolocation algorithm

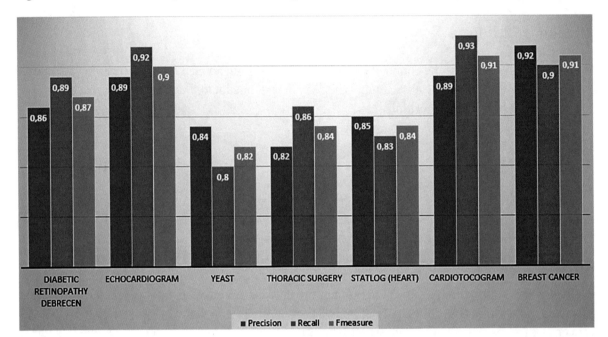

Social Bees' Algorithm

Table 3 shows the obtained results using social bees' algorithm:

Accuracy presents the percentage of correctly classified examples in the dataset. As seen in Table 3, Social bees' algorithm gave a good accuracy, from 77.9% for classification of Thoracic surgery vectors up to 91.2% for classification of Breast cancer image vectors. social bees' algorithm gave an accuracy lower than bat echolocation, this is because it is based on combination of three distances, where the Chebyshev distance affected the final similarity which affected the obtained results.

Precision is a measure used to evaluate the average of correctly classified vectors among all newly classified vectors, if it converges to one we can say that our system responds very well. In our cases, precision varied from 0.78 for classification of Thoracic surgery up to 0.91 for classification of Breast

Table 3. Obtained results by social bees algorithm

Data Set	Accuracy %	Precision	Recall	Fmeasure
Diabetic Retinopathy Debrecen	86.1	0.86	0.84	0.85
Echocardiogram	83.9	0.84	0.89	0.86
Yeast	84.6	0.85	0.79	0.82
Thoracic Surgery	77.9	0.78	0.80	0.79
Statlog (Heart)	86.4	0.86	0.87	0.86
Cardiotocogram	80.23	0.85	0.85	0.85
Breast Cancer	91.2	0.91	0.95	0.93

cancer, this means that 82% of the classified Thoracic surgery vectors were correctly classified while for Diabetic Retinopathy Debrecen, Statlog data, or Cardiotocogram data, the amount of correctly classified vectors was more than 85%, and for breast cancer vectors.

As precision, recall presents the amount of correctly classified vectors, but this time, it calculates the correctly classified vectors from the original classification given by experts. Table 3 shows the recall obtained using social bees' algorithm, Yeast data got the bad recall (about 80%), while bat echolocation algorithm could predict more than 85% of the other dataset.

Fmeasure is the harmonic average of precision and recall, it is used to evaluate in the same time the newly predicted classes and the amount of correctly classified vectors from the original data set. As seen in Table 3, the fmeasure values were varied between 0.79 up to 0.93, which means that social bees' algorithm proved its efficiency for medical data classification.

Figure 4 shows the comparison of precision, recall and fmeasure obtained by classification of the seven data sets using social bees' algorithm.

Evolutionary Algorithm

Table 4 shows the obtained results using evolutionary algorithm.

Evolutionary algorithm implemented in this study was used to generate classification rules. As seen in Table 3, evolutionary algorithm gave accuracy less than bat algorithm or social bees' algorithm, from 70% for classification of statlog vectors up to 85.2% for classification of Breast cancer image vectors. social bees' algorithm gave an accuracy lower than bat echolocation, this is because evolutionary algorithm used here generates rules for classification rather than calculation of similarity.

Figure 4. Obtained results by social bees' algorithm

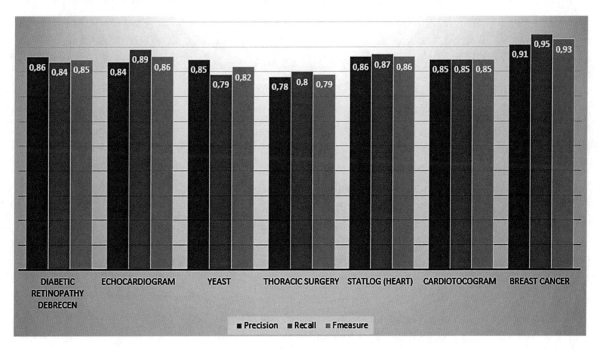

Table 4. Obtained results by evolutionary algorithm

Data Set	Accuracy	Precision	Recall	Fmeasure
Diabetic Retinopathy Debrecen	85.2	0.85	0.88	0.87
Echocardiogram	86.1	0.86	0.87	0.86
Yeast	79.8	0.79	0.80	0.79
Thoracic Surgery	73.5	0.74	0.78	0.76
Statlog (Heart)	70	0.71	0.67	0.69
Cardiotocogram	73.1	0.72	0.76	0.74
Breast Cancer	81.6	0.82	0.79	0.80

Precision is a measure used to evaluate the average of correctly classified vectors among all newly classified vectors, if it converges to one we can say that our system responds very well. In our cases, precision varied from 0.71 for classification of statlog up to 0.86 for classification of echocardiogram, this means that 71% of the classified echocardiogram vectors were correctly classified while for Diabetic Retinopathy Debrecen, Statlog data, or Cardiotocogram data, the amount of correctly classified vectors was between 72 to 86%.

As precision, recall presents the amount of correctly classified vectors, but this time, it calculates the correctly classified vectors from the original classification given by experts. Table 4 shows the recall obtained using evolutionary algorithm, statlog data got the bad recall (about 67%), while evolutionary algorithm could predict more than 75% of the other datasets.

Fmeasure is the harmonic average of precision and recall, it is used to evaluate in the same time the newly predicted classes and the amount of correctly classified vectors from the original data set. As seen in Table 3, the fmeasure values were varied between 0.69 up to 0.87.

Figure 5 shows the comparison of precision, recall and fmeasure obtained by classification of the seven data sets using evolutionary algorithm.

Local Search Algorithm

Table 5 shows the obtained results using local search algorithm.

Local search algorithm implemented in this study was used to generate classification rules. As seen in Table 5, local search algorithm gave accuracy less than bat algorithm or social bees' algorithm but better than evolutionary algorithm, it gave an accuracy between 79.4% for classification of statlog vectors up to 90.1% for classification of Echocardiogram vectors, this is because local search algorithm implemented is like evolutionary algorithm, it generates rules for classification rather than calculation of similarity.

In our cases, precision varied from 0.78 for classification of either statlog or cardiotocogram up to 0.87 for classification of echocardiogram, this means that 78% of the classified statlog and cardiotocogram vectors were correctly classified while for Diabetic Retinopathy Debrecen, echocardiogram, yeast, thoracic, or breast cancer, the amount of correctly classified vectors was between 83 to 87%.

As precision, recall presents the amount of correctly classified vectors, but this time, it calculates the correctly classified vectors from the original classification given by experts. Table 5 shows the recall obtained using local search algorithm, cardiotocogram data got the bad recall (about 80%), while local search algorithm could predict more than 81% of the other datasets.

Figure 5. Obtained results by evolutionary algorithm

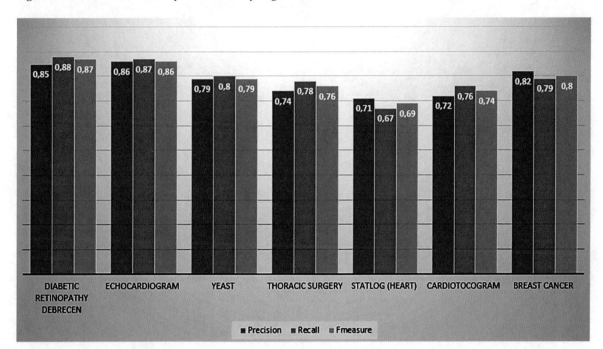

Table 5. Obtained results by local search algorithm

Data Set	Accuracy	Precision	Recall	Fmeasure
Diabetic Retinopathy Debrecen	89.3	0.84	0.89	0.86
Echocardiogram	90.1	0.87	0.91	0.89
Yeast	87.6	0.83	0.87	0.85
Thoracic Surgery	82.3	0.83	0.82	0.82
Statlog (Heart)	79.4	0.78	0.81	0.80
Cardiotocogram	80.1	0.78	0.80	0.79
Breast Cancer	86.5	0.85	0.89	0.87

Fmeasure is the harmonic average of precision and recall, it is used to evaluate in the same time the newly predicted classes and the amount of correctly classified vectors from the original data set. As seen in table 5, the fmeasure values were varied between 0.79 up to 0.87, which means that local search algorithm proved its efficiency for medical data classification.

Figure 6 shows the comparison of precision, recall and fmeasure obtained by classification of the seven data sets using local search algorithm.

Comparison Study

In this section, we compared the different obtained results of application of the four algorithms mentioned above on classification of the seven data sets in terms of fmeasure, we chose fmeasure because

Figure 6. Obtained results by local search algorithm

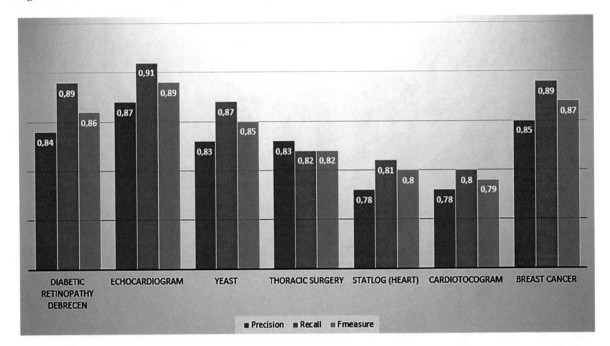

it combines precision and recall, which allowed us to evaluate the newly predicted classes and the old classes. Figure 7 shows the comparison of the algorithms.

As seen in Figure 7, for all cases, bat algorithm and social bees' algorithm gave results better than either evolutionary algorithm or local search algorithm, because bat algorithm classifies vectors based on calculation of distance and a frequency by calculating the difference between their average, while social bees' algorithm classifies vectors based on combination of three distances, so these two algorithms classify vectors based on exact calculation of similarity. Evolutionary algorithm and local search algo-

Figure 7. comparison between the four algorithms applied on each dataset

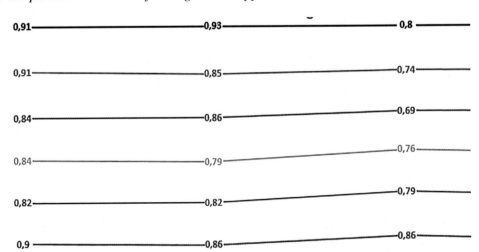

rithm were used to construct rules for classification, the problem of these two algorithms is that they are based on random calculation or generation of population, which cannot assure that results have gotten are good, and rules constructed are good as model used for classification of medical data. However, all algorithms proved their efficiency in classification of real medical data.

CONCLUSION

Medical data mining has high potential for exploring the hidden patterns in the data sets of the medical domain. These patterns can be utilized for clinical diagnosis for widely distributed in raw medical data which is heterogeneous in nature and voluminous. This collected data can be integrated to form information system for a hospital.

The objective of this work is study of application of bio inspired algorithms in one of the major real life issues, medical data analysis. We have applied four bio inspired algorithms on seven different medical datasets, obtained results showed a high efficiency for supervised classification, two of the algorithms were based on similarity calculation while the other two were based on random generation of rules for classification, randomness of evolutionary algorithm or local search algorithm affected the results in manner we have gotten good results but not better than algorithms based on similarity calculation, because those last used mathematic exact calculation in order to classify medical data.

For future work, we planned to implement more bio inspired algorithms for medical data analysis, because this study belongs to a series of studies in order to develop an intelligent system for medical data analysis that will help doctors in future.

REFERENCES

Chaurasia, V., & Pal, S. (2014). A novel approach for breast cancer detection using data mining techniques. *International Journal of Innovative Research in Computer and Communication Engineering*, *2*(1), 2456–2465.

Vijiyarani, S., & Sudha, S. (2013). Disease prediction in data mining technique–a survey. *International Journal of Computer Applications & Information Technology*, *2*, 17–21.

Kaur, A. R. (2013). A study of detection of lung cancer using data mining classification techniques. *International Journal (Toronto, Ont.)*, *3*(3).

Nedjar. (2012). *Design a classifier Blur Using Bee Colony On For Medical Diagnostics* (Master thesis). University Aboubeker Belkaid.

Ansari, A. Q., & Gupta, N. K. (2011, December). Automated diagnosis of coronary heart disease using neuro-fuzzy integrated system. In *Information and Communication Technologies (WICT), 2011 World Congress on* (pp. 1379-1384). IEEE. doi:10.1109/WICT.2011.6141450

Antal, B., & Hajdu, A. (2014). An ensemble-based system for automatic screening of diabetic retinopathy. *Knowledge-Based Systems*, *60*, 20–27. doi:10.1016/j.knosys.2013.12.023

Bellazzi, R., & Abu-Hanna, A. (2009). Data mining technologies for blood glucose and diabetes management. *Journal of Diabetes Science and Technology*, *3*(3), 603–612. doi:10.1177/193229680900300326 PMID:20144300

Bouarara, H. A., Hamou, R. M., & Amine, A. (2015). Text Clustering using Distances Combination by Social Bees: Towards 3D Visualisation Aspect. *International Journal of Information Retrieval Research*, *4*(3), 34–53. doi:10.4018/IJIRR.2014070103

Brown, G. (2004). *Diversity in neural network ensembles*. University of Birmingham.

Dash, M., Choi, K., Scheuermann, P., & Liu, H. (2002). Feature selection for clustering-a filter solution. In *Data Mining, 2002. ICDM 2003. Proceedings. 2002 IEEE International Conference on* (pp. 115-122). IEEE. doi:10.1109/ICDM.2002.1183893

Divina, F., & Marchiori, E. (2005). Handling continuous attributes in an evolutionary inductive learner. *IEEE Transactions on Evolutionary Computation*, *9*(1), 31–43. doi:10.1109/TEVC.2004.837752

Han, J., Pei, J., & Kamber, M. (2011). *Data mining: Concepts and techniques*. Elsevier.

Horton, P., & Nakai, K. (1996, June). A probabilistic classification system for predicting the cellular localization sites of proteins. In ISMB (Vol. 4, pp. 109-115). Academic Press.

Ishibuchi, H., & Yamamoto, T. (2004). Fuzzy rule selection by multi-objective genetic local search algorithms and rule evaluation measures in data mining. *Fuzzy Sets and Systems*, *141*(1), 59–88. doi:10.1016/S0165-0114(03)00114-3

Kaski, S., & Peltonen, J. (2003). Informative discriminant analysis. In ICML (pp. 329-336). Academic Press.

Kononenko, I., Šimec, E., & Robnik-Šikonja, M. (1997). Overcoming the myopia of inductive learning algorithms with RELIEFF. *Applied Intelligence*, *7*(1), 39–55. doi:10.1023/A:1008280620621

Melli, G. (1998). *A Lazy Model-Based Approach to On-Line Classification* (Doctoral dissertation). Simon Fraser University.

Popescul, A., Pennock, D. M., & Ungar, L. H. (2003). *Mixtures of conditional maximum entropy models*. Academic Press.

Rahmani, M. E., Amine, A., Hamou, R. M., Rahmani, A., Menad, H., Bouarara, H. A., & Boudia, M. A. (2016). A Novel Bio Inspired Algorithm Based on Echolocation Mechanism of Bats for Seismic Hazards Detection. In *Modelling and Implementation of Complex Systems* (pp. 77–89). Springer International Publishing. doi:10.1007/978-3-319-33410-3_6

Rahmani, M. E., Bouarara, H. A., Amine, A., Hamou, R. M., & Menad, H. (2016). New Supervised Approach for Plant Leaves Classification using Artificial Social Bees. *International Journal of Organizational and Collective Intelligence*, *6*(1), 15–28. doi:10.4018/IJOCI.2016010102

Salzberg, S. L. (1988). *Exemplar-based learning: Theory and implementation*. Harvard University, Center for Research in Computing Technology, Aiken Computation Laboratory.

Sammut, C., & Webb, G. I. (Eds.). (2011). *Encyclopedia of machine learning*. Springer Science & Business Media.

Sebban, M., Nock, R., & Lallich, S. (2002). Stopping criterion for boosting-based data reduction techniques: From binary to multiclass problem. *Journal of Machine Learning Research*, *3*(Dec), 863–885.

Sen, A. K., Patel, S. B., & Shukla, D. P. (2013). A data mining technique for prediction of coronary heart disease using neuro-fuzzy integrated approach two level. *International Journal of Engineering and Computer Science*, *2*(9), 1663–1671.

Shouman, M., Turner, T., & Stocker, R. (2012). Applying k-nearest neighbour in diagnosing heart disease patients. *International Journal of Information and Education Technology (IJIET)*, *2*(3), 220–223. doi:10.7763/IJIET.2012.V2.114

Soni, J., Ansari, U., Sharma, D., & Soni, S. (2011). Predictive data mining for medical diagnosis: An overview of heart disease prediction. *International Journal of Computers and Applications*, *17*(8), 43–48. doi:10.5120/2237-2860

Street, W. N., Wolberg, W. H., & Mangasarian, O. L. (1993, July). Nuclear feature extraction for breast tumor diagnosis. In *IS&T/SPIE's Symposium on Electronic Imaging: Science and Technology* (pp. 861-870). International Society for Optics and Photonics.

Wang, P., Weise, T., & Chiong, R. (2011). Novel evolutionary algorithms for supervised classification problems: An experimental study. *Evolutionary Intelligence*, *4*(1), 3–16. doi:10.1007/s12065-010-0047-7

Yang, X. S. (2010). A new metaheuristic bat-inspired algorithm. In Nature inspired cooperative strategies for optimization (NICSO 2010) (pp. 65-74). Springer Berlin Heidelberg. doi:10.1007/978-3-642-12538-6_6

Zięba, M., Tomczak, J. M., Lubicz, M., & Świątek, J. (2014). Boosted SVM for extracting rules from imbalanced data in application to prediction of the post-operative life expectancy in the lung cancer patients. *Applied Soft Computing*, *14*, 99–108. doi:10.1016/j.asoc.2013.07.016

Chapter 15
Comparative Study Between Two Swarm Intelligence Automatic Text Summaries:
Social Spiders vs. Social Bees

Mohamed Amine Boudia
Dr. Tahar Moulay University of Saida, Algeria

ABSTRACT

This chapter is a comparative study between two bio-inspired approach based on the swarm intelligence for automatic text summaries: Social Spiders and Social Bees. The authors use two techniques of extraction, one after the other: scoring of phrases and similarity that aims to eliminate redundant phrases without losing the theme of the text. While the optimization uses the bio-inspired approach to perform the results of the previous step, the objective function of the optimization is to maximize the sum of similarity between phrases of the candidate summary in order to keep the theme of the text and minimize the sum of scores in order to increase the summarization rate. This optimization will also give a candidate's summary where the order of the phrases changes compared to the original text. For the third and final step concerning choosing a best summary from all candidate summaries generated by optimization layer, the authors opted for the technique of voting with a simple majority.

INTRODUCTION AND PROBLEM

The quantity of electronic textual information increase day after day making more difficult the access to relevant information without the use of special tools. The software and hardware infrastructure to access to the content of information, are an obstacle, and the major problem is the exponential quantity of textual information electronically. This requires the use of more specific tools i.e. access to the content of texts by rapid and effective means has become a necessary task. Current requirements of users continue to increase in addition to the quality of the results, he wants to get these results very quickly.

DOI: 10.4018/978-1-5225-3004-6.ch015

A summary of a text is an effective way to represent the contents of the texts and allow quick access to their semantic content (Boudia et al, 2016). The purpose of a summarization is to produce an abridged text covering most of the content from the source text. As a matter of fact, a summary of the text has rewritten the text in smaller way under constraint kept the semantics of a document that is minimized entropy semantics to help the reader to identify interesting information for him/her without reading the entire document (Boudia et al, 2016).

Automatic summaries can be used to reduce the search time to find the relevant documents or to reduce the treatment of long texts by identifying the key information e(Boudia et al, 2016). Automatic summaries can be used to reduce the search time to find the relevant documents or to reduce the treatment of long texts by identifying the key information.

To make an automatic summary, the current literature presents three approaches: by extraction, by understanding and by classification. Our current work uses automatic summarization by extraction as it is a simple method to implement that gives good results; Noting that they are three mains techniques in this approach: Scoring, similarity and prototype.

Our study focuses on comparative study between two approaches based on bio-inspired and more precisely a swarm intelligence that we have already proposed: Social spiders for automatic summarization by extraction vs Social bees for automatic summarization by extraction

Before stating in a comparative study, we will give a brief explanation of each method, and then we will identify the experiment environment and present the results of each method. It concludes with a comparison of four methods' using the same corpus, this comparison is based on execution time, confusion matrix for each method, that will be used to construct a podium according to Recall, Precision, F-measure and ROUGE.

The first part contribution of our work is to use two methods of summarization at the same time on the quality of summary. The second part and the most important of this work is the proposition to use a bio-inspired based on the swarm intelligence whether the social spiders or social bees to the automatic summary. We aim to evaluate the impact of them on the quality of summary.

STATE OF THE ART

Automatic summarization appeared earlier as a field of research in computer science from the axis of NLP (automatic language processing), HP Luhn (1958) proposed in 1958 a first approach to the development of automatic abstracts from extracting phrases.

In the early 1960s, HP Edmundson and other participants in the project TRW (Thompson Ramo Wooldridge Inc.) (Edmundson et al, 1960) Proposed a new system of automatic summarization where it combined several criteria to assess the relevance of phrases to extract.

These works were made to identify the fundamental ideas around the automatic summarization, such as problems caused by extraction to build summaries (problems of redundancy, incompleteness, break, etc..), the theoretical inadequacy of the use of statistics, or the difficulties to understand a text (from semantic analysis) to summarize.

Other projects were based on the same technique to build the abstract; otherwise, they were based on the extraction of phrases from the evaluation of the relevance of each of these phrases. Consideration of the evaluating of a phrase was a plus: its relationship with the rest of the text has grown steadily, and if it is extracted, checked this link with the preceding phrases for example, the presence of connector's start of phrases.

From the 1980s, theories have emerged to describe the various treatments involved in the human cognitive system in the activities of reading and text understanding, in particular the model of Kintsch and Van Dijk (Van Dijk, 1985) explained in more construction of a summary.

These theories had then greatly inspired the architecture of the automatic summary of the time. The influence of psychological theories constituted a new step in the automatic summarization compared to the previous techniques, henceforth we "understand" the text, using the knowledge from deeper cognitive structures like scripts, scheme, frames... one of these early works inspired by research in psychology was that of G. DeJong with the FRUMP system (Kintsch & Van Dijk, 1978; DeJong, 1982). Other important works continued to appear at that time such as SUSY, TOPIC, SCISSOR and PAULINE.

Systems for automatic summarization by an understanding of this era were strongly influenced by all the works that are done on reading comprehension and knowledge representation in cognitive psychology and artificial intelligence. Thus, researchers attempt to copy the human activity of summarizing on their system even if it was difficult and practically less applicable. Indeed, all these systems were often dependent on which thematic field of the original texts. Some works, such as SUSY (Fum et al, 1982; Salton et al, 1997), where even very ambitious, they considered many treatments (syntactic, semantic, etc..) Which, even today, have never been fully made, for example, the implementation of the propositional representation of text.

In the late of the 90s, looking for information began to grow considerably, especially with the come on the Internet and search engines. The amount of information to be processed has become so large and heterogeneous that research needs the information has exploded, especially for automatic summarization. The needles are then oriented to rapid methods broadly applicable; that is to say, independent of areas.

Obviously, the automatic summarization returned largely to the development of systems for extraction, which in fact were less heavy, and generally independent from domains.

The extensive use of statistical and numerical methods, as there were in search of classical information, is naturally inserted in the automatic summarization since quite suited to the needs expressed, see e.g. (Mitra et al, 1997; Teufel et al, 1999).

In some cases, the same system is evaluated multiple times with different combinations of evaluation criteria (Mani et al, 1999), changes in coefficients of importance, changes in coefficients for learning, etc. The evaluation then participated fully in the construction of the system and no longer intervenes only at the end of it.

Automatic summarization systems assimilate in some cases real black boxes where only assessments help guide them in the correct configuration. These are not always theoretical or cognitive considerations that guide choices in the right combination of criteria pertinences, the values of coefficients of importance, etc.

This phenomenon is even more pronounced in techniques with learning. An important event during the 90s was the TIPSTER program, led mainly by DARPA (Defense Advanced Research Projects Agency), which began in 1991 by studying the different information retrieval techniques (algorithms, software architecture, etc..). In its third and final phase, from 1996 to 1998, the TIPSTER program was interested in automatic summarization and has an "official" evaluation of proposed at the time in the field solutions (Mani et al, 2002). In 1998, the first major evaluation SUMMAC (TIPSTER Text Summarization Evaluation) has been done on different systems by defining two frames of evaluation. The first part consisted of traditional evaluation of indicative summaries generated automatically while the second consisted of the evaluation of abstracts, after reading them, should allow the reader to be able to categorize the original document. The results then showed that reading summaries with a low ratio (10 and 17% in this case) was generally as effective as reading the original texts to find information on the content, and that. Moreover, these summaries provided a considerable saving of time (> 40%) in the decision-making such as the categorization of a document by a human (Mani et al, 2001).

Finally, for the years 2003 and 2004, there seems to be a slowdown in the field of automatic summarization as well in academia, where jobs are scarcer than in firms that do not innovate in this area (see the quiet development of their product). This fact is also obviously observable in the reduction of seminars or conferences on this domain. Since 2001, following the work of Inderjeet Mani (1999), no reference on automatic summarization has been created in English. In 2004, a number of the French journal TAL (Minel, 2004) appeared in the automatic summarization works, but only gather some articles on some very specific works, and does not offer a sufficient overview of the French area.

Thus, there is still no reference book which is currently available in French on the subject. With regard to companies, only little software are available for the French including Relevance Mining, Copernic Summarizer, and Subject Search Summarizer.

Although key phrases are useful for multiple tasks, very few documents are provided, because of the high cost of production thereof, in terms of time and human resources. Actually, many researchers are interested in the automatic extraction of these campaigns and some assessments, such as DEFT (Litvak et al, 2008) SemEval and (Kim et al, 2010), in which they propose tasks Automatic extraction of key terms in order to compare the different systems. To do this, the data and the method of evaluation are the same for all systems. Other researchers use their synthetic virtues in construction methods of automatic summaries (Boudin et al; Lin et al).

In recent years, large-scale assessments, independent designers, systems have emerged and several evaluation measures have been proposed. As regards the evaluation of automatic summary, two evaluation campaigns have already been conducted by the U.S. DARPA (Defense Advanced Research Projects Agency). The first, entitled SUMMAC, run from 1996 to 1998 under the TIPSTER (Mani et al, 2002), program, and the second, entitled DUC (Document Understanding Conferences) followed from 2000 to 2007. Since 2008 it is the Text Analysis Conference Such measures may be applied to the distribution of units in the summaries of the systems P and those of Q. The reference value is used to assign a score summary product (Hovy et al, 2006).

The method was evaluated by (Donaway et al, 2000) on the corpus DUC'02 for tasks mono and multi-document summary. A good correlation was found between measures of divergence and the two rankings obtained with ROUGE and ROUGE-SM and coverage.

DATA REPRESENTATION

The machine learning algorithms cannot process directly the unstructured data: image, video, and of course the texts written in natural language. Thus, we are obliged to pass by an indexing step. Indexing step is simply a representation of the text as a vector where each entry corresponds to a different word and the number at that entry corresponds to how many times that word was present in the document (or some function of it); this is very delicate and very important at the same time: a poor or bad representation will lead certainly to bad results (Chhabra et al, 2006).

We will represent each text as a vector where each entry corresponds to a different word and the number at that entry corresponds to how many times that word was present in the document (or some function of it).

In this way, we shall have a vector which represents the text and which is exploitable by machine learning algorithms at the same time (Chhabra et al, 2006).

Several approaches for the representation of texts exist in the literature, among whom the bag-of-words representation which is the simplest and the most used, the bag-of-sentences representation, lexical-roots representation and of course the n-gram representation which is a representation independent from the natural language (Chhabra et al, 2006).

Stop words will not be removed, because the method of automatic summarization by extraction aims to extract the most informative phrases without modifying them: if we remove Stop words without information on their morph syntactic impact on the phrases, we risk having an inconsistent summary in a morphological part. Then cleaning is to remove emoticons, to replace spaces with "_" and remove special characters (#, \, [,] ....).

For automatic summarization by extraction, we will need two representations: Bag of words representation or Bag of sentences representation.

Both representations are introduced in the vector model.

The first representation consists to transform the text i into a vector v_i (w_1, w_2,...., $w_{|T|}$) where T is the number of all words that appear at least once in the text i, The weight w_k indicated the occurrence of the word t_k in the text i.

The second representation consists to transform the text i into a vector v_i (w_1, w_2,...., $w_{|T|}$) where T is the number of all phrases that appear at least once in the text i, The weight w_k indicated the occurrence of the word t_k in the text i.

And finally the "word-phrases" occurrence matrix will be generated after the two previous performances, the size of this matrix is equal to (the number of words in the text) X (the number of words in the text), p_{ik} weight is the number occurrence of the word i in the phrase j;

Once the "Word-Phrase" matrix is ready, we calculate the weighting of "Word-Phrase" matrix by using one of the encodings (tf-idf, or tfc) with a small modification to adapt it with the concept of a mono-document summarization.

$$TfIdf(tk, i) = Nb * \log(A / B) \tag{2}$$

Nb: The number of occurrences of the term t_k in the text i;
A: The total number of phrase in the text;
B: The number of phrase in which the t_k term appears at least once.

$$tfc\left(t_k, p_i\right) = \frac{tf - idf\left(t_k, p_i\right)}{\sqrt{\sum_{i=1}^{|p|} tf - idf\left(t_k, p_i\right)^2}} \tag{3}$$

After calculating the frequency of each word, a weight is assigned to each phrase. The generated summary is then generated by displaying the highest score of the source document phrases.

FIRST PROPOSED APPROACH: SOCIAL SPIDERS (BOUDIA ET AL, 2015)

The approach that we have presented in our previous article (Boudia et al, 2015) obeys the following steps that the Figure 1 indicates.

In step 1 the classic technique of automatic summarization is used: scoring and similarity at the end of this step we can draw an non-oriented complete graph where we considers the extracts textual unit will be represented by the summit and the similarity between this textual unit will be represented by the weight of the arc (wire) between two summit. In step two, a meta-heuristic is used, which is a bio-inspired method in case the social spiders, knowing that social spiders were shown their power in graph theory, and that the canvas can be the counterpart of our textual graph. What makes our approach hybridization between the classical method of automatic summarization and meta-heuristic bio-inspired social spiders (see Figure 2).

After the pretreatment, we will have a weighting "Word-Phrase" matrix, that contains the score of each phrase; The generated summary is then generated by displaying the highest score of the source document phrases.

This score of a phrase is equal to the sum of the words in this phrase:

Figure 1. Process of the proposed approach

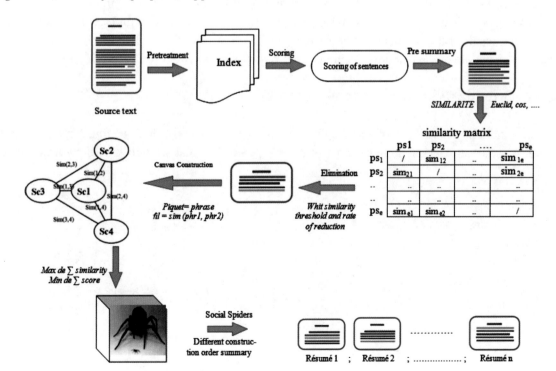

$$SCORE\left(p_i\right) = \sum_{k=0}^{nbr\_word} Mik \qquad (1)$$

Step 1: Pre-Summary

Suggested process claims on the principle that high-frequency words in a document are important words. (Shannon, 1948)

The final step is to select the N first phrases that have the highest score which are considered the most relevant. We can also extracting the first N phrases by defined a threshold, in this case, the score of the phrase must be greater than or equal to the threshold in order that this phrase will be extracted.

Similarity Method Summarization by Extraction

The result of the previous step is a set of phrases which is a high score. Just we have a possibility that two or more phrases have a high score but they are similar, so we proceed to the elimination of phrases that resembling. The similarity between the phrases that have been selected at the end of the previous step with known metrics (cosine Euclidean ......).

We have one parameter which is used to adjust the elimination of repetitions: similarity threshold: defined the point that we can consider two phrases as similar, When the similarity between two phrases is greater than similarity threshold: we chose the phrase that has the highest score and remove the other phrase.

The similarity is also used to detect the phrase that has more relation with the theme of the text. According to the domain experts, it is the phrase which is most similar to the other phrases door themed text.

The final result of this step is a set of textual unit and an array of textual similarity between these units. As it is two items we can draw a graph as the figure above shows (See Figure 2).

Step 2: Optimization Using Social Spiders

To understand who we will use of social spider to automatic summarization, we must first provide an overview on the natural functioning model of social spider after that we will then draw up a model-

Figure 2. Drawing a textual graph

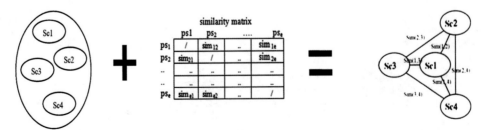

ing table that will show how we spend natural to the artificial, and finally we will explain in detail the artificial model.

Natural Model

Environment is a set of pickets which serve weaving wire brackets, this pickets have different sizes.
Spiders have three features:

- **Weaving:** Weaving creates a wire between the current and the last visited picket stake.
- **Movement:** Movement allows the spider to move in the environment on the wire woven by her or by others spider in the same canvas. The selection of the new position dependent upon a finite number of criteria.

The wire has a flexibility F which represents the maximum weight with a correction relative to its diameter that can be held by the wire, is one of the major criteria of movement of the spider.

- **Communication:** Social spiders communicate with the others in the weaving task, movement or capture prey; communication can be done by two different methods; by vibration on the wire or by the concentration of hormonal substances that spider left on a wire.
- **System Dynamics:** It is built on the principle of stigmergy: the behavior of agents have effects on the environment (wire-laying) in return behavior is influenced by the context of the agent (environment).

Artificial Model

Our Artificial model is described as follow (see Table 1).
Environment is a graph drawing in the end of step 1(final result of step 1) where each pickets is representing a phrase, the pickets have different sizes that representing the score of the corresponding phrase. Initially, all the wires are woven so as to have a complete graph; the diamater of wire between two pickets represent the similarity between the two phrase that are representing by this two pickets.

Table 1. Modeling table (natural model vs. artificial model)

	Natural Model	**Artificial Model**
Environment	A set of pickets having different sizes	A textual graph: pickets = phrases, wire = similarity between phrase
Weaving	A wire between the current and the last visited picket stake.	Weaving a complete graph
Movement	To move in the environment on the wire woven by her or by others spider in the same canvas. The selection of the new position dependent upon a finite number of criteria.	Movement of the spider is incremental and random. Every spider save in its memory every way which she followed. sum of score and sum of similarity to doing a choose.
Communication	By vibration on the wire or by the concentration of hormonal substances that spider left on a wire.	Hormonal comminucation: to ensures diversity between different summaries candidate to avoid the repetition of phrases in the same summary

The number of spiders is equal to or less than the number of phrase, initially each spider is placed on a picket (phrase) randomly.

- **Weaving:** The wires are woven in the beginning of each iteration in order to have a complete graph. The similarity sxy between two phrases phx phy represents the diameter of wire woven between the two picket x and y associate respectively to phrases phx to and phy, as given the similarity is commutative (s (x, y) = s (y, x)): the diameter of wire woven between the two picket x and y will be a uniform.
- **Movement:** Movement of the spider is incremental and random; Every spider save in its memory every way which she followed. To save result, a weight of path should be: Superior to the "lower threshold of the summary rate" and Less the "upper threshold of the summary of rates."

We associated to the social spider i in iteration j a Pij weight initialized to zero and it equal to the sum of the weights of k SCORE phrases (size of pickets) whose social spider i have visited during the iteration j.

The wire has a flexibility F that depends on its diameter: is constant and represents the maximum weight that can load on itself, with artificial model F is defined as follows

$$Flexible\left(fil_{ij}\right) = upper\ threshold\ of\ summarization\ rate * diametre\left(wire_{ij}\right) \quad (4)$$

$$diametre\left(wire_{ij}\right) = similarity\left(phrase_i, phrase_j\right) \quad (5)$$

Noting That: Upper threshold of summarization rate is constant.

If i social spider during iteration j with P_{ij} weight passes through the wire (x, y), it will execute this pseudo-algorithm:

If P_{ij} is lower than F(x,y) then
The spider will go to the wire (x,y)
Updating the current path
Update the weight P_{ij},
Else the wire is torn //and path will be considered unnecessary,

Social spider i will go into pause state waiting for the end of the iteration j.
We will give these two observations:

- F(x,y) is higher than F(w,z) is equivalent to say that the similarity between the phrase x and the phrase y is greater than the similarity between the phrase w and the phrase z because "upper threshold of the summary of rates" is constant.
- The interpretation of F(x,y) is higher than F(w,z), is that by optimizing with social spider: if choice between wire (x,y) and the wire (w,z) the spider will choose the first wire because it safe for her.

From observations A and B, we can deduce that the optimization is to minimize the weight of the summary in order to minimize the summarization rate, and maximize the similarity in order to preserve the theme of the candidate summary.

- **The Utility Constraint:** Produce a summary Automatically with the summarization rate higher than "upper threshold of summarization rate" is not helpful.
- **The Semantic Constraint:** Produce a summary Automatically with summarization rate smaller than "lower threshold of summarization rate" Leads to losing a lot of semantics.
  - ○ **End of Iteration:** When all the spider will be in the pause state, the iteration j will be declared finished, the spiders will rewoven the spiders rendomly choose their new start position and start the iteration j + 1.
  - ○ **Communication:** Each spider leaves a hormonal trace on each visited picket so that other spiders will not take this part of the way. First it ensures diversity between different summaries candidate: spiders take in consideration in this movement, the number of picket that they share with the others spiders that operates on the canvas, and moves with the constraint to not exceeding M picket in the same iteration with another spider.

Secondly, communication is used to avoid the repetition of phrases in the summary. In cases where social spider returns while moving on a picket that it been already have been visited by itself in current iteration it makes a flashback and continues his trip without considering this visit.

The duration of evaporation of communication hormone is equal to an iteration, it should be noted that the hormone density cannot be cumulative.

- **System Dynamics:** It is built on the principle of stigmergy: the behavior of agents have effects on the environment. In return behavior is influenced by the context of the agent.

Each spider keeps in mind, the best visited paths, after a number of spider iterations, every spider returns the best paths.

- **Path:** It is a series of picket visited in chronological order, and is a summarization. Recall that each picket is a phrase (See the initial state).
- **End of the Optimisation of the Social Spiders:** When the number of iterations performed reached the maximum number of iterations, each spider returns all paths (each path, is a candidate summary) and was associated with each path (candidate summary) a set of evaluations indices and launching a voting algorithm compared these evaluation indices to choose the best candidate summary as final result in the next layer.

Final Step: Evaluation and Vote

Candidates summaries generated by the previous layer will be evaluated by several evaluations metric, and then we will classify by pairs. R1 and R2 are two candidate summaries rate by N metric evaluation, the number of associated point to R1 represents the number of evaluation indicating that the quality of

R1 is greater than or equal to R2(respectively to R2). The summary with most points will win the duel and will face another until there are no more challenger. Summary will be declared the winner as the best summary.

SECOND PROPOSED APPROACH (BOUDIA ET AL, 2015)

First Step: Primitive Summary

To create a summary by extraction, it is necessary to identify textual units (phrases, clauses, phrases, paragraphs) considered salient (relevant), then we select the textual units that carry the main ideas of the document content with some order to finally build a resume.

After a vectorization of text like we have seen in previous section (Pretreatment and Weighting), a weight or score is assigned to each phrase. The generated summary is then generated by displaying the highest score of the source document phrases.

This score of a phrase is equal to the sum of the words in this phrase:

$$SCORE\left(p_i\right) = \sum_{k=0}^{nbr\_word} Mik \tag{6}$$

The last step is to select the N first phrases that have the highest weight and which are considered the most relevant. The process of extracting the first N phrases intended to build the summary is defined either by a threshold, in this case, the score of the phrase must be greater than or equal to the threshold in order that this phrase will be extracted the second method is to fix a number N of phrase to be extracted, all phases will be ranked in descending order according of their score, and we take only the first N phrases.

Elimination of Rehearsals and Theme Detection: Using Similarity Method Summarization by Extraction

The result of the previous sub-step is a set of phrases which is a high score. Just we have a possibility that two or more phrases have a high score but they are similar, so we proceed to the elimination of phrases that resembling. The similarity between the phrases that have been selected at the end of the previous step with known metrics (cosine Euclidean ......).

Two parameters are used to adjust the elimination of repetitions: similarity threshold and reduction rate, the first parameter defined the point that we can consider two phrases as similar, and the second parameter indicates the number of resemblance to eliminate, to decrease the entropy of information. When the similarity between two phrases is greater than similarity threshold: we chose the phrase that has the highest score and remove the other phrase.

The similarity is also used to detect the phrase that has more relation with the theme of the text. According to the domain experts, it is the phrase which is most similar to the other phrases door themed text.

Second Step: Optimization Using Saving Energy Model of Bees

Natural Model

According to the lifestyle of the species, there are several types of bees. As a definition, the term "bee" is one of the common names of the European honeybee (Apis mellifera). It can also be used for any other domesticated bee by humans.

The term "social bee" means a species of bee that lives in colonies, if it is a "solitary bee" constituting rather aggregations of individual burrows. Other species are "parasitic bees" that practice the kleptoparasitism. Among all categories of bees exist (Boudia et al, 2015).

Such as ants, bees are social insects; they cannot have an isolated existence and need to live in colonies. A very highly organized colony always composed of workers, drones and one queen. The workers are exclusively female bees, the most numerous of the colony (about 30,000 to 70,000 per hive). In the colony, where they work tirelessly, they are responsible for all tasks related to the proper functioning of the hive. Unlike ants who does one specific task throughout their lives, the bees perform all successively, in a life that, on average, lasts only a few weeks (about 45 days).

During the first four days of its life, the worker cleans and maintains the hive. From 5th to the 11th day, it is the nurse and gave larvae royal jelly of the royal cells. At the 11th and 13th days, it becomes storekeeper: its role is to store pollen and nectar in the cells and to ventilate the hive, waving its wings quickly, so as to maintain a constant temperature. From the 14th to the 17th day, the wax glands of its abdomen is being developed, it becomes waxy, and builds the shelves. From the 18th to the 21st day, it becomes sentry and stands guard at the entrance of the hive to chase all intruders, wasps, butterflies and even drones. From the 22nd day and until his death, she will go from flower to flower to collect nectar, pollen and propolis. Consequently, it becomes forager and brings food to the hive.

In the life cycle of bee workers, the largest labs time is during the period of collecting the nectar, pollen and propolis in the flower field. During the exercise of this task, the bee should mark the territory of the hive from which it originated. Thus, it has to travel and cover the greater part of the field of flowers.

The worker bee uses a model to save energy that is spent to keep high efficiency. Roughly, is done as follows:

- Choose the flowers that initially are of low or no pheromone to start collecting.
- Minimize the weight that she carries to every flower and look for flower with less pollen.
- Select the next flower in its movement in order to minimize the distances that are traveled.
  - **Environment:** A field of flowers
  - **Pollen Collection:** It takes the nectar and pollen where the propolis of the flower is on her body.
  - **Movement:** Movement allows the bees to move in the environment. The selection of the new position dependent upon a finite number of criteria.
  - The weight that bee carries and the distance between the current and the next flower are the main criteria for choosing the new position
  - **Communication:** A social bees communicate with the others in the taking pollen task, movement or attack; communication can be done by two different methods; by dance move or by the concentration of hormonal substances. Each dance or each concentration of substances has a specific meaning to others bees.

The Artificial Model

As it is known in physics, the energy is computed in term of power by time (equation 7). Also the power is equal to the applied force multiplied by the rate of distance by time (equation 8).

$$Energy = power * time \tag{7}$$

$$Power = \sum force * \frac{\sum Distance}{Time} \tag{8}$$

From this two previous equations we can conclude that the final law of energy is equal to force multiplied by the distance (equation 9)

$$Energy = \sum force * \sum distance \tag{9}$$

Our inspiration is based on the force that a bee applies to stay stable in a specific level. As it known that the force applied on the bee is the gravity force which is generally related to the weight of the bee and the pollen which he collect. For that the bee must apply at least the same force on the opposite way in order to preserve its current level.

F' will be not take we will not focus on F ' because it is not our purpose in this paper (See Figure 3).

Weight of pollen represents in our artificial model a sum score of sentence that the bee holds. From that we conclude that the force of an artificial bee in equal to the score of a phrase. Meanwhile, there is another known law that links the distance to the similarity of two objects. Simply the similarity is equal to the rate of 1 by the given distance (equation 10)

$$\sum Similarity = \frac{1}{\sum Distance} \tag{10}$$

Figure 3. Force apply on a bee in collection of pollen task

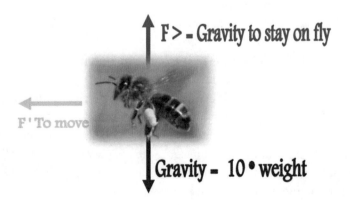

However, for good functioning of such bee, it must conserve the maximum of its energy. To do that, a natural bee tries to get the nectar from the most closed flowers to each other. In other words, it tries to minimize distance between sources. Consequently, by looking to the equations 3 and 4, and the inspiration we made in the previous paragraph, we conclude a new fitness function for automatic summarization approach using bees' algorithm. This function is based on minimizing loss of energy of a bee using the similarity between phrases and its scores. Our fitness function is demonstrated in equation 11 below.

$$\text{energy} = R * \frac{\sum score_{phrase}}{\sum similarity} \tag{11}$$

Where R is a constant that represents minimum carrying capacity that a bee could transfer. The objective of using this constant is to keep the fitness function in a positive position and avoid a fitness that is equal to 0.

Energy $\sum score_{phrase}$

The minimization of energy is equivalent to minimizing the sum of the scores of phrases in order to minimize the summarization rate, and maximize the similarity and to preserve the theme of the candidate summary, while respecting the dice constrained utility and semantics represented by the interval:[lower threshold of summarization rate, upper threshold of summarization rate] noting that the lower and upper thresholds of summarization rate are determined and fixed by the experts.

- **The Utility Constraint:** Produce a summary automatically with the summarization rate higher than "upper threshold of summarization rate" is not helpful.
- **The Semantic Constraint:** Produce a summary Automatically with summarization rate smaller than "lower threshold of summarization rate" Leads to losing a lot of semantics.

Our Artificial model is described as follow:

- **Environment:** A flower grid (N * N). N is the square root of the number of phrases after step 1 (pre-summary and the elimination of similar phrases) where each flower is representing a phrase, the pickets have different sizes that representing the score of the corresponding phrase. Initially, there is not pheromones in environment;

The number of bees is equal to or less than the number of phrase, initially each bee is placed on a flower (phrase) randomly.

- **Pollen Collection and Movement:** According to the fitness function (energy), taken Pollen and movement will be made.

We associated to the worker bee i in iteration j a Pij weight initialized to zero and it equal to the sum of the weights of k SCORE phrases whose worker bee i have visited during the iteration j.

- **Communication:** Each bee leaves a hormonal trace on each visited flower so that other bees will not take this part of the way. First it ensures diversity between different summaries candidate: bees take in consideration in this movement, the number of flower that they share with the others bees of the hive, and moves with the constraint to not exceeding M flower in the same iteration with another bees. Secondly, communication is used to avoid the repetition of phrases in the summary. In cases where worker bee returns while moving on a flower that it been already have been visited by itself in current iteration it makes a flashback and continues his trip without considering th is visit.

The duration of evaporation of communication hormone is equal to one iteration, it should be noted that the hormone density cannot be cumulative.

Each bess keeps in mind, the best visited paths, after a number of bees iterations, every bee returns the best paths.

- **Path:** It is a series of flower visited in chronological order, and is a summarization. Recall that each flower is a phrase (See the artificial environment).
- **End of the Optimisation of the Workers Bees:** When the number of iterations performed reached the maximum number of iterations, each bee returns all paths (each path, is a candidate summary) and was associated with each path (candidate summary) a set of evaluations indices and launching a voting algorithm compared these evaluation indices to choose the best candidate summary as final result in the next layer.

Step 3: Evaluation and Vote

Candidates summaries generated by the previous layer will be evaluated by several evaluations metric, and then we will classify by pairs. R1 and R2 are two candidate summaries rate by N metric evaluation, the number of associated point to R1 represents the number of evaluation indicating that the quality of R1 is greater than or equal to R2(respectively to R2).

The summary with most points will win the duel and will face another until there are no more challengers. Summary will be declared the winner as the best summary.

EXPERIMENTATION

Our methods are oriented for the moment to the generation of generic mono-document summaries using a an hybridization between classical technique: scoring and similarity with two biomimetic approach Social Spider or Social Bees that are a field of Swarm intelligence .

Used Corpus

It was used as the text corpus "Hurricane" in English, which contains a title and 20 phrases and 313 words. We have use three references summaries produced successively by Summarizer CORTEX, Essential Summarizer, and a summary produced by a human (see Table 2).

Figure 4. Process of the proposed approach

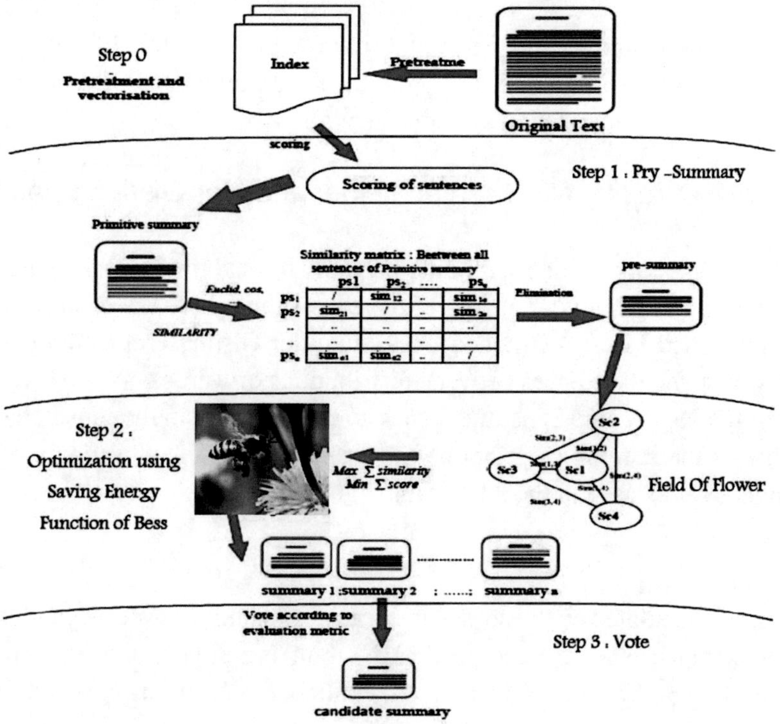

Table 2. Reference summary used in evaluation step

Essential Summarizer
"There is no need for alarm," Civil Defense Director Eugenio Cabral said in a television alert shortly after midnight Saturday. Cabral said residents of the province of Barahona should closely follow Gilbert's movement. On Saturday, Hurricane Florence was downgraded to a tropical storm, and its remnants pushed inland from the U.S. Gulf Coast. Residents returned home, happy to find little damage from 90 mph winds and sheets of rain.
Cortex
Hurricane Gilbert Swept toward the Dominican Republic Sunday, and the Civil Defense alerted its heavily populated south coast to prepare for high winds, heavy rains, and high seas. The National Hurricane Center in Miami reported its position at 2 a.m. Sunday at latitude 16.1 north, longitude 67.5 west, about 140 miles south of Ponce, Puerto Rico, and 200 miles southeast of Santo Domingo. The National Weather Service in San Juan, Puerto Rico, said Gilbert was moving westward at 15 mph with a "broad area of cloudiness and heavy weather" rotating around the center of the storm. Strong winds associated with the Gilbert brought coastal flooding, strong southeast winds, and up to feet to Puerto Rico's south coast.
Expert Humain
Hurricane Gilbert is moving toward the Dominican Republic, where the residents if the south coast, especially the Barahona Province, have been alerted to prepare for heavy rain, and high winds and seas. Tropical storm Gilbert formed in the eastern Caribbean and became a hurricane on Saturday night. By 2am Sunday it was about 200 miles southeast of Santo Domingo and moving westward at 15 mph with of 75 mph. Flooding is expected in Puerto Rico and the Virgin Islands. The second hurricane of the season, Florence, is now over the southern United States and downgraded to a tropical storm.

Validation

We evaluated the summaries produced by this algorithm with the metric ROUGE (Lin 2004) which compares a candidate summary (automatically produced) and Summary Reference (created by human experts or other automatic summarization systems known).

The Evaluation Measure Recall: Oriented Understudy for Gisting Evaluation

The evaluation of abstracts can be done semi-automatically through measures of similarities computed between a candidate summary and one or more reference summaries. We evaluate the results of this work by the measure called Recall - Oriented Understudy for Gisting Evaluation (ROUGE) proposed by (Lin, 2004) involving the differences between distributions of words.

Heavily used in the DUC campaigns, these measures are increasingly considered standard by the community because of their strong correlation with manual ratings. Two variants of ROUGE will be developed, it is the measures used in the DUC campaigns.

ROUGE (N).

Measurement of return calculated on the co-occurrences of N-grams between a candidate summary R_{can} and a set of reference summaries R_{ref} Co-occurrences (N-gram) is the maximum number of co-occurrences N-grams and R_{ref} in R_{can} number and (N-grams) to the number of N-grams appearing in the abstract

$$OUGE(N) = \frac{\sum_{s \in R_{ref}} \sum_{s \in R_{can}} Co - occurences\left(R_{ref}, R_{can}, N\right)}{Nbr - NGramme(N)_{R_{ref}}} \quad (12)$$

ROUGE-SU (M)

Adaptation of ROUGE-2 using bigrams hole (skip units (SU)) maximum size M and counting unigrams.

F-Measure for the Evaluation of Automatic Extraction Summaries

We have proposed in our work before an adaptation of the F-measure for the validation of automatic summarization by extraction, as this technique is based on phrases to keep and delete the other has in a certain philosophy (scoring, detection, thematic ...) this can be regarded as a two-class classification, which justifies our adaptation of F-measure is as shown in Table 3.

From the confusion matrix, we can calculate: the recall, precision than we combined the two measures to calculate the F-Measure like that:

$$F - Measure = \frac{2 * \left(Precision * Recall\right)}{\left(Precision + Recall\right)} \quad (13)$$

Table 3. Confusion matrix for automatic text summary task

Automatic Summary		Candidate Summary	
		Word K	**Word R**
Reference Summary	**Word K**	X	Y
	Word R	Z	W

Word K: number of words to keep
Word R: number of words to remove

Result

Results of Step 1: Before Optimisation

After experiments we have grouped the results in Table 4.

Results of Step 2: After Optimization With the Social Spider/Social Bees and VOTE

We used two social spiders parameter combined: We have fixed some parameters: Number of iterations = 500 and Number of spiders = 10 and Maximum number of common stake in the same order = 5.

Table 4. Result of Step 1: before optimization with social spider or social bees

Threshold Similarity		Phrases Score											
		0.60						0.65					
Threshold Similarity	**Evaluation Metric**	**REG**	**Cortex**	**Humain**	**Nbr Word**	**Nbr Phrase**	**Reduce Rate**	**REG**	**Cortex**	**Humain**	**Nbr Word**	**Nbr Phrase**	**Reduce Rate**
0.60	ROUGE-SU(2)	0,67	0,71	0,55	245	15	21,72%	0,67	0,68	0,52	224	13	28,43%
	F-Measure	0,49	0,46	0,32				0,55	0,50	0,47			
0.65	ROUGE-SU(2)	0,65	0,69	0,55	232	14	25,87%	0,72	0,68	0,53	221	12	29,39%
	F-Measure	0,51	0,49	0,37				0,58	0,54	0,52			
0.70	ROUGE-SU(2)	0,61	0,68	0,51	230	14	26,51%	**0,71**	**0,69**	**0,56**	**208**	**10**	**33,54%**
	F-Measure	0,57	0,51	0,44				**0,64**	**0,62**	**0,55**			
0.60	ROUGE-SU(2)	0,71	0,70	0,52	193	10	38,33%	0,67	0,67	0,58	123	6	60,70%
	F-Measure	0,60	0,61	0,53				0,43	0,64	0,45			
0.65	ROUGE-SU(2)	0,61	0,70	0,57	180	8	42,49%	0,68	0,68	0,58	113	5	63,89%
	F-Measure	0,58	0,59	0,56				0,42	0,45	0,41			
0.70	ROUGE-SU(2)	0,71	0,68	0,54	143	7	54,31%	0,71	0,74	0,64	110	4	64,85%
	F-Measure	0,57	0,55	0,55				0,39	0,45	0,38			

- *In Italic:* The local optimal candidate summary before optimization, quoted just for illustration, but will not be used for optimization with social spiders.
- **In Bold:** Global optimal candidate summary before optimization, which will be used for optimization with social spiders,

And we change this parameter:

- **Best Combine:** (see Table)
  - Threshold higher discount rate 55% = 0,55.
  - Threshold lower discount rate 27,50% = 0,275.
- **Worst Combine:** (see Table)
  - Threshold higher discount rate 50% = 0,50.
  - Threshold lower discount rate 30% = 0,30.

We used two parameter combinations of Social Bees: we have use ten Bees with this combine of set

- Best Combine:
  - Threshold higher discount rate 75% = 0,75.
  - Threshold lower discount rate 50% = 0,65.
  - Number of iterations = 500.
- Worst Combine:
  - Threshold higher discount rate 50% = 0,80.
  - Threshold lower discount rate 30% = 0,50.
  - Number of iterations = 500.

We conducted a series of experiments to find and fix the most optimal parameters of social spiders. According to the experimental set of results when we set the target parameter values, it has turn out that:

1. Increasing number of iterations and the increase in social spiders or social bees influences the execution time, the candidate summary quality is not reached by the change of these two parameters.
2. Maximum number of common stake in the same order minimizes the number of abstracts same candidate before the vote and can cover the maximum possible case.

INTERPRETATION AND COMPARISON STUDY

We experimented document "Hurricane" using the coding TFC for the first step (pre-summary) and several similarity distances to try to detect the sensitive parameters to have the best results, we validated the result by the metric ROUGE by comparing our candidates suummaries with the references summaries produced by REG, COTREX and a human expert. All tests on data representation parameters were performed to avoid a wrong judgment on our new approach based on a biomimetic approach in this case social spiders.

ROUGE is a metric intrinsic semi-automatic evaluation based on the number of co-occurrence between a summary candidate and one or more reference summaries divided by the size of the latter. Its weakness is that it is based on the summary references and neglects the original text.

The values given in ROUGE for a summary, a negligible reduction rate is high. This high value is due to the increased number of term co-occurrence between the candidate summary and abstract references.

Table 5. Final result: after optimization with social spider/social bees and vote

	Evaluation Matric	REG	Cortex	Humain	Nbr Words	Nbr Phrases	Reduce Rate	Execution Time
Before optimisation	ROUGE-SU(2)	0,71	0,69	0,56	208	10	33,54%	819ms
	F-Measure	0,64	0,62	0,55				
Optimization by social spider (combine 1)	*ROUGE-SU(2)*	*0,72*	*0,73*	*0,60*	*205*	*9*	*35,31%*	*3602ms*
	F-Measure	*0,66*	*0,67*	*0,57*				
Optimization by social spider (combine 1)	ROUGE-SU(2)	0,72	0,75	0,61	195	9	37,69%	2762ms
	F-Measure	0,68	0,72	0,66				
Optimization by social bees (combine 1)	**ROUGE-SU(2)**	**0.78**	**0.79**	**0.63**	**207**	**13**	**34,50%**	**3146 ms**
	F-Measure	**0.68**	**0.69**	**0.62**				
Optimization by social bees (combine 2)	ROUGE-SU(2)	0.72	0.71	0.59	195	12	37,69%	3119 ms
	F-Measure	0.69	0.63	0.58				

- *In Italic:* The worst optimization result.
- **In Bold:** The best optimization result,

The F-measure is one of the most robust metric used for the evaluation of classification; the F-measure is a combination of Recall and precision. For adaptation that is added to the F-measure of the strength that made, we will proceed with an extrinsic evaluation at the beginning, and continues with an intrinsic valuation: thus, a hybrid evaluation.

For automatic summary reduced rate of reduction, F-Measure offers better feedback than ROUGE because it takes into account the absence of the term. Unlike ROUGE evaluation summary, high reduction rate candidate can be distorted because the false negative maximum value is what will give good evaluations for generally poor summary (high reduction rate leads to an increase in entropy of information). The accuracy indicates the purity of the candidate summary while the reminder interprets the candidate summary resemblance to the summary reference.

In the Figure 5 the four graphs show that the quality of the summary candidate high reduction rate.

The first sub-graph (top left corner) indicates incoherence between the F-Measure evaluation metric and ROUGE. This incoherence is resulting from a false evaluation of ROUGE because the ROUGE metric is weak against summary with negligible reduction rate: in fact a summary has low reduction rate will have a big number of occurrences between him and a set of reference summaries (more larger than a summary has greatly reduced rates).

The second sub-graph (top right corner) and the third sub-graph (bottom left) sub-graph shows complete coherence between the three evaluation indexes: reduction rate, F-Measure and ROUGE. While the 4th sub graph shows another inconsistency between the evaluation ROUGE and F-Measure; because F-Measure is weakness against summary with a very high reduction ratio: the number of true negative is the maximal value, then F-Measure is high but that does not really reflect the quality of summary candidate who has lost much of semantic because it was much reduced.

Figure 6 shows explicitly that the second combine of parameter optimization with social spiders return results better compared to the first combine. This is explained by the given interval of "utility and semantics" represented by two thresholds: upper and lower discount rate is reduced, which allows well-directed the socials spiders .

Figure 5. Summary evaluation graph before optimization

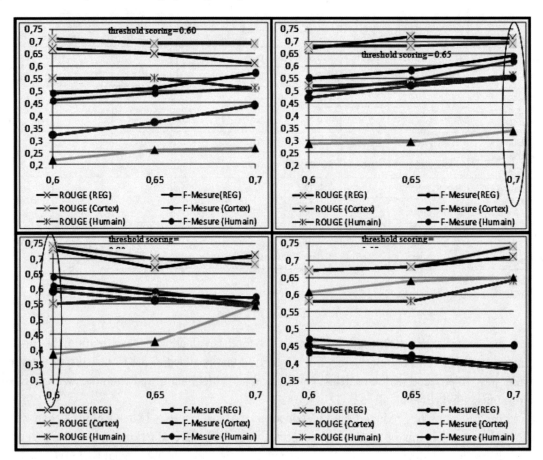

Figure 6. Optimization by social spider

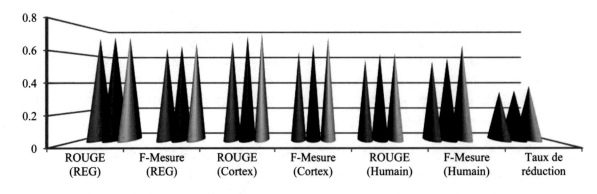

■ Layer 0 : Before Optimization   ■ Optimizing social spider (Combine 1)   ■ Optimizing social spider (Combine 2)

From the two graphs, it is suggested that the interval of "utility and semantics" must be as wide as possible in order to have a better optimization of social spiders and generate automatic summarization with the most superior quality possible.

We note that the execution time (see Figure 7), optimization combined with the first is greater than the second combines this means that the search field first combines is greater than the second combination.

Table 1 and Table 2 show that the quality of the summary candidate high reduction rate. In Table 1: first sub-table (top left corner) indicates incoherence between the F-Measure evaluation metric and ROUGE. This incoherence is resulting from a false evaluation of ROUGE because the ROUGE metric is weak against summary with negligible reduction rate: in fact a summary has low reduction rate will have a big number of occurrences between him and a set of reference summaries (more larger than a summary has greatly reduced rates).

Always in Table 1: the second sub-table (top right corner) and the third sub-table (bottom left) shows complete coherence between the three evaluation indexes: reduction rate, F-Measure and ROUGE. While the 4th sub table shows another inconsistency between the evaluation ROUGE and F-Measure; because F-Measure is weakness against summary with a very high reduction ratio:

The number of true negative is the maximal value, then F-Measure is big but that does not really reflect the quality of summary candidate who has lost much of semantic because it was much reduced.

The graphs show explicitly that the first combine of parameter optimization with bees return results better com-pared to the first combine. This is explained by the given interval of "utility and semantics" represented by two thresholds: upper and lower discount rate is reduced, which allows well-directed the bees.

Figure 7. Execution time optimization by social spider

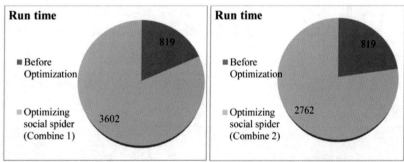

Figure 8. Execution time optimization by social bees

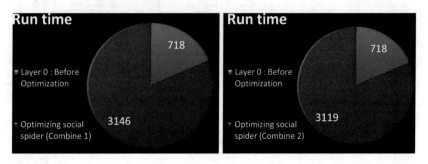

From the graphs, it is suggested that the interval of "utility and semantics" must be as wide as possible in order to have a better optimization of social Bees and generate automatic summarization with the most superior quality possible.

We note that the execution time optimization combined with the first is greater than the second combines this means that the search field first combines is greater than the second combination.

Based on some evaluation criteria, Table 3 is presented for comparison between the two algorithms studied. In terms of results and based on several evaluation measure, we find that our model based on Saving Energy Function of Workers Bees for automatic summarization gives the best results even in the worst case .

CONCLUSION AND PERSPECTIVE

In this article, we presented new ideas. Firstly, we have used two techniques of extraction summary after another to improve the rate of reduction without loss of semantics.

The second idea is the use of two biomimetic approach that has the representation of strength graph; social spiders and social bees can almost total coverage on a graph using the communication module.

Given the results obtained, our approach based on two biomimetic approach can help solve one of the problems of textual data exploration and visualization will. We find also that the model based on Saving Energy Function of Workers Bees for automatic summarization gives the best results even in the worst case than the second approach based on the social bees.

In the light of these results, facts and opinions, we will try to improve this approach using the Word-Net thesaurus, and use a summary based on feelings using the SentiWordNet. For nature still has not revealed all the secrets, we will also try to explore other biomimetic methods.

Looking ahead, we will try to improve automatic summarization by extraction based on the detection of opinion by the application of technical and other conventional method such as detection thematic.

Table 6. Result of evaluation of the two approaches (our approach (bee algorithm), social spider for summarization)

	The Worst Case		The Best Case	
	Bee Algorithm (Our Approach)	**Social Spider for Summarization**	**Bee Algorithm (Our Approach)**	**Social Spider for Summarization**
F-Measure (Cortex)	0.7153	0.66	0.7924	0.78
ROUGE(Cortex)	0.6339	0.62	0.6821	0.66
F-Measure (REG)	0.7211	0.68	0.7859	0.75
ROUGE(REG)	0.6912	0.64	0.6831	0.65
F-Measure (Human)	0.5949	0.47	0.6338	0.62
ROUGE(Human)	0.5814	0.55	0.6289	0.60
Reduce Rate	39,06%	40,25%	35,31%	39,29%

REFERENCES

Boudia, M. A., Hamou, R. M., & Amine, A. (2016). A New Approach Based on the Detection of Opinion by SentiWordNet for Automatic Text Summaries by Extraction. *International Journal of Information Retrieval Research, 6*(3), 19–36. doi:10.4018/IJIRR.2016070102

Boudia, M. A., Hamou, R. M., Amine, A., & Rahmani, A. (2015). A New Biomimetic Method Based on the Power Saves of Social Bees for Automatic Summaries of Texts by Extraction. *International Journal of Software Science and Computational Intelligence, 7*(1), 18–38. doi:10.4018/IJSSCI.2015010102

Boudia, M. A., Hamou, R. M., Amine, A., Rahmani, M. E., & Rahmani, A. (2015). Hybridization of Social Spiders and Extractions Techniques for Automatic Text Summaries. *International Journal of Cognitive Informatics and Natural Intelligence, 9*(3), 65–86. doi:10.4018/IJCINI.2015070104

Boudia, M. A., Hamou, R. M., Amine, A., Rahmani, M. E., & Rahmani, A. (2015, May). A New Multi-layered Approach for Automatic Text Summaries Mono-Document Based on Social Spiders. In *IFIP International Conference on Computer Science and its Applications_x000D_* (pp. 193-204). Springer International Publishing. doi:10.1007/978-3-319-19578-0_16

Boudia, M. A., Rahmani, A., Rahmani, M. E., Djebbar, A., Bouarara, H. A., Kabli, F., & Guandouz, M. (2016). Hybridization Between Scoring Technique and Similarity Technique for Automatic Summarization by Extraction. *International Journal of Organizational and Collective Intelligence, 6*(1), 1–14. doi:10.4018/IJOCI.2016010101

Boudin, F., & Morin, E. (2013, June). Keyphrase Extraction for N-best re-ranking in multi-phrase compression. In *North American Chapter of the Association for Computational Linguistics*. NAACL.

Buckley, C., Singhal, A., & Cardie, C. (1997, June). An Analysis of Statistical and Syntactic Phrases. In RIAO (Vol. 97, pp. 200-214). Academic Press.

Cuevas, E., Cienfuegos, M., Zaldívar, D., & Pérez-Cisneros, M. (2013). A swarm optimization algorithm inspired in the behavior of the social-spider. *Expert System with Applications, 40*(16), 6374-6384.

DeJong, G. (1982). An overview of the FRUMP system. *Strategies for Natural Language Processing*, 113.

Donaway, R. L., Drummey, K. W., & Mather, L. A. (2000, April). A comparison of rankings produced by summarization evaluation measures. In *Proceedings of the 2000 NAACL-ANLP Workshop on Automatic summarization* (vol. 4, pp. 69-78). Association for Computational Linguistics. doi:10.3115/1117575.1117583

Edmundson, H. P. (1963). *Automatic Abstracting. Thompson Ram Wooldridge* Inc.

Fum, D., Guida, G., & Tasso, C. (1982, July). Forward and backward reasoning in automatic abstracting. In *Proceedings of the 9th conference on Computational linguistics* (vol. 1, pp. 83-88). Academia Praha. doi:10.3115/991813.991826

Hamou, R. M., Boudia, M. A., & Amine, A. (n.d.). *A new approach based on the detection of opinion by sentiwordnet for automatic text summaries by extraction*. Academic Press.

Hamou, R. M., Amine, A., & Boudia, A. (2013). A New Meta-Heuristic Based on Social Bees for Detection and Filtering of Spam. *International Journal of Applied Metaheuristic Computing, 4*(3), 15–33. doi:10.4018/ijamc.2013070102

Hamou, R. M., Amine, A., & Lokbani, A. C. (2012). The Social Spiders in the Clustering of Texts: Towards an Aspect of Visual Classification. *International Journal of Artificial Life Research, 3*(3), 1–14. doi:10.4018/jalr.2012070101

Hamou, R. M., Amine, A., & Rahmani, M. (2012). A new biomimetic approach based on social spiders for clustering of text. In Software Engineering Research, Management and Applications 2012 (pp. 17-30). Springer Berlin Heidelberg. doi:10.1007/978-3-642-30460-6_2

Hovy, E., Lin, C. Y., Zhou, L., & Fukumoto, J. (2006, May). Automated summarization evaluation with basic elements. In *Proceedings of the Fifth Conference on Language Resources and Evaluation (LREC 2006)* (pp. 604-611). Academic Press.

Kim, S. N., Medelyan, O., Kan, M. Y., & Baldwin, T. (2010, July). Semeval-2010 task 5: Automatic keyphrase extraction from scientific articles. In *Proceedings of the 5th International Workshop on Semantic Evaluation* (pp. 21-26). Association for Computational Linguistics.

Kintsch, W., & Van Dijk, T. A. (1978). Toward a model of text comprehension and production. *Psychological Review, 85*(5), 363–394. doi:10.1037/0033-295X.85.5.363

Lin, C. Y., Cao, G., Gao, J., & Nie, J. Y. (2006, June). An information-theoretic approach to automatic evaluation of summaries. In *Proceedings of the main conference on Human Language Technology Conference of the North American Chapter of the Association of Computational Linguistics* (pp. 463-470). Association for Computational Linguistics. doi:10.3115/1220835.1220894

Litvak, M., & Last, M. (2008, August). Graph-based keyword extraction for single-document summarization. In *Proceedings of the workshop on Multi-source Multilingual Information Extraction and Summarization* (pp. 17-24). Association for Computational Linguistics. doi:10.3115/1613172.1613178

Louis, A., & Nenkova, A. (2009, August). Automatically evaluating content selection in summarization without human models. In *Proceedings of the 2009 Conference on Empirical Methods in Natural Language Processing* (vol. 1, pp. 306-314). Association for Computational Linguistics. doi:10.3115/1699510.1699550

Luhn, H. P. (1958). The automatic creation of literature abstracts. *IBM Journal of Research and Development, 2*(2), 159–165. doi:10.1147/rd.22.0159

Mani, I. (2001). *Automatic summarization* (Vol. 3). John Benjamins Publishing. doi:10.1075/nlp.3

Mani, I., House, D., Klein, G., Hirschman, L., Firmin, T., & Sundheim, B. (1999, June). The TIPSTER SUMMAC text summarization evaluation. In *Proceedings of the ninth conference on European chapter of the Association for Computational Linguistics* (pp. 77-85). Association for Computational Linguistics. doi:10.3115/977035.977047

Mani, I., Klein, G., House, D., Hirschman, L., Firmin, T., & Sundheim, B. (2002). SUMMAC: A text summarization evaluation. *Natural Language Engineering, 8*(01), 43–68. doi:10.1017/S1351324901002741

Minel, J. (2004). Le résumé automatique de textes: solutions et perspectives. *Traitement automatique des langues, 45*(1), 14.

Paroubek, P., Zweigenbaum, P., Forest, D., &Grouin, C. (2012). *Indexation libre et contrôlée d'articles scientifiques Pré-sentation et résultats du défi fouille de textes DEFT2012*. Actes du huitième DÉfi Fouille de Textes.

Pereira, D. R., Pazoti, M., Pereira, L., & Papa, J. P. (2014, December). A social-spider optimization approach for support vector machines parameters tuning. In *Swarm Intelligence (SIS), 2014 IEEE Symposium on* (pp. 1-6). IEEE. doi:10.1109/SIS.2014.7011769

Saffre, F., Furey, R., Krafft, B., & Deneubourg, J. L. (1999). Collective decision-making in social spiders: Dragline-mediated amplification process acts as a recruitment mechanism. *Journal of Theoretical Biology, 198*(4), 507–517. doi:10.1006/jtbi.1999.0927 PMID:10373351

Salton, G., Singhal, A., Mitra, M., & Buckley, C. (1997). Automatic text structuring and summarization. *Information Processing & Management, 33*(2), 193–207. doi:10.1016/S0306-4573(96)00062-3

Teufel, S., &Moens, M. (1999). Argumentative classification of extracted phrases as a first step towards flexible abstracting. *Advances in Automatic Text Summarization, 155*, 171.

Van Dijk, T. A. (1985). Handbook of discourse analysis. Discourse and Dialogue.

APPENDIX

Corpus: Hurricane

Hurricane Gilbert heads toward Dominican Coast. By Ruddy Gonzalez. Associated Press Writer .Santo Domingo, Dominican Republic (AP).

Hurricane Gilbert Swept toward the Dominican Republic Sunday, and the Civil Defense alerted its heavily populated south coast to prepare for high winds, heavy rains, and high seas. The storm was approaching from the southeast with sustained winds of 75 mph gusting to 92 mph. "There is no need for alarm," Civil Defense Director Eugenio Cabral said in a television alert shortly after midnight Saturday. Cabral said residents of the province of Barahona should closely follow Gilbert's movement.

An estimated 100,000 people live in the province, including 70,000 in the city of Barahona, about 125 miles west of Santo Domingo. Tropical storm Gilbert formed in the eastern Caribbean and strengthened into a hurricane Saturday night. The National Hurricane Center in Miami reported its position at 2 a.m. Sunday at latitude 16.1 north, longitude 67.5 west, about 140 miles south of Ponce, Puerto Rico, and 200 miles southeast of Santo Domingo. The National Weather Service in San Juan, Puerto Rico, said Gilbert was moving westward at 15 mph with a "broad area of cloudiness and heavy weather" rotating around the center of the storm. The weather service issued a flash flood watch for Puerto Rico and the Virgin Islands until at least 6 p.m. Sunday. Strong winds associated with the Gilbert brought coastal flooding, strong southeast winds, and up to 12 feet to Puerto Rico's south coast. There were no reports on casualties. San Juan, on the north coast, had heavy rains and gusts Saturday, but they subsided during the night. On Saturday, Hurricane Florence was downgraded to a tropical storm, and its remnants pushed inland from the U.S. Gulf Coast. Residents returned home, happy to find little damage from 90 mph winds and sheets of rain. Florence, the sixth named storm of the 1988 Atlantic storm season, was the second hurricane. The first, Debby, reached minimal hurricane strength briefly before hitting the Mexican coast last month.

Chapter 16
Complex Biological Data Mining and Knowledge Discovery

Fatima Kabli
Dr. Tahar Moulay University of Saida, Algeria

ABSTRACT

The mass of data available on the Internet is rapidly increasing; the complexity of this data is discussed at the level of the multiplicity of information sources, formats, modals, and versions. Facing the complexity of biological data, such as the DNA sequences, protein sequences, and protein structures, the biologist cannot simply use the traditional techniques to analyze this type of data. The knowledge extraction process with data mining methods for the analysis and processing of biological complex data is considered a real scientific challenge in the search for systematically potential relationships without prior knowledge of the nature of these relationships. In this chapter, the authors discuss the Knowledge Discovery in Databases process (KDD) from the Biological Data. They specifically present a state of the art of the best known and most effective methods of data mining for analysis of the biological data and problems of bioinformatics related to data mining.

INTRODUCTION

In recent years, Bioinformatics has experienced important development, linked the culmination of many works of sequencing, which having led to the arrival of enormous biological quantity of data with different type (DNA, proteins, RNA), all these data are grouped in a variety of databases in their volume and nature. So, it is necessary to implement computer strategies to gain maximum knowledge. The application of data mining techniques in the genomic data is considered as a particular difficult task, represents a real scientific challenge, based on an exploratory analysis of data, to search the systematically potential relationships without prior knowledge of the relationships nature; in order to help the biologist to understand the function of genes and their structures. The biological data mining help the biologist to solve the essential questions for understand the function of genes: what is the role of a gene in which biological process it is involved? How the genes are regulated? What are the genes involved in a particular disease? And many other questions about the structures and functions of genes and proteins.

DOI: 10.4018/978-1-5225-3004-6.ch016

Many data mining techniques have been applied to answer these questions; the classification, clustering, association rules and text mining, this chapter is structured around four stages:

(1) An introduction to biological information with different types of representation format and biological databases available on the internet, (2) A state of the art of bioinformatics and its application fields, (3) the KDD biological process steps with biological data mining methods, (4) the relation among the bioinformatics problems and data mining. Finally, we conclude our chapter.

BIOLOGICAL DATA

Molecular Sequences

To understand the bioinformatics fields, it is necessary to have a rudimentary biology knowledge. This section gives a brief introduction to some basic concepts of molecular biology that are relevant to bioinformatics problems.

Our body consists many organs. Each organism consists of a number of tissues, and each tissue considered as a collection of similar cells that perform a specialized function.

The individual cell is the minimum auto reductive unit in all living species. It performs two different functions:

- Storage and transmission of genetic information to keep life from one generation to another, this information is stored in the form of bi-catenary DNA
- Perform the necessary chemical reactions to keep our life, through proteins that are produced by the transcription of DNA portions to ARN to protein.

The three basic types of molecules are deoxyribonucleic acid (DNA), ribonucleic acid (RNA) and proteins are present in a cell, in this section we discuss these three main molecules.

DNA

Deoxyribonucleic acid (DNA) is the genetic material of all organisms (with the exception of certain viruses), it stores the instructions necessary for the cell to perform the vital functions.

The correct structure of the DNA was deduced by (J.D.Watson and F.H.C.Crick, 1953), they deduced that the DNA consists of two antiparallel strands that are wound around each other to form a double helix. Each strand is a chain of small molecules called nucleotides.

The types of nucleotides depend on the type of the nitrogenous bases, which are adenine (A), guanine (G), cytosine (C), thymine (T).

According to the analysis of E.Charga and colleagues, it is deduced that the concentration of Thymine is always equal to the concentration of adenine and the concentration of cytosine is always equal to the concentration of guanine. This observation strongly suggests that A and T as well as C and G have some fixed relation.

Figure 1. Double helix of DNA

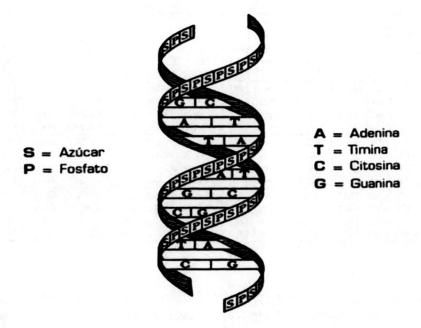

S = Azúcar
P = Fosfato

A = Adenina
T = Timina
C = Citosina
G = Guanina

RNA

Ribonucleic acid (RNA) is the nucleic acid produced during Transcription (obtaining the RNA sequence from the DNA sequence). Exceptionally, RNA is used as genetic material instead of DNA, in some organisms, such as viruses.

The RNA uses the U-base instead of the T-base of DNA. The base U is chemically similar to T. In particular, U is also complementary to A.

Protein

A protein is a very large biological molecule composed of a chain of smaller molecules called amino acids. There are 20 types of amino acids and each one has different chemical properties. The 20 amino acids obtained after the translation of three nucleotides, is specified by a translation table called "genetic code". The genetic code is universal for all organisms.

The length of a protein in the range of 20 to more than 5000 amino acids. On average, contains about 350 amino acids, there are four levels of protein structure: primary, secondary, tertiary and quaternary structures.

Biological Databases

The origin of bioinformatics field has been associated with the need of databases containing biological, biochemical and clinical data, a biological database is a large organized body of persistent data, with different types of sequences (DNA, RNA, Proteins), experimental data, etc.

Table 1. Genetic code

		T	C	A	G	
T		TTT Phe [F] TTC Phe [F] TTA Leu [L] TTG Leu [L]	TCT Ser [S] TCC Ser [S] TCA Ser [S] TCG Ser [S]	TAT Tyr [Y] TAC Tyr [Y] TAA Ter [end] TAG Ter [end]	TGT Cys [C] TGC Cys [C] TGA Ter [end] TGG Trp [W]	T C A G
C		CTT Leu [L] CTC Leu [L] CTA Leu [L] CTG Leu [L]	CCT Pro [P] CCC Pro [P] CCA Pro [P] CCG Pro [P]	CAT His [H] CAC His [H] CAA Gln [Q] CAG Gln [Q]	CGT Arg [R] CGC Arg [R] CGA Arg [R] CGG Arg [R]	T C A G
A		ATT Ile [I] ATC Ile [I] ATA Ile [I] ATG Met [M]	ACT Thr [T] ACC Thr [T] ACA Thr [T] ACG Thr [T]	AAT Asn [N] AAC Asn [N] AAA Lys [K] AAG Lys [K]	AGT Ser [S] AGC Ser [S] AGA Arg [R] AGG Arg [R]	T C A G
G		GTT Val [V] GTC Val [V] GTA Val [V] GTG Val [V]	GCT Ala [A] GCC Ala [A] GCA Ala [A] GCG Ala [A]	GAT Asp [D] GAC Asp [D] GAA Glu [E] GAG Glu [E]	GGT Gly [G] GGC Gly [G] GGA Gly [G] GGG Gly [G]	T C A G

Historically, the biological sequencing process began with amino acid sequences in proteins, there are many bioinformatics projects involving database technology, these databases include "public" repositories of genetic data and "private" databases such as those used by research groups or Held by biotechnology companies

Currently, there is rapid growth in the volume of data stored in biological databases, which are also increasing. There are dense links between different databases, since they often contain information about several aspects. In addition, there are a considerable number of Internet resources related to search and navigation in databases and certain algorithms processing and data inference.

In recent years, the number of biological sequences (protein, DNA and RNA) and experimental data have grown exponentially (doubling every 18 months), these sequences are submitted to banks of biological data; in this part we have referred to some types of databases of biological sequences.

Genomic Databases (DNA)

GenBank is the most well-known genomic database, maintained by NCBI (National Center for Biotechnology Information) (https://www.ncbi.nlm.nih.gov/), It contains all nucleic acid and amino acid sequences, its content is reflected by two other databases, EMBL (http://www.ebi.ac.uk/) and DDBJ (http://www.ddbj.nig.ac.jp/) .

Many databases contain more specialized information on genomic sequences. As the SNP (Single Nucleotide Polymorphisms) database, it is a database of the consortium for biomedical research (http://snp.cshl.org/), the promoter gene database and cisRED regulatory sequences, (http://meme.sdsc.edu/meme/intro.html, and also the database for the standardization of the no-menclature of genes (http://www.gene.ucl.ac.uk/nomenclature/index.html).

Protein Databases

On account of the correspondence between the amino acid sequences and the codon sequences, there are strong links between the protein and nucleotide databases, both types of sequences are available in GenBank (https://www.ncbi.nlm.nih.gov/genbank/) Data of amino acid sequences, taxonomy, functional aspects, families and protein domains, classification, secondary and 3D structures of proteins, are stored in protein databases (http://scop.mrc-lmb.cam.ac.uk/).

KDD PROCESS AND BIO-DATA MINING

Biological KDD Process

With the recent development of proteomic and genomic studies, Biological data have increased considerably and diversified. These data are then presented in the form of sequences or information that come from direct submissions by the authors, via the Internet or other appropriate electronic means.

We then find

- Sequences and gene expression data (DNA, RNA, Protein).
- Annotation information (functions) of genes, proteins, etc.

Although, the general process of KDD (Knowledge Discovery in Databases) is particularly standard. It nevertheless presents specific treatments from one stage to another relative to the nature of the data processed, in this section we will present the KDD process includes the following five steps: data selection, pre-processing, transformation, data mining, knowledge evaluation and interpretation, showing from one stage to another, (see Figure 2).

Figure 2. Knowledge discovery process

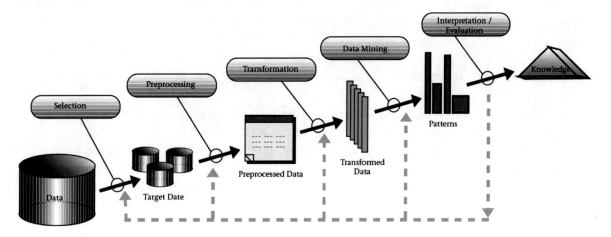

Data Selection

Access to data over the Internet via specialized interfaces for download the selected experimental samples according to criteria set by the user. use the data access and retrieval system, which allows to interrogate a collection of sequences available in deferent format (detailed above), it also allows the retrieval and extraction of data relating to nucleotide or protein sequences, associated bibliographic references, and collections of genomic and structural sequences, by means of a simple interrogation of the server.

Pre-Processing of Data

Pre-processing step involves to formatting and cleaning data in an appropriate format for efficient exploitation help to manage all types of biological data and improve their quality. The Basic data pre-processing methods can be organized in categories: the data Cleaning methods are used to detect and delete redundant, outliers and incomplete data, the data Transformation methods, help to Transform the data from a space of large dimension to a small dimension for reduce the effort in the phase of data mining, Data Discretization methods are consist to convert the continuous value variables into discrete values to represent the original variables because some learning algorithms can only adapted with discrete value variables.

Data Mining

This is the core of the KDD biological process. The extraction of knowledge is Made from this step. Consists in deriving a set of knowledge from the pre-processed data. Using a set of algorithms and machine learning techniques detailed in the 3.2 step.

Knowledge Evaluation and Interpretation

In most cases, the knowledge extracted in the data mining step is not all profitable. Indeed, it is difficult to have directly valid knowledge usable by the human user, Therefore, for most data mining techniques, there are many techniques for evaluate the extracted models. These techniques help to correct the models, and adjust them to data. Depending on the accuracy degree of the knowledge returned, the domain expert decides to stop the KDD process or restart it from a specific step until the biological knowledge obtained is new, interpretable, valid and useful to the Data Miner.

BIOLOGICAL DATA MINING

The complexity of the enormous biological information available on the Internet and its evolution continues over time, it become very difficult to analyze it, so it is necessary to apply effective approaches to solve the problems of biological information processing that detailed in the previous bioinformatics step. while, the traditional approaches of biological data analysis are not effective and produce only a very limited information compared to many current mechanisms, the knowledge extraction and biological data mining methods can answer to these new trends.

In the following; we will present the most used and more efficient techniques and algorithms in deferent aspects of data mining (clustering, classification, association rules and text mining) for the analysis and processing of biological data.

- **Clustering of Biological Data:** Clustering has been recognized as one of the most commonly used data mining techniques, helps to analyze and extract knowledge hidden in biological data. Large number of methods have been developed, and several research studies have been conducted in order to cluster analysis particularly for biological data.

The complex relationships between genes or proteins can participate to determine the biological function, when we want to define the function of new biological data with one of the clustering methods, the similar genomic or proteomic sequences are clustered according to a similarity measure, the sequences that share similar properties included in the same cluster, this task is also referred to as segmentation. In machine learning, it is necessary that the number of clusters and categories are not known in advance.

The main challenges concerning the application of clustering to biological sequences are:

Defining the Appropriate Distance Between Objects

The similarity between the objects is defined by the distance between them. The choice of the distance plays an important role in the cluster analysis. Several distance measurements (Euclidean, Manhattan, Chebyshev, etc.) (J.Han and M.Kamber, 2000) can be calculated, depending on the problem studied. However, these distance measures are not always adequate to detect correlations between objects (H.Wang et al, 2002),which measure the similarity between the forms of two expression gene patterns. However, they are not robust with outlier values. The cosine correlation was found to be more robust on the aberrant values because it computes the cosine of the angle between the expression gene value vectors.

The Choice of the Clustering Algorithm

Several algorithms were previously designed for the clustering of gene expression data in order to solve different biological problems. Some of these algorithms have proved to be good in the biological domain, achieve good results and accelerate the analysis process. As they divide the data samples into different groups. (1) the data samples in the same cluster are similar and (2) the data samples of different clusters are dissimilar.

There are many clustering algorithms in the literature. That can be classified into different categories. Among the existing clustering algorithms, the most widely used methods are partitioning methods, hierarchical methods, self-organizing map (SOM), and new algorithms, which specifically address gene expression data, have been proposed (Datta & Datta, 2006).

Classification of Biological Data

The classification decides the class of an unclassified data sample. There must be at least two predefined classes. Therefore, to classify a sample it is necessary to define its attributes and the classification model to decide at the end the class to which the sample of data belongs.

Classification of biological samples is an important technique for data mining, especially in the context of cancer research, diagnosis of a tissue sample from its phenotype, pattern recognition, medical diagnosis, prediction Defects in industry and biological applications etc.

The most widely used classification algorithms to gene data analysis belong four categories: Random forest (RF), Bayesian classifiers, neural networks and support vector machines (SVM).

Random Forest (RF)

In the applications of bioinformatics for the classification of biological data, the RF algorithm is widely used, Because the application of RF gives a high precision and provide additional information about the functionality of genes and proteins. RF is an evolution of the decision tree exploited for the analysis of biological data (Breiman, 2001) characterized by a set of individual decision trees, where each tree in the forest builds with a random subset of data samples. Therefore, to predict the class of a new sample, each decision tree in the forest launches an unweighted vote for the sample, the majority vote determines the class of the sample. Díaz-Uriart and Alvarez (2006) showed good RF performance for noisy and multi-class genomic.

Support Vector Machines (SVM)

SVM is a learning algorithm, introduced by Vapnik (1998), aims to separate the two sets of data by a separation hyperplane (one class is defined as the positive class and another class is called the negative class). SVM has been applied to a number of tasks, that involve the classification of yeast genes into functional categories by Brown et al. (2000), describe the application of SVM to the recognition of colon cancer tissues) (Moller et al., 2000; Carter et al., 2001). The application of SVM to the problem of recognition of functional RNAs in genomic DNA (Segal et al., 2003) also use SVM to develop a genome-based classification scheme for clear cell sarcoma and several Other tasks (William Stafford Noble, 2003).

Neural Networks (ANN)

A network of artificial neurons is a mathematical model schematically inspired by the operation of biological neurons, allow to create rapid classifications, it is defined as a set of artificial neurons (units) that are organized in layers. The input layer is simply composed of the original data, and the output layers represent the classes. Units that can connected, that belong to two consecutive layers. A unit receives information from several units belonging to the previous layer.

The ANNs have been applied to a number of bioinformatics tasks, which are proven to be very effective. In the context of microarray analysis, (Linder, 2007) presented a review of the advantages and disadvantages of neural networks, other works presented a multi-class protein classification system based on neural networks. ANNs were also applied to predict the tertiary structure of proteins, ANN-based technique applied for predicting secondary protein structure.

Bayesian Classifiers

Bayesian classifier Based on the idea of estimate the probability that a document belongs to a category, know the probability that a category corresponds to this document, Using the Bayes theorem. The Naïve Bayes classifier is known to be a robust method, can be trained efficiently in a supervised learning context and shows on average a good performance in terms of classification accuracy.

Vijayarani and Deepa (2014) applied the naïve Bayesian method for the classification of protein sequences of diseases. The KNN approach (Fix et al., 1949) has been popular in the Biological, (Deshpande et al., 2002; Lu et al., 2003) Given a database of pre-classified sequences, classifying a new sequence by searching for k similar sequences in the database. The class that contains the majority of these k sequences is the class assigned to the new unclassified sequence. HMM-based approaches (Rabiner, 1989) for protein sequences classification have demonstrated their efficacy for the detection of residue patterns conserved in a set of protein sequences. (Eddy et al., 1995; Hughey et al., 1996).

Extraction of Association Rules From the Biological Data

The extraction of association rules is a descriptive method of data mining. It can be defined as the search of relationships between Items in a data set. This technique is widely used for the analysis of baskets, In its most common version, an association rule is characterized as follows A={a1,a2,...,am} set of items, and T={i1,i2,...,in} a set of transactions, Each transaction is assigned a subset of A, an association rule is defined by: X → Y, wherein X,Y ⊆ A and X∩Y=∅. Each rule induces two concepts, the support and confidence, measure respectively the scope and the precision of the rule. The most used algorithms are Apriori, AIS, FP-Growth, (Agrawal et al., 1993), AIS (Agrawal et Srikant, 1994)

Algorithm Apriori

Apriori is used to construct frequent candidate itemsets and then verifies which of them are frequent. For the generation frequent k-itemsets, the set of (k-1) frequent candidates is exploited, the process of extracting frequent items presents four steps:

1. Generate the set of items candidate Ci.
2. Calculate the frequencies (support) of generated itemsets.
3. Keep the itemset with the support value higher than the minimum support threshold (minsup).
4. Keep the rules with a confidence value higher than the minimum threshold (MinConf).

FP-Growth Algorithm

The main disadvantages of the APRIORI algorithm is not only the generation of a large number of candidate itemset, but also runs the database several times, (Han et al, 2000) proposed an algorithm, called FP-GROWTH, without the generation of candidates. The FP-Growth adopts a division-and-conquer strategy to discover all frequent items, Based on the tree data structure. FP-Growth allows to discover the frequent itemsets by two stages:

1. The construction of the tree FP-Tree.
2. Extraction of frequent itemset from the FP-tree.

Other type of recent algorithms for association rules extraction, based on the special treatment of the genomic data, the most known is GenMiner (Martinez et al., 2008), is an implementation of association rules discovering, appropriate to the treatment of the genomic data, It measures sets from multiple data sources taking into account the discrete values, such as gene annotations, and continuous values, Genminer integrate two algorithms NorDi and close, measure respectively the (normalizing and discretizing) continuous values and select the non-redundant association rules. other works Based on several genetic sources (Carmona-Saez, 2006), with the possibility of analyzing genes annotated in different ways, whereas the authors (Pei et al., 2007), tried to cross heterogeneous data. For enhance the relevance of the results.

BIOINFORMATICS

Definition

Bioinformatics is the science of managing, analyzing, extracting and interpreting information from sequences and biological molecules. Is an area of active research since the late 1980s. Combines the technologies of computing, statistics and optimization, Therefore, the objectives of bioinformatics are:

1. Organize and save the biological data.
2. Develop tools to facilitate data analysis and management.
3. Use biological data to analyze and interpret results biologically.

Fields of Bioinformatics

The real challenge in bioinformatics is: how to solve the scientific problems posed by the biologist. Due to the complexity of biological data, there are many challenging research questions in bioinformatics, but it is very difficult to provide a complete problems categorization. In general, the problems associated with data analysis in bioinformatics can be divided into three classes according the type of biological data: sequences, structures and networks.

Sequences Bioinformatics

The primary sequences of DNA, RNA and proteins have an importance in the life sciences, Bioinformatics of sequences, help to analyze the data derived from the genetic information contained in these three types of sequences.

Numerous bioinformatics problems, focus on sequence studies, by multiple analysis and comparison of sequences, identification of sequences from experimental data, Identification of similarities between sequences, Sequences classification and regression, identifying genes or biologically relevant regions in DNA or proteins, Based on the base components (nucleotides, amino acids).

Sequence Analysis and Comparison

Many fields of modern molecular biology, based on the multiple analysis and comparison of biological sequences, which are considered as a fundamental bioinformatics problem

Similarity

This is the percentage of conservative identities and / or substitutions between sequences. The degree of similarity is quantified by a score. The result of the search for a similarity can be used to infer the homology of sequences.

Homology

Two sequences are homologous if they have a common ancestor. Homology is measured by similarity: significant similarity is a sign of homology unless the sequences have a low complexity that is defined as regions that contain few different characters.

The Alignment

Sequence alignment based on the arranging of DNA, RNA, or protein sequences to identify similar regions that may be a consequence of structural, functional, or evolutionary relationships between sequences.

The alignment process based on the insertion of the "holes" in one of the two sequences where there are non-identical letters (amino acids or nucleotides), what is called "mismatches". In order to maximize the number of coincidences of characters between the two sequences.

Some methods represent the alignment by a matrix (N, M), N defines the sequences and M defines the sequences components (amino acids or nucleotides), The values of the matrix defined by three deferent scores (match = + 2, mismatch = -1, grap = -2), Signified (identical, not identical, hole) respectively. Therefore, the similarity between two sequences is defined by the alignment score value, which is calculated by a similarity function, the best known of which is SUM-OF-PAIR (SP). The distance SP is defined as som ($1 \leq i < j \leq k$ dM (S'i, S'j)) where dM (S'i, S 'j) is equal to the sum of the distance score of each pair Aligned.

Pairwise Alignment

Pairwise sequence alignment, as suggested by its name, is a comparison of two biological sequences (protein or nucleic acid) only.

Multiple Alignment

Multiple alignment is a comparison of many biological sequences together to identify regions of similarity that may indicate functional, structural or evolutionary relationships.

Example

S1=ACG_ _GAGA

S2=_CGTTGACA

S3=AC_T_GA_A

S4=CCGTTCAC_

THE HOMOLOGOUS ANALYSIS

The identification of homologous genes, is one of the main applications of sequence alignment, while living organisms share a large number of genes derived from common ancestors and have been maintained in different organisms according to its functionality, but accumulate the differences that have diverged from each other.

Identification of the Sequences From the Experimental Data

The Identification of sequences from the experimental data it is an important problem of bioinformatics, determine the biological sequences from the data generated by experiments in wet laboratories. Due to the significant differences between the technologies and the methods used to generate experimental data. The sequence identification problem has several variants which are totally different in calculation point of view. In order to better understand, we discus below about the problems of identification of DNA sequences and protein sequences.

Identification of DNA Sequence From Sequencing Data

The Identification of DNA sequences technology is widely used. In DNA sequencing, many copies of the original DNA sequence are cut into millions of fragments, each copy is cut in a different way. So, a fragment of one copy can overlap fragments of another. For a given set of fragments, the sequence assembly consists of aligning and fusing fragments to reconstitute the original DNA sequence.

Biological Sequence Classification

In molecular biology, there is some correlation between the primary sequence of DNA, functional and structural properties of proteins, that poses a problem of sequences properties prediction and relationships that are not fully understood, so we must call in this case the methods of computational prediction and machine learning.

The Biological Sequence classification is an important problem in computational biology. Helps to identify protein domains from their Structures which are linked to a particular biological function, to identify also the interest regions of the particular sequence, detection of homology between proteins etc.

Numerous effective classification approaches that are called in many works, specifically to solve the biological classification problem. Such as the generative models (ex HMMs (Krogh, 1994), discriminative models (Jaakkola et al 2000; Leslie et al, 2003).

SVMs have better prediction performance on biological sequence data than other methods (Jaakkola et al 2000; Leslie et al, 2003; Liao & Stafford, 2002; Weston, 2005) In addition, it has been shown in Weston (2005) that random-walk kernels (Szummer & .Jaakkola, 2002) and empirical-map kernels (Scholkopf et al, 2001) have produced good results on the detection of homology between the proteins based on classification process.

STRUCTURAL BIOINFORMATICS

One of the most important branches of molecular biology is structural biology, many bioinformatics researchers focus on the study of the tertiary structures of macromolecules such as RNA and proteins.

The problems of bioinformatics related to the tertiary structure of macromolecules can be divided into three different classes: Multiple structure analysis, structure prediction, and structure-based prediction.

Multiple Structure Analysis

Many applications in the life science focus on the comparison of multiple structures and the discovery of common models from a set of structures (RNA / Protein). To reveal the relationships between protein sequences, structures and functions, and characterizing families of proteins that are functionally or structurally related. We call the multiple structure analysis

Two major problems of bioinformatics in this category are structural alignment and structural motifs discovery:

- **Structural Alignment:** Helps to establish the homology Between two or more structures based on their three-dimensional structure. This process is usually applied to protein tertiary structures but can also be used for large RNA molecules. Which can transfer the information about a well-known protein to unknown proteins that can be structurally aligned to it.
- **Structural Motif Discovery:** The structural motif discovery process helps to detect global and local motifs in a proteins database without the need to multiple structure or sequence alignments and without relying on prior classification of proteins into families, such Motifs are useful for reveal interesting evolution and functional relationships among proteins when the sequence similarity between proteins is very low.

Structure Prediction

Due to the difficulty to obtain the tertiary structure of RNA and protein primary sequences by wet laboratory experiments. Large number of prediction tools have been developed over the past 20 years, these tools adopt different principles such as modeling by homology, threading of proteins, And ab initio methods.

Structure-Based Prediction

The functions of proteins in the cell are determined just by the tertiary structure, so this structure is important information in several bioinformatics applications that can be called "structure-based prediction" as the prediction of protein- Proteins, drug targets and prediction of protein functions.

NETWORK BIOINFORMATICS

Complex biological systems are generally presented and analyzed as networks, which are concerned as interactions between genes, proteins, cells, organisms, where the biological units represent the vertices of network and interactions between units represent the arcs. This part of the bioinformatic feeds in particular data from high-throughput analysis technologies such as proteomics or transcriptomics to analyze genetic or metabolic flows. There are three axes of research in bioinformatics networks are: (1) network analysis, (2) network inference, and (3) network assisted prediction.

BIOINFORMATICS PROBLEMS RELATED TO DATA MINING

Gene Prediction

Hidden Markov models are involved in many sequence analysis algorithms, whether for the detection of genes. Inference and pattern detection, or the search for exceptional words. The HMM2 hidden Markov models have a great utility in the segmentation of large DNA sequences in large classes deduced from short sequences rich in biological semantics. This segmentation is used to produce sets of co-regulated genes that are likely to have related functions (Hergalant et al., 2002).

Finding Frequent Patterns

The search for repeated sequences (frequent patterns), in tandem or repeated and in dispersion over the whole genome, such as tandem search is defined as a sequence of several adjacent nucleotide patterns in a DNA sequence and which Repeat identically. For example: ATTCGATTCGATTCG contains three tandem repeats of the pattern of five ATTCG nucleotides. On the other hand, the repeating patterns in dispersion are repeated at several places on the chromosomes, (Hergalant et al., 2002) used Hidden Markov Models of order 2 to classify a residue or a group of nucleotide residues.

Heterogeneity Search

One of the main methods of detecting a pathogen in a genome is the detection of heterogeneous areas in genes, (Hergalant et al., 2002), based on hidden Markov models and showed a high capacity for detect the heterogeneity.

Search for Similarities and Alignment Study

Its aim is to identify places where identical or very close regions exist between two sequences, also to deduce those which are significant and which correspond to a biological meaning by a simple comparison between sequences can be local (Local Alignment) or global (Global Alignment) with a database. Several programs have been created that are best known and most used by biologists are FASTA and BLAST (Chervitz et al., 1999).

Identification of Coding and Non-Coding Genes

It is necessary to identify significant DNA subunits for functional genomic exploitation, Data mining methods have been used to allow the segmentation of large DNA sequences into different classes, and analyze these classes.

The Extraction of Frequent Patterns and Search for Association

The extraction of frequent patterns methods has shown good results, has been widely used for the extraction of association rules and genetic profiles for a disease, (Benabdeslem et al., 2007) is based on learning the rules to know the various factors involved in a cancer of the nasopharynx, also, another study in this direction was made on the STANISLAS cohort (Maumus et al., 2005).

Prediction of Diseases

The application of data mining methods to predict the risks of major diseases such as cancers, cardiovascular diseases or cognitive decline, remains a crucial issue, A study was carried out in this direction on a population of 8000 participants, and has shown good predictions of coronary heart disease risk (Maumus et al., 2005). By the application of Bayesian networks.

CONCLUSION

This chapter shows a state of the art of biological KDD (knowledge extraction process from biological data) which consists in analyzing the biological information for the extraction of the appropriate information; we presented several data mining methods, clustering classification, association and illustrate how these methods help to solve the bioinformatics problems.

REFERENCES

Agrawal, R., Swami, A., & Imielinski, T. (1993). Mining Association Rules Between Sets of Items in Large Databases. *Proceedings ACM SIGMOD International Conference on Management of Data*, 207. doi:10.1145/170035.170072

Agrawal, R., & Srikant, R. (1994). Fast Algorithms for Mining Association Rules. *Proceedings of the 20th International Conference on Very Large Data Bases (VLDB'94)*, 487-499.

Krogh, A., Brown, M., & Saira Mian, I. (1994). Hidden markov models in computational biology: Applications to protein modeling. *Journal of Molecular Biology*, *235*(5), 1501–1531. doi:10.1006/jmbi.1994.1104 PMID:8107089

Benabdeslem, K., Lebbah, M., Aussem, A., & Corbex, M. (2007). Approche connexionniste pour l'extraction de profils cas-témoins du cancer du Nasopharynx à partir des données issues d'une étude épidémiologique. *EGC 2007, RNTI, 2007*.

Scholkopf, B., & Smola, A. J. (2001). Learning with Kernels. In Support Vector Machines, Regularization, Optimization, and Beyond. MIT Press.

Carmona-Saez, P., Chagoyen, M., Rodriguez, A., Trelles, O., Carazo, J. M., & Pascual-Montano, A. (2006). Integrated analysis of gene expression by association rules discovery. *BMC Bioinformatics*, *7*(1), 54. doi:10.1186/1471-2105-7-54 PMID:16464256

Chervitz, S. A. Hester, E.T., Ball, C., Dolinski, K., Dwight, S.S., Haris, M.A., … Botstein, D. (1999). Using the Sacharomyces genome databases (SGD) for analysis of protein similarities and structure. Nucleic Acids Research, 27(1).

Leslie, C., Eskin, E., Weston, J., & Noble, W. S. (2003). Mismatch string kernels for SVM protein classification. In S. Becker, S. Thrun, & K. Obermayer (Eds.), *NIPS 2002* (Vol. 15, pp. 1441–1448). Cambridge, MA: MIT Press.

Moler, E. J., Chow, M. L., & Mian, I. S. (2000). Analysis of molecular profile data using generative and discriminative methods. *Physiological Genomics*, *4*, 109–126. PMID:11120872

Fix, E., & Hodges, J. L. (1949). *Discriminatory Analysis, Non-Parametric Discrimination: Consistency Properties* (Technical Report 21-49-004). USAF School of Aviation Medicine.

Han, J., Pei, J., & Yin, Y. (2000). Mining Frequent Patterns without Candidate Generation. *Proceedings of the 2000 ACM-SIGMOD Int'l Conf. on Management of Data*.

Hergalant, S., Aigle, B., Leblond, P., Mari, J. F., & Decaris, B. (2002). Fouille de données à l'aide de HMM: Application à la détection de réitérations intragénomiques. *JOBIM*, *2*, 269–273.

Wang, H., Wang, W., Yang, J., & Yu, P. S. (2002). Clustering by pattern Similarity in large datasets. In *Proceedings of the 2002 ACM SIGMOD International conference on Management of data*. ACM.

Watson, J. D., & Crick, F. H. (1953). Molecular structure of nucleic acids: A structure for deoxyribose nucleic acid. *Nature*, *171*(4356), 737–738. doi:10.1038/171737a0 PMID:13054692

Han, J., & Kamber, M. (2000). *Data Mining: Concepts and Techniques*. San Francisco: Morgan Kaufmann.

Weston, Leslie, Ie, Zhou, Elisseeff, & Noble. (2005). Semi-supervised protein classification using cluster kernels. *Bioinformatics, 21*(15), 3241–3247.

Breiman, L. (2001). Random forests. *Machine Learning, 45*(1), 5–32. doi:10.1023/A:1010933404324

Liao, L., & Stafford Noble, W. (2002). Combining pairwise sequence similarity and Support Vector Machines for remote protein homology detection. Journal of Computational Biology, 225–232. doi:10.1145/565196.565225

Rabiner, L. R. (1989). A tutorial on hidden Markov models and selected applications in speech recognition. *Proceedings of the IEEE, 77*(2), 257–286. doi:10.1109/5.18626

Brown, M. P. S., Grundy, W. N., Lin, D., Cristianini, N., Sugnet, C., & Furey, T. S. Jr. (2000). Knowledge-based analysis of microarray gene expression data using support vector machines. *Proceedings of the National Academy of Sciences of the United States of America, 97*(1), 262–267. doi:10.1073/pnas.97.1.262

Martinez, R., Pasquier, N., & Pasquier, C. (2008). GenMiner: mining non-redundant association rules from integrated gene expression data and annotations. Bioinformatics, 24, 2643-2644. doi:10.1093/bioinformatics/btn490

Szummer & Jaakkola. (2002). Partially labeled classification with markov random walks. In *Advances in Neural Information Processing Systems* (pp. 945–952). MIT Press.

Deshpande, M., & Karypis, G. (2002). Evaluation of techniques for classifying biological sequences. *PAKDD, 2002*, 417–431.

Segal, N. H., Pavlidis, P., Noble, W. S., Antonescu, C. R., Viale, A., Wesley, U. V., & Houghton, A. N. et al. (2003). Classification of clear cell sarcoma as melanoma of soft parts by genomic profiling. *Journal of Clinical Oncology, 21*, 1775–1781. doi:10.1200/JCO.2003.10.108 PMID:12721254

Pei, W., Williams, P.H., Clark, M.D., Stemple, D.L., & Feldman, B. (2007). Environmental and genetic modifiers of squint penetrance during zebrafish embryogenesis. *Development Biology, 308*(2), 368-78.

Díaz-Uriart, R., & Alvarez, S. (2006). Gene selection and classification Of microarray data using random forest. *BMC Bioinformatics, 7*(1), 3. doi:10.1186/1471-2105-7-3 PMID:16398926

Hughey, R., & Krogh, A. (1996). Hidden Markov models for sequence analysis: Extension and analysis of the basic method. *Computer Applications in the Biosciences, 12*, 95–107. PMID:8744772

Linder, R., Richards, T., & Wagner, M. (2007). Microarray data classified by Artificial neural networks. *Methods in Molecular Biology Clifton Then to Towa, 382*, 345–372. doi:10.1007/978-1-59745-304-2_22 PMID:18220242

Datta, S., & Datta, S. (2006). Evaluation of clustering algorithms for gene Expression data. *BMC Bioinformatics, 7*(Suppl4), S17. doi:10.1186/1471-2105-7-S4-S17 PMID:17217509

Eddy. (1995). Multiple alignment using hidden Markov models. *ISMB*, 114–120.

Vijayarani & Deepa. (2014). Naïve Bayes Classification for Predicting Diseases in Haemoglobin Protein Sequences. *International Journal of Computational Intelligence and Informatics, 3*(4).

Jaakkola, Diekhans, & Haussler. (2000). *A discriminative framework for detecting remote protein homologies*. Academic Press.

Vapnik, V. (1998). *Statistical learning theory*. Wiley-Interscience.

Noble. (2003). Support vector machine applications in computational biology. Kernal Methods in Computational Biology, 71-92.

Lu, Y., & Han, J. (2003). Cancer classification using gene expression data. *Information Systems*, *28*(4), 243–268. doi:10.1016/S0306-4379(02)00072-8

Chapter 17
Big Data Analytics in Bioinformatics

Dharmendra Trikamlal Patel
Charotar University of Science and Technology, India

ABSTRACT

Voluminous data are being generated by various means. The Internet of Things (IoT) has emerged recently to group all manmade artificial things around us. Due to intelligent devices, the annual growth of data generation has increased rapidly, and it is expected that by 2020, it will reach more than 40 trillion GB. Data generated through devices are in unstructured form. Traditional techniques of descriptive and predictive analysis are not enough for that. Big Data Analytics have emerged to perform descriptive and predictive analysis on such voluminous data. This chapter first deals with the introduction to Big Data Analytics. Big Data Analytics is very essential in Bioinformatics field as the size of human genome sometimes reaches 200 GB. The chapter next deals with different types of big data in Bioinformatics. The chapter describes several problems and challenges based on big data in Bioinformatics. Finally, the chapter deals with techniques of Big Data Analytics in the Bioinformatics field.

1.0 INTRODUCTION TO BIG DATA ANALYTICS

In last several years, the volume, variety and velocity of data generating in any organization whether big or small reaches to unprecedented level. Such kind of voluminous data is termed as Big Data. Few major trends that is responsible and management of this situation are:

- Internet that has made the information available to everyone. Through Internet people send e-mails, likes face book comments, send tweets, upload photos in face book etc. The data transit via Internet is in voluminous amount and has in variety of types. Internet has given the birth of Internet of Things (IoT) that is one kind of network of manmade things embedded with electronics products, software and sensors which enable things to collect and exchange data. According to Gartner, information technology research and advisory company, revenue generated for IoT things would exceed $300 billion by 2020. IoT and big data are basically considered as two sides

DOI: 10.4018/978-1-5225-3004-6.ch017

of the same coin. Extraction and management of IoT data is the biggest challenge for most of all organization in the world. To manage and extract IoT data properly, organization should set up a proper analytics platform that give performance and can be expanded in future.

- Ubiquitous devices have helped people to connect with everyone and for personal computing activities such as social networking, photo sharing, micro blogging etc. The rise of big data increasingly demanded that data analytics should be supported through ubiquitous devices to enable decision making from anywhere without barrier of specific workplace.
- Cloud Computing has provided infinite computing power with cheapest rate. The cloud is an ideal place for big data because of its scalable storage space, infinite computing power and elastic resources.

Big Data (Bryant et al.,2008) is broad and very complex term for data sets(J. Becla et al.,2009) so traditional way of analytics is inadequate for that. Big Data Analytics is a new way of analytics that is used to make analysis of Big Data. Following is a complete definition of Big Data Analytics.

Big Data Analytics is the proactive process of examining quantitative and qualitative big data to identify useful, hidden, valid, previously unknown patterns and correlations that can be used to make better decisions for any organization.

Basically, analytics have four main approaches and they falls either in reactive or proactive category.

1. Business Intelligence is a reactive approach to generate standard and ad hoc business reports based on certain analytics when they are demanded. This kind of analytics generates reports based on static past.
2. Big Data Business Intelligence (McAfee et al.,2012) is a similar approach as Business Intelligence but applicable on huge data sets.
3. Big Analytics is a proactive approach of analytics (Sandryhaila et al.,2014) that does optimization, text mining, forecasting, statistical analysis, predictive analysis etc. However, it is not applicable on Big Data as traditional storage environment (Balazinska et al.,2009).
4. Big Data Analytics is a proactive approach that is applicable on Big Data. It is helpful for determining hidden, unknown and useful information from terabytes, petabytes and exabytes.

Big Data Analytics deals with Big Data so understanding of Big Data terminology is vital for analysis and interpretation. Next section will deal with the Big Data thoroughly.

1.1 Big Data Overview

There is no specific rule about exactly what size of dataset requires to be considered as "Big". However certain things require defining Big Data such as (a) the requirement for new techniques (Chen et al.,2014) and tools (Shvachko et al.,2010) in order to be able to process it (b) the requirement of software programs that span multiple physical or virtual machines in order to process data efficiently and timely.

Big Data is characterized by four important vectors – volume, variety, velocity and veracity.

- **Volume:** The sheer volume of data is generated and stored in different types of system today. The volume of data is detonation. Mobile devices, Internet of Things(IoT), cloud computing and open source initiatives are major driving factors to generate such kind of voluminous data. Organizations are unaware about how to manage them. Organizations need techniques and tools to manage such sheer volume of data.
- **Variety:** It refers to poly structure nature of recent data. The recent data is not limited to only relational data but also semi structured and unstructured web server log data, web pages, sensor data, social media, e-mail etc. Organizations should setup logical infrastructure in order to analyze all types of data i.e. structured, unstructured and semi structured.
- **Velocity:** It refers how quickly the data is process and retrieval. Traditional databases do not deliver data in quick manner, which is expected to achieve high velocity. Organization need database management system that support high amount of velocity.
- **Veracity:** It refers that the quality of data needs to test as is sourced from many different places. Veracity is most important vector as it affects the overall analytics result.

Based on above discussion, Big Data is defined as "Large and complex data sets, which is voluminous, have wider variety in data which needs velocity and veracity and most importantly traditional tools and techniques are not enough to process them."

1.2 Importance of Big Data

If organizations are able to process Big Data (Zikopoulos et al., 2011) in efficiently and effective manner can lead to improve efficiency in their processes, reduced cost, increased sales; provided better service to customers and improved product and service.

Retailers can know who buys their products. By using social media data and server log data of their e-commerce sites help them to understand buying patterns of their customers. They are able to know who did not buy their products. Retailers are able to achieve targeted marketing campaign.

Financial service providers are able to improve their analysis of customers and able to give improved and quality services to their existing customers. They are also able to identify potential customers as well. Financial institutions like banking need Big Data visibility to cope up from problems of fraud. Big Data is helpful for banking to calculate credit score and set interest rates. Insurance companies can analyze hundreds of dynamic variables to assess the risk and to decide appropriate price of their products.

Due to modern technologies like smart phone and GPS devices have opened up new doors for advertisers. Based on analysis of GPS and smart phone like data, advertisers can pick up targeted customers when there are close to certain venues such as hotel, store, bar etc.

Manufactures collect voluminous real time data from sensors and that is very important to decrease production cost and help to minimize waste by receiving instant alerts. In addition to this, real time analysis of manufacturing data helps to improve visibility from raw materials through finished product. It is very useful to increase useful life of equipment.

Healthcare providers are able to improve the quality of life, avoid preventable deaths, and predict deadly disease. Big data solutions help pharmaceutical companies to track drug importance and reduce drug development cycle.

Using Big Data solutions, media and entertainment industry is able to indentifying audience interest. They are able to understand when customers are most likely to view content with which device. They are able to develop the best promotional strategies to attract and retain customers.

The importance of Big Data is huge for telecommunication industry. Telecommunication companies are able to attract and retain their mobile customers. They understand customer location and travel pattern in order to support real time promotions and advertisement. Due to increase demand of smart devices and growing use of IP based networks; communications related fraud is common for telecommunication industries and those can be eliminated by proper analysis of Big Data.

Big Data can help education industry to reform educational delivery and to help in improving learning experience (Barbu et al.,2013). It is able to equip students with appropriate skills for their upcoming careers.

Travel companies are able to decrease cost and deliver a more electrifying travel experience to their customers. Big Data can help to make travel more approachable and paying attention around travelers' requirements and fondness.

Big Data is very crucial for all kind of industry whether small or big. Cost reduction, Invention of new service and product; and faster, better and improved decision making are three crucial advantages industry get from proper analysis of big data.

1.3 Role of Big Data Analytics

For several years companies have been applying data analytics in order to achieve better decision making. However, most of such kind of analytics (Singh et al.,2012) typically has been for the time being and specific to certain problem. Due to advancement of Information Technology and software tools, companies have started using ever-more sophisticated tools (Bagyamathi et al.,2015) for their daily decision making. In recent times, the growth of digital technologies allows companies to gather gigantic amounts of data. Companies require more powerful techniques to process those data and that gave birth of new era analytics- Big Data Analytics.

Role of Big Data Analytics (Danyel Fisher et al.,2012) is enormous in development of company's growth. Following are several important roles of Big Data Analytics in context to the growth of any organization:

- To create an organizational capability to retort more rapidly to changes.
- Allows organizations to incorporate various data sources with relatively little effort in very small time frame.
- To make business decision making process more intellectual.
- To facilitate organization to recommend more appropriate services to their customers customized to their specific needs.
- To generate outcome that is advantageous to ample range of stake holders across the organization.
- To give insights into errors that help organization reacting rapidly to drift the effect of an operational problem.
- To track competitors more efficiently. New strategies of competitors are perceived immediately.
- To improve service of an organization that leads to more revenue generation for organization.
- To monitor risk competently (Ihaka et al.,1996). Organization can take immediately appropriate action based on detecting risk by analytics.

- To save money of an organization. For example, the cost of storing one terabyte for one year is more than $35,000 for traditional relational kind of databases but for through Big Data technologies it is only nearby $2,000.

2.0 BIG DATA AND BIOINFORMATICS

In Bioinformatics field, large amounts of genomic information become to be obtainable and for that more proficient and specific analysis becomes decisive and significant. Massive genomic information is extremely difficult to analyze using conventional way of analytics. Big Data Analytics is proficient in terms of analyzing voluminous data; that are dramatically increasing in bioinformatics field recently. EBI (European Bioinformatics Institute) had large warehouse of bioinformatics related data and their total storage size is doubling-up every year. Institutes like NCBI (National Center for Biotechnology Information) and NIG (National Institute of Genetics) also had gigantic data about bioinformatics. In such circumstances, the role of Big Data Analytics is crucial in bioinformatics field. The next section of this chapter will deal with different types of Big Data in Bioinformatics field.

2.1 Types of Big Data in Bioinformatics

There are many types of data that are colossal in size and extensively used in bioinformatics field. Table 1 describes main types of Big Data in bioinformatics field with their characteristics.

The next section will deal with in detail about first five types of Big Data as they are immense in size and used profoundly in bioinformatics research.

2.2 Data Based on Gene Expression

Gene Expression data (Ben-Dor, et.al, 2003) is very crucial to investigate the appearance level of thousands of genes over different circumstances. A microarray based databases that consist of microarray gene expression data are used to hoard the quantity data, handle a searchable catalog, and construct the data available to other applications for examination and explanation. Following Figure 1 describes the microarray databases in several distinct classes. Public repositories stick on to precise standards and considered to be used by many analysis applications and groups. A specialized repository allied principally with the product of a particular being, an application outfit, an issue or an examination method, whether it is profit-making, non-profit, or intellectual.

Gene Expression Omnibus (GEO) is a microarray based public repository that freely distributes high-throughput purposeful genomic data presented by the scientific community. GEO contains variety types of data such as microarray based gene expression profiling data; microarray based non-coding RNA profiling data, genome variation profiling by array, serial analysis of Gene Expression, protein array, genome methylation profiling etc. The following Figure 2 indicates the volume and variety of data available in GEO.

The data of GEO is gigantic and contains wide variety of data. Big data analytics is obliging for scientists to drill down through innately strident expression data to genes that are appropriate. Using big data analytics tools and techniques, such a bulky collection of data accessible and analyzing using common edges that could add priceless exploratory extent.

Table 1. Types and characteristics of Big Data in bioinformatics

Sr. No.	Type of Big Data	Characteristics
1.	Gene Expression	A Gene is an elongate of DNA. Gene Expression data sets are huge; consists of more than thousand rows corresponding to the genes and several columns one for each experimental condition measured.
2.	Sequence Data (DNA,RNA, Protein)	Sequence data is used to find out sequence of individual genes, bigger genetics province and whole genomes. Sequencing presents the order of individual nucleotides present in molecules of DNA, RNA or Protein.
3.	PPI data (Protein-Protein Interaction)	It refers to physical associates establish amid two or more proteins as a result of biochemical episode. Proteins seldom act unaided. Many molecular processes inside a cell are carried out by molecular machines that are built from a huge number of protein components organized by their PPIs.
4.	Pathway data	Pathway data is very helpful to identify genes and proteins in order to achieve several biological tasks such as predicting drug targets.
5.	GO (Gene Ontology)	Gene Ontology is helpful for biological processes and molecular functions. They are structured and dynamic related to specific gene ontology.
6.	HDN (Human Disease Network)	It is a plan of human diseases relations; referring generally to disease genes. It is a hefty range human disease network with indication to their genetic origins or other features.
7.	DGAN(Disease Gene Association Network)	It is connection that organizes gigantic amount of medical data about human diseases. It is a kind of map that describes most human diseases with known human genetics.

Figure 1. Microarray based distinct classes

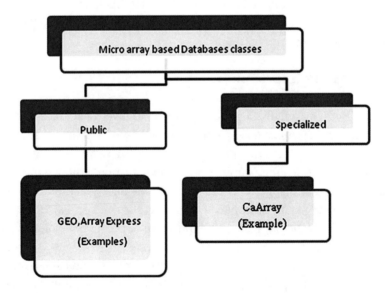

Array Express is another repository suggested by major technical journals to records functional genomics data to carry reproducible research. Array Express consists of different kinds of data which is depicts in following Figure 3. Array Express also contains variety of data so big data analytics techniques and tools are really helpful for such kind of repository.

CaArray is a specialized repository produced by The National Cancer Institute (NCI) Center for Biomedical Informatics and Information Technology (CBIIT). It provides the functionalities of a microarray repository, allowing researchers to share microarray experiment annotations and data. It contains

Figure 2. Volume and variety of data in GEO

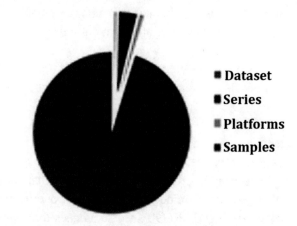

- Dataset
- Series
- Platforms
- Samples

Figure 3. Different kinds of data in Array Express

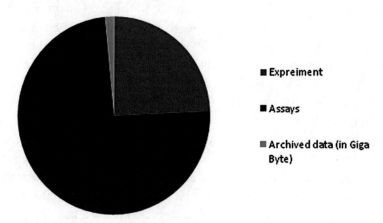

- Expreiment
- Assays
- Archived data (in Giga Byte)

183 microarray experiments. Most of the data are derived from sample of human diseases. It contains variety types of data such as gene expression, Exon, MicroRNA, Methylation, Comparative genomic hybridization etc. To analyze CaArray dataset, techniques and tools of Big Data analytics seems vital as it contains voluminous datasets.

2.3 DNA, RNA, and Protein Sequence Data

Sequence data is one category of biological datasets that is poised of a large set of digital sequences stored on a computer. Sequence databases are produced based on extensive varieties of sources from individual researchers to enormous genome sequencing hub.

UniProt is a best example of sequence database based on protein. It is a wide ranging, premium and freely available database of protein sequence. It contains voluminous quantity of information about biological purpose of proteins derivative from the research literature. UniProt is divided among number of categories such as (a) UniProt Knowledgebase (b) UniProt reference (c) UniParc and (d) Proteomes and (e) Supporting data.

UniProt Knowledgebase is a hub that consists of functional information on proteins with precise, reliable and affluent annotation. It has two main sections: manually annotated and computationally analyzed. Following Figure 4 describes the proportion of annotation in UniProt Knowledgebase. Total number of annotations reaches to 5, 58, 20,795 *.

The UniProt Reference Clusters offer clustered sets of series from the UniProt Knowledgebase and chosen UniParc records. This conceals duplicate sequences and obtains complete exposure of the sequence space at three decrees:

1. **UniRef100:** Mixes matching sequences and sub-fragments with 11 or more filtrates from any organism into a single UniRef entry.
2. **UniRef90:** Assembles by clustering UniRef100 sequences such that each cluster is poised of sequences that have at least 90% sequence uniqueness to, and 80% overlie with, the longest sequence.
3. **UniRef50:** Assembles by clustering UniRef90 seed sequences that have at least 50% sequence identity to, and 80% overlap with, the longest sequence in the cluster.

Total number of sequences is 124,987,186*. The proportion of three categories is depicts in Figure 5.

UniParc is a complete and non-duplicate database that contains a large amount of the openly available protein sequences. Proteins may subsist in different source databases and in numerous replicas in the identical database. UniParc evades such duplication by storing each unique sequence only once. UniParc includes merely protein sequences. All other information regarding the protein must be recovered from the source databases using the database cross-references. Total number of protein sequence in this database is 11, 03, 48,070*.

A proteome is the set of proteins contemplation to be uttered by an organism. Proteomes are divided into mainly two categories: reference and others. Reference proteomes are derived manually and algorithmically. In this database 3,226 * reference and 28,036* other proteomes are available.

Supporting data is also crucial in the research of bioinformatics. This database also contains several supporting data such as literature citations, cross reference databases, taxonomy, diseases, keywords, sub cellular locations etc.

Figure 4. Proportion of annotations in UniProt Knowledgebase

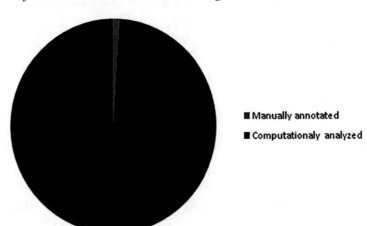

Figure 5. Proportions of categories of UniProt Reference

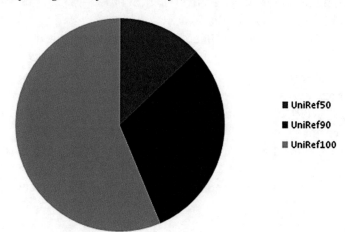

- ■ UniRef50
- ■ UniRef90
- ▩ UniRef100

2.4 Ontology Based on Gene

Gene Ontology (GO) is a main bioinformatics to combine the depiction of gene and gene product features across all species. This gigantic database serves three main purposes:

1. Retains and grows glossary of gene and gene products.
2. Interpret gene and gene product also incorporate and circulate data.
3. Easy access of data based on appropriate tools and techniques.

Gene Ontology is based on collaboration of three gigantic databases such as Flybase, Saccharomyces Genome Database (SGD) and the Mouse Genome Database (MGD). Flybase is a database of drosophila genes and genomes. A wide range of data is presented in different formats. The database proposes numerous diverse query tools in order to give efficient access to the data offered and ease the discovery of momentous associations within the database. The *Saccharomyces* Genome Database (SGD) offers wide-ranging incorporated biological information for the budding yeast *Saccharomyces cerevisiae* along with explore and investigation tools to discover these data, enabling the finding of functional relationships linking sequence and gene products in fungi and higher organisms. Mouse Genome Database (MGD) is a key mold creature for understanding the human genome (E. S. Lander et al.,2001)and human biology. MGD curates and presents the consent depiction of genotype to phenotype information including greatly exhaustive information regarding genes and gene products.

2.5 Protein Based Interaction Data

Protein based interaction data are the foundation of different diseases such as cancer. Protein based interaction data are widely used in the research of bioinformatics.

DIP (Database of Interacting Protein) is a genetic repository which registers experimentally determined relations between proteins. This repository is anticipated to make available the technical society with a wide-ranging and integrated tool for browsing and competently digging out information about protein relations and communication networks in biological processes. The statistics of this repository in context to variety of information depicts in Figure 6.

STRING (Search Tool for the Retrieval of Interacting Genes) is a genetic repository and web resource of well-known and predicted protein-protein interactions. The recent version contains information of 9.6 * millions proteins from more than 2000* organisms. The STRING interactions come from physical and functional associations and derived from genomic context, high throughput experiments, co expression and previous knowledge. STRING quantitatively amalgamates interaction data from these sources for a huge quantity of organisms.

BioGRID (Biological General Repository for Interaction Datasets) is an open access genetic and protein interaction repository contains 9,71,115* genetic relations, 27,034* chemical relations and 38,559 * post translational adaptation from major model organism species and humans.

2.6 Pathway Data

Pathway data is helpful for understanding molecular origin of an illness. It is also very valuable for recognition of genes and proteins associated with an etiology of a disease. To predict drug targets and to conduct targeted literature searches are vital tasks of pathway data analysis.

KEGG (Kyoto Encyclopedia of Genes and Genomes) is a voluminous repository for understanding sophisticated utilities of the genetic organism. It deals with systems, genomic, chemical and health information. System information includes pathway records for cellular functions, modules of genes and hierarchical classifications of biological entities. Genome information deals with genomes, genes and ortholog groups of genes. Chemical information includes chemical reactions, enzyme nomenclature and glycans. Health information consists of human diseases and approved drugs.

Reactome is a repository of pathways and retorts in creature biology. This repository supports genome analysis, modeling, system biology and research. The database contains voluminous annotations that cover diversity of topics such as metabolism, cell motility, neural function, immune function etc. Reactome contains voluminous datasets of species, proteins, complexes, reactions, pathways etc. Figure 7 describes the statistics of this gigantic repository.

Figure 6. Statistics of variety of information of DIP

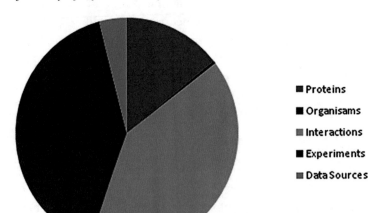

Pathway Commons is a set of openly accessible pathway information from multiple organisms. This gigantic repository contains 31,698* pathways, 11, 51,476* interactions and 18* different sources. Pathways common can comprise biochemical effects, multifarious assembly, transport and catalysis events, physical connections involving proteins, DNA, RNA, miniature molecules and complexes, gene directive actions and genetic connections involving genes.

3.0 PROBLEMS AND CHALLENGES OF BIG DATA IN BIOINFORMATICS

Bioinformatics research needs large data sets in order to achieve efficient analysis and interpretation. There are basically two main categories of problems exist in term of Big Data in bioinformatics as (a) either entire network or related data are analyzed and (b) evolutionary research is going on and as a result adaption and evolution is needed.

3.1 Data and Network Based Data Analysis

In bioinformatics research, big data analytics is used mainly in microarray data analysis, pathway data analysis, protein-protein Interaction data analysis, sequence data analysis, gene-gene based network analysis and diseases network analysis.

The micro array data analysis presents a commanding approach to the study of gene expression. The main trouble of gene expression experiments are having intricate datasets that are very complex to analyze and interpret. Microarray tests are very costly too. There is also a difficulty that microarray data analysis consequences will direct to unexpected outcome due to usage of conventional approach of analysis and not enough sample size. It requires extensive training to design efficient microarray based experiment. Different statistical analysis approaches are required based on study objective.

Figure 7. Statistics of Reactome

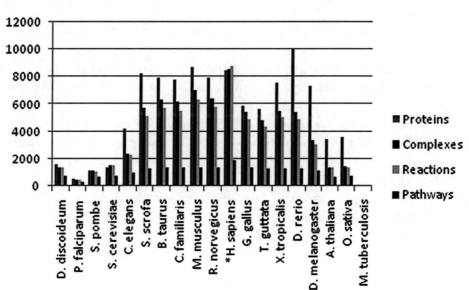

Pathway data have increasing rapidly so association analysis on gigantic volume is the main problem for Big Data community. Pathways are created manually from biological experiments or automatically using some computational techniques. Manual work is more accurate and reliable in comparison with automatic computations. The challenge for Big Data analytics is provide efficient tools that do atomization with more accuracy and reliability.

Protein-protein data analysis is very crucial in diverse fields of life sciences with making of capacious data. Protein-protein data analytics is very intricate due to huge quantity, diversity and necessity of faster access of data which creates a real Big Data problem.

In a recent joint study, researchers have combined two publicly available 'omics' catalogues to create a new catalogue of 'cancer drivers'. The researchers used cancer transformation and protein structure databases to identify transformation in patient tumors that modify typical protein-protein interaction (PPI) interfaces. This research is successful due to Big Data of genomic, clinical, and molecular data. Big Data Analytics is used to predict patient outcomes, as well as to discovery new drug objectives to avoid, indulgence, and potentially cure cancer. Researchers integrated tumor data from almost 6,000 patients in The Cancer Genome Atlas (TCGA) with more than 18,000 three-dimensional protein structures from the Protein Data Bank (PDB). The algorithm considers whether structural variation of PPI interfaces is improved in cancer mutations, and can therefore identify candidate driver genes.

Due to gigantic DNA data derived from diverse sources, the conventional sequencing tools are not adequate. Design and development of tools that fulfills demand of modern Big Data is the main concern in Bioinformatics field. RNA technologies have taken the place of micro array based technologies but it requires complex machine learning techniques(. The problem with Big Data Analytics is to design and develop more sophisticated machine learning techniques in order to analyze RNA sequence efficiently.

Different gene-gene network exist from gene expression analysis and data derived from it is voluminous in quantity. To analyze such large amount of data in effective way is a main problem of Big Data Analytics. To find the abnormal networks is also a challenging task for Big Data Community. The interpretation of results from genome expressions is a challenging and main important problem in bioinformatics research.

Gene disease associations are increasing in rapid manner and they are generally in heterogeneous nature. To derive associations from such heterogeneous networks are very crucial for understanding the relationship among diseases. Conventional network based analysis is not enough and efficient for such variety and voluminous datasets. Velocity of such huge data ensures of analyzing more datasets.

The University of Texas at Austin has developed one research project based on Gene-Diseases Prediction using link prediction approach. The prediction problem can be posed a link prediction in a heterogeneous network consisting of bipartite gene-disease network, gene-interactions network and disease similarity network. Supervised technique is used to classify known positive associations from negative associations. In the project, instead of complex machine learning techniques, network based techniques, partial supervision and inductive matrix completion methods are used. In the project, predicting associations between genes and diseases is viewed as a link prediction problem. Project dealt with number of heterogeneous networks and identifies relationships between gene nodes, causal relationships between gene and disease nodes, etc. Katz similarity technique is used to determine the path similarity between gene and disease node. The project used a huge amount of data from diversified networks and produced high speed results.

3.2 Evolutionary Research

In the recent advancement of bioinformatics research, scientists need huge and diversified datasets in order to achieve efficient results. Bioinformatics becomes a platform of Big Data Analytics. Bioinformatics deals with large amount of genomic information so efficient analysis of data is critical. In DNA sequencing, different analysis is carried out to find out how it is prepared into bigger building blocks and how it narrates to other sequence data. This gives out as the foundation for the learning of biological evolution and development. The detonation of the data in the biomedical research demands fast and efficient clarifications so Big Data analytics play a crucial role in it. Healthcare requires integration with biomedical data (Wang et al.,2010) in order to encourage personalized medicine (Fernald et al.,2011) and to offer improved treatments. Hospitals started considering Big Data solutions in order to provide quick and reliable treatment for their patients. Genome sequencing, microarrays, and metabolomics related projects generate enormous quantity of data and conventional analytics are inadequate for them. Big Data has brought dynamic changes in the field of bioinformatics. Big Data fulfills the need of analyzing voluminous and variety types of biological Big Data. Big Data solutions are also efficient to integrate large heterogeneous data sets. Big Data is a future and realistic solution of upcoming research in bioinformatics.

4.0 TECHNIQUES OF BIG DATA ANALYTICS FOR BIOINFORMATICS

There are three main Big Data Analytics techniques, i.e. supervised, unsupervised and hybrid, used widely in all types of applied research and that is also applicable for bioinformatics research. Supervised technique is appropriate when target value is clearly defined and intention is to predict data so it is also known as *predictive* (Fania et al.,2013) or *directed* technique. Unsupervised technique does not focus on predefined attributes and any targeted value so it is known as descriptive or undirected. Hybrid technique provides features of both supervised and unsupervised techniques.

4.1 Supervised Techniques

Classification, regression and anomaly detection are three main techniques of Big Data analytics in context to supervised learning. Supervised techniques accept independent variables as an input and generate dependent variables as an output. The supervised techniques methods can be applied in diversity of areas including bioinformatics.

The main objective of classification technique is to organize substances into number of predefined classes. There are two levels of it: construction of classes and usage of classifier. Prediction model based on classification needs several things in order to achieve efficient outcome. In supervised classification Decision Tree, Support Vector Machine, Naïve Bayes, Neural network, Genetic Algorithms and Nearest Neighbor are well known classifiers.

Decision tree is an analytical modeling approach used in multidiscipline. Decision trees used in large sets of data and having two main categories: classification and regression. In classification, outcome is the predefined class while in regression outcome is any real number. There are numbers of algorithms are available in literature related to Decision Tree such as ID3, CART,C4.5, CHAID, MARS, Inference Tree etc. Decision tree based algorithms are well suited for Big Data as they perform well with large datasets. Decision tree based algorithms are easiest to implement, easy to customize and fastest in execution. Decision trees based algorithms are widely used in research of bioinformatics field to predict certain aspects from gigantic datasets. Gene expression microarray based projects use decision trees because their ability of appropriate gene assortment and scalability, as well as model accurateness and simple elucidation. The most popular algorithms of decision trees based on bioinformatics research are C4.5 and CART. C4.5 builds decision trees based on concept of information entropy. According to C4.5; trait with the top normalize information gain is selected to make the decision. CART is a non-parametric decision tree algorithm that gives outcome as classification or regression tree depended on category of variable.

Revoscale package of R programming language by Revolution Analytics provides fast and scalable predictive analytics on Big Data. Function rxDTree( ) of this package contains facility to estimate decision tree proficiently on very huge data sets. The function is based on binning based recursive partitioning algorithms. This function is very helpful for bioinformatics research which needs to classify datasets in different predefined classes .rxDTree( ) function includes approximations, summarization methods and parallelism(Y. Low et al.,2014) like all other algorithms. rxDTree( ) offers an supplementary factor: maxNumBins that indicates the maximum number of bins to use in building histograms and hence, controls the accurateness of the algorithm. rxDTree( ) is also very vital for small data as well.

Support vector machine is another well known supervised learning technique extensively used for Big Data. It is best suited for applications in which binary classes are formed. According to which data is linearly separated into two classes. However several variations of SVM exists that separates the data in non-linear fashion also. Training time of standard Support Vector Machine technique is $O(N^3)$ that is not suited for large data sets. However by applying clustering techniques on SVM, it becomes suitable for large data sets. One of the major tasks for bioinformatics is prediction and classification of biological data and SVM provides best result of prediction. SVMs are designed to exploit the margin to divide two classes so that the trained model simplifies well on hidden and valid data.

Naïve Bayes classification is one of the important classification techniques that can be programmed in form of MapReduce to process the data in parallel. Naïve Bayes classification is extremely fast supervised learning technique compare to other technique and it is based on Bayes theorem of probability in order to predict the class of unknown data sets. In bioinformatics particularly in biomedical science things are uncertain and they are difficult to predict. Naïve Bayes classification is the boon in such situations. Naïve Bayes uses posterior probability in order to predict certain things. It is considered as optimal classifiers as chance of misclassification is very small.

Neural network is yet another supervised learning technique that predicts the data without requiring in-memory access to gigantic amount of data. Neural network type of learning is best suited for Big Data. Neural Network is non-parametric model while most of others are parametric which requires knowledge of statistics. Due to rapid growth of numerous biological databases, neural network has become the essential technique in bioinformatics. The most common application of neural network is prediction in bioinformatics field. Neural network has two main advantages on Big Data of bioinformatics (a) Prediction is very efficient compare to other machine learning algorithms and (b) Computations are very fast.

Genetic algorithms optimize search consequences for problems with bulky data sets. Genetic algorithms have been applied to gene expression, mass spectrometry data analysis and several other regions of bioinformatics that have huge and computationally costly problems.

The Nearest Neighbor Networks algorithm is a precious classification method that have been applied to many applications of bioinformatics such as effectively groups genes that are likely to be functionally related. Nearest Neighbor produces small and precise clusters that spans to wider variety of biological processes. Nearest Neighbor produces high precision result of biological interest in comparison of other algorithms.

4.2 Unsupervised Techniques

The supremacy of unsupervised machine learning is that it can mark prominent correlations and connections among data points that no person would have thought to look for. Unsupervised Learning is often well thought-out more difficult than supervised learning because there is no matching response variable for each surveillance. Unsupervised means clustering algorithms are classified into many classifications: (1) Hierarchical Clustering (2) Partitioning methods and (3) Grid based methods. Hierarchical algorithms do not revisit clusters once they build so generally they are not so useful in the context of unsupervised research. Partitioning clustering technique has different relocation schemes so optimization in cluster formation is achieved, but is not suitable for categorical data and it requires mentioning k clusters for the formation of sub clusters. According to grid based algorithms, space is divided into a set of connected components and based on density; functional cluster formation is to be done. Generally, such kinds of algorithms are useful for spatial data.

Unsupervised learning techniques are most common technique for analyzing huge amount of microarray data. K-windows algorithm is the most common algorithm of this context. Clustering methods can be used to group co-expressed genes, shedding light on gene function and co-regulation. Unsupervised machine learning techniques have number of applications in bioinformatics field such as sequence alignment, gene finding, multiple sequence alignment, protein domain analysis, protein folding prediction etc.

4.3 Hybrid Techniques

Big Data Analytics tools such as R, SAS and Matlab are very vital for data scientist but they are not sufficient as alone. Data scientist needs system with three main options (a) replace traditional analytics tools with system that ranges from traditional relational databases to newer data processing platform based on Big Data such as map reduce kind of paradigm (b) enlarged version of analytic tool is needed that improve performance on Big Data (c) Integration of analytic tool with Big Data tool.

Agrios is a hybrid approach to big array analytics. It stands for A Generalized R Interface Over SciDB. The components of Agrios system are R and SciDB. R is a language and computing environment modeled after S-Plus, and is intentionally designed for analysis of structured data. R is extensible, through the inclusion of user-developed packages. There are thousands of such packages, their functionality ranging from database connectivity, to pretty printing, to sophisticated machine-learning algorithms. SciDB is a scalable database system built explicitly to handle extremely large array-modeled datasets. All of SciDB's components – including its optimizer, query processor, storage manager – are designed around arrays. The storage and processing power of SciDB scales through the addition of computing nodes, intended to be simple off-the-shelf commercial systems. R and SciDB are natural candidates for hybrid system components, for many reasons. Their data models are similar, so translating expressions over data objects from one language to the other is relatively straightforward. The functions ex-posed by both systems also include simple commands applicable to complex objects such as arrays. The code of R and SciDB is publicly available, and both systems are extensible. These hybrid systems present familiar functionality to data scientists, while extending the capability of the analytic tool to include analyses on large, disk-resident datasets. Unlike other hybrid approaches, Agrios automates the management of inter-component data movement, minimizing the amount of data transferred through three techniques. Agrios' stager minimizes data movement by using a top-down memorization algorithm to identify the optimal execution locations for the operations in an analytic script. Staging is rendered more effective through the accumulation of expressions, and the rewriting of expressions through trans-formation rules.

5.0 CONCLUSION

The chapter started with the introduction of Big Data Analytics where major trends for generating Big Data are identified and explained. It also described approaches of analytics in modern context. The chapter rightly dealt with overview of Big Data with their important characteristics and definition. Big Data has importance in many sectors and that is exhaustively described by taking examples of all sectors. The chapter also dealt with role of Big Data analytics compare to traditional ways of analysis. Bioinformatics is one of the leading sectors where gigantic volume of data are generated and managed. The chapter described different types of big data in bioinformatics with explanation and characteristics. The chapter dealt with problems and challenges of Big Data in bioinformatics field. Several illustrations are given based on problems and challenges of Big Data in bioinformatics field. At last the chapter described the techniques of Big Data analytics such as supervised, unsupervised and hybrid in context to bioinformatics field. Several illustrations of different techniques are given in the chapter.

NOTE

* indicates figure at the time of writing

REFERENCES

Bagyamathi, M., & Inbarani, H. H. (2015). *A novel hybridized rough set and improved harmony search based feature selection for protein sequence classification. In Big Data in Complex Systems* (pp. 173–204). Springer.

Balazinska, Becla, Cudre-Mauroux, DeWitt, Heath, Kimura, … Zdonik. (2009). A demonstration of SciDB: A science-oriented DBMS. *VLDB*, 87-100.

Barbu, A., She, Y., Ding, L., & Gramajo, G. (2013). *Feature selection with annealing for big data learning.* arXiv preprint arXiv:1310.2880

Becla, DeWitt, Lim, Maier, Ratzesberger, Stonebraker, & Zdonik. (2009). Requirements for science data bases and SciDB. *CIDR Perspectives*, 202-214.

Ben-Dor, A., Chor, B., Karp, R., & Yakhini, Z. (2003). Discovering local structure in gene expression data: The Order-Preserving sub matrix problem. *Journal of Computational Biology*, *10*(3-4), 373–384. doi:10.1089/10665270360688075 PMID:12935334

Bryant, R., Katz, R., & Lazowska, E. (2008). *Big Data Computing: Creating revolutionary breakthroughs in commerce, science and society.* Washington, DC: Computing Community Consortium.

Chen, C. P., & Zhang, C.-Y. (2014). Data-intensive applications, challenges, techniques and technologies: A survey on big data. *Information Sciences*, *275*, 314–347. doi:10.1016/j.ins.2014.01.015

Fania, M., Peiravi, P., Chandramouly, A., & Yalla, C. (2013). *Predictive Analytics and Interactive Queries on Big Data* (White Paper). Intel Reference Architecture, Big Data Analytics.

Fernald, G. H., Capriotti, E., Daneshjou, R., Karczewski, K. J., & Altman, R. B. (2011). Bioinformatics challenges for personalized medicine. *Bioinformatics (Oxford, England)*, *27*(13), 1741–1748. doi:10.1093/bioinformatics/btr295 PMID:21596790

Fisher, D., DeLine, R., Czerwinski, M., & Drucker, S. (2012). *Interaction with Big data analytics.* Interactions Cover Story.

Ihaka, R., & Gentelman, R. (1996). R: A language for data analysis and graphics. *Journal of Computational and Graphical Statistics*, 299–314.

Lander, E. S., Linton, L. M., Birren, B., Nusbaum, C., Zody, M. C., Baldwin, J., & Morgan, M. J. et al. (2001). Initial sequencing and analysis of the human genome. *Nature*, *409*(6822), 860–921. doi:10.1038/35057062 PMID:11237011

Low, Y., Gonzalez, J. E., Kyrola, A., Bickson, D., Guestrin, C. E., & Hellerstein, J. (2014). *Graphlab: A new framework for parallel machine learning.* arXiv preprint arXiv:1408.2041

McAfee, A., Brynjolfsson, E., Davenport, T. H., Patil, D. J., & Barton, D. (2012). Big data: The management revolution. *Harvard Business Review, 90*(10), 60–68. PMID:23074865

Sandryhaila, A., & Moura, J. M. F. (2014). Big data analysis with signal processing on graphs: Representation and processing of massive data sets with irregular structure. *IEEE Signal Processing Magazine, 31*(5), 80–90. doi:10.1109/MSP.2014.2329213

Shvachko, K., Kuang, H., Radia, S., & Chansler, R. (2010). The hadoop distributed file system. In *Mass Storage Systems and Technologies (MSST), IEEE 26th Symposium on*. IEEE.

Singh, S., & Singh, N. (2012). Big Data Analytics. *IEEE International Conference on Communication, Information and Computing Technology (ICCICT)*.

Wang, F., Ercegovac, V., & Syeda-Mahmood, T. (2010). Large-scale multimodal mining for healthcare with mapreduce. In *Proceedings of the 1st ACM International Health Informatics Symposium*. ACM. doi:10.1145/1882992.1883067

Zikopoulos, P., Eaton, C., deRoos, D., Deutsch, T., & Lapis, G. (2011). *Understanding Big Data: Analytics for Enterprise Class Hadoop and Streaming Data*. McGraw-Hill Osborne Media.

Chapter 18
Multimodal Information Systems

Zakaria Bendaoud
University of Saida, Algeria

Yachba Khadidja
University of Oran, Algeria

Bouamrane Karim
University of Oran, Algeria

ABSTRACT

The number of individuals using public transportation is increasing. Transport companies want to ensure, at best, the satisfaction of the travellers. Nevertheless, a significant number of these companies sometimes pushes the travellers to confusion to compose their itineraries and obtain the required information. The authors suggest in this chapter integrating several traveller information systems into the same global system. This chapter aims to provide information to the traveller without concern for their location and optimize processing by limiting the number of involved nodes. They opted for a multi-agent system associated with the Voronoï decomposition of the global network.

INTRODUCTION

The third world countries experience an expansion in a variety of domains. Algeria, being one of these nations; is facing nowadays different challenges in terms of or related to logistics, management and transportations. As a matter of fact, collective migration to big cities for economic and social reasons occurring in the country have contributed in making competition harder, enterprises continue to multiply and innovate do that to meet the needs of the travelers.

The public transportation field nowadays, is part of the domains that are mostly concerned with this trend. The management of the transport network can be perceived according to two different angles. The first point concerns the companies of transport itself; it is about finding the best modeling of the network and the best combinations in order to implement a decisional support system (DSS) that serves

DOI: 10.4018/978-1-5225-3004-6.ch018

the objectives of the company. The second point concerns the travelers; it consists of satisfying their requirements and offering them the required information on the right time. In order to meet their needs, the transportation companies often, deploy on internet a passenger information system (PIS) so that to interact well with passengers.

In this chapter, we give an overview of the basic notions of public transport, and we explain the different tasks and situations that should be undertaken by an enterprise of public transport.

MULTIMODALITY

Before going deep into the rest of the chapter, it is necessary to define some basic concepts concerning modes of transport:

1. **Intermodality:** Defined by the successive use of the modes of transport to rally or join the starting point to the arrival point. It has to do with a variety of means of public transport (Eg: Bus, Tramway then Plane), it can also take the form of a succession of private transport mode then public transport mode (Eg: personal car then train). The intermodality is characterized by the notion of chaining that ought to be respected.
2. **The Multimodality:** Also called intermodality alternative, it is the use of various modes of transport for the same path. It is characterized by the notion of choice. The traveler can manage his ride according to days and reasons of the trip.
3. **The Multimodal Information:** Its main objective is to inform the passenger on the modes of transport that he attempts to take or on the eventual disturbance that might affect a given rode. This information might take two forms: either static if it is about a constant information (Eg: a touristic site), either dynamic if it depends on the state of the network (Eg: the leakage time in case of disturbance). The multimodal information deals with: itinerary calculations, leakage time, circulation conditions, information on fees and information on the waiting time.
4. **The Broadcasting Channels of Multimodal Information:** Multimodal information could be broadcasted through various means of communication. Due to the developments of web technologies, the undebatable first channel is internet. Each enterprise suggest its own route calculator via a web page. The cellular also permit an interaction in real time between companies of transport and the clients, the pieces of information that are broadcasted so often concern the disturbance of the network. Eventually, or finally, the boards help to display the timing of the modes of transport.

So, we can classify the companies of public transport in accord to their type of network:

1. **Multimodal Companies:** They are enterprises that include various modes of transport within their network.
2. **Monomodal Companies:** Unlike multimodals, they manage one mode of transport in their network only. It is nonetheless important to distinguish the line modes of transport. One mode of transport may operate on various lines linking two different points (departure and arrival).

THE ENTREPRISING SIDE OF TRANSPORT

Within the sphere of public transport, transportation companies seek to highly satisfy the expectations and the preferences of the passengers yet at lower investing costs so that to optimize incomes. This is why transportation companies handle this problem through two phases:

Phase 1: Courses Planning

This task consists of doing a market study so that to set up courses and circuits based on the requests of the passengers. It is true that high number of transportation means offer a better quality of service to the clients, but it considerably increases expenditure due to maintenance and fuel. On the other hand, the use of a limited number of means of transport affect the quality of services offered to the passengers since it causes a consequent waiting time. Then, It would be better to find a good compromise between the number of cars and the requirements of the passengers so that satisfy clients on one hand, and optimize incomes on the other (Huisman et al., 2002). This planning is undertaken generally once a year and it is based only on the previsions of the demand and on the periods of the journeys between the stops of the network. Its main objective is to establish a provisional supply of transport that is adjusted to the demand. This allows to elaborate an approximation on the leakage time of each car in the stations that are part of the network. This approximation is presented in a form of tables called "timetable" (Laïchour, 2002).

Beyond the planning of the journeys, this step allows to assign the stuff to the right structures and establish the timing files for the drivers to assign them to the cars for which they will be responsible. Planning issues is the object of a variety of works, they are referred to tasks and arrangements issues.

According to (Zgaya, 2007), this issue is generally dealt with by bus transportation companies. The tool that is frequently used is HASTUS developed in the 80s (Rousseau & Blais, 1985).

Phase 2: Network Regulation

Tasks planning allows obtaining an approximation on the leakage hours of cars to the stations. The timetables represent an estimation done preliminary. Planning is, in fact, a theoretical study of the demand and the leakage hours of the cars. It does not always coincide with reality, in fact it is so often that there would be disturbances in the roads that might be due to different reasons:

- Technical reasons related to cars
- Natural reasons (rain, bad weather…)
- Saturation of the network
- External reasons concerning works of engineering

In this way, it is mandatory to foresee a management of the network and the traffic in real time. This step is known as "regulation process" whose objective is to minimize discrepancies between the anticipated time during planning and reality. These regulation measures allow a better exploitation of the network when it goes to a degraded state. The regulator's mission is to analyze the state of the network, better evaluate the solutions that satisfy the constraints related to the state of the network and come up with the best option possible.

Therefore, there should be a forecast of support solutions so that to meet the anticipations of the passengers as quickly as possible. These manipulations of regulation are done in real time, they contribute in making fluid the traffic in a way to better respect the theoretical timetables dispatched during the planning step.

TRANSPORT CLIENT SIDE

The achieved research in this sense deals with the quality of the offered service to the passengers. Their objective is to facilitate the acquisition of the information to the passengers through a supply of information system capable of extracting, composing and calculating the required itineraries according to the client's preferences. The set-up of these information systems is so often launched by transportation companies so that to offer the best services and compete with companies that operate in the same sector. This operation, despite being costy to the enterprises, offers great comfort and a good quality service to passengers. Great efforts have been done in this sense.

For instance, Petit-Roze et al (2004) have introduced a multi-agent system as aid for travelling based on the notion of context. The latter has three types:

1. **Identical:** It corresponds to the characteristics related to the identity of the passenger, his preferences and his objectives
2. **Spatial:** It consists of localizing the passenger during his interaction with the information system.
3. **Temporary:** Consists of taking into consideration the time during which the request has has been done by the passenger and determining the acceptable time of response so that to manage the treatment of priorities.

Taking into consideration these three types of context offer a response more adequate to the requirements of the passengers for the treatment takes into consideration the passengers profiles rather than the context in which the request has been expressed.

Zidi and Hammadi (2005) have introduced a support system in normal mode as well as in degraded mode. The objective of this system is to minimize the waiting time of the passengers during perturbations and to assure them as much as possible the continuity during their journeys. Zgaya (2007) has suggested an information system that permits data management in an important flow, the request is then decomposed into many tasks

This sort of projects could also be initiated by the authorities so that to combine the networks of all transport enterprises in one global system, this permits a good management of public transport as the network becomes on a larger scale. Moreover, this composition of different information systems in one and unique system facilitates access to the information and highly encourages tourism that represents nowadays a major factor in economy.

MULTIMODAL INFORMATION SYSTEM

An information system (IS) is an organized series of resources (materials, softwares, stuff, data and procedures) that permits to collect, regroup, classify, treat and broadcast information in a given environment (De Courcy, 1992). Then, the ISs are articulated around the following five points:

1. The reception and collection of information
2. The classification and grouping of information according to needs
3. The treatment of information
4. The determination of the use of information
5. The partition of the information and its representation according to the user.

The Aid Information Systems for Exploitation (AISE) are information systems dedicated to transport enterprises so that to facilitate to them some tasks. A SISE manage the following functions:

1. Support to the analysis of the offer and the service given.
2. Support to regulations of the network in real time in case of perturbations.
3. Support to the maintenance of material infrastructures
4. Support to bill management.
5. Support to passengers.

The aid information systems to the movements of the passengers (AISMP) are but a special module of exploitation support systems. They permit the assistance of the passenger during his travel through a suggestion of diverse itineraries and if possible to direct him during perturbations. On the other hand, the multimodal information system (MIS) are support information systems to the decision (AISD) that integrate many transportation companies. The MISs produce and supply to passengers a multimodal information that provides information on different modes of travelling possible in a given geographical perimeter (Perreau, 2002).

The number of passengers who use public transport know an important rise, the same as the number transport companies that multiplies. This opening strategy –conducted by Algeria- so that to assure the citizen the right to travel in the best conditions hit the organizational bewilderment et often push the passenger to difficulties for the composition of its multimodal information. With the technological developments, many enterprises are on the road spreading their aid information system on internet. These websites of the enterprises such the one of SNTF or SOGRAL express their ambition to best organize their technology watch.

Notwithstanding, the constant growth of public transportation companies and the transition that the world of information is experiencing by means of digitization of information create a real ditch between the transport companies and the passengers. In fact, the latter has to have a perfect knowledge on all the enterprises operating in the market, their itineraries and the pricings of each of them. It is clear the deployment of information systems on internet has simplified this task but this requires a knowledge of computing tools and memorization of the websites of all enterprises. Moreover, the comparisons between the itineraries and the fees between the different enterprises require the availability of the passengers.

One of the objectives of the multimodal information systems is to supply a unique platform that would integrate many support information systems to movements of many enterprises. This globalization of multimodal data would avoid to passengers to do manual researches so that to find the best possible itinerary between two points or in order to identify the lowest pricing.

THE EXISTING MULTIMODAL INFORMATION SYSTEMS

Many systems have been developed – mainly in Europe – in order to integrate many support systems for exploitation in one and unique system in order to facilitate access to multimodal information. If the reference modals are "DELFI" and "Direct Transport" developed respectively in Germany and UK and which are based on a distributed architecture, other countries such as Switzerland and Netherlands choose a centralized architecture.

« Delfi »: The German Modal

Germany is federal republican. There are many domains that do not depend on the national law, but rather on regional law, that of « Länder" (German States). Transports management is then divided between a national ministry and 16 ministries of Lander. So often, they are gathered with other ministries. Eg: "Ministry of Economy and Transports" or else "Ministry of Transports and Urbanism", etc.. (Danflous, 2000).

Delfi is the first European project that aims at a better organization of transport of passengers in Germany. It is a multimodal information system extended to all national territory. It has been initiated by the German Federal Ministry of transport in 1996. This project is considered as a reference in literature since it has been the first national information system implemented on the web.

This system permits the research and the composition of the itinerary from door to door on the whole German territory. Its objective is to supply multimodal information to the passenger even if it depends on many operators. The user can consult the website that serve as an interface and ask the system on the routes or the information that he wants to obtain. He doesn't have to know the names and the networks of all companies. The final answer to his query will offer him all the necessary details for his journey. On the other hand, Delfi is considered an "open" modal for it keeps the information system of the market and the multimodal information open to existing systems through encouraging new partnerships with new suppliers o information. All designers of information systems and research of itineraries already existing in Germany have participated in the development of this project (Zgaya, 2007). Delfi is based on the architecture CORBA (Common Object Request Broker) (Geib et al, 1997) that, unlike traditional architectures, operate on three level modal based on clients, application servers and servers of data. The clients communicate with object servers via API (Application and Programming Interface) who access required services and who are standardized interfaces for the programming of the described applications IDL, an independent language from programming language IDL(Interface Definition Language). Hence, There are many components expanded on many servers capable of realizing many tasks.

DELFI is composed of the following modal (Danflous, 2000):

1. **A Common Base of Information:** It is a common data base between the servers, it is copied on different local systems. It is meta-base that contains many pieces of information. It is to do the

translations and the transformations between different languages used by the different systems that integrate DELFI. Moreover, it possesses a table "responsibility" that helps to know which servers permit the treatment of a given data.

2. **A Local Core:** That helps to calculate the requested itineraries by the passengers. Each server implements its own methods and algorithm of calculation according to the concerned Länder (s)
3. An identification module of origin-destinations.
4. **Principal Composer:** It is a super mechanism that helps to do the apportioned treatments.

Like each system, Delfi has been designed in three steps. First, the passengers need analysis that resulted in a global conception of the system. The second step has permitted to extract the first prototypes of the system. Finally, the third step helped to do the tests on the network on a large scale. The Figure 1 introduces the global architecture of Delfi (Danflous, 2000).

When a passenger decides to travel through the help of the Delfi system, he connects to one of his servers via his internet address. Based on the nouns of cities of origins and the destination dispatched by the passenger and tables of responsibilities, the system selects the main server and the server of destination responsible on the treatment of the request. Once the addresses or the names of the stops are validated, the principal composer selects the intermediate servers responsible on the treatment of the request, then claim the transitional points to go from zone to another. The request is then devised into sub-requests according to the transitional points and each server calculates the itinerary for which his is responsible. A complete list of itineraries is set up and the principal composer defines the itinerary that better meets the passenger's expectations.

« Direct Transport »: The English Modal

The English modal « Direct Transport » has been launched by the English government so that to fight against congestion and deregulation of the public transport network by offering the best quality service on a national multimodal network. "direct Transport" is registered in the development register that aims at improving transport of passengers, it represents an improvement to the project of "Traveline" that has been designed couple of years ago. The aims of the project Direct Transport were (Danflous, 2003):

Figure 1. The architecture of DELFI

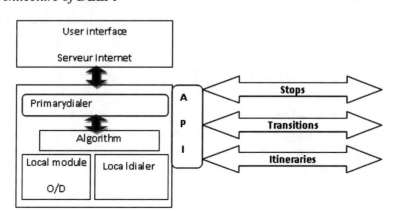

1. The comparison of modes of transport and the possible solutions throughout the network, moreover, the passenger could choose the itinerary and the modes of transports the most adequate to his preferences.
2. The possibility of making a booking and payment of the course from the planning without being obliged to go to specific counters in order to make things easier for the passenger.
3. Inform the passenger in real time on all information that concerns his movement, these pieces of information could be about perturbations that might happen or modifications on the itineraries.

Despite the fact that « Traveline » fills these tasks, « Direct Transport » aims at a good coverage of the national network and the availability of the information. This information had to be multimodal and multi-operators. This ambitious project made the information services a pillar. It is true that the implementation of such a system requires an important collection of information and data. Nevertheless, this task has been simplified since a big part of this work has been done during the project of "traveline". The organization of these data has been done in a way that access be as soon as possible, the data have been divided according to 11 regions distributed geographically according to cities of the British territory.

« Direct Transport » uses the protocol JourneyWeb (Danflous, 2003), the latter – which is open and independent- permit the itinerary calculators to question and to communicate in order to compose a final itinerary through concatenating the ends of itineraries supplied by calculators who belong to different information systems. This protocol uses XML (McLaughlin, 2001) and TCP/IP (Caicoya & Saury, 2013) for the transfer of data, its functioning depends on the availability of two data base:

1. A national repertory (National Public Transport Gazetteer: NPTG) that contains the names of all places (cities, villages, points of interest) so that to identify the systems to be contacted in case of long distance journey. In fact, the calculation of a long distance itinerary requires – in the majority- the invocation of many itinerary calculators.
2. A local repertoire (National Public Transport Access Node: NaPTAN). That contains the group of points that cover a local itinerary calculator and that permits access to the network. These points could be (stops, stations, etc.)

When a user sends a request to the itinerary calculator, the local server consult the data base NPTG and NaPTAN so that to determine the servers in charge of calculating this itinerary and the exchange poles that permit access to servers. It calculates the itinerary between the source and the adequate exchange pole then concatenates the ends of itinerary acquired by the servers responsible on the treatment of this request. Finally, the final itinerary is suggested by the passenger. Figure 2 introduces the architecture of Direct Transport (Danflous, 2003).

« Gofas »: The Switzerland Modal

Unlike the two previous systems « Delfi » and « Transport Direct », Switzerland opted for a centralized modal for integrating data. This choice is explained by the limited geographical territory of this country. In fact, it is easier to manage a series of restricted data on a centralized architecture than on an expanded architecture. The figure 3 Illustrates this architecture (Danflous, 2001)

Gofas is composed of two sub-systems (Danflous, 2001):

Figure 2. The architecture of transport direct

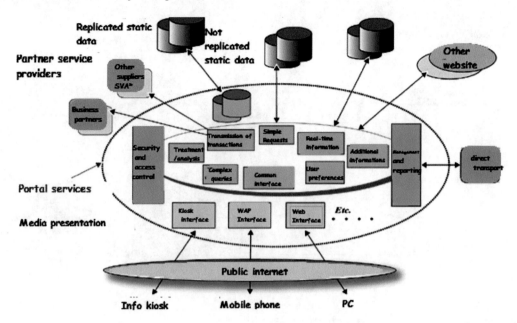

1.   **Infopool:** It permits the importation and collection of multimodal information from the data base of different operators to construct a centralized data base that hosts a series of multimodal information on the territory. This multimodal information concerns the timing of leakage and the list of all the geocoded stations associated to their correspondence. The timings are provided by the operators in an electronic form once a year. It is true that each operator uses his own codification and representation form, this system convert them to a specific forma transform so that to be able to exploit them.

2.   **Internet-GIS:** Once the data base Infopool is constructed, it is first transferred to an intermediate server available on the network intranet. The latter permits to do the tests on new updates of the application and on the improvements done. It also helps to increase the application through new functions or by new multimodal information such as points of interest, businesses, hotels …

The heart of the system is the itinerary calculator that operates on the Infopool data base. The treatment is done from a station to another only. The calculation of one address to another include the innovation of a supplementary software layer that permits the visualization of cards via internet. Once the system is approved, the application is replicated on two identical and interchangeable machines that serves the applications servers and that permits the interaction with passengers. The aim of using two similar machines is to face breakdowns and facilitate access to passengers. In afct, one is dedicated to clients whose mother tongue is Deutch whereas the second is dedicated to clients whose first language is French or Italian.

Figure 3. The architecture of GOFAS

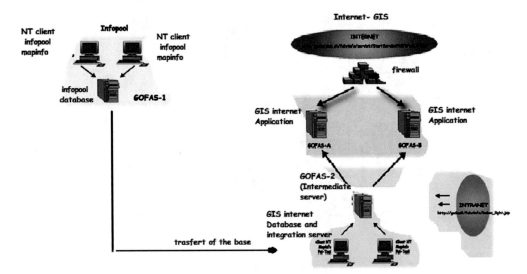

« 9292 »: The Example of Netherlands

It is a system that supplies a multimodal information on movement and about perturbation (Danflous, 2006). Each year during December, all enterprises supply series of timing and information on their networks. There isn't a specific form to respect for the representation of timing. The system is responsible on modifying and converting data in a way that is exploitable. On the other hand, a data base of geocoded addresses is used to calculate the door to door addresses

THE CHALLENGES OF MULTIMODAL INFORMATION SYSTEMS

The multimodal information represents a crucial data for all aid information systems for exploitation in the domain of transports. Many works have been done in order to offer the best services to passengers. In fact, many transportation companies employ nowadays their information system on internet. This measure is translated by the possibility of the calculator of itineraries driving from point A to point B by simply consulting a website. Then, it is difficult to find an information system for help to travel on an extended geographical territory taking into consideration all possible modes of transport. The composition of multimodal information is a big challenge, since beyond technical difficulties, it comes up against various obstacles that are mentioned below:

1. **Organizational Reasons:** Many actors operate in the domain of public transport in Algeria. As explained, when the country has opened up, it has encouraged individuals to invest in the domain of transport. Then there should be a cooperation between these actors.
2. **Economic Reasons:** In addition to the fact that the production of information is costly, the multimodal information represents a major rivalry assent to the enterprises. Its broadcasting helps to attract more passengers, the multimodal information then, can quickly become a key to dominating the market.

3. **Legal Reasons:** The provision of the information really causes an issue of ownership. Moreover, the attached responsibility to this information in case of uncertainty is hardly discernible.
4. **Technical Reasons:** The diversity of information generates an issue related to the homogeneity of data. Each company possesses its own conceptual modal of data and it refers to a given norm. on the other hand, the updates of data by the companies in case of perturbation can be a difficult task as far as access has to be rapid so that to assure the accuracy of the information for the passenger.

The invocation of the existing multimodal information system imply: either the invocation of all its network in case architecture is based on an integration of data. (Eg: the modal GOFAS). - or the useless invocation of some networks of companies who are not concerned with request in case architecture is based on the decentralization of data. (Eg: the modal DELFI). In both types of architecture, we should note that the networks of companies who are not concerned with requests might be invoked.

The multimodal information systems must assure the composition of the multimodal information between many companies of transport and which adapt to the context of the market. In fact, the detonators of the multimodal information are divers, they change from one mode of transport to another and from one company to another. This problematic has two stakes, on one hand producing useful multimodal information for passengers so that to make an encouraging asset for tourism, on the other, protect companies of transport from competition so that to encourage them to adhere to the system.

The multimodal information systems have to answer the two following questions: "how to produce multi-operators information for the passenger within encouraging the enterprises to adhere to a system and bringing up their autonomy?" And "how to minimize the number of the invoked knots during the treatment of a request related to itinerary calculation?"

CONCLUSION

The multimodal information is the foundation of SIAD, the setup of this information for the profit of the passengers make easier for them the movements and encourages them to go hand in hand with new technologies for its acquisition. Many enterprises set up their itinerary calculator, the strategies and the algorithm of these calculations change from a company to another. Nevertheless, it is difficult to compose an itinerary when we call for many companies to reach a destination. The passenger has to have the necessary information for the composition of the lines of the network and the timing of all the enterprises of the concerned sector. In order or remedy this issue, the multimodal information systems have been suggested, they permit integration to the aid information systems for the movement in the same system. If the context and the techniques of integration change from a region to another, it is frequent in the existing systems – that the networks of the enterprises who are not concerned by the treatment of the request might be invoked.

Unlike the perceived ideas, the multimodal information is not summed up to itinerary calculations. This notion which is rather widespread could be explained by the fact that the information mostly researched by the passenger concerns the itinerary calculations. The multimodal information treats, in fact, the diverse services linked to transport (itinerary, timing, touristic information etc). A multimodal information system should treat the itinerary calculations and the touristic information while minimizing the number of the invoked knots.

REFERENCES

Caicoya, S., & Saury, Jg. (2013). TCP/IP - Le guide complet, Maîtrisez les principes de la communication réseau sous Windows. *Edition Micro Application.*

Danflous, D. (2000). Déploiement national des Systèmes d'information Multimodale, Delfi: l'exemple allemand. Rapport du Centre d'études sur les réseaux, les transports, l'urbanisme et les constructions publiques. France.

Danflous, D. (2001). Déploiement national des Systèmes d'Information Multimodale, GOFAS: l'exemple Suisse. Rapport du Centre d'études sur les réseaux, les transports, l'urbanisme et les constructions publiques. France.

Danflous, D. (2003). Déploiement national des Systèmes d'Information Multimodale, Transport Direct: l'exemple Anglais. Rapport du Centre d'études sur les réseaux, les transports, l'urbanisme et les constructions publiques. France.

De Courcy, R. (1992). Les systèmes d'information en réadaptation. Réseau international CIDIH et facteurs environnementaux, 5, 7-10.

Geib, J., Gransart, C., & Merle, P. (1997). *CORBA: des concepts à la pratique*. Edition Masson.

Huisman, D., Freling, R., & Wagelmans, A. (2002). *A Dynamic Approach to Vehicle Scheduling*. Rapport de l'Insititut économoque, Université Erasmus, Rotterdam, Pays-Bas.

Laïchour, H. (2002). *Modélisation mutli-agent et aide à la décision: application à la régulation des correspondances dans les réseaux de transport urbai*. (Thèse de doctorat). Université des sciences et technologies de Lille. France.

Mclaughlin, B. (2001). Java & XML (2nd ed.). O'Reilly.

Perreau, C. (2002). *Les Systèmes d'Information Multimodale* (Thèse de doctorat). Institut d'Etudes Politiques de Paris, France.

Petit-Roze, C., Anli, A., Grislin-Lestrugeon, E., Abed, M., & Uster, G. (2004). Système d'information transport personnalisée à base d'agents logiciels. *Revue Génie Logiciel, 70*, 29–38.

Rousseau, Jm., & Blais, Jy. (1985). HASTUS: An interactive systems for buses and crew scheduling. *Computer Scheduling of Public Transport, 2*, 45–60.

Zgaya, H. (2007). *Conception et optimisation distribuée d'un système d'information d'aide à la mobilité urbaine: Une approche multi-agent pour la recherche et la composition des services liés au transport* (Thèse de doctorat). Université de Lille. France.

Zidi, K., & Hammadi, S. (2005). DMAS: Distributed Multi-Agents System for assist users in the multimodal travels. *International Conference on Industrial Engineering and Systems Management (IESM 2005)*.

Chapter 19
Brain–Machine Interfaces:
Advanced Issues and Approaches

Kijpokin Kasemsap
Suan Sunandha Rajabhat University, Thailand

ABSTRACT

This chapter indicates the overview of Brain-Machine Interfaces (BMIs); the aspects of BMIs; BMIs, human-machine interfaces, and electrooculography interfaces; BMIs, Amyotrophic Lateral Sclerosis (ALS), and stroke motor recovery; speech BMIs; BMIs and neuroplasticity; and BMIs and transcranial doppler (TCD). BMIs are the computerized approaches to gaining the brain signals, investigating them, and translating them into computerized functions in order to organize the required practices. BMIs can allow people to manipulate computerized networks and various electrical devices. With the support of modern technologies, BMIs are functional and able to operate in operational settings. The chapter argues that applying BMIs has the potential to increase organizational performance and reach strategic goals in the digital age.

INTRODUCTION

The improvement of the resolution of brain signal and the ability to control external device has been the most important goal in the brain-machine interfaces (BMIs) research field (Li, Hong, Zhang, & Guo, 2014). BMIs are the advanced systems that allow individuals to interact with a computer by means of their brain signals. BMIs open new horizons for the treatment of paralyzed people, giving hope for the artificial restoration of lost physiological functions (Tankus, Fried, & Shoham, 2014). BMIs read brain signals and directly transmit them to a computer, bypassing the neuromuscular system through which individuals interact with the world. BMIs consist of a computer, an amplifier, and a skullcap, and include any form of a direct interface between brain and artificial device regarding computations (Oweiss & Badreldin, 2015). BMIs offer an alternative method of communication for individuals who are cognitively aware but unable to speak or gesture as a consequence of severe physical impairments (Lu, Mamun, & Chau, 2015).

DOI: 10.4018/978-1-5225-3004-6.ch019

BMI technology makes direct communication between the brain and a machine possible by means of electrodes (Jebari, 2013). Electrodes serve as the first critical interface to the biological organ system (Patil & Thakor, 2016). BMIs are the modern machines that can decode the physiological signals from the brain and convert them into actions in an effective manner that reflects the brain's intention (Moran, 2010). BMIs can be divided into three classes: sensory interfaces, which artificially activate the human sensory system; cognitive interfaces, which try to reestablish the communication of the neural networks; and motor interfaces, which translate the brain activity into the control commands for a device of interest (Sanchez & Principe, 2007).

BMI may take the pattern of a brain-computer interface (BCI), a direct neural interface, a brain-machine application, or a deep brain stimulating electrode (Demetriades, Demetriades, Watts, & Ashkan, 2010). Alonso-Valerdi et al. (2015) stated that motor BMI is a state-of-the-art technology that is known as BCI. BMI can translate a specific brain activity into computer command, thus establishing a direct connection between human brain and external device (Zhang, Zhou, Jin, Wang, & Cichocki, 2015). BMIs utilize the neuroelectric and metabolic brain activities to activate the peripheral devices and computers without the mediation of the motor system (Birbaumer & Chaudhary, 2015). Research using BMI technology significantly proposes the development of interfaces based on the interaction of neural networks with artificial tools to restore the motor control and full mobility of the injured area (Gongora et al., 2013).

This chapter focuses on the literature review through a thorough literature consolidation of BMIs. The extensive literature of BMIs provides a contribution to practitioners and researchers by describing the perspectives of BMIs in order to maximize the medical and technological impacts of BMIs in the robotic age.

BACKGROUND

Biomedical engineering technologies (e.g., BMIs and neuroprosthetics) are the advancements which assist human beings in various ways (Lee, 2016). Current state and availability of BMI systems urge a broader societal discourse on the pressing ethical challenges associated with the advancements in neurotechnology and BMI research (Birbaumer, Gallegos-Ayala, Wildgruber, Silvoni, & Soekadar, 2014). BMI system detects the electrical signals produced from the human brain and converts them into the control signals to operate a device by reading the user's thoughts (Choi & Kang, 2014). The electrical activities of the brain and heart have been recorded and analyzed for the diverse clinical and pathological purposes (Kim et al., 2014).

BMIs can be classified by the type of mental activity generating the BMI signals (Coffey, Brouwer, Wilschut, & van Erp, 2010). Zander et al. (2008) suggested the distinction among active BMIs, passive BMIs, and reactive BMIs. Active BMIs are those used for the direct control of devices which are based on signals intentionally generated by the user, for example a wheelchair steered by signals that correspond with motor imagery tasks performed by the user (Zander et al., 2008). Motor imagery is recognized as a dynamic state during which a subject mentally repeats a specific movement (sequence), without any overt motor output (Jeannerod, 1995). Motor imagery shares many of the same neural mechanisms with actual movement execution, with an emphasis on the prefrontal cortex, which is responsible for the creation and maintenance of an explicit representation used in thought and action (Decety, 1996).

Regarding active BMIs, the success in the motor imagery-based BMI can be attributed to the underlying neurophysiological phenomena accompanying motor imagery, termed event-related desynchronization and event-related synchronization (Xu, Zhou, Wang, & Huang, 2009). Processing of motor commands or somatosensory stimuli causes an attenuation of the rhythmic activity termed event-related desynchronization, while an increase in the rhythmic activity is termed event-related synchronization (Pfurtscheller & Aranbibar, 1979). Passive BMIs are used for supporting systems rather than directly controlling devices (Zander et al., 2008). Passive BMIs are not based on intentional thoughts, but on the spontaneously generated states of the user's cognition that do not require the directed attention of the user or otherwise interfere with the ongoing mental or motor activities. Reactive BMIs are based on brain signals that are automatically generated upon the perception of certain external stimuli. Reactive BMIs can be considered more active or passive depending on the degree of intentional involvement of the user (Zander et al., 2008).

Efferent BMIs read the neural activity from descending neural pathways utilizing a sensing device by extracting the spike event rates from the well-isolated neurons (Fetz, 1969), or from the multiple single units (Aghagolzadeh & Oweiss, 2009), that are subsequently decoded to generate the control signals that actuate the end effector. This can be the natural impaired limb (Ethier, Oby, Bauman, & Miller 2012), or an artificial limb (Collinger et al., 2013). Afferent BMIs (Harrison, 1987) can extract the features from the control signals using an encoder which subsequently modulates the stimulation patterns in order to evoke the artificial percepts (Liu, Khalil, & Oweiss, 2011).

BMI technology has been used to realize the direct control of prosthetic devices, such as robot arms, computer cursors, and paralyzed muscles (Yu et al., 2010). Prosthetic devices (i.e., an artificial substitute for a missing part, such as an eye, limb, or tooth, used for functional or cosmetic reasons, or both). Prosthetic devices for restoring the lost body functions can be controlled by brain signals (Rotermund, Ernst, & Pawelzik, 2006). With the goal of improving the quality of life for people suffering from various motor control disorders, BMIs provide the direct neural control of prosthetic devices by translating neural signals into control signals (Zhang & Chase, 2015). BMI efforts have been focused on utilizing either invasive implanted electrodes or training-extensive conscious manipulation of brain rhythms to control the prosthetic devices (Georgopoulos, Langheim, Leuthold, & Merkle, 2005).

IMPORTANT PERSPECTIVES ON BRAIN-MACHINE INTERFACES

This section provides the overview of BMIs; the aspects of BMIs; BMIs, human-machine interfaces, and electrooculography interfaces; BMIs, ALS, and stroke motor recovery; speech BMIs; BMIs and neuroplasticity; and BMIs and TCD.

Overview of Brain-Machine Interfaces

BMIs have demonstrated lots of successful arm-related reach decoding in past decades, which provide a new hope for restoring the lost motor functions for the disabled people (Hao et al., 2013). BMIs are based on the processing of brain signals in order to generate commands to control the external devices (Gao, Dignfeng, Cheng, & Gao, 2003). Reliability, scalability and clinical viability are of importance in the design of wireless BMI systems (Zhang, Aghagolzadeh, & Oweiss, 2012). An evoked BMI reflects the automatic response of the brain to the external stimuli (Iturrate, Antelis, Kubler, & Minguez, 2009). On the other hand, in spontaneous BMIs, the users execute the mental task on their own will (Millan,

Renkens, Mourino, & Gerstner, 2004). Radio frequency (RF) is a viable option for communicating with BMIs for clinical applications (Ibrahim, Abraham, & Rennaker, 2007).

Brain signals can be registered using invasive or noninvasive methods. Invasive methods are based on the using of microelectrodes implanted directly in the brain (Ubeda, Ianez, Azorin, & Perez-Vidal, 2013). Invasive systems require surgery to implant electrodes on or near the surface of the brain. Careful analysis of brain signals allows them to be utilized to control various technologies (e.g., prosthetics and muscle stimulators) that restore the lost functionality caused by injury (Kim, Reyes, Garza, & Choi, 2015). The implantable microsystem requires the hybrid circuit technology for BMIs (Li, 2009). Invasive methods have been used in animals to determinate the movement intention (Chapin, Moxon, Markowitz, & Nicolelis, 1999) or to control a cursor in a screen (Serruya, Harsopoulos, Paninski, Fellows, & Donoghue, 2002). Invasive BMIs hold promise to improve the bandwidth by utilizing multichannel recordings from ensembles of brain neurons (Lebedev, 2014).

Regarding noninvasive techniques, electrodes are placed on the scalp of the patient to obtain the electroencephalographic signals. Noninvasive BMIs can be used to move a wheelchair, to detect mental illnesses, and to control web browsers (Iscan, Dokur, & Demiralp, 2011). Noninvasive techniques are divided into endogenous and exogenous (Ubeda et al., 2013). Concerning exogenous perspectives, the brain reacts against different external stimulus. The user can send synchronous commands depending on the stimulus received. There are many BMI-related studies based on the visual evoked potentials to control the virtual environments, web browsers, and a robot arm (Sirvent, Ianez, Ubeda, & Azorin, 2012). Evoked potential is an electrical response recorded from the nervous system after the presentation of a stimulus (Abdulkader, Atia, & Mostafa, 2015). Regarding endogenous perspectives, the user can perform the voluntary cognitive commands to control the external devices (Ubeda et al., 2013) and the user does not depend on external stimulus and can willingly generate the control commands (Millan, Ferrez, Galan, Lew, & Chavarriaga, 2008).

BMI helps the sensory-motor integration system reintegrate the sensory-motor loop toward accessing to brain information (Alonso-Valerdi et al., 2015). When the sensory-motor integration system is malfunctioning, it provokes a wide variety of neurological disorders, such as stroke, epilepsy, chronic pain, Parkinson's disease, schizophrenia, anxiety disorders, and attention deficit hyperactivity disorder (Alonso-Valerdi et al., 2015). Chronic pain is recognized as a disease state that involves changes in brain function (Saab, 2013). In healthy individuals, the sensory-motor integration system records sensory information to generate the motor actions according to internal factor (e.g., learning) and external factor (e.g., number of tasks to attend) (Wood, 2001). Artificial sensations can be produced by the direct brain stimulation of sensory areas through the implanted microelectrodes (Fridman, Blair, Blaisdell, & Judy, 2010). Deep brain stimulation promises the clinical benefits for the severely suffering patients (Clausen, 2013). Regarding BMIs, the feedback control of deep brain stimulation in Parkinson's disease has great potential to improve efficacy, reduce side effects, and decrease the cost of treatment (Little & Brown, 2012). Chai et al. (2014) indicated that lack of reliable sensory feedback is the biggest defect to sophisticated prosthetic hands, greatly hindering their usefulness and perceptual embodiment.

Aspects of Brain-Machine Interfaces

There are two main strategies pursued to restore function after stroke utilizing BMIs (Soekadar, Birbaumer, Slutzky, & Cohen, 2015). The first strategy aims at bypassing nonfunctional cortico-spinal pathways to allow for the continuous and permanent control of robotic devices (Collinger et al., 2013) or functional electric stimulation (FES) of paralyzed muscles (Ethier et al., 2012). By substituting for lost motor functions, the assistive BMIs have demonstrated the recovery of versatile motor control in daily life activities (Hochberg et al., 2006). The second strategy aims at the facilitation of neuroplasticity and motor learning to enhance motor recovery (rehabilitative BMIs) (Dobkin, 2007)

While deriving from different research traditions, both strategies involve the same neural mechanisms for BMI learning and control, mainly operant conditioning and feedback learning independent of the invasiveness of the approach and both involve the cortico-striatal loop (Koralek, Jin, Long, Costa, & Carmena, 2012). In noninvasive BMIs, six types of brain signals have been explored: sensori-motor rhythms (SMR, 8–15 Hz, also termed rolandic alpha or mu-rhythm depending on the context) (Soekadar, Birbaumer, & Cohen, 2011); slow cortical potentials (SCP) (Birbaumer et al., 1999); event-related potentials (Farwell & Donchin, 1988); steady state visually or auditory evoked potentials (SSVEP/SSAEP) (Sakurada et al., 2013); blood-oxygenation level dependent (BOLD)-contrast imaging utilizing the functional magnetic resonance imaging (Weiskopf et al., 2003); and concentration changes of oxy/deoxy hemoglobin utilizing the functional near-infrared spectroscopy (Mihara et al., 2013).

Event-related potential is the measured brain response that is the direct result of an event, such as the presentation of a visual stimulus (Luck, 2005). Functional magnetic resonance imaging helps mapping activities to the corresponding used brain areas which is known as source localization problem, and depends on the fact that any usage of brain part requires the increase of incoming blood flow (Abdulkader et al., 2015). Near-infrared spectroscopy is the emerging neuroimaging modality which employs the near-infrared light to investigate the cerebral oxygenation changes in the neurologically challenged adults and children (Strangman, Boas, & Sutton, 2002). Near-infrared spectroscopy has reasonable spatial (about 1 cm) and good temporal (about 1 ms) resolution and is relatively robust to motion artifact, thus enabling it to be suitable for investigating everyday tasks (Strangman et al., 2002).

Neural recording requires the use of precise, low-noise amplifier systems to acquire and condition the weak neural signals that are transduced through electrode interfaces (Ng, Greenwald, Xu, & Thakor 2016). EEG stands for electroencephalogram (i.e., the recording of the electrical changes occurring in the brain, produced by placing the electrodes on the scalp and amplifying the electrical potential developed). BMI requires a medium of communication represented by an event that evokes an EEG response (Kumar & Sahin, 2015). Brain patterns are classified from EEG signals and correspond to the situations of low and high mental workload (Heger, Putze, & Schultz, 2011).

Low signal to noise ratio's, low processing speed, and huge variability currently call for the addition of intelligence to the applications, in order to compensate for errors in the production and the decoding of brain signals (Haselager, 2013). Due to the low signal-to-noise ratio of the EEG signals, the detection of ERPs requires efficient and robust pattern recognition techniques that can deal with the non-stationarity of the signal and the specificity of each subject (Cecotti, 2015). One of the main problems related to EEG-based BMI systems is the non-stationarity of the underlying EEG signals (Shin et al., 2015). EEG-based BMIs capture the EEG signal by means of electrodes or channels disposed on the subjects scalp (Aler & Galvan, 2015). The EEG signal is recorded from the electrodes, then the signal is preprocessed using the different kinds of filters and, finally, it is classified. The result of the classification can be used to control a device (Aler & Galvan, 2015).

Implantable medical devices technologically integrated with muscles, peripheral nerves, and the brain have been developed for many applications over the last decades (Stieglitz, 2010), and are well-suited to many novel applications (Udoekwere, Oza, & Giszter, 2014). Implantable BMIs, in contrast, require the surgical implantation of epidural, subdural, or intracortical electrode arrays. In order to make assistive BMIs reliable in daily life environments, stable decoding of brain activity for controlling the high degree-of-freedom output is necessary.

Implantable BMIs have effectively utilized the local field potentials (LFPs) inside the cortex (Hwang & Andersen, 2009) or on the surface (Schalk, Brunner, Gerhardt, Bischof, & Wolpaw, 2008) and action potentials (spikes) (Taylor, Tillery, & Schwartz, 2002). LFP reflects a variety of electrophysiological processes and is a fundamental signal used to enhance knowledge about neuroscience (Waldert, Lemon, & Kraskov, 2013). LFPs arise from transmembrane currents driven by combinations of spiking, sub-threshold synaptic currents, electrical interactions, and the biophysical properties of cell membranes (Donoghue, Nurmikko, Black, & Hochberg, 2007). The different frequency components in the LFP play different roles in kinematics decoding (Zhang et al., 2011).

Brain-Machine Interfaces, Human-Machine Interfaces, and Electrooculography Interfaces

Electrooculography (EOG) is based on the fact that the eye acts as an electrical dipole between the cornea (positive potential) and the retina (negative potential) (Hortal, Ianez, Ubeda, Perez-Vidal, & Azorin, 2015). The foundation of surgical robotics is in the development of the robotic arm (Moran, 2007). BMI and EOG interfaces have been combined in order to perform the complex tasks, such as the pick-and-place operations in the three-dimensional (3D) workspace utilizing the robotic arm.

Through the detection of vertical and horizontal eye movements, EOG interface can control the movements of the robotic arm in the horizontal plane (Hortal et al., 2015). Each 0.5 second, the EOG and EEG signals are processed to obtain the gaze direction or the blink and the mental task. Both commands are combined to interact with the robotic arm.

EEG signals are recorded to distinguish between two different mental states. Each of them controls the height of the robot making the gripper move upward or downward according to the detected mental state. EEG reflects the collective activity of large populations of cortical neurons located underneath the sensor position (Li et al., 2014), and has low spatial resolution and provides only the noisy overview of ongoing brain activity (Scherer et al., 2013). The EOG interface is used to control the movement of the robot in the horizontal plane (XY plane). The BMI controls the height (Z axis) of the robot end effector. To activate the gripper, the user must perform two consecutive blinks to close or open it depending on its current position

BMIs and EOG interfaces are the well-known examples of the type of human-machine interfaces (HMIs) (Hortal et al., 2015). BMIs allow generating the control commands for an external device from the brain activity of a person (Nicolelis, 2001). BMIs have been utilized to control wheelchairs (Diez et al., 2013), computer interfaces (Perez-Marcos, Buitrago, & Velasquez, 2011), robots (Hortal, Ubeda, Ianez, & Azorin, 2014), and prosthetic devices (McFarland & Wolpaw, 2008), among other devices. EOG interfaces utilize the eye movements to generate the control commands (Hortal et al., 2015). EOG interfaces can detect the eye movements by measuring the difference of potential between the cornea and the retina. EOG interfaces have been utilized to control the different systems, such as a computer (Postelnicu, Girbacia, & Talaba, 2012), video games (Berta, Bellotti, de Gloria, Pranantha, & Schatten, 2013), a wheelchair (Tanaka, Matsunaga, & Wang, 2005), and a robot (Chae, Jeong, & Jo, 2012).

Brain-Machine Interfaces, Amyotrophic Lateral Sclerosis, and Stroke Motor Recovery

BMIs utilize brain activity to control external devices and represent a promising strategy to establish communication with paralyzed amyotrophic lateral sclerosis (ALS) patients as it does not need muscle engagement for its utilization (Chaudhary, Birbaumer, & Curado, 2015). ALS is a progressive motor disease of the lower and often upper motor neurons that affects the sensory or cognitive functions (Chaudhary et al., 2015), leads to the neurodegeneration of the motor system, causing severe physical disabilities that involve all limbs, swallowing, breathing, and speech (Liberati et al., 2015), and leads to the complete paralysis within five years (McCane et al., 2015). Kim et al. (2012) indicated that BMI can provide a communication pathway for patients with ALS. Distinct BMI techniques have been explored to evaluate brain neurophysiology in order to control BMI for patients' communication, especially EEG and near-infrared spectroscopy.

Stroke is one of the most leading causes of acquired disability in the adult population worldwide (Beaglehole, Irwin, & Prentice, 2003). BMI training for stroke motor recovery involves the repetitive motor tasks with the paretic limb through decoding of brain signals related to processing of motor information (e.g., actual movement and motor imagery) and contingent movement of the paretic limb guided by an external device providing sensory (visual and kinesthetic) feedback. Bauer et al. (2015) stated that motor imagery can be understood as the planning of a movement, with its overt execution being inhibited.

The brain signal used to control BMI for stroke motor recovery is the sensorimotor rhythm (SMR), an oscillatory brain activity located over the sensorimotor cortex in the range of 8–13 Hz (Pfurtscheller & da Silva, 1999). The SMR-BMI training with contingent feedback can improve BMI performance and motor learning, thus enhancing SMR desynchronization during motor imagery. During BMI training, response planning constantly adapts itself to decrease the difference between the anticipated feedback and the actual feedback upon the response (Ziessler, Nattkemper, & Frensch, 2004).

BMI for neurorehabilitation involves the recording and decoding of local brain signals generated by the patients, as they try to perform the particular tasks (van Dokkum, Ward, & Laffont, 2015). BMI and robotic rehabilitative devices can enhance stroke neurorehabilitation, accelerate functional recovery, and improve quality of life (Venkatakrishnan, Franciscok, & Contreras-Vidal, 2014). Kondo et al. (2015) stated that the correlation of motor command generation and BMI can augment rehabilitation gains in stroke patients by activating corticomotor networks, providing sensory feedback to close the sensory motor loop. While for patients with incomplete hand paralysis-related repetitive motor tasks may restore motor function (Luft et al., 2004), patients with severe hand paresis do not gain the health care-related profit from the current rehabilitation strategies as they are not able to perform the therapeutic movements. For those patients, BMI training represents the promising strategy to recover the motor function (Chaudhary et al., 2015).

Speech Brain-Machine Interfaces

Speech is the clearest example of a combination of cognitive and motor processes (Tankus et al., 2014). Restoring the ability to artificially communicate again is a natural procedure for allowing paralyzed individuals to express their high level thoughts directly to other people, and can improve the quality of life of ALS patients during the late stages of the disease (Tankus et al., 2014). Speech production involves the large network as described by multiple imaging, lesion, and stimulation studies (Hickok, Houde, & Rong, 2011).

The speech production network includes areas in charge of speech comprehension, such as the bilateral superior temporal gyri (STG), inferior temporal cortex, left angular gyrus, pars orbitalis, and the bilateral superior temporal sulci (Price, 2010). The transition from percepts to actual motor output involves word retrieval (left middle frontal cortex) and articulatory planning (left anterior insula), with the initiation and execution of speech controlled by the left putamen, presupplementary motor area (pre-SMA), SMA, and motor cortex (Price, 2010).

Both the rostral anterior cingulate cortex (Sahin, Pinker, Cash, Schomer, & Halgren, 2009) and the STG (Peeva et al., 2010) participate in the basic control of speech production, while the medial-frontal orbitofrontal cortex is involved in speech comprehension (Sabri et al., 2008) and reading (Kujala et al., 2007). Anterior cingulate cortex is more active for speech than non-speech vocalization (Chang, Kenney, Loucks, Poletto, & Ludlow, 2009), and participates in speech motor control in both human (Wise, Greene, Buchel, & Scott, 1999) and monkey's vocalizations (Paus, 2001).

Brain-Machine Interfaces and Neuroplasticity

Neuroplasticity is the major approach to the operation of BMIs and is the direct communication pathway between the brain and the man-made computing device (Oweiss & Badreldin, 2015). While early efferent BMI work has focused on exhibiting the phenomenological aspects of neuroplasticity (i.e., the brain's ability to change its function during development and recovery from injury), recent work has focused on the technical aspects of the system design, such as the fabrication of BMI devices and the control of multiple degrees of freedom with increasing dexterity in robotic arm control (Collinger et al., 2013).

Neuroplasticity is the ability of nervous system to reorganize its structure, function, and connections in response to BMI training (van Dokkum et al., 2015). The type and extent of neuroplasticity is task-specific, highly time-sensitive, and strongly influenced by environmental factors as well as motivation and attention. Emphasizing the mechanisms of neuroplasticity, particularly at the cellular and subcellular levels, remains essential because it may provide guidance to BMI design and training protocols to manage neuroplasticity in ways that supersede traditional physical rehabilitation exercises.

Brain-Machine Interfaces and Transcranial Doppler

BMIs enable the generation of a control command through mental activity alone, thus bypassing the need for motor involvement (Tai, Blain, & Chau, 2008). Many portable brain monitoring modalities have been explored for BMI development (Lu et al., 2015). Although EEG has been the most popular modality (Wolpaw, Birbaumer, McFarland, Pfurtscheller, & Vaughan, 2002), recent studies have suggested the potential of hemodynamic-based brain monitoring, such as near-infrared spectroscopy (Falk, Guirgis, Power, & Chau, 2011) and transcranial doppler (TCD). TCD is an emerging BMI modality and is a noninvasive ultrasound technology that detects the changes in cerebral blood flow velocity (CBFV) (Lu et al., 2015).

Clinical applications include intracranial pressure monitoring in neurocritical care, evaluation of subarachnoid hemorrhage, detection of micro-embolisms, and monitoring of cerebral circulation during cardiopulmonary bypass (Tsivgoulis, Alexandrov, & Sloan, 2009). TCD has been deployed in functional brain imaging to examine the effects of mental tasks on blood flow velocities, primarily in the middle cerebral arteries (MCAs) (Lu et al., 2015). TCD-BMI system has the potential to become a bedside access technology that enables the activities of daily living for severely nonverbal but cognitively capable individuals (Lu et al., 2015). TCD is robust to ambient lighting, which can encumber near-infrared spectroscopy-BMIs. TCD fulfills a gap where users have sufficient literacy skills to do mental spelling, but may be unable to utilize the electrical and optical alternatives due to excessive myogenic noise (i.e., noise that comes from muscles when they contract) and light absorption by dark hair (Lu et al., 2015).

FUTURE RESEARCH DIRECTIONS

The classification of the extensive literature in the domains of BMIs will provide the potential opportunities for future research. Neuroscience involves several scientific subjects concerning the development, function, chemistry, pharmacology, and pathology of the nervous system (Kasemsap, 2017a). Cognitive neuroscience can help individuals understand how the human brain encourages the perception, affection, and various aspects of cognition and behavior (Kasemsap, 2017b). Utilizing human-computer interaction (HCI) can improve the interactions between users and computers by making computerized devices more receptive to the individual's requirements (Kasemsap, 2018a). Regarding advanced technology, the Internet of Things (IoT) can control many sophisticated tasks without human intervention (Kasemsap, 2018b). Exploring the relationships among BMIs, neuroscience, cognitive neuroscience, HCI, and the IoT would be viable for future research efforts.

CONCLUSION

This chapter explained the overview of BMIs; the aspects of BMIs; BMIs, human-machine interfaces, and electrooculography interfaces; BMIs, ALS, and stroke motor recovery; speech BMIs; BMIs and neuroplasticity; and BMIs and TCD. BMIs are the computerized approaches to gaining the brain signals, investigate them, and translate them into the computerized functions in order to organize the required practices. BMIs can allow people to manipulate computerized networks and various electrical devices. With the support of modern technologies, BMIs are functional and able to operate in operational settings. Applying BMIs has the potential to increase organizational performance and reach strategic goals in the digital age.

REFERENCES

Abdulkader, S. N., Atia, A., & Mostafa, M. S. M. (2015). Brain computer interfacing: Applications and challenges. *Egyptian Informatics Journal*, *16*(2), 213–230. doi:10.1016/j.eij.2015.06.002

Aghagolzadeh, M., & Oweiss, K. (2009). Compressed and distributed sensing of neuronal activity for real time spike train decoding. *IEEE Transactions on Neural Systems and Rehabilitation Engineering*, *17*(2), 116–127. doi:10.1109/TNSRE.2009.2012711 PMID:19193517

Aler, R., & Galvan, I. M. (2015). Optimizing the number of electrodes and spatial filters for brain–computer interfaces by means of an evolutionary multi-objective approach. *Expert Systems with Applications*, *42*(15/16), 6215–6223. doi:10.1016/j.eswa.2015.03.008

Alonso-Valerdi, L. M., Salido-Ruiz, R. A., & Ramirez-Mendoza, R. A. (2015). Motor imagery based brain–computer interfaces: An emerging technology to rehabilitate motor deficits. *Neuropsychologia*, *79*, 354–363. doi:10.1016/j.neuropsychologia.2015.09.012 PMID:26382749

Bauer, R., Fels, M., Vukelić, M., Ziemann, U., & Gharabaghi, A. (2015). Bridging the gap between motor imagery and motor execution with a brain–robot interface. *NeuroImage*, *108*, 319–327. doi:10.1016/j.neuroimage.2014.12.026 PMID:25527239

Beaglehole, R., Irwin, A., & Prentice, T. (2003). *The world health report 2003: Shaping the future*. Geneva, Switzerland: World Health Organization.

Berta, R., Bellotti, F., de Gloria, A., Pranantha, D., & Schatten, C. (2013). Electroencephalogram and physiological signal analysis for assessing flow in games. *IEEE Transactions on Computational Intelligence and AI in Games*, *5*(2), 164–175. doi:10.1109/TCIAIG.2013.2260340

Birbaumer, N., & Chaudhary, U. (2015). Learning from brain control: Clinical application of brain–computer interfaces. *e-Neuroforum*, *6*(4), 87–95.

Birbaumer, N., Gallegos-Ayala, G., Wildgruber, M., Silvoni, S., & Soekadar, S. R. (2014). Direct brain control and communication in paralysis. *Brain Topography*, *27*(1), 4–11. doi:10.1007/s10548-013-0282-1 PMID:23536247

Birbaumer, N., Ghanayim, N., Hinterberger, T., Iversen, I., Kotchoubey, B., Kübler, A., & Flor, H. et al. (1999). A spelling device for the paralysed. *Nature*, *398*(6725), 297–298. doi:10.1038/18581 PMID:10192330

Cecotti, H. (2015). Toward shift invariant detection of event-related potentials in non-invasive brain–computer interface. *Pattern Recognition Letters*, *66*, 127–134. doi:10.1016/j.patrec.2015.01.015

Chae, Y., Jeong, J., & Jo, S. (2012). Toward brain-actuated humanoid robots: Asynchronous direct control using an EEG-based BCI. *IEEE Transactions on Robotics*, *28*(5), 1131–1144. doi:10.1109/TRO.2012.2201310

Chai, G. H., Sui, X. H., Li, P., Liu, X. X., & Lan, N. (2014). Review on tactile sensory feedback of prosthetic hands for the upper-limb amputees by sensory afferent stimulation. *Journal of Shanghai Jiaotong University (Science)*, *19*(5), 587–591. doi:10.1007/s12204-014-1546-y

Chang, S. E., Kenney, M. K., Loucks, T. M. J., Poletto, C. J., & Ludlow, C. L. (2009). Common neural substrates support speech and non-speech vocal tract gestures. *NeuroImage*, *47*(1), 314–325. doi:10.1016/j.neuroimage.2009.03.032 PMID:19327400

Chapin, J. K., Moxon, K. A., Markowitz, R. S., & Nicolelis, M. A. L. (1999). Real-time control of a robot arm using simultaneously recorded neurons in the motor cortex. *Nature Neuroscience*, *2*(7), 664–670. doi:10.1038/10223 PMID:10404201

Chaudhary, U., Birbaumer, N., & Curado, M. R. (2015). Brain–machine interface (BMI) in paralysis. *Annals of Physical and Rehabilitation Medicine, 58*(1), 9–13. doi:10.1016/j.rehab.2014.11.002 PMID:25623294

Choi, S. J., & Kang, B. G. (2014). Prototype design and implementation of an automatic control system based on a BCI. *Wireless Personal Communications, 79*(4), 2551–2563. doi:10.1007/s11277-014-1861-5

Clausen, J. (2013). Bonding brains to machines: Ethical implications of electroceuticals for the human brain. *Neuroethics, 6*(3), 429–434. doi:10.1007/s12152-013-9186-8

Coffey, E. B. J., Brouwer, A. M., Wilschut, E. S., & van Erp, J. B. F. (2010). Brain–machine interfaces in space: Using spontaneous rather than intentionally generated brain signals. *Acta Astronautica, 67*(1/2), 1–11. doi:10.1016/j.actaastro.2009.12.016

Collinger, J. L., Wodlinger, B., Downey, J. E., Wang, W., Tyler-Kabara, E. C., Weber, D. J., & Schwartz, A. B. et al. (2013). High-performance neuroprosthetic control by an individual with tetraplegia. *Lancet, 381*(9866), 557–564. doi:10.1016/S0140-6736(12)61816-9 PMID:23253623

Decety, J. (1996). The neurophysiological basis of motor imagery. *Behavioural Brain Research, 77*(1/2), 45–52. doi:10.1016/0166-4328(95)00225-1 PMID:8762158

Demetriades, A. K., Demetriades, C. K., Watts, C., & Ashkan, K. (2010). Brain–machine interface: The challenge of neuroethics. *The Surgeon: Journal of the Royal Colleges of Surgeons of Edinburgh and Ireland, 8*(5), 267–269. doi:10.1016/j.surge.2010.05.006 PMID:20709284

Diez, P. F., Muller, S. M. T., Mut, V. A., Laciar, E., Avila, E., Bastos-Filho, T. F., & Sarcinelli-Filho, M. (2013). Commanding a robotic wheelchair with a high-frequency steady-state visual evoked potential based brain–computer interface. *Medical Engineering & Physics, 35*(8), 1155–1164. doi:10.1016/j.medengphy.2012.12.005 PMID:23339894

Dobkin, B. H. (2007). Brain–computer interface technology as a tool to augment plasticity and outcomes for neurological rehabilitation. *The Journal of Physiology, 579*(3), 637–642. doi:10.1113/jphysiol.2006.123067 PMID:17095557

Donoghue, J. P., Nurmikko, A., Black, M., & Hochberg, L. R. (2007). Assistive technology and robotic control using motor cortex ensemble-based neural interface systems in humans with tetraplegia. *The Journal of Physiology, 579*(3), 603–611. doi:10.1113/jphysiol.2006.127209 PMID:17272345

Ethier, C., Oby, E. R., Bauman, M. J., & Miller, L. E. (2012). Restoration of grasp following paralysis through brain-controlled stimulation of muscles. *Nature, 485*(7398), 368–371. doi:10.1038/nature10987 PMID:22522928

Falk, T. H., Guirgis, M., Power, S., & Chau, T. T. (2011). Taking NIRS-BCIs outside the lab: Towards achieving robustness against environment noise. *IEEE Transactions on Neural Systems and Rehabilitation Engineering, 19*(2), 136–146. doi:10.1109/TNSRE.2010.2078516 PMID:20876031

Farwell, L. A., & Donchin, E. (1988). Talking off the top of your head: Toward a mental prosthesis utilizing event-related brain potentials. *Electroencephalography and Clinical Neurophysiology, 70*(6), 510–523. doi:10.1016/0013-4694(88)90149-6 PMID:2461285

Fetz, E. E. (1969). Operant conditioning of cortical unit activity. *Science*, *163*(3870), 955–958. doi:10.1126/science.163.3870.955 PMID:4974291

Fridman, G. Y., Blair, H. T., Blaisdell, A. P., & Judy, J. W. (2010). Perceived intensity of somatosensory cortical electrical stimulation. *Experimental Brain Research*, *203*(3), 499–515. doi:10.1007/s00221-010-2254-y PMID:20440610

Gao, X., Dignfeng, X., Cheng, M., & Gao, S. (2003). A BCI-based environmental controller for the motion-disabled. *IEEE Transactions on Neural Systems and Rehabilitation Engineering*, *11*(2), 137–140. doi:10.1109/TNSRE.2003.814449 PMID:12899256

Georgopoulos, A. P., Langheim, F. J. P., Leuthold, A. C., & Merkle, A. N. (2005). Magnetoencephalographic signals predict movement trajectory in space. *Experimental Brain Research*, *167*(1), 132–135. doi:10.1007/s00221-005-0028-8 PMID:16044305

Gongora, M., Peressutti, C., Machado, S., Teixeira, S., Velasques, B., & Ribeiro, P. (2013). Progress and prospects in neurorehabilitation: Clinical applications of stem cells and brain–computer interface for spinal cord lesions. *Neurological Sciences*, *34*(4), 427–433. doi:10.1007/s10072-012-1232-5 PMID:23161257

Hao, Y. Y., Zhang, Q. S., Zhang, S. M., Zhao, T., Wang, Y. W., Chen, W. D., & Zheng, X. X. (2013). Decoding grasp movement from monkey premotor cortex for real-time prosthetic hand control. *Chinese Science Bulletin*, *58*(20), 2512–2520. doi:10.1007/s11434-013-5840-0

Harrison, R. V. (1987). Cochlear implants: A review of the principles and important physiological factors. *The Journal of Otolaryngology*, *16*(5), 268–275. PMID:3316687

Haselager, P. (2013). Did I do that? Brain–computer interfacing and the sense of agency. *Minds and Machines*, *23*(3), 405–418. doi:10.1007/s11023-012-9298-7

Heger, D., Putze, F., & Schultz, T. (2011). An EEG adaptive information system for an empathic robot. *International Journal of Social Robotics*, *3*(4), 415–425. doi:10.1007/s12369-011-0107-x

Hickok, G., Houde, J., & Rong, F. (2011). Sensorimotor integration in speech processing: Computational basis and neural organization. *Neuron*, *69*(3), 407–422. doi:10.1016/j.neuron.2011.01.019 PMID:21315253

Hochberg, L. R., Serruya, M. D., Friehs, G. M., Mukand, J. A., Saleh, M., Caplan, A. H., & Donoghue, J. P. et al. (2006). Neuronal ensemble control of prosthetic devices by a human with tetraplegia. *Nature*, *442*(7099), 164–171. doi:10.1038/nature04970 PMID:16838014

Hortal, E., Ianez, E., Ubeda, A., Perez-Vidal, C., & Azorin, J. M. (2015). Combining a brain–machine interface and an electrooculography interface to perform pick and place tasks with a robotic arm. *Robotics and Autonomous Systems*, *72*, 181–188. doi:10.1016/j.robot.2015.05.010

Hortal, E., Ubeda, A., Ianez, E., & Azorin, J. M. (2014). Control of a 2 DoF robot using a brain–machine interface. *Computer Methods and Programs in Biomedicine*, *116*(2), 169–176. doi:10.1016/j.cmpb.2014.02.018 PMID:24694722

Hwang, E. J., & Andersen, R. A. (2009). Brain control of movement execution onset using local field potentials in posterior parietal cortex. *The Journal of Neuroscience*, *29*(45), 14363–14370. doi:10.1523/JNEUROSCI.2081-09.2009 PMID:19906983

Ibrahim, T. S., Abraham, D., & Rennaker, R. L. (2007). Electromagnetic power absorption and temperature changes due to brain machine interface operation. *Annals of Biomedical Engineering*, *35*(5), 825–834. doi:10.1007/s10439-007-9264-3 PMID:17334681

Iscan, Z., Dokur, Z., & Demiralp, T. (2011). Classification of electroencephalogram signals with combined time and frequency features. *Expert Systems with Applications*, *38*(8), 10499–10505. doi:10.1016/j.eswa.2011.02.110

Iturrate, I., Antelis, J. M., Kubler, A., & Minguez, J. (2009). A non-invasive brain-actuated wheelchair based on a P300 neurophysiological protocol and automated navigation. *IEEE Transactions on Robotics*, *25*(3), 614–627. doi:10.1109/TRO.2009.2020347

Jeannerod, M. (1995). Mental imagery in the motor context. *Neuropsychologia*, *33*(11), 1419–1432. doi:10.1016/0028-3932(95)00073-C PMID:8584178

Jebari, K. (2013). Brain machine interface and human enhancement: An ethical review. *Neuroethics*, *6*(3), 617–625. doi:10.1007/s12152-012-9176-2

Kasemsap, K. (2017a). Investigating the roles of neuroscience and knowledge management in higher education. In S. Mukerji & P. Tripathi (Eds.), *Handbook of research on administration, policy, and leadership in higher education* (pp. 112–140). Hershey, PA: IGI Global. doi:10.4018/978-1-5225-0672-0.ch006

Kasemsap, K. (2017b). Mastering cognitive neuroscience and social neuroscience perspectives in the information age. In M. Dos Santos (Ed.), *Applying neuroscience to business practice* (pp. 82–113). Hershey, PA: IGI Global. doi:10.4018/978-1-5225-1028-4.ch005

Kasemsap, K. (2018a). The fundamentals of human-computer interaction. In M. Khosrow-Pour (Ed.), Encyclopedia of information science and technology (4th ed.; pp. 4199–4209). Hershey, PA: IGI Global. doi:10.4018/978-1-5225-2255-3.ch364

Kasemsap, K. (2018b). Multifaceted applications of the Internet of Things. In M. Khosrow-Pour (Ed.), *Encyclopedia of information science and technology* (4th ed.; pp. 7775–7784). Hershey, PA: IGI Global. doi:10.4018/978-1-5225-2255-3.ch676

Kim, B., Reyes, A., Garza, B., & Choi, Y. (2015). A microchannel neural interface with embedded microwires targeting the peripheral nervous system. *Microsystem Technologies*, *21*(7), 1551–1557. doi:10.1007/s00542-014-2340-3

Kim, D. W., Lee, J. C., Park, Y. M., Kim, I. Y., & Im, C. H. (2012). Auditory brain–computer interfaces (BCIs) and their practical applications. *Biomedical Engineering Letters*, *2*(1), 13–17. doi:10.1007/s13534-012-0051-1

Kim, J., Lee, M., Rhim, J. S., Wang, P., Lu, N., & Kim, D. H. (2014). Next-generation flexible neural and cardiac electrode arrays. *Biomedical Engineering Letters*, *4*(2), 95–108. doi:10.1007/s13534-014-0132-4

Kondo, T., Saeki, M., Hayashi, Y., Nakayashiki, K., & Takata, Y. (2015). Effect of instructive visual stimuli on neurofeedback training for motor imagery-based brain–computer interface. *Human Movement Science*, *43*, 239–249. doi:10.1016/j.humov.2014.08.014 PMID:25467185

Koralek, A. C., Jin, X., Long, J. D. II, Costa, R. M., & Carmena, J. M. (2012). Corticostriatal plasticity is necessary for learning intentional neuroprosthetic skills. *Nature*, *483*(7389), 331–335. doi:10.1038/nature10845 PMID:22388818

Kujala, J., Pammer, K., Cornelissen, P. L., Roebroeck, P., Formisano, E., & Salmelin, R. (2007). Phase coupling in a cerebro-cerebellar network at 8–13 Hz during reading. *Cerebral Cortex*, *17*(6), 1476–1485. doi:10.1093/cercor/bhl059 PMID:16926241

Kumar, S., & Sahin, F. (2015). A framework for a real time intelligent and interactive brain computer interface. *Computers & Electrical Engineering*, *43*, 193–214. doi:10.1016/j.compeleceng.2015.03.024

Lebedev, M. (2014). Brain–machine interfaces: An overview. *Translational Neuroscience*, *5*(1), 99–110. doi:10.2478/s13380-014-0212-z

Lee, J. (2016). Cochlear implantation, enhancements, transhumanism and posthumanism: Some human questions. *Science and Engineering Ethics*, *22*(1), 67–92. doi:10.1007/s11948-015-9640-6 PMID:25962718

Li, H. (2009). A compensability RF CMOS mixed-signal interface for implantable system. *Analog Integrated Circuits and Signal Processing*, *61*(3), 301–307. doi:10.1007/s10470-009-9311-0

Li, T., Hong, J., Zhang, J., & Guo, F. (2014). Brain–machine interface control of a manipulator using small-world neural network and shared control strategy. *Journal of Neuroscience Methods*, *224*, 26–38. doi:10.1016/j.jneumeth.2013.11.015 PMID:24333753

Liberati, G., Pizzimenti, A., Simione, L., Riccio, A., Schettini, F., Inghilleri, M., & Cincotti, F. et al. (2015). Developing brain-computer interfaces from a user-centered perspective: Assessing the needs of persons with amyotrophic lateral sclerosis, caregivers, and professionals. *Applied Ergonomics*, *50*, 139–146. doi:10.1016/j.apergo.2015.03.012 PMID:25959328

Little, S., & Brown, P. (2012). What brain signals are suitable for feedback control of deep brain stimulation in Parkinson's disease? *Annals of the New York Academy of Sciences*, *1265*(1), 9–24. doi:10.1111/j.1749-6632.2012.06650.x PMID:22830645

Liu, J., Khalil, H. K., & Oweiss, K. G. (2011). Neural feedback for instantaneous spatiotemporal modulation of afferent pathways in bi-directional brain–machine interfaces. *IEEE Transactions on Neural Systems and Rehabilitation Engineering*, *19*(5), 521–533. doi:10.1109/TNSRE.2011.2162003 PMID:21859634

Lu, J., Mamun, K. A., & Chau, T. (2015). Pattern classification to optimize the performance of transcranial doppler ultrasonography-based brain machine interface. *Pattern Recognition Letters*, *66*, 135–143. doi:10.1016/j.patrec.2015.07.020

Luck, S. J. (2005). *An introduction to the event-related potential technique*. Cambridge, MA: MIT Press.

Luft, A. R., McCombe-Waller, S., Whitall, J., Forrester, L. W., Macko, R., Sorkin, J. D., & Hanley, D. F. et al. (2004). Repetitive bilateral arm training and motor cortex activation in chronic stroke: A randomized controlled trial. *Journal of the American Medical Association*, *292*(15), 1853–1861. doi:10.1001/jama.292.15.1853 PMID:15494583

McCane, L. M., Heckman, S. M., McFarland, D. J., Townsend, G., Mak, J. N., Sellers, E. W., & Vaughan, T. M. et al. (2015). P300-based brain-computer interface (BCI) event-related potentials (ERPs): People with amyotrophic lateral sclerosis (ALS) vs. age-matched controls. *Clinical Neurophysiology, 126*(11), 2124–2131. doi:10.1016/j.clinph.2015.01.013 PMID:25703940

McFarland, D. J., & Wolpaw, J. R. (2008). Brain–computer interface operation of robotic and prosthetic devices. *Computer, 41*(10), 52–56. doi:10.1109/MC.2008.409

Mihara, M., Hattori, N., Hatakenaka, M., Yagura, H., Kawano, T., Hino, T., & Miyai, I. (2013). Near-infrared spectroscopy-mediated neurofeedback enhances efficacy of motor imagery-based training in poststroke victims: A pilot study. *Stroke, 44*(4), 1091–1098. doi:10.1161/STROKEAHA.111.674507 PMID:23404723

Millan, J. R., Ferrez, P. W., Galan, F., Lew, E., & Chavarriaga, R. (2008). Non-invasive brain–machine interaction. *International Journal of Pattern Recognition and Artificial Intelligence, 22*(5), 959–972. doi:10.1142/S0218001408006600

Millan, J. R., Renkens, F., Mourino, J., & Gerstner, W. (2004). Non-invasive brain-actuated control of a mobile robot by human EEG. *IEEE Transactions on Biomedical Engineering, 51*(6), 1026–1033. doi:10.1109/TBME.2004.827086 PMID:15188874

Moran, D. (2010). Evolution of brain–computer interface: Action potentials, local field potentials and electrocorticograms. *Current Opinion in Neurobiology, 20*(6), 741–745. doi:10.1016/j.conb.2010.09.010 PMID:20952183

Moran, M. E. (2007). Evolution of robotic arms. *Journal of Robotic Surgery, 1*(2), 103–111. doi:10.1007/s11701-006-0002-x PMID:25484945

Ng, K. A., Greenwald, E., Xu, Y. P., & Thakor, N. V. (2016). Implantable neurotechnologies: A review of integrated circuit neural amplifiers. *Medical & Biological Engineering & Computing, 54*(1), 45–62. doi:10.1007/s11517-015-1431-3 PMID:26798055

Nicolelis, M. A. L. (2001). Actions from thoughts. *Nature, 409*(6818), 403–407. doi:10.1038/35053191 PMID:11201755

Oweiss, K. G., & Badreldin, I. S. (2015). Neuroplasticity subserving the operation of brain–machine interfaces. *Neurobiology of Disease, 83*, 161–171. doi:10.1016/j.nbd.2015.05.001 PMID:25968934

Patil, A. C., & Thakor, N. V. (2016). Implantable neurotechnologies: A review of micro- and nanoelectrodes for neural recording. *Medical & Biological Engineering & Computing, 54*(1), 23–44. doi:10.1007/s11517-015-1430-4 PMID:26753777

Paus, T. (2001). Primate anterior cingulate cortex: Where motor control, drive and cognition interface. *Nature Reviews. Neuroscience, 2*(6), 417–424. doi:10.1038/35077500 PMID:11389475

Peeva, M. G., Guenther, F. H., Tourville, J. A., Nieto-Castanon, A., Anton, J. L., Nazarian, B., & Alario, F. X. (2010). Distinct representations of phonemes, syllables, and supra-syllabic sequences in the speech production network. *NeuroImage, 50*(2), 626–638. doi:10.1016/j.neuroimage.2009.12.065 PMID:20035884

Perez-Marcos, D., Buitrago, J. A., & Velasquez, F. D. G. (2011). Writing through a robot: A proof of concept for a brain–machine interface. *Medical Engineering & Physics, 33*(10), 1314–1317. doi:10.1016/j.medengphy.2011.06.005 PMID:21741290

Pfurtscheller, G., & Aranbibar, A. (1979). Evaluation of event-related desynchronization preceding and following voluntary self-paced movement. *Electroencephalography and Clinical Neurophysiology, 46*(2), 138–146. doi:10.1016/0013-4694(79)90063-4 PMID:86421

Pfurtscheller, G., & da Silva, F. H. L. (1999). Event-related EEG/MEG synchronization and desynchronization: Basic principles. *Clinical Neurophysiology, 110*(11), 1842–1857. doi:10.1016/S1388-2457(99)00141-8 PMID:10576479

Postelnicu, C. C., Girbacia, F., & Talaba, D. (2012). EOG-based visual navigation interface development. *Expert Systems with Applications, 39*(12), 10857–10866. doi:10.1016/j.eswa.2012.03.007

Price, C. J. (2010). The anatomy of language: A review of 100 fMRI studies published in 2009. *Annals of the New York Academy of Sciences, 1191*(1), 62–88. doi:10.1111/j.1749-6632.2010.05444.x PMID:20392276

Rotermund, D., Ernst, U. A., & Pawelzik, K. R. (2006). Towards on-line adaptation of neuro-prostheses with neuronal evaluation signals. *Biological Cybernetics, 95*(3), 243–257. doi:10.1007/s00422-006-0083-7 PMID:16802156

Saab, C. (2013). Visualizing the complex brain dynamics of chronic pain. *Journal of Neuroimmune Pharmacology, 8*(3), 510–517. doi:10.1007/s11481-012-9378-8 PMID:22684310

Sabri, M., Binder, J. R., Desai, R., Medler, D. A., Leitl, M. D., & Liebenthal, E. (2008). Attentional and linguistic interactions in speech perception. *NeuroImage, 39*(3), 1444–1456. doi:10.1016/j.neuroimage.2007.09.052 PMID:17996463

Sahin, N. T., Pinker, S., Cash, S. S., Schomer, D., & Halgren, E. (2009). Sequential processing of lexical, grammatical, and phonological information within Broca's area. *Science, 326*(5951), 445–449. doi:10.1126/science.1174481 PMID:19833971

Sanchez, J. C., & Principe, J. C. (2007). *Brain–machine interface engineering*. New York, NY: Morgan & Claypool Publishers.

Schalk, G., Brunner, P., Gerhardt, L. A., Bischof, H., & Wolpaw, J. R. (2008). Brain–computer interfaces (BCIs): Detection instead of classification. *Journal of Neuroscience Methods, 167*(1), 51–62. doi:10.1016/j.jneumeth.2007.08.010 PMID:17920134

Scherer, R., Faller, J., Balderas, D., Friedrich, E. V. C., Pröll, M., Allison, B., & Müller-Putz, G. (2013). Brain–computer interfacing: More than the sum of its parts. *Soft Computing, 17*(2), 317–331. doi:10.1007/s00500-012-0895-4

Serruya, M. D., Harsopoulos, N. G., Paninski, L., Fellows, M. R., & Donoghue, K. (2002). Instant neural control of a movement signal. *Nature, 416*(6877), 141–142. doi:10.1038/416141a PMID:11894084

Shin, Y., Lee, S., Ahn, M., Cho, H., Jun, S. C., & Lee, H. N. (2015). Simple adaptive sparse representation based classification schemes for EEG based brain–computer interface applications. *Computers in Biology and Medicine*, *66*, 29–38. doi:10.1016/j.compbiomed.2015.08.017 PMID:26378500

Sirvent, J. L., Ianez, E., Ubeda, A., & Azorin, J. M. (2012). Visual evoked potential-based brain–machine interface applications to assist disabled people. *Expert Systems with Applications*, *39*(9), 7908–7918. doi:10.1016/j.eswa.2012.01.110

Soekadar, S. R., Birbaumer, N., & Cohen, L. G. (2011). Brain–computer interfaces in the rehabilitation of stroke and neurotrauma. In L. Cohen & K. Kansaku (Eds.), *Systems neuroscience and rehabilitation* (pp. 3–18). Berlin, Germany: Springer–Verlag. doi:10.1007/978-4-431-54008-3_1

Soekadar, S. R., Birbaumer, N., Slutzky, M. W., & Cohen, L. G. (2015). Brain–machine interfaces in neurorehabilitation of stroke. *Neurobiology of Disease*, *83*, 172–179. doi:10.1016/j.nbd.2014.11.025 PMID:25489973

Stieglitz, T. (2010). Manufacturing, assembling and packaging of miniaturized neural implants. *Microsystem Technologies*, *16*(5), 723–734. doi:10.1007/s00542-009-0988-x

Strangman, G., Boas, D. A., & Sutton, J. P. (2002). Non-invasive neuroimaging using near-infrared light. *Biological Psychiatry*, *52*(7), 679–693. doi:10.1016/S0006-3223(02)01550-0 PMID:12372658

Tai, K., Blain, S., & Chau, T. (2008). A review of emerging access technologies for individuals with severe motor impairments. *Assistive Technology*, *20*(4), 204–221. doi:10.1080/10400435.2008.101319 47 PMID:19160907

Tanaka, K., Matsunaga, K., & Wang, H. (2005). Electroencephalogram-based control of an electric wheelchair. *IEEE Transactions on Robotics*, *21*(4), 762–766. doi:10.1109/TRO.2004.842350

Tankus, A., Fried, I., & Shoham, S. (2014). Cognitive-motor brain–machine interfaces. *Journal of Physiology, Paris*, *108*(1), 38–44. doi:10.1016/j.jphysparis.2013.05.005 PMID:23774120

Taylor, D. M., Tillery, S. I. H., & Schwartz, A. B. (2002). Direct cortical control of 3D neuroprosthetic devices. *Science*, *296*(5574), 1829–1832. doi:10.1126/science.1070291 PMID:12052948

Tsivgoulis, G., Alexandrov, A. V., & Sloan, M. A. (2009). Advances in transcranial doppler ultrasonography. *Current Neurology and Neuroscience Reports*, *9*(1), 46–54. doi:10.1007/s11910-009-0008-7 PMID:19080753

Ubeda, A., Ianez, E., Azorin, J. M., & Perez-Vidal, C. (2013). Endogenous brain–machine interface based on the correlation of EEG maps. *Computer Methods and Programs in Biomedicine*, *112*(2), 302–308. doi:10.1016/j.cmpb.2013.01.012 PMID:23453295

Udoekwere, U. I., Oza, C. S., & Giszter, S. F. (2014). A pelvic implant orthosis in rodents, for spinal cord injury rehabilitation, and for brain machine interface research: Construction, surgical implantation and validation. *Journal of Neuroscience Methods*, *222*, 199–206. doi:10.1016/j.jneumeth.2013.10.022 PMID:24269175 van Dokkum, L. E. H., Ward, T., & Laffont, I. (2015). Brain computer interfaces for neurorehabilitation: Its current status as a rehabilitation strategy post-stroke. *Annals of Physical and Rehabilitation Medicine*, *58*(1), 3–8. doi:10.1016/j.rehab.2014.09.016 PMID:25614021

Venkatakrishnan, A., Franciscok, G. E., & Contreras-Vidal, J. L. (2014). Applications of brain–machine interface systems in stroke recovery and rehabilitation. *Current Physical Medicine and Rehabilitation Reports*, *2*(2), 93–105. doi:10.1007/s40141-014-0051-4 PMID:25110624

Waldert, S., Lemon, R. N., & Kraskov, A. (2013). Influence of spiking activity on cortical local field potentials. *The Journal of Physiology*, *591*(21), 5291–5303. doi:10.1113/jphysiol.2013.258228 PMID:23981719

Weiskopf, N., Veit, R., Erb, M., Mathiak, K., Grodd, W., Goebel, R., & Birbaumer, N. (2003). Physiological self-regulation of regional brain activity using real-time functional magnetic resonance imaging (fMRI): Methodology and exemplary data. *NeuroImage*, *19*(3), 577–586. doi:10.1016/S1053-8119(03)00145-9 PMID:12880789

Wise, R. J., Greene, J., Buchel, C., & Scott, S. K. (1999). Brain regions involved in articulation. *Lancet*, *353*(9158), 1057–1061. doi:10.1016/S0140-6736(98)07491-1 PMID:10199354

Wolpaw, J. R., Birbaumer, N., McFarland, D. J., Pfurtscheller, G., & Vaughan, T. M. (2002). Brain–computer interfaces for communication and control. *Clinical Neurophysiology: Official Journal of the International Federation of Clinical Neurophysiology*, *113*(6), 767–791. doi:10.1016/S1388-2457(02)00057-3 PMID:12048038

Wood, I. K. (2001). *Neuroscience: Exploring the brain*. Philadelphia, PA: Lippincott Williams & Wilkins.

Xu, Q., Zhou, H., Wang, Y. J., & Huang, J. (2009). Fuzzy support vector machine for classification of EEG signals using wavelet-based features. *Medical Engineering & Physics*, *31*(7), 858–865. doi:10.1016/j.medengphy.2009.04.005 PMID:19487151

Yu, Y., Zhang, S. M., Zhang, H. J., Liu, X. C., Zhang, Q. S., Zheng, X. X., & Dai, J. H. (2010). Neural decoding based on probabilistic neural network. *Journal of Zhejiang University. Science. B.*, *11*(4), 298–306. doi:10.1631/jzus.B0900284 PMID:20349527

Zander, T., Kothe, C., Welke, S., & Roetting, M. (2008). *Enhancing human– machine systems with secondary input from passive brain– computer interfaces*. Paper presented at the 4th International Brain–Computer Interface Workshop and Training Course, Graz, Austria.

Zhang, F., Aghagolzadeh, M., & Oweiss, K. (2012). A fully implantable, programmable and multimodal neuroprocessor for wireless, cortically controlled brain-machine interface applications. *Journal of Signal Processing Systems for Signal, Image, and Video Technology*, *69*(3), 351–361. doi:10.1007/s11265-012-0670-x PMID:23050029

Zhang, S., Jiang, B., Zhu, J., Zhang, Q., Chen, W., Zheng, X., & Zhao, T. (2011). A study on combining local field potential and single unit activity for better neural decoding. *International Journal of Imaging Systems and Technology*, *21*(2), 165–172. doi:10.1002/ima.20287

Zhang, Y., & Chase, S. M. (2015). Recasting brain-machine interface design from a physical control system perspective. *Journal of Computational Neuroscience, 39*(2), 107–118. doi:10.1007/s10827-015-0566-4 PMID:26142906

Zhang, Y., Zhou, G., Jin, J., Wang, X., & Cichocki, A. (2015). Optimizing spatial patterns with sparse filter bands for motor-imagery based brain–computer interface. *Journal of Neuroscience Methods, 255*, 85–91. doi:10.1016/j.jneumeth.2015.08.004 PMID:26277421

Ziessler, M., Nattkemper, D., & Frensch, P. A. (2004). The role of anticipation and intention in the learning of effects of self-performed actions. *Psychological Research, 68*(2/3), 163–175. doi:10.1007/s00426-003-0153-6 PMID:14634810

ADDITIONAL READING

Asano, H., Sagami, T., & Ide, H. (2013). The evaluation of the emotion by near-infrared spectroscopy. *Artificial Life and Robotics, 17*(3), 452–456. doi:10.1007/s10015-012-0083-8

Belov, D. R., Stepanova, P. A., & Kolodyazhnyi, S. F. (2015). Traveling waves in the human EEG during voluntary hand movements. *Neuroscience and Behavioral Physiology, 45*(9), 1043–1054. doi:10.1007/s11055-015-0184-7

Buller, T. (2013). Neurotechnology, invasiveness and the extended mind. *Neuroethics, 6*(3), 593–605. doi:10.1007/s12152-011-9133-5

Choi, K. (2012). Control of a vehicle with EEG signals in real-time and system evaluation. *European Journal of Applied Physiology, 112*(2), 755–766. doi:10.1007/s00421-011-2029-6 PMID:21667185

Chou, N., Byun, D., & Kim, S. (2014). MEMS-based microelectrode technologies capable of penetrating neural tissues. *Biomedical Engineering Letters, 4*(2), 109–119. doi:10.1007/s13534-014-0133-3

Claussen, J. C., & Hofmann, U. G. (2012). Sleep, neuroengineering and dynamics. *Cognitive Neurodynamics, 6*(3), 211–214. doi:10.1007/s11571-012-9204-2 PMID:23730352

Dubrovskii, D. I. (2013). Subjective reality and the brain: An essay on a theoretical solution to the problem. *Herald of the Russian Academy of Sciences, 83*(1), 59–69. doi:10.1134/S101933161301005X

Eagles, J. S., Carlsen, A. N., & MacKinnon, C. D. (2015). Neural processes mediating the preparation and release of focal motor output are suppressed or absent during imagined movement. *Experimental Brain Research, 233*(5), 1625–1637. doi:10.1007/s00221-015-4237-5 PMID:25744055

Ekusheva, E. V., & Damulin, I. V. (2015). Post-stroke rehabilitation: Importance of neuroplasticity and sensorimotor integration processes. *Neuroscience and Behavioral Physiology, 45*(5), 594–599. doi:10.1007/s11055-015-0117-5

Frolov, A. A., Biryukova, E. V., Bobrov, P. D., Mokienko, O. A., Platonov, A. K., Pryanichnikov, V. E., & Chernikova, L. A. (2012). Principles of neurorehabilitation based on the brain–computer interface and biologically adequate control of the exoskeleton. *Human Physiology*, *39*(2), 196–208. doi:10.1134/S0362119713020035

Glannon, W. (2014). Neuromodulation, agency and autonomy. *Brain Topography*, *27*(1), 46–54. doi:10.1007/s10548-012-0269-3 PMID:23322211

Gulrez, T., & Tognetti, A. (2014). A sensorized garment controlled virtual robotic wheelchair. *Journal of Intelligent & Robotic Systems*, *74*(3), 847–868. doi:10.1007/s10846-013-9839-1

Hosain, M. K., Kouzani, A., & Tye, S. (2014). Closed loop deep brain stimulation: An evolving technology. *Australasian Physical & Engineering Sciences in Medicine*, *37*(4), 619–634. doi:10.1007/s13246-014-0297-2 PMID:25195055

Izeboudjen, N., Larbes, C., & Farah, A. (2014). A new classification approach for neural networks hardware: From standards chips to embedded systems on chip. *Artificial Intelligence Review*, *41*(4), 491–534. doi:10.1007/s10462-012-9321-7

Jebari, K., & Hansson, S. O. (2013). European public deliberation on brain machine interface technology: Five convergence seminars. *Science and Engineering Ethics*, *19*(3), 1071–1086. doi:10.1007/s11948-012-9425-0 PMID:23263902

Johnson, B. D. (2014). Brain machines. *Personal and Ubiquitous Computing*, *18*(4), 811–817. doi:10.1007/s00779-013-0681-z

Lee, Y., & Jun, S. B. (2014). Strategies for minimizing glial response to chronically-implanted microelectrode arrays for neural interface. *Biomedical Engineering Letters*, *4*(2), 120–128. doi:10.1007/s13534-014-0134-2

Machado, A. (2013). New frontier: The brain machine interface. *Neuromodulation: Technology at the Neural Interface*, *16*(1), 6–7. doi:10.1111/ner.12021 PMID:23373814

Putintsev, N. I., Vishnevsky, O. V., & Vityaev, E. E. (2015). Development of artificial cognitive systems based on models of the brain of living organisms. *Russian Journal of Genetics: Applied Research*, *5*(6), 589–600. doi:10.1134/S207905971506012X

Ramos-Murguialday, A., García-Cossio, E., Walter, A., Cho, W., Broetz, D., Bogdan, M., & Birbaumer, N. et al. (2015). Decoding upper limb residual muscle activity in severe chronic stroke. *Annals of Clinical and Translational Neurology*, *2*(1), 1–11. doi:10.1002/acn3.122 PMID:25642429

Schmitz, S. (2012). The neurotechnological cerebral subject: Persistence of implicit and explicit gender norms in a network of change. *Neuroethics*, *5*(3), 261–274. doi:10.1007/s12152-011-9129-1

Seif, Z., & Daliri, M. R. (2015). Evaluation of local field potential signals in decoding of visual attention. *Cognitive Neurodynamics*, *9*(5), 509–522. doi:10.1007/s11571-015-9336-2 PMID:26379801

Shen, H. M., Lee, K. M., Hu, L., Foong, S., & Xu, X. (2016). Effects of reconstructed magnetic field from sparse noisy boundary measurements on localization of active neural source. *Medical & Biological Engineering & Computing, 54*(1), 177–189. doi:10.1007/s11517-015-1381-9 PMID:26358243

So, K., Ganguly, K., Jimenez, J., Gastpar, M. C., & Carmena, J. M. (2012). Redundant information encoding in primary motor cortex during natural and prosthetic motor control. *Journal of Computational Neuroscience, 32*(3), 555–561. doi:10.1007/s10827-011-0369-1 PMID:22042443

Tehovnik, E. J., & Chen, L. L. (2015). Brain control and information transfer. *Experimental Brain Research, 233*(12), 3335–3347. doi:10.1007/s00221-015-4423-5 PMID:26319545

Uno, Y., Amano, K., & Takeda, T. (2013). Development of a generative model of magnetoencephalography noise that enables brain signal extraction from single-epoch data. *Medical & Biological Engineering & Computing, 51*(8), 937–951. doi:10.1007/s11517-013-1069-y PMID:23657832

Wu, Z. H. (2014). Brain–machine interface (BMI) and cyborg intelligence. *Journal of Zhejiang University Science C, 15*(10), 805–806. doi:10.1631/jzus.C1400325

Zephaniah, P. V., & Kim, J. G. (2014). Recent functional near infrared spectroscopy based brain computer interface systems: Developments, applications and challenges. *Biomedical Engineering Letters, 4*(3), 223–230. doi:10.1007/s13534-014-0156-9

KEY TERMS AND DEFINITIONS

Brain: The element of neural system located in the skull.

Brain-Machine Interface: The computerized consolidation that can help user communicate data through brain signals.

Computer: The modern appliance that collects, controls, and produces information.

Electrode: The conductor used to transfer, receive, accumulate, and execute the electric charge carriers.

Information: The data that can be executed for the important tasks.

Neural Network: The artificial intelligence method that emulates the application of human brain.

Robot: The modern machine equipped with various sensors to accomplish many sophisticated functions.

Signal: The electronic procedure that can transfer the data in an effective manner.

Technology: The utilization of modern methods and systems for gaining the improved products and services.

Chapter 20
Efficient Implementation of Hadoop MapReduce–Based Dataflow

Ishak H. A. Meddah
Oran University of Science and Technology – Mohamed Boudiaf, Algeria

Khaled Belkadi
Oran University of Science and Technology – Mohamed Boudiaf, Algeria

ABSTRACT

MapReduce is a solution for the treatment of large data. With it we can analyze and process data. It does this by distributing the computation in a large set of machines. Process mining provides an important bridge between data mining and business process analysis. This technique allows for the extraction of information from event logs. Firstly, the chapter mines small patterns from log traces. Those patterns are the representation of the traces execution from a business process. The authors use existing techniques; the patterns are represented by finite state automaton; the final model is the combination of only two types of patterns that are represented by the regular expressions. Secondly, the authors compute these patterns in parallel, and then combine those patterns using MapReduce. They have two parties. The first is the Map Step. The authors mine patterns from execution traces. The second is the combination of these small patterns as reduce step. The results are promising; they show that the approach is scalable, general, and precise. It minimizes the execution time by the use of MapReduce.

INTRODUCTION

Many techniques have been proposed that mine such patterns from execution traces. However; most existing techniques mine only simple patterns, or they mine a single complex pattern that is restricted to a particular set of manually selected events, patterns are the work flow of the process.

Recent work has recognized that patterns can be specified as regular languages (Ammons et al., 2002). This allows the compact representation of patterns as regular expressions or finite state automata, and it allows the characterization of the pattern mining as a language learning problem.

DOI: 10.4018/978-1-5225-3004-6.ch020

Current approaches are fundamentally similar; each takes as input a static program or a dynamic traces or profile and produces one or more compact regular languages that specify the pattern representation or the workflow. However; the individual solutions differ in key ways.

In this paper, we present a new general approach to pattern mining that addresses several of the limitations of current techniques. Our insight is twofold. First, we recognize that instances of smaller patterns can be composed in parallel into larger patterns. Second, we observed also that the composition of small pattern can be in parallel.

We then leverage this insight to divide our work into two parts; The first one, we use a technique how we can mine two types of small patterns and we compose them by using standard algorithms for finite state automaton manipulation (Gabel & Su, 2008), and some special rules using by M. Gabel and Z. Su (2008), the mining is also performed by symbolic mining algorithm (Gabel & Su, 2008, May).

The second one, we use the framework MapReduce in mining and composing micropatterns; those patterns have been shown as regular expressions or their finite state automatons, in this party we mine small patterns using the same symbolic mining algorithm but in parallel as Map step, and we compute these small patterns into larger pattern in parallel as reduce step.

Our approach has been implemented in the java programming language with the log file of two application; the SKYPE and VIBER applications. The size of those applications log file is more than 10 Go, who are generated by log file generator.

We have tested our approach in two clusters in a cloud, the first regroup five machines, and the second regroups ten machines, the traces in our applications are the call, the answer, and the messages.

RELATED WORK

Many techniques are suggested in the domain of process mining, we quote:

M. Gabel and al (Gabel & Su, 2008) present a new general technique for mining temporal specification, they realized their work in two steps, firstly they discovered the simple patterns using existing techniques, then combine these patterns using the composition and some rules like Branching and Sequencing rules.

Temporal specification expresses formal correctness requirement of an application's ordering of specific actions and events during execution, they discovered patterns from traces of execution or program source code; The simples patterns are represented using regular expression (ab)* or (ab*c)* and their representation using finite state automaton, after they combine simple patterns to construct a temporal specification using a finite state automaton.

G.Greco and al (Greco et al., 2006) discovered several clusters by using a clustering technique, and then they calculate the pattern from each cluster, they combine these patterns to construct a final model, they discovered a workflow scheme from, and then they mine a workflow using a Mine Workflow Algorithm, after they define many clusters from a log traces by using clustering technique and Process Discover Algorithm and some rules cluster.

Then they use a Find Features Algorithm to find a patterns of each cluster, finally they combine these patterns to construct a completely hierarchical workflow model.

In their clustering algorithm, clusters reflect only structural similarities among traces; they say that in future works extending their techniques to take care of the environment so that clusters may reflect not only structural similarities among traces, but also information about, e.g., users and data values.

H.R.Motahari-Nezhed and al (Motahari-Nezhad, et al., 2008) use a service conversation log; first they split a log into several partitions, 2ⁿᵈ they discovered a model from each partition, and 3ʳᵈ, they annotate the discover protocol model with various metadata to construct a protocol model from real-word service conversation logs.

The protocol is the specification of all possible conversations that a service can have with its partners and the conversation consists of a sequence of messages exchanged between two or more services.

During the split they discovered a simple precise protocol models by analyzing messages sequences in the log, they eliminate conversations considered noisy or not presented in the log; they augment discovered protocol with various metadata including state and transition supports to get a final protocol model of the log a most generalized model based splitting.

MAPREDUCE

Since its introduction just a few years ago, the MapReduce framework (Dean & Ghemawat, 2008; Seki, Jinno, & Uehara, 2013) has become extremely popular for analyzing large datasets in cluster environments. The success of MapReduce stems from hiding the details of parallelization, fault tolerance, and load balancing in a simple programming framework; it is increasingly being used to analyze large volume of data. Having several small process, meaning these small processes or called also patterns can be computed in parallel.

This framework is implemented in the C programming language, there is an open sources implementation called Hadoop, it uses a distributed processing architecture in which a task is mapped to a set of servers in then reduced down a single output set, one node, designed as the master node, controls the distribution of tasks. The following diagram shows a Hadoop cluster with the master node directing a group of slave nodes, which process the data.

MapReduce (Dean & Ghemawat, 2008) was originally proposed and used by Google engineers to process the large amount of data they must analyze on a daily basis; The input data for MapReduce consists of a list of key/value pairs. Mappers accept the incoming pairs, and map them into intermediate key/value pairs. Each group of intermediate data with the same key is then passed to a specific set of reducers, each of which performs computations on the data and reduce it to one single key/values pair. The sorted output of the reducers is the final result of the MapReduce process (Itkar, & Kulkarni, 2013; Seki, Jinno, & Uehara, 2013).

To illustrate MapReduce, we consider an example MapReduce process, which counts the frequency of word lengths in a book. The example process is shown in figure 3. Mappers accept every single word from the book and make keys for them. Because we want to count the frequency of all words with different length, a typical approach would be to use the length of the word as key. So, for the word "hello", a mapper will generate a key/value pair of"5/hello". Afterwards, the key/value pairs with the same key are grouped and sent to reducers. A reducer, which receives a list of values with the same key, can simply count the size of this list, and keep the key in its output. If a reducer receives a list with key "5", for example, it will count the size of the list of all the words that have as length "5", if the size is "n", it outputs an output pair "5/n" which means there are "n" words with length "5" in the book (Seki, Jinno, & Uehara, 2013; Koundinya et al., 2012).

The power and challenge of the MapReduce (Shang et al, 2009; Bhuiyan, & Al Hasan, 2015; Tsourakakis, 2010) model reside in its ability to support different mapping and reducing strategies. For example, an alternative mapper implementation could map each input value (i.e, word) based on its first letter and its length. Then the reducers would process those words starting with one or a small number of different letters (keys), and perform the counting. This MapReduce strategy permits an increasing number of reducers that can work in parallel on the problem. However; the final output needs additional post-processing in the comparison to the first strategy. In short, both strategies can solve the problem, but each strategy has different performance and implementation benefits and challenges.

The open source implementation of MapReduce "Hadoop" (Stewart, et al., 2011; Itkar, & Kulkarni, 2013; Koundinya et al., 2012; Aridhi et al., 2014)] is supported by yahoo and used by Amazon, AOL, Baidu and a number of other companies for their distributed solutions. Hadoop can run on various operating systems such as Linux, Windows, FreeBSD, Mac OSX and OpenSolaris. It doesn't only implement the MapReduce model, but also provides a distributed file system, called the Hadoop Distributed File System (HDFS). Hadoop supplies java interfaces to simplify the MapReduce model and to control the HDF programmatically. Another advantage for users is that Hadoop by default comes with some basic and widely used mapping and reducing methods, for example to split files into lines, or to split a directory into files. With these methods, users occasionally do not have to write new code to use MapReduce.

We used Hadoop as our MapReduce implementation for the following four reasons:

Hadoop is easy to use. Researchers do not want to spend considerable time on modifying their mining program to make it distributed. The simple MapReduce java interface simplifies the process of implementing the mappers and reducers. (Bhuiyan, & Al Hasan, 2015)

Hadoop runs on different operating systems. Academic research labs tend to have a heterogeneous network of machines with different hardware configurations and varying operating systems. Hadoop can run on most current operating systems and hence to exploit as much of the available computing power as possible (Itkar, & Kulkarni, 2013; Koundinya et al., 2012).

Hadoop runs on commodity machines. The largest computation resources in research labs and software development companies are desktop computers and laptops. This characteristic of Hadoop permits these computers to join and leave the computing cluster in a dynamic and transparent fashion without user intervention (Bhuiyan, & Al Hasan, 2015; Seki, Jinno, & Uehara, 2013).

Hadoop is mature and an open source systems. Hadoop has been successfully used in many commercial projects. It is actively developed with new features and enhancements continuously being added. Since Hadoop is free to download and redistribute, it can be installed on multiple machines without worrying about costs and per seat licensing (Itkar, & Kulkarni, 2013; Tsourakakis, 2010).

Based on these points, we consider Hadoop as the most suitable MapReduce implementation for our research.

PROCESS MINING

Recently, process mining has become an interesting research area (Van der Aalst et al., 2004; Van der Aalst, Weijters, & Maruster, 2004). The basic idea of process mining is to diagnose business processes by mining event logs for knowledge. Process mining techniques and tools provide the means for discovering process, control, data, organizational, and social structures from event logs (Van der Aalst, 2004).

It provides an important bridge between data mining and business process analysis (Weske, M, 2012; Gao, X, 2013), and even allow for extracting information from event logs.

The idea is that process mining is:

- **Process Discovery:** What processes are executed in our company, supported by enterprise information systems (ERP, BPM, total ad-hoc, e-mail).
- **Conformance Checking:** Business processes are executed according to the rules defined, or human variants exist.
- **Performance Analysis:** Where are the bottlenecks?
- **Process Prediction:** When will the process end?
- **Process Improvement:** How to redesign a process?

For example, the audit trails of a workflow management system or the transaction logs of an enterprise resource planning system can be used to discover models describing processes, organizations, and products. Moreover, it is possible to use process mining to monitor deviations (e.g., comparing the observed events with predefined models or business rules in the context of SOX)." (Versteeg & Bouwman, 2006)

In addition, Process mining is interesting (Versteeg & Bouwman, 2006):

In enterprise architecture, when analysts and people who work in your company lost time for processes that exist, in order to establish process and system architecture. Process Mining plays an indispensable role in the discovery of true enterprise architecture.

- **Process Conformity:** How many times people discovered that the processes are not performed according to the rules (our human nature love finding new ways to execute). This does not mean that the process should be executed according to the rules, because sometimes the rules were not correctly set up.
- **Process Optimization:** People that has the experience to perform process analysis by looking at process flows usually indicate easily where are the bottleneck, duplication, repetition, but nowadays (!) in the world of knowledge management where flows do not dictate the manner of execution is necessary to sit side by side with the people who perform work to understand what are the obstacles (in a large company this is a daunting task). But it is also true that normally escapes analysis teams some of the problem sources, or because there are based opinions, or simply … bad reasoning. (V.D.Aalst, W, 2004)

Business Intelligence helps to understand how we do things, but does have predictive capabilities needed to understand how work could be performed.

BUSINESS PROCESS

Business process is a set of activities occurring within a company that lead to a specific end. Most often, it focuses on meeting the needs of the customer and delivering a good or service that will fulfill that need. This process is actually often a collection of interrelated processes that function in a logical sequence to achieve the ultimate goal (Van Der Aalst, 2013; De Weerdt et al, 2013).

The log files correspond to the actions or traces of the business process. The following example, which is very simple, represents a sequence of characters:

1x Case1 A B C D E G

1x Case2 A C B D G

1x Case3 A E D

Simple Log File

A= Send e-mail, B= check credit, C= calculate capacity, D= check system, E= accept, F= reject, G=send e-mail.

There are many techniques to discover micro patterns from event log or process traces, the next section describes how we mine small patterns from business process.

IMPLEMENTATION AND RESULTS

Implementation and Experimental Setup

We implemented our approach in the java programing language. The first phase, which consist of mining micro patterns, is performed by an existing symbolic specification-mining algorithm (Gabel & Su, 2008, May). This algorithm leverages Binary Decision Diagrams (Bryant, 1986) to maintain a compact state throughout its execution, despite simultaneously tracking up to billions of potential micro patterns. This algorithm is currently the most scalable pattern-based approach, and it is the only algorithm capable of scalably mining micro patterns with alphabets of size three.

Our Hadoop installation is divided into two steps; first is deployed on five computers in a local network. The five computers have an Intel Core I5 3210M @ 2.5 GHz CPU with 8 GB Ram memory. The second phase is deployed on ten computers. The ten computers have the same characteristics of the five computers.

Our small patterns were represented by using regular expression or their finite state automaton, to compose these small patterns, we use the standard algorithm for finite state automaton, using the following rules:

- **Definition (Projection):** The projection π of a string s over an alphabet $\sum$, $\pi_{\sum}$ (s), is defined as s with all letters not in $\sum$ deleted.

  The projection of a language L over $\sum$ is defined as $\pi_{\sum} (L) = \{\pi_{\sum} (s) \mid s \in L\}$.

- **Definition (Specification Pattern):** A specification pattern is a finite state automaton A= $(Q, \sum,$ $\delta, q_0, F)$, where Q is a finite set of states, $\sum$ is a set of input symbols, $\delta: Q$ x $\sum \rightarrow Q$ is the transition function, q_0 is the single starting state, and F is a set of final states. A pattern is satisfied over a trace T with alphabet $\sum' \supseteq \sum$ if $\pi_{\sum} (T) \in L (A)$.

- **Definition (Expansion) [Gabel and Su, (Gabel, M & Su, Z, 2008, May) §2.6]:** Assume a regular language defined by finite state automaton A= $(Q, \sum, \delta, q_0, F)$. The expansion of $(L (A))$ over an arbitrary alphabet $\sum'$, written $E_{\sum'} (L (A))$, is the maximal language over $\sum \cup \sum'$ whose projection over $\sum$ is $L (A)$.

An automaton accepting $E_{\sum'} (L (A))$ can be constructed by first duplicating A and then adding a looping transition $\delta (q, a) = q$ to each state q for each letter a $\in \sum' \backslash \sum$.

Expansion can be thought of maximal inverse of projection. For example, an expression corresponding to $E_{\{a, b, c\}} ((a b)^*)$ is $c^*(a c^*b c^*)^*$.

Note that projecting this new language over {a, b} yields the original language, (a b)*. The composition of two patterns is defined as follows:

- **Definition (Composition):** The composition of two patterns A_1 and A_2 is the intersection of the expansion of each pattern over their combined alphabets, $E_{\sum 1} (A_1) \cap E_{\sum 2} (A_2)$

Intuitively, the composition of two patterns defines a language of traces in which both patterns hold.

We could use this general definition to arbitrary compose patterns by using standard algorithms for finite state automaton manipulation. However, in general, performing these pairwise compositions directly is undesirable. Given a reasonably large set of patterns, the finite state expansion, intersection, and minimization operations become more expensive as the automata grow.

There is some difficulty of treatment with the use of those rules, however, we use some other rules used by Gabel and Su (2008) in their framework Javert.

They recognize special cases of composition in which the result of composition is compact and intuitive. Then they formulate these cases as inference rules, which leads to straightforward implementation in which composition is a constant time operation.

They suggest two rules: the branching rule and the sequencing rule:

Branching Rule describes the composition of two patterns with identical "endpoint", i.e., the first and the last letters of a single iteration of the pattern. Defining $\sum'$ as {a, b} $\cup \sum_{L1} \cup \sum_{L2}$, the correctness of the branching rule follows:

$E_{\sum'}(aL_1{}^*b)^* \cap E_{\sum'} (aL_2{}^*b)^* = (a(L_1|L_2)^*b)^*$ (Gabel, M., & Su, Z, 2008) §3.5]

This rule performs the composition, of two patterns that describe legal operations at the same logical state. For example, from the patterns: [Call answer* Close]*, and [Call not answer* Close]*

We can infer a third pattern [Call (answer | not answer)* Close]*

Sequencing Rule describes the sequencing of two patterns with compatible endpoints.as with the previous rule, L_1 and L_2 must have disjoint alphabets, which must in turn be disjoint from {a, b,c}. Redefining $\sum'$ as {a, b, c} $\cup \sum_{L1} \cup \sum_{L2}$, the correctness of the sequencing rule follows from the following fact:

$E_{\sum'}(a L_1 b)^* \cap E_{\sum'}(b L_2 c)^* \cap E_{\sum'}(a c)^* = (a L_1 b L_2 c)^*$ (Gabel, M., & Su, Z, 2008) §3.6]

Continuing the earlier example, from the patterns:

[Call (answer | not answer)* Close]*, [Connect Call]*, and [Connect close]*

We can infer a fourth pattern [Connect Call (answer | not answer)* Close]*

Both of these rules are general; they apply to both micro patterns and any intermediate assembly thereof.

For the second party, we computed and composed the small patterns in parallel with the use of MapReduce framework (Braun et al., 2014; (Deng, & Lv, 2015).

In the MapReduce implementation, we have two steps: the Map step and the Reduce step; we consider the mining Patterns as the Map step, and compose patterns as the Reduce step.

As an input we have log file of two applications, in this log file we have all applications traces, from those traces we mine in parallel small patterns, having <P, Value>, Patterns as the key and their values. In the Map step we mine all possible patterns, there are two types of patterns (ab)* and (ab*c)*; P is a small pattern and value is the number of patterns, in this step we have many cases of <P, Value>. In the reduce step we have only the result of patterns <P1, Value> and <P2, Value>, after we compose them in parallel in order to get the final pattern that represents the whole model of the process, this model generates a lot of cases, Unfortunately there are two cases can't be generated by our approach.

Our algorithm is an amelioration of existing techniques by using MapReduce:

```
Repeat the process for all application
Input
Process Traces or the log files of Applications
Mapper
Pattern 1, value
................                        /*Pattern 1= (ab)*            */
Pattern 2, value
................                          /*Pattern 2= (ab*c)*        */
Reducer
Pattern 1, Values
Pattern 2, Values
Composition
Compose the patterns using standard Algorithms of finite state automaton, and
the sequencing, branching rules
Output
The workflow how represents the actions of users for three web applications.
```

The following figure represents our MapReduce approach; P1 and P2 are the small mining patterns. The next section presents our result in all steps.

Results

The Table 1 presents the result of our approach without using MapReduce; we used a log file of size more than 10 GB of two Applications Skype and Viber. The number of traces is the actions effected, and total trace events are the number of all actions contained in the log file, we know that we have two steps; the pattern mining and the composition of patterns whom are executed in limited times.

The Table 2 presents the result of our approach using MapReduce distributed in five (05) computers with the same applications and the log file size.

The Table 3 presents the result of our approach using MapReduce distributed in ten (10) computers with the same applications and the log file size.

CONCLUSION AND FUTURE WORK

A scalable patterns mining solution should be efficient, scalable. In this paper, we propose to use MapReduce as a general framework to mining micro patterns from process traces. To validate our approach, we presented our experience of mining small patterns and compose them. Our experiments demonstrate that our solution reduces the execution time, and we conclude that the parallel compute have an inverse relationship with the execution time, with the grow of the machines, the time execution decreases. In addition to the existence of a proportional relationship between the grow of computers and the efficiency of treatment.

There are a number of directions for future work, including and evaluating our method in a big number of computers in cloud, also for big log file size of different applications.

REFERENCES

Ammons, G., Bodík, R., & Larus, J. R. (2002). Mining specifications. *ACM SIGPLAN Notices*, *37*(1), 4–16. doi:10.1145/565816.503275

Aridhi, S., D'Orazio, L., Maddouri, M., & Mephu, E. (2014, June). A novel MapReduce-based approach for distributed frequent subgraph mining. In *Reconnaissance de Formes et Intelligence Artificielle*. RFIA.

Bhuiyan, M. A., & Al Hasan, M. (2015). An iterative MapReduce based frequent subgraph mining algorithm. *Knowledge and Data Engineering. IEEE Transactions on*, *27*(3), 608–620.

Braun, P., Cameron, J. J., Cuzzocrea, A., Jiang, F., & Leung, C. K. (2014). Effectively and efficiently mining frequent patterns from dense graph streams on disk. *Procedia Computer Science*, *35*, 338–347. doi:10.1016/j.procs.2014.08.114

Bryant, R. E. (1986). Graph-based algorithms for Boolean function manipulation. Computers. *IEEE Transactions on*, *100*(8), 677–691.

De Weerdt, J., Schupp, A., Vanderloock, A., & Baesens, B. (2013). Process Mining for the multi-faceted analysis of business processes—A case study in a financial services organization. *Computers in Industry*, *64*(1), 57–67. doi:10.1016/j.compind.2012.09.010

Dean, J., & Ghemawat, S. (2008). MapReduce: Simplified data processing on large clusters. *Communications of the ACM*, *51*(1), 107–113. doi:10.1145/1327452.1327492

Deng, Z. H., & Lv, S. L. (2015). PrePost+: An efficient N-lists-based algorithm for mining frequent itemsets via Children–Parent Equivalence pruning. *Expert Systems with Applications, 42*(13), 5424–5432. doi:10.1016/j.eswa.2015.03.004

der Aalst, W., Weijters, T., & Maruster, L. (2004). Workflow mining: Discovering process models from event logs. *Knowledge and Data Engineering. IEEE Transactions on, 16*(9), 1128–1142.

Gabel, M., & Su, Z. (2008, November). Javert: fully automatic mining of general temporal properties from dynamic traces. In *Proceedings of the 16th ACM SIGSOFT International Symposium on Foundations of software engineering* (pp. 339-349). ACM. doi:10.1145/1453101.1453150

Gabel, M., & Su, Z. (2008, May). Symbolic mining of temporal specifications. In *Proceedings of the 30th international conference on Software engineering* (pp. 51-60). ACM.

Gao, X. (2013). Towards the next generation intelligent BPM–in the era of big data. In *Business Process Management* (pp. 4–9). Springer Berlin Heidelberg. doi:10.1007/978-3-642-40176-3_2

Greco, G., Guzzo, A., Pontieri, L., & Sacca, D. (2006). Discovering expressive process models by clustering log traces. *Knowledge and Data Engineering. IEEE Transactions on, 18*(8), 1010–1027.

Itkar, S. A., & Kulkarni, U. V. (2013). Distributed Algorithm for Frequent Pattern Mining using Hadoop-Map Reduce Framework. *Proc. of Int. Conf. on Advances in Computer Science, AETACS.*

Koundinya, A. K., Sharma, K. A. K., Kumar, K., & Shanbag, K. U. (2012). *Map/Reduce Deisgn and Implementation of Apriori Alogirthm for handling voluminous data-sets.* arXiv preprint arXiv:1212.4692

Motahari-Nezhad, H. R., Saint-Paul, R., Benatallah, B., & Casati, F. (2008). Deriving protocol models from imperfect service conversation logs. *Knowledge and Data Engineering. IEEE Transactions on, 20*(12), 1683–1698.

Seki, K., Jinno, R., & Uehara, K. (2013). Parallel distributed trajectory pattern mining using hierarchical grid with MapReduce. *International Journal of Grid and High Performance Computing, 5*(4), 79–96. doi:10.4018/ijghpc.2013100106

Shang, W., Jiang, Z. M., Adams, B., & Hassan, A. E. (2009). *Mapreduce as a general framework to support research in mining software repositories.* MSR.

Stewart, R. J., Trinder, P. W., & Loidl, H. W. (2011). Comparing high level mapreduce query languages. In *Advanced Parallel Processing Technologies* (pp. 58–72). Springer Berlin Heidelberg. doi:10.1007/978-3-642-24151-2_5

Tsourakakis, C. E. (2010). *Data Mining with MAPREDUCE: Graph and Tensor Algorithms with Applications* (Doctoral dissertation). Carnegie Mellon University.

van der Aalst, W. (2004). Discovering coordination patterns using process mining. *Workshop on Petri Nets and Coordination*, 49-64.

Van Der Aalst, W. (2013). Service mining: Using process mining to discover, check, and improve service behavior. *Services Computing. IEEE Transactions on*, *6*(4), 525–535.

Van der Aalst, W. M., & Weijters, A. J. M. M. (2004). Process mining: A research agenda. *Computers in Industry*, *53*(3), 231–244. doi:10.1016/j.compind.2003.10.001

Versteeg, G., & Bouwman, H. (2006). Business architecture: A new paradigm to relate business strategy to ICT. *Information Systems Frontiers*, *8*(2), 91–102. doi:10.1007/s10796-006-7973-z

Weske, M. (2012). *Business process management: concepts, languages, architectures*. Springer Science & Business Media. doi:10.1007/978-3-642-28616-2

APPENDIX

Figure 1. Principal of MapReduce
(Dean, J., & Ghemawat, S., 2008)

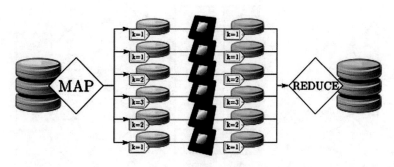

Figure 2. Master node directing a group of slave nodes
(Shang, W and al, 2009)

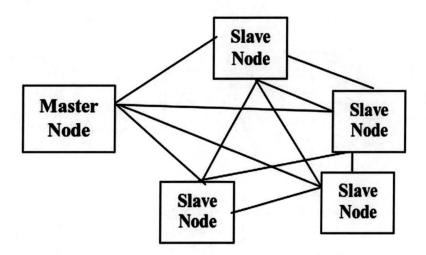

Figure 3. Example MapReduce process for counting the frequency of word lengths in a book
(Shang et al, 2009; Koundinya et al., 2012)

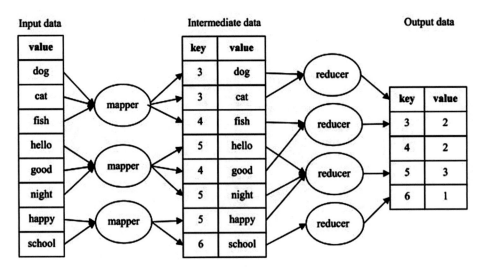

Figure 4. The approach architecture using MapReduce

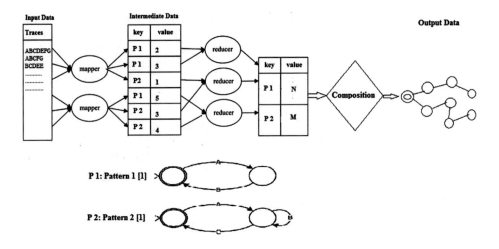

Table 1. Trace data and analysis times

Execution Time				
Application	**Num. of Traces Total**	**Trace Events**	**Pattern Mining**	**Composition**
Skype	11	825,458,970	5432,8s	462,0s
Viber	8	332,697,321	3951,0s	589,4s

Table 2. Trace data and analysis times with using MapReduce in five machines

Execution Time				
Application	**Num. of Traces Total**	**Trace Events**	**Pattern Mining**	**Composition**
Skype	11	825,458,970	892,5s	98,0s
Viber	8	332,697,321	901,0s	122,1s

Table 3. Trace data and analysis times with using MapReduce in ten machines

Execution Time				
Application	**Num. of Traces Total**	**Trace Events**	**Pattern Mining**	**Composition**
Skype	11	825,458,970	431,3s	53,0s
Viber	8	332,697,321	352,8s	62,7s

Compilation of References

Abbass, H. A., & Sarker, R. (2002). The Pareto Differential Evolution Algorithm. *International Journal of Artificial Intelligence Tools*, *11*(4), 531–552. doi:10.1142/S0218213002001039

Abdessemed, M. R., Slimane, M., Aupetit, S., & Bilami, A. (2009, March). Une approche de groupement orienté dans un entourage de robots homogènes. *5th international conference SETIT: Sciences of Electronic, Technologies of Information and Telecommunications.*

Abdulkader, S. N., Atia, A., & Mostafa, M. S. M. (2015). Brain computer interfacing: Applications and challenges. *Egyptian Informatics Journal*, *16*(2), 213–230. doi:10.1016/j.eij.2015.06.002

Abou-Taleb, Mohamedet, Mohamed, & Abedelhalim. (2013c). Hybridizing Filters and Wrapper Approaches for Improving the Classification Accuracy of Microarray Dataset. *International Journal of Soft Computing and Engineering*, *3*(3), 155-159.

Aggarwal, G. P. (2001). *Nonlinear Fiber Optics* (2nd ed.). San Diego, CA: Academic Press.

Aghagolzadeh, M., & Oweiss, K. (2009). Compressed and distributed sensing of neuronal activity for real time spike train decoding. *IEEE Transactions on Neural Systems and Rehabilitation Engineering*, *17*(2), 116–127. doi:10.1109/TNSRE.2009.2012711 PMID:19193517

Agrawal, R., & Srikant, R. (1994). Fast Algorithms for Mining Association Rules. *Proceedings of the 20th International Conference on Very Large Data Bases (VLDB'94)*, 487-499.

Agrawal, R., Swami, A., & Imielinski, T. (1993). Mining Association Rules Between Sets of Items in Large Databases. *Proceedings ACM SIGMOD International Conference on Management of Data*, 207. doi:10.1145/170035.170072

Ahmed & Zeeshan. (2014a). Applying weka towards machine learning with genetic algorithm and back propagation neural networks. *International Journal of Soft Computing and Engineering*, *3*(3), 155-159.

Alanou, L. M. V. (1996). *Détection d'intrusion dans un système informatique: méthodes et outils*. Academic Press.

Alaoui, A. (2012). *Application des techniques des métaheuristiques pour l'optimisation de la tâche de la classification de la fouille de données* (Doctoral dissertation). USTO, Oran, Algeria.

Aler, R., & Galvan, I. M. (2015). Optimizing the number of electrodes and spatial filters for brain–computer interfaces by means of an evolutionary multi-objective approach. *Expert Systems with Applications*, *42*(15/16), 6215–6223. doi:10.1016/j.eswa.2015.03.008

Alloui, T., Boussebough, I., & Chaoui, A. (2015). A Particle Swarm Optimization Algorithm for Web Information Retrieval: A Novel Approach. *International Journal of Intelligent Information Technologies*, *11*(3), 15–29. doi:10.4018/IJIIT.2015070102

Alonso-Valerdi, L. M., Salido-Ruiz, R. A., & Ramirez-Mendoza, R. A. (2015). Motor imagery based brain–computer interfaces: An emerging technology to rehabilitate motor deficits. *Neuropsychologia*, *79*, 354–363. doi:10.1016/j.neuropsychologia.2015.09.012 PMID:26382749

Amin, A. H. M., & Khan, A. I. (2013). One-shot Classification of 2-D Leaf Shapes Using Distributed Hierarchical Graph Neuron (DHGN) Scheme with k-NN Classifier. *Procedia Computer Science*, *24*, 84–96. doi:10.1016/j.procs.2013.10.030

Ammons, G., Bodík, R., & Larus, J. R. (2002). Mining specifications. *ACM SIGPLAN Notices*, *37*(1), 4–16. doi:10.1145/565816.503275

Anderson, D., Frivold, T., Tamaru, A., & Valdes, A. (1994). *Next generation intrusion detection expert system (nides), software users manual*. Academic Press.

Anh, V. N., & Moffat, A. (2005). Inverted index compression using word-aligned binary codes. *Information Retrieval*, *8*(1), 151–166. doi:10.1023/B:INRT.0000048490.99518.5c

Ansari, A. Q., & Gupta, N. K. (2011, December). Automated diagnosis of coronary heart disease using neuro-fuzzy integrated system. In *Information and Communication Technologies (WICT), 2011 World Congress on* (pp. 1379-1384). IEEE. doi:10.1109/WICT.2011.6141450

Antal, B., & Hajdu, A. (2014). An ensemble-based system for automatic screening of diabetic retinopathy. *Knowledge-Based Systems*, *60*, 20–27. doi:10.1016/j.knosys.2013.12.023

Aridhi, S., D'Orazio, L., Maddouri, M., & Mephu, E. (2014, June). A novel MapReduce-based approach for distributed frequent subgraph mining. In *Reconnaissance de Formes et Intelligence Artificielle*. RFIA.

Arun Kumar, R. (2016, November). Digital Image Watermarking using Fuzzy Logic and Genetic Algorithm. *International Journal of Computer Trends and Technology*, *41*(02), 101–105.

Atkinson, M. D., Santoro, N., & Urrutia, J. (1986). Integer Sets with Distinct Sums and Differences and Carrier Frequency Assignments for Nonlinear Repeaters. *IEEE Transactions on Communications*, *34*(6), 614–617. doi:10.1109/TCOM.1986.1096587

Ayari, N., Luong, T. V., & Jemai, A. (2010). A Hybrid Genetic Algorithm for Golomb Ruler Problem. *Proceedings of ACS/IEEE International Conference on Computer Systems and Applications (AICCSA–2010)*, 1–4. doi:10.1109/AICCSA.2010.5586955

Azar, A. T., & Hassanien, A. E. (2015). Hybrid TRS-PSO clustering approach for Web2. 0 social tagging system. *International Journal of Rough Sets and Data Analysis*, *2*(1), 22–37. doi:10.4018/ijrsda.2015010102

Azizi, R. (2014). *Empirical study of artificial fish swarm algorithm*. arXiv preprint arXiv:1405.4138

Babcock, W. (1953). Intermodulation Interference in Radio Systems. *The Bell System Technical Journal*, *32*(1), 63–73. doi:10.1002/j.1538-7305.1953.tb01422.x

Bagyamathi, M., & Inbarani, H. H. (2015). *A novel hybridized rough set and improved harmony search based feature selection for protein sequence classification. In Big Data in Complex Systems* (pp. 173–204). Springer.

Balazinska, Becla, Cudre-Mauroux, DeWitt, Heath, Kimura, … Zdonik. (2009). A demonstration of SciDB: A science-oriented DBMS. *VLDB*, 87-100.

Bansal, S., Jain, P., Singh, A. K., & Gupta, N. (2016). Improved Multi–Objective Firefly Algorithms to Find OGR Sequences for WDM Channel–Allocation. International Journal of Mathematical, Computational, Physical, Electrical and Computer Engineering, 10(7), 315–322.

Bansal, S., Kumar, S., & Bhalla, P. (2013). A Novel Approach to WDM Channel Allocation: Big Bang–Big Crunch Optimization. *Proceeding of Zonal Seminar on Emerging Trends in Embedded System Technologies (ETECH–2013)*, 80–81.

Bansal, S., Singh, A. K., & Gupta, N. (2017a). Optimal Golomb Ruler Sequences Generation: A Novel Parallel Hybrid Multi–Objective Bat Algorithm. *Journal of The Institution of Engineers (India): Series B, 98*(1), 43–64, doi:10.1007/s40031-016-0249-1

Bansal, S. (2014). Optimal Golomb Ruler Sequence Generation for FWM Crosstalk Elimination: Soft Computing Versus Conventional Approaches. *Applied Soft Computing, 22*, 443–457. doi:10.1016/j.asoc.2014.04.015

Bansal, S., Chauhan, R., & Kumar, P. (2014). A Cuckoo Search based WDM Channel Allocation Algorithm. *International Journal of Computers and Applications, 96*(20), 6–12. doi:10.5120/16908-6988

Bansal, S., Gupta, N., & Singh, A. K. (2017b). Nature-Inspired Metaheuristic Algorithms to Find Near–OGR Sequences for WDM Channel Allocation and their Performance Comparison. *Open Mathematics, 15*(1), 520–547. doi:10.1515/math-2017-0045

Bansal, S., Kumar, S., Sharma, H., & Bhalla, P. (2011). Golomb Ruler Sequences Optimization: A BBO Approach. *International Journal of Computer Science and Information Security, 9*(5), 63–71.

Bansal, S., & Singh, K. (2014). A Novel Soft–Computing Algorithm for Channel Allocation in WDM Systems. *International Journal of Computers and Applications, 85*(9), 19–26. doi:10.5120/14869-3244

Barbu, A., She, Y., Ding, L., & Gramajo, G. (2013). *Feature selection with annealing for big data learning*. arXiv preprint arXiv:1310.2880

Barrón-Cedeño, A., Vila, M., Martí, M. A., & Rosso, P. (2013). Plagiarism meets paraphrasing: Insights for the next generation in automatic plagiarism detection. *Computational Linguistics, 39*(4), 917–947. doi:10.1162/COLI_a_00153

Basile, C. (2009). A plagiarism detection procedure in three steps: Selection, matches and squares. In *Proceeding of the SEPLN '09 pan 09 3rd workshop and 1st international compétition on plagiarism* (pp. 19-23). IEEE.

Basturk, B., & Karaboga, D. (2006, May). An artificial bee colony (ABC) algorithm for numeric function optimization. In IEEE swarm intelligence symposium (Vol. 8, No. 1, pp. 687-697). IEEE.

Bauer, R., Fels, M., Vukelić, M., Ziemann, U., & Gharabaghi, A. (2015). Bridging the gap between motor imagery and motor execution with a brain–robot interface. *NeuroImage, 108*, 319–327. doi:10.1016/j.neuroimage.2014.12.026 PMID:25527239

Beaglehole, R., Irwin, A., & Prentice, T. (2003). *The world health report 2003: Shaping the future*. Geneva, Switzerland: World Health Organization.

Beauquier, D., Berstel, J., & Chrétienne, P. (1992). *Éléments d'algorithmique* (Vol. 8). Paris: Masson.

Becla, DeWitt, Lim, Maier, Ratzesberger, Stonebraker, & Zdonik. (2009). Requirements for science data bases and SciDB. *CIDR Perspectives*, 202-214.

Belayachi, N., Yachba, K., Gelareh, S., & Bouamrane, K. (2017). Storage the logistic of empty containers' return in the liner-shipping network. *Tansport and Telecommunication Journal, 18*(3), 207–219.

Bellazzi, R., & Abu-Hanna, A. (2009). Data mining technologies for blood glucose and diabetes management. *Journal of Diabetes Science and Technology, 3*(3), 603–612. doi:10.1177/193229680900300326 PMID:20144300

Benabdeslem, K., Lebbah, M., Aussem, A., & Corbex, M. (2007). Approche connexionniste pour l'extraction de profils cas-témoins du cancer du Nasopharynx à partir des données issues d'une étude épidémiologique. *EGC 2007, RNTI, 2007*.

Ben-Dor, A., Bruhn, L., Friedman, N., Nachman, I., Schummer, M., & Yakhini, Z. (2000a). Classification with Gene Expression Profiles. *Proceedings of the 4th Annual International Conference on Computational Molecular Biology*, *7*(3/4), 559-84.

Ben-Dor, A., Chor, B., Karp, R., & Yakhini, Z. (2003). Discovering local structure in gene expression data: The Order-Preserving sub matrix problem. *Journal of Computational Biology*, *10*(3-4), 373–384. doi:10.1089/10665270360688075 PMID:12935334

Berta, R., Bellotti, F., de Gloria, A., Pranantha, D., & Schatten, C. (2013). Electroencephalogram and physiological signal analysis for assessing flow in games. *IEEE Transactions on Computational Intelligence and AI in Games*, *5*(2), 164–175. doi:10.1109/TCIAIG.2013.2260340

Bhardwaj, A., Kaur, M., & Kumar, A. (2013). Recognition of plants by Leaf Image using Moment Invariant and Texture Analysis. *International Journal of Innovation and Applied Studies*, *3*(1), 237–248.

Bhattacharya, S. (2014). Watermarking Digital Image Using Fuzzy Matrix Compositions and Rough Set. *International Journal of Advanced Computer Science and Applications*, *5*(06), 135–140. doi:10.14569/IJACSA.2014.050621

Bhattacharya, S. (2014, November). Survey on Digital Watermarking- A Digital Forensics & Security Application. *International Journal of Advanced Research in Computer Science and Software Engineering*, *4*(11), 1–6.

Bhuiyan, M. A., & Al Hasan, M. (2015). An iterative MapReduce based frequent subgraph mining algorithm. *Knowledge and Data Engineering. IEEE Transactions on*, *27*(3), 608–620.

Birbaumer, N., & Chaudhary, U. (2015). Learning from brain control: Clinical application of brain–computer interfaces. *e-Neuroforum*, *6*(4), 87–95.

Birbaumer, N., Gallegos-Ayala, G., Wildgruber, M., Silvoni, S., & Soekadar, S. R. (2014). Direct brain control and communication in paralysis. *Brain Topography*, *27*(1), 4–11. doi:10.1007/s10548-013-0282-1 PMID:23536247

Birbaumer, N., Ghanayim, N., Hinterberger, T., Iversen, I., Kotchoubey, B., Kübler, A., & Flor, H. et al. (1999). A spelling device for the paralysed. *Nature*, *398*(6725), 297–298. doi:10.1038/18581 PMID:10192330

Bloom, G. S., & Golomb, S. W. (1977). Applications of Numbered Undirected Graphs. *Proceedings of the IEEE*, *65*(4), 562–570. doi:10.1109/PROC.1977.10517

Blum, A., & Langley, P. (1997c). Selection of relevant features and examples in machine learning. *Artificial Intelligence*, *97*(1-2), 245–271. doi:10.1016/S0004-3702(97)00063-5

Blum, E. J., Biraud, F., & Ribes, J. C. (1974). On Optimal Synthetic Linear Arrays with Applications to Radio Astronomy. *IEEE Transactions on Antennas and Propagation*, *22*(1), 108–109. doi:10.1109/TAP.1974.1140732

Bodri, B. (2001). A neural-network model for earthquake occurrence. *Journal of Geodynamics*, *32*(3), 289–310. doi:10.1016/S0264-3707(01)00039-4

Bouarara, H. A., Hamou, R. M., & Amine, A. (2014). Text Clustering using Distances Combination by Social Bees: Towards 3D Visualisation Aspect. *International Journal of Information Retrieval Research*, *4*(3), 34–53. doi:10.4018/IJIRR.2014070103

Bouarara, H. A., Hamou, R. M., & Amine, A. (2015). A Novel Bio-Inspired Approach for Multilingual Spam Filtering. *International Journal of Intelligent Information Technologies*, *11*(3), 45–87. doi:10.4018/IJIIT.2015070104

Bouarara, H. A., Hamou, R. M., & Amine, A. (2015). New Swarm Intelligence Technique of Artificial Social Cockroaches for Suspicious Person Detection Using N-Gram Pixel with Visual Result Mining. *International Journal of Strategic Decision Sciences*, *6*(3), 65–91. doi:10.4018/IJSDS.2015070105

Bouarara, H. A., Hamou, R. M., Rahmani, A., & Amine, A. (2015). Boosting Algorithm and Meta-Heuristic Based on Genetic Algorithms for Textual Plagiarism Detection. *International Journal of Cognitive Informatics and Natural Intelligence*, *9*(4), 65–87. doi:10.4018/IJCINI.2015100105

Bouchekara, H. R. (2013). Optimal design of electromagnetic devices using a black-hole-based optimization technique. *IEEE Transactions on Magnetics*, *49*(12), 5709–5714. doi:10.1109/TMAG.2013.2277694

Bouchekara, H. R. E. H. (2014). Optimal power flow using black-hole-based optimization approach. *Applied Soft Computing*, *24*, 879–888. doi:10.1016/j.asoc.2014.08.056

Boudia, M. A., Hamou, R. M., Amine, A., Rahmani, M. E., & Rahmani, A. (2015, May). A New Multi-layered Approach for Automatic Text Summaries Mono-Document Based on Social Spiders. In *IFIP International Conference on Computer Science and its Applications_x000D_* (pp. 193-204). Springer International Publishing. doi:10.1007/978-3-319-19578-0_16

Boudia, M. A., Hamou, R. M., & Amine, A. (2015). A New Meta-Heuristic based on Human Renal Function for Detection and Filtering of SPAM. *International Journal of Information Security and Privacy*, *9*(4), 26–58. doi:10.4018/IJISP.2015100102

Boudia, M. A., Hamou, R. M., & Amine, A. (2016). A New Approach Based on the Detection of Opinion by SentiWordNet for Automatic Text Summaries by Extraction. *International Journal of Information Retrieval Research*, *6*(3), 19–36. doi:10.4018/IJIRR.2016070102

Boudia, M. A., Hamou, R. M., & Amine, A. (2017). A New Meta-Heuristics for Intrusion Detection System Inspired from the Protection System of Social Bees. . *International Journal of Information Security and Privacy*, *11*(1), 18–34. doi:10.4018/IJISP.2017010102

Boudia, M. A., Hamou, R. M., Amine, A., & Rahmani, A. (2015). A New Biomimetic Method Based on the Power Saves of Social Bees for Automatic Summaries of Texts by Extraction. *International Journal of Software Science and Computational Intelligence*, *7*(1), 18–38. doi:10.4018/IJSSCI.2015010102

Boudia, M. A., Hamou, R. M., Amine, A., Rahmani, M. E., & Rahmani, A. (2015). Hybridization of Social Spiders and Extractions Techniques for Automatic Text Summaries. *International Journal of Cognitive Informatics and Natural Intelligence*, *9*(3), 65–86. doi:10.4018/IJCINI.2015070104

Boudia, M. A., Rahmani, A., Rahmani, M. E., Djebbar, A., Bouarara, H. A., Kabli, F., & Guandouz, M. (2016). Hybridization Between Scoring Technique and Similarity Technique for Automatic Summarization by Extraction. *International Journal of Organizational and Collective Intelligence*, *6*(1), 1–14. doi:10.4018/IJOCI.2016010101

Boudin, F., & Morin, E. (2013, June). Keyphrase Extraction for N-best re-ranking in multi-phrase compression. In *North American Chapter of the Association for Computational Linguistics*. NAACL.

Boystov, L. (2012). *Clueweb09 posting list data set*. Retrieved from http://boytsov.info/datasets/clueweb09gap/

Brandes, U., Delling, D., Gaertler, M., Görke, R., Hoefer, M., Nikoloski, Z., & Wagner, D. (2006). *Maximizing modularity is hard*. arXiv preprint physics/0608255

Braun, P., Cameron, J. J., Cuzzocrea, A., Jiang, F., & Leung, C. K. (2014). Effectively and efficiently mining frequent patterns from dense graph streams on disk. *Procedia Computer Science*, *35*, 338–347. doi:10.1016/j.procs.2014.08.114

Breiman, Friedman, Olshen, & Stone. (1984). *Classification and Regression Trees*. Wadsworth.

Breiman, L. (2001). Random forests. *Machine Learning*, *45*(1), 5–32. doi:10.1023/A:1010933404324

Brown & Grundy. (2000). Knowledge-based analysis of microarray gene expression data by using support vector machines. *International Journal of Web Engineering and Technology*, *97*(1), 262-267.

Brown, G. (2004). *Diversity in neural network ensembles*. University of Birmingham.

Brown, M. P. S., Grundy, W. N., Lin, D., Cristianini, N., Sugnet, C., & Furey, T. S. Jr. (2000). Knowledge-based analysis of microarray gene expression data using support vector machines. *Proceedings of the National Academy of Sciences of the United States of America*, *97*(1), 262–267. doi:10.1073/pnas.97.1.262

Bryant, R. E. (1986). Graph-based algorithms for Boolean function manipulation. *Computers. IEEE Transactions on*, *100*(8), 677–691.

Bryant, R., Katz, R., & Lazowska, E. (2008). *Big Data Computing: Creating revolutionary breakthroughs in commerce, science and society*. Washington, DC: Computing Community Consortium.

Buckley, C., Singhal, A., & Cardie, C. (1997, June). An Analysis of Statistical and Syntactic Phrases. In RIAO (Vol. 97, pp. 200-214). Academic Press.

Caicoya, S., & Saury, Jg. (2013). TCP/IP - Le guide complet, Maîtrisez les principes de la communication réseau sous Windows. *Edition Micro Application*.

Cai, Q., Ma, L., Gong, M., & Tian, D. (2016). A survey on network community detection based on evolutionary computation. *International Journal of Bio-inspired Computation*, *8*(2), 84–98. doi:10.1504/IJBIC.2016.076329

Carmona-Saez, P., Chagoyen, M., Rodriguez, A., Trelles, O., Carazo, J. M., & Pascual-Montano, A. (2006). Integrated analysis of gene expression by association rules discovery. *BMC Bioinformatics*, *7*(1), 54. doi:10.1186/1471-2105-7-54 PMID:16464256

Cecotti, H. (2015). Toward shift invariant detection of event-related potentials in non-invasive brain–computer interface. *Pattern Recognition Letters*, *66*, 127–134. doi:10.1016/j.patrec.2015.01.015

Chae, Y., Jeong, J., & Jo, S. (2012). Toward brain-actuated humanoid robots: Asynchronous direct control using an EEG-based BCI. *IEEE Transactions on Robotics*, *28*(5), 1131–1144. doi:10.1109/TRO.2012.2201310

Chai, G. H., Sui, X. H., Li, P., Liu, X. X., & Lan, N. (2014). Review on tactile sensory feedback of prosthetic hands for the upper-limb amputees by sensory afferent stimulation. *Journal of Shanghai Jiaotong University (Science)*, *19*(5), 587–591. doi:10.1007/s12204-014-1546-y

Chaki, J., & Parekh, R. (2011). Plant leaf recognition using shape based features and neural network classifiers. *International Journal of Advanced Computer Science and Applications*, *2*(10). doi:10.14569/IJACSA.2011.021007

Chan, C. Y., & Ioannidis, Y. E. (1998, June). Bitmap index design and evaluation. *SIGMOD Record*, *27*(2), 355–366. doi:10.1145/276305.276336

Chang, S. E., Kenney, M. K., Loucks, T. M. J., Poletto, C. J., & Ludlow, C. L. (2009). Common neural substrates support speech and non-speech vocal tract gestures. *NeuroImage*, *47*(1), 314–325. doi:10.1016/j.neuroimage.2009.03.032 PMID:19327400

Chapin, J. K., Moxon, K. A., Markowitz, R. S., & Nicolelis, M. A. L. (1999). Real-time control of a robot arm using simultaneously recorded neurons in the motor cortex. *Nature Neuroscience*, *2*(7), 664–670. doi:10.1038/10223 PMID:10404201

Chatterjee, A. (2015). A Comparative Analysis of Three Important Data Hiding Schemes in Steganography. *International Journal of Innovative Trends In Engineering*, *11*(2), 61–65.

Chatterjee, A. (2015). A Survey on Different Digital Media Based Steganography Techniques Using Genetic Algorithms. *International Journal of Innovative Research in Computer and Communication Engineering, 3*(12), 12990–12998.

Chaudhary, U., Birbaumer, N., & Curado, M. R. (2015). Brain–machine interface (BMI) in paralysis. *Annals of Physical and Rehabilitation Medicine, 58*(1), 9–13. doi:10.1016/j.rehab.2014.11.002 PMID:25623294

Chaurasia, V., & Pal, S. (2014). A novel approach for breast cancer detection using data mining techniques. *International Journal of Innovative Research in Computer and Communication Engineering, 2*(1), 2456–2465.

Chebli, K. (2011). Optimisation des mouvements des conteneurs dans un terminal maritime, mémoire présenté en vue de l'obtention du diplôme de maîtrise des sciences appliquées (Génie Industriel). École polytechnique de Montréal, Canada.

Chen, C. P., & Zhang, C.-Y. (2014). Data-intensive applications, challenges, techniques and technologies: A survey on big data. *Information Sciences, 275*, 314–347. doi:10.1016/j.ins.2014.01.015

Chen, M., Kuzmin, K., & Szymanski, B. K. (2014). Community detection via maximization of modularity and its variants. *IEEE Transactions on Computational Social Systems, 1*(1), 46–65. doi:10.1109/TCSS.2014.2307458

Chervitz, S. A. Hester, E.T., Ball, C., Dolinski, K., Dwight, S.S., Haris, M.A., … Botstein, D. (1999). Using the Sacharomyces genome databases (SGD) for analysis of protein similarities and structure. Nucleic Acids Research, 27(1).

Chhabra, S., Yerazunis, W. S., & Siefkes, C. (2004, November). Spam filtering using a markov random field model with variable weighting schemas. In *Data Mining, 2004. ICDM'04. Fourth IEEE International Conference on* (pp. 347-350). IEEE. doi:10.1109/ICDM.2004.10031

Choi, S. J., & Kang, B. G. (2014). Prototype design and implementation of an automatic control system based on a BCI. *Wireless Personal Communications, 79*(4), 2551–2563. doi:10.1007/s11277-014-1861-5

Chou, C. H., Sinha, A. P., & Zhao, H. (2008). A text mining approach to Internet abuse detection. *Information Systems and e-Business Management, 6*(4), 419–439. doi:10.1007/s10257-007-0070-0

Chraplyvy, A. R. (1990). Limitations on Lightwave Communications Imposed by Optical–Fiber Nonlinearities. *Journal of Lightwave Technology, 8*(10), 1548–1557. doi:10.1109/50.59195

Cikala, F., Lataix, R., & Marmeche, S. (2005). *Les IDS/IPS.* Intrusion Detection/Prevention Systems.

Clausen, J. (2013). Bonding brains to machines: Ethical implications of electroceuticals for the human brain. *Neuroethics, 6*(3), 429–434. doi:10.1007/s12152-013-9186-8

Clauset, A., Newman, M. E., & Moore, C. (2004). Finding community structure in very large networks. *Physical Review. E, 70*(6), 066111. doi:10.1103/PhysRevE.70.066111 PMID:15697438

Clune, T., & Rood, R. (2011). Software testing and verification in climate model development. *IEEE Software, 28*(6), 49–55. doi:10.1109/MS.2011.117

Coffey, E. B. J., Brouwer, A. M., Wilschut, E. S., & van Erp, J. B. F. (2010). Brain–machine interfaces in space: Using spontaneous rather than intentionally generated brain signals. *Acta Astronautica, 67*(1/2), 1–11. doi:10.1016/j.actaastro.2009.12.016

Colannino, J. (2003). *Circular and Modular Golomb Rulers.* Available at http://cgm.cs.mcgill.ca/~athens/cs507/Projects/2003/JustinColannino/

Collinger, J. L., Wodlinger, B., Downey, J. E., Wang, W., Tyler-Kabara, E. C., Weber, D. J., & Schwartz, A. B. et al. (2013). High-performance neuroprosthetic control by an individual with tetraplegia. *Lancet, 381*(9866), 557–564. doi:10.1016/S0140-6736(12)61816-9 PMID:23253623

Cope, J. S., Remagnino, P., Barman, S., & Wilkin, P. (2010). Plant texture classification using gabor co-occurrences. In *Advances in Visual Computing* (pp. 669–677). Springer Berlin Heidelberg. doi:10.1007/978-3-642-17274-8_65

Cotta, C., Dotu, I., Fernandez, A. J., & Hentenryck, P. V. (2007). Local Search–Based Hybrid Algorithms for Finding Golomb Rulers. Kluwer Academic Publishers.

Cotta, C., Dotú, I., Fernández, A. J., & Hentenryck, P. V. (2006). *A Memetic Approach to Golomb Rulers. In* Lecture Notes in Computer Science: Vol. 4193. *Parallel Problem Solving from Nature–PPSN IX* (pp. 252–261). Springer–Verlag Berlin Heidelberg. doi:10.1007/11844297_26

Cotta, C., & Fernández, A. J. (2005). *Analyzing Fitness Landscapes for the Optimal Golomb Ruler Problem.* In J. Gottlieb & G. Raidl (Eds.), *In* Lecture Notes in Computer Science: *Evolutionary Computation in Combinatorial Optimization* (Vol. 3448, pp. 68–79). Springer–Verlag Berlin. doi:10.1007/978-3-540-31996-2_7

Cotta, C., & Hemert, J. V. (2008). Recent Advances in Evolutionary Computation for Combinatorial Optimization. *Studies in Computational Intelligence, Springer, 153.* doi:10.1007/978-3-540-70807-0

Cuevas, E., Cienfuegos, M., Zaldívar, D., & Pérez-Cisneros, M. (2013). A swarm optimization algorithm inspired in the behavior of the social-spider. *Expert System with Applications, 40*(16), 6374-6384.

Cuevas, E., Oliva, D., Zaldivar, D., Pérez-Cisneros, M., & Sossa, H. (2012). Circle detection using electro-magnetism optimization. *Information Sciences, 182*(1), 40–55. doi:10.1016/j.ins.2010.12.024

da Cruz, J. M. M. (2009). Méthodologie d'évaluation des filtres anti-spam. *Journées Réseaux, Nante du, 1.*

Dagorn, N. (2006). Détection et prévention d'intrusion: présentation et limites. *HAL archives-ouvertes.*

Dai, J. J., Lieu, L., & Rocke, D. (2006a). TDimension reduction for classification with gene expression microarray data. *Statistical Applications in Genetics and Molecular Biology, 5*(1), 1–19. doi:10.2202/1544-6115.1147 PMID:16646870

Danflous, D. (2000). Déploiement national des Systèmes d'information Multimodale, Delfi: l'exemple allemand. Rapport du Centre d'études sur les réseaux, les transports, l'urbanisme et les constructions publiques. France.

Danflous, D. (2001). Déploiement national des Systèmes d'Information Multimodale, GOFAS: l'exemple Suisse. Rapport du Centre d'études sur les réseaux, les transports, l'urbanisme et les constructions publiques. France.

Danflous, D. (2003). Déploiement national des Systèmes d'Information Multimodale, Transport Direct: l'exemple Anglais. Rapport du Centre d'études sur les réseaux, les transports, l'urbanisme et les constructions publiques. France.

Dasgupta, D., & Michalewicz, Z. (Eds.). (2013). *Evolutionary algorithms in engineering applications.* Springer Science & Business Media.

Dash, M., Choi, K., Scheuermann, P., & Liu, H. (2002). Feature selection for clustering-a filter solution. In *Data Mining, 2002. ICDM 2003. Proceedings. 2002 IEEE International Conference on* (pp. 115-122). IEEE. doi:10.1109/ICDM.2002.1183893

Dash, M., & Liu, H. (1997b). Feature selection for classification. *Intelligent Data Analysis, 1*(1-4), 131–156. doi:10.1016/S1088-467X(97)00008-5

Datta, S., & Datta, S. (2006). Evaluation of clustering algorithms for gene Expression data. *BMC Bioinformatics, 7*(Suppl4), S17. doi:10.1186/1471-2105-7-S4-S17 PMID:17217509

David, Saeb, & Al Rubeaan. (2013a). Comparative Analysis of Data Mining Tools and Classification Techniques using WEKA in Medical Bioinformatics. *International Journal of Computer Engineering and Intelligent Systems, 4*(13), 28-38.

De Courcy, R. (1992). Les systèmes d'information en réadaptation. Réseau international CIDIH et facteurs environnementaux, 5, 7-10.

de Ru, W. G. (1997). Enhanced Password Authentication through Fuzzy Logic. *IEEE Intelligent Systems*, 38–45.

De Vel, O., Anderson, A., Corney, M., & Mohay, G. (2001). Mining e-mail content for author identification forensics. *SIGMOD Record*, *30*(4), 55–64. doi:10.1145/604264.604272

De Weerdt, J., Schupp, A., Vanderloock, A., & Baesens, B. (2013). Process Mining for the multi-faceted analysis of business processes—A case study in a financial services organization. *Computers in Industry*, *64*(1), 57–67. doi:10.1016/j.compind.2012.09.010

Dean, J., & Ghemawat, S. (2008). MapReduce: Simplified data processing on large clusters. *Communications of the ACM*, *51*(1), 107–113. doi:10.1145/1327452.1327492

Debar, H. (1993). *Application des reseaux de neurones a la detection d'intrusions sur les systemes informatiques* (Doctoral dissertation).

Debar, H., Becker, M., & Siboni, D. (1992, May). A neural network component for an intrusion detection system. In *Research in Security and Privacy, 1992. Proceedings., 1992 IEEE Computer Society Symposium on* (pp. 240-250). IEEE. doi:10.1109/RISP.1992.213257

Deb, K. (1999). Evolutionary Algorithms for Multi–Criterion Optimization in Engineering design. In *Evolutionary Algorithms in Engineering and Computer Science* (pp. 135–161). New York: Wiley.

Deb, K. (2001). *Multi-Objective Optimization Using Evolutionary Algorithms*. New York: Wiley.

Deb, K. (2001). *Multi–Objective Optimization Using Evolutionary Algorithms*. New York: Wiley.

Decety, J. (1996). The neurophysiological basis of motor imagery. *Behavioural Brain Research*, *77*(1/2), 45–52. doi:10.1016/0166-4328(95)00225-1 PMID:8762158

DeJong, G. (1982). An overview of the FRUMP system. *Strategies for Natural Language Processing*, 113.

Demetriades, A. K., Demetriades, C. K., Watts, C., & Ashkan, K. (2010). Brain–machine interface: The challenge of neuroethics. *The Surgeon: Journal of the Royal Colleges of Surgeons of Edinburgh and Ireland*, *8*(5), 267–269. doi:10.1016/j.surge.2010.05.006 PMID:20709284

Deng, Z. H., & Lv, S. L. (2015). PrePost+: An efficient N-lists-based algorithm for mining frequent itemsets via Children–Parent Equivalence pruning. *Expert Systems with Applications*, *42*(13), 5424–5432. doi:10.1016/j.eswa.2015.03.004

Denning, D. E. (1987). An intrusion-detection model. *Software Engineering, IEEE Transactions on*, (2), 222-232.

Derrac, J., García, S., Molina, D., & Herrera, F. (2011). A Practical Tutorial on the Use of Nonparametric Statistical Tests as A Methodology for Comparing Evolutionary and Swarm Intelligence Algorithms. *Swarm and Evolutionary Computation*, *1*(1), 3–18. doi:10.1016/j.swevo.2011.02.002

Deshpande, M., & Karypis, G. (2002). Evaluation of techniques for classifying biological sequences. *PAKDD, 2002*, 417–431.

Dewdney, A. (1985). Computer Recreations. *Scientific American*, *253*(2), 16–26. doi:10.1038/scientificamerican0885-16

Dewdney, A. (1986). Computer recreations. *Scientific American*, *255*(3), 14–21. doi:10.1038/scientificamerican0986-14

Díaz-Uriart, R., & Alvarez, S. (2006). Gene selection and classification Of microarray data using random forest. *BMC Bioinformatics*, *7*(1), 3. doi:10.1186/1471-2105-7-3 PMID:16398926

Diez, P. F., Muller, S. M. T., Mut, V. A., Laciar, E., Avila, E., Bastos-Filho, T. F., & Sarcinelli-Filho, M. (2013). Commanding a robotic wheelchair with a high-frequency steady-state visual evoked potential based brain–computer interface. *Medical Engineering & Physics, 35*(8), 1155–1164. doi:10.1016/j.medengphy.2012.12.005 PMID:23339894

Dimitromanolakis, A. (2002). *Analysis of the Golomb Ruler and the Sidon Set Problems, and Determination of Large, Near–Optimal Golomb Rulers* (Master's thesis). Department of Electronic and Computer Engineering, Technical University of Crete.

Dimitromanolakis, A. (2002). *Analysis of the Golomb Ruler and the Sidon Set Problems, and Determination of Large, Near–Optimal Golomb Rulers* (Master's Thesis). Department of Electronic and Computer Engineering, Technical University of Crete.

Distributed.net. (2017). *Project OGR*. Retrieved January 2017 from http://www.distributed.net/ogr

Divina, F., & Marchiori, E. (2005). Handling continuous attributes in an evolutionary inductive learner. *IEEE Transactions on Evolutionary Computation, 9*(1), 31–43. doi:10.1109/TEVC.2004.837752

Dkhil, H. (2015). *Optimisation des systèmes de stockage de conteneurs dans les terminaux maritimes automatisés* (Doctoral thesis). Mathématiques générales [math.GM], Université du Havre.

Dobkin, B. H. (2007). Brain–computer interface technology as a tool to augment plasticity and outcomes for neurological rehabilitation. *The Journal of Physiology, 579*(3), 637–642. doi:10.1113/jphysiol.2006.123067 PMID:17095557

Dollas, A., Rankin, W. T., & McCracken, D. (1998). A New Algorithm for Golomb Ruler Derivation and Proof of the 19 Mark Ruler. *IEEE Transactions on Information Theory, 44*(1), 379–382. doi:10.1109/18.651068

Domnic, S., & Glory, V. (2012). Inverted file compression using EGC and FEGC. *Procedia Technology, 6*, 493–500. doi:10.1016/j.protcy.2012.10.059

Donaway, R. L., Drummey, K. W., & Mather, L. A. (2000, April). A comparison of rankings produced by summarization evaluation measures. In *Proceedings of the 2000 NAACL-ANLP Workshop on Automatic summarization* (vol. 4, pp. 69-78). Association for Computational Linguistics. doi:10.3115/1117575.1117583

Donoghue, J. P., Nurmikko, A., Black, M., & Hochberg, L. R. (2007). Assistive technology and robotic control using motor cortex ensemble-based neural interface systems in humans with tetraplegia. *The Journal of Physiology, 579*(3), 603–611. doi:10.1113/jphysiol.2006.127209 PMID:17272345

Dorigo, M., Birattari, M., & Stutzle, T. (2006). Ant colony optimization. *IEEE Computational Intelligence Magazine, 1*(4), 28–39. doi:10.1109/MCI.2006.329691

Dotú, I., & Hentenryck, P. V. (2005). A Simple Hybrid Evolutionary Algorithm for Finding Golomb Rulers. *Proceedings of 2005 IEEE Congress on Evolutionary Computation, 3*, 2018–2023. doi:10.1109/CEC.2005.1554943

Drakakis, K. (2009). A Review of The Available Construction Methods for Golomb Rulers. *Advances in Mathematics of Communications, 3*(3), 235–250. doi:10.3934/amc.2009.3.235

Drakakis, K., & Rickard, S. (2010). On the Construction of Nearly Optimal Golomb Rulers by Unwrapping Costas Arrays. *Contemporary Engineering Sciences, 3*(7), 295–309.

Drucker, H., Wu, S., & Vapnik, V. N. (1999). Support vector machines for spam categorization. *Neural Networks. IEEE Transactions on, 10*(5), 1048–1054. PMID:18252607

Dubreuil, J. (2008). La logistique des terminaux portuaires de conteneurs, Centre interuniversitaire de recherche sur les réseaux d'entreprise. Mémoire, Centre Universitaire de Recherche sur les Réseaux d'Entreprise la Logistique et Transport, Montréal, Canada.

Duch, W. (2006). *Feature extraction, foundations and applications*. Springer.

Duda & Hart. (1973). *Pattern Classification and scene analysis*. Wiley.

Dudoit, S. (2002b). Comparison of discrimination methods for the classification of tumors using gene expression data. *Journal of the American Statistical Association, 97*(457), 77-87.

Dutt, D., Hedge, V., & Borse, P. T. (2015). AAKRITI[ed]: An Image and Data Encryption-Decryption Tool. *International Journal of Computer Science and Information Technology Research, 02*(02), 264–268.

Duvaland & Hao. (1999). *Advances in metaheuristics for gene selection and classification of Microarray data*. Addison-Wesley.

Easterbrook, S. M. (2010, November). Climate change: a grand software challenge. In *Proceedings of the FSE/SDP workshop on Future of software engineering research* (pp. 99-104). ACM. doi:10.1145/1882362.1882383

Easterbrook, S. M., & Johns, T. C. (2009). Engineering the software for understanding climate change. *Computing in Science & Engineering, 11*(6), 64–74. doi:10.1109/MCSE.2009.193

Eberhart, R. C., & Kennedy, J. (1995, October). A new optimizer using particle swarm theory. In *Proceedings of the sixth international symposium on micro machine and human science* (Vol. 1, pp. 39-43). doi:10.1109/MHS.1995.494215

Eddy. (1995). Multiple alignment using hidden Markov models. *ISMB*, 114–120.

Edmundson, H. P. (1963). *Automatic Abstracting. Thompson Ram Wooldridge* Inc.

El-bayoumy, M. A., Rashad, M. Z., Elsoud, M. A., & El-dosuky, M. A. (2014). Job Scheduling in Grid Computing with Fast Artificial Fish Swarm Algorithm. *International Journal of Computers and Applications, 96*(14).

Elias, P. (1975). Universal codeword sets and representations of the integers. *IEEE Transactions on Information Theory, 21*(2), 194–203. doi:10.1109/TIT.1975.1055349

Elith, J., & Leathwick, J. R. (2009). Species distribution models: Ecological explanation and prediction across space and time. *Annual Review of Ecology Evolution and Systematics, 40*(1), 677–697. doi:10.1146/annurev.ecolsys.110308.120159

Erol, O. K., & Eksin, I. (2006). A New Optimization Method: Big Bang–Big Crunch. *Advances in Engineering Software, 37*(2), 106–111. doi:10.1016/j.advengsoft.2005.04.005

Ethier, C., Oby, E. R., Bauman, M. J., & Miller, L. E. (2012). Restoration of grasp following paralysis through brain-controlled stimulation of muscles. *Nature, 485*(7398), 368–371. doi:10.1038/nature10987 PMID:22522928

Evangelista, T. (2004). *Les IDS: les systèmes de détection d'intrusions informatiques*. Dunod.

Falk, T. H., Guirgis, M., Power, S., & Chau, T. T. (2011). Taking NIRS-BCIs outside the lab: Towards achieving robustness against environment noise. *IEEE Transactions on Neural Systems and Rehabilitation Engineering, 19*(2), 136–146. doi:10.1109/TNSRE.2010.2078516 PMID:20876031

Faloutsos, C. (1985). Access methods for text. *ACM Computing Surveys, 17*(1), 49–74. doi:10.1145/4078.4080

Faloutsos, M., Faloutsos, P., & Faloutsos, C. (1999, August). On power-law relationships of the internet topology. *Computer Communication Review, 29*(4), 251–262. doi:10.1145/316194.316229

Fang, R. J. F., & Sandrin, W. A. (1977). Carrier Frequency Assignment for Non–Linear Repeaters. *C.O.M.S.A.T. Technical Review, 7,* 227–245.

Fania, M., Peiravi, P., Chandramouly, A., & Yalla, C. (2013). *Predictive Analytics and Interactive Queries on Big Data* (White Paper). Intel Reference Architecture, Big Data Analytics.

Farwell, L. A., & Donchin, E. (1988). Talking off the top of your head: Toward a mental prosthesis utilizing event-related brain potentials. *Electroencephalography and Clinical Neurophysiology, 70*(6), 510–523. doi:10.1016/0013-4694(88)90149-6 PMID:2461285

Farzi, S. (2009). Efficient job scheduling in grid computing with modified artificial fish swarm algorithm. *International Journal of Computer Theory and Engineering, 1*(1), 13.

Faynberg, I., Lu, H. L., Perlman, R., & Zeltsan, Z. (2010). *U.S. Patent No. 7,752,440.* Washington, DC: U.S. Patent and Trademark Office.

Fernald, G. H., Capriotti, E., Daneshjou, R., Karczewski, K. J., & Altman, R. B. (2011). Bioinformatics challenges for personalized medicine. *Bioinformatics (Oxford, England), 27*(13), 1741–1748. doi:10.1093/bioinformatics/btr295 PMID:21596790

Fetz, E. E. (1969). Operant conditioning of cortical unit activity. *Science, 163*(3870), 955–958. doi:10.1126/science.163.3870.955 PMID:4974291

Fisher, D., DeLine, R., Czerwinski, M., & Drucker, S. (2012). *Interaction with Big data analytics.* Interactions Cover Story.

Fix, E., & Hodges, J. L. (1949). *Discriminatory Analysis, Non-Parametric Discrimination: Consistency Properties* (Technical Report 21-49-004). USAF School of Aviation Medicine.

Forghieri, F., Tkach, R. W., & Chraplyvy, A. R. (1995). WDM Systems with Unequally Spaced Channels. *Journal of Lightwave Technology, 13*(5), 889–897. doi:10.1109/50.387806

Forghieri, F., Tkach, R. W., Chraplyvy, A. R., & Marcuse, D. (1994). Reduction of Four–Wave Mixing Crosstalk in WDM Systems Using Unequally Spaced Channels. *IEEE Photonics Technology Letters, 6*(6), 754–756. doi:10.1109/68.300184

Forrest, S., Hofmeyr, S. A., Somayaji, A., & Longstaff, T. A. (1996, May). A sense of self for unix processes. In *Security and Privacy, 1996. Proceedings., 1996 IEEE Symposium on* (pp. 120-128). IEEE. doi:10.1109/SECPRI.1996.502675

Fortunato, S. (2010). Community detection in graphs. *Physics Reports, 486*(3), 75–174. doi:10.1016/j.physrep.2009.11.002

Fortunato, S., & Barthelemy, M. (2007). Resolution limit in community detection. *Proceedings of the National Academy of Sciences of the United States of America, 104*(1), 36–41. doi:10.1073/pnas.0605965104 PMID:17190818

Fournier-Viger, P., Gomariz, A., Šebek, M., & Hlosta, M. (2014). VGEN: fast vertical mining of sequential generator patterns. In Data Warehousing and Knowledge Discovery (pp. 476-488). Springer International Publishing. doi:10.1007/978-3-319-10160-6_42

Fox, B., Xiang, W., & Lee, H. P. (2007). Industrial applications of the ant colony optimization algorithm. *International Journal of Advanced Manufacturing Technology, 31*(7-8), 805–814. doi:10.1007/s00170-005-0254-z

Fridman, G. Y., Blair, H. T., Blaisdell, A. P., & Judy, J. W. (2010). Perceived intensity of somatosensory cortical electrical stimulation. *Experimental Brain Research, 203*(3), 499–515. doi:10.1007/s00221-010-2254-y PMID:20440610

Fukunaga, K. (1990). *Statistical pattern recognition* (2nd ed.). Morgan Kaufmann.

Fum, D., Guida, G., & Tasso, C. (1982, July). Forward and backward reasoning in automatic abstracting. In *Proceedings of the 9th conference on Computational linguistics* (vol. 1, pp. 83-88). Academia Praha. doi:10.3115/991813.991826

Gabel, M., & Su, Z. (2008, May). Symbolic mining of temporal specifications. In *Proceedings of the 30th international conference on Software engineering* (pp. 51-60). ACM.

Gabel, M., & Su, Z. (2008, November). Javert: fully automatic mining of general temporal properties from dynamic traces. In *Proceedings of the 16th ACM SIGSOFT International Symposium on Foundations of software engineering* (pp. 339-349). ACM. doi:10.1145/1453101.1453150

Gale, W. J., Heasley, K. A., Iannacchione, A. T., Swanson, P. L., Hatherly, P., & King, A. (2001, January). Rock damage characterisation from microseismic monitoring. In *DC Rocks 2001, The 38th US Symposium on Rock Mechanics (USRMS)*. American Rock Mechanics Association.

Galinier, P., Jaumard, B., Morales, R., & Pesant, G. (2001). A constraint–Based Approach to the Golomb Ruler Problem. *Proceedings of 3rd International Workshop on Integration of AI and OR Techniques (CP–AI–OR 2001)*.

Gao, X. (2013). Towards the next generation intelligent BPM–in the era of big data. In *Business Process Management* (pp. 4–9). Springer Berlin Heidelberg. doi:10.1007/978-3-642-40176-3_2

Gao, X., Dignfeng, X., Cheng, M., & Gao, S. (2003). A BCI-based environmental controller for the motion-disabled. *IEEE Transactions on Neural Systems and Rehabilitation Engineering, 11*(2), 137–140. doi:10.1109/TNSRE.2003.814449 PMID:12899256

Geib, J., Gransart, C., & Merle, P. (1997). *CORBA: des concepts à la pratique*. Edition Masson.

Gent, P. R., Danabasoglu, G., Donner, L. J., Holland, M. M., Hunke, E. C., Jayne, S. R., & Worley, P. H. et al. (2011). The community climate system model version 4. *Journal of Climate, 24*(19), 4973–4991. doi:10.1175/2011JCLI4083.1

Georgopoulos, A. P., Langheim, F. J. P., Leuthold, A. C., & Merkle, A. N. (2005). Magnetoencephalographic signals predict movement trajectory in space. *Experimental Brain Research, 167*(1), 132–135. doi:10.1007/s00221-005-0028-8 PMID:16044305

Ghaffarzadeh, N., & Heydari, S. (2015). Optimal Coordination of Digital Overcurrent Relays using Black Hole Algorithm. *World Applied Programming, 5*(2), 50–55.

Gibowicz, S. J., & Lasocki, S. (2001). Seismicity induced by mining: Ten years later. *Advances in Geophysics, 44*, 39–181. doi:10.1016/S0065-2687(00)80007-2

Girvan, M., & Newman, M. E. (2002). Community structure in social and biological networks. *Proceedings of the National Academy of Sciences of the United States of America, 99*(12), 7821–7826. doi:10.1073/pnas.122653799 PMID:12060727

Giveki, D., Salimi, H., Bahmanyar, G., & Khademian, Y. (2012). *Automatic detection of diabetes diagnosis using feature weighted support vector machines based on mutual information and modified cuckoo search*. arXiv preprint arXiv:1201.2173

Glory, V., & Domnic, S. (2013). Re-Ordered FEGC and Block Based FEGC for Inverted File Compression. *International Journal of Information Retrieval Research, 3*(1), 71–88. doi:10.4018/ijirr.2013010105

Goel, A., & Mishra, A. (2015, January). Survey on Watermarking Schemes using Adaptive Soft Computing Techniques. *International Journal of Computers and Applications, 110*(04), 4–8. doi:10.5120/19302-0751

Gog, A., Dumitrescu, D., & Hirsbrunner, B. (2007, September). Community detection in complex networks using collaborative evolutionary algorithms. In *European Conference on Artificial Life* (pp. 886-894). Springer Berlin Heidelberg. doi:10.1007/978-3-540-74913-4_89

Goldstein, J., Ramakrishnan, R., & Shaft, U. (1998). Compressing relations and indexes. In *Data Engineering, 1998. Proceedings., 14th International Conference on* (pp. 370-379). IEEE. doi:10.1109/ICDE.1998.655800

Golomb, S. W. (1966). Run Length Coding. *IEEE Transactions on Knowledge and Data Engineering, 12*(3), 399–401.

Golub, T. R. (1999a). Molecular classification of cancer: Class discovery and class prediction by gene expression monitoring. *Science, 286*(5439), 531–539. doi:10.1126/science.286.5439.531 PMID:10521349

Gong, M., Cai, Q., Li, Y., & Ma, J. (2012, June). An improved memetic algorithm for community detection in complex networks. In *2012 IEEE Congress on Evolutionary Computation* (pp. 1-8). IEEE.

Gong, M., Fu, B., Jiao, L., & Du, H. (2011). Memetic algorithm for community detection in networks. *Physical Review. E, 84*(5), 056101. doi:10.1103/PhysRevE.84.056101 PMID:22181467

Gongora, M., Peressutti, C., Machado, S., Teixeira, S., Velasques, B., & Ribeiro, P. (2013). Progress and prospects in neurorehabilitation: Clinical applications of stem cells and brain–computer interface for spinal cord lesions. *Neurological Sciences, 34*(4), 427–433. doi:10.1007/s10072-012-1232-5 PMID:23161257

Gorman, R. P., & Sejnowski, T. J. (1988). Analysis of hidden units in a layered network trained to classify sonar targets. *Neural Networks, 1*(1), 75–89. doi:10.1016/0893-6080(88)90023-8

Greco, G., Guzzo, A., Pontieri, L., & Sacca, D. (2006). Discovering expressive process models by clustering log traces. *Knowledge and Data Engineering. IEEE Transactions on, 18*(8), 1010–1027.

Grozea, C., Gehl, C., & Popescu, M. (2009, September). ENCOPLOT: Pairwise sequence matching in linear time applied to plagiarism detection. *3rd PAN Workshop. Uncovering Plagiarism, Authorship and Social Software Misuse*, 10.

Guimera, R., Sales-Pardo, M., & Amaral, L. A. N. (2004). Modularity from fluctuations in random graphs and complex networks. *Physical Review. E, 70*(2), 025101. doi:10.1103/PhysRevE.70.025101 PMID:15447530

Guoqiang, C., & Xiaofang, G. (2010, December). A genetic algorithm based on modularity density for detecting community structure in complex networks. In *Computational Intelligence and Security (CIS), 2010 International Conference on* (pp. 151-154). IEEE. doi:10.1109/CIS.2010.40

Gupta, G., Mazumdar, C., & Rao, M. S. (2004). Digital Forensic Analysis of E-mails: A trusted E-mail Pro-tocol. *International Journal of Digital Evidence, 2*(4).

Guyet, T., & Quiniou, R. (2011, July). Extracting temporal patterns from interval-based sequences. In *IJCAI Proceedings-International Joint Conference on Artificial Intelligence* (Vol. 22, No. 1, p. 1306). Academic Press.

Guyon, I., & Elisseeff, A. (2003). An introduction to variable and feature selection. *Journal of Machine Learning Research, 3*, 1157–1182.

Guyon, I., Weston, J., Barnhill, S., & Vapnik, V. (2002a). Gene selection for cancer classification using support vector machine. *SMachine Learning., 46*(13), 389–422. doi:10.1023/A:1012487302797

Guzella, T. S., & Caminhas, W. M. (2009). A review of machine learning approaches to spam filtering. *Expert Systems with Applications, 36*(7), 10206–10222. doi:10.1016/j.eswa.2009.02.037

Hamdadou, D., & Bouamrane, K. (2007). A Multicriterion SDSS for the Space Process Control: Towards a Hybrid Approach, MICAI 2007. *Advances in Artificial Intelligence, 1611*(3349), 139–150.

Hamidi, Y. N. E. (2015). *L'utilisation de l'approche boosting pour le diagnostic du diabéte* (Doctoral dissertation). Tlemcen university, Algeria.

Hamou, R. M., Amine, A., & Rahmani, M. (2012). A new biomimetic approach based on social spiders for clustering of text. In Software Engineering Research, Management and Applications 2012 (pp. 17-30). Springer Berlin Heidelberg. doi:10.1007/978-3-642-30460-6_2

Hamou, R. M., Boudia, M. A., & Amine, A. (n.d.). *A new approach based on the detection of opinion by sentiwordnet for automatic text summaries by extraction*. Academic Press.

Hamou, R. M., Amine, A., & Boudia, A. (2013). A New Meta-Heuristic Based on Social Bees for Detection and Filtering of Spam. *International Journal of Applied Metaheuristic Computing, 4*(3), 15–33. doi:10.4018/ijamc.2013070102

Hamou, R. M., Amine, A., & Lokbani, A. C. (2012). The Social Spiders in the Clustering of Texts: Towards an Aspect of Visual Classification. *International Journal of Artificial Life Research, 3*(3), 1–14. doi:10.4018/jalr.2012070101

Hamou, R. M., Amine, A., & Lokbani, A. C. (2013). Study of Sensitive Parameters of PSO Application to Clustering of Texts. *International Journal of Applied Evolutionary Computation, 4*(2), 41–55. doi:10.4018/jaec.2013040104

Han, J., & Kamber, M. (2000). *Data Mining: Concepts and Techniques*. San Francisco: Morgan Kaufmann.

Han, J., Pei, J., & Kamber, M. (2011). *Data mining: concepts and techniques*. Elsevier.

Han, J., Pei, J., & Kamber, M. (2011). *Data mining: Concepts and techniques*. Elsevier.

Han, J., Pei, J., & Yin, Y. (2000). Mining Frequent Patterns without Candidate Generation. *Proceedings of the 2000 ACM-SIGMOD Int'l Conf. on Management of Data*.

Haouzia, A., & Noumeir, R. (2007). Methods for image authentication: A survey. *Multimed Tools Appl.*, 1-46.

Hao, Y. Y., Zhang, Q. S., Zhang, S. M., Zhao, T., Wang, Y. W., Chen, W. D., & Zheng, X. X. (2013). Decoding grasp movement from monkey premotor cortex for real-time prosthetic hand control. *Chinese Science Bulletin, 58*(20), 2512–2520. doi:10.1007/s11434-013-5840-0

Harding, , & Leitner, , & Schmidhuber. (2013). Cartesian Genetic Programming for Image Processing. *Genetic and Evolutionary Computation: Genetic Programming Theory and Practice, 10*, 1–17.

Harrison, R. V. (1987). Cochlear implants: A review of the principles and important physiological factors. *The Journal of Otolaryngology, 16*(5), 268–275. PMID:3316687

Haselager, P. (2013). Did I do that? Brain–computer interfacing and the sense of agency. *Minds and Machines, 23*(3), 405–418. doi:10.1007/s11023-012-9298-7

Hassan & Abou-Taleb. (2013). A hybrid feature selection approach of ensemble multiple Filter methods and wrapper method for Improving the Classification Accuracy of Microarray Data Set. *International Journal of Computer Science and Information Technology and Security, 3*(2).

Hatamlou, A. (2013). Black hole: A new heuristic optimization approach for data clustering. *Information Sciences, 222*, 175–184. doi:10.1016/j.ins.2012.08.023

He, D., Wang, Z., Yang, B., & Zhou, C. (2009, November). Genetic algorithm with ensemble learning for detecting community structure in complex networks. In *Computer Sciences and Convergence Information Technology, 2009. ICCIT'09. Fourth International Conference on* (pp. 702-707). IEEE. doi:10.1109/ICCIT.2009.189

Hearst, M. A., Dumais, S. T., Osman, E., Platt, J., & Scholkopf, B. (1998). Support vector machines. *Intelligent Systems and their Applications, IEEE, 13*(4), 18-28.

Heger, D., Putze, F., & Schultz, T. (2011). An EEG adaptive information system for an empathic robot. *International Journal of Social Robotics*, *3*(4), 415–425. doi:10.1007/s12369-011-0107-x

Heidari, A. A., & Abbaspour, R. A. (2014). Improved black hole algorithm for efficient low observable UCAV path planning in constrained aerospace. *Advances in Computer Science: an International Journal*, *3*(3), 87–92.

Hergalant, S., Aigle, B., Leblond, P., Mari, J. F., & Decaris, B. (2002). Fouille de données à l'aide de HMM: Application à la détection de réitérations intragénomiques. *JOBIM*, *2*, 269–273.

Hernandez, J. (2007). *A Genetic Embedded Approach for Gene Selection and Classification of Microarray Data*. EvoBIO.

Hickok, G., Houde, J., & Rong, F. (2011). Sensorimotor integration in speech processing: Computational basis and neural organization. *Neuron*, *69*(3), 407–422. doi:10.1016/j.neuron.2011.01.019 PMID:21315253

Hoad, T. C., & Zobel, J. (2003). Methods for identifying versioned and plagiarized documents. *Journal of the American Society for Information Science and Technology*, *54*(3), 203–215. doi:10.1002/asi.10170

Hochachka, W. M., Caruana, R., Fink, D., Munson, A. R. T., Riedewald, M., Sorokina, D., & Kelling, S. (2007). Data-mining discovery of pattern and process in ecological systems. *The Journal of Wildlife Management*, *71*(7), 2427–2437. doi:10.2193/2006-503

Hochberg, L. R., Serruya, M. D., Friehs, G. M., Mukand, J. A., Saleh, M., Caplan, A. H., & Donoghue, J. P. et al. (2006). Neuronal ensemble control of prosthetic devices by a human with tetraplegia. *Nature*, *442*(7099), 164–171. doi:10.1038/nature04970 PMID:16838014

Holland, J. H., & Reitman, J. S. (1977). Cognitive systems based on adaptive algorithms. *ACM SIGART Bulletin*, (63), 49-49.

Holland, J. H. (1992). Genetic algorithms. *Scientific American*, *267*(1), 66–72. doi:10.1038/scientificamerican0792-66

Holm, S. (1979). A Simple Sequentially Rejective Multiple Test Procedure. *Scandinavian Journal of Statistics*, *6*(2), 65–70.

Hortal, E., Ianez, E., Ubeda, A., Perez-Vidal, C., & Azorin, J. M. (2015). Combining a brain–machine interface and an electrooculography interface to perform pick and place tasks with a robotic arm. *Robotics and Autonomous Systems*, *72*, 181–188. doi:10.1016/j.robot.2015.05.010

Hortal, E., Ubeda, A., Ianez, E., & Azorin, J. M. (2014). Control of a 2 DoF robot using a brain–machine interface. *Computer Methods and Programs in Biomedicine*, *116*(2), 169–176. doi:10.1016/j.cmpb.2014.02.018 PMID:24694722

Horton, P., & Nakai, K. (1996, June). A probabilistic classification system for predicting the cellular localization sites of proteins. In ISMB (Vol. 4, pp. 109-115). Academic Press.

Hovy, E., Lin, C. Y., Zhou, L., & Fukumoto, J. (2006, May). Automated summarization evaluation with basic elements. In *Proceedings of the Fifth Conference on Language Resources and Evaluation (LREC 2006)* (pp. 604-611). Academic Press.

Hu, J., Zeng, X., & Xiao, J. (2010, December). Artificial fish school algorithm for function optimization. In *Information Engineering and Computer Science (ICIECS), 2010 2nd International Conference on* (pp. 1-4). IEEE. doi:10.1109/ICIECS.2010.5678350

Huang, Z., & Chen, Y. (2015). Log-linear model based behavior selection method for artificial fish swarm algorithm. *Computational Intelligence and Neuroscience*, *2015*, 10. doi:10.1155/2015/685404 PMID:25691895

Hughey, R., & Krogh, A. (1996). Hidden Markov models for sequence analysis: Extension and analysis of the basic method. *Computer Applications in the Biosciences*, *12*, 95–107. PMID:8744772

Huisman, D., Freling, R., & Wagelmans, A. (2002). *A Dynamic Approach to Vehicle Scheduling*. Rapport de l'Insititut économoque, Université Erasmus, Rotterdam, Pays-Bas.

Hwang, B., & Tonguz, O. K. (1998). A Generalized Suboptimum Unequally Spaced Channel Allocation Technique—Part I: In IM/DDWDMsystems. *IEEE Transactions on Communications, 46*(8), 1027–1037. doi:10.1109/26.705403

Hwang, E. J., & Andersen, R. A. (2009). Brain control of movement execution onset using local field potentials in posterior parietal cortex. *The Journal of Neuroscience, 29*(45), 14363–14370. doi:10.1523/JNEUROSCI.2081-09.2009 PMID:19906983

Ibrahim, T. S., Abraham, D., & Rennaker, R. L. (2007). Electromagnetic power absorption and temperature changes due to brain machine interface operation. *Annals of Biomedical Engineering, 35*(5), 825–834. doi:10.1007/s10439-007-9264-3 PMID:17334681

Ihaka, R., & Gentelman, R. (1996). R: A language for data analysis and graphics. *Journal of Computational and Graphical Statistics*, 299–314.

Ilgun, K., Kemmerer, R. A., & Porras, P. A. (1995). State transition analysis: A rule-based intru-sion detection approach. *Software Engineering. IEEE Transactions on, 21*(3), 181–199.

Iscan, Z., Dokur, Z., & Demiralp, T. (2011). Classification of electroencephalogram signals with combined time and frequency features. *Expert Systems with Applications, 38*(8), 10499–10505. doi:10.1016/j.eswa.2011.02.110

Ishibuchi, H., & Yamamoto, T. (2004). Fuzzy rule selection by multi-objective genetic local search algorithms and rule evaluation measures in data mining. *Fuzzy Sets and Systems, 141*(1), 59–88. doi:10.1016/S0165-0114(03)00114-3

Itkar, S. A., & Kulkarni, U. V. (2013). Distributed Algorithm for Frequent Pattern Mining using HadoopMap Reduce Framework. *Proc. of Int. Conf. on Advances in Computer Science, AETACS*.

Iturrate, I., Antelis, J. M., Kubler, A., & Minguez, J. (2009). A non-invasive brain-actuated wheelchair based on a P300 neurophysiological protocol and automated navigation. *IEEE Transactions on Robotics, 25*(3), 614–627. doi:10.1109/TRO.2009.2020347

Jaakkola, Diekhans, & Haussler. (2000). *A discriminative framework for detecting remote protein homologies*. Academic Press.

Jade, R. K., Verma, L. K., & Verma, K. (2013). *Classification using Neural Network & Support Vector Machine for Sonar dataset*. Academic Press.

Jain, A., & Zongker, D. (1997a). Feature selection: Evaluation, application, and small sample performance. *IEEE Transactions on Pattern Analysis and Machine Intelligence, 19*(2), 153–157. doi:10.1109/34.574797

Jain, P., Bansal, S., Singh, A. K., & Gupta, N. (2015). Golomb Ruler Sequences Optimization for FWM Crosstalk Reduction: Multi–population Hybrid Flower Pollination Algorithm. *Proceeding of Progress in Electromagnetics Research Symposium (PIERS)*, 2463–2467.

Jantawan & Tsai. (2014). A Comparison of Filter and Wrapper Approaches with Data Mining Techniques for Categorical Variables Selection. *International Journal of Innovative Research in Computer and Communication Engineering, 2*(6).

Jeannerod, M. (1995). Mental imagery in the motor context. *Neuropsychologia, 33*(11), 1419–1432. doi:10.1016/0028-3932(95)00073-C PMID:8584178

Jebari, K. (2013). Brain machine interface and human enhancement: An ethical review. *Neuroethics, 6*(3), 617–625. doi:10.1007/s12152-012-9176-2

Jiang, M., & Cheng, Y. (2010, July). Simulated annealing artificial fish swarm algorithm. In *Intelligent Control and Automation (WCICA), 2010 8th World Congress on* (pp. 1590-1593). IEEE.

Joshi, M., & Srivastava, P. R. (2013). Query optimization: An intelligent hybrid approach using cuckoo and tabu search. *International Journal of Intelligent Information Technologies, 9*(1), 40–55. doi:10.4018/jiit.2013010103

Kabiesz, J. (2006). Effect of the form of data on the quality of mine tremors hazard forecasting using neural networks. *Geotechnical and Geological Engineering, 24*(5), 1131–1147. doi:10.1007/s10706-005-1136-8

Kadir, A., Nugroho, L. E., Susanto, A., & Santosa, P. I. (2011). *A comparative experiment of several shape methods in recognizing plants.* arXiv preprint arXiv:1110.1509

Kadushin, C. (2012). *Understanding social networks: Theories, concepts, and findings.* OUP USA.

Kågström, J. (2005). *Improving naive Bayesian spam filtering* (Doctoral dissertation). Mid Sweden University.

Kameche, Z. (2011). *Sélection des Web Services à Base Des Essaimes Particulaires.* Tlemcen University.

Kang, N., Gelbukh, A., & Han, S. (2006, September). PPChecker: Plagiarism pattern checker in document copy detection. In Text, Speech and Dialogue (pp. 661-667). Springer Berlin Heidelberg.

Kanungo, D. P., Nayak, J., Naik, B., & Behera, H. S. (2016). Hybrid Clustering using Elitist Teaching Learning-Based Optimization: An Improved Hybrid Approach of TLBO. *International Journal of Rough Sets and Data Analysis, 3*(1), 1–19. doi:10.4018/IJRSDA.2016010101

Karabatak, M., & Ince, M. C. (2009). An expert system for detection of breast cancer based on association rules and neural network. *Expert Systems with Applications, 36*(2), 3465–3469. doi:10.1016/j.eswa.2008.02.064

Karaboga, D., & Basturk, B. (2007). A powerful and efficient algorithm for numerical function optimization: Artificial bee colony (ABC) algorithm. *Journal of Global Optimization, 39*(3), 459–471. doi:10.1007/s10898-007-9149-x

Kasemsap, K. (2018a). The fundamentals of human-computer interaction. In M. Khosrow-Pour (Ed.), Encyclopedia of information science and technology (4th ed.; pp. 4199–4209). Hershey, PA: IGI Global. doi:10.4018/978-1-5225-2255-3.ch364

Kasemsap, K. (2017a). Investigating the roles of neuroscience and knowledge management in higher education. In S. Mukerji & P. Tripathi (Eds.), *Handbook of research on administration, policy, and leadership in higher education* (pp. 112–140). Hershey, PA: IGI Global. doi:10.4018/978-1-5225-0672-0.ch006

Kasemsap, K. (2017b). Mastering cognitive neuroscience and social neuroscience perspectives in the information age. In M. Dos Santos (Ed.), *Applying neuroscience to business practice* (pp. 82–113). Hershey, PA: IGI Global. doi:10.4018/978-1-5225-1028-4.ch005

Kasemsap, K. (2018b). Multifaceted applications of the Internet of Things. In M. Khosrow-Pour (Ed.), *Encyclopedia of information science and technology* (4th ed.; pp. 7775–7784). Hershey, PA: IGI Global. doi:10.4018/978-1-5225-2255-3.ch676

Kashan, A. H. (2014). League Championship Algorithm (LCA): An algorithm for global optimization inspired by sport championships. *Applied Soft Computing, 16*, 171–200. doi:10.1016/j.asoc.2013.12.005

Kaski, S., & Peltonen, J. (2003). Informative discriminant analysis. In ICML (pp. 329-336). Academic Press.

Kasprzak, J., Brandejs, M., & Kripac, M. (2009, September). Finding plagiarism by evaluating document similarities. In *Proc. SEPLN* (*Vol. 9*, pp. 24-28). Academic Press.

Kaur, A. R. (2013). A study of detection of lung cancer using data mining classification techniques. *International Journal (Toronto, Ont.)*, *3*(3).

Kefi, G. M. (2008). *Optimisation Heuristique Distribuée du Problème de Stockage de Conteneurs dans un Port* (Doctoral thesis). l'Ecole Centrale de Lille, France.

Kim, B., Reyes, A., Garza, B., & Choi, Y. (2015). A microchannel neural interface with embedded microwires targeting the peripheral nervous system. *Microsystem Technologies*, *21*(7), 1551–1557. doi:10.1007/s00542-014-2340-3

Kim, D. W., Lee, J. C., Park, Y. M., Kim, I. Y., & Im, C. H. (2012). Auditory brain–computer interfaces (BCIs) and their practical applications. *Biomedical Engineering Letters*, *2*(1), 13–17. doi:10.1007/s13534-012-0051-1

Kim, J. H. (2009, July). Interleaved Hop-by-Hop Authentication using fuzzy logic to defend against of False Report Injection by Replaying an attack. *International Journal of Computer Science and Network Security*, *9*(7), 91–96.

Kim, J., Lee, M., Rhim, J. S., Wang, P., Lu, N., & Kim, D. H. (2014). Next-generation flexible neural and cardiac electrode arrays. *Biomedical Engineering Letters*, *4*(2), 95–108. doi:10.1007/s13534-014-0132-4

Kim, K., & Kim, H. (1997). A routing algorithm for a single transfer crane to load export containers onto a containership. *Computers & Industrial Engineering*, *33*(3-4), 673–676. doi:10.1016/S0360-8352(97)00219-2

Kim, S. N., Medelyan, O., Kan, M. Y., & Baldwin, T. (2010, July). Semeval-2010 task 5: Automatic keyphrase extraction from scientific articles. In *Proceedings of the 5th International Workshop on Semantic Evaluation* (pp. 21-26). Association for Computational Linguistics.

Kintsch, W., & Van Dijk, T. A. (1978). Toward a model of text comprehension and production. *Psychological Review*, *85*(5), 363–394. doi:10.1037/0033-295X.85.5.363

Kobayashi, M., & Takeda, K. (2000). Information retrieval on the web. *ACM Computing Surveys*, *32*(2), 144–173. doi:10.1145/358923.358934

Kohavi, R., & John, G. H. (1997). Wrappers for feature subset selection. *Artificial Intelligence*, *97*(1-2), 273–334. doi:10.1016/S0004-3702(97)00043-X

Koller, D., & Sahami, M. (1996). Toward optimal feature selection. *13th International conference on machines learning*, 1-15.

Kondo, T., Saeki, M., Hayashi, Y., Nakayashiki, K., & Takata, Y. (2015). Effect of instructive visual stimuli on neurofeedback training for motor imagery-based brain–computer interface. *Human Movement Science*, *43*, 239–249. doi:10.1016/j.humov.2014.08.014 PMID:25467185

Kononenko, I., Šimec, E., & Robnik-Šikonja, M. (1997). Overcoming the myopia of inductive learning algorithms with RELIEFF. *Applied Intelligence*, *7*(1), 39–55. doi:10.1023/A:1008280620621

Koralek, A. C., Jin, X., Long, J. D. II, Costa, R. M., & Carmena, J. M. (2012). Corticostriatal plasticity is necessary for learning intentional neuroprosthetic skills. *Nature*, *483*(7389), 331–335. doi:10.1038/nature10845 PMID:22388818

Korbaa, O., & Yim. (2004). Container Assignment to stock in a fluvial port. *Proceedings of The International Conference on Systems, Man and Cybernetics*. doi:10.1109/ICSMC.2004.1401369

Kornowski, J. (2003). Linear prediction of aggregated seismic and seismoacoustic energy emitted from a mining longwall. *ACTA Montana*, *129*, 5–14.

Koundinya, A. K., Sharma, K. A. K., Kumar, K., & Shanbag, K. U. (2012). *Map/Reduce Deisgn and Implementation of Apriori Alogirthm for handling voluminous data-sets.* arXiv preprint arXiv:1212.4692

Koza, J. R. (1994). Genetic programming II: Automatic discovery of reusable subprograms. Cambridge, MA: Academic Press.

Koziel, S., & Yang, X.-S. (2011). *Computational Optimization, Methods and Algorithms.* Springer. doi:10.1007/978-3-642-20859-1

Krogh, A., Brown, M., & Saira Mian, I. (1994). Hidden markov models in computational biology: Applications to protein modeling. *Journal of Molecular Biology, 235*(5), 1501–1531. doi:10.1006/jmbi.1994.1104 PMID:8107089

Kujala, J., Pammer, K., Cornelissen, P. L., Roebroeck, P., Formisano, E., & Salmelin, R. (2007). Phase coupling in a cerebro-cerebellar network at 8–13 Hz during reading. *Cerebral Cortex, 17*(6), 1476–1485. doi:10.1093/cercor/bhl059 PMID:16926241

Kumar, S., & Spafford, E. H. (1994). *An application of pattern matching in intrusion detection.* Purdue University. Computer Science Technical Reports.

Kumari, N., Singh, T., & Bansal, S. (2016). Optimal Golomb Ruler Sequences as WDM Channel–Allocation Algorithm Generation: Cuckoo Search Algorithm with Mutation. *International Journal of Computers and Applications, 142*(9), 21–27. doi:10.5120/ijca2016909910

Kumar, S., & Sahin, F. (2015). A framework for a real time intelligent and interactive brain computer interface. *Computers & Electrical Engineering, 43*, 193–214. doi:10.1016/j.compeleceng.2015.03.024

Kwong, W. C., & Yang, G. C. (1997). An Algebraic Approach to the Unequal–Spaced Channel–Allocation Problem in WDM Lightwave Systems. *IEEE Transactions on Communications, 45*(3), 352–359. doi:10.1109/26.558698

Laïchour, H. (2002). *Modélisation mutli-agent et aide à la décision: application à la régulation des correspondances dans les réseaux de transport urbai.* (Thèse de doctorat). Université des sciences et technologies de Lille. France.

Lakshmi, R. D., & Radha, N. (2010, September). Spam classification using supervised learning techniques. In *Proceedings of the 1st Amrita ACM-W Celebration on Women in Computing in India* (p. 66). ACM.

Lam, A. W., & Sarwate, D. V. (1988). On Optimal Time–Hopping Patterns. *IEEE Transactions on Communications, 36*(3), 380–382. doi:10.1109/26.1464

Lancichinetti, A., Fortunato, S., & Radicchi, F. (2008). Benchmark graphs for testing community detection algorithms. *Physical Review. E, 78*(4), 046110. doi:10.1103/PhysRevE.78.046110 PMID:18999496

Lande, P. U. (2010). Robust image adaptive watermarking using fuzzy logic an FPGA approach. *International Journal of Signal Processing, Image Processing and Pattern Recognition, 3*(4), 43–54.

Lander, E. S., Linton, L. M., Birren, B., Nusbaum, C., Zody, M. C., Baldwin, J., & Morgan, M. J. et al. (2001). Initial sequencing and analysis of the human genome. *Nature, 409*(6822), 860–921. doi:10.1038/35057062 PMID:11237011

Lasocki, S. (2005, March). Probabilistic analysis of seismic hazard posed by mining induced events. In *Proc. Sixth Int. Symp. on Rockburst and Seismicity in Mines "Controlling Seismic Risk"* (pp. 9-11). Academic Press.

Lavanya & Usha Rani. (2011). Analysis of feature selection with classification: Breast Cancer Datasets. *Indian Journal of Computer Science and Engineering, 2.*

Lavoie, P., Haccoun, D., & Savaria, Y. (1991). New VLSI Architectures for Fast Soft-Decision Threshold Decoders. *IEEE Transactions on Communications, 39*(2), 200–207. doi:10.1109/26.76456

Lebedev, M. (2014). Brain–machine interfaces: An overview. *Translational Neuroscience, 5*(1), 99–110. doi:10.2478/s13380-014-0212-z

Lee, J. (2016). Cochlear implantation, enhancements, transhumanism and posthumanism: Some human questions. *Science and Engineering Ethics*, *22*(1), 67–92. doi:10.1007/s11948-015-9640-6 PMID:25962718

Leitao, T. (2004). Evolving the Maximum Segment Length of a Golomb Ruler. *Proceedings of Genetic and Evolutionary Computation Conference.*

Lemire, D., & Boystov, L. (2013). *FastPFOR Java code, 2013*. Retrieved from https://github.com/lemire/JavaFastPFOR

Lemire, D., & Boytsov, L. (2015). Decoding billions of integers per second through vectorization. *Software, Practice & Experience*, *45*(1), 1–29. doi:10.1002/spe.2203

Lenin, K., Reddy, B. R., & Kalavathi, M. S. (2014). Black Hole Algorithm for Solving Optimal Reactive Power Dispatch Problem. *International Journal of Research in Management, Science & Technology, 2*, 10-15.

Leslie, C., Eskin, E., Weston, J., & Noble, W. S. (2003). Mismatch string kernels for SVM protein classification. In S. Becker, S. Thrun, & K. Obermayer (Eds.), *NIPS 2002* (Vol. 15, pp. 1441–1448). Cambridge, MA: MIT Press.

Leśniak, A., & Isakow, Z. (2009). Space–time clustering of seismic events and hazard assessment in the Zabrze-Bielszowice coal mine, Poland. *International Journal of Rock Mechanics and Mining Sciences*, *46*(5), 918–928. doi:10.1016/j.ijrmms.2008.12.003

Liao, L., & Stafford Noble, W. (2002). Combining pairwise sequence similarity and Support Vector Machines for remote protein homology detection. Journal of Computational Biology, 225–232. doi:10.1145/565196.565225

Liberati, G., Pizzimenti, A., Simione, L., Riccio, A., Schettini, F., Inghilleri, M., & Cincotti, F. et al. (2015). Developing brain-computer interfaces from a user-centered perspective: Assessing the needs of persons with amyotrophic lateral sclerosis, caregivers, and professionals. *Applied Ergonomics*, *50*, 139–146. doi:10.1016/j.apergo.2015.03.012 PMID:25959328

Li, H. (2009). A compensability RF CMOS mixed-signal interface for implantable system. *Analog Integrated Circuits and Signal Processing*, *61*(3), 301–307. doi:10.1007/s10470-009-9311-0

Lin, C. Y., Cao, G., Gao, J., & Nie, J. Y. (2006, June). An information-theoretic approach to automatic evaluation of summaries. In *Proceedings of the main conference on Human Language Technology Conference of the North American Chapter of the Association of Computational Linguistics* (pp. 463-470). Association for Computational Linguistics. doi:10.3115/1220835.1220894

Linder, R., Richards, T., & Wagner, M. (2007). Microarray data classified by Artificial neural networks. *Methods in Molecular Biology Clifton Then to Towa*, *382*, 345–372. doi:10.1007/978-1-59745-304-2_22 PMID:18220242

Lindqvist, U., & Porras, P. A. (1999). Detecting computer and network misuse through the pro-duction-based expert system toolset (P-BEST). In *Security and Privacy, 1999. Proceedings of the 1999 IEEE Symposium on* (pp. 146-161). IEEE.

Li, T., Hong, J., Zhang, J., & Guo, F. (2014). Brain–machine interface control of a manipulator using small-world neural network and shared control strategy. *Journal of Neuroscience Methods*, *224*, 26–38. doi:10.1016/j.jneumeth.2013.11.015 PMID:24333753

Little, S., & Brown, P. (2012). What brain signals are suitable for feedback control of deep brain stimulation in Parkinson's disease? *Annals of the New York Academy of Sciences*, *1265*(1), 9–24. doi:10.1111/j.1749-6632.2012.06650.x PMID:22830645

Litvak, M., & Last, M. (2008, August). Graph-based keyword extraction for single-document summarization. In *Proceedings of the workshop on Multi-source Multilingual Information Extraction and Summarization* (pp. 17-24). Association for Computational Linguistics. doi:10.3115/1613172.1613178

Liu, H., & Yu, L. (2005). Toward Integrating Feature Selection Algorithms for Classification and Clustering. *IEEE Trans. on Knowledgeand Data Engineering.*, *17*(4), 491–502. doi:10.1109/TKDE.2005.66

Liu, J., Khalil, H. K., & Oweiss, K. G. (2011). Neural feedback for instantaneous spatiotemporal modulation of afferent pathways in bi-directional brain–machine interfaces. *IEEE Transactions on Neural Systems and Rehabilitation Engineering*, *19*(5), 521–533. doi:10.1109/TNSRE.2011.2162003 PMID:21859634

Li, Z., Zhang, S., Wang, R. S., Zhang, X. S., & Chen, L. (2008). Quantitative function for community detection. *Physical Review. E*, *77*(3), 036109. doi:10.1103/PhysRevE.77.036109 PMID:18517463

Lokbani, A. C., Lehireche, A., & Hamou, R. M. (2013). Experimentation of Data Mining Technique for System's Security: A Comparative Study. In *Advances in Swarm Intelligence* (pp. 248–257). Springer Berlin Heidelberg. doi:10.1007/978-3-642-38715-9_30

Louis, A., & Nenkova, A. (2009, August). Automatically evaluating content selection in summarization without human models. In *Proceedings of the 2009 Conference on Empirical Methods in Natural Language Processing* (vol. 1, pp. 306-314). Association for Computational Linguistics. doi:10.3115/1699510.1699550

Low, Y., Gonzalez, J. E., Kyrola, A., Bickson, D., Guestrin, C. E., & Hellerstein, J. (2014). *Graphlab: A new framework for parallel machine learning.* arXiv preprint arXiv:1408.2041

Lozano, S., Duch, J., & Arenas, A. (2007). Analysis of large social datasets by community detection. *The European Physical Journal. Special Topics*, *143*(1), 257–259. doi:10.1140/epjst/e2007-00098-6

Lucas, D. D., Klein, R., Tannahill, J., Ivanova, D., Brandon, S., Domyancic, D., & Zhang, Y. (2013). Failure analysis of parameter-induced simulation crashes in climate models. *Geoscientific Model Development*, *6*(4), 1157–1171. doi:10.5194/gmd-6-1157-2013

Luck, S. J. (2005). *An introduction to the event-related potential technique.* Cambridge, MA: MIT Press.

Lueg, Mueller, & Scott. (2009). *Fight Spam on the Internet!* Retrieved from spam.abuse.net

Lueg, C., & Martin, S. (2007, July). Users dealing with spam and spam filters: some observations and rec-ommendations. In *Proceedings of the 8th ACM SIGCHI New Zealand chapter's International Conference on Computer-Human Interaction: Design Centered HCI* (pp. 67-72). ACM.

Luft, A. R., McCombe-Waller, S., Whitall, J., Forrester, L. W., Macko, R., Sorkin, J. D., & Hanley, D. F. et al. (2004). Repetitive bilateral arm training and motor cortex activation in chronic stroke: A randomized controlled trial. *Journal of the American Medical Association*, *292*(15), 1853–1861. doi:10.1001/jama.292.15.1853 PMID:15494583

Luhn, H. P. (1958). The automatic creation of literature abstracts. *IBM Journal of Research and Development*, *2*(2), 159–165. doi:10.1147/rd.22.0159

Lu, J., Mamun, K. A., & Chau, T. (2015). Pattern classification to optimize the performance of transcranial doppler ultrasonography-based brain machine interface. *Pattern Recognition Letters*, *66*, 135–143. doi:10.1016/j.patrec.2015.07.020

Lusseau, D., Schneider, K., Boisseau, O. J., Haase, P., Slooten, E., & Dawson, S. M. (2003). The bottlenose dolphin community of Doubtful Sound features a large proportion of long-lasting associations. *Behavioral Ecology and Sociobiology*, *54*(4), 396–405. doi:10.1007/s00265-003-0651-y

Lu, Y., & Han, J. (2003). Cancer classification using gene expression data. *Information Systems*, *28*(4), 243–268. doi:10.1016/S0306-4379(02)00072-8

Mallah, C., Cope, J., & Orwell, J. (2013). Plant leaf classification using probabilistic integration of shape, texture and margin features. Signal Processing. *Pattern Recognition and Applications*, 5, 1.

Mani, I. (2001). *Automatic summarization* (Vol. 3). John Benjamins Publishing. doi:10.1075/nlp.3

Mani, I., House, D., Klein, G., Hirschman, L., Firmin, T., & Sundheim, B. (1999, June). The TIPSTER SUMMAC text summarization evaluation. In *Proceedings of the ninth conference on European chapter of the Association for Computational Linguistics* (pp. 77-85). Association for Computational Linguistics. doi:10.3115/977035.977047

Mani, I., Klein, G., House, D., Hirschman, L., Firmin, T., & Sundheim, B. (2002). SUMMAC: A text summarization evaluation. *Natural Language Engineering*, 8(01), 43–68. doi:10.1017/S1351324901002741

Martinez, R., Pasquier, N., & Pasquier, C. (2008). GenMiner: mining non-redundant association rules from integrated gene expression data and annotations. Bioinformatics, 24, 2643-2644. doi:10.1093/bioinformatics/btn490

Matignon, L. (2013). *UML: Unified Modeling Language, Diagrammes dynamiques.* Lyon: Université Claude Bernard.

McAfee, A., Brynjolfsson, E., Davenport, T. H., Patil, D. J., & Barton, D. (2012). Big data: The management revolution. *Harvard Business Review*, 90(10), 60–68. PMID:23074865

McCallum, A., & Nigam, K. (1998, July). A comparison of event models for naive bayes text classification. In AAAI-98 workshop on learning for text categorization (Vol. 752, pp. 41-48). Academic Press.

McCane, L. M., Heckman, S. M., McFarland, D. J., Townsend, G., Mak, J. N., Sellers, E. W., & Vaughan, T. M. et al. (2015). P300-based brain-computer interface (BCI) event-related potentials (ERPs): People with amyotrophic lateral sclerosis (ALS) vs. age-matched controls. *Clinical Neurophysiology*, 126(11), 2124–2131. doi:10.1016/j.clinph.2015.01.013 PMID:25703940

McFarland, D. J., & Wolpaw, J. R. (2008). Brain–computer interface operation of robotic and prosthetic devices. *Computer*, 41(10), 52–56. doi:10.1109/MC.2008.409

Mclaughlin, B. (2001). Java & XML (2nd ed.). O'Reilly.

Mei, Shen, & Ye. (2009a). Hybridized KNN and SVM for gene expression data classification. *Life Science Journal*, 6(1), 61-65.

Melli, G. (1998). *A Lazy Model-Based Approach to On-Line Classification* (Doctoral dissertation). Simon Fraser University.

Memarsadegh, N. (2013). Golomb Patterns: Introduction, Applications, and Citizen Science Game. *Information Science and Technology (IS&T), Seminar Series NASA GSFC*. Available at http://istcolloq.gsfc.nasa.gov/fall2013/presentations/memarsadeghi.pdf

Meyer, C., & Papakonstantinou, P. A. (2009). On the complexity of constructing Golomb Rulers. *Discrete Applied Mathematics*, 157(4), 738–748. doi:10.1016/j.dam.2008.07.006

Mihara, M., Hattori, N., Hatakenaka, M., Yagura, H., Kawano, T., Hino, T., & Miyai, I. (2013). Near-infrared spectroscopy-mediated neurofeedback enhances efficacy of motor imagery-based training in poststroke victims: A pilot study. *Stroke*, 44(4), 1091–1098. doi:10.1161/STROKEAHA.111.674507 PMID:23404723

Millan, J. R., Ferrez, P. W., Galan, F., Lew, E., & Chavarriaga, R. (2008). Non-invasive brain–machine interaction. *International Journal of Pattern Recognition and Artificial Intelligence*, 22(5), 959–972. doi:10.1142/S0218001408006600

Millan, J. R., Renkens, F., Mourino, J., & Gerstner, W. (2004). Non-invasive brain-actuated control of a mobile robot by human EEG. *IEEE Transactions on Biomedical Engineering*, 51(6), 1026–1033. doi:10.1109/TBME.2004.827086 PMID:15188874

Minel, J. (2004). Le résumé automatique de textes: solutions et perspectives. *Traitement automatique des langues, 45*(1), 14.

MIT Lincoln Labs. (1998). *DARPA Intrusion Detection Evaluation*. Available on: http://www.ll.mit.edu/mission/communications/ist/corpora/ideval/ index.html

Moffat, A., & Stuiver, L. (2000). Binary interpolative coding for effective index compression. *Information Retrieval, 3*(1), 25–47. doi:10.1023/A:1013002601898

Moler, E. J., Chow, M. L., & Mian, I. S. (2000). Analysis of molecular profile data using generative and discriminative methods. *Physiological Genomics, 4*, 109–126. PMID:11120872

Moran, D. (2010). Evolution of brain–computer interface: Action potentials, local field potentials and electrocorticograms. *Current Opinion in Neurobiology, 20*(6), 741–745. doi:10.1016/j.conb.2010.09.010 PMID:20952183

Moran, M. E. (2007). Evolution of robotic arms. *Journal of Robotic Surgery, 1*(2), 103–111. doi:10.1007/s11701-006-0002-x PMID:25484945

Morrison, D. R. (1968). PATRICIA—practical algorithm to retrieve information coded in alphanumeric. *Journal of the Association for Computing Machinery, 15*(4), 514–534. doi:10.1145/321479.321481

Motahari-Nezhad, H. R., Saint-Paul, R., Benatallah, B., & Casati, F. (2008). Deriving protocol models from imperfect service conversation logs. *Knowledge and Data Engineering. IEEE Transactions on, 20*(12), 1683–1698.

Murphy, K., Travers, P., & Walport, M. (2008). *Janeway's immunology*. Garland Science.

Murty, K. G., Liu, J., Wan, Y. W., & Linn, R. (2005). A decision support system for operations in a container shipping terminal. *Decision Support Systems, 39*(3), 309–332. doi:10.1016/j.dss.2003.11.002

Naser, A. M. A., & Alshattnawi, S. (2014). An Artificial Bee Colony (ABC) Algorithm for Efficient Partitioning of Social Networks. *International Journal of Intelligent Information Technologies, 10*(4), 24–39. doi:10.4018/ijiit.2014100102

Nawab, R. M. A., Stevenson, M., & Clough, P. (2011). External Plagiarism Detection using Information Retrieval and Sequence Alignment-Notebook for PAN at CLEF 2011. *Proceedings of the 5th International Workshop on Uncovering Plagiarism, Authorship, and Social Software Misuse*.

Ndèye, F. N. (2014). A Branch-and-Cut Algorithm to Solve the Container Storage Problem. In *Proceedings of The Ninth International Conference on Systems*. University of Le Havre.

Nedjar. (2012). *Design a classifier Blur Using Bee Colony On For Medical Diagnostics* (Master thesis). University Aboubeker Belkaid.

Neshat, M., Sepidnam, G., Sargolzaei, M., & Toosi, A. N. (2014). Artificial fish swarm algorithm: A survey of the state-of-the-art, hybridization, combinatorial and indicative applications. *Artificial Intelligence Review*, 1–33.

Newman, M. E. (2004). Fast algorithm for detecting community structure in networks. *Physical Review. E, 69*(6), 066133. doi:10.1103/PhysRevE.69.066133 PMID:15244693

Newman, M. E. (2006). Modularity and community structure in networks. *Proceedings of the National Academy of Sciences of the United States of America, 103*(23), 8577–8582. doi:10.1073/pnas.0601602103 PMID:16723398

Newman, M. E., & Girvan, M. (2004). Finding and evaluating community structure in networks. *Physical Review. E, 69*(2), 026113. doi:10.1103/PhysRevE.69.026113 PMID:14995526

Ng, K. A., Greenwald, E., Xu, Y. P., & Thakor, N. V. (2016). Implantable neurotechnologies: A review of integrated circuit neural amplifiers. *Medical & Biological Engineering & Computing, 54*(1), 45–62. doi:10.1007/s11517-015-1431-3 PMID:26798055

Ng, W. K., & Ravishankar, C. V. (1997). Block-oriented compression techniques for large statistical databases. *IEEE Transactions on Knowledge and Data Engineering, 9*(2), 314–328. doi:10.1109/69.591455

Nicolelis, M. A. L. (2001). Actions from thoughts. *Nature, 409*(6818), 403–407. doi:10.1038/35053191 PMID:11201755

Noble. (2003). Support vector machine applications in computational biology. Kernal Methods in Computational Biology, 71-92.

O'Brien, C., & Vogel, C. (2003, September). Spam filters: Bayes vs. chi-squared; letters vs. words. In *Proceedings of the 1st international symposium on Information and communication technologies* (pp. 291-296). Trinity College Dublin.

Obied, A., & Alhajj, R. (2009). Collection and Analysis of Web-based Exploits and Malware. *Journal of Applied Intelligence, 30*(2), 112–120. doi:10.1007/s10489-007-0102-y

Oda, T., & White, T. (2005). Immunity from spam: An analysis of an artificial immune system for junk email detection. In *Artificial Immune Systems* (pp. 276–289). Springer Berlin Heidelberg. doi:10.1007/11536444_21

Odum, E. P., Odum, H. T., & Andrews, J. (1971). *Fundamentals of ecology* (Vol. 3). Philadelphia: Saunders.

Oweiss, K. G., & Badreldin, I. S. (2015). Neuroplasticity subserving the operation of brain–machine interfaces. *Neurobiology of Disease, 83*, 161–171. doi:10.1016/j.nbd.2015.05.001 PMID:25968934

Paroubek, P., Zweigenbaum, P., Forest, D., &Grouin, C. (2012). *Indexation libre et contrôlée d'articles scientifiques Pré-sentation et résultats du défi fouille de textes DEFT2012.* Actes du huitième DÉfi Fouille de Textes.

Patel, M. (2015, August). A Robust DCT Based Digital Image Watermarking Using Fusion of Computational Intelligence Techniques. *Oriental Journal of Computer Science and Technology, 8*(2), 146–153.

Patil, A. C., & Thakor, N. V. (2016). Implantable neurotechnologies: A review of micro- and nanoelectrodes for neural recording. *Medical & Biological Engineering & Computing, 54*(1), 23–44. doi:10.1007/s11517-015-1430-4 PMID:26753777

Patil, N., Toshniwa, D., & Garg, K. (2013b). *Genome data classification based on fuzzy matching.* Addison-Wesley.

Paus, T. (2001). Primate anterior cingulate cortex: Where motor control, drive and cognition interface. *Nature Reviews. Neuroscience, 2*(6), 417–424. doi:10.1038/35077500 PMID:11389475

Peeva, M. G., Guenther, F. H., Tourville, J. A., Nieto-Castanon, A., Anton, J. L., Nazarian, B., & Alario, F. X. (2010). Distinct representations of phonemes, syllables, and supra-syllabic sequences in the speech production network. *NeuroImage, 50*(2), 626–638. doi:10.1016/j.neuroimage.2009.12.065 PMID:20035884

Pei, W., Williams, P.H., Clark, M.D., Stemple, D.L., & Feldman, B. (2007). Environmental and genetic modifiers of squint penetrance during zebrafish embryogenesis. *Development Biology, 308*(2), 368-78.

Peng, D. T., Shin, K. G., & Abdezaher, T. F. (1997). Assignment and Scheduling communicating periodic tasks in distributed real time systems. *Software Engineering, 23*(12), 745–758. doi:10.1109/32.637388

Percher, J. M., & Jouga, B. (2003). Détection d'intrusions dans les réseaux Ad hoc. *Projet.*

Pereira, D. R., Pazoti, M., Pereira, L., & Papa, J. P. (2014, December). A social-spider optimization approach for support vector machines parameters tuning. In *Swarm Intelligence (SIS), 2014 IEEE Symposium on* (pp. 1-6). IEEE. doi:10.1109/SIS.2014.7011769

Perez-Marcos, D., Buitrago, J. A., & Velasquez, F. D. G. (2011). Writing through a robot: A proof of concept for a brain–machine interface. *Medical Engineering & Physics*, *33*(10), 1314–1317. doi:10.1016/j.medengphy.2011.06.005 PMID:21741290

Perreau, C. (2002). *Les Systèmes d'Information Multimodale* (Thèse de doctorat). Institut d'Etudes Politiques de Paris, France.

Petit-Roze, C., Anli, A., Grislin-Lestrugeon, E., Abed, M., & Uster, G. (2004). Système d'information transport personnalisée à base d'agents logiciels. *Revue Génie Logiciel*, *70*, 29–38.

Pfurtscheller, G., & Aranbibar, A. (1979). Evaluation of event-related desynchronization preceding and following voluntary self-paced movement. *Electroencephalography and Clinical Neurophysiology*, *46*(2), 138–146. doi:10.1016/0013-4694(79)90063-4 PMID:86421

Pfurtscheller, G., & da Silva, F. H. L. (1999). Event-related EEG/MEG synchronization and desynchronization: Basic principles. *Clinical Neurophysiology*, *110*(11), 1842–1857. doi:10.1016/S1388-2457(99)00141-8 PMID:10576479

Pizzuti, C. (2008, September). Ga-net: A genetic algorithm for community detection in social networks. In *International Conference on Parallel Problem Solving from Nature* (pp. 1081-1090). Springer Berlin Heidelberg. doi:10.1007/978-3-540-87700-4_107

Popescul, A., Pennock, D. M., & Ungar, L. H. (2003). *Mixtures of conditional maximum entropy models*. Academic Press.

Postelnicu, C. C., Girbacia, F., & Talaba, D. (2012). EOG-based visual navigation interface development. *Expert Systems with Applications*, *39*(12), 10857–10866. doi:10.1016/j.eswa.2012.03.007

Price, C. J. (2010). The anatomy of language: A review of 100 fMRI studies published in 2009. *Annals of the New York Academy of Sciences*, *1191*(1), 62–88. doi:10.1111/j.1749-6632.2010.05444.x PMID:20392276

Price, K., Storn, R., & Lampinen, J. (2005). *Differential Evolution–A Practical Approach to Global Optimization*. Berlin, Germany: Springer.

Provost, J. (1999). *Naıve-Bayes vs. Rule-Learning in Classification of Email*. University of Texas at Austin.

Quinlan. (1993). C4.5: programs for machine learning. Morgan Kaufmann Publishers Inc.

Rabiner, L. R. (1989). A tutorial on hidden Markov models and selected applications in speech recognition. *Proceedings of the IEEE*, *77*(2), 257–286. doi:10.1109/5.18626

Rahmani, M. E., Amine, A., & Hamou, R. M. (2017). A Novel Bio Inspired Algorithm Based on Echolocation Mechanism of Bats for Seismic States Prediction. *International Journal of Swarm Intelligence Research*, *8*(3), 1–18. doi:10.4018/IJSIR.2017070101

Rahmani, M. E., Amine, A., & Hamou, R. M. (2017). New Approach based on Termite's Hill Building for Prediction of Successful Simulations in Climate Models. *International Journal of Swarm Intelligence Research*, *8*(3), 30–60. doi:10.4018/IJSIR.2017070103

Rahmani, M. E., Amine, A., & Hamou, R. M. (in press). Sonar Data Classification Using a New Algorithm Inspired from Black Holes Phenomenon. *International Journal of Information Retrieval Research*.

Rahmani, M. E., Amine, A., Hamou, R. M., Rahmani, A., Menad, H., Bouarara, H. A., & Boudia, M. A. (2016). A Novel Bio Inspired Algorithm Based on Echolocation Mechanism of Bats for Seismic Hazards Detection. In *Modelling and Implementation of Complex Systems* (pp. 77–89). Springer International Publishing. doi:10.1007/978-3-319-33410-3_6

Rahmani, M. E., Bouarara, H. A., Amine, A., Hamou, R. M., & Menad, H. (2016). New Supervised Approach for Plant Leaves Classification using Artificial Social Bees. *International Journal of Organizational and Collective Intelligence*, *6*(1), 15–28. doi:10.4018/IJOCI.2016010102

Rajasekaran, S., & Pai, G. A. V. (2004). *Neural Networks, Fuzzy Logic, and Genetic Algorithms–Synthesis and Applications*. New Delhi: Prentice Hall of India Pvt. Ltd.

Rana, S., Jasola, S., & Kumar, R. (2011). A review on particle swarm optimization algorithms and their applications to data clustering. *Artificial Intelligence Review*, *35*(3), 211–222. doi:10.1007/s10462-010-9191-9

Randhawa, R., Sohal, J. S., & Kaler, R. S. (2009). Optimum Algorithm for WDM Channel Allocation for Reducing Four–Wave Mixing Effects. *Optik (Stuttgart)*, *120*(17), 898–904. doi:10.1016/j.ijleo.2008.03.023

Ranjan, J., & Bhatnagar, V. (2010). Application of data mining techniques in the financial sector for profitable customer relationship management. *International Journal of Information and Communication Technology*, *2*(4), 342–354. doi:10.1504/IJICT.2010.034976

Ranjan, J., & Bhatnagar, V. (2011). Role of knowledge management and analytical CRM in business: Data mining based framework. *The Learning Organization*, *18*(2), 131–148. doi:10.1108/09696471111103731

Rankin, W. T. (1993). *Optimal Golomb Rulers: An Exhaustive Parallel Search Implementation* (M.S. Thesis). Duke University. Available at http://people.ee.duke.edu/~wrankin/golomb/golomb.html

Rankin, W. T. (1993). *Optimal Golomb Rulers: An Exhaustive Parallel Search Implementation* (Master's thesis). Duke University. Available at http://people.ee.duke.edu/~wrankin/golomb/golomb.html

Rao, R. V., Savsani, V. J., & Vakharia, D. P. (2011). Teaching–learning-based optimization: A novel method for constrained mechanical design optimization problems. *Computer Aided Design*, *43*(3), 303–315. doi:10.1016/j.cad.2010.12.015

Rashedi, E., Nezamabadi-Pour, H., & Saryazdi, S. (2009). GSA: A gravitational search algorithm. *Information Sciences*, *179*(13), 2232–2248. doi:10.1016/j.ins.2009.03.004

Rice, R. F. (1979). *Some practical universal noiseless coding techniques*. Academic Press.

Ritu, B. (2016). A Novel Bat Algorithm for Channel Allocation to Reduce FWM Crosstalk in WDM Systems. *International Journal of Computers and Applications*, *136*(4), 33–42. doi:10.5120/ijca2016908459

Robinson, J. P. (1979). Optimum Golomb Rulers. *IEEE Transactions on Computers*, *28*(12), 183–184.

Robinson, J. P. (2000). Genetic Search for Golomb Arrays. *IEEE Transactions on Information Theory*, *46*(3), 1170–1173. doi:10.1109/18.841202

Robinson, J. P., & Bernstein, A. J. (1967). A Class of Binary Recurrent Codes with Limited Error Propagation. *IEEE Transactions on Information Theory*, *IT–13*(1), 106–113. doi:10.1109/TIT.1967.1053951

Rotermund, D., Ernst, U. A., & Pawelzik, K. R. (2006). Towards on-line adaptation of neuro-prostheses with neuronal evaluation signals. *Biological Cybernetics*, *95*(3), 243–257. doi:10.1007/s00422-006-0083-7 PMID:16802156

Rousseau, Jm., & Blais, Jy. (1985). HASTUS: An interactive systems for buses and crew scheduling. *Computer Scheduling of Public Transport*, *2*, 45–60.

Ruan, G., & Tan, Y. (2010). A three-layer back-propagation neural network for spam detection using artifi-cial immune concentration. *Soft Computing*, *14*(2), 139–150. doi:10.1007/s00500-009-0440-2

Rudajev, V., & Čiž, R. (1999). Estimation of mining tremor occurrence by using neural networks. *Pure and Applied Geophysics, 154*(1), 57-72.

Saab, C. (2013). Visualizing the complex brain dynamics of chronic pain. *Journal of Neuroimmune Pharmacology, 8*(3), 510–517. doi:10.1007/s11481-012-9378-8 PMID:22684310

Saaid, N. M. (2010). Nonlinear Optical Effects Suppression Methods in WDM Systems with EDFAs: A Review. *Proceedings of International Conference on Computer and Communication Engineering (ICCCE–2010)*, 1–4. doi:10.1109/ICCCE.2010.5556802

Sabri, M., Binder, J. R., Desai, R., Medler, D. A., Leitl, M. D., & Liebenthal, E. (2008). Attentional and linguistic interactions in speech perception. *NeuroImage, 39*(3), 1444–1456. doi:10.1016/j.neuroimage.2007.09.052 PMID:17996463

Sadollah, A., Bahreininejad, A., Eskandar, H., & Hamdi, M. (2013). Mine blast algorithm: A new population based algorithm for solving constrained engineering optimization problems. *Applied Soft Computing, 13*(5), 2592–2612. doi:10.1016/j.asoc.2012.11.026

Saffre, F., Furey, R., Krafft, B., & Deneubourg, J. L. (1999). Collective decision-making in social spiders: Dragline-mediated amplification process acts as a recruitment mechanism. *Journal of Theoretical Biology, 198*(4), 507–517. doi:10.1006/jtbi.1999.0927 PMID:10373351

Sahami, M., Dumais, S., Heckerman, D., & Horvitz, E. (1998, July). A Bayesian approach to filtering junk e-mail. In *Learning for Text Categorization: Papers from the 1998 workshop* (Vol. 62, pp. 98-105). Academic Press.

Sahin, N. T., Pinker, S., Cash, S. S., Schomer, D., & Halgren, E. (2009). Sequential processing of lexical, grammatical, and phonological information within Broca's area. *Science, 326*(5951), 445–449. doi:10.1126/science.1174481 PMID:19833971

Saidi, M. (2011). *Traitement de données médicales par un Système Immunitaire Artificiel Reconnaissance Automatique du Diabète.* Tlemcen University.

Salomon, D. (2004). *Data compression: the complete reference.* Springer Science & Business Media.

Salomon, D. (2007). *Variable-length codes for data compression.* Springer Science & Business Media. doi:10.1007/978-1-84628-959-0

Salton, G., Singhal, A., Mitra, M., & Buckley, C. (1997). Automatic text structuring and summarization. *Information Processing & Management, 33*(2), 193–207. doi:10.1016/S0306-4573(96)00062-3

Salzberg, S. L. (1988). *Exemplar-based learning: Theory and implementation.* Harvard University, Center for Research in Computing Technology, Aiken Computation Laboratory.

Sammut, C., & Webb, G. I. (Eds.). (2011). *Encyclopedia of machine learning.* Springer Science & Business Media.

Sanchez, J. C., & Principe, J. C. (2007). *Brain–machine interface engineering.* New York, NY: Morgan & Claypool Publishers.

Sandryhaila, A., & Moura, J. M. F. (2014). Big data analysis with signal processing on graphs: Representation and processing of massive data sets with irregular structure. *IEEE Signal Processing Magazine, 31*(5), 80–90. doi:10.1109/MSP.2014.2329213

Sanz, E. P., Gómez Hidalgo, J. M., & Cortizo Pérez, J. C. (2008). Email spam filtering. *Advances in Computers, 74*, 45–114. doi:10.1016/S0065-2458(08)00603-7

Sardesai, H. P. (1999). A Simple Channel Plan to Reduce Effects of Nonlinearities In Dense WDM Systems. Proceedings of Lasers and Electro–Optics (CLEO '99), 183-184. doi:10.1109/CLEO.1999.834058

Sayad, D. S. (2010). *decision_tree*. Retrieved November 20, 2013, from saedsayad: http://www.saedsayad.com/

Schalk, G., Brunner, P., Gerhardt, L. A., Bischof, H., & Wolpaw, J. R. (2008). Brain–computer interfaces (BCIs): Detection instead of classification. *Journal of Neuroscience Methods*, *167*(1), 51–62. doi:10.1016/j.jneumeth.2007.08.010 PMID:17920134

Scherer, R., Faller, J., Balderas, D., Friedrich, E. V. C., Pröll, M., Allison, B., & Müller-Putz, G. (2013). Brain–computer interfacing: More than the sum of its parts. *Soft Computing*, *17*(2), 317–331. doi:10.1007/s00500-012-0895-4

Scholkopf, B., & Smola, A. J. (2001). Learning with Kernels. In Support Vector Machines, Regularization, Optimization, and Beyond. MIT Press.

Sculley, D., & Wachman, G. M. (2007, July). Relaxed online SVMs for spam filtering. In *Proceedings of the 30th annual international ACM SIGIR conference on Research and development in information retrieval* (pp. 415-422). ACM.

Sebastiani, F. (2002). Machine learning in automated text categorization. *ACM computing surveys (CSUR)*, *34*(1), 1-47.

Sebban, M., Nock, R., & Lallich, S. (2002). Stopping criterion for boosting-based data reduction techniques: From binary to multiclass problem. *Journal of Machine Learning Research*, *3*(Dec), 863–885.

Segal, N. H., Pavlidis, P., Noble, W. S., Antonescu, C. R., Viale, A., Wesley, U. V., & Houghton, A. N. et al. (2003). Classification of clear cell sarcoma as melanoma of soft parts by genomic profiling. *Journal of Clinical Oncology*, *21*, 1775–1781. doi:10.1200/JCO.2003.10.108 PMID:12721254

Seki, K., Jinno, R., & Uehara, K. (2013). Parallel distributed trajectory pattern mining using hierarchical grid with MapReduce. *International Journal of Grid and High Performance Computing*, *5*(4), 79–96. doi:10.4018/ijghpc.2013100106

Sen, A. K., Patel, S. B., & Shukla, D. P. (2013). A data mining technique for prediction of coronary heart disease using neuro-fuzzy integrated approach two level. *International Journal of Engineering and Computer Science*, *2*(9), 1663–1671.

Serruya, M. D., Harsopoulos, N. G., Paninski, L., Fellows, M. R., & Donoghue, K. (2002). Instant neural control of a movement signal. *Nature*, *416*(6877), 141–142. doi:10.1038/416141a PMID:11894084

Shang, W., Jiang, Z. M., Adams, B., & Hassan, A. E. (2009). *Mapreduce as a general framework to support research in mining software repositories*. MSR.

Shannon, C. E. (1948). *A Mathematical Theory of Communication'-BSTJ*. Juillet et Octobre.

Shearer, J. B. (2001a). *Golomb Ruler Table*. Mathematics Department, IBM Research. Available at http://www.research.ibm.com/people/s/shearer/grtab.html

Shearer, J. B. (2001b). *Smallest Known Golomb Rulers*. Mathematics Department, IBM Research. Available at http://www.research.ibm.com/people/s/shearer/gropt.html

Shearer, J. B. (1990). Some New Optimum Golomb Rulers. *IEEE Transactions on Information Theory*, *36*(1), 183–184. doi:10.1109/18.50388

Shearer, J. B. (1998). Some New Disjoint Golomb Rulers. *IEEE Transactions on Information Theory*, *44*(7), 3151–3153. doi:10.1109/18.737546

Shet, K. C., & Acharya, U. D. (2012). Semantic plagiarism detection system using ontology mapping. *Advances in Computers*, *3*(3).

Shi, Z., Liu, Y., & Liang, J. (2009, November). PSO-based community detection in complex networks. In *Knowledge Acquisition and Modeling, 2009. KAM'09. Second International Symposium on* (Vol. 3, pp. 114-119). IEEE.

Shin, Y., Lee, S., Ahn, M., Cho, H., Jun, S. C., & Lee, H. N. (2015). Simple adaptive sparse representation based classification schemes for EEG based brain–computer interface applications. *Computers in Biology and Medicine, 66*, 29–38. doi:10.1016/j.compbiomed.2015.08.017 PMID:26378500

Shouman, M., Turner, T., & Stocker, R. (2012). Applying k-nearest neighbour in diagnosing heart disease patients. *International Journal of Information and Education Technology (IJIET), 2*(3), 220–223. doi:10.7763/IJIET.2012.V2.114

Shvachko, K., Kuang, H., Radia, S., & Chansler, R. (2010). The hadoop distributed file system. In *Mass Storage Systems and Technologies (MSST), IEEE 26th Symposium on.* IEEE.

Si, A., Leong, H. V., & Lau, R. W. (1997, April). Check: a document plagiarism detection system. In *Proceedings of the 1997 ACM symposium on Applied computing* (pp. 70-77). ACM. doi:10.1145/331697.335176

Sikder, I. U., & Munakata, T. (2009). Application of rough set and decision tree for characterization of premonitory factors of low seismic activity. *Expert Systems with Applications, 36*(1), 102–110. doi:10.1016/j.eswa.2007.09.032

Silvestri, F., & Venturini, R. (2010). VSEncoding: efficient coding and fast decoding of integer lists via dynamic programming. In *Proceedings of the 19th ACM international conference on Information and knowledge management* (pp. 1219-1228). ACM. doi:10.1145/1871437.1871592

Simon, D. (2008). Biogeography-based optimization. *IEEE Transactions on Evolutionary Computation, 12*(6), 702–713. doi:10.1109/TEVC.2008.919004

Singhal, A. (2001). Modern information retrieval: A brief overview. *IEEE Data Eng. Bull., 24*(4), 35–43.

Singh, K., & Bansal, S. (2013). Suppression of FWM Crosstalk on WDM Systems Using Unequally Spaced Channel Algorithms–A Survey. *International Journal of Advanced Research in Computer Science and Software Engineering, 3*(12), 25–31.

Singh, R., & PancholiBhavan, K. (2016). A Nobel Technique for Digital Image Watermarking Authentication Using Fuzzy Mean Clustering. *International Journal of Science and Research, 5*(4), 207–209.

Singh, S., Singh, M., & Markou, M. (2002). Feature selection for face recognition based on data partitioning. *ICPR, 1*, 680–683.

Singh, S., & Singh, N. (2012). Big Data Analytics. *IEEE International Conference on Communication, Information and Computing Technology (ICCICT).*

Sirvent, J. L., Ianez, E., Ubeda, A., & Azorin, J. M. (2012). Visual evoked potential-based brain–machine interface applications to assist disabled people. *Expert Systems with Applications, 39*(9), 7908–7918. doi:10.1016/j.eswa.2012.01.110

Smith, R. L., & Smith, T. M. (2012). *Elements of ecology.* Benjamin Cummings.

Soekadar, S. R., Birbaumer, N., & Cohen, L. G. (2011). Brain–computer interfaces in the rehabilitation of stroke and neurotrauma. In L. Cohen & K. Kansaku (Eds.), *Systems neuroscience and rehabilitation* (pp. 3–18). Berlin, Germany: Springer–Verlag. doi:10.1007/978-4-431-54008-3_1

Soekadar, S. R., Birbaumer, N., Slutzky, M. W., & Cohen, L. G. (2015). Brain–machine interfaces in neurorehabilitation of stroke. *Neurobiology of Disease, 83*, 172–179. doi:10.1016/j.nbd.2014.11.025 PMID:25489973

Soliday, S. W., Homaifar, A., & Lebby, G. L. (1995). Genetic Algorithm Approach to the Search for Golomb Rulers. *Proceedings of the Sixth International Conference on Genetic Algorithms (ICGA–95)*, 528–535.

Somasundaram, K., & Domnic, S. (2007). Extended golomb code for integer representation. *IEEE Transactions on Multimedia*, *9*(2), 239–246. doi:10.1109/TMM.2006.886260

Soni, J., Ansari, U., Sharma, D., & Soni, S. (2011). Predictive data mining for medical diagnosis: An overview of heart disease prediction. *International Journal of Computers and Applications*, *17*(8), 43–48. doi:10.5120/2237-2860

Sridevi, T., & Sameena Fathima, S. (2013). Digital Image Watermarking using Fuzzy Logic approach based on DWT and SVD. *International Journal of Computers and Applications*, *74*(13), 16–20. doi:10.5120/12945-0014

Stein, B. (2007). Principles of Hash-Based Text Retrieval. *30th Annual International ACM SIGIR Conference*, 527–534.

Stephen, B., Arpita, G., & Alessandro, M. (2003). *Branch and Bound Methods*. Notes for EE392o, Stanford University. Available from: https://web.stanford.edu/class/ee364b/lectures/bb_slides.pdf

Stewart, R. J., Trinder, P. W., & Loidl, H. W. (2011). Comparing high level mapreduce query languages. In *Advanced Parallel Processing Technologies* (pp. 58–72). Springer Berlin Heidelberg. doi:10.1007/978-3-642-24151-2_5

Stieglitz, T. (2010). Manufacturing, assembling and packaging of miniaturized neural implants. *Microsystem Technologies*, *16*(5), 723–734. doi:10.1007/s00542-009-0988-x

Storn, R., & Price, K. V. (1997). Differential Evolution—A Simple and Efficient Heuristic for Global Optimization Over Continuous Spaces. *Journal of Global Optimization*, *11*(4), 341–359. doi:10.1023/A:1008202821328

Strangman, G., Boas, D. A., & Sutton, J. P. (2002). Non-invasive neuroimaging using near-infrared light. *Biological Psychiatry*, *52*(7), 679–693. doi:10.1016/S0006-3223(02)01550-0 PMID:12372658

Street, W. N., Wolberg, W. H., & Mangasarian, O. L. (1993, July). Nuclear feature extraction for breast tumor diagnosis. In *IS&T/SPIE's Symposium on Electronic Imaging: Science and Technology* (pp. 861-870). International Society for Optics and Photonics.

Suaris, P. R., & Kedem, G. (1988). An algorithm for quadrisection and its application to standard cell placement. *IEEE Transactions on Circuits and Systems*, *35*(3), 294–303. doi:10.1109/31.1742

Szummer & Jaakkola. (2002). Partially labeled classification with markov random walks. In *Advances in Neural Information Processing Systems* (pp. 945–952). MIT Press.

Tabakov, P. Y. (2011). Big Bang–Big Crunch Optimization Method in Optimum Design of Complex Composite Laminates, *World Academy of Science, Engineering and Technology, International Journal of Mechanical, Aerospace, Industrial Mechatronic and Manufacturing Engineering*, *5*(5), 835–839.

Tai, K., Blain, S., & Chau, T. (2008). A review of emerging access technologies for individuals with severe motor impairments. *Assistive Technology*, *20*(4), 204–221. doi:10.1080/10400435.2008.10131947 PMID:19160907

Tamane, S. C., & Deshmukh, R. R. (2012). Blind 3d model watermarking based on multi-resolution representation and fuzzy logic. *International Journal of Computer Science & Information Technology*, *4*(01), 117–126. doi:10.5121/ijcsit.2012.4110

Tan, P. J., & Dowe, D. L. (2004, December). MML inference of oblique decision trees. In *Australasian Joint Conference on Artificial Intelligence* (pp. 1082-1088). Springer Berlin Heidelberg.

Tan, Y., Deng, C., & Ruan, G. (2009, June). Concentration based feature construction approach for spam detection. In *Neural Networks, 2009. IJCNN 2009. International Joint Conference on* (pp. 3088-3093). IEEE. doi:10.1109/IJCNN.2009.5178651

Tanaka, K., Matsunaga, K., & Wang, H. (2005). Electroencephalogram-based control of an electric wheelchair. *IEEE Transactions on Robotics, 21*(4), 762–766. doi:10.1109/TRO.2004.842350

Tankus, A., Fried, I., & Shoham, S. (2014). Cognitive-motor brain–machine interfaces. *Journal of Physiology, Paris, 108*(1), 38–44. doi:10.1016/j.jphysparis.2013.05.005 PMID:23774120

Tasgin, M., Herdagdelen, A., & Bingol, H. (2007). *Community detection in complex networks using genetic algorithms.* arXiv preprint arXiv:0711.0491

Taylor, D. M., Tillery, S. I. H., & Schwartz, A. B. (2002). Direct cortical control of 3D neuroprosthetic devices. *Science, 296*(5574), 1829–1832. doi:10.1126/science.1070291 PMID:12052948

Teufel, S., &Moens, M. (1999). Argumentative classification of extracted phrases as a first step towards flexible abstracting. *Advances in Automatic Text Summarization, 155,* 171.

Thing, V. L. L., Rao, M. K., & Shum, P. (2003). Fractional Optimal Golomb Ruler Based WDM Channel Allocation. *Proceedings of the 8th Opto-Electronics and Communication Conference (OECC–2003), 23,* 631–632.

Thing, V. L. L., Shum, P., & Rao, M. K. (2004). Bandwidth–Efficient WDM Channel Allocation for Four–Wave Mixing–Effect Minimization. *IEEE Transactions on Communications, 52*(12), 2184–2189. doi:10.1109/TCOMM.2004.838684

Tonguz, O. K., & Hwang, B. (1998). A Generalized Suboptimum Unequally Spaced Channel Allocation Technique—Part II: In coherent WDM systems. *IEEE Transactions on Communications, 46*(9), 1186–1193. doi:10.1109/26.718560

Tsivgoulis, G., Alexandrov, A. V., & Sloan, M. A. (2009). Advances in transcranial doppler ultrasonography. *Current Neurology and Neuroscience Reports, 9*(1), 46–54. doi:10.1007/s11910-009-0008-7 PMID:19080753

Tsourakakis, C. E. (2010). *Data Mining with MAPREDUCE: Graph and Tensor Algorithms with Applications* (Doctoral dissertation). Carnegie Mellon University.

Ubeda, A., Ianez, E., Azorin, J. M., & Perez-Vidal, C. (2013). Endogenous brain–machine interface based on the correlation of EEG maps. *Computer Methods and Programs in Biomedicine, 112*(2), 302–308. doi:10.1016/j.cmpb.2013.01.012 PMID:23453295

Udoekwere, U. I., Oza, C. S., & Giszter, S. F. (2014). A pelvic implant orthosis in rodents, for spinal cord injury rehabilitation, and for brain machine interface research: Construction, surgical implantation and validation. *Journal of Neuroscience Methods, 222,* 199–206. doi:10.1016/j.jneumeth.2013.10.022 PMID:24269175

van der Aalst, W. (2004). Discovering coordination patterns using process mining. *Workshop on Petri Nets and Coordination,* 49-64.

Van Der Aalst, W. (2013). Service mining: Using process mining to discover, check, and improve service behavior. *Services Computing. IEEE Transactions on, 6*(4), 525–535.

van der Aalst, W. M. (2015). Extracting event data from databases to unleash process mining. In *BPM-Driving innovation in a digital world* (pp. 105–128). Springer International Publishing. doi:10.1007/978-3-319-14430-6_8

Van der Aalst, W. M., & Weijters, A. J. M. M. (2004). Process mining: A research agenda. *Computers in Industry, 53*(3), 231–244. doi:10.1016/j.compind.2003.10.001

Van der Aalst, W., Weijters, T., & Maruster, L. (2004). Workflow mining: Discovering process models from event logs. *Knowledge and Data Engineering. IEEE Transactions on, 16*(9), 1128–1142.

Van Dijk, T. A. (1985). Handbook of discourse analysis. Discourse and Dialogue.

van Dokkum, L. E. H., Ward, T., & Laffont, I. (2015). Brain computer interfaces for neurorehabilitation: Its current status as a rehabilitation strategy post-stroke. *Annals of Physical and Rehabilitation Medicine, 58*(1), 3–8. doi:10.1016/j.rehab.2014.09.016 PMID:25614021

Van Staden, F., & Venter, H. S. (2009). The State of the Art of Spam and Anti-Spam Strategies and a Possi-ble Solution using Digital Forensics. ISSA, 437-454.

Vapnik, V. (1998). *Statistical learning theory.* Wiley-Interscience.

Vartak, R., & Deshmukh, S. (2014, July). Survey of Digital Image Authentication Techniques. *International Journal of Research in Advent Technology, 2*(7), 176–179.

Venkatakrishnan, A., Franciscok, G. E., & Contreras-Vidal, J. L. (2014). Applications of brain–machine interface systems in stroke recovery and rehabilitation. *Current Physical Medicine and Rehabilitation Reports, 2*(2), 93–105. doi:10.1007/s40141-014-0051-4 PMID:25110624

Versteeg, G., & Bouwman, H. (2006). Business architecture: A new paradigm to relate business strategy to ICT. *Information Systems Frontiers, 8*(2), 91–102. doi:10.1007/s10796-006-7973-z

Vijayarani & Deepa. (2014). Naïve Bayes Classification for Predicting Diseases in Haemoglobin Protein Sequences. *International Journal of Computational Intelligence and Informatics, 3*(4).

Vijiyarani, S., & Sudha, S. (2013). Disease prediction in data mining technique–a survey. *International Journal of Computer Applications & Information Technology, 2,* 17–21.

Vyas, J., Bansal, S., & Sharma, K. (2016). Generation of Optimal Golomb Rulers for FWM Crosstalk Reduction: BB–BC and FA Approaches. In *Proceeding of 2016 International Conference on Signal Processing and Communication (ICSC–2016).* Jaypee Institute of Information Technology. doi:10.1109/ICSPCom.2016.7980551

Waldert, S., Lemon, R. N., & Kraskov, A. (2013). Influence of spiking activity on cortical local field potentials. *The Journal of Physiology, 591*(21), 5291–5303. doi:10.1113/jphysiol.2013.258228 PMID:23981719

Wallace, C. S., & Dowe, D. L. (1999). Minimum message length and Kolmogorov complexity. *The Computer Journal, 42*(4), 270–283. doi:10.1093/comjnl/42.4.270

Wang, F., Ercegovac, V., & Syeda-Mahmood, T. (2010). Large-scale multimodal mining for healthcare with mapreduce. In *Proceedings of the 1st ACM International Health Informatics Symposium.* ACM. doi:10.1145/1882992.1883067

Wang, H., Wang, W., Yang, J., & Yu, P. S. (2002). Clustering by pattern Similarity in large datasets. In *Proceedings of the 2002 ACM SIGMOD International conference on Management of data.* ACM.

Wang, P., Weise, T., & Chiong, R. (2011). Novel evolutionary algorithms for supervised classification problems: An experimental study. *Evolutionary Intelligence, 4*(1), 3–16. doi:10.1007/s12065-010-0047-7

Wang, X. L., Jing, Z., & Yang, H. Z. (2011a). Service selection constraint model and optimization algorithm for web service composition. *Journal of Information Technology, 10*(5), 1024–1030. doi:10.3923/itj.2011.1024.1030

Watson, J. D., & Crick, F. H. (1953). Molecular structure of nucleic acids: A structure for deoxyribose nucleic acid. *Nature, 171*(4356), 737–738. doi:10.1038/171737a0 PMID:13054692

Wei, X. X., Zeng, H. W., & Zhou, Y. Q. (2010, October). Hybrid artificial fish school algorithm for solving ill-conditioned linear systems of equations. In *Intelligent Computing and Intelligent Systems (ICIS), 2010 IEEE International Conference on* (Vol. 1, pp. 290-294). IEEE. doi:10.1109/ICICISYS.2010.5658678

Weimar, B.-U. (2009, September 10). *webis groupe weimer*. Retrieved november 9, 2013, from webis: http://www.webis. de/research/events/pan-09

Weiskopf, N., Veit, R., Erb, M., Mathiak, K., Grodd, W., Goebel, R., & Birbaumer, N. (2003). Physiological self-regulation of regional brain activity using real-time functional magnetic resonance imaging (fMRI): Methodology and exemplary data. *NeuroImage, 19*(3), 577–586. doi:10.1016/S1053-8119(03)00145-9 PMID:12880789

Weisstein, E. W. (2017a). *Perfect Ruler from MathWorld--A Wolfram Web Resource*. Available at http://mathworld. wolfram.com/PerfectRuler.html

Weisstein, E. W. (2017b). *Golomb Ruler from MathWorld--A Wolfram Web Resource*. Available at http://mathworld. wolfram.com/GolombRuler.html

Weske, M. (2012). *Business process management: concepts, languages, architectures*. Springer Science & Business Media. doi:10.1007/978-3-642-28616-2

Weston, Leslie, Ie, Zhou, Elisseeff, & Noble. (2005). Semi-supervised protein classification using cluster kernels. *Bioinformatics, 21*(15), 3241–3247.

White, B., Yeh, T., Lin, J., & Davis, L. (2010, July). Web-scale computer vision using mapreduce for multimedia data mining. In *Proceedings of the Tenth International Workshop on Multimedia Data Mining* (p. 9). ACM. doi:10.1145/1814245.1814254

Williams, H. E., & Zobel, J. (2002). Indexing and retrieval for genomic databases. *IEEE Transactions on Knowledge and Data Engineering, 14*(1), 63–78. doi:10.1109/69.979973

Wise, R. J., Greene, J., Buchel, C., & Scott, S. K. (1999). Brain regions involved in articulation. *Lancet, 353*(9158), 1057–1061. doi:10.1016/S0140-6736(98)07491-1 PMID:10199354

Wolpaw, J. R., Birbaumer, N., McFarland, D. J., Pfurtscheller, G., & Vaughan, T. M. (2002). Brain–computer interfaces for communication and control. *Clinical Neurophysiology: Official Journal of the International Federation of Clinical Neurophysiology, 113*(6), 767–791. doi:10.1016/S1388-2457(02)00057-3 PMID:12048038

Wood, I. K. (2001). *Neuroscience: Exploring the brain*. Philadelphia, PA: Lippincott Williams & Wilkins.

Wu, F., & Huberman, B. A. (2004). Finding communities in linear time: A physics approach. *European Physical Journal. B, Condensed Matter and Complex Systems, 38*(2), 331–338. doi:10.1140/epjb/e2004-00125-x

Xiaodong, D., Cunrui, W., Xiangdong, L., & Yanping, L. (2008, June). Web community detection model using particle swarm optimization. In *2008 IEEE Congress on Evolutionary Computation (IEEE World Congress on Computational Intelligence)* (pp. 1074-1079). IEEE. doi:10.1109/CEC.2008.4630930

Xiao-li, C., Pei-yu, L., Zhen-fang, Z., & Qiu, Y. (2009, August). A method of spam filtering based on weighted support vector machines. In *IT in Medicine & Education, 2009. ITIME'09. IEEE International Symposium on* (Vol. 1, pp. 947-950). IEEE.

Xiong, M., Jin, L., & Li, W. (2000b). Computational methods for gene expression-based tumor classification. *BioTechniques, 29*(6), 264–268, 1270. PMID:11126130

Xu, Q., Zhou, H., Wang, Y. J., & Huang, J. (2009). Fuzzy support vector machine for classification of EEG signals using wavelet-based features. *Medical Engineering & Physics, 31*(7), 858–865. doi:10.1016/j.medengphy.2009.04.005 PMID:19487151

Yachba, K. (2017). *Vers une contribution dans le transport maritime de marchandises: Optimisation de placement des conteneurs dans un port maritime* (PhD thesis). Computer Science Department, University of Oran1 Ahmed Benbella.

Yachba, K., Bouamrane, K., & Gelareh, S. (2015). Containers storage optimization in a container terminal using a multimethod multi-level approach. *Proceedings of The 45th International Conference on Computers & Industrial Engineering (CIE45)*.

Yachba, K., Gelareh, S., & Bouamrane, K. (2016). Storage management of hazardous containers using the genetic algorithm. *Transport and Telecommunication Journal, 17*(4), 371–383. doi:10.1515/ttj-2016-0033

Yang, Chuang, & Yang. (2009). A Hybrid Filter/Wrapper Method for Feature Selection of Microarray Data. *International Journal of Medical and Biological Engineering, 30*(1), 23-28.

Yang, X. S. (2010). A new metaheuristic bat-inspired algorithm. In Nature inspired cooperative strategies for optimization (NICSO 2010) (pp. 65-74). Springer Berlin Heidelberg. doi:10.1007/978-3-642-12538-6_6

Yang, X.-S. (2010c). Firefly Algorithm, Levy Flights and Global Optimization. In Research and Development in Intelligent Systems XXVI. Springer London.

Yang, X.-S. (2012). Flower Pollination Algorithm for Global Optimization. In Lecture Notes in Computer Science: Vol. 7445. Proceeding of Unconventional Computation and Natural Computation (UCNC 2012). Springer. doi:10.1007/978-3-642-32894-7_27

Yang, X.–S. (2012). Nature–Inspired Mateheuristic Algorithms: Success and New Challenges. *Journal of Computer Engineering and Information Technology, 1*(1), 1–3. doi:104172/2324-9307.1000e101

Yang, J., & Honovar, V. (1998). feature subset selection using a genetic algorithm. *IEEE Intelligent Systems, 13*(2), 44–49. doi:10.1109/5254.671091

Yang, X.-S. (2009). Firefly Algorithms for Multimodal Optimization. In Lecture Notes in Computer Science: Vol. 5792. *Stochastic Algorithms: Foundations and Applications (SAGA–2009)* (pp. 169–178). Berlin: Springer–Verlag. doi:10.1007/978-3-642-04944-6_14

Yang, X.-S. (2010). *Nature–Inspired Metaheuristic Algorithms* (2nd ed.). Luniver Press.

Yang, X.-S. (2010b). Firefly Algorithm, Stochastic Test Functions and Design Optimisation. *International Journal of Bio-inspired Computation, 2*(2), 78–84. doi:10.1504/IJBIC.2010.032124

Yang, X.-S. (2011). Bat Algorithm for Multi–objective Optimization. *International Journal of Bio-inspired Computation, 3*(5), 267–274. doi:10.1504/IJBIC.2011.042259

Yang, X.-S. (2013). Multiobjective Firefly Algorithm for Continuous Optimization. *Engineering with Computers, 29*(2), 175–184. doi:10.1007/s00366-012-0254-1

Yang, X.-S. (2013). Optimization and Metaheuristic Algorithms in Engineering. In X. S. Yang, A. H. Gandomi, S. Talatahari, & A. H. Alavi (Eds.), *Metaheursitics in Water, Geotechnical and Transport Engineering* (pp. 1–23). Elsevier. doi:10.1016/B978-0-12-398296-4.00001-5

Yang, X.-S., Karamanoglu, M., & He, X. S. (2014). Flower Pollination Algorithm: A Novel Approach for Multiobjective Optimization. *Engineering Optimization, 46*(9), 1222–1237. doi:10.1080/0305215X.2013.832237

Yan, H., Ding, S., & Suel, T. (2009). Inverted index compression and query processing with optimized document ordering. In *Proceedings of the 18th international conference on World wide web* (pp. 401-410). ACM. doi:10.1145/1526709.1526764

Yazdani, D., Toosi, A. N., & Meybodi, M. R. (2010, December). Fuzzy adaptive artificial fish swarm algorithm. In *Australasian Joint Conference on Artificial Intelligence* (pp. 334-343). Springer Berlin Heidelberg.

Yegin, A. E., & Watanabe, F. (2005). Authentication, Authorization, and Accounting. *Next Generation Mobile Systems 3G and Beyond*, 315-343.

Yeh, W. C. (2012). Novel swarm optimization for mining classification rules on thyroid gland data. *Information Sciences*, *197*, 65–76. doi:10.1016/j.ins.2012.02.009

Yerazunis, W. S. (2004, January). The spam-filtering accuracy plateau at 99.9% accuracy and how to get past it. *Proceedings of the 2004 MIT Spam Conference.*

Yin, H., Li, J., & Niu, Y. (2014). Detecting Local Communities within a Large Scale Social Network Using Mapreduce. *International Journal of Intelligent Information Technologies*, *10*(1), 57–76. doi:10.4018/ijiit.2014010104

Yu, L., & Liu, H. (2004a). Efficient feature selection via analysis of relevance and redundancy. *Journal of Machine Learning Research*, *5*, 1205–1224.

Yu, Y., Zhang, S. M., Zhang, H. J., Liu, X. C., Zhang, Q. S., Zheng, X. X., & Dai, J. H. (2010). Neural decoding based on probabilistic neural network. *Journal of Zhejiang University. Science. B.*, *11*(4), 298–306. doi:10.1631/jzus.B0900284 PMID:20349527

Zachary, W. W. (1977). An information flow model for conflict and fission in small groups. *Journal of Anthropological Research*, *33*(4), 452–473. doi:10.1086/jar.33.4.3629752

Zander, T., Kothe, C., Welke, S., & Roetting, M. (2008). *Enhancing human– machine systems with secondary input from passive brain– computer interfaces.* Paper presented at the 4th International Brain–Computer Interface Workshop and Training Course, Graz, Austria.

Zdziarski, J. A. (2005). *Ending spam: Bayesian content filtering and the art of statistical language classifica-tion.* No Starch Press.

Zgaya, H. (2007). *Conception et optimisation distribuée d'un système d'information d'aide à la mobilité urbaine: Une approche multi-agent pour la recherche et la composition des services liés au transport* (Thèse de doctorat). Université de Lille. France.

Zhang, F., Aghagolzadeh, M., & Oweiss, K. (2012). A fully implantable, programmable and multimodal neuroprocessor for wireless, cortically controlled brain-machine interface applications. *Journal of Signal Processing Systems for Signal, Image, and Video Technology*, *69*(3), 351–361. doi:10.1007/s11265-012-0670-x PMID:23050029

Zhang, L., Zhu, J., & Yao, T. (2004). An evaluation of statistical spam filtering techniques. *ACM Transactions on Asian Language Information Processing*, *3*(4), 243–269. doi:10.1145/1039621.1039625

Zhang, S., Jiang, B., Zhu, J., Zhang, Q., Chen, W., Zheng, X., & Zhao, T. (2011). A study on combining local field potential and single unit activity for better neural decoding. *International Journal of Imaging Systems and Technology*, *21*(2), 165–172. doi:10.1002/ima.20287

Zhang, Y., & Chase, S. M. (2015). Recasting brain-machine interface design from a physical control system perspective. *Journal of Computational Neuroscience*, *39*(2), 107–118. doi:10.1007/s10827-015-0566-4 PMID:26142906

Zhang, Y., & Li, X. (2014). Relative Superiority of Key Centrality Measures for Identifying Influencers on Social Media. *International Journal of Intelligent Information Technologies*, *10*(4), 1–23. doi:10.4018/ijiit.2014100101

Zhang, Y., Li, X., & Wang, T. W. (2013). Identifying influencers in online social networks: The role of tie strength. *International Journal of Intelligent Information Technologies*, *9*(1), 1–20. doi:10.4018/jiit.2013010101

Zhang, Y., Zhou, G., Jin, J., Wang, X., & Cichocki, A. (2015). Optimizing spatial patterns with sparse filter bands for motor-imagery based brain–computer interface. *Journal of Neuroscience Methods, 255*, 85–91. doi:10.1016/j.jneumeth.2015.08.004 PMID:26277421

Zhu, K. K., Jiang, M., & Cheng, Y. (2010, October). Niche artificial fish swarm algorithm based on quantum theory. In *Signal Processing (ICSP), 2010 IEEE 10th International Conference on* (pp. 1425-1428). IEEE.

Zhu, K., & Jiang, M. (2010, July). Quantum artificial fish swarm algorithm. In *Intelligent Control and Automation (WCICA), 2010 8th World Congress on* (pp. 1-5). IEEE.

Zidi, K., & Hammadi, S. (2005). DMAS: Distributed Multi-Agents System for assist users in the multimodal travels. *International Conference on Industrial Engineering and Systems Management (IESM 2005)*.

Zięba, M., Tomczak, J. M., Lubicz, M., & Świątek, J. (2014). Boosted SVM for extracting rules from imbalanced data in application to prediction of the post-operative life expectancy in the lung cancer patients. *Applied Soft Computing, 14*, 99–108. doi:10.1016/j.asoc.2013.07.016

Ziessler, M., Nattkemper, D., & Frensch, P. A. (2004). The role of anticipation and intention in the learning of effects of self-performed actions. *Psychological Research, 68*(2/3), 163–175. doi:10.1007/s00426-003-0153-6 PMID:14634810

Zikopoulos, P., Eaton, C., deRoos, D., Deutsch, T., & Lapis, G. (2011). *Understanding Big Data: Analytics for Enterprise Class Hadoop and Streaming Data*. McGraw-Hill Osborne Media.

Zobel, J., & Moffat, A. (2006). Inverted files for text search engines. *ACM Computing Surveys, 38*(2), 6, es. doi:10.1145/1132956.1132959

Zukowski, M., Heman, S., Nes, N., & Boncz, P. (2006). Super-scalar RAM-CPU cache compression. In *22nd International Conference on Data Engineering (ICDE'06)* (pp. 59-59). IEEE. doi:10.1109/ICDE.2006.150

About the Contributors

Reda Mohamed Hamou received an engineering degree in computer Science from the Computer Science department of Djillali Liabes University of Sidi-Belabbes-Algeria and PhD (Artificial intelligence) from the same University. He has several publications in the field of BioInspired and Metaheuristic. His research interests include Data Mining, Text Mining, Classification, Clustering, computational intelligence, neural networks, evolutionary computation and Biomimetic optimization method. He is a head of research team in GecoDe laboratory. Dr. Hamou is an associate professor in technology faculty in UTMS University of Saida-Algeria.

* * *

Abdelmalek Amine received an engineering degree in Computer Science, a Magister diploma in Computational Science and PhD from Djillali Liabes University in collaboration with Joseph Fourier University of Grenoble. His research interests include data mining, text mining, ontology, classification, clustering, neural networks, and biomimetic optimization methods. He participates in the program committees of several international conferences and on the editorial boards of international journals. Prof. Amine is the head of GeCoDe-knowledge management and complex data-laboratory at UTM University of Saida, Algeria; he also collaborates with the "knowledge base and database" team of TIMC laboratory at Joseph Fourier University of Grenoble.

Shonak Bansal is a doctoral student at PEC University of Technology, Chandigarh, India in Electronics and Communication Engineering department. He holds M.Tech. and B. Tech. in Electronics and Communication Engineering department from Maharishi Markandeshwar University, Mullana, and Kurukshetra University, Kurukshetra, respectively in India. His areas of research interest are in Soft computing algorithms, Optical communication, Fuzzy logic, and Nanophotonics etc. Shonak Bansal has published his research in journals such as Applied Soft Computing, International Journal of Computer Applications, Journal of The Institution of Engineers (India): Series B, Open Mathematics, among others. He has also published a book on Digital System Design with VHDL: Programming by Examples in LAP LAMBERT Academic Publishing, Germany. He is also working as a reviewer in Journal of The Institution of Engineers (India), Applied Soft Computing, Open Mathematics, International Journal of Applied Metaheuristic Computing, International Journal of Applied Evolutionary Computation, and International Journal of Innovative Research in Science & Engineering.

Zakaria Bendaoud (born in Tlemcen, Algeria) is a Teacher (Assistant Professor) in Computer sciences departement of Saida University and a research assistant at LIO Laboratory, Oran, Algeria. He received his Ph. D. in road transport at University of Oran 1, Ahmed Benbella in 2015. His research interests are in Decision Support Systems (urban, road, maritime transportation, and health), Optimization, Simulation, Cooperative and Distributed System, Knowledge bases and Multi Criteria Decision Making. Zakaria Bendaoud has published in journals such as transport and telecommunication.

Karim Bouamrane is an Engineer in Computer Science (1991), Computer Science Institute of Oran; Master of Artificial Intelligence (1996), Phd Thesis in Artificial Intelligence, Computer Science department, Oran University since 2006, Head of Computer science department since 2010. He participates in several scientific committees international/national conferences in Algeria and others countries in the same domain and collaborate in Algerian-French scientific projects. Publications: more than 30 scientific publications. Fields of research: decision support system (urban, road, maritime transportation, and health), traveler information system, optimization, cooperative and distributed system, Knowledge bases.

Hadj Ahmed Bouarara received a licence degree in computer Science and Master diploma in computer modeling of knowledge and reasoning from the Computer Science department of Tahar Moulay University of Saida Algeria. Now Hadj Ahmed BOUARARA is a phd student in Web and Knowledge Engineering in Dr. Tahar Moulay University. His research interests Data Mining, Knowledge Discovery, Metaheuristic, Bio-inspired techniques, Retrieval Information, Cloud Computing and images processing.

Mohamed Amine Boudia is an Assistant Teacher of computer sicence in the Computer Science department of Tahar Moulay University of Saïda-Algeria, He received his PhD, in Web and knowledge engineering from the Computer Science department of Tahar Moulay University of Saïda-Algeria He is a member of GeCoDe laboratory. His research interests include Data Mining, Text Mining, Classification, Clustering. He has published in several relevant journal as IJISP, IJIRR, IJAMC.., and participated in several international conference, and he is Editorial Review Board and ad-Hoc Reviewer at IGI-Global for many journal.

Ayan Chatterjee, MCA, is an assistant professor of D.EL.ED section at Sarboday Public Academy, Purba Medinipur, India. He holds a Master's degree in Computer Application from Vidyasagar University, India. Before that, he did B.Sc (Hons.) degree in Mathematics from University of Calcutta, India. Mr. Chatterjee started his professional career since January, 2016. In his academic career, he published some research papers with good impact factors. His Master's thesis is on optimization technique of Travelling Salesman Problem (TSP) using Artificial Neural Network under supervision of Dr. Asit Kumar Das, IIEST, India. His areas of interests are Software Engineering, Computational Methodology, Soft Computing, Steganography and Cryptography.

Mohamed Guendouz received his Bachelor's degree in computer science from the Dr.Tahat Moulay University of Saïda, Algeria in 2012, he received his Master's degree from the same university. Now, Mohamed Guendouz is a PhD student at Dr. Tahar Moulay University of Saïda and a researcher at the GeCoDe Research Laboratory, he works on Big Data and Social Networks Analysis, he participated in several international conferences in Algeria as an author.

Fatima Kabli received the Master degree in software engineering from the University of Ahmed Ben bella Oran. She is currently pursuing the Ph.D. Degree in computer science with GeCoDe Laboratory in UTMS University of Saida-Algeria. Her current Researches include complex data mining and analysis, bioinformatics.

Kijpokin Kasemsap received his BEng degree in Mechanical Engineering from King Mongkut's University of Technology, Thonburi, his MBA degree from Ramkhamhaeng University, and his DBA degree in Human Resource Management from Suan Sunandha Rajabhat University. Dr. Kasemsap is a Special Lecturer in the Faculty of Management Sciences, Suan Sunandha Rajabhat University, based in Bangkok, Thailand. Dr. Kasemsap is a Member of the International Economics Development and Research Center (IEDRC), the International Foundation for Research and Development (IFRD), and the International Innovative Scientific and Research Organization (IISRO). Dr. Kasemsap also serves on the International Advisory Committee (IAC) for the International Association of Academicians and Researchers (INAAR). Dr. Kasemsap is the sole author of over 250 peer-reviewed international publications and book chapters on business, education, and information technology. Dr. Kasemsap is included in the TOP 100 Professionals–2016 and in the 10th edition of 2000 Outstanding Intellectuals of the 21st Century by the International Biographical Centre, Cambridge, England.

Ahmed Chouaki Lokbani received an engineering degree in computer Science from the Computer Science department of Djillali Liabes University of Sidi-Belabbes-Algeria and PhD (security by data mining) from the same University. His research interests include security, IDS, Classification, Data mMining and Biomimetic optimization. He is an associate professor and a head of computer Science of Dr. Tahar Moulay University of Saida-Algeria.

Ishak H. A. Meddah is a PHD Student at the USTO MB university, Oran, Algeria. He is interested in Data Mining, and the Parallel and distributed Treatment.

Norreddine Mekour is a Researcher at the Gestion Complex Knowledge and Data Management (GeCoDe) Laboratory, doctor Tahar Moulay University of Saïda, Algeria. He received his Master in Computer Science from Saida University, Algeria, in 2013. He is a PhD candidate in Computer Science Department at Saida University. His research interests are in Biomimicry and data mining in genomics.

Hanane Menad received a licence degree in computer Science from the Computer Science department of Dr. Tahar Moulay University of Saida-Algeria, received the Master diploma in Data mining and knowledge management from same university. Now Hanane Menad is a researcher. Her research interests include Data Mining, knowledge extraction, bioinspired algorithms, medical data analysis.

Dharmendra Patel received Bachelor Degree in Industrial Chemistry- BSc. (Industrial Chemistry) from North Gujarat University, Gujarat, India and Master Degree in Computer Applications(MCA) from North Gujarat University, Gujarat, India. He completed his Ph.D., in the field of Web Usage Mining. He is HOD of MCA Department at Smt. Chandaben Mohanbhai Patel Institute of Computer Applications, under Charusat University of Science and Technology (CHARUSAT), Changa, Gujarat, India.

Amine Rahmani received a licence degree in computer Science from the Computer Science department of Dr. Tahar Moulay University of Saida-Algeria, received the Master diploma in Network, System and Security Informatics from Djillali Liabes University. Now Amine Rahmani is a PhD student in Web and Knowledge Engineering in Dr. Tahar Moulay University. His research interests include Big Data, Privacy Preserving, Informatics Security, Data Mining, Cloud Computing, Big Data analytics, Access Control, and Cryptography.

Mohamed Elhadi Rahmani received a licence degree in computer Science from the Computer Science department of Dr. Tahar Moulay University of Saida-Algeria, received the Master diploma in Data mining and knowledge management from same university. Now Mohamed Elhadi Rahmani is a PhD student in Web and Knowledge Engineering in Dr. Tahar Moulay University. His research interests include Data Mining, Cloud Computing, Big Data analytics, Ecological issues, Ecosystem.

Mahendra Rong, M.Sc., PhD, is working as an Assistant Professor in Mathematics at Bangabasi Evening College under University of Calcutta, India. He is also handling a UGC (India) Minor Research Project. His fields of interest are optimization, operations research, fuzzy-random mathematics, etc. He has publications in international journals such as European Journal of Operational Research, Applied Mathematical Modelling, Central European Journal of Operation Research, etc.

Domnic S. received the B.Sc. and M.C.A degrees from Bharathidasan University, Tiruchirappalli, India, in 1998 and 2001, respectively, and the Ph.D. degree from Gandhigram Rural University, Dindigul, India, in 2008. He is currently an Assistant Professor with the Department of Computer Applications, National Institute of Technology at Tiruchirappalli, Tiruchirappalli. His current research interests are data compression, image/video processing, and information retrieval.

Kuldeep Sharma is a doctoral student and research assistant at the PEC University of Technology, Chandigarh, India. He holds a M.Tech. and B.E. in Electronic and Communication engineering from NIT, Jalandhar and University of Rajsthan, Jaipur, respectively in India. His research interests are RF MEMS Switch, UWB antenna, soft computing algorithms and Biomedical. Kuldeep Sharma has published in various national and international journals and conferences.

Glory V. received the B.Sc degree in computer science from Madurai Kamaraj University and the M.C.A degree from Kalasalingam University, India, in 2007 and 2010, respectively and the Ph.D degree from National Institute of Technology, Tiruchirappalli, India, in 2015. She is currently working as a Teaching Assistant in the Department of Computer Science, Periyar University, Salem. Her research interest is in information retrieval.

Index

G

Gene Expression 66-67, 309, 325, 327, 331-332, 334-335

genetic algorithm 66, 71, 75, 130-131, 137, 215, 220, 222, 265

Golomb ruler 2-5, 9, 13, 16, 18-19, 176-178, 184, 191, 201, 203

I

Information 18, 27-28, 39-40, 43, 45, 62, 66, 70-71, 73, 75, 78-79, 82, 90, 95, 103, 105, 112-113, 116, 133, 135, 141-142, 144, 155, 161, 164, 166, 173, 204, 212-214, 216, 224, 226, 230, 246, 248, 251-258, 273, 276-280, 286, 295, 303-304, 306-308, 310, 312, 316-317, 324-331, 333-334, 339-340, 342-344, 346, 348-349, 354, 357, 371-373, 376

Information Retrieval 39-40, 90, 105, 135, 161, 164, 248, 278

Information Security 212, 216

Integer Encoders 92

Integer List Encoders 93

Integrity 212-214, 216

intrusion detection system 26-29, 31-32

Inverted Index 90-91

IT Security 26-27, 38

K

KDD Process 307-308

kidney 46-49, 154

Knowledge discovery 226, 251-252, 303, 307

Knowledge extraction 303, 308, 317

M

Machine learning 39-40, 42-43, 71, 73, 103, 105-106, 108, 117, 229, 252, 255, 279-280, 308-309, 314, 332, 335

machine learning tool 73

Medical data analysis 251-252, 273

Medical data classification 267, 269, 271

meta heuristics 46, 155, 173, 226, 251

Meta-Heuristic 26, 28, 39, 41, 118, 155, 281

N

Nephron 49-50, 57

Neural Network 41, 214, 222, 228-229, 253, 255, 333-335, 371

n-Gram 38, 43, 103, 105, 280, 292

O

Optimal Golomb ruler 2, 5, 176

Optimization 1-3, 5-6, 8-9, 11-12, 19-20, 49-50, 58, 71, 81, 95, 109, 121-123, 125, 130-131, 133, 135-139, 143-144, 154-155, 173, 175-176, 179, 181-182, 184, 186, 204-205, 213, 222, 226, 254, 264, 276, 282, 285, 287, 293, 295-298, 312, 335

Optimization Methods 138

P

Pareto front 2, 7, 11, 17, 176, 180, 185

Patient 252, 256-257, 332, 354

Peak Signal to Noise Ratio (PSNR) 217, 224

Plagiarism Detection 103, 105-106, 110, 115, 117

Protein 257, 303, 305-308, 310-311, 313-316, 325, 327-328, 330, 332, 335

R

Renal System 40, 46-48, 62

Robot 353-354, 356, 371

ROUGE 277, 279, 292, 294-295, 297

S

scenario approach 29

Scoring 49, 276-277, 281, 290, 292

Signal 2, 31, 45, 217, 224, 230, 234, 243, 261, 351, 355-357, 371

similarity 51, 54, 58, 105, 134, 144, 216, 239, 251, 262, 267-270, 272-273, 276-277, 281-283, 285-286, 288-290, 294, 309, 313, 332-333

social 26-29, 31-32, 38-41, 44-47, 54, 60, 62, 80-82, 118, 133-135, 147, 149, 154, 212, 231-232, 235-236, 243, 251, 262, 264, 268-270, 272, 276-277, 281-282, 284-285, 287, 290, 293-298, 323, 339, 375

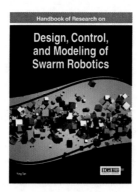

Stay Current on the Latest Emerging Research Developments

Become an IGI Global Reviewer for Authored Book Projects

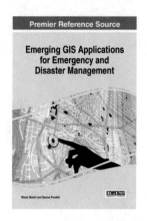

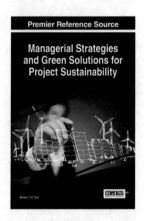

The overall success of an authored book project is dependent on quality and timely reviews.

In this competitive age of scholarly publishing, constructive and timely feedback significantly decreases the turnaround time of manuscripts from submission to acceptance, allowing the publication and discovery of progressive research at a much more expeditious rate. Several IGI Global authored book projects are currently seeking highly qualified experts in the field to fill vacancies on their respective editorial review boards:

Applications may be sent to:
development@igi-global.com

Applicants must have a doctorate (or an equivalent degree) as well as publishing and reviewing experience. Reviewers are asked to write reviews in a timely, collegial, and constructive manner. All reviewers will begin their role on an ad-hoc basis for a period of one year, and upon successful completion of this term can be considered for full editorial review board status, with the potential for a subsequent promotion to Associate Editor.

If you have a colleague that may be interested in this opportunity, we encourage you to share this information with them.

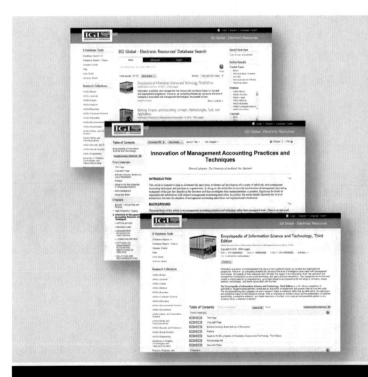